Motivation: Theory, Research, and Applications

Third Edition

Herbert L. Petri
Towson State University
Baltimore, Maryland

Wadsworth Publishing Company
Belmont, California
A Division of Wadsworth, Inc.

*T*his book is dedicated to the memory of Mom and Pop,
and with love to my wife, Jan,
and my children, Stephanie, Kathleen, and Estelle.

Psychology Editor: Kenneth King
Editorial Assistant: Cynthia Campell
Production Editor: Rosaleen Bertolino, Bookman Productions
Print Buyer: Randy Hurst
Designer: Hal Lockwood
Technical Illustrators: Christine Dettner, Darwen and Vally
  Hennings, Cyndie Clark-Huegel
Compositor: Auto-Graphics
Signing Representative: Marilee Morris
Cover: *Growing, 1940,* Josef Albers; oil on masonite, 15 × 17
  3/4 inches; San Francisco Museum of Modern Art, gift of
  Mrs. Charlotte Mack.

Printed in the United States of America

1 2 3 4 5 6 7 8 9 10—95 94 93 92 91 90

Library of Congress Cataloging in Publication Data

Petri, Herbert L.
  Motivation : theory and research / Herbert L. Petri.—3rd
    ed. p.   cm.
  Includes bibliographical references.
  Includes index.
  ISBN 0-534-14364-4
  1. Motivation (Psychology)   I. Title.
BF503.P47 1990
153.8—dc20
                                            90-38988
                                            CIP

Preface to the Third Edition

I have found the study of motivation to be one of the most fascinating and complex topics in psychology. It is fascinating because people want to know why they behave the way they do—to understand the processes that activate their behavior. It is complex because it cuts across many specialty areas within psychology and draws from each of them. Thus you will find in this book physiological, conditioning, and cognitive explanations of behavior.

My own motives for writing this text are also complex. First, I have felt for some time that a motivation text should cover in detail the major approaches suggested by theorists of varying specialties and backgrounds. What I found, however, was that some texts emphasized the cognitive or personality aspects but not the biological aspects. I believe this book provides a more even coverage of the current thinking about motivational processes. Second, when surveying the various texts available, I found that they often presented a particular point of view (usually the author's) on which approaches were the "best." It seems to me that a book designed for a first course in motivation ought to put forward, as far as possible, an unbiased view of motivational theory. Therefore, I have tried to present the material in this text as objectively as possible, including both the advantages and disadvantages of each of the approaches discussed.

In addition, I have observed that students need to be presented with the basic ideas within a given area, as well as some conclusions about those ideas. Students too often become "lost in the data" and miss the major points. For this reason, I have purposely avoided an encyclopedic presentation of the major areas. Instead, I have tried to focus on the kinds of research conducted to test the major ideas. As I see it, a textbook on motivation should provide the basic information necessary for a good background in motivational processes, while at the same time allowing instructors the freedom to present additional material of their own choosing related to the various areas. This book is intended to provide the basic information instructors can build on.

The book is divided into three major areas: approaches to motivation that emphasize its biological components, approaches that emphasize its learned components, and approaches that emphasize its cognitive components. Within each of these areas I have tried to present the material in such a way that understanding the later chapters does not depend on having read the earlier chapters. The independence of the chapters allows each instructor to select whichever ones best fit in with his or her particular approach to motivation. This independence also means that chapters can be assigned in any order that is deemed appropriate.

Motivational theory is sometimes difficult for students because it requires modes of thinking that may be quite far removed from everyday experience. For this reason, I have used examples drawn from day-to-day life wherever possible. I have also tried to keep the language simple and direct.

It hardly seems possible that ten years have passed since the publication of the first edition of this text. During those ten years the book has been updated in a second edition (1986), and it is now time to update it again.

The third edition represents a refinement of the progression of topics found in the second edition. The order of the chapters remains the same with the exception that Chapter Fourteen on work motivation has been deleted from the third edition. Because many psychology programs now include a course in organizational psychology, the inclusion of this chapter was deemed less crucial than was the case earlier.

Major changes in the third edition include coverage of several new topics (e.g., pain motivation; the biological basis of shyness) and expanded coverage of sexual and aggressive motivation. Research on sexual motivation and aggressive motivation appears in several chapters. The unifying concept is that many motives are best understood as complex behaviors influenced by a variety of factors. Thus, for example, sexual behavior can be understood as having genetic, arousal, regulatory, drive, incentive, and learning components. Attempting to study sexual behaviors without considering this combination of factors will lead to an incomplete understanding of sexual motivation. Aggressive behaviors, and ultimately all motives, are probably best understood as resulting from a complex interaction of factors.

Other changes in the third edition include the reorganization of Chapter One, including a new section on the changing concepts within motivational theory from the 1800s to the present. This section was written to give the student a better understanding of how motivational concepts have changed across the years. This section also provides a general outline for the chapter sequence. In general, the order of

the chapters follows the flow of ideas from mechanistic to cognitive explanations described in this brief historical overview.

As was the case with the second edition, the third edition has been considerably updated. The third edition now contains nearly 1,000 references, a 20% increase over the second edition. About 46% of these new references were published after the second edition went to press, so a substantial amount of recent material has been added to the third edition.

The third edition contains new information on a number of important topics of interest to students, such as sleep, stress, eating disorders, helping behavior, attributions, and emotion. Each of these research areas has experienced considerable growth in the past several years. Thus the instructor familiar with the second edition will find the sequence and topics similar but updated with more recent research.

No one writes a book without a great deal of help and support from many people. I thank God and my parents for whatever talents I possess that have allowed this book to become a reality. My parents provided an atmosphere during my youth that instilled in me a love of knowledge and a desire to teach it to others. That the book is now in its third edition attests to their success.

As is the case with any endeavor of this size, many people have contributed time, effort, and expertise to this project. I would particularly like to thank the user-reviewers for their thoughtful and thought-provoking suggestions. These reviewers were Harold Babb of SUNY, Binghamton; David Lopatto of Grinnell College; Aaron Ettenberg of the University of California, Santa Barbara; Richard O. Straub of the University of Michigan, Dearborn; and Marvin Dunn of Florida International University.

I am also grateful to Towson State University for supporting this project and providing the necessary materials for developing the manuscript of the third edition. To the many students in my classes who have been subjected to varying renditions of this material, I say thank you. You helped me determine what would work and what would not. Many colleagues have shared books, articles, and expertise. I thank each of them for their help.

The staff at Wadsworth has provided excellent support over the years. Ken King, psychology editor, has been a constant source of support and has urged me on during the development of the third edition. Through his selection of reviewers and timely advice, he has strengthened the third edition immeasurably. He is a writer's editor, providing encouragement without undue pressure, thus allowing creativity and innovation. Many of Ken's own ideas have found their way into the text in one form or another.

Finally, I must express my greatest appreciation to my family, who have now endured the writing process yet a third time. First and foremost, my wife, Jan, who is always there to provide support and encouragement when I need it, and my children, Stephanie, Kathleen, and Estelle, who have often had to wait while I wrote. Without the family's support the project would have been largely meaningless. My daughter Kathy deserves a special thank-you for typing and rearranging the reference section. She volunteered many hours of her time to help me meet my deadline.

It is my hope that faculty and students alike will find the third edition of this text as interesting and informative to read as I have found it challenging to write.

Herbert L. Petri
January 1990

A Note About the Author

HERBERT L. PETRI was born in Hamilton, Ohio, in
1944. He received his A.B. degree from Miami University, Oxford, Ohio, in 1967 and M.A. and Ph.D.
degrees from Johns Hopkins University in 1969 and
1972, respectively. He has taught at Towson State
University since receiving his doctorate and has
been recognized on five separate occasions for his
excellent teaching. Dr. Petri also occasionally teaches
the motivation course at Johns Hopkins University.

Brief Contents

Contents

I

OVERVIEW

Chapter One

Introduction

CHAPTER PREVIEW

This chapter is concerned with the following questions:

1. What is motivation?

2. What are the philosophical and physiological roots of motivation?

3. How is motivation studied?

4. What are the major constructs in motivation?

5. What is the plan of this book?

INTRODUCTION

Teresa has a problem. As a baby she was excessively fat, and today, at 14, she is tormented by her weight problem. Teresa's life is also full of stress. Her mother is always nagging Teresa about her weight, and her two younger brothers tease her constantly. Teresa has also had more than her share of abuse at school. In elementary school the other children taunted her; now, as an adolescent, she is either ignored or is the butt of jokes by the others. All these factors in Teresa's life make her miserable, and when Teresa is miserable, she eats. Thus a vicious cycle is initiated that starts with eating and leads to more eating. As we shall see later, the story of Teresa illustrates some of the complexities of motivation. Now, however, we need to examine the concept of motivation.

THE CONCEPT OF MOTIVATION

Motivation is the concept we use when we describe the forces acting on or within an organism to **initiate** and **direct** behavior. We also use the concept of motivation to explain differences in the **intensity** of behavior. More intense behaviors are considered to be the result of higher levels of motivation. Additionally, we often use the concept of motivation to indicate the **direction** of behavior. When we are hungry, we direct our behavior in ways to get food.

Why does the study of behavior need a concept of motivation? One reason often suggested by both casual and scientific observation is that "something" triggers behavior. Sometimes we behave in a certain way and at other times we do not. What was different from the one time to the others? Presumably motivation was present when we behaved but was absent (or perhaps a different motive was active) when we did not. The concept of motivation helps to explain why behavior occurs in the one situation but not in the others. To the extent that such a concept increases our ability to understand and predict behavior, the concept is useful. As readers will discover throughout the remainder of this book, many psychologists have found the concept of motivation useful.

THE MEASUREMENT OF MOTIVATION

As scientists we almost never measure motivation directly. Instead we manipulate some stimulus (S) condition and then measure some behavior in the form of a response (R). Sup-

pose, for example, that we take food away from a rat for 48 hours (a form of **deprivation**) as our stimulus change (S) and observe how fast that rat subsequently runs in a maze (R) in order to get food at the goal box (see Figure 1.1). Further, suppose that we observe that our rat runs faster after 48 hours of deprivation than when not deprived. In this hypothetical experiment we manipulated hours without food and measured speed of running, neither of which is motivation. Motivation, however, can be *inferred* from the change in behavior that occurred, and an indication of its strength can be observed in the rat's speed of responding in the maze. Thus the concept of motivation helps us understand the change in the animal's behavior (assuming of course that some other alternative cannot better explain the change), and we might label the inferred motivational state as hunger. The concept of motivation in this example serves as an **inter-**

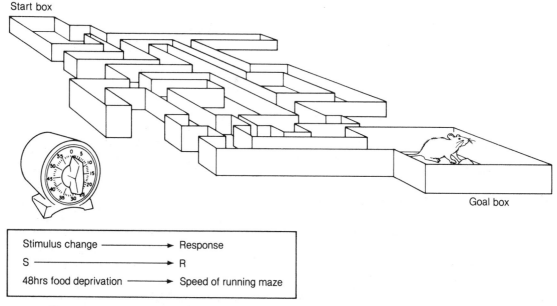

Figure 1.1   *Stimulus-response analysis of motivation. Motivation is inferred when changes in responding follow from changes in stimulus conditions.*

vening variable.* An intervening variable comes between a stimulus and a response and serves to link the two together. Thus motivation serves to link the stimulus change (deprivation) to the behavior change (increased speed of running) and provides a possible explanation for the relationship between the stimulus and response, as shown in Figure 1.2.

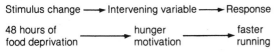

Figure 1.2 *Motivation as an intervening variable.*

The intervening nature of motivational processes is one reason that motivation is difficult to study. A second difficulty stems from the temporary nature of motivation. Psychologists typically describe the temporary nature of motivation by pointing out that motivation is a **performance variable**. When enough motivation is present, behavior is performed; when motivation is absent, behavior is absent. Motivation as a performance variable is often contrasted with learning, where more permanent changes in behavior occur. We learn many things not immediately demonstrated in behavior, but the demonstration of learned behavior depends upon adequate motivation. Indeed every specialty area within psychology analyzes situations that involve the combination of specific processes and the performance of these processes in behavior.

CHARACTERISTICS OF MOTIVATION

We have, after a fashion, discussed motivation as if we knew what it is. Certainly each of us has some intuitive feeling for what is called motivation, and yet it has proven to be rather difficult to define. Kleinginna and Kleinginna

*A variable is any factor that can have more than one value; for example, we can be a little hungry, moderately hungry, or ravenously hungry.

(1981), for example, have gathered 102 defining or criticizing statements concerning motivation. Though textbooks on the topic differ somewhat in their definitions, one commonly held characteristic of motivation is its activating properties.

Activation

The activating property of motivation is most easily seen in the production of behavior. Is the observed organism behaving in some way? If it is, then at least some minimal amount of motivation is assumed to be present. If no overt behavior is observed, then the motivational level of the organism may be insufficient to trigger behavior. While the occurrence of overt behavior is generally taken as evidence for motivation, its absence does not necessarily mean that no motivation is present. For example, consider a rabbit that freezes when in close proximity to a predator. Is the rabbit unmotivated by the presence of this threat? Probably not. In fact, while overt behavior may be virtually absent in this situation, behavioral indexes such as heart rate, adrenalin output, and so forth would probably be high. The moral is clear—though motivation is considered to be behaviorally activating, the behavior activated may not always be overt. We must therefore be very cautious in assuming a lack of motivation when no overt responding is apparent; perhaps we are not measuring the response or responses that are being activated. Fortunately, for many motivational states, changes in motivation do lead to changes in overt behavior.

A second characteristic that is often mentioned in regard to the activating properties of motivation is **persistence**. Hungry animals persist in their attempts to get food. Similarly, humans often persist in behaving in particular ways even when the chances of success are vanishingly small. Observation of this continued persistence has led many psychologists to regard it as an index of motivation. This index, however, is also not free of problems. How persistent a behavior is depends at least in part on what alternative behaviors are available. Suppose, for example, that a hungry monkey has been taught to press a lever for food. For several hours each day, the monkey is placed in an experimental chamber that contains only the lever. Of course the monkey does not have to press the lever, but there is little else for it to do, and if lever pressing has been learned, it will tend to persist. On the other hand, suppose the monkey is placed in a chamber where several different responses in addition to lever pressing are possible. If these alternative responses lead to different outcomes (for example, a peek out a window, a sweet-tasting fluid, and so on), lever pressing may become less persistent. In multiple response situations (as often occur in naturalistic situations) continued persistence probably does accurately reflect motivational strength, but as Beck (1983) points out, motivational research has not typically examined persistence in situations where more than one response is possible. Thus, although persistence does seem to be one index of motivation, it is important to realize that other factors may also contribute to the persistence of behavior.

Both casual observation and the laboratory suggest that energetic behavior is more motivated than hesitant behavior. One rat that runs faster than another through a maze may also be more motivated. Such a hypothesis is more likely to be true if we also know that the two rats differ in how hungry they are but not in how well they have learned to run the maze. **Vigor** of responding, then, is another characteristic typically associated with the presence of motivation. But as with the other characteristics we have examined, vigorous responses do not always mean high motivation. It is possible, for example, to teach a rat that the correct response to obtain food is to push down on a lever with a certain amount of force. Suppose that someone designed an

experiment where hungry rats had to press the response lever with a good deal of force for food pellets to be delivered. If we were to unknowingly observe these "forceful" rats, we might conclude that they were highly motivated as they banged away at the response lever. However, in this instance we would be wrong because the vigorous responding may not index motivation alone; factors such as learning may also be involved.

Overt responding, persistence, and vigor are characteristics of the activation properties of motivation, assuming that other factors can be ruled out, and are, under appropriate conditions, reasonable indexes of the presence of motivation. Activation is usually considered one of the two major components of motivation; however Birch, Atkinson, and Bongort (1974) suggest that the activation of behavior should not be a major concern of motivational analyses because organisms are continually active. These researchers propose that motivational analyses should examine the conditions that lead the organism to change from one activity to another. In other words, the directionality of behavior is what is important.

Direction

When we are hungry we go the refrigerator, and when we are thirsty we go to the water faucet. How do we decide to direct our behavior in one way versus another? Questions of this type involve a consideration of which mechanism (or mechanisms) directs behavior. Although the specific way in which this directionality is achieved is debated by theorists, many psychologists have argued that motivation is involved. **Directionality**, then, is often considered an index of motivational state. The direction that a particular behavior takes is usually obvious, as in going to the refrigerator when we are hungry; however, when several choices are possible, directionality is sometimes not so clear. Suppose that we have two bottles, each filled with a solution of water and sucrose (table sugar) but with different concentrations. Will the rat be more motivated by one of the two concentrations? To determine which is the more motivating, we would run a **preference test**. The rat is given the opportunity to lick fluid from either bottle, and we measure the amount consumed. If we were to conduct such a test, we would discover that the rat preferred the more concentrated sugar solution (Young & Greene, 1953), and we would have some evidence that more concentrated solutions of sucrose are more motivating. In some situations preference testing is the best way to determine which of several alternatives is most motivating, because indexes such as persistence or vigor may not indicate differences. Indeed Beck (1983) considers preference to be the most basic motivational index.

THE STUDY OF MOTIVATION: CATEGORIES OF ANALYSIS

As you proceed through the chapters of this text, you will discover that motivation has been studied from many different points of view. In general we can order these views along at least four dimensions, each containing

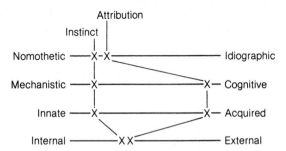

Figure 1.3 *Categories of analysis. Four dimensions along which analysis of motivation may differ. As shown, motivation from an instinctive perspective is nomothetic, mechanistic, innate, and in response to both internal and external cues. Motivation from the point of view of attribution theory is nomothetic, cognitive, acquired, and also in response to both internal and external cues.*

points representing opposing views, as shown in Figure 1.3. Although these dimensions overlap in some respects, the following analysis attempts to provide a framework within which the student can understand these differing points of view. Certainly other frameworks are possible.

Nomothetic Versus Idiographic

Research may be classified as falling along a continuum that proceeds from strictly **nomothetic** approaches at one extreme to strictly **idiographic** approaches at the other. The nomothetic approach involves the development of general or universal laws (*Webster's New World Dictionary*, 1962). Typically, research of this type studies groups of people or animals and determines how they are *similar*. For example, identifying brain structures such as the hypothalamus that are involved in motivation is nomothetic because research has shown that the hypothalamus is involved in motivation not only in a single rat but also in rats in general. Further, it is often assumed that the general rules uncovered by studying one species will also apply to other species. Although this assumption is sometimes incorrect and is always open to critical review, the nomothetic approach attempts to discover general laws applicable to the widest range of situations. In the study of motivation the nomothetic approach predominates. In opposition to nomothetic analyses is the idiographic approach, which proposes that we can understand behavior by looking at how people differ from each other, that is, by examining those properties that make each person *unique*. In motivation the idiographic approach is most clearly seen in the humanist and actualization theorists (see Chapter Twelve).

Innate Versus Acquired

Psychologists have debated for almost 100 years the contribution that innate versus acquired tendencies make to behavior, and motivation, as a specialty area within psychology, has not escaped this contention. Early theorists such as McDougall (reprinted in Russell, 1970) and James (1890) saw motivation as primarily controlled by innate motives they termed **instincts**. Although these early approaches did not last, modern research on the innate components of motivation is being pursued by animal behaviorists and ethologists. During the middle portion of the twentieth century, psychology was dominated by research on the factors involved in learning. Theorists and researchers studied how behavior is acquired, and much of what has been discovered is also applicable to the acquisition of motive states. Perhaps the most important motivational notion to develop from this work was the concept of incentive motivation. We will examine incentive motivation in Chapter Six; suffice it to say here that analyses emphasizing both innate and acquired motives continue today.

Internal Versus External

Another dimension along which motivation may be studied concerns the source of the motivation, that is, internal versus external sources of motivation. One prevalent approach to the study of motivation has involved the idea that different motive states can be conceptualized as **needs** that, when active, promote behaviors to reduce those needs. Needs are usually viewed as internal sources of motivation that activate and direct behavior to items in the environment that alleviate some state of deprivation. In this context needs are often couched in physiological terms (for example, the need for food and water, the avoidance of pain, and so forth), although some theorists also include social and psychological needs within their frameworks (see, for example, Lewin, 1936, 1938). In contrast to need theorists, others emphasize exter-

nal sources of motivation. These theorists generally examine the motivating effects of either various goal objects or social relationships. According to this point of view, motivation can be activated by changes in the external environment. For example, helping behavior often depends upon the number of other people present. Research has shown (see Chapter Ten) that the presence of other people often inhibits helping responses.

Mechanistic Versus Cognitive

How do the processes that control motivation work? Are they blind and mechanical, triggered automatically by changes in internal or external states, or are they controlled by rational, purposive thought? As you can probably guess, theorists have forcefully defended both sides. Some theorists argue that such motives as hunger, thirst, and sex are triggered automatically by changes in factors such as blood sugar level, fluid balance, and hormonal concentrations. This **mechanistic** approach assumes that changes in specific factors activate circuits that in turn motivate the organism to engage in appropriate behavior. Neither conscious awareness nor intent on the part of the organism is assumed. Researchers who embrace the mechanistic view are often interested in internal need states and innate patterns of behavior. In contrast, other researchers, more often interested in externally motivated states and acquired motives, believe that motivational processes are cognitive in nature. The **cognitive** approach assumes that the manner in which information is interpreted influences motive states. For example, attributing failure at a task to its difficulty is likely to have a different influence on future motivation than attributing failure to lack of ability.

The complexity of motivation is such that it is probably safe to assume that all the approaches mentioned above have some validity. In certain situations behavior seems best understood as motivated by internal states that activate the organism to respond in genetically determined ways. Other behaviors seem clearly the result of external information that is acted upon based on acquired experiences. Various combinations of approaches fit our observations of still other behaviors. To summarize, at this time no one approach would appear to be better than any other in explaining motivation in its entirety. Some approaches explain particular motive states better than others; however, depending on the motive studied, the best explanation may be nomothetic or idiographic, innate or acquired, internal or external, mechanistic or cognitive, or some combination of these.

LEVELS OF ANALYSIS

Before closing this discussion of the ways in which motivation is analyzed, we should mention the different levels at which it may be studied. Because motivation cuts across so many specialty areas within psychology, the number of levels (and sublevels within levels) at which it is studied is quite large. For the sake of brevity, however, we will group these various levels into the four main categories of physiological analysis, individual analysis, social analysis, and philosophical analysis.

Physiological Analysis

Though physiological analyses of motivation have been conducted using both humans and animals, research with animals is the most prevalent. Typically, this level of analysis is concerned with the brain's control of motivated states. Researchers, for example, are interested in the various brain structures involved in the triggering of motivation, the way in which motivationally important infor-

mation is processed by a group of cells, and even in which chemicals within the brain are involved in the alteration of motivational states. Thus we can identify many sublevels within the physiological analysis of motivation.

Studies of the role of the nervous system in motivation often require electrical, chemical, or surgical manipulation of carefully mapped brain areas. For example, in 1954 James Olds and Peter Milner conducted a study on rats in which thin wires called **electrodes** were introduced into various parts of the brain. These electrodes were designed so that portions of the brain could be stimulated electrically by the experimenters.

The experimental situation was so arranged that if the rats pressed a lever, current would be applied to the electrode. To everyone's amazement, rats with electrodes implanted in the **septal** region would press the lever many hundreds of times per hour in order to receive this weak electrical current. By conventional standards of conditioning, the electrical stimulation would have to be judged as a powerful reward. One rat pressed the lever more than 7,500 times in a 12-hour period while another responded 1,920 times in 1 hour. When the electrical current was turned off, bar pressing quickly ceased; when it was turned on again, bar pressing quickly resumed. The rats appeared to be highly motivated to obtain the electrical stimulation and worked for long periods of time to obtain it. The subjective impression one gained from observing these self-stimulating rats was that the electrical stimulation was quite pleasurable.

Since the discovery of self-stimulation sites in the brain by Olds and Milner, hundreds of additional studies have been conducted. The effects have proven to be much more complex than first supposed; for our purposes in this chapter, however, this research indicates one method of gaining knowledge about motivation. Direct manipulation of the brain by electrical stimulation has shown us that brain circuits exist that may be active when reward occurs. Circuits that appear to have a punishing effect on behavior have also been noted (e.g., Delgado, Roberts, & Miller, 1954).

Electrical stimulation of the brain is only one of several techniques used in the study of motivation at the physiological level. Researchers can also study motivation by **chemically stimulating** the brain after inserting a minute tube (called a **canula**) into a specific brain region, injecting a solution, and noting how motivation changes as a result. Additionally, researchers sometimes create a **lesion** within the brain by surgically removing some portion of it and observing how (or if) motivation is altered. These techniques have revealed that a wide range of motivated behaviors, including feeding, drinking, sexual arousal, fear, and aggression, can be altered by manipulation of specific brain areas. Finally, we should note that it is possible to **record** the brain's natural electrical activity during various motivated states. The general activity of large groups of brain cells (called **neurons**) can be recorded by an **electroencephalograph (EEG)**, while small groups of cells and even single neurons can be recorded through the use of **depth electrodes**. Though a particular researcher will often use only one or two physiological techniques, data gathered by all these techniques should be consistent. If lesion techniques have shown that a brain area is involved with feeding, then chemical or electrical stimulation of this area in other experimental subjects ought to elicit food-related activities. Similarly, recordings from this brain area during feeding behavior should indicate altered activity within these cells. Unfortunately, the convergence of information from different experimental techniques has not always been as consistent as one would like. The reasons for this lack of consistency are complex and remain a problem for understanding motivation at a physiological level of analysis.

Individual Analysis

The study of motivation at the level of the individual involves research aimed at understanding motivational changes that occur to a person as a result of internal or external conditions. Analysis at this level occurs about equally often in animal and human research. In animal research **deprivation** is often used to alter the motivational state of the organism; for example, one might deprive a rat of food for 48 hours and observe how its behavior changes as a result. In research conducted with humans, researchers may attempt to **induce** a motivational state through specific instructions. In some achievement studies, for example, researchers stimulated the need for achievement by telling the subjects that they had failed an important task (McClelland et al., 1949). More simply, human subjects are sometimes asked, using a survey technique such as a questionnaire, to indicate their own motives as they perceive them. One such technique developed by Rotter (1966) has provided theorists with considerable insight into how people view themselves.

Even though research at this level is conducted in order to provide insight into the important motivational factors that influence the behavior of the individual, most research of this type is actually done with groups of individuals. Testing several individuals increases the likelihood of finding an effect and taking the nomothetic approach; it is proper to presume that behavioral changes detected in several individuals are also present in people in general. An example of just such an approach is research conducted by Bandura and his associates concerning how aggression may be learned in children (e.g., Bandura, 1973).

In one study Bandura showed a group of nursery school children a film in which an adult attacked a life-size Bobo doll in unusual ways. For example, the adult hit the Bobo doll with a large mallet while saying such things as

"Socko!" and "Pow!" A second group of children saw the same behaviors performed by a cartoon character (actually an adult dressed up in a cat suit). A third group observed the aggressive behaviors performed by a live adult model, while a fourth group saw a live model behave in a calm, nonaggressive manner toward the Bobo doll.

Shortly afterward, the children were led to a room containing several different toys, among them the Bobo doll. The children's behavior was observed both for the novel forms of aggression depicted by the adult and for overall aggression. Results of the experiment showed that the live model's behavior was imitated more often than the filmed or cartoon models' behavior. However, significant imitation of the aggressive behavior of both the filmed model and the cartoon character also occurred. Of particular interest was the finding that the children not only modeled the observed aggressive behaviors, they also performed many aggressive behaviors of their own. The group that had observed the nonaggressive model, however, showed little aggressive behavior. Bandura's research is important for an understanding of motivation at the level of the individual because it strongly suggests that some motivated behaviors are learned, quite simply, through observation. Thus, if our parents or peers behave aggressively, we will learn to behave this way also. If, on the other hand, the models we observe show us that they are motivated to work hard, pursue excellence, and be successful, we are likely to be motivated in similar ways.

Social Analysis

A moment's reflection should quickly reveal that our behavior often differs when we are in the company of others. Behavior in the classroom is generally predictable: students take notes, ask questions, and sometimes fall asleep; professors lecture, answer questions, and tend to write illegibly on the chalkboard. These same individuals, however, behave rather differently at parties. Students and professors may drink alcoholic beverages, dance, argue politics, and play idiotic games that they would not even consider in other circumstances. Our motivations for engaging in these rather different sets of behavior are often studied by social psychologists. These psychologists tell us that our behaviors are considerably influenced by both **situational factors** (such as whether we are in the classroom or at a party) and by the **presence** of other people. As just one example, conformity studies conducted by Solomon Asch (1952, 1965) showed that approximately 80% of the subjects he tested conformed to a group decision at least once even though that decision was clearly wrong. When interviewed after the experiment, many subjects indicated that they did not question the group's decision but rather wondered why they differed from the group. These subjects also expressed a strong desire to conform. Studies such as those conducted by Asch indicate that the presence of others whose opinions differ from our own generates within us motivation to conform. Motivation, then, may be analyzed not only at the physiological or individual level but also at the level of groups. Groups can influence our motives and, in conjunction with situational variables, alter the ways in which we behave.

Philosophical Analysis

One final level of analysis should be mentioned. Motivational theory is infused with philosophical assumptions that are often subtle. Theorists sometimes view motivation in a negative way; that is, they see the presence of motivation as an **aversive** state that behavior seeks to overcome. Freud perhaps represents a good example of this particular philosophy of motivation. According to Freud, motivational states create a condition of tension that the individual then seeks to reduce. Further, Freud thought that individuals have little control over the innate conditions that generate this motivational tension, and as a result, the ego must repeatedly control behavior to keep the tension within the id low.

Humanist psychologists present a sharp contrast to the negative view of motivation espoused by Freud. Unlike Freud, who regarded our behavior as the result of strong inner forces of which we are largely unaware, theorists such as Rogers and Maslow have proposed that our behavior is directed toward **self-actualization**. Motivation, from this point of view, is a positive force pushing the individual to become all that she or he can become. I regard the approaches of both Freud and the humanists as examples of philosophical analysis because (1) the descriptions of motivation and its effects depend upon the theorists' philosophy (humans are basically evil versus humans are basically good), and (2) the theories are couched in terms that make them difficult to test experimentally. As a result, one must usually accept or reject their propositions based on the philosophical arguments they provide rather than on empirical data. I do not mean to imply, however, that these approaches should be dismissed because empirical data is less available; I have included them in this text because I believe that they do have something to add to our understanding of motivation.

ANALYSIS OF TERESA'S PROBLEM

Let us return now to the story that began this chapter. Teresa has a weight problem. Why? We can analyze Teresa's problem at any (or all) of the four levels we have just discussed. At the physiological level, Teresa may have a genetic predisposition to gain weight. This could be due to an excess of fat cells or to a metabolic disorder that prevents her from using energy at the same rate as other people. It is even possible, although unlikely, that she may have damage to brain structures that would normally control appetite so that she may be abnormally hungry or lack mechanisms that normally inhibit food intake. At the physiological level of analysis, we would look for the basis of Teresa's problem in physiological changes that have disrupted the processes that normally keep body weight stable.

At the individual level of analysis, we might investigate the possibility that Teresa had learned to overeat when she was anxious. Perhaps as a baby she was given a bottle whenever she cried, regardless of whether she was hungry or not. If Teresa came to associate eating with anxiety that triggered crying and eating reduced her anxiety somewhat (perhaps by making her lethargic or sleepy), then she would repeat the eating behavior whenever she became anxious. As she grew older and was teased by her brothers and playmates and nagged by her mother, the anxiety about her weight could have triggered a terrible cycle in which being heavy leads to anxiety, which in turn leads to eating, which in turn increases weight and, as a result, anxiety. To understand Teresa's problem at the individual level, we would attempt to discover what conditions motivate her to eat. Does she eat in some circumstances but not in others? Does she eat because of anxiety? Do past experiences play a part in her eating problem? Answers to any or all of these questions might provide insight into the reasons for her overeating.

At the social level, we might examine Teresa's family life more closely. Perhaps her mother has always fixed large meals and expects everyone to clean their plates. Teresa may have learned to eat even when she was not hungry because she was not allowed to leave the table until her plate was clean. Because she wanted her mother's approval, she complied and ate when she was not hungry. Now she overeats because she no longer pays attention to her internal state of hunger. Additionally, because Teresa does not have a very good self-image, she may have a strong need to conform. If she is out with others and they eat fattening foods, it could prove very difficult for her to resist doing the same. Other conformity situations may arise within her family. Her brothers, who are physically active, may eat ice cream and cake and other sweets without gaining weight. It will be very difficult for Teresa to avoid desserts if everyone else in the family is eating them. The group analysis of Teresa's problem would look to the interactions she has with her parents, siblings, and peers. Do compliance and conformity play a part in her eating problem? If so, family counseling might prove useful.

From a philosophical point of view such as Freud's, Teresa's problem might be viewed as a result of sexual anxiety. If any type of sexuality is frowned upon in her family, then her normal sexual drives might become locked up in the id and only allowed dissipation (by the ego) through displacement into eating behavior. Or perhaps Teresa did not get enough oral satisfaction during the first year of life and as a result continues to compensate by overeating. The humanist psychologists, on the other hand, might see Teresa's overeating as the result of lack of positive regard. If Teresa's parents led her to believe that she was only loved when she behaved correctly (conditional positive regard), then her tendency toward growth and full functioning would become stunted. Teresa would channel energy normally used for this growth into defenses to protect her self-image from the anxiety resulting from the conditional positive regard. Overeating, then, may be analyzed as the result of distortion of the growth tendency by anxiety.

As you can see, the reasons one might suggest for Teresa's overeating depend, at least in part, on the level of analysis one chooses. In actuality, Teresa's overeating is probably the result of a complex set of physiological, individual, social, and philosophical factors. It is worth noting that even a seemingly simple behavior such as eating can be the result of a terribly complex set of motivational factors.

MAJOR CONSTRUCTS IN MOTIVATION

A number of major constructs are frequently used in motivational theory. An understanding of some of these major constructs can be useful for comparing the different theories because the theories differ in regard to the way these constructs are handled.

Energy

Many of the theories discussed in this book assume the existence of some source of energy that drives behavior. Some theorists have proposed that just one source of energy exists for all behavior, that the energy behind behavior is **general**. Assumptions of a general energy source require the existence of some additional mechanism that can direct this energy in different ways at different times. Other researchers have proposed that the force behind particular behaviors is **specific**. For these theorists the energy-activating behavior can also serve a directing function because each behavior has its own energy source. During hunger, for example, food-getting behavior would be activated and directed, while water-directed behaviors would occur during thirst.

While some motivational theories do not explicitly postulate a source of energy for behavior, such a source is implied by many theories. Several theorists have proposed that an energy concept is unnecessary and that one can understand the motivation of behavior without having to assume some energy existing behind behavior. Thus the concept of energy is more important in some theories than in others.

Heredity

Several different mechanisms have been proposed as constructs to help explain motivation. One general approach has been to assume that such motivational mechanisms are genetically programmed or "wired in" to the organism. This biological approach has usually taken one of two forms.

The **instinct** approach proposes that energy accumulates within the organism and leads to a motivated state. Preprogrammed behaviors then occur to reduce the motivation. The triggering of these "wired-in" behaviors is usually attributed to specific stimuli in the environment that have the effect of releasing the behavior.

The second biological approach proposes that circuits within the brain **monitor** the state of the body and activate behaviors when changes are detected. The activation of these circuits then leads to the motivation of responses, which may be either innate or learned.

Learning

The role of learning in motivated behavior has also been important. Clark Hull developed a theory in the 1940s that outlined the interrelationships of learning and motivation in generating behavior. Later theorists have stressed the role of incentives in controlling goal-directed behavior. Research has also examined the ways in which classical and operant conditioning may be involved in the development of motive states. Some motives also seem to be learned through observation; this process, termed **modeling**, may be the basis for much of human motivation behavior.

Social Interaction

Our interactions with others can also be motivating. Research in social psychology has pointed to the power of the group in motivating us to conform and to the power of authority figures in motivating us to obey. Also, the presence of others often reduces the likelihood that an individual will provide help in an emergency situation. Social situations have a large influence on our behavior because the presence of others alters our motivation.

Cognitive Processes

The role of cognitive processes in motivation has become increasingly recognized. The kinds of information we take in and the ways in which that information is processed have important influences on our behavior. Theories such as Heider's balance theory, Festinger's cognitive dissonance theory, and Bem's self-perception theory emphasize the role of **active information processing** (i.e., thinking) in the control of behavior.

Attribution theory had also emphasized the role of cognition in the interpretation of others' (and our own) behaviors and indicates that our behavior will, to a large extent, be based on these interpretations.

The Activation of Motivation

Another major construct of motivational theory concerns the triggering of motivation. Research in this area has investigated the mechanisms that monitor the state of the organism and that trigger motivation when the body is out of balance. Early theories emphasized the role of **peripheral** (also called **local**) receptors in the monitoring of physical states. Thus an empty, cramping stomach or a dry mouth were thought to be the cues that told an individual that he or she was hungry or thirsty.

As evidence against the local theories accumulated, emphasis shifted to the **central** receptors in the brain that monitor conditions such as blood glucose or blood osmolarity, which might trigger appropriate motivational states. For some theorists the emphasis has begun to shift again back to the periphery with the discovery of stomach, intestine, and liver receptors that seem to monitor specific conditions.

Though the debate over the location of the receptors that monitor bodily states is far from resolved, there may actually be several monitoring systems, some located in the internal organs of the body and others in the brain.

Homeostasis

Theorists have also presented differing views regarding the purpose for motivation. Perhaps the most commonly accepted purpose is to maintain **homeostasis** (i.e., the idea that an optimal level exists for various states of the body). When the body deviates too far from this optimal level, motivational circuits are triggered by the receptors monitoring these states, and behaviors that will bring the body back to its optimal level are begun. Certainly, some motive states seem homeostatic. Others, however, are not easily explained by the concept of homeostasis.

Hedonism

Perhaps the oldest explanation for the purpose of motivated behavior is the idea of **hedonism**, which assumes that we are motivated by pleasure and pain. We learn to approach situations that are pleasurable and similarly learn to avoid situations that are painful. Modern hedonistic explanations propose that pleasure and pain exist along a continuum and that what is pleasurable (or painful) will change as conditions change. For example, the offer of a seven-course dinner immediately after one has finished a large meal is not pleasurable.

Though hedonism may explain some motive states, it does not provide a satisfactory explanation for motivations that result in self-destructive or self-painful behaviors.

Growth Motivation

The third major approach to understanding the purpose of motivation is the concept of growth motivation. Growth motivation stresses the idea that humans are motivated to reach their full potential—physically, psychologically, and emotionally. Rogers discusses this growth motivation in relation to the fully functioning individual, while Maslow uses the term **self-actualization** to describe the motivation to strive for personal fulfillment.

One aspect of growth motivation is the need to control or have an effect on our environment. This has been called **effectance motivation** by some and **personal causation** by others. By whatever name, all growth motivation theories suggest that humans are strongly motivated to test and improve their capacities.

PHILOSOPHICAL AND PHYSIOLOGICAL ROOTS OF MOTIVATIONAL THEORY

Modern psychology is the product of philosophical thought that can be traced back to Greek philosophers such as Aristotle and to developments within the study of physiology, many of which occurred between 1800 and 1850 (Boring, 1950). These two approaches to understanding heavily influenced early psychological thought and indeed continue to influence our understanding of psychological processes today. As will become clearer, the study of motivation is a complex blend of philosophical and physiological concepts. While some theorists have attempted to understand motivation almost exclusively from the point of view of physiology, others have approached it from a more philosophical direction (see Chapter Twelve). Both philosophy and physiology have much to offer psychologists who attempt to unravel the complex motives that activate and direct human behavior. It is important, therefore, to briefly review some ideas within philosophy and physiology that have influenced modern psychological thought.

Philosophical Antecedents

Aristotle The Greek philosopher Aristotle proposed two important ideas that even today continue to have an influence within the study of motivation. Aristotle argued that the *soul is free* and that the mind at birth is a *blank slate* (Boring, 1950). Aristotle's first idea is often contrasted to the idea of **determinism**, which proposes that all behavior is the result of conditions that precede the behavior. (In psychology these preceding conditions are known as **antecedent variables**.)

Each of us has some opinion about the free will versus determinism controversy, but psychology, for the most part, has chosen to disagree with Aristotle and embrace determinism. Determinism as it applies to psychology assumes that every behavior has a cause. If behavior Y occurs, some antecedent condition X must have caused it. Thus if I observe someone eating, I might assume that an antecedent condition called hunger led to the eating behavior. Though the antecedent conditions that determine behavior are often not observable, psychology nevertheless assumes that some previous condition caused those responses to occur. The concept of motivation is often proposed as the antecedent condition

that leads to responding. This deterministic point of view is necessary if one is to study behavior.

Suppose for a moment that behavior is truly free (random) and not the result of antecedent conditions. If this were so, it would be impossible to study behavior because no rules could be developed for predicting when certain behaviors would occur. In fact, though most of us entertain the idea of free will, we do not usually assume that either our own behavior or that of others is random, for we often ask such questions as "Why did she do that?" or "Why did he do that to me?" Such questions imply that behavior is caused and therefore deterministic.

Students are often perplexed by determinism because they feel it allows them no freedom to choose how to behave. But the assumption that determinism denies one the ability to make a choice is mistaken. For example, I decided to write about the influence of philosophy on motivational theory this afternoon rather than work on my still unfinished patio. At one level of analysis, I would seem to have free will because I chose to write instead of working on my patio. My choice, however, was influenced by several antecedent conditions, such as deadlines for getting the manuscript prepared, how long it had been since I last sat down to write, and so forth. Though I subjectively feel that I chose to write this afternoon, my choice was actually determined by those antecedent conditions. People who know me well might have predicted that I would engage in writing rather than work on the patio if they also knew the antecedent conditions. Thus, although we have freedom to choose, our choices are ultimately determined by antecedent conditions associated with those choices.

Though modern psychology has generally chosen determinism over free will, Aristotle's idea that the mind is a blank slate (upon which experience writes) had a tremendous influence on psychological theory. Aristotle's concept led to the proposal that most behaviors are learned. The acquisition of behavior through experience is one side of a longstanding argument in psychology known as the **nature-nurture controversy**. Psychologists who accepted Aristotle's premise believed that experience (nurture) is the major force in the development of behavior. In opposition to the nurture psychologists, others proposed that much of our behavior is programmed into us by heredity (nature). This latter group argued that nature provides ready-made behaviors that are executed when conditions are appropriate. Psychological thought on the nature-nurture problem has alternated back and forth several times, and the controversy has never been resolved to everyone's satisfaction. Most psychologists today, however, recognize that both sides were right; behavior is a combination of both nature and nurture.

The nature-nurture controversy is important to the study of motivation because both nature and nurture play roles in the activation of motive states. As you will discover in later chapters, some motives seem best understood as the result of genetically programmed sequences, while others are clearly learned. Further, motivation may also result from a complex blend of nature and nurture.

Descartes   Aristotle, of course, was only one of many philosophers who influenced psychological thought. René Descartes was equally influential. Descartes is best known for his arguments concerning the dualistic nature of humans. **Dualism** proposes that human behavior is partly the result of a free, rational soul and partly the result of automatic, nonrational processes of the body. Humans, being the only possessors of souls, are motivated by both the soul (motives of this type were often called **will**) and the body (motives of this type

were later attributed to **instinct**). Animals, however, have no souls and are therefore essentially **automatons** (mechanical beings). This mechanistic approach and Descartes's proposal of **innate ideas** (a view similar to Plato's) became one basis for the instinct psychology that was popular around the turn of the twentieth century. Thus in many respects the nature-nurture controversy can be seen as an outgrowth of the philosophies of Aristotle and Descartes.

Locke   Before we leave this necessarily brief exposition of the philosophical roots of motivation, we need to examine some contributions of the British school of philosophy. Two ideas proposed by British philosophers became especially important for psychology. These two ideas concern the importance of sensory experience and the association of ideas. We shall consider the philosophy of John Locke as representative of the British approach, although there were many other noted philosophers within this same framework. Locke proposed that ideas are the elementary units of the mind (Boring, 1950). Further, he thought that these ideas come from experience (nurture again) in one of two ways. One source of ideas is the conversion of **sensation** into **perception**. For example, the conversion of the sensation of light of 521 nanometers leads to the perception of the color green. The idea of green, then, results from experience with particular wavelengths of light, namely, those near 521 nanometers. The second source of ideas, according to Locke, is **reflection**, which occurs when the mind obtains knowledge of its own operations. Thus one can generate ideas from sensory information or from understanding *how* one manipulates and works with ideas. This second source amounts to "ideas about ideas and the manner of their occurrence" (Boring, 1950, p. 172).

Ideas, according to Locke, can be *simple* or *complex*. Because a simple idea is the elementary unit of thought, it is not further analyzable, but a complex idea can be reduced to simple ideas. The concept of complex ideas composed of simple ideas leads naturally to a concept of association. Complex ideas are nothing more than the association of simple ideas to one another. The concept of association is one of the most fundamental axioms within psychology. For example, the association of stimulus to stimulus, stimulus to response, response to response, and response to reward have all been offered as the basis for learning. Associationism is equally important to motivation because many motives, especially those peculiar to humans, appear to be learned through association. These "higher" motives are often quite complex but are assumed to gain their motivating properties through earlier association with more basic motives. Through repeated association these motives can become so strong that the more basic motives with which they were originally paired are no longer necessary. The independence of these higher motives appears similar to Allport's (1937) concept of **functional autonomy**.

Other philosophical approaches have contributed to our understanding of motivation, many more than we have time to consider here. (For the student interested in the philosophical underpinnings of psychology, Boring [1950] is still one of the best references.) It is time to move on to a brief look at discoveries in physiology that have also affected motivational thought.

Physiological Antecedents

Sensory and Motor Nerves   Modern conceptions of the role of brain mechanisms in motivation are largely outgrowths of discoveries about how the nervous system gains information and controls behavior. At one time it was thought that nerves allowed the flow of animal spirits from one part of the body to another. The concept of reflex and its close companion, instinct, are outgrowths of the idea that animal spirits coming from the sense organs along one pathway are sent back to the muscles along a separate pathway (Boring, 1950). Galen (ca. A.D. 129–199) had correctly guessed that separate **sensory and motor nerves** must exist, but more than 600 years passed before Charles Bell (1811, as cited by Boring, 1950) was able to show that the sensory fibers of a mixed nerve enter the spinal cord on the posterior side, while the motor fibers exit the cord on the anterior side. In 1822 Magendie made the discovery independent of Bell (Boring, 1950). The discovery of separate sensory and motor fibers led to the study of sensation on one hand and responses on the other. Indeed one might argue that the stimulus-response analysis of behavior, once so popular in psychology, could not exist before this fundamental fact of physiology was known.

Specific Nerve Energies   Once sensory and motors fibers were shown to exist, it was only a short intellectual step to the realization that different fibers must carry different kinds of information. This idea, usually associated with Müller, eventually became known as the **doctrine of specific nerve energies** (Boring, 1950) and was important (1) because it implied that the nerves send specific coded messages rather than allowing for the flow of animal spirits and (2) that these codes determine the content of the information (for example, different energies for different colors, tones, and so on). Thus the nervous system becomes an active, interpreting mechanism rather than a passive conduit for ill-defined and mysterious vapors.

Electrical Nature of the Nerve Impulse   In 1780 Galvani had discovered that a frog's leg could be made to twitch when the muscle of the leg was connected to what amounted to a primitive battery (Boring, 1950). Galvani's experiment suggested that the energy passing through a nerve might be electrical in nature, and somewhat later (1848–1849), du Bois-Reymond used a galvanometer to show that the energy passing along the nerve is indeed electrical. Helmholtz measured the speed of this electrical wave down a nerve and found it to be less than 100 miles per hour. As noted by Boring (1950), Helmholtz's discovery showed that it is possible to study the function of the nervous system through experimental procedures.

Localization of Function Sometimes theories are important for the development of a science even though they are ultimately proven wrong. One such case was the phrenology of Gall in the early 1800s. Gall proposed the idea that particular mental abilities are located in specific regions of the brain. Any excess in a particular ability would lead to an enlargement of that portion of the brain, and as a result, a bump would be created on the skull. According to Gall, one could determine a person's special abilities by feeling the bumps on his or her head (see Figure 1.4). Though Gall's ideas concerning the "reading" of a person's abilities from the bumps on his or her head have been thoroughly discredited, his ideas did promote the further examination of the **localization of function** within various areas of the brain. Today we know a great deal about the function of specific areas of the brain, and motivational theory has been strengthened by the discovery that activity within the **hypothalamus** (a region within the brain) is related to changes in motivational state. Even though Gall's phrenology is no longer useful, his emphasis on the study of the localization of function within the brain has been very important.

The study of motivation, as you can see, has roots in both philosophy and physiology. Further, motivation has been analyzed both as an act of the will and as the result of activity in specialized brain centers. In Part II of this book we examine theories that have emphasized the biological or physiological aspects of motivation. In Part III we examine theories that have emphasized the role of experience, while in Part IV we examine social motivation and approaches that are more philosophical in nature. Rogers and Maslow, for example, have both proposed theories of motivation that are more philosophical than experimental. The complex nature of motivation has resulted in the development of theories from many differing points of view. As we shall see, there is room within motivational theory for physiological, experiential, and philosophical approaches.

THE FLOW OF IDEAS ABOUT MOTIVATION

In order to better understand some of the topics examined later in this book, it is useful to take a brief look at how concepts about motivation have changed across time.

As we have just seen, modern motivational theory is rooted in earlier philosophical ideas and physiological discoveries. One final historical note, about the changing perspectives researchers have taken over the last 100 years, is worthy of our examination. In the 1800s it was common to distinguish between the behavior of animals and humans using Descartes's dualistic distinction. Animals, having no rationality, were instinctively motivated to behave in appropriate ways, whereas humans, having both rationality and instinctive motives, might behave as a result of either of these mechanisms.

In the late 1800s theorists such as William

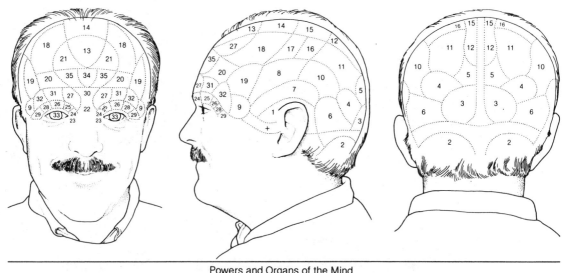

Powers and Organs of the Mind			
Affective	9. Constructiveness	19. Ideality	26. Coloring
	II. Sentiments	20. Mirthfulness	27. Locality
I. Propensities	10. Cautiousness	21. Imitation	28. Order
1. Destructiveness	11. Approbativeness		29. Calculation
2. Amativeness	12. Self-esteem	Intellectual	30. Eventuality
3. Philoprogenitiveness	13. Benevolence		31. Time
4. Adhesiveness	14. Reverence	I. Perceptive	32. Tune
5. Inhabitiveness	15. Firmness	22. Individuality	33. Language
6. Combativeness	16. Conscientiousness	23. Configuration	II. Reflective
7. Secretiveness	17. Hope	24. Size	34. Comparison
8. Acquisitiveness	18. Marvelousness	25. Weight and Resistance	35. Causality

Figure 1.4 *A phrenology chart showing the locations of presumed abilities. (Adapted from Spurzheim 1908.)*

James (1890) and William McDougall (1970) argued that much of human behavior could be regarded as instinctive, thus playing down the mentalistic concept of a rational soul or will. Behaviorists beginning with John Watson (1914), while for the most part rejecting the instinct notion in favor of a learning analysis, also vehemently opposed what they considered the mentalistic approaches common to psychology at that time. As a result, in the early 1900s a strong behaviorist position developed that emphasized the idea that behavior was largely a reaction to the environment and **S-R (stimulus-response)** psychology was born. Thorndike's

(1913) studies of the importance of the consequences of a response to future behavior were a strong argument in favor of the S-R type of analysis.

The motivation of behavior, then, could be argued to result from the **consequences** of previous behavior: pleasurable consequences would be sought again, while aversive consequences would be avoided if possible. The behaviorism of the early 1900s was, in many ways, a return to the concept of hedonism espoused by some Greek philosophers more than 2,000 years earlier. The behaviorists, however, had experimental data to show that behaviors did indeed change as a result of their consequences.

By the end of the 1920s the instinct theories of James and others had been roundly criticized and largely rejected (although as we shall discover, this rejection was probably premature). Behaviorism was the dominant theme in psychology, and a new motivational concept, known as **drive theory**, was touted as the primary motivational concept. The drive concept, first introduced by Woodworth (1918), proposed that motivated behavior was in response to changing bodily needs that were acted upon by finding those items in the environment that would reduce the drive.

Drive theory reached its zenith of popularity with the publications of Clark Hull (1943, 1951, 1952). Hull proposed a quasi-mathematical theory that indicated the crucial components for the activation of behavior and how these components interacted to produce behavior. In addition, Hull's theory provided the groundwork for analyzing the contribution of learning to motivation and was partially responsible (as was Tolman and his colleagues) for the eventual development of the concept of incentive motivation.

Eventually Hull's theory was shown to be inadequate, but the research spawned by the search for the basis of drive led to a greater understanding of how brain mechanisms control, and learning influences, behavior. Indeed, much of the initial physiological research on motivation was a search for the physiological basis of various drive states.

Although behaviorism was the dominant theme in psychology until about 1960, some psychologists took exception to the strong S-R bias during this time. Researchers such as Köhler (1925) and Tolman (1932) argued, and provided experimental data, for an analysis of behavior based on the active processing of information, rather than S-R connections. These forerunners of modern cognitive psychology led the way for those who came later to examine motivation as resulting from an organism's ability to anticipate future events, choose between alternatives, and act in a purposive way.

This alternative view of motivation has proven fruitful in a number of ways. Research on the motivational consequences of attributions of cause-effect has led to a greater understanding of behaviors associated with the need to achieve, fear of success, and even emotion. Similarly, research on the purposive and goal-oriented nature of motivated behavior has led to the development of **expectancy-value theory**, a concept that has proven useful in understanding achievement behavior, social learning, and motivation in the workplace.

The changing approaches to motivation that have occurred during the last 100 years have molded the way motivation is studied today. Motivational research today may be conveniently divided into three major areas: the biological, the behavioral, and the cognitive. The **biological** approach continues to try to understand the physical underpinnings of motivated behavior; it is the legacy of both the early instinct approaches and drive theory. The **behavioral** approach examines the relation of motivation to other concepts such as learning in the activation of motivated behavior. The concepts of drive, incentive motivation, and learned motives are the central concern of the behavioral approach. The **cognitive** approach encompasses a loosely connected group of concepts which have in common the assumption that organisms can act in purposive ways to pursue anticipated goals. Areas of motivational research that fall within the cognitive approach are expectancy-value theory, consistency theory, self-perception theory, social-learning theory, actualization theories, and attribution theory.

The remainder of this text will examine in some detail each of the three major motivational areas of research. We will first examine theory and research on the biological nature of some motives. This section will be followed by an analysis of theory and research on the behaviorist contributions to motivation. Finally, the book will conclude by examining cognitive theory and research on motivation.

THE AUTHOR'S BIAS

It is important at the outset for the reader to understand my own point of view, because the rest of the book will reflect my personal bias to a greater or lesser extent. From my vantage point, no one theory can explain all the data on motivation. Explanations of hunger will differ from explanations of achievement. I think it is naive to believe that one comprehensive theory can explain all motivational states. The reason for my belief is, quite simply, that motivation is multiply determined. The processes that undergird the physiologically important motives are different from the processes that undergird psychological motives.

Motivation is also, in my opinion, overdetermined. Like a NASA rocket, the human body has "backup systems" that come into play if one mechanism fails. One example of this is seen in a rat that has been lesioned in its ventromedial hypothalamus. After destruction of this part of the brain, the rat eats and eats and eats, sometimes increasing its weight by 100%. It does not, however, eat until it explodes. At some point, a new stable body weight (albeit obese) is reached, and its weight becomes regulated around this new point. The apparent conclusion is that a second mechanism regulating body weight at the new, higher level has become activated.

The approach of this book, then, is eclectic. I will present the various approaches and point out both their basic assumptions and basic problems. Cited research will be representative of these various approaches. I will not attempt an exhaustive review of any particular research literature because that is not the purpose of this book. Extensive reviews can be found in various journals (e.g., *Psychological Bulletin, Psychological Review*), as well as in the *Annual Review of Psychology* and more specialized texts.

Because motivation cuts across so many different subfields within psychology, its study often seems rather disjointed, with the various theories having little relationship to one another. Although such a perception is in some cases at least partially correct, the unity of motivation as a field of study comes from attempting to determine how these differing motivational factors (biological, behavioral, cognitive) interact to produce behavior. In an attempt to provide a unifying theme to the studies within this text, I will include in appropriate chapters information about sexual and aggressive motivation as understood from the point of view of theories within those chapters. I hope that, as a result, readers will understand that every motivated behavior has many components and only when we understand these various components, and how they interact, can we hope to understand why people behave as they do.

SUGGESTIONS FOR FURTHER READING

Boring, E. G. (1950). *A History of experimental psychology*. New York: Appleton-Century-Crofts. This is still one of the best references for understanding the relationship of psychology to philosophy and physiology.

Kalat, J. W. (1981). *Biological psychology*. Belmont, Calif.: Wadsworth. Excellent introduction to philosophical considerations of physiological psychology in Chapter 2.

II

BIOLOGICAL APPROACHES TO MOTIVATION

Chapter Two

Genetic Contributions to Motivated Behavior

CHAPTER PREVIEW

This chapter is concerned with the following questions:

1. How did motivated behavior develop?

2. Are some motives genetic?

3. What did early instinct theories emphasize?

4. How do modern instinct theories explain behavior?

5. Do humans have instincts?

As I walk down the hall toward my office, I noticed a group of students talking near the exit. Upon hearing my footsteps, they glance my way. Three of them, whom I do not know, return their attention to their friends. The fourth, a student who attended one of my classes last semester, smiles, briefly raises his eyebrow, then also returns his attention to the conversations.

This brief encounter can be used to illustrate the major thrust of this chapter, which is that some motivated behaviors are instinctive. Considerable research on the instinctive components of behavior has been conducted by a group of biologists who call themselves **ethologists.** Though most of this research has used birds, fish, and other nonhuman animals as subjects, some research on human instinctive behavior has been conducted. This research indicates that some of the hallway behaviors mentioned are instinctive.

For example, Eibl-Eibesfeldt (1972) has found that when one human recognizes another as familiar, a set pattern of behaviors occurs. A person recognizing someone as familiar smiles and briefly raises the eyebrows. These behaviors serve as a signal to the other person that he or she has been recognized as familiar; usually that person responds by also smiling and briefly raising the eyebrows. Eibl-Eibesfeldt has found that this greeting ceremony is universal across all the cultures (both primitive and advanced) that he studied. It is a bit of genetically preprogrammed behavior that communicates recognition between humans and probably also serves to reduce the possible threat involved in approaching someone.

In this chapter we will examine the various instinctive explanations for motivated behavior that have been proposed. We will begin by examining the concept of evolution as it applies to motivated behavior and then proceed to examine early instinct approaches.

EVOLUTION

Evolution can be defined as the progressive change of organisms across time (Solbrig, 1966). The theory of evolution is usually credited to Charles Darwin (1899), though Alfred Wallace independently developed the same idea. Both men presented papers on the topic at the same meeting in 1858. Richard Dawkins (1976) has noted that the theory of evolution is really another way of expressing the idea that those elements that are the most stable will continue to exist. Some members of a group of organisms will be less able to cope with the rigors of the environment in which they live and will thus die. Other members of the group will be better adapted to the environment and will be able to survive and therefore pass on their characteristics to the succeeding generation.

The environment is important in determining which members of a group survive. Through a process that Darwin termed **natural selection,** the environment influences the progression of genetic change. Those individuals who inherited genes that give them an advantage in the environment will live long enough to reproduce, while those with inherited genes that put them at a disadvantage will die, and the disadvantageous genes will be removed from the characteristics of the species.

Obviously all of this is basically a random process. We cannot select the genes we possess; that is determined at the moment of conception. Natural selection is entirely a mechanical process that has the effect of altering species over time as the conditions of the environment change.

Evolution not only influences the physical characteristics of an individual but also influences behavior. Genes that control the development of certain types of behavior will be exposed to natural selection in the same way as any other characteristic. For example, the behavior of a mother hen running to a chick that is making distress calls is advantageous for both the chick and the species. Natural selection works toward behaviors that increase the survival of the organism. Hens that lack the genes controlling this behavior would be likely to lose chicks to predators or to the elements; over a period of time, therefore, the behavior of not responding to a chick in distress would be eliminated along with the chickens lacking those genes.

The point of course is that natural selection will lead to the survival of organisms that cope best with their environment. Thus genes that control the expressions of particular behaviors will be continued in a species if the behaviors expressed are adaptive.

Not all behaviors are genetically determined. Many are learned through interactions of the organism with its environment during its lifetime. These behaviors are not passed on to the next generation because genes are not altered by experience. However, the ability to learn new behaviors during one's lifetime must surely be genetically determined. The ability to learn has enabled some organisms to survive because it makes them more adaptable to possible change in their environment. Thus we can see that even the ability to learn must have a genetic basis.

What all this means is that some types of behaviors may be genetically determined, such as a moth's attraction to light (called **positive phototaxis**), while other behaviors may be the result of experience, such as remembering where you last found food. Motivated behaviors, therefore, might be expected to include both types (i.e., either relatively fixed and rigid or relatively flexible and open to modification), and indeed blends of both types might also be predicted.

Genetically motivated behaviors have

often been analyzed under the topic of instinct. An instinct can be regarded as a genetically programmed bit of behavior that occurs when circumstances are appropriate and that requires no learning of the behavior. As we shall see, early instinct approaches were often vague; but later instinct theories, such as those of the ethologists, have been much more carefully and clearly defined.

EARLY INSTINCT THEORIES

Instinct as an explanation for motivated behavior in both humans and animals reached its peak of popularity in the late 1800s and early 1900s. Beach (1955) noted that the popularity of the concept was due in part to its use as a theoretical bridge between humans and animals. This bridge was important for any development of the idea that evolution applied to both humans and animals and to both physical structure and mind. Thus, for some theorists, animals were seen as having some rationality in addition to instinctive behaviors, and humans were seen as having some instinctively controlled behavior in addition to a rational mind.

As the concept of instinct grew in popularity, attempts to "explain" all behaviors as instinctive became fashionable. This led to what has been called the **nominal fallacy** (i.e., that simply naming something an instinct does not explain the behavior). For example, if we saw someone behaving aggressively, we might try to "explain" that behavior in terms of an aggressive instinct. The problem, however, is that we really have not explained anything; we have merely labeled the behavior we observed. To explain the behavior, we must do more than label it. We must understand what conditions led to the behavior and what consequences resulted from it. Explanation presumes a cause-and-effect relationship, and labeling a behavior does not give causal information.

Also, instinctive behaviors were not clearly separated from learned behaviors because a confusion of definition existed. These problems, along with several others, eventually led to virtual elimination of the instinct concept.

Nevertheless, the early instinct approaches were important because they emphasized the continuity of human and animal behavior and because they provided a base from which the later ethological theories could build. They also helped develop the modern theories of instinctive behavior through their mistakes. The problems they encountered eventually brought the definitions and study of instinct to much more careful and narrow refinement.

To gain some feeling for these early approaches, we will now examine the instinct theories of William James and William McDougall, noting similarities between them and also problems in their approaches.

James

William James, whose writing spanned both philosophical and psychological thought, believed that instincts are similar to reflexes, are elicited by sensory stimuli, and occur blindly the first time (James, 1890). To James, "occurring blindly" meant that the behavior occurs automatically under the appropriate conditions and without knowledge of the end or goal toward which the behavior leads. He argued that "every instinct is an impulse," which puts instinct squarely into the domain of motivation (i.e., a force acting on or within the organism to initiate behavior). Though James believed that the first occurrence of an instinct is blind, he felt that memory interacts with instincts so that subsequent behavior is no longer blind; in other words, he believed that instinctive behavior changes through experience. He maintained that an instinct is not uniform but is only a tendency to act in a particular way (although, on the average, the resulting behavior will be relatively constant).

Thus, for James, the instinct of "modesty" might cause one to blush and turn away automatically if one accidentally stumbles into a nude sunbather on a beach. On the other hand, one who frequents nude bathing beaches might no longer automatically blush or turn away but might become blasé about nudity, so that one's "modesty instinct" would then be **inhibited** (i.e., held back) by experience. At any rate, this somewhat exaggerated example indicates the idea that instincts for James could be altered by experience.

James explained the variability of instincts through two principles. The first principle stated that habit (i.e., learning) can inhibit an instinct. The second principle proposed that some instincts are transitory, useful only at certain times or during certain developmental periods. James proposed that learning may inhibit an instinct by restricting the range of objects involved in an instinctive activity. Thus learning was thought to limit the extent to which an instinct can develop or be used. For example, the triggering of the instinct of fear by a teacher might lead to a student's poor academic performance—because another instinct, such as inquisitiveness, could become blocked (by learning) or limited to nonacademic situations. The transitory nature of instincts implies that some instincts are only present at a specific time in development and then become inactive, such as when a newly hatched chick learns to follow the first moving object it sees during its first day of life but runs away from a moving object after the first day. These two principles proposed by James were important forerunners of the ethological concepts of critical period and imprinting, which will be detailed later in this chapter.

James saw instinctive behavior as intermediate between reflexes and learning, shading into each at the extremes. Unlike some of his contemporaries, James did not propose to explain all behavior through instinctive processes. In his view instincts provide a base upon which experience can build through the development of habits. The concept of instinct was not reserved just for nonhuman animals. James believed that people possess all the instincts of other animals plus many exclusively human ones. He proposed a classification of human instincts that included the following:

rivalry	curiosity
pugnacity	sociability
sympathy	shyness
hunting	secretiveness
fear	cleanliness
acquisitiveness	modesty
constructiveness	jealousy
play	parental love

James thought that by describing various instincts and how these might have been adaptive during the evolution of humans, he was explaining how behavior is motivated. Unfortunately, he did not clearly describe how one could distinguish between a reflex, an instinct, and a learned behavior.

McDougall

William McDougall was a theorist who viewed instincts somewhat differently from James. Writing around the turn of the century, McDougall did not view instincts as basically reflexive because he believed that *all* behavior is instinctive. He felt that the primary task of the psychologist is to discover and classify the various instincts in order to understand motivation.

McDougall argued that instincts are more than just dispositions to react in a particular way. He saw every instinct as consisting of three components: the **cognitive**, the **affec-**

tive, and the **conative** (McDougall, 1970). The cognitive aspect of the instinct is the "knowing" of an object that can satisfy the instinct. The affective component is the feeling (i.e., emotion) that the object arouses in the organism. The conative aspect of the instinct is a striving toward or away from the object. Therefore every behavior consists of (1) thoughts concerning those goals that will satisfy the motive, (2) subjective emotions that are aroused by the behavior, and (3) purposive striving aimed at reaching the goal. Using McDougall's approach, we would expect that a hungry rat would have some understanding of an object that would satisfy its hunger, would show an emotional arousal when hungry, and would strive persistently toward obtaining the object that would relieve its hunger.

McDougall saw striving toward a goal as an example of the purposiveness of instinctive behavior. He believed that one can identify the activated instinct by determining the goal toward which the behavior is directed. For example, if one observes a monkey actively attempting to take apart a puzzle made of interlocking blocks, one can conclude that the behavior aroused was the instinct of curiosity. Such an analysis is said to be teleological. **Teleology** is the idea that a behavior serves some ultimate purpose. While this type of explanation is not entirely unreasonable for humans who can foresee or predict where their behavior is likely to lead, it has not been a very popular explanation for animal behavior; and many theorists, including Freud, have argued that even humans are often largely unaware of the reasons for their behavior.

Like James, McDougall compiled a long list of instinctive behaviors. Some of these include the following:

parental care	sympathy
combat	self-assertion
curiosity	submission
food seeking	mating
repulsion	constructiveness
escape	appeal
gregariousness	

According to McDougall, an instinct can be altered in four ways. First, an instinct may be activated not only by some specific external object but also by the *idea* of that object or by other external objects or their ideas. Thus the kinds of objects or ideas that might elicit an instinct could change. For example, milk might initially activate food seeking in the infant. As the child grows, other foods would also activate this instinct, as would the thought of food. In fact, a good TV commercial might lead one to think of what is in the refrigerator and thus to the activation of food-seeking behavior (there are of course other valid explanations for this chain of events).

Second, the movements through which the instinctive behavior occurs can be modified. The instinct of curiosity might initially involve exploring one's local environment, as when an infant crawls about the room. Later this same instinct might be satisfied by reading in the sciences. Though the curiosity instinct remained, the behaviors involved in its expression changed.

Third, several instincts may be triggered simultaneously, and the resulting behavior will be a blend of the excited instincts. Thus McDougall might argue that the sexual behavior of teenagers is a blend of curiosity and mating instincts, and the "petting" that occurs is a compromise behavior reflecting both of these instincts. Contemporary theorists, as we will see later, have argued that such situations may lead to ambivalent behaviors (Burghardt, 1973) or to displacement behaviors (Tinbergen, 1951).

Finally, instinctive behaviors may become organized around particular objects or ideas and thus become less responsive in other situations. For example, people may sometimes be self-assertive (an instinct, according to McDougall) in their jobs but submissive (also an instinct) at home, so that the instinctive behavior occurs only in certain situations. In some respects this is similar to Freud's concept of fixation.

McDougall's method of analysis was very **anthropomorphic**. He believed he could infer the feelings of other organisms by asking himself how he would feel in similar circumstances. For example, if McDougall saw a dog licking the wounds of another, he might conclude that the first dog was feeling sympathy for the second. Anthropomorphism (i.e., the attribution of human characteristics to objects or animals) is very common in our everyday thinking. For example, the person who says "my cat feels guilty for killing the robin" is being anthropomorphic. Whether the cat experiences guilt in the human sense is questionable. Guilt may not even be experienced in animals other than humans. Anthropomorphism is generally recognized today as an inadequate method of analysis. In fact experimenters go to great extremes to avoid biasing their studies with their own subjective experiences.

In addition to the problem of anthropomorphism, McDougall (like James) did not clearly distinguish between instinct and learning. In many cases the two concepts overlapped (as in modifiable instincts), and this led to confusion. This was not a problem, of course, as far as McDougall himself was concerned, because he believed that all behavior is instinctive.

Criticisms of the Early Instinct Theories

Kuo (1921) attempted to destroy the concept of instinct completely in an article titled "Giving Up Instincts in Psychology." Of the several criticisms he leveled at the instinct concept,

among the most important are the following three. First, he wrote, there is no agreement concerning what types of or how many instincts exist. He maintained that compiled lists of instincts are arbitrary and depend upon each writer's interests. Second, Kuo argued that behaviors called instinctive are not innate but learned. He felt that behavior is built from random responses, some of which are reinforced and retained, others of which are unreinforced and extinguished. He felt that psychologists like McDougall were guilty of ignoring the responses that had to be learned in order to reach the goal toward which the behavior is directed. Finally, Kuo insisted that instincts are not the motive forces underlying behavior because behavior is aroused by external stimuli. By his emphasis on the external control of behavior, Kuo rejected the assumptions made by the instinctivists that behaviors are largely the result of genetic programming. Kuo felt strongly that the instinct concept had little usefulness, and he argued persuasively that the concept ought to be dropped.

Tolman (1923) also carefully reviewed the concept of instinct and pointed out several criticisms. Unlike Kuo, however, Tolman felt that the concept could be saved if the criticisms he noted could be met. First, Tolman noted that the arbitrary designation of behaviors as instinctive robs the concept of any explanatory value. In other words, instincts such as curiosity, playfulness, and pugnacity are merely descriptive labels that do not explain the causes of the behavior. Second, no clear criteria exist for determining which behaviors are instinctive and which are not. Theorists, quite simply, had not bothered to state clearly how one could identify an instinctive behavior. Third, the concept, as presented, sounds very similar to Plato's doctrine of innate ideas (i.e., the concept that all knowledge is present in every individual and only awaits discovery). Tolman noted, however, that this is not a valid criticism because instinctive behavior may have evolved to such an extent that it now appears intelligent (i.e., the organism has some foresight of the goals toward which it strives). Finally, he pointed out the confusion between instincts and habits (i.e., learning) that we have already seen in the theories of James and McDougall.

Tolman believed that the instinct concept could be saved by reconstructing it in behavioral rather than subjective terms. His emphasis was on the behavioral ends toward which the behavior is directed; he believed that those ends (i.e., goals) are fixed or instinctive but that the means of obtaining them can vary and are thus modifiable through learning. Therefore, behaving in order to get food when hungry is instinctive, but the behavior necessary to obtain the food is flexible and learned.

Unfortunately for the original instinct concept, the criticisms of Kuo, Tolman, and others proved too damaging, and the term disappeared from psychology texts for many years. It is still not unusual for introductory psychology texts, as well as texts on motivation, to ignore the topic of instinctive behaviors. However, though the concept of instinct disappeared from American psychology, it remained alive in a branch of European biology know as ethology.

ETHOLOGY

Ethology, as a specialized branch of biology, is concerned with the evolution, development, and function of behavior. While the ethological approach is not limited to the study of instinctive behaviors, much ethological research has emphasized instinct. Ethologists have carefully defined the concept and have analyzed the various components of such behaviors. We will therefore examine such concepts as appetitive and consummatory behaviors, fixed action patterns, key stimuli, vacuum activity, intention movements, con-

flict behavior, reaction chains, and imprinting. Much of the early work in ethology was conducted by Konrad Lorenz and Niko Tinbergen in the 1930s.

Lorenz argued persuasively that we must observe organisms in their natural setting if we are to understand the function of their behavior (Lorenz, 1971a, 1971b). Ethology has done just as Lorenz suggested, stressing the careful observation of an organism's full range of behaviors before attempting to interpret that behavior. Considerable time is spent compiling lists of observed behaviors for each species studied. Such a list is called an **ethogram** (Tinbergen, 1951).

Ethological Terms

The ethological approach is firmly based on Darwin's theory of evolution. Instinctive behaviors exist because they have or had survival value for the species in question. Another important aspect of the ethological approach to motivated behavior is seen in the concepts of **consummatory** and **appetitive** behavior, first proposed by Wallace Craig (1918). Craig noted that behaviors can be divided into well-coordinated, fixed patterns of responding to specific stimuli, which he called consummatory behavior, and restless, searching behavior that is flexible and adaptive to the environment, which he called appetitive behavior. Appetitive behavior is subject to modification through learning (e.g., when a rat learns where food can be found in its environment). Consummatory behavior is innate and stereotyped (e.g., the chewing and swallowing of food).

The ethological approach also assumes that each behavior has its own source of energy called **action specific energy (ASE)**. Each behavior is also inhibited from occurring, however, by the **innate releasing mechanism (IRM)**, which works much like a lock that can be opened by the proper key (Lorenz,

1950; Tinbergen, 1951). The "key" that allows the behavior to occur is a biologically important stimulus that may be either environmental or the result of the behavior of a species member. Environmental stimuli are called **key stimuli** or **sign stimuli**, while stimuli that involve behavior of another member of the species are called **releasers** or **social releasers** (Mortenson, 1975). Social releasers are key stimuli that serve a communicative function between species members. For example, postures, conspicuous plumage, or coloration indicating sexual readiness are often social releasers.

Key Stimuli   Key stimuli are usually simple stimuli or simple configurational relationships between stimuli. For example, the red belly of the male three-spined stickleback releases aggressive behavior in other male sticklebacks who have set up territories; yet the same males will tolerate a female in their territories because she does not have the red coloration.

Sometimes the normal key stimulus is not the optimal stimulus for releasing a given

behavior. The ringed plover, for example, lays eggs that are light brown with darker brown spots. If, however, we present plovers with a choice between their own eggs and eggs that are white with black spots, they choose to incubate the black and white eggs (Tinbergen, 1951). Oystercatchers also prefer abnormally large eggs over their own smaller eggs. These examples are particularly interesting because they show not only that an artificial stimulus may be preferred to a natural one but also that the stimuli may be configurational (for example, dark spots on a light background) rather than single stimuli. Activation of behavior triggered by an unnatural stimulus also indicates the rigid nature of the behavior; the behavior occurs when a stimulus releases it and does not depend upon the organism learning about the stimulus. Stimuli that release behavior more effectively than the normal stimulus are called **supernormal stimuli** or **superoptimal stimuli**. An example of a supernormal stimulus is shown in Figure 2.1.

Rowland (1989c) provides an interesting example of a preference for supernormal stim-

Figure 2.1 *Oystercatcher showing a preference for an egg larger than its own as a result of the large egg's action as a supernormal stimulus. (From Tinbergen, 1948. Used by permission.)*

uli. Sexually receptive female three-spined sticklebacks were presented with two dummy male sticklebacks, one of normal size (50 mm) and the other 1.5 times larger (75 mm). The dummy males were connected to a motorized carousel that caused them to move in a circular path, simulating male courtship movements. Rowland observed receptive females' choices and found that the females showed a significant preference for the larger (i.e., the supernormal) dummy, even though the size of this dummy exceeded the size of any males in the natural population from which the females were drawn.

Rowland suggests that preference for a supernormal male stimulus could provide several advantages for a female stickleback. First of all, large males compete more successfully for breeding territories (Rowland, 1989a) and would therefore be expected to have greater success in raising offspring (male sticklebacks hatch and care for the young). Females who chose larger males should increase the chances of survival of their eggs.

Second, Rowland suggests that larger males might be expected to fan the eggs more effectively (fanning provides oxygen to the eggs) and/or to defend the nest and eggs better than smaller males.

Third, larger males might be less subject to predation and would therefore be more likely to survive to provide paternal care to the offspring to the point of their independence.

In a related study Rowland (1989b) has shown that male sticklebacks prefer dummy females with excessive abdominal distension or excessive body size. Thus it appears that mate size is an important variable in the mating behavior of sticklebacks. Rowland's research suggests that supernormal stimulus effects may occur more often in nature than had been formerly assumed and that preference for supernormal stimuli may, in some cases, provide an evolutionary advantage.

Fixed Action Patterns   The response that a key stimulus releases is called a **fixed action pattern (FAP)**. Fixed action patterns are species-specific motor patterns that are rigid, stereotyped, and, for all practical purposes, "blind." The occurrence of a fixed action pattern depends upon a key stimulus and is not influenced by learning.

Moltz (1965) has noted four empirical properties of a fixed action pattern:

1.   The fixed action pattern is stereotyped. Though this term implies that the behavior itself is invariable, and though this seems generally true, some variability in the performance of fixed action patterns does exist (Burghardt, 1973).

2.   The fixed action pattern is independent of immediate external control. Once the fixed action pattern is activated, it continues to completion regardless of changes in the external environment. The graylag goose, for example, retrieves eggs that have rolled from its nest. This behavior consists of two components: a fixed action pattern involving the drawing of the egg toward the nest with the bill, and lateral (i.e., side to side) movements of the bill that keep the nonsymmetrical egg from rolling off to one side (see Figure 2.2). The lateral movements depend upon sensory feedback back from the egg as it rolls unequally. They are compensatory and keep the egg in line with the nest. These lateral bill movements are an example of a class of behavior known as **taxes**. Taxes are similar to FAPs in that they are unlearned; however, unlike FAPs they are responsive to environmental change (Mortenson, 1975). The fixed action pattern component of the behavior, however, continues to completion (even if a devious experimenter removes the egg!). Once released, then, the fixed action pattern appears to

Figure 2.2   *Graylag goose retrieving an egg that has rolled from the nest. (From Lorenz & Tinbergen, 1938. Used by permission.)*

be independent of external changes in stimulation. But there must be some limitations of independence of fixed action patterns from the environment—the sparrow, when attacked by a cat, does not continue to feed on grain. Obviously some mechanism must exist that can short-circuit or stop a fixed action pattern when environmental conditions demand.

3. Fixed action patterns are spontaneous. In addition to external stimulation, internal motivation is necessary for the occurrence of a fixed action pattern. The longer the interval since the last occurrence of the fixed action pattern, the more "ready" it is to occur. Spontaneity refers to the fact that when energy has built up sufficiently, the behavior may occur **in vacuo** (i.e, without being released by a key stimulus). Burghardt (1973) has noted that the spontaneity of fixed action patterns is often cited as evidence for central nervous system structures that control behavior independent of experience.

4. Fixed action patterns are independent of learning. Specifically, the fixed action pattern appears to be nonmodifiable through learning. Hailman (1969) has shown that this is not entirely true. We will examine Hailman's research in the section of this chapter on new directions in ethology.

Theoretical Models

The motivational models generated by ethologists have emphasized internal sources of motivation as opposed to external ones. As we will see in later chapters, external conditions can become powerful motivators of behavior. Ethologists, however, have usually chosen to limit their theorizing to internally motivated, genetically programmed behaviors. The basis of the ethological approach is the concept of energy, which builds within the nervous system and motivates behavior designed to release it.

Both Lorenz (1950) and Tinbergen (1951) have proposed models of instinctive behavior. While both theorists admit the tentative nature of their models, the models do provide a framework for thinking about instinctive behavior.

Lorenz's Hydraulic Model   In many respects, Lorenz's view of motivation is similar to Freud's. Both use the concept of energy buildup to "explain" the motivation underlying behavior. The buildup of energy is often conceived as similar to the accumulation of water in a reservoir. As it accumulates, it motivates the organism to behave in such a way as to release the energy. Additionally, as energy builds up, the stimulus necessary to release a behavior becomes less, so that the threshold that must be reached for a particular behavior to occur becomes progressively lower.

Energy may sometimes accumulate to the point that the threshold for stimulation reaches zero and the behavior occurs spontaneously. Such behavior has been termed **vacuum activity** (Tinbergen, 1951). Lorenz discusses a tame flycatcher that would fly about the room behaving exactly as if catching flies. This particular behavior is normally triggered by the stimuli of flies, but in this instance, it occurred in the absence of the "correct" stimulus. Normally, however, a particular behavior is inhibited or "held back" from occurring until the correct stimulus releases it.

Lorenz's model is shown in Figure 2.3. As can be seen, action-specific energy (ASE) is conceptualized as accumulating in a reservoir. The accumulation of energy in the reservoir stimulates appetitive behavior in the organism, eventually leading to a stimulus situation that will activate the innate releasing mechanism (IRM) depicted in the drawing as the spring-loaded washer. The key stimulus is represented by the weight on the scale pan; in conjunction with the pressure from the accumulating energy, it works to open the valve so that energy may run off in the form of fixed action patterns (FAPs). The scale in the diagram measures the intensity of the behavior that results from two factors: the amount of pressure exerted by the ASE and the appropriateness of the key stimulus for opening the valve wide. The energy is conceived as falling into a sloping pan with openings in the bottom. The sloping pan represents the idea that the

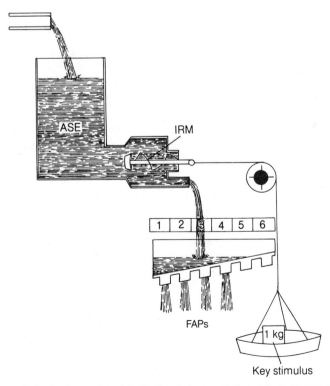

Figure 2.3 *Lorenz's hydraulic model of instinctive behavior. (Adapted from Lorenz, 1950. Used by permission.)*

more intense the motivation (and thus energy), the more complete the consummatory behavior; each opening in the bottom of the pan represents an additional component of the behavior. Thus a small accumulation of energy might lead to only a partial response, whereas a large accumulation of energy would lead to a full-blown response. For example, aggressive action-specific energy will accumulate in a male stickleback that has established a breeding territory. The presence of the red belly of another male in his territory serves as a key stimulus (i.e., the weight on the scale pan) to open the valve (IRM), and the fixed action patterns of attack occur.

This model can also explain vacuum activity. If the appropriate key stimulus is not present to activate the IRM, the energy may continue to build to the point where it overcomes the force of the spring holding the washer closed, and the fixed action pattern occurs just as spontaneously as in Lorenz's flycatcher.

Finally, we should note that each fixed action pattern has its own hydraulic system with an appropriate reservoir and releasing mechanism. Lorenz also noted that the size of the reservoirs for some behaviors could be smaller than for other behaviors so that they would "fill" more quickly and thus be highly probable responses. It is also possible to assume that the rate of energy flow into the reservoir can differ for different motives and thus lead to a difference in the probabilities of behaviors. Thus a highly probable response such as grooming (licking the fur or preening the feathers) could be analyzed as resulting from either a small reservoir that fills quickly or a high rate of energy flow.

Tinbergen's Hierarchical Model Tinbergen's model is more detailed than that of Lorenz and proposes a series of centers connected to one another. The highest center controls those below it, the next center con-

trols those below it, and so on down to the lowest centers, which control the movements involved in the fixed action patterns. Such a stepwise model is called a **hierarchy** because each level controls those below it but is, in turn, controlled by those above it. Figure 2.4 may help explain this model.

Tinbergen proposed that a separate hierarchy exists for each general class of instinctive behavior. Thus separate hierarchies exist for reproductive behavior, feeding, body care, and so on.

The highest center in the hierarchy controls the activation of the general class of behaviors (e.g., reproduction). Separate centers at the next lower level would control more specific types of behavior related to reproduction (e.g., driving off intruders, courting, nestbuilding, fanning the eggs), each center controlling only one type of activity.

Even lower centers control the release of specific fixed action patterns. Thus, at this level, centers control specific types of behavior (e.g., aggressive patterns—chasing, biting, ramming) that would be activated by a higher center involved with driving off intruders.

The energy in the top center is held back or inhibited from activating its lower centers by an IRM. In the case of the reproductive instinct in fish, the key stimulus releasing the block might be water temperature or length of day. Energy then flows to the next level, where it is again blocked. Here the presence of another male would serve as a releaser of the innate mechanism for aggressive behavior, allowing energy to flow down to the next level, where various types of aggressive behavior are held in check by the IRMs.

Specific behaviors of the intruder then serve as releasers of specific FAPs of aggression. If the intruding male attacks, the territory holder will attack in return; if the intruder now flees, the territory "owner" will chase, and so on. If the territorial intruder is a

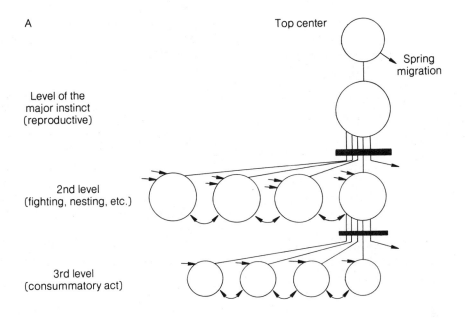

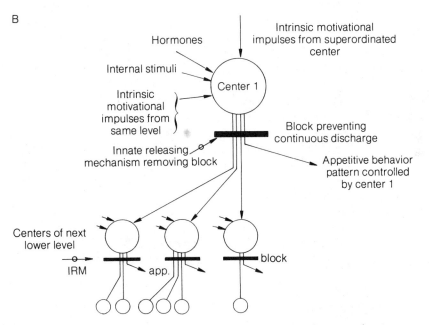

Figure 2.4 A.—Hierarchical organization of centers involved in the reproductive instinct; B.—intermediate center in the hierarchy showing the influence of internal and external stimuli on the center. (Adapted from Tinbergen, 1951. Used by permission.)

female, a different series of centers will be activated. As their IRMs are triggered, energy flows into the specific FAPs associated with mating.

Each center is influenced by additional factors besides the center above it and the key stimuli, which release energy to the next lower level. One such factor is hormonal changes, which may make a center more or less sensitive to key stimuli. For example, sexual behavior may not occur in the male, even though the appropriate key stimulus is present, if androgen is missing.

A second factor influencing the sensitivity of the centers is internal sensory information. Basically this is feedback from the body indicating the "state" of the organism. For example, an aroused cat is more likely to attack or flee (depending on the circumstances) than a relaxed cat. The feedback that indicates arousal serves to sensitize the centers involved with defense and perhaps inhibit other centers such as feeding or drinking.

Third, the activity of the nervous system influences the centers of Tinbergen's model. Thus vacuum activity can be explained as the spontaneous activation of centers controlling behavior patterns, even though the key stimulus may be absent.

Each center at a given level is connected to other centers at the same level. These connections serve the primary purpose of inhibiting the other centers when one center is activated (e.g., when the aggression center is activated, the mating center is inhibited, and vice versa). However, these circuits allow displacement behaviors to occur when two centers are simultaneously activated and inhibit each other. The energy from the blocked impulse "sparks over" to an unrelated center and activates its fixed action pattern. An example of this is seen in male sticklebacks at the edges of a common boundary between territories. At the boundary, the centers controlling attack and flight are both activated, and they inhibit one another. The energy

often "sparks over" into displacement nest-building. Of course, if this displacement behavior occurs frequently enough and is adaptive, it may become a social releaser indicating that the stickleback is in a "balanced state," in which the two strong motives of attack and flight are equal.

In Tinbergen's model, appetitive behavior occurs when a center is activated but the proper key stimulus is not present to trigger the IRM. When this happens, the organism begins a restless searching activity through its environment. Past experiences, learning, and memories guide this flexible, adaptive, appetitive behavior. When the proper key stimulus is encountered, the block is removed and the next lower center is activated. If the proper key stimulus for this new lower center is not present, appetitive behavior begins again. Eventually the correct stimulus is encountered and the consummatory behavior (i.e., fixed action pattern) reduces the motivation.

The models of Lorenz and Tinbergen serve as useful frames to help us think about instinctive behavior. Both scientists have based their models on great amounts of research, and both have defined the terms they use in ways that can be tested. The theoretical models of Lorenz and Tinbergen have stimulated a great deal of research, some of which has focused on analyzing more complex forms of behavior as combinations of simpler components. In the next section we examine some of the results of these studies.

Intention Movements and Social Releasers

Lorenz (1971b) pointed out that before a fixed action pattern occurs, one can observe **intention movements**. These movements are low-intensity, incomplete responses indicating that energy is beginning to accumulate in an instinctive behavior system. These intention movements may also become social releasers over the evolutionary history of the species. Initially the intention movements are noncommunicative, but through a process termed **ritualization** they begin to serve a communicative function. For example, many threat gestures seem to have evolved from attack responses and serve to indicate the motivational readiness of the organism for combative behavior (Mortenson, 1975). Intention movements that have become social releasers are usually exaggerated forms of the original response. The movements then serve as key stimuli for the release of fixed action patterns in the **conspecific** (i.e., member of the same species) toward which they are directed.

Do humans make intention movements that serve as social signals? Lockard, Allen, Schielle, and Wiemer (1978) believe that they do. In their initial experiment these researchers recorded the postural stance of subjects who were engaged in conversation with another person. They found that at the beginning of a social interaction between two people, their subjects tended to stand with their weight distributed equally to both legs. Near the close of the interaction, however, the subjects stood with most of their weight borne on one leg. This result suggested to Lockard and co-workers that shifts in weight may serve as an intention movement for departure.

A second experiment revealed that the frequency of unequal weight stances increased before departure, as did weight shifts in general. In addition, weight shifts that increased the distance between the individuals also occurred just prior to departure. Shifts in weight, then, are apparently intention movements that serve as a signal that an individual is about to leave.

These researchers produced additional evidence for the signal function of weight shifts from the fact that weight shifts were exaggerated in situations where people departed alone, as compared to situations where the two persons departed together. The weight shift exaggeration would be expected if it serves as a signal of imminent departure, since persons departing together would have little need to signal their coming departure to each other.

Several popular books have been written on body language in the past several years. The work of ethologists suggests that body language has some validity because changes in posture, position, or weight can serve as intention movements that signal the future behavior of an individual.

Lorenz (1971b) has maintained that relationships between species members tend to be instinctive, with learning playing a minor role. However, some behaviors, such as individual recognition within closed groups and dominance orders, appear to be learned. Lorenz further suggested that learning is primarily useful in relationships with the external environment and that these differences are also seen in human behavior. Nonverbal communication, discussed in Chapter Thirteen, may exemplify human intention movements that have become ritualized into social releasers.

Conflict Behavior

An interesting question arises if we consider the possibility that two or more sign stimuli could be present at the same time. Which fixed action pattern would occur? Such situations involve a motivational conflict.

Conflict behavior has been divided into four categories: **successive ambivalent behavior, simultaneous ambivalent behavior, redirected behavior,** and **displacement** (Hess, 1962).

Successive ambivalent behavior involves the alternation of incomplete responses representing the two motivational states. For example, a male stickleback may alternate between attack and escape responses when it meets an intruding male stickleback at the border of its territory.

Simultaneous ambivalent behavior occurs in conflict situations where both motivational states can be expressed in behavior at the same time. For example, Leyhausen (cited in Burghardt, 1973) has argued that the arched back of the cat is the result of the simultaneous expression of the motives to attack (rear feet forward) and to flee (front feet drawn backward).

Redirected behavior is conceptually similar to the Freudian concept of displacement (Burghardt, 1973). In redirected behavior the appropriate responses (e.g., attack) occur but not to the appropriate object, because of a conflicting motive (e.g., fear). Such redirected behavior is often focused on a nearby organism or inanimate object. The husband who has been reprimanded by his boss and comes home to "take it out" on the wife or children instead of reacting aggressively to the boss might be analyzed as displaying redirected behavior.

Displacement occurs when two equally strong motives are in conflict and are inhibiting each other. The energies associated with the two motives continue to accumulate but cannot be expressed through their normal behavorial outlets. Displacement behaviors are responses that differ from either of the motives in conflict. The displacement activities are themselves, however, fixed action patterns (Tinbergen, 1951). For example, the motives of attack and flight balanced against each other in the male stickleback may lead to displaced nestbuilding behavior, a fixed action pattern normally released by different stimulus conditions than the conflict between flight and attack. According to Tinbergen, the energy accumulating in the blocked instinctive behaviors may "spark over" to another instinct center and find its outlet through that center's fixed action patterns. Tinbergen also notes that displacement behaviors may take on communicative value, just as intention movements do. Thus displacement nestbuilding becomes a ritualized threat gesture in male sticklebacks.

Reaction Chains

We now turn from the analysis of responses released by patterns of stimuli to an examination of behavior sequences. We will discover that quite complex behavior patterns may be built from simpler key-stimuli–fixed-action-pattern relationships.

Most behaviors are more complex than a single fixed action pattern released by a single key stimulus. Behaviors frequently involve a sequence of responses in which each response is released by its appropriate stimulus. Such a situation is known as a **reaction chain**. A reaction chain often consists of alternating stimuli and fixed action patterns in a particular sequence until the behavior comes to an end, as in the case of the stickleback mating behavior shown in Figure 2.5. The release of a fixed action pattern often causes the next key stimulus to appear; thus the next part of the sequence is released, and so on. As shown in Figure 2.5, the appearance of the female releases the zigzag dance in the male, which in turn serves as a social releaser for courting behavior in the female. Courting behavior releases leading (to the nest) behavior in the male, and the chain of releasers and fixed action patterns continues until fertilization of the eggs occurs. Lorenz (1970) pointed out that sometimes there are gaps in these chains of behavior that can be filled by learned behaviors such as **imprinting** (see below). Such situations result in a series of behaviors, some learned and others innate. These sequences of instinctive and learned behaviors have been termed **instinct-conditioning intercalcation** by Lorenz.

Imprinting

One area in which instinct and learning seem to intercalcate is in the process known as imprinting, first brought to the attention of researchers by Lorenz, although the process had been recognized and described by Spauld-

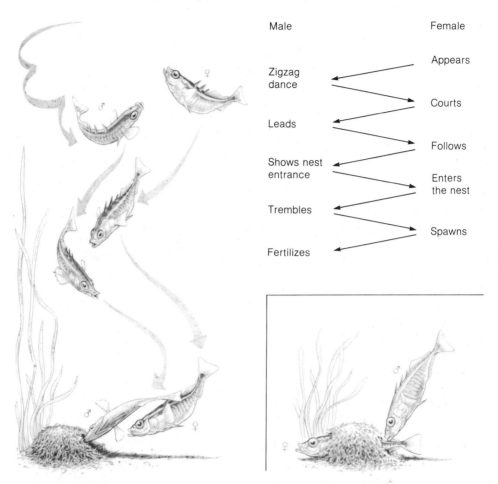

Figure 2.5 Mating behavior of the three-spined stickleback showing the reaction chain that is produced when the female appears. (From Tinbergen, 1951. Used by permission.)

ing in 1873 (Mortenson, 1975) and, as noted by Burghardt (1973), was also described by More in 1516. Nevertheless, our understanding of the variables involved in imprinting date from the introduction of the concept by Lorenz.

Imprinting is generally considered a socialization process in which a young organism forms an attachment to its parents (Mortenson, 1975). The process of imprinting has been studied most extensively in birds (Sluckin, 1973), although imprinting occurs in other species as well, including mammals (Klopfer, 1971).

The imprinting process itself seems to include both instinctive and learned components. For example, a newly hatched chick will try to follow the first moving object it sees. Normally this is the mother hen, but it will also follow a human, a toy train, or a moving red rubber ball. The chick follows and forms an attachment to the object to which it is exposed. Thus the object of the attachment is learned; however, the process of becoming attached appears to be innate.

Lorenz described what he believed to be the major characteristics of imprinting. First, he noted that the attachment process only occurs during a very limited, critical period in the organism's life. In support of his assertion Ramsay and Hess (1954) showed that the strength of imprinting peaks between 13 to 16 hours after hatching for mallard ducklings. But apparently instead of a critical period when the learning does or does not occur, there exists a **sensitive period** within which imprinting occurs more readily than before or after this period (Mortenson, 1975).

Second, Lorenz felt that the imprinting process is permanent and irreversible; once established, it does not extinguish. In particular Lorenz suggested that the initial attachment formed by imprinting leads to intraspecific identification and that the sexual preferences of the adult result from this attachment. Lorenz imprinted some graylag geese on himself at the time of hatching. When adult, these geese ignored sexually receptive members of their own species but made sexual displays toward Lorenz! Most of the evidence, however, suggests that formation of an irreversible bond is the exception in imprinting rather than the rule. The reversibility of imprinting in birds may depend upon whether the species is **nidifugous** (i.e., leaves the nest shortly after hatching) or **nidicolous** (i.e., remains in the nest for an extended period). Nidicolous species show a more permanent attachment to the imprinted object, sometimes preferring that object sexually to members of their own species. Imprinting to nonspecies members in nidifugous birds, however, does not prevent them from mating with their own species (Mortenson, 1975). The extended period in the nest of nidicolous species may allow the more permanent attachment to originate from factors other than imprinting (e.g., reinforcement by parent birds).

The third characteristic of imprinting noted by Lorenz is its **independence from reward**. The process of imprinting apparently occurs automatically rather than in a trial-and-error fashion that would suggest a gradual process of learning to follow. This finding has been generally supported, and several studies have shown that a response (e.g., following) is not even necessary for imprinting to occur (Burghardt, 1973). Of possible theoretical importance is the finding that although reinforcement is unnecessary for the process of imprinting to occur, an imprinted stimulus can be used to reinforce other behaviors, such as jumping on a lever in order to obtain a brief appearance of the imprinted object (Bateson & Reese, 1969; Hoffman et al., 1966).

Apparently not all stimulus objects are equally effective in establishing imprinting. For example, Figler, Mills, and Petri (1974), in a study of stimulus generalization in imprinting, concluded that color is a more dominant aspect of the imprinting object than shape. Other researchers have shown that the characteristic maternal call of a species is preferred over that of other species, while species-typical visual stimuli are not thus preferred (Gottlieb, 1972).

Some work has also been conducted on the effect that imprinting may have on other social behaviors. Hoffman and Boskoff (1972) obtained results suggesting that imprinting may be involved in aggressive pecking in ducklings. Other studies by Petri and Mills (1977) and Rajecki, Ivins, and Rein (1976) show that aggressive pecking in young chicks is probably due to isolation and not to imprinting per se.

Criticisms of the Ethological Approach

The ethological view of motivation has been criticized both from within ethology (Hinde, 1966, 1971) and from without (Lehrman, 1970). These criticisms have been amply summarized by others (Alcock, 1975; Bolles, 1975; Burghardt, 1973), and we will note only the major criticisms.

As with the early instinct theories, the distinction between learned and instinctive behaviors is still not clear. It has become increasingly clear that instinctive behaviors depend upon the proper developmental and environmental conditions. Basically a behavior is considered innate if *no* learning has been demonstrated in its development. Hinde, however, argued that all behaviors depend upon both innate mechanisms and the environment. To say that a behavior is simply innate, then, is to oversimplify the situation. As an example of the interaction of the innate and the acquired, Hailman (1969) has shown that the innate pecking response of the laughing gull changes developmentally, becoming more accurate and efficient, and is released by increasingly more specific objects as the chick matures. Hailman suggests that the peck appears stereotyped and innate in nature because all laughing gulls share similar environments that modify their behavior in similar ways.

Another major criticism of the ethological view involves the energy concept. Classical ethologists have argued that both displacement and vacuum activity indicate the presence of an energy buildup within the organism. Antagonists of the energy concept argue that displacement and vacuum activity can be explained by assuming a hierarchy of responses, with some responses being more probable than others. Thus, if an innate behavior is blocked from occurring, the next most probable response whose stimuli are present will occur. Displacement behavior may occur not because of energy "sparking over" but because of occurrence of the next most probable response. Thus displacement scratching shown by fighting cocks is analyzed as simply a highly probable response, associated with feeding, that occurs when the motives of attack and fight are balanced. Similarly, vacuum activity need not result from energy overflowing the reservoir but may result from stimulus generalization (i.e., the range of stimuli that can elicit a response is probably wider than generally believed).

Thus, for example, the female of the species is only one of a number of stimuli that may elicit sexual behavior from the male.

One major criticism of the ethological models of Lorenz and Tinbergen is that their models do not allow for feedback. They provide no indication that ongoing behavior is influenced by characteristics of the stimulus situation. Both scientists believed that motivation can only be reduced by the occurrence of the fixed action pattern that consumes the energy. A mouse attacked by a predator, however, doesn't continue feeding until the energy in its feeding system is reduced—it flees, if possible. Obviously some sort of mechanism is needed that can quickly alter patterns of behavior from one type to another. As we shall see, newer theories have begun to incorporate the idea of feedback into their models.

The conceptual models presented by Lorenz and Tinbergen have also been criticized because they do not correspond with what is known about the functioning of the nervous system. This argument, however, is not entirely fair, because neither Lorenz nor Tinbergen conceived their models as accurate representations of nervous activity but as frameworks to guide our thinking about motivated behavior.

Even though ethology has been criticized, clearly the naturalistic approach to understanding behavior has much to offer. It is also becoming increasingly clear that some behaviors are genetically preprogrammed.

NEW DIRECTIONS IN ETHOLOGY

Some of the newer directions in ethology indicate both a sensitivity to the criticisms offered and a broadened scope of the behaviors being studied. Although we cannot hope to do justice to the many current research endeavors here, we should at least mention them. Three basic areas of current research concern (1) recent modifications to the basic models of instinctual behavior, (2) control mechanisms of instinctual behavior, and (3) human ethology.

Modifications to the Basic Ideas of Ethology

First, research has begun to reform our notions about the stimuli involved in releasing instinctive behavior. Konishi (1971) provided an interesting neurobiological analysis of sign stimuli in terms of stimulus filtering—the fact that our sensory systems are "tuned" to respond to certain kinds of stimuli and not to others. For example, the eye of the frog has receptors that respond to small, roundish, moving objects (e.g., insects) and release the response of the tongue snapping out to grasp the potential prey (Maturana et al., 1960). Konishi noted that the concept of "releasers" fits well with data on filtering at the receptor level, but he argued that stimulus filtering also occurs in more central regions of the brain.

In both Lorenz's and Tinbergen's models, stimulus-processing, releasing, and motivating functions are controlled by separate systems. Konishi believed that at least for some types of behavior, a central processing network can perform all three functions. He also believed that a control systems approach involving feedback and corrective action is useful in analyzing instinctive behavior. Additionally, he suggested that some behaviors are more "open" (i.e., to modification through learning) than others; such a behavioral system would compare ongoing behavior against some internal criterion (either innate or learned) and modify the response depending upon its relationship to the criterion. An example of such a feedback process is song learning in many species of birds. Song sparrows develop abnormal songs if they are deafened as chicks, yet they develop normal sparrow songs if raised only with canaries! Thus the "song" of the song sparrow is apparently innate but requires

auditory feedback in order to develop properly.

Konishi was not the only one to take a systems approach. Mayr (1974) provided an analysis of behavior based on what he called **open and closed programs**. According to Mayr, a program is a series of behaviors that are determined genetically. The difference between an open and a closed program is that an open program can be modified by experience, while a closed program (i.e., instinct) cannot. Both open and closed programs are genetically established, but only an open program is modifiable through experience. Open programs would not be considered "blank slates," however, because some types of information are more easily acquired than others. The concept of open programs is remarkably similar to the concept of preparedness proposed by Seligman (1970) and Seligman and Hager (1972). **Prepared** behaviors are either instinctive or very easily and quickly learned. Organisms possessing genes that allowed them to behave in this way were favored in the struggle to survive. **Contraprepared** behaviors are very difficult, perhaps impossible, to learn because they were "prepared against" during the evolutionary history of the organism. Between these extremes are what Seligman calls **unprepared** behaviors, which involve the associations between events in the environment and appropriate responding; the associations formed, however, tend to be arbitrary (e.g., teaching a rat to press a lever to obtain food), and learning will not be as quick as with more prepared responses. What Seligman and his colleagues pointed out is that what can be learned is **biologically constrained** (i.e., limited).

Mayr suggested that organisms with short life spans (and therefore less chance to profit from experience) should tend to have more closed programs, while longer lived organisms would tend to have more open programs. In addition, he believed it possible to correlate open or closed behaviors with their function for the organism. He noted that behaviors serving a communicative function, whether within or between species, tend to be closed programs (as Lorenz has also suggested), while noncommunicative behaviors are more likely to be open programs. Thus it would be adaptive for behaviors such as threat gestures and submissive signals to be generated by closed programs, for the chance of "misunderstanding" the signals is then avoided. On the other hand, it would be adaptive for behaviors that involve interaction with the environment (e.g., foraging for food) to be controlled by open programs so that behaviors could adapt as conditions changed.

Baerends (1976) provided a complex, modified version of Tinbergen's hierarchical model that emphasizes negative feedback as part of a system for controlling certain behaviors. Much research cited by Baerends requires the addition of a feedback system that corrects ongoing behavior or interrupts it if conditions change. This is the basis for the concept of a negative feedback system. Similarly, Hailman (1969) has shown how the improvement in the laughing gull's pecking accuracy as a chick is a result of visual negative feedback provided by the pecks that miss their mark. Thus the original idea that a behavior once released is uninfluenced by external conditions seems incorrect.

Hailman's analysis suggests the close interaction of innate and acquired patterns of behavior. For example, he believed that the gull chick has only a very rough innate representation of the parent that becomes sharpened through experience. Newly hatched chicks respond primarily to the parent's bill and initially do not discriminate between models of their own parents and those of a related species. By one week of age, however, the chicks are sensitive to small differences in the details of beak and head and can easily discriminate differences between new models

and models with which they were raised. This discrimination seems based on a type of learning known as **classical conditioning**.

Though models of innate behavior such as Baerends's are too complex for inclusion here, it is important to note that theorists such as Baerends, Mayr, and Hailman have emphasized the interaction between instinctive and learned behaviors and also the modification of instinctive behaviors through experience.

Physiological Control of Innate Behavior

Both Lorenz's and Tinbergen's models rely ultimately on changes in the activity of the nervous system. Though little evidence was available to them at the time about how the nervous system might perform the sequences of behavior they described, recent research has begun to advance our understanding of the physiology of instinctive behavior.

One example of research on the physiology of instinctive behavior is the work of Willows (1971) and Willows and Hoyle (1969) on escape behavior in the sea slug (*Tritonia diomedia*). The sea slug's innate response to contact with certain species of predatory starfish consists of alternating contractions of muscles on its back and underside. This escape response seems to be triggered by a chemical cue from the tentacles of the starfish that is sensed by chemoreceptors on the surface of the slug's body. Because the nervous system of the sea slug consists of only a few hundred cells, Willows was able to trace the electrical activity involved in the escape response (see Figure 2.6). When a sufficient number of receptors have been stimulated by the chemical from the starfish, the slug brain area receiving the input from these receptors becomes active. This area causes the sea slug to elongate in preparation for escape and also stimulates three other areas of the sea slug's brain. The first area causes contractions of the

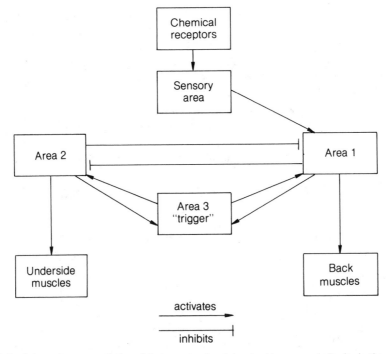

Figure 2.6   Schematic representation of the neural network involved in escape behavior in the sea slug.

muscles along the back of the sea slug, causes the area controlling the muscles of the underside to be inhibited, and stimulates a third area that acts as a trigger for further activating Areas 1 and 2. The first brain region is active for a set length of time and then stops. When it stops, the third area stimulates Area 2 to become active. Area 2 causes the muscles along the underside to contract, inhibits Area 1, and finally also activates Area 3. After a set period of time, Area 2 stops its activity and Area 3 now activates Area 1 so that the back muscles are again contracted, and the whole cycle starts over again. The activity of these three areas thus results in a series of alternating back muscle contractions followed by underside contractions that together serve to propel the sea slug from the vicinity of the starfish.

Willows's research has thus provided us with insight into how the nervous system controls innate behavior.

Human Ethology

Perhaps the greatest amount of research on human instinctive behavior patterns has been conducted by Eibl-Eibesfeldt, summarized in his book *Love and Hate: The Natural History of Behavior Patterns* (1972), which points out many human behavior patterns that he believes are innate. His conclusions were based on considerable study of both technologically advanced and primitive cultures in addition to behaviors of blind, deaf, and severely retarded children.

Facial Expressions   Eibl-Eibesfeldt pointed out that many facial expressions are universal and do not seem to be learned. Smiling, laughing, weeping, and frowning are observed in the appropriate circumstances across all cultures. Additionally, children born blind, deaf, or retarded also smile or laugh when happy and frown or cry when unhappy. Figure 2.7 shows some of these behaviors in a deaf-blind child.

Another interesting behavior that Eibl-Eibesfeldt believed innate is the eyebrow flick, which consists of a very brief lifting of the eyebrow upon greeting an acquaintance. This response is shown from three different cultures in Figure 2.8. The behavior is essentially

a greeting signal of recognition and perhaps a nonthreat or appeasement gesture.

Joseph Hager and Paul Ekman (1979) have examined the ability of people to recognize specific facial signals at varying distances. They chose six emotional expressions (happiness, sadness, fear, anger, surprise, and disgust) that were previously shown to be reliably associated with specific facial movements. Hager and Ekman then taught two individuals (a man and a woman) how to consistently make these facial movements. Photographs were taken of each individual making each facial movement.

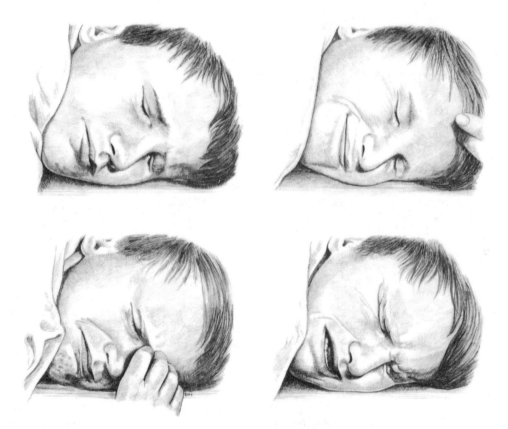

Figure 2.7 *Facial expressions of a deaf-blind girl. Top left, relaxed mood; top right, smiling. Bottom left and right, crying. (Adapted from* Love and Hate *by Irenaus Eibl-Eibesfeldt. Copyright © 1971, 1972 by Methuen and Co. Ltd. and Holt, Rinehart and Winston. Reprinted by permission of Henry Holt and Company, Inc.)*

Figure 2.8 *Examples of the eyebrow flick from three different cultures. Left, before recognition; right, after recognition. Cultures from top to bottom: Waika Indian, Balinese, Papuan. (Adapted from* Love and Hate *by Irenaus Eibl-Eibesfeldt. Copyright © 1971, 1972 by Methuen and Co. Ltd. and Holt, Rinehart and Winston. Reprinted by permission of Henry Holt and Company, Inc.)*

Then other subjects in the experiment were asked to observe either a photograph of one of the individuals (blown up to life size) or the actual individual at varying distances from 30 to 45 m. The observers had three seconds in which to view the facial expression and then had to select the specific expression they believed was being conveyed.

The results indicated that every observer performed significantly better than chance, even at the furthest distance (45 m). Of the six expressions, happiness and surprise were the easiest to recognize, and some preliminary results reported by these researchers suggested that these two expressions can be accurately recognized as much as 100 m distant.

The results also indicated that in general, observers' judgments were more accurate for male than for female expressions, whether live or photographed.

Hager and Ekman believed that their results showed that the face is a long-distance transmitter of emotion. Apparently our ability to judge a person's expression from a considerable distance is quite good. As Hager and Ekman noted, the upper limit for the distance that a hand-propelled object (e.g., a rock) can be thrown is approximately 95 m. If some facial expressions can be understood at 100 m, facial expression could have served as a signal of emotional state beyond the distance limits of primitive physical combat. Thus such long-distance recognition should have had considerable survival value.

Shyness Some behaviors that we often assume have resulted from childhood experiences may in fact have a biological basis. Kagen, Reznick, and Snidman (1988) provide evidence that extreme shyness has a genetic basis expressed in differences in arousibility. Children who inherit a low threshold of arousibility are more likely to become inhibited in social situations. Furthermore, the differences between these inhibited children and less restrained, socially interactive children is consistent at both two years and seven years of age.

Kagen et al. further suggest, however, that this inherited tendency toward shyness requires some form of chronic environmental stress to cause it to develop. These researchers suggest

that being later born and thus being exposed to the stress of older siblings who may take toys, tease, or yell could be sufficient stress to trigger the behavioral inhibition. Indeed, two-thirds of the inhibited children in their sample were later born, while two-thirds of the uninhibited children were first born.

The Kagen et al. study is important because it points out that genetically determined predispositions to behave in a particular way often still require appropriate environmental circumstances for their expression. Stephen Suomi (Adler, 1989) has uncovered a similar set of biological-environmental interactions in rhesus monkeys. He has found that about 20% of his free-roaming colony of 200 monkeys are genetically predisposed to react to separation with depressed behavior and high levels of stress. Similar to Kagen's research, Suomi finds that the stresses of separation can be influenced by environmental circumstances. The presence of friendly peers and a nurturing foster mother can reduce the stress produced by separation from the biological mother. Genetic-environmental interactions in other behaviors have been shown in other species (e.g., Greene,

Figure 2.9 Examples of stimuli that release "cuddling" in adults. Note the chubby cheeks, large eyes, and large head in relation to body. (Adapted from Love and Hate *by Irenaus Eibl-Eibesfeldt. Copyright © 1971, 1972 by Methuen and Co. Ltd. and Holt, Rinehart and Winston, Publishers. Reprinted by permission of Henry Holt and Company, Inc.)*

1989; Oakley, 1983), so it is not too surprising that primates, humans and rhesus, also should be subject to such interactions. Further study of such interactions could provide useful insights into why particular behaviors such as shyness or stress reactions occur in some individuals more than others.

Additional Innate Behaviors Eibl-Eibesfeldt also mentioned several key stimuli that release human instinctive behavior (see also Sternglanz, Gray, & Murakami, 1977). For example, he suggested that the infant's chubby cheeks, large eyes, small mouth, and large head release "cuddling" behavior in adults. Toy manufacturers and cartoonists sometimes employ these characteristics to endear us to their products (see Figure 2.9).

At the adult level, female flirting was considered by Eibl-Eibesfeldt as a type of innate ritualized foreplay that involves flight as one component. Flirting behavior (i.e., eye contact, smile, lowering of head, and closing of eyes or looking away) was analyzed as a type of ritualized flight that invites pursuit by the male. Although this may seem a little far-fetched, ritualized flight is a common behavior pattern in many species during mating (Eibl-Eibesfeldt, 1972).

Eibl-Eibesfeldt believed that kissing is a ritualized form of feeding behavior derived from the feeding of the infant. Since for most of our evolutionary history baby foods have not come neatly packaged in small glass containers, it was common for parents to chew food well and then push it into the child's mouth with the tongue. Along similar lines, Eibl-Eibesfeldt noted that lovers often talk "baby talk" to each other. He believed that this is done to elicit cherishing behavior of the individual, much as with a child, and thus strengthens the bond between the lovers.

Eibl-Eibesfeldt (1979) has also noted that humans use many of the same basic behavior patterns used by chimpanzees when threatening attack or making fighting movements. For example, both chimpanzees and humans stamp their feet when angry, slap surfaces with the flat of the hand, and threaten conspecifics with objects such as sticks. When threatened we also tend to stand erect and inhale, which increases our apparent size. We sometimes also use clothing for intimidation to make us look more formidable. For example, military uniforms often exaggerate the shoulders of the wearer, making them appear larger. A good example of how a change in the shoulders can alter our perception of an individual occurs when a man puts on football shoulder pads. With pads in place, the man looks much more imposing.

Staring is not only rude but is probably also an innate threat gesture (Eibl-Eibesfeldt, 1977, 1979; Andrew, 1965). In primates the stare is a frequently used threat gesture (Tinbergen & Tinbergen, 1972). Ellsworth, Carlsmith, and Henson (1972) conducted a series of field experiments involving an individual on a motor scooter staring at automobile drivers stopped at a red light. They found that those drivers who were stared at crossed the intersection significantly faster when the light turned green than drivers who were not stared at. While this experiment does not demonstrate that staring is an innate threat gesture, it does fit with observations of other primates. Incidentally, it is also possible that we consider staring to be rude because we innately recognize it for what it is—an intention movement indicating potential attack.

Eye contact is a complex topic; staring is only one of several types of eye contact. As summarized by Kleinke (1986), eye contact can serve a variety of functions in addition to threat, such as providing information, indicating liking or attraction, indicating competence, and communicating feelings. We must therefore be careful not to overgeneralize and assume that all eye contacts indicate threat.

Ethological methods have also been applied to the study of early childhood autism by Tinbergen and Tinbergen (1972). They noted that several characteristics usually associated with autism (e.g., gaze aversion) are seen in normal children in certain circumstances. Such circumstances involve the social interaction of the normal child with a stranger. The Tinbergens argued that an encounter between a child and a stranger creates a motivational conflict between approaching and avoiding the stranger. In the autistic child, because of past environmental conditions and perhaps a genetic predisposition toward shyness, the key stimuli of the stranger cause withdrawal behavior, even when the stimuli are normally ones that would elicit approach. In this respect even the parents of the child are reacted to as strangers. Thus the autistic child is analyzed as one hungry for social interactions but inhibited by strong withdrawal tendencies that are elicited by virtually all social releasers, particularly eye contact. While the Tinbergens' analysis is still very tentative, it is a provocative theory that should be seriously researched.

The ethological method has also been successfully used in the assessment of depressive disorders. Fossi, Faravelli, and Paoli (1984) studied the behavior of 29 inpatients who were diagnosed as having a major depressive disorder. Depressed patients were found to differ in several behaviors before and after treatment. Eye contact, exploration of their environment, and social behaviors were all lower before treatment than after, whereas crying, nonsocial behaviors, and pathological behaviors were higher before treatment than after. Their data indicate that a pattern of behaviors specific to depression does exist and corresponds closely to the behaviors identified by clinical assessment. Fossi et al. suggest that the ethological methods of observation could prove useful in assessing maladaptive behaviors such as depression. Ethological observations also provide an objective alternative method of assessment separate from the clinical interview, which could prove useful in determining the effects of various treatments.

Speech Other ethologists have pointed out the possible genetic character of speech (Marler, 1970; Mattingly, 1972). But ethologists have not been the only researchers to argue for a biological component to language. For example, Lenneberg (1960, 1967) has persuasively argued that language must be biologically constrained. Marler has also pointed out several parallels between song development in birds and the development of speech in humans. For example, both birds and children display a critical period during which the ability to learn is at its maximum, and both bird and human vocalizations are controlled by one dominant side of the brain. Both of these findings suggest a genetic component to birdsong and speech because critical periods are genetically determined and the localization of vocal function within the brain is also under genetic control. Marler also noted that language is biologically constrained; children do not imitate all the sounds they hear but only the ones involved in speech. This suggests that children innately recognize that some sounds are species specific, and they imitate these sounds.

Recently Liberman and Mattingly (1989) have suggested that a specialization for the perception of speech has evolved in humans. In their terms a *phonetic module* has evolved which analyzes auditory information and extracts that information necessary for the determination of phonetic segments (which they call **phonetic gestures**).

Mattingly also believed that certain speech cues are innate and serve as key stimuli. He noted that synthetic speech sounds are correctly identified even though the sounds themselves are unnatural in character. That we perceive synthetic speech sounds (e.g., those produced by a sound spectrograph) suggests that some sort of innate recognition of these sounds occurs. Mattingly believed that prior to the development of language, vocalizations served as key stimuli for the release of social behavior in humans, much as they still do in many animals. Language allowed us to represent the world around us semantically, but the older social releaser system was not lost. Mattingly argued that language serves two purposes: it provides a representation of our experiences, and it is a phonetic releaser system. Perhaps the social releaser system is what allows us to "read between the lines" when we listen to someone talk, providing us with insight into that individual beyond what is being said.

Sex and Aggression

Sexual activity and aggressive behavior are viewed by ethologists as largely innate. For example, sexual behavior in many animals involves reaction chains of ritualized courtship behavior in which social releasers trigger the appropriate fixed action patterns. Ritualized feeding is often a component of these reaction chains, as seen in the domestic chicken (*Gallus gallus*) where the rooster scratches and pecks at the ground while calling to the hen. The hen, enticed by the feeding responses, approaches the rooster (Eibl-Eibesfeldt, 1970). Similarly, songbirds feed one another in a manner similar to that of an adult feeding the young. Indeed Eibl-Eibesfeldt (1970, 1972) argued that courtship behaviors, including those of humans, are derived from the parental care instinct.

In a book entitled *On Aggression*, Lorenz (1967) developed the idea that aggressive behavior has been adaptive. Two major types of aggressive behavior are noted: **interspecific** (aggressive behavior between members of different species) and **intraspecific** (aggressive behavior between members of the same species). Interspecific aggression may further be broken into the categories of **predatory attack, mobbing behavior**, and **critical reaction**. Predatory attack is essentially food-getting behavior and is characterized by a lack of emotionality. Lorenz suggests that an equilibrium normally exists between predator and prey so that the extinction of one species by another does not usually occur. Mobbing behavior occurs when the prey turn the tables on the predator and attack it as a group. Mobbing behavior can be observed in certain species of birds; for example, crows have been known to attack a cat as a group (Lorenz, 1967). The third major type of interspecific aggression, critical reaction, involves intense aggressive behavior motivated by fear and instigated by an inability to escape. Such behavior occurs when the cornered animal is approached closer than some critical distance. Heidiger (cited by Lorenz, 1967) pointed out that lion tamers get their lions to perform by approaching and withdrawing from this critical distance. When the tamer gets within the critical distance, the lion approaches as if to attack; when the tamer withdraws, the lion stops or retreats.

Intraspecific aggression may actually serve a useful purpose in species that participate in this type of behavior. Lorenz believes that intraspecific aggression may be advantageous in three different ways. One effect of aggressive encounters among conspecifics (members of a species) is to spread out members more evenly over a given area, thereby affording each member, at least statistically, a better chance for survival. Indeed Lorenz believes that this spacing function is the most important advantage of intraspecific aggression because it provides adequate territory for breeding and food gathering. Territorial aggression, therefore, increases the chances for survival because it leads to better management of scarce resources.

A second advantage of intraspecific aggression is that it provides the strongest animals with the best territories and the first choice of mates. The characteristics that make the "winners" of these rival fights most dominant have a better chance of being passed on to the next generation because the conditions for their survival are better than they are for the traits of the "losers," who by losing are forced to take less desirable territories and mates. This second advantage suggests that aggressive and sexual motivation interact in complex ways to promote survival. As just one such example, Guhl (1956) has shown that the dominant rooster in a flock of chickens accounts for the greatest percentage of fertilized eggs. Obviously the rooster's dominance promotes the continued expression of this aggressive behavior in future generations. As we shall see shortly, the interaction of sexual and aggressive motives is complex.

The third major advantage of intraspecific aggression is protection of the young from predators. As noted above, intraspecific aggression will promote aggressiveness as a general trait within the species. Such increased aggressiveness should be advantageous in protecting the young. Increased survival of the young, in turn, promotes the survival of the species.

Eibl-Eibesfeldt (1961) notes that intraspecific aggression very rarely leads to death or even serious injury of the opponents, and in fact would be maladaptive if such were the case. It is typical for conflicts between conspecifics to involve highly ritualized tournaments. Animals that have specialized weapons (such as horns) usually do not use them to full advantage during these ritualized combats. Rattlesnakes, for example, do not attempt to bite when attacking each other but rather determine the stronger by wrestling until the weaker snake is pinned.

Serious injury from intraspecific conflict is also often avoided through the use of a special class of social releasers called **appeasement gestures**. The loser of an intraspecific conflict usu-

ally performs behaviors that inhibit further attacks by the winner. These behaviors are often submissive in appearance. For example, male cichlid fish engage in intraspecific combat with raised fins and beat at each other with currents of water directed by the tail fin. They may then "jaw lock," each fish grasping the other's mouth with its own, and a shoving match ensues. Eventually the loser submits by folding its fins and swimming away, the winner allowing the loser to escape (Eibl-Eibesfeldt, 1961). Folding of the fins appears to be a social releaser which inhibits further aggressive behavior. Dogs inhibit further aggression by rolling on their backs and presenting the vulnerable belly region to the more dominant dog, sometimes also urinating slightly at the same time. Such behaviors usually inhibit further aggression but can be disconcerting to a dog owner who is trying to get his or her pet to behave in a particular way. In such cases genetically determined behaviors intrude and often disrupt the behaviors to be learned. Breland and Breland (1961) provide some interesting insights into those situations where learned and instinctive behaviors interact.

A particularly interesting finding in regard to dominance has been noted by Simpson and Simpson (1982). These researchers examined the relationship between the social rank of female rhesus monkeys and the sex of their offspring. They found that high-ranking females gave birth to twice as many females as males, while for lower-ranking females, male infants were more common. Further, it was found that the daughters of high-ranking females themselves ranked high in social dominance. Though it is not at all evident how these differing sex ratios are accomplished, it is hypothesized that high-ranking females improve their own fitness by giving birth to high-ranking daughters, who remain within the colony, rather than to sons, who often migrate at puberty to other groups. Thus it would appear that aggressiveness not only may be favored as a trait, it also may lead to one gender being favored over another.

From the data we have examined so far, it is apparent that aggressive and sexual motivation are intimately related. Many such relationships are known; for example, female ducks will incite males to threaten intruders (Lorenz, 1967). Eibl-Eibesfeldt (1970) has suggested that this inciting behavior acts to separate out a particular male from a group of courting males for mating. Figler and his associates (Figler, 1973; Figler, Klein, & Thompson, 1975; Klein, Figler, & Peeke, 1976; Cole et al., 1980) have provided considerable support for the hypothesis that sexual and aggressive behaviors are mutually inhibitory (see Sevenster, 1961; Peeke, 1969) in some species of fish.

In one study (Cole et al., 1980) male and female convict cichlids were exposed to either male or female target fish (behind a plexiglas partition) for a period of 24 hours. The four groups so formed (male-male, male-female, female-female, and female-male) were all initially aggressive toward their targets; however, as the aggressive behaviors began to habituate, sexual behaviors became more prevalent. Although the two opposite-sexed groups showed the most sexual behavior, sexual behaviors were observed in the same-sexed pairs to a smaller degree. Using a sophisticated statistical procedure (principle components analysis), the researchers were able to show that these sexual and aggressive behaviors were inversely related to each other. As they point out, the most straightforward interpretation of their results is that "frequent performance of sexual behavior...decreases the likelihood of aggressive behavior being performed and vice versa"(Cole et al., 1980, p. 13). One possible conclusion we might draw from this study is that in order for successful mating to occur, aggressive responses toward a potential mate must first be reduced to levels that allow the emergence of sexual responses. In turn, once sexual responses have become

frequent enough, aggression toward the mate is largely inhibited. Such a mechanism can help us understand how an animal that behaves aggressively toward its neighbors nevertheless lives peacefully with its mate.

Research with humans concerning the relationship of aggression to sexuality is much less clear. For example, Zillmann and his associates have found that exposure to erotic or pornographic material may lead to increased aggressiveness in individuals who have been previously provoked (Zillmann & Bryant, 1982; Ramirez, Bryant, & Zillmann, 1982). Other researchers, however, have obtained results indicating that provoked individuals are less aggressive after exposure to erotic materials (Baron, 1974a, 1974b; Baron & Bell, 1977; Donnerstein, Donnerstein, & Evans, 1975). As noted by Sapolsky and Zillmann (1981), the only point on which these different sets of studies agree is that the aggressiveness of unprovoked individuals is relatively unaffected by exposure to erotica.

The innate character of aggressiveness in humans is a matter of much debate among theorists. Most ethologists have argued that human aggressiveness is innate (see, for example, Lorenz, 1967; Tinbergen, 1977; Eibl-Eibesfeldt, 1979). Lorenz, for example, believes that human aggressiveness was adaptive during the early Stone Age but became maladaptive with the invention of weapons. Tinbergen, noting that some species defend group territories, has suggested that war may result from this innate group territoriality in humans. Similarly, Eibl-Eibesfeldt has proposed that war developed as a cultural mechanism of groups competing for space and raw materials but that aggressiveness as a behavior is innate.

The complexity of human sexual and aggressive behaviors is such that·it seems likely both innate and learned tendencies play a role. As we shall see in later chapters, there is considerable evidence that physiology and environment are important influences on sexual and aggressive behaviors.

SUMMARY

The concept of instinct has had a long and varied career. Early formulations were often subjective and in many cases no more than descriptive labels. Problems arose with the early theories because they confused learned and instinctive behaviors. Additionally, these early theories were guilty of the nominal fallacy—naming behaviors without explaining them.

The ethologists helped us understand motivation from the viewpoint of naturally occurring behavior and evolution. They also attempted to define the various components of motivated behavior in ways that could be experimentally verified. Concepts such as key stimulus, fixed action pattern, innate releasing mechanism, and action-specific energy help us understand how some behaviors are motivated by genetically controlled programs. More complex behaviors can be understood with such concepts as reaction chains, intention movements, and conflict behavior.

Newer approaches have begun to investigate these ideas in more detail, and physiological research suggests that the ethological concepts have some validity. An interest in understanding human behavior from an ethological perspective has begun to develop and may eventually provide insight into how language is learned, certain social behaviors, and even some abnormal behaviors.

Though the concept of instinct cannot explain all that we know about the motivation of behavior, certain types of behavior in humans as well as other animals appear to be genetically programmed. Genetic programming, then, is one source of the activation and direction of behavior. Further study of this source of motivation is needed, particularly in humans.

SUGGESTIONS FOR FURTHER READING

Eibl-Eibesfeldt, I. (1972). *Love and hate: The natural history of behavior patterns* (trans. Geoffrey Strachan). New York: Holt, Rinehart & Winston. The best compilation of information on human instinctive behavior patterns currently available.

Eibl-Eibesfeldt, I. (1979). *The biology of peace and war*. Britain: Thames and Hudson. Presents evidence for the instinctive aspects of aggressive behavior in humans.

Gould, J. L. (1982). *Ethology: The mechanisms and evolution of behavior*. New York: Norton. A comprehensive introduction to the field of ethology.

Lorenz, K. Z. (1967). *On aggression*. New York: Bantam. Presents the ethological position on the innate character of aggression in man and animals.

Lorenz, K. Z. (1981). *The foundations of ethology*. New York: Springer-Verlag. An overview of the field of ethology by one of its founders.

Chapter Three

Physiological Mechanisms of Arousal

CHAPTER PREVIEW

This chapter is concerned with the following questions:

1. Can motivation and emotion be explained as a result of the arousal of an organism?

2. Which brain mechanisms are involved in arousal?

3. What are the properties, mechanisms, and functions of sleep?

4. What is stress and how does it influence the body?

5. Are changes in the events of an individual's life related to stress and illness?

6. How can we deal with stress?

Toward the end of each semester, an interesting phenomenon occurs. Students get sick. At first I attributed this phenomenon to attempts by certain students to avoid taking exams that would probably finalize grades lower than they desired. After observing this late-semester-illness phenomenon and also observing a similar phenomenon in myself and my colleagues during periods of acute stress, I

have concluded that it is not malingering or an attempt to postpone the inevitable but a result of stress. For the student, stresses increase toward the end of the semester as exams are scheduled, projects near completion, and reports or term papers come due. For faculty, stresses more often involve deadlines for submission of articles for publication, the necessity of preparing grant proposals, or preparation of new courses.

My own observation is that such stresses seem to accumulate until at some yet unspecific point, our bodies succumb to whatever variety of flu or other such malady this year brings us. Apparently we tend to get sick precisely when we can least afford to.

INTRODUCTION

Fortunately I am not alone in thinking that stress is related to illness; a considerable amount of research has been conducted that suggests a link between the two. We will examine some of this research toward the end of this chapter.

Stress is often conceptually located at the extreme end of a continuum of arousal. If arousal levels are too low, we sleep or may even be in a coma. At more moderate levels of arousal, we are awake and alert, while at the high end of the continuum, anxiety and stress appear. In this chapter we examine theory and research that attempts to explain motivated behavior as a result of changes in arousal. Much of this research has focused on the brain mechanisms of arousal—about which, as we shall see, much is known.

For some reason, statistics, foreign languages, and physiological brain structures strike fear into the hearts of students. What is common to these three, perhaps, is that they require students to think (and to use strange, new terms) in ways that are different from their normal approach to learning. Therefore the material in this chapter and the next is presented as nontechnically as possible, even though learning new terms and something about how changes in brain activity lead to changes in behavior will be necessary.

It is ironic that humans have progressed to the point where they can successfully send men and women into outer space but still know little about the "inner space" of the nervous system. This is partially because of the complexity of the nervous system and perhaps also because it is easier to control our external environment, and therefore study it, than to control and study the nervous system. Ultimately, however, everything we are capable of doing, every behavior from brushing our teeth to solving differential equations, is the result of the activity of our nervous system.

In this chapter we will examine the ideas and research put forth to explain the arousal or activation of behavior. We will begin by examining early notions of how the brain accomplishes this activation and then proceed to theories and research showing that the automatic processes of the brain (i.e., the autonomic nervous system) are intimately involved. We will then examine in some detail Hebb's theory of activation as representative of the thinking on arousal that was current in the 1950s. This will lead us into a more detailed examination of brain arousal mechanisms, particularly to a structure called the **reticular activating system**. We will examine theory and research indicating the involvement of this structure in arousal (from sleep to active attention) and then proceed to examine information on one aspect of arousal—sleep.

High states of arousal lead to stress, and we will look at research indicating that high arousal or stress influences our adaptive ability to our environment. In particular we will examine Selye's general adaptation syndrome and more recent research on stress and susceptibility to illness.

We will find that the concept of emotion weaves itself in and out of the research we will examine and that it is usually difficult to separate motivation, emotion, and arousal. For the purposes of this chapter, in fact, we might say that motivation = emotion = arousal—although this approach also has its pitfalls.

EARLY FORMULATIONS OF EMOTIONAL AROUSAL

Prior to the 1884 publication of William James's article on emotion, it was felt that the arousal of behavior was the last step in a three-step process that began with the perception of some stimulus (e.g., a barking dog), which led to the development of an emotion (e.g., fear) and culminated in behavior (e.g., running away). Figure 3.1a depicts the sequence of events leading from perception to behavior as they were understood prior to 1884.

The James-Lange Theory

James in 1884 and Lange in 1885 independently proposed that the feelings of emotion did not occur immediately after the perceptions of some event in the environment but as a result of our bodily responses to the object. Their approach became known as the **James-**

Sequence of events triggering arousal and subsequent behavior.

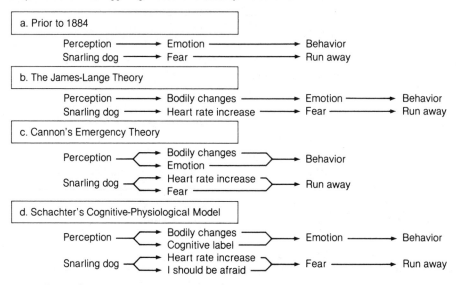

Figure 3.1   *Four models of the relationship between events, emotion, and behavior.*

Lange theory of emotion. For James the experience of emotion occurs as follows: the perception of an environmental stimulus (e.g., a barking dog) leads to changes in the body (e.g., increased heart rate, rapid breathing, and so on), which, in turn, are fed back to the brain indicating a "changed state." The change in the physical state (particularly of the internal organs) is the experience of emotion. In other words, our perception of changes in our body leads to an emotional experience. The sequence of events leading from perception to behavior is noted in Figure 3.1b.

For example, if an automobile almost runs us down as we are jogging along the roadside, we react by changes in muscle tension and glandular secretion, and we become angry (perhaps making an obscene gesture)— in that order.

James thought that without the bodily changes, emotions would not exist or, at most, would be cold or intellectualized (e.g., "I know I should feel angry, but I don't").

The James-Lange theory of emotion was very popular because it agreed with common sense, and it was generally regarded as "truth" until W. B. Cannon (1929, 1968) began to question it experimentally. Based on his own research and that of others, he criticized the James-Lange theory on five counts.

First, Cannon argued that the bodily changes supposed to provide feedback to the brain and thus provide emotional quality to experience could be completely eliminated without disturbing the emotions of an organism. He denervated cats so that no changes in the body could occur. These cats, however, still showed normal rage behavior in the presence of a barking dog.

Second, Cannon noted that the bodily changes occurring in emotional states are very nearly the same regardless of the emotion shown. For example, he noted that in both fear and rage the heart accelerates, blood sugar levels increase, the pupils of the eyes dilate, and hair stands erect. Thus feedback from these kinds of changes could not be determining the emotional state of the organism. He further noted that these same bodily changes occur in response to changes in temperature (e.g., in exposure to extreme cold or heat).

Third, Cannon claimed that the internal organs (i.e., viscera) supposed to provide feedback to the brain for the experience of emotion are not very sensitive structures. The number of sensory nerve fibers (i.e., afferents) coming from these structures (stomach, intestines, heart, and so on) are often only $1/10$ the number of motor nerve fibers coming to them from the brain (i.e., efferents). Cannon noted that we are usually unaware of the movements and changes of our internal organs (for example, what is your small intestine doing at this moment?). He noted that one can cut, tear, crush, or even burn the components of the digestive system, in fact, with no discomfort to unanesthetized humans—which, of course, suggests that these organs do not play a prominent role in providing feedback.

Fourth, Cannon felt that the changes occurring in the internal organs are too slow to provide the experience of emotion. He observed that the experience of emotion is sometimes immediate, but the triggering of the internal organs and feedback to the brain concerning their change may take several seconds. Cannon felt, therefore, that the state of emotion exists before feedback from the viscera can occur.

Fifth, Cannon noted that artificial induction of an aroused emotional state does not lead to an emotional "feeling." Thus injections of adrenalin (a hormone released by the adrenal glands during an emotional episode) did not make injected persons emotional even though adrenalin alters bodily functioning in ways associated with emotionality. Injected subjects reported feeling "as if" they should be emotional but without the emotional experience itself. In a very small number of cases

reported by Maranon (cited in Cannon, 1927), real emotions were produced, but this only occurred in individuals who had been induced into an emotional state by talking about their sick children or dead parents before the injection. In one case reported by Maranon, emotion was experienced after an injection of adrenalin in a patient who was diagnosed as having a hyperthyroid condition. But hyperthyroidism results in various changes to metabolic processes and to the endocrine system, so it is difficult to conclude that the experienced emotion resulted only from the injection.

These five criticisms of the James-Lange theory led Cannon to propose an alternative theory of emotion termed the **emergency theory**.

The Emergency Theory of Emotional Arousal

To understand Cannon's theory fully, we must briefly examine the autonomic nervous system.

The Autonomic Nervous System The autonomic nervous system (ANS) is basically involved with the regulation of vegetative processes (Carlson, 1977); that is, the ANS controls those processes that we do not voluntarily control, such as heartbeat, blood vessel constriction or dilation, glandular secretion, and so on. The ANS is composed of two subsystems, the **sympathetic** and **parasympathetic nervous systems**, which tend to have opposite effects upon the body.

The sympathetic nervous system (SNS) is most active when energy stores of the body are being expended. When activated, the SNS causes increased blood flow to the muscles, secretion of adrenalin (today the term **epinephrine** is more commonly used) from the adrenal glands, increased heart rate, and release of additional blood sugar by the liver.

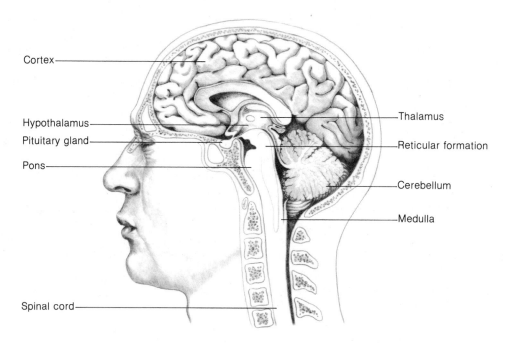

Cortex

Hypothalamus

Pituitary gland

Pons

Spinal cord

Thalamus

Reticular formation

Cerebellum

Medulla

Figure 3.2   *Major structures of the brain. Note the locations of the thalamus, hypothalamus, and reticular formation.*

The SNS in general prepares the organism to deal with emergency situations such as attack or flight.

The parasympathetic nervous system (PNS) is most active when the body is in the process of storing energy for future use. It decreases heart rate, dilates blood vessels, and causes saliva flow to the mouth when one is eating food. It also increases stomach and intestinal activity and directs the flow of blood away from the muscles to the digestive system. It is the system most active when we are quiet and relaxed after a large holiday meal.

The ANS also controls the endocrine system, which consists of glands that secrete their hormones directly into the bloodstream (e.g., pituitary, thyroid, and adrenal glands). This system will be discussed later when we examine its relationship to stress.

The SNS and PNS do not work in strict opposition to one another, because the organs they innervate are often different. It is, however, a useful simplification to view them as opposing one another from a motivational point of view, and this is essentially what Cannon did.

Cannon believed that emotion is associated with activation of the SNS. He argued that the control of emotion is based on a brain structure called the **thalamus**, which receives information from the various senses throughout the body and is located as shown in Figure 3.2. Cannon believed that various emotional response patterns (e.g., anger and fear) are activated by the thalamus when the external sensory information it received is relayed to the cortex. He argued that the emotional behaviors activated by the thalamus are held in check by the cortex (see Figure 3.2). When the cortex receives appropriate sensory information, it releases the thalamus to trigger emotional responses. Cannon thought the thalamus was also responsible for SNS activation leading to the bodily changes considered so important by the James-Lange theory. Thus Cannon saw the expression of emotion as simultaneous with activation of the body, not the result of it (see Figure 3.1c).

Schachter's Cognitive-Physiological Theory of Emotion

Stanley Schachter has proposed a theory of emotion that involves both physiological arousal and cognitive attributions (Schachter, 1964; Schachter & Singer, 1962). Basically the theory assumes that both physiological arousal and a cognitive label are necessary for the full experience of emotion. If either is absent, the subjective state experienced will be incomplete.

Schachter and Singer devised a novel experiment to test the idea that both arousal and cognitive labeling are necessary for the experience of emotion. In most everyday circumstances, the physiological arousal that occurs is clearly defined by the situation, so that we do not perceive the cognitive label and the arousal as distinct. What would happen, Schachter and Singer wondered, if some subjects were artificially aroused through the injection of a substance normally present when a person is in an aroused state? They surmised that subjects experiencing physiological arousal for which there was no adequate explanation would search their environment for cues to help them label (i.e., attribute) the arousal they felt.

Male subjects who participated in the experiment were told that the experiment involved the effects of a new vitamin supplement on vision. This supplement was to be given by injection, after which the subjects

would wait 20 minutes for it to begin to act and then would be given a vision test. Actually the injections were either epinephrine (i.e., a chemical released by the body during arousal that leads to changes in heart rate, accelerated breathing, flushing, and hand tremors) or a harmless and inactive salt solution (i.e., saline placebo). Some subjects were correctly told what to expect from the injection of epinephrine, while another group was misinformed that their feet would feel numb and that they might experience itching and a slight headache. A third group of subjects was given no information about what to expect from the epinephrine injection. Subjects in the placebo condition were also given no information concerning the injection.

In order to provide an experimentally induced cognitive label, half of the subjects in each group waited to take the eye test in a room with another subject (actually a confederate of the experimenter), who acted either euphoric (e.g., sailing paper airplanes, shooting paper wads, using a hula hoop) or angry (e.g., at being asked to take an injection, at filling out a questionnaire, and finally tearing up the questionnaire and storming from the room). The seven groups and the conditions under which they were run were as follows:

Euphoria

epinephrine informed
epinephrine ignorant
epinephrine misinformed*
placebo

Anger

epinephrine informed
epinephrine ignorant
placebo

*Note that this group was run only in the euphoria condition. This list of seven groups and conditions is from Schachter and Singer, 1962. Copyright 1962 by the American Psychological Association. Reprinted by permission.

Schachter and Singer expected that the epinephrine-informed condition would not lead to the experience of the emotions of euphoria or anger because these subjects should already have been able to attribute the bodily changes they experienced to the epinephrine injection. Likewise the placebo condition should not have led to much emotional experience because there should have been no physiological arousal. Both the epinephrine-ignorant and the epinephrine-misinformed groups, however, could be expected to search their environment for cues concerning the bodily reactions they would feel. The presence of a euphoric or angry companion (whom the subject thought also had been injected) should have led the subject to attribute his own experiences to either euphoria or anger. In other words, the confederate should have provided cues that would have allowed the subject to cognitively label the feeling he was experiencing as either euphoric or angry.

The results of the experiment supported Schachter and Singer's hypothesis. The euphoria or anger experienced by the epinephrine-ignorant group was greater than for the epinephrine-informed condition. Likewise the epinephrine-misinformed group showed more euphoria than the epinephrine-informed group. One problem with the results was that the subjects of the placebo condition experienced emotion intermediate to the epinephrine-ignorant and the epinephrine-informed conditions and did not differ from the epinephrine-ignorant condition. Schachter and Singer believed that the lack of difference between the epinephrine-ignorant and the placebo conditions resulted from the fact that some subjects in the epinephrine-ignorant condition attributed their feelings to the injection, even though they had not been specifically told that the injection would have an effect. These "self-informed" subjects should therefore have been less influenced by the euphoric or angry model, and the effect of

the confederate on their emotion would tend to be reduced. Schachter and Singer were able to determine which subjects were self-informed by their answers to an open-ended question. When these subjects were eliminated from the analysis, the epinephrine-ignorant group and the placebo group differed significantly in emotionality.

Schachter and Singer's data support the notion that subjective feelings of emotion require both physiological arousal and a cognitive label that attributes the aroused state to particular causes. Normally the cues for labeling the aroused state are clear to us; however, if a physiological state is aroused and we have no ready explanation for it, we then search our environment for cues that will help us attribute (i.e., label) the arousal we experience.

Schachter's analysis of emotion suggests that if a cognitive label exists in the absence of physiological arousal, the experience of emotion should also be incomplete. Such an experience would perhaps resemble a cold anger or an "as if" state; that is, the person might feel "as if" he or she should be angry or sad but the subjective state would lack the full-blown feeling of true emotion.

One way in which to test the contribution of physiological arousal to emotionality would be to interview patients with spinal cord damage. The nearer the break in the spinal cord to the brain, the less information will be available to judge one's state of arousal. Schachter (1964) cited a study conducted by Hohmann (1962) revealing that the closer a spinal break was to the brain, the greater the decrease in emotion. This decrease in emotionality applied to sexual excitement, fear, anger, and grief but not to sentimentality. Several of the accident victims also reported that their feelings of emotionality were more cognitive or "mental" than before.

In many respects Schachter's model of emotion is a combination and modification of the James-Lange theory and Cannon's emergency theory of emotion. Schachter's theory, like the James-Lange theory, proposes that bodily changes are involved in the experience of emotion. In a fashion similar to Cannon, however, Schachter also proposes that the interpretation of an event is important for the full experience of emotion. But Schachter goes beyond the earlier theories in proposing that both physiological change *and* cognitive labeling are necessary for the full experience of emotion. Schachter's model has proven enormously popular since its introduction in 1964. In addition to its initial purpose as an explanation of emotion, the theory has also spawned a large literature on the misattribution of arousal, particularly as misattribution relates to the reduction of fear and anxiety. We will examine some aspects of the misattribution research in Chapter Eleven.

Although Schachter's theory has both generated and suggested several new lines of research, the support for the theory itself is modest. Cotton (1981) reviewed research on the model and noted that the original study upon which the model was based (Schachter & Singer, 1962) has been criticized on both methodological and empirical grounds (see, e.g., Plutchik & Ax, 1967). Additionally, several attempts to replicate the Schachter and Singer study have been unsuccessful (Marshall & Zimbardo, 1979; Maslach, 1979; Rogers & Deckner, 1975), although Erdmann and Janke (1978) have provided support for the model as a result of their research. Research by Lazarus (1968) and Weiner, Russell, and Lerman (1978) suggests that the cognitive component alone may be both necessary and sufficient for the arousal of emotion. As should be evident at this point, there is considerable debate among psychologists concerning the conditions necessary for the instigation of emotion. Over the past several decades, analyses of emotion have increasingly emphasized the cognitive component to a greater degree than the physiological component. Whether cognition alone will pro-

vide sufficient explanation of emotion remains to be determined; however, much of what is known today about arousal grew out of research on the physiology of emotion. It is to the ideas and research on arousal that we now turn.

AROUSAL THEORY

The arousal approach tends to emphasize the organism as a whole (Duffy, 1966) and argues that we can best understand behavior by understanding how the organism becomes activated.

The basic idea underlying arousal theory is that we can understand emotion and motivation by viewing them on a continuum of behavioral activation. This continuum ranges from low levels of arousal (e.g., coma or sleep) to very high levels (e.g., rage). Basically arousal theory regards emotion as the result of the individual's arousal level.

Arousal theory assumes that behavior will change as we become more aroused. Some changes in arousal, as from sleep to alert wakefulness, will result in increased efficiency of performance, but other arousal changes, as from alert wakefulness to extreme emotional arousal, will interfere with efficient responding. This reasoning suggests that an optimal level of arousal exists at which behavior will be most efficient, as depicted in Figure 3.3.

The curve in Figure 3.3 is called an **inverted U function** and indicates that increasing arousal improves performance only up to a point, after which continued increases in arousal actually begin to interfere with responding. This arousal-performance relationship, sometimes called the **Yerkes-Dodson law**, is easily seen. In order to study objectively for an exam, we must be sufficiently aroused; on the other hand, if we become "too emotional" about the exam, our anxiety may interfere with our studying to the point that we cannot learn the material.

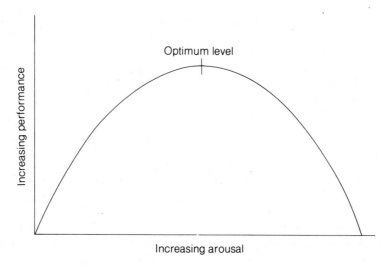

Figure 3.3 *The inverted U function relating performance to arousal. As arousal increases, so does performance up to a point; beyond the optimum level, increases in arousal lead to reduced levels of performance. (Adapted from Hebb, 1955.)*

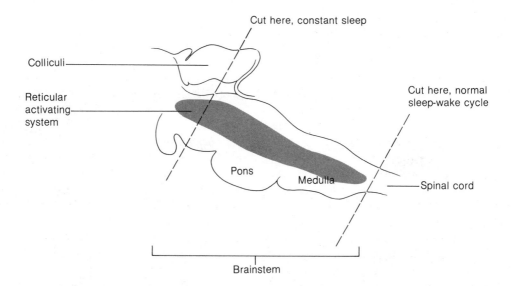

Figure 3.4 *Brainstem cuts made by Bremer. Note location of the reticular activating system.*

Hokanson (1969) noted that the proposed relationship between arousal and performance holds for some types of tasks but not for others. For example, Freeman (1940) obtained an inverted U function between arousal (as measured by skin conductance) and reaction time, but Hokanson did not obtain inverted U functions for tasks such as symbol matching and concept formation. Thus the relationship between arousal and behavior is apparently more complex and task specific than arousal theory has indicated.

If emotion and motivation result from activation of the nervous system, as arousal theory suggests, there should be structures in the nervous system that trigger this activation. Bremer (1937) has shown that if we cut through the brainstem of an animal between the medulla and the spinal cord (see Figure 3.4), the animal continues to go through its normal sleep-wake cycle even though the body has been deprived of all its higher cortical brain tissue (Bremer called this preparation **encephale isolé**). On the other hand, if we cut higher up the brainstem at the level of the colliculi, the sleep-wake cycle is abolished and the animal sleeps constantly, showing no spontaneous waking (called the **cerveau isolé**).

Taken together, the results of Bremer's two cuts suggest that some brain structure (or structures) located between the two cuts may control changes in the arousal level involved in moving from sleeping to waking. Further, such a structure is probably located in the vicinity of the pons (see Figure 3.4).

The Reticular Activating System

Arousal theory received a big boost with the discovery by Moruzzi and Magoun (1949) of the role of the reticular activating system in arousal. The reticular activating system (RAS) is a group of neurons (i.e., nerve cells) located in the brainstem's central core, which runs from the level of the medulla through the

thalamus, as shown in Figure 3.4 (Carlson, 1977). Moruzzi and Magoun found that electrical stimulation of the RAS led to changes in the electrical activity of the cortex (recorded by the **electroencephalogram** or **EEG**) that were indistinguishable from changes seen when external stimuli (e.g., a loud noise) were being paid attention to. In order to understand the role of the RAS in arousal, we must briefly examine what is shown by an EEG.

An individual resting quietly shows a regular pattern of cortical electrical activity that can be measured by means of the EEG. The electrical activity of the cells in this relaxed state tends to occur simultaneously (i.e., they are **synchronous**) and leads to a pattern of electrical activity known as **alpha waves**. If we make a loud sound, however, the individual will open the eyes and look around in an alert manner, and the pattern of the EEG during this alert behavior is very different. The cells of the cortex tend now to be active independently of one another (i.e., they are **desynchronized**), which leads to a new EEG pattern sometimes called **alpha blocking**. Alpha blocking is associated with alert, attentive, and aroused individuals ready to deal with changes in their environment.

Moruzzi and Magoun found that stimulation of the RAS leads to alpha blocking just as environmental stimuli do. Therefore it seemed reasonable that the RAS is responsible for the activation of the organism to begin with. Support for this idea was provided in a number of different ways. First, the RAS receives sensory input from the external sensory systems as well as from the muscles and internal organs (Hokanson, 1969); thus it has the necessary inputs to trigger arousal. Second, Lindsley (1951) cut all the brain structures surrounding the RAS in experimental animals and found that the animals still displayed normal sleep-wake cycles. But when he cut the RAS, leaving everything else intact, the result was a permanently sleeping animal, just as in Bremer's cerveau isolé preparation. Finally, the RAS is known to send fibers diffusely to the whole cortex. Apparently, therefore, the RAS is the brain structure that serves to arouse the organism from sleep to wakefulness. Thus the RAS most likely determines where on the arousal continuum we find ourselves.

The discovery of the role of the RAS in arousal led activation theorists to argue that emotion and motivation were equivalent to cortical arousal (e.g., see Lindsley, 1950, 1951). Perhaps one of the best-reasoned theories was put forth by Donald Hebb (1955), and to his theory we now turn.

Hebb's Theory

Hebb believed that sensory information serves two purposes: to provide information, or what he termed the **cue function** of a stimulus, and to arouse the individual (i.e., the **arousal function**). If the individual's cortex is not aroused, the cue function of a stimulus will have no effect (e.g., we do not react to the sound of a passing car when we are asleep because the cortex is not aroused by the RAS).

Sensory stimuli picked up by a person are sent to both the RAS and the cortex via the thalamus. Hebb believed that the stimulus effect at the RAS level is to activate or "tone up" the cortex so that the stimulus information coming from the thalamus can be processed by the cortex. Motivation, for Hebb, is the activation of the cortex by the RAS.

It is also known that the cortex sends fibers down to the RAS (Magoun, 1963). Thus the cortex can also activate the RAS and keep arousal high if no external or internal stimulation is present. This fact provides a possible explanation for how thoughts could be motivating. Lying in bed and thinking about tomorrow's exam activates one's RAS, which in turn keeps the cortex aroused, and sleep becomes difficult. Thus thoughts as well as

external stimuli can lead to the arousal of an individual. More research on this aspect of arousal might prove very useful to our understanding of the way in which thoughts influence behavior.

Psychophysiological Measures

Arousal theory is based on the assumption that one can measure arousal by monitoring the activity of the brain or changes in the autonomic nervous system and correlating these with changes in behavior. As researchers soon discovered, however, these correlations were often minimal (although usually positive). The lack of substantial correlations between different indexes of arousal has created problems for arousal theory and led Lacey (1967) to propose that more than one type of arousal exists. Thus we may see **behavioral arousal** as indicated by a responding organism, **autonomic arousal** as shown by changes in bodily functions, or **cortical arousal** as evidenced by desynchronized, fast brain waves. Lacey proposed that although these three arousals often occur together, they do not have to and are in fact independent. He noted, for example, that certain chemicals (e.g., atropine) produce EEG activity akin to sleep in cats and dogs, which nevertheless respond behaviorally in a normal, awake manner. Other chemicals (e.g., physostigmine) produce EEG activity like that of an alert animal, but the animal behaves as if drowsy. Comatose patients sometimes show "normal" EEGs, and normal responding is sometimes observed in individuals with sleep-like EEGs. Lacey also reported several studies indicating that sometimes little relationship exists between central nervous system activity and autonomic changes. As a result of these problems, he proposed that arousal is multidimensional. He believed that different situations produce different patterns of somatic responses (e.g., heart rate).

Feedback from the periphery of the body is also important in Lacey's model of arousal.

For example, he reported research showing that distention of the carotid sinus (a mechanism in the carotid artery) causes EEG activity to change from alert, high-frequency activity to low-frequency activity generally associated with sleep. This change indicates that feedback from various systems of the body can directly influence the arousal system and suggests that bodily systems may also play a role in the length of arousal episodes.

To summarize, RAS research indicates a physiological mechanism that is involved with arousal of the organism, the sleep-wake cycle, and alert attention to the environment. These conclusions fit nicely with arousal theory's concept of motivation and emotion as equivalent to arousal.

Problems with Arousal Theory

Unfortunately, several problems with arousal theory remain. One major problem is the lack of a strong relationship between measures of behavioral, cortical, and autonomic arousal. A second problem specific to Lacey's theory is that it assumes different patterns of bodily responses, yet clear differences remain to be shown. Some studies have indicated that the adrenal hormone norepinephrine may be related to anger or aggression and epinephrine to fear or anxiety (Schildkraut & Kety, 1967). However, further work is needed to determine if Lacey's theory can account for different emotions in terms of different bodily response patterns. Of particular interest in this regard is a study by Ekman, Levenson, and Friesen (1983) indicating that changes in autonomic activities are discernible for the emotions of disgust, anger, fear, and sadness when careful control procedures are employed. Ekman and associates suggest that the autonomic changes may be instigated by contraction of the facial muscles into the universal signals for these emotions. Facial muscular patterns may even provide the different bodily response patterns that arousal theory dictates

and may yet revive the James-Lange theory of emotion.

Another problem with arousal theory is its general assumption that cortical arousal, as evidenced by the EEG, indicates a motivated or emotional state. As Lacey pointed out, this relationship is not always found. It is not presently clear that cortical arousal is equivalent to motivated behavior; but even if we were to make that assumption, it is also not clear how this arousal directs behavior. One final problem is the assumption that an understanding of arousal requires only an understanding of the underlying physiological mechanisms. This may be incorrect. A full understanding of arousal may also require a knowledge of environmental factors and the past history of the organism.

Research concerned with arousal theory has added much to our understanding of behavior. Arousal is present during emotional episodes, and emotionally aroused persons are motivated. But major problems with an arousal theory of emotion and motivation remain to be solved. Research to date has only suggested that different physiological states or chemical balances may accompany various emotions. Clearly, for arousal theory to be viable, we must be able to understand how different types of emotions are activated.

SLEEP

Most arousal theories regard sleep as either the absence or a low state of arousal. But sleep itself consists of more than one state and in some respects closely resembles waking activity.

Anyone who has gone for any lengthy period of wakefulness realizes that sleep can become an overpowering motive, easily overriding such motives as hunger or sex. This observation is supported by research indicating that sleep shows characteristics of a motivated need state (Dement, 1972).

Sleep research can be traced as far back as

the late 1800s, but systematic research only began with Nathaniel Kleitman's studies in the early 1920s (Kleitman, 1963). Much is known about the sleep process (see, e.g., Long, 1987; Pressman, 1986), yet the reasons for sleep remain obscure. For example, it is known that the effects of sleep deprivation are specific to the type of task required of a sleep-deprived individual (Johnson, 1983). Webb (1986) found that going without sleep for approximately 48 hours led to problems of *sustaining* performance on a long, complex task requiring high levels of attention and cognitive processing. There were, however, no clear indications that *accuracy* of performance declined. In the following sections we will explore what is known about sleep, what physiological structures seem to be involved, and what the function of sleep is thought to be.

General Properties of Sleep

We spend roughly one third of our lives in the state of sleep. On that basis alone, sleep must be considered an important behavior to understand. Even though a large portion of our lives is spent sleeping, large variations exist among individuals in the amount of sleep needed. While most people sleep seven to eight hours per night, others are able to get along with less. Dement (1972) reported his study of two individuals who regularly slept less than three hours per night without apparent ill effects.

Common sense indicates that we sleep when we are fatigued. This cannot be the entire explanation, however, because people confined to bed 24 hours per day sleep approximately the same amount of time that they would have slept if they had been up and active. Dement suggested that we may sleep because we are least efficient at certain times. Our bodies go through cyclic changes that often approximate 24 hours in length; these cycles are called **circadian rhythms** (from the Latin *circa*, about, and *diem*, a day). Many of

these circadian rhythms operate in the lowest part of their cycle during sleep, and Dement proposed that sleep may protect us from engaging in behavior at a time when we are least efficient. Webb and Agnew (1973) similarly suggested that sleep is adaptive because it keeps organisms from responding at unnecessary or dangerous times. Meddis (1975) made a similar proposal based on an evolutionary perspective. Several lines of research suggest that circadian rhythms and sleep are closely linked (Czeisler et al., 1989; Pool, 1989). A more complete understanding of the role of circadian rhythms in the sleep process may prove useful in treating sleep disorders and jet lag.

Different animals spend different amounts of time in sleep, as the following data from Webb and Agnew (1973) show:

donkey, 3.1 hours
rabbit, 10.8 hours
chimpanzee, 11.0 hours
rat, 13.5 hours
cat, 14.4 hours
bat, 18.0 hours
opossum, 19.4 hours

This variation seems to fit with Webb and Agnew's idea of the adaptiveness of sleep, because different animals would be expected to differ in the durations of time when responding would be disadvantageous to them.

In humans the length of time spent in sleep decreases with age. Infants who are three days old sleep approximately 14 to 16 hours a day, while 5-year-olds sleep about 11 hours. By age 20 the average individual sleeps about $6\frac{1}{2}$ to 7 hours per night. Generally, in the aged, a further small decrease in sleep time occurs, although the most striking thing about sleep in the aged is its variability. Some aged people sleep more than they did when younger, while others sleep considerably less (Webb & Agnew, 1973).

Consider how we fall asleep. Sleep seems to come gradually; that is, we "drift off" slowly into sleep. Actually, EEG recordings of the brain during the act of falling asleep indicate that our perception is incorrect—we fall asleep abruptly (Dement, 1972).

The EEG has been a powerful tool in helping researchers to study sleep. It is used to identify different stages or levels of sleep, and we now turn to these stages.

Stages of Sleep

As defined by electrical activity of the brain, sleep proceeds through five stages during the night. The alpha wave activity that characterizes relaxed wakefulness is replaced by fast, irregular waves of low amplitude in **Stage 1** of sleep, which lasts for about 10 to 15 minutes. Then the EEG pattern starts to show brief periods of **sleep spindles** (14 hz/sec waves),

and the subject is now in **Stage 2** of sleep. As Stage 2 continues (approximately 15 minutes), the amplitude of the waves becomes larger and slower ($\frac{1}{2}$ to $3\frac{1}{2}$ hz/sec). When these slow waves become frequent enough, the person is said to be in **Stage 3** of sleep (15 minutes). **Stage 4**, in which the slow, high-amplitude waves become dominant, will be reached approximately 30 to 45 minutes after falling asleep. After some time in Stage 4 sleep, the EEG pattern begins to change again to Stage 3, then to Stage 2, and finally to Stage 1. At Stage 1 the individual's eyes usually begin moving rapidly under the lids, and muscle tone, as measured at the jaw muscle, is very low. This is the fifth stage of sleep, generally called **REM sleep** (for rapid eye movements), and is the time during sleep when dreaming occurs (Webb & Agnew, 1973; Carlson, 1977). Examples of the various EEG patterns of the sleep stages are shown in Figure 3.5.

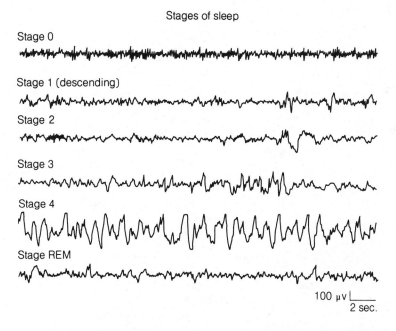

Stages of sleep

Stage 0

Stage 1 (descending)

Stage 2

Stage 3

Stage 4

Stage REM

100 µv
2 sec.

Figure 3.5 EEG patterns associated with the various stages of sleep. Stage 0 is relaxed wakefulness. Note how the waves become slower and larger as sleep progresses through the stages until stage REM. (From Webb & Agnew, 1968. Used by permission.)

REM and NREM Sleep Sleep Stages 1 through 4 are generally called NREM (for non-REM) sleep because eye movements are not evident during these stages. Non-REM sleep is also sometimes called **slow-wave** sleep to point out the predominance of the high-amplitude, slow waves (called **delta waves**) seen in Stages 3 and 4.

Some researchers believe that NREM sleep serves a restorative function, giving the body a chance to rebuild resources. We know, however, that Stage 4 sleep decreases with age, showing a sharp decline after age 30 and in some individuals disappearing altogether by age 50 (Webb & Agnew, 1973; but see Webb, 1982, for another view). Hayashi and Endo (1982) have also found large reductions in sleep Stages 3 and 4 in healthy aged persons. Their results indicate a forward shifting of

REM toward earlier portions of the night, perhaps, Hayashi and Endo suggest, because of the reduction in Stages 3 and 4.

Snoring, if it occurs, typically does so during NREM sleep, and a person awakened during NREM sleep does not usually report dreaming. Typically he or she reports random thoughts, usually of a nonemotional sort, similar to waking thoughts.

Sleep time is not equally divided among the five stages of sleep, nor do the stages occur evenly throughout the night. Approximately 5% of total sleep is spent in Stage 1, while almost 50% is spent in Stage 2. Stage 3 occupies only about 6% of total sleep time, and Stage 4 amounts to approximately 14%. REM sleep accounts for about 25% of sleep time.

Of the various stages, Stage 4 and REM sleep have been studied most extensively. A

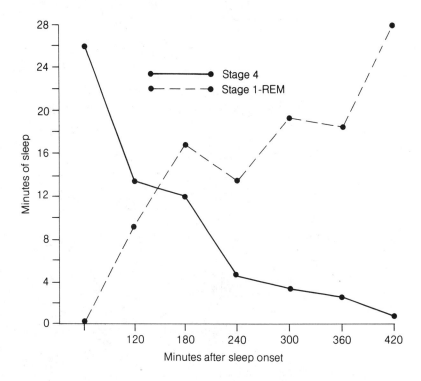

Figure 3.6   *Time spent in Stage 4 and REM sleep as a function of time since falling asleep. As can be seen, Stage 4 occurs primarily early in the night, while REM sleep increases as the night progresses. (From Webb & Agnew, 1973. Used by permission.)*

greater proportion of Stage 4 sleep occurs early in the night, and most REM sleep occurs later. Figure 3.6 shows the difference in sleep time for these two stages.

Rapid eye movement (REM) sleep was discovered by Aserinsky and Kleitman in 1955 (see also Aserinsky, 1987). It quickly became apparent to researchers that REM sleep correlated with reports of dreaming. For example, Dement (1972) noted that reports of dreaming from individuals awakened during REM sleep are approximately 80%, while reports of dreaming from persons awakened from Stage 4 are only about 7%. Some controversy exists concerning the percentage of dreams reported in REM and NREM sleep. This controversy certainly results from differences in how various researchers define dreaming—and, indeed, from the difficulty of defining dreaming in operational terms. The major difference, however, between dreams reported in REM and NREM sleep is apparently that REM dreams are more often bizarre, emotionally loaded, or lifelike, while dreams reported during NREM sleep are more likely to be described as nonemotional, random thoughts.

During REM sleep the EEG activity of the cortex is in Stage 1 and is, in many respects, similar to the EEG activity seen in a person who is awake and alert. In fact the EEG activity that occurs during REM sleep in cats is virtually indistinguishable from their waking EEG activity (Jouvet, 1976). But even though the electrical activity of the cortex appears to be close to that of waking behavior, arousing someone from REM sleep is difficult. For this reason, REM sleep has sometimes been called **paradoxical sleep** (the paradox being that the EEG appears aroused, yet strong stimulation is required to wake the individual).

Besides rapid eye movements in REM sleep, there is also a loss of muscle tone. This is apparently caused by inhibition of motor neurons in the brain and actually amounts to a temporary paralysis (Dement, 1972). The loss of muscle tone is actually the best indicator of "dream" or REM sleep. REM sleep normally occurs about once every 90 minutes throughout the night. REM periods become longer throughout the night, so that by morning one may be in a REM period for as long as an hour (Dement, 1972).

REM sleep, like Stage 4 sleep, tends to decline with age; however, REM sleep stabilizes at about age 20 and remains relatively constant thereafter. Newborn infants spend approximately 50% of their sleep time in REM sleep, while it is known that premature babies spend up to 75% of their sleep in the REM stage. The sleep of kittens, puppies, and rat pups is 100% REM (Dement, 1972). All these findings have led Dement to speculate that REM sleep may organize connections within the brain. In support of this hypothesis, Dement noted that guinea pigs, which are more mature than kittens at birth, show very little REM sleep.

The fact that animals show REM sleep in a fashion similar to humans raises the question of whether animals dream. Though we know that REM sleep and dreaming are correlated in humans, we cannot be sure that the same is true for other species. Thus, while the question is tantalizing, there is presently no good answer. Our knowledge of evolutionary processes, however, may lend support to the possibility that some animals, such as primates and perhaps dogs and cats, do dream.

Clearly the most exciting aspect of REM sleep research was the finding that it coincides with dreaming. For the first time, sleep scientists could begin to study objectively the very subjective state of dreaming.

Dreams

Although some people do not believe that they dream, research has shown that everyone dreams. This is easily shown by having a "nondreamer" sleep for several nights while connected to EEG apparatus and to equipment that measures eye movements and muscle tone. The adamant nondreamer falls asleep and eventually enters a period of REM activity. If awakened during this REM period, the "nondreamer" discovers to great amazement that he or she has been dreaming vividly!

The average individual spends about 100 minutes per night in dreaming (Webb & Agnew, 1973). It seems to be true, however, that one doesn't remember one's dreams unless one awakes soon after they have occurred. This is why we tend to remember the dreams we had just before the alarm went off but do not remember dreams that occurred earlier in the night.

Research has shown that although most dreams are brief, they can sometimes last up to an hour (Dement, 1972). Most dreams occur in ordinary, everyday settings and are usually not terribly emotional. When emotion is present in dreams, however, it tends to be negative; about 65% of emotional dreams are of this sort. Dement also noted that dreams early in the night tend to draw on the events of the previous day, while later dreams draw more from stored memories.

Sleep Deprivation

As noted earlier, the effects of sleep deprivation vary with the type of task. Short tasks performed under sufficient motivation often show only minor effects of sleep deprivation. Long, boring tasks requiring high motivation do, however, show deficits in sustaining attention (Webb, 1986).

Although common sense would seem to indicate that the effects of sleep deprivation are negative when they occur, research has shown that sleep deprivation can have therapeutic properties for some depressed individuals. As little as one complete night without sleep has an antidepressant effect on between ⅓ to ½ of de-

pressed patients (Roy-Byrne, Uhde, & Post, 1986).

Dream Deprivation William Dement pioneered research in dream deprivation. His procedure was to observe the recordings of sleeping persons for rapid eye movements and, when they occurred, quickly awaken the sleeper. Dement found that in order to deprive sleepers of REM sleep, it was necessary to awaken them more and more often. He noted that it was as if a "pressure" was building up that could only be expressed through REM sleep. When Dement let his subjects sleep normally, he discovered a now well-established phenomenon known as **REM rebound**. He found that when dream-deprived subjects were allowed to sleep, they dreamed much more than normal, as if the REM periods were rebounding from their imposed low level. Indeed this overshooting of the normal amount of dreaming continued for several days after the period of deprivation.

Dement noted that his REM-deprived subjects appeared irritable and anxious and had trouble concentrating. This suggested to him that REM sleep may be necessary for psychological well-being. Unfortunately, other investigators have not found anxiety or irritability in their REM-deprived subjects; therefore little can be concluded about the necessity of dreaming for psychological health.

REM deprivation can sometimes occur from drug usage. Many drugs (particularly barbiturates, if taken beyond recommended levels) suppress REM sleep. If the drugs are abruptly withdrawn, REM rebound occurs, and the person shows increased dreaming with vivid nightmares. Amphetamines, which act on the reticular formation to maintain arousal and wakefulness, also suppress REM when sleep finally occurs. Webb and Agnew (1973) noted that withdrawal of amphetamines leads to prolonged REM rebound, sometimes lasting up to two weeks, accompanied by vivid nightmares. Even alcohol, if taken in sufficient doses, leads to REM suppression. It is possible that the vivid hallucinations sometimes experienced in alcohol withdrawal (termed **delirium tremens** or "d.t.'s") may result from REM rebound intruding on waking behavior (Dement, 1972; Webb & Agnew, 1973). It seems clear that some "cures" for sleeplessness, like heavy barbiturate use, may turn out to be worse than sleep loss (Palca, 1989).

Much research has been conducted on both REM and NREM sleep. Though we know a good deal about sleep characteristics, we are just beginning to gain some understanding of the brain systems involved with sleep. The research is complex and sometimes contradictory; nevertheless, several brainstem and forebrain structures have been identified as important in sleep maintenance.

Physiology of Sleep

The autonomic nervous system changes its activity during sleep. During NREM sleep, blood pressure, heart rate, and respiration decline, and the veins and arteries dilate (**vasodilation**). During REM sleep, blood pressure, heart rate, and respiration generally increase but also become much more variable. There is also an increased flow of blood to the brain and penile erection in males occurs (Williams, Holloway, & Griffiths, 1973); the presence of an erection does not seem to bear any relationship to the content of the dream! In REM sleep the electrical activity of the cortex, as you remember, changes from slow, high-amplitude delta waves to fast, low-amplitude waves similar to those present during waking.

Most research has been aimed at explaining how structures within the brainstem may be related to changes in cortical activity. A considerable amount of research also exists, however, that suggests that forebrain areas also exert control over the sleep process. We

will now examine research concerned with brainstem structures.

Brainstem Mechanisms In discussing the reticular formation we examined the work of Bremer. You will recall that when he cut through the brain at the level of the colliculi, his cats no longer showed the normal sleep-wake cycle. When the cut was lower, between the medulla and the spinal cord, normal sleep-wake cycles were observed. These transections are shown in Figure 3.7.

If a cut is made approximately midway between Bremer's two cuts (through the middle of the pons), the animal shows insomnia. This suggests that the area between the collicular cut and the midpontine cut is normally involved in wakefulness. If this area is disconnected from the rest of the brain, as in Bremer's collicular cut, the animal sleeps; if the area remains connected, as in the midpontine cut, wakefulness is maintained and sleep is disrupted. Below this arousal center (RAS), in the general area of the pons, lies a structure that must normally suppress the RAS so that sleep can occur. But the RAS can no longer be suppressed if this structure is disconnected from the RAS (by the midpontine cut), and the animal cannot sleep. If the cut is made lower, between the medulla and the spinal cord as done by Bremer, both systems are left intact and connected to the cortex so that the normal sleep-wake cycle occurs (see Figure 3.7).

These findings led to an intense study of the area of the pons in order to discover which structures control the activity of the midbrain RAS and thus control arousal. At least three structures within this area have been implicated in the production of sleep (Carlson, 1977). The three structures are the **raphé nucleus**, and **locus coerulus**, and the **gigantocellular tegmental field** (see Figure 3.7).

Jouvet (1976) destroyed the cells within the raphé nucleus of the pons and medulla and found that insomnia was produced, just as in

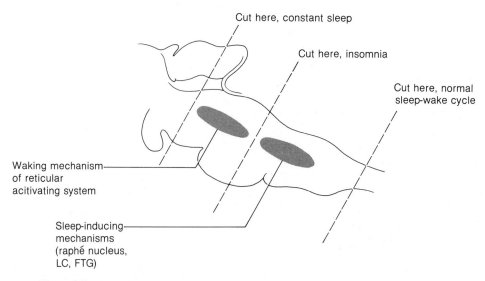

Figure 3.7 *Approximate locations of brainstem mechanisms involved in the control of sleep.*

the midpontine cut mentioned earlier. Thus it appeared to Jouvet that the raphé system is responsible for suppressing the activity of the midbrain reticular system (which is responsible for arousal and wakefulness). Following the terminology of Jouvet, we can think of the raphé nucleus as a "brake" on wakefulness.

More recent research suggests that the locus coerulus (hereafter called LC and located in the pons) and the gigantocellular tegmental field (called FTG and also located in the pons) work in a reciprocal fashion to determine periods of REM and NREM sleep (Carlson, 1977; Hobson, 1977; Hobson, McCarley, & Wyzinski, 1975; McCarley & Hobson, 1975).

Other structures within the brainstem are also known to influence arousal and sleep. For example, the nucleus of the solitary tract (located in the medulla) seems to suppress the activity of the RAS under certain conditions (Carlson, 1977). Interestingly, this nucleus receives input from the tongue and various internal organs; as Carlson noted, its presence might explain why large meals make us drowsy. Thus the physiological mechanisms that control waking behavior and sleep are

quite complex. To add even more complexity, there is considerable evidence that forebrain structures such as the frontal cortex, thalamus, hypothalamus, and preoptic areas also play a role in sleep (Williams, Holloway, & Griffiths, 1973).

A Sleep Chemical If you have ever gone without sleep for any length of time, you know how overpowering the desire to sleep can become. There now exists some evidence that the body makes a chemical that promotes sleep during periods of wakefulness.

Evidence for a sleep chemical was provided by Henri Pieron in the early 1900s (Pappenheimer, 1976). Pieron found that when he injected normal dogs with the cerebrospinal fluid of dogs deprived of sleep for ten days or more, the recipients slept for several hours following the injection. This suggested to Pieron that some sort of sleep-promoting chemical may develop during periods of prolonged wakefulness. Pieron's techniques left much to be desired, and although his early research was interesting, little progress was made until much later.

In 1976 John Pappenheimer at Harvard Medical School developed techniques whereby cerebrospinal fluid could easily be tapped or administered through carefully placed canulas (tubes). Pappenheimer deprived goats of sleep for 48 hours and withdrew some cerebrospinal fluid. This fluid was then injected into the cerebrospinal fluid of laboratory cats. Pappenheimer found that the cats became drowsy. In a series of experiments, Pappenheimer refined his techniques and was able to show that rats injected with cerebrospinal fluid taken from sleep-deprived goats also became significantly less active. Recording the electrical activity of the brains in his rats revealed an increase in the slow-wave patterns seen during normal sleep.

Pappenheimer's work strongly suggests that some chemical substance that promotes sleep is generated during wakefulness. In a sense we may be drugging ourselves to sleep by staying awake. Pappenheimer and his colleagues are trying to isolate this sleep-promoting chemical. Though considerable progress has been made, the amounts of the chemical generated by wakefulness are extremely small, perhaps as little as one-millionth of a gram. Krueger, Pappenheimer, and Karnovsky (1982) have also isolated a chemical in human urine that appears to be sleep promoting.

Other chemicals that have been implicated in the sleep process are cytokines such as interleukin-1, the prostaglandin D_2, and the neurotransmitter acetylcholine (for REM sleep) (Palca, 1989). The work of Pappenheimer and others is exciting because it provides both an increased understanding of how sleep occurs and eventual hope of a natural cure for insomnia.

Possible Functions of Sleep

Although researchers are beginning to piece together an understanding of the brain structures involved in the sleep process, our understanding of the function of sleep is still largely a mystery. Recently several hypotheses have

been offered, however, and some research is beginning to accumulate. The ideas are tantalizing, so let's consider a few.

What functions have been attributed to sleep? From among many proposals, probably the most common is that it provides a restorative function. Hartmann (1973) believed that Stages 3 and 4 are primarily restorative in nature and may also promote the synthesis of chemical compounds for use during REM sleep (e.g., proteins or ribonucleic acid—RNA). Hartmann further suggested that REM sleep may also serve a restorative function in regard to attention and emotion. He pointed out that more REM sleep seems to occur after days full of worry, stress, or intense learning. From Hartmann's point of view, REM sleep may help us cope with stressful situations by allowing us to attend to our environment more efficiently when awake. As noted earlier, several studies indicate the restorative nature of NREM sleep (e.g., Shapiro et al., 1981; Bunnell, Bevier, & Horvath, 1983; Shapiro, 1982). Further, Greenberg and associates (1983) have reported that REM deprivation decreases access to emotionally important memories but not to nonpersonal memories. Based on their results, Greenberg and associates suggest that REM sleep may be involved in making a connection between present emotionally important experiences and emotional memories related to these present experiences. Thus it would appear that REM sleep may indeed be important in regard to emotionality. Further suggestive evidence for the importance of REM sleep in emotionality comes from research showing that depression and initial REM onset are positively correlated (see, e.g., Kupfer, 1976; Knowles, MacLean, & Cairns, 1982; McCarley, 1982).

A problem with any theory that argues for a restorative function for sleep, however, is that both Stage 4 and REM sleep decline with age. Many theorists have suggested that Stage

4 is primarily a restorative sleep process, yet some individuals (as noted earlier) do not show Stage 4 sleep by age 50. Any theory of restorative function must be able to deal with this discrepancy.

Dement (1972) has proposed that sleep, particularly REM sleep, may be involved in the organization of the brain. Dement based this idea on the fact that young mammals show much more REM than adult mammals. Therefore REM may be an internal source of stimulation that helps to "set up" the young brain correctly. REM sleep in the adult may be nothing more than a **vestigial** (i.e., no longer useful but still existing) system that serves no real purpose.

Though it is possible that REM sleep and dreaming are not necessary in the adult, REM deprivation studies seem to suggest otherwise. Why would REM pressure increase with deprivation if the system is unimportant in the adult? The organization of the young brain may indeed be part of the function of sleep, but there must be more to that function than only the initial programming of the brain.

Several theorists (e.g., Bertini, 1973; Dewan, 1970) have proposed that REM sleep serves as a programming device. New material learned during waking is seen as being incorporated into and changing the existing organization of the brain during REM sleep. Dewan has likened the process to that of a self-programming computer. During REM sleep the programs are altered and reorganized based on new information received. Part of this reprogramming, of course, requires the storing of new information in the proper location.

Broughton and Gastaut (1973), Greenberg (1970), and Pearlman (1970) have emphasized the idea that REM sleep may be involved in the consolidation of memories. Greenberg, for example, believed that dreaming enables material to be transferred from short-term to long-term memory. Bertini, Dewan, Greenberg, and Pearlman all believed that the storage process may be based on the emotional aspects of the information, thus explaining why emotionality occurs in dreams. The particular emotion felt during the learning process may serve as a "tag" or label that determines where and with what other memories a piece of information is stored. The research of Greenberg and associates (1983) also supports this notion.

Stern (1970) discussed research suggesting that REM deprivation interferes with the learning of responses and also with the retention of tasks learned prior to the deprivation. In addition, Pearlman cited evidence of interference in adaptation to anxiety-provoking events by REM deprivation. An anxiety-provoking film was shown to subjects who were then deprived of REM sleep for one night. Then they viewed the film a second time. Normal subjects showed much less anxiety on a second viewing, while the REM-deprived subjects were as anxious during the second viewing as during the first. Pearlman's results suggest that dreaming may allow us to incorporate anxiety-producing situations and thus habituate to them.

REM sleep may also play a part in the storage of complex associative information. Scrima (1982), for example, found recall of complex associative material to be significantly better after isolated REM periods than after either isolated NREM periods or wakefulness in a group of ten narcoleptics. (Narcolepsy is a sleep disorder in which the individual often falls asleep quickly during the day and in which REM often occurs at sleep onset rather than after the normal NREM period.)

Chronic alcoholic patients sometimes show a set of symptoms called Korsakoff's syndrome, part of which involves disruption of memory. Greenberg (1970) studied patients suffering from Korsakoff's syndrome and found that those who had recently developed the syndrome showed increased REM states, which, however, tended to be fragmentary. Greenberg believed that alcohol-induced brain lesions interrupt both memory and dreaming processes and that the increased REM is an attempt by the brain to compensate.

One of the most interesting pieces of research on the possible relationship of memory and sleep was conducted by Zornetzer, Gold, and Boast (1977). In their series of experiments, consolidation (i.e., storage time) of memory was altered by destruction of the locus coerulus (LC). As you remember, the LC is apparently part of the mechanism involved in the activation and inhibition of REM and NREM sleep. The researchers found that damage to the LC prolongs the amount of time in which new information is susceptible to memory disruption. Essentially, it appears that the LC plays a role in limiting the length of time in which memory can be interfered with. Zornetzer and associates also noted several anatomical relationships suggesting that the LC is involved in the memory process. Though the data are far from clear, an increasingly apparent conclusion is that one very important function of sleep and dreaming may be to store information, particularly of an emotional sort.

Sleep is generally considered to be located at the low end of the arousal continuum. As we have seen, this is probably an oversimplified point of view because cortical activity differs from stage to stage, as do autonomic activity and muscle control. Lacey's (1967) argument for several types of arousal seems appropriate in view of the data on waking and sleeping behavior that we have examined, but much remains to be done in order to understand the arousal of behavior.

We will now examine research dealing with what is usually considered the high end of the arousal continuum, generally called stress.

STRESS

When our arousal level is high, we are being stressed. Often the term **stress** is equated with distress (e.g., Arnold, 1967). It seems clear, however, that we are also stressed when "good" things happen to us, such as a promotion or marriage.

A more general way of looking at the concept is to think of stress as occurring when the body is forced to cope with or adapt to a changed situation, which may be either good or bad. Thus any situation that causes a marked deviation from our normal state would be considered stressful.

Stress is an integral part of life; we cannot escape it, for as Selye notes, "complete freedom from stress is death" (1973, p. 693). In order to understand motivated behavior, it is important to know how stress affects our bodies and our behavior. In this section we will examine research on stress as it relates to motivation and emotion, and we will also examine ways of coping with stress.

Definition of Stress

The concept of stress has proven particularly hard to define. This is perhaps because of the multitude of situations that can trigger stress in an individual. Nevertheless, let us try to formulate a rough definition to use in examining the research on stress.

Selye (1973) has defined stress as *a nonspecific response of the body to any demand made upon it*. Basically Selye assumed that some optimal level of bodily functioning exists and that stressors (i.e., stimuli or situations that create stress in the person) cause a movement away from this optimum level. The stress response, then, is seen as an adaptive behavior that attempts to return the body to its normal state. As such, stress is a homeostatic mechanism. Either systemic or psychological stress, then, can be viewed as an adaptive response designed to return the individual to a more optimal condition.

Systemic and Psychological Stress

Systemic stress involves some challenge to the integrity of the physical body (Appley & Trumbull, 1967). The body reacts to invasions (e.g., bacteria, viruses, heat, cold, and so on) by a generalized response that helps combat the challenge. We will soon examine this response in detail.

But stress does not require a physical challenge to the body in order to occur; it can occur for purely psychological reasons. Worry about a sick mother or anxiety about losing a job can likewise create stress. And the body's reaction to psychological stress, interestingly, is virtually identical to its systemic stress reaction. Even anticipation of the future can create stress. For example, the anticipation of a parachute jump is more stressful to an experienced jumper than the actual jump (Tanner, 1976). The presence of emotion is usually considered a sign of psychological stress; another typical sign is the disruption of ongoing behavior (Appley & Trumbull, 1967).

The effects of stress are not always bad, though we usually tend to study the negative side of stress. A certain amount of stress seems necessary for creativity and performance. Moderate amounts of stress improve performance (Tanner, 1976). We all know individuals who seem unable to accomplish anything unless stressed by an impending deadline. For these individuals, moderate stress seems to help. We should keep in mind, however, that large differences exist in the ability to tolerate stress, and it is sometimes useful to ask ourselves under what condition our own behavior is most efficient.

Endocrine System Activity and Stress

In order to understand some of the effects of stress, we must know something about the reactions of the body when a stressor is encountered. One of the major effects of a stressor is on the endocrine system.

The endocrine system is a set of glands located throughout the body that secrete their substances directly into the bloodstream. The substances are called **hormones** and can be thought of as chemical signals that regulate or coordinate the activity of distant organs (Seyle, 1956). The major gland within this system is the **pituitary**, which has been called the master gland because of its role in controlling the other glands. The pituitary is located at the base of the brain and is controlled by the brain structure known as the hypothalamus. The hypothalamus is active in many motivated activities, as we shall see in the next chapter. It manufactures hormones that have the effect of causing the pituitary to release its substances (Guillemin & Burgus, 1976; Levine, 1971).

Besides the pituitary, the other major gland of interest to us in the study of stress is the adrenal gland. The adrenal gland (one located on top of each kidney) is composed of two parts that serve different functions. The outer covering of the adrenal gland (called the **adrenal cortex**) secretes hormones called **17-hydroxycorticoids**. While several of these corticoids exist in humans, most of the secretion of the adrenal cortex is **hydrocortisone**. The adrenal cortex also secretes small quantities of another hormone called **aldosterone**, whose main effect is on water and electrolyte balance (Oken, 1967). The center portion (the **adrenal medulla**) secretes two substances, **epinephrine** and **norepinephrine**. Now let's put all this highly technical data together and try to understand what happens when we are stressed (see Figure 3.8).

Information about the "state" of the body is constantly being gathered by external sensory systems (e.g., eyes, ears, nose) and by internal sensory systems (e.g., the condition of internal organs, blood changes, and so on). This information is monitored by the brain,

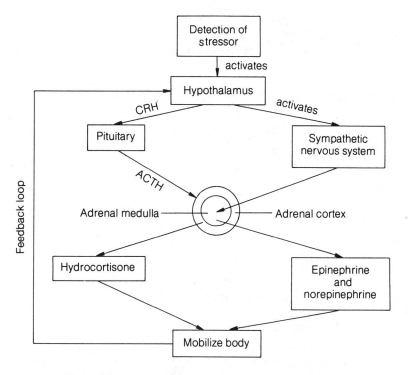

Figure 3.8 Flowchart of mechanisms triggered by a stressor.

and when a stressor is detected, systems within the hypothalamus are activated. The posterior portion of the hypothalamus activates sympathetic nervous system activity, which stimulates the adrenal medulla to secrete epinephrine and norepinephrine. At the same time, other systems within the hypothalamus secrete a substance called **corticotropin releasing hormone (CRH)**, which causes the pituitary gland to secrete a substance into the bloodstream called **adrenocorticotropic hormone (ACTH)** (Vale et al., 1981; Roberts et al., 1982). ACTH is important because it travels through the bloodstream to the adrenal glands, where it causes the adrenal cortex to secrete hydrocortisone as well as small quantities of aldosterone into the bloodstream (Oken, 1967).

The release of epinephrine and hydrocortisone into the bloodstream has the effect of mobilizing the body for action (by increasing blood sugar, heart rate, and blood pressure) so that we can better deal with the stressor. Some sort of feedback mechanism must also exist because, as blood levels of hydrocortisone increase, the brain shuts off the production of ACTH and, therefore, hydrocortisone.

When the stressor is overcome or disappears, the activity of the pituitary-adrenal system is reduced, and we return to a more "relaxed" state. The anterior (front) portion of the hypothalamus seems to be important in this respect and may act to inhibit the posterior (back) portion, which is active when we are stressed (Bovard, 1967).

The individual most responsible for

advancing the study of stress is Hans Selye (1950, 1956, 1973), who has proposed a three-part system of response to stress, and to this system we now turn.

The General Adaptation Syndrome

In 1925 an 18-year-old medical student named Hans Selye got his first look at the symptoms of infectious disease. It was probably his youthfulness, as he pointed out, that allowed him to see the common symptoms that all the patients possessed rather than the specific symptoms he was supposed to see (Seyle, 1956).

Still unbiased by the current medical thinking, Selye noticed that most diseases have a common set of symptoms. The patient looks and feels sick, has a coated tongue, complains of aches and pains in the joints, and has loss of appetite and fever. Imposed on this general set of symptoms are more specific symptoms, which allow one to determine the actual disease. Though the medical practitioners of the day were interested in the specific symptoms (because they enable diagnosis of the illness), Selye was intrigued by the large degree of overlap in the general symptoms from one disease to another.

Not until ten years later did Selye begin to fit these early observations together and arrive at the concept of stress. He had been conducting research in sex hormones and found that injecting his animals with ovarian or placental hormones caused a series of changes, including enlargement of the adrenal cortex, shrinkage of the thymus gland and lymph nodes, and ulceration of the gastrointestinal tract. He soon discovered that injections of any noxious or foreign material caused the same effects. In other words, the bodily responses that he was observing were **nonspecific** (i.e., they didn't change if different agents were injected), just as the symptoms he had observed in medical school were nonspecific.

These results led Selye to study the reactions of the body when subjected to stressors.

He soon discovered that the changes he noted in the adrenal glands, lymph system, and gastrointestinal tract are the initial response of the body to a stressor. He named this response the **alarm reaction**.

During the alarm reaction the forces of the body are mobilized so that life can be maintained while local adaptive responses (e.g., inflammation at a point of infection) progress. The corticoids of the adrenal cortex are secreted into the bloodstream in order to help prepare the body for attack by the stressor. Epinephrine is secreted by the adrenal medulla and travels to all parts of the body, increasing the efficiency of the muscle synapses, accelerating breathing, increasing heart rate, and so on. During the early phase of the alarm reaction, our resistance to stress is actually below normal, but it quickly rises above normal.

Once local adaptive responses have been established, a second stage, which Selye termed the **stage of resistance**, develops. During this period the processes accelerated during the alarm reaction drop back almost to normal levels (e.g., corticoid levels decrease to just slightly above normal). Rather than mobilizing the entire body for action, as in the alarm reaction, the stage of resistance mobilizes only that part of the body under attack. Ability to adapt to the stressor is greater than normal during the stage of resistance.

If, however, the local defenses are inadequate or fail to limit the effects of the stressor, resistance finally gives way to the third stage, which Selye termed the **stage of exhaustion**. In this stage the reaction to the stressor becomes general again. Corticoid levels rise very similarly to their rise during the alarm reaction. Life at this stage can continue only as long as the extra defenses brought in by activation of the whole system can last. If the stressor is not eliminated or removed, the bodily defenses are exhausted and death occurs (see Figure 3.9).

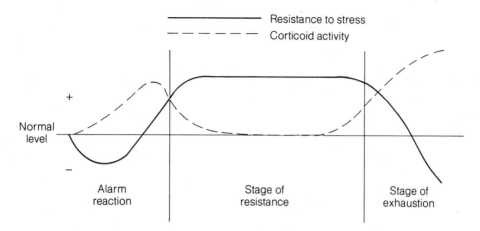

Figure 3.9 Changes in resistance to stress and changes in corticoid levels in the three stages of the general adaptation syndrome.

The three stages together comprise the body's reaction to stress, and this reaction has been termed the **general adaptation syndrome (GAS)**.

The GAS, then, is a set of responses that is triggered by a stressor and designed to eliminate or contain the stressing element so that the body can maintain life. The physiological changes associated with the GAS are essentially what we experience as "stress" (Selye, 1956, 1973).

The GAS is activated not only by physical stresses such as infection but also by psychological stresses such as anxiety, loud noises, or crowding. The body reacts in the same way (i.e., with the GAS) to all stressors. Because stressors such as anxiety cannot be easily escaped, they may cause us damage by keeping the GAS active. In this regard, problems such as ulcers, high blood pressure, and even certain types of kidney disease may be the result of psychological stress. Thus the GAS response is not always adaptive; for some reason, the response may not be appropriate to the problem. When this occurs, we suffer, in Selye's term, **diseases of adaptation**.

Diseases of Adaptation

Sometimes the responses of the body may be inadequate or inappropriate to the stressor. For example, one of the most basic processes in the control of a physical stressor is inflammation. Inflammation provides a barrier that limits the spread of a stressor (e.g., infection). If, however, the body reacts to a foreign particle, the inflammation may cause more harm than the particle. This seems to be what happens in allergic reactions to pollen. Selye believed that many common diseases are, in part, diseases of adaptation, in which the body reacts incorrectly to a potential stressor.

One novel aspect of Selye's theory is the idea that each of us possesses only a certain amount of what he called **adaptive energy**. Adaptive energy is a hypothetical substance that is used up when we are stressed. Selye believed that aging and death result from the using up of this adaptive energy; that we can use it up quickly by living highly stressful, short lives; or that we can parcel it out frugally and live long lives of low stress. At present there is little evidence to support the existence of adaptive energy.

One problem of Selye's theory concerns the triggering of the alarm reaction. Clearly something triggers that alarm reaction, but the actual processes remain unclear. Oken (1967) believed that the trigger for the GAS may be emotion, because almost any emotionally arousing stimulus leads to activation of the pituitary-adrenal component of the GAS. Research for the signal or signals that may activate the stress response is clearly a complex task.

Selye's research has generated thousands of additional studies on stress. A thorough understanding of how physical or psychological stress influences behavior is clearly very important. Stress, on the one hand, can motivate creativity; on the other hand, it can create high blood pressure and ulcers.

One arena in which stress has been studied is its relationship to significant life changes on the one hand and to illness on the other. We turn now to an examination of these topics.

Life Change, Stress, and Illness

One area of research that has attempted to untangle the web of relationships between stress and illness is on the topic of life change. Life-change research, like most of the literature on stress, can be traced back to Walter Cannon (Dohrenwend & Dohrenwend, 1974). The "life charts" constructed by Adolph Meyer in the 1930s constituted one of the earliest attempts to associate changes in the lives of patients with illness. Meyer's research pioneered modern studies of the relationship between stress and illness.

The basic idea underlying change research is that the events of our lives influence our susceptibility to physical and mental illness. Research has focused primarily on attempts to scale various life changes in terms of the amount of adjustments these changes require of us and then to correlate these life changes with the incidence of illness or the seeking of professional help.

Long-term studies were conducted by Hinkle (1974), who examined health and work records of telephone company employees over a 20-year span. His results showed that some people were much more likely to become ill than others. People experiencing the most missed days of work had more diseases of both a minor and major nature. Illness also tended to cluster around certain periods of an individual's life. This clustering tended to occur during times in people's lives when their social environment or interpersonal relationships made large demands on them. The stress-illness relationship was not invariable, however, because Hinkle noticed that many other people had experienced considerable stress and yet had not become ill. He suggested that healthy individuals seem able to "emotionally insulate" themselves from drastic life changes that occur to them.

Thomas Holmes and his associates developed a scale of major life changes that they found to be clinically related to illness (see Holmes & Masuda, 1974; Ruch & Holmes, 1971). The 43 items of the scale (called the **Social Readjustment Rating Scale** or **SRRS**) were rated by people in terms of the amount of adjustment these events would require in their lives. Not all of the items were negative (although the majority were); some were positive events such as marriage or Christmas. However, all of them required some coping or adaptation on the part of the person experiencing the change.

Scaling of the 43 items led to a determination of which items required the most coping or adjustment. As can be seen in Table 3.1 (Holmes & Rahe, 1967), death of a spouse requires the most adaptation, followed by divorce, marital separation, and so on.

The SRRS has been given to various groups (e.g., adults, college students, adoles-

Table 3.1   The Social Readjustment Rating Scale

	Life Event	Mean Value
1.	death of spouse	100
2.	divorce	73
3.	marital separation	65
4.	jail term	63
5.	death of a close family member	63
6.	personal injury or illness	53
7.	marriage	50
8.	fired at work	47
9.	marital reconciliation	45
10.	retirement	45
11.	change in health of family member	44
12.	pregnancy	40
13.	sex difficulties	39
14.	gain of new family member	39
15.	business readjustment	39
16.	change in financial state	38
17.	death of close friend	37
18.	change to different line of work	36
19.	change in number of arguments with spouse	35
20.	mortgage over $10,000	31
21.	foreclosure of mortgage or loan	30
22.	change in responsibilities at work	29
23.	son or daughter leaving home	29
24.	trouble with in-laws	29
25.	outstanding personal achievement	28
26.	wife begins or stops work	26
27.	begin or end school	26
28.	change in living conditions	25
29.	revision of personal habits	24
30.	trouble with boss	23
31.	change in work hours or conditions	20
32.	change residence	20
33.	change in schools	20
34.	change in recreation	19
35.	change in church activities	19
36.	change in social activities	18
37.	mortgage or loan less than $10,000	17
38.	change in sleeping habits	16
39.	change in number of family get-togethers	15
40.	change in eating habits	15
41.	vacation	13
42.	Christmas	12
43.	minor violations of the law	11

See T. H. Holmes and R. H. Rahe: The Social Readjustment Rating Scale, *Journal of Psychosomatic Research II:* 213–218, 1967, for complete wording of the items. Copyright 1967, Pergamon Press, Ltd. Reprinted by permission.

cents), and agreement on the amount of adjustment required by the various life experiences is very consistent, even cross-culturally (Holmes & Masuda, 1974; Isherwood & Adam, 1976).

Researchers have found that life changes tend to cluster significantly in the two years prior to the onset of an illness. Studies showed that with increase in the number of life-change units (termed LCUs: the measure of the amount of life change in a given unit of time, such as six months or a year), the probability of illness also increased.

Many of the investigations into life change and illness are called **retrospective studies**, in which individuals are asked to indicate when illnesses and also life changes occurred. The researchers then look for relationships between illness and life changes that may have preceded the illness. LCU scores ranging from 150 to 199 in one year were considered mild life crises, and it was found that 37% of the individuals scoring within this range reported a major health change. LCU scores between 200 to 299 were defined as moderate life crises, and the percentage of persons reporting a major health change rose to 79% (Holmes & Masuda, 1974). Holmes believed that the onset of illness after a major life change occurs in about a year, presumably because it takes that amount of time for the stress of the life changes to show its effects. Research into these relationships, however, is hampered by problems of the subject's memory for events that may have occurred several years earlier.

Prospective studies, in which individuals supply information about recent life changes and are questioned later (usually six months to a year) about changes in health, have also been attempted. The point of such studies is to see if changes in life events can effectively predict future health changes. Holmes and Masuda cited several studies indicating that life changes do predict future illness. In one study

86% of those individuals scoring above 300 LCUs had a major health change sometime during the next two years (48% who scored between 200 to 299 and 33% who scored between 150 to 199 had a major health change).

One of the most interesting prospective studies involved prediction of performance based on recent life-change scores, in a prolonged competitive stress situation (Popkin et al., 1976). The competitive event was a dog sled race that covered 1,049 miles between Anchorage and Nome, Alaska. The researchers found that a significant negative correlation existed between life-change scores and order of finish in the race; the larger the number of recent life changes that had occurred to an individual, the poorer that person finished in the race. Though the number of subjects was small (25), the results may be revealing.

Roskies, Iida-Miranda, and Strobel (1975) studied life change and illness in a group of Portuguese immigrants to Canada. Their findings are of interest in two respects. First, 68% of the subjects fell into the moderate or major life crisis categories, yet this Portuguese sample showed no greater incidence of illness than the population of Canada as a whole. Suffering the major life change of immigration does not, then, necessarily put one into a high-risk category for illness, even though these researchers did find a significant correlation between life change and illness.

The second, more interesting finding was that significant sex differences existed in regard to life change and illness among this immigrant group. Immigrant women were more likely than immigrant men to become ill, and the correlation between life change and illness for the women was much stronger (although still only .24). No significant relationship between life change and illness was found for the men. And for a subgroup of the men (young or highly educated or both), the relationship was negative, indicating that for them life change was associated with health! The possibility that sex differences exist in the relationship between life change and health change needs systematic study.

Bedell and associates (1977) studied the life changes of children who attended a three-week camp for the chronically ill. These children were given a battery of personality tests and a children's version of the SRRS. The children were classified into two groups based on their life-change scores: a low-stress group whose scores approximated those of normal children, and a high-stress group whose scores were far above normal. The results of the questionnaires showed that the high-stress group, compared to the low-stress group, had poorer self-concepts, perceived themselves as poorly behaved, said they were less attractive and less popular, and felt they were less successful in school. The highly stressed, chronically ill child thus tended to make negative self-evaluations.

The study also found that the high-stress group had significantly more day-to-day health problems than the low-stress group. During the three-week period of the camp, 69 episodes of illness occurred in the high-stress group, compared to only 19 in the low-stress group. Since the two groups were matched for types and severity of illness, the high-stress group was apparently more vulnerable to acute episodes of illness. One wonders whether chronically ill children are less able to adapt to the additional stresses of life change and are therefore more susceptible to acute illnesses.

Problems of Life-Change Research   Several studies have begun to question the utility of the SRRS in predicting illness (Bieliauskas & Webb, 1974; Bieliauskas & Strugar, 1976; Caplan, 1975; Cleary, 1981; Garrity, Marx, & Somes, 1977a, 1977b; Mechanic, 1974; Schroeder & Costa, 1984 [but see also Maddi, Bartone, & Puccetti, 1987]; Wershow & Reinhart, 1974).

There seems little doubt that a relationship between life changes and health changes does exist, but the correlations, though significant, are often very small and account for very little of the total variance within the experiments. What this means is that the SRRS can predict general changes in health resulting from changes across large groups of people, but it predicts very little about the chances of illness for any particular individual as a result of life changes.

Individual differences have always been the biggest problem in attempting to understand how life events relate to illness. The same events simply do not affect people similarly. Rahe (1974) pointed out that we need to understand more about how people cope with life changes both psychologically and physiologically before we can hope to understand why life changes affect one person but not another.

Buffering the Effects of Life Change and Stress   That some individuals endure numerous life changes and yet do not become ill suggests that these people may be able to reduce the stressing effects of life changes. Research examining the buffering effects of personality variables and various stress-reducing strategies has supported this idea. A number of studies have identified some of the variables that appear to play a role. Some of the suggested variables are hardiness, exercise, social support, sex-role orientation, self-complexity, humor, and optimism (Cohen & Wills, 1985; Fisher, 1988; House, Landis, & Umberson, 1988; Kobasa, Maddi, & Puccetti, 1982; Labott & Martin, 1987; Linville, 1987; Peterson, Seligman, & Vaillant, 1988; Roos & Cohen, 1987). For example, Kobasa, Maddi, and Puccetti (1982) examined the effect of two variables on the stress-illness relationship. The first variable was a personality style they termed **hardiness** (Kobasa, 1979). Hardiness is conceived as a combination of three personality characteristics—**commitment, control,** and **challenge**—that serve to buffer the effects of stress because they are associated with curiosity and interest in the experiences of life. Further, hardy individuals believe that they can control what happens to them and that change is natural. These attitudes seem to help buffer the effects of stress because they help individuals keep the changing life events in perspective (Kobasa, Maddi, & Puccetti, 1982). The second variable studied by Kobasa and associates was exercise. Though exercise has most often been examined relative to the cardiovascular system these researchers were interested in the effect of exercise as a buffer for life-change-induced stress.

In this carefully conducted study, the researchers found that both hardiness and exercise decreased the likelihood of illness as a result of stressing life changes in a sample of 137 male, middle- and upper-level management personnel. Additionally, the buffering effects of hardiness and exercise were independent and additive. The greatest buffering effect was seen in those subjects who were high in both hardiness and exercise. These researchers propose that the buffering effect of these two variables is on differing aspects of the life-change–stress-illness relationship. They believe that hardiness serves to transform the stressing events and thus decrease their stressfulness, while exercise decreases the psychological and physiological strain on the individual by these events. Thus the proposed buffering effects of these two variables are quite different; one reduces the stressfulness of the events themselves, while the other reduces the deleterious effects of the stress on the person. As a result of their differing points of action, hardiness and exercise are additive in reducing the effect of life changes on illness.

The results of the study by Kobasa and associates (1982) are consistent with a general body of research that shows that the controllability-uncontrollability dimension of stressing life events is important in determining the effects of life change on illness. For example,

Johnson and Sarason (1978) have shown that subjects indicating a belief in an internal locus of control (a measure of how we view our ability to control the events of our lives) show a lower correlation between life changes and subsequent illness than subjects indicating a belief in an external locus of control. Similarly, Stern, McCants, and Pettine (1982) found that items on the SRRS rated as uncontrollable by subjects were more highly associated with illness than were items rated as controllable. Additionally, they found that those items considered uncontrollable were also rated as more stressing. It should be noted, however, that subjects' agreement on how controllable different events were was widely divergent; what one subject considered controllable was often considered uncontrollable by another. Similar results have been reported by Suls and Mullen (1981), who found that undesirability and uncontrollability were related to the incidence of psychological distress symptoms. Perhaps the low correlation between life change and illness is partly due to these differing perceptions of controllability. As Stern and associates have noted, event uncontrollability may prove to be a better index of stress than life changes. The research noted above suggests that a belief that one can control the events of his or her life is an important adaptive mechanism for coping with stress.

Our social relationships can influence our health (House, Landis, & Umberson, 1988). It has been known for some time that death rates from all causes are higher among the unmarried as compared to the married. Similarly, unmarried and socially isolated persons have higher rates of tuberculosis, accidents, and psychiatric disorders.

The correlation between social relationships and health has led some researchers to propose that social relationships might promote health by buffering the effects of stress (Cassel, 1976; Cobb, 1976; see Cohen & Wills, 1985, and House et al., 1988, for reviews). One buffering aspect of social interaction that has been studied is its supportive nature. **Social support theory** proposes that social relationships buffer the effects of stress through the encouragement an individual or individuals can offer to the person experiencing the stress. Social support might promote better health through practical help, emotional comfort, provision of a sense of meaning and coherence to life, facilitation of good health behaviors (e.g., proper sleep, diet, exercise, and so forth), promotion of positive affect, development of feelings of self-worth, or some combination of these.

Interestingly, social support may be more effective as a buffer for men (House et al., 1988) or for persons displaying masculine sex-role orientation (Roos & Cohen, 1987).

Other characteristics in addition to social support appear to have a buffering effect on the stress-illness relationship. Peterson and associates (1988) report that **explanatory style** (the ways we explain events) is predictive of health status 20 to 30 years later. Specifically, they found that a pessimistic explanatory style (attributing bad events to stable, global, and internal factors) at age 25 predicted poor health at ages 45 through 60. Those subjects in this study who accounted for the bad events in their lives using a more optimistic explanatory style (attributing those events to unstable, specific, and external causes) were healthier than the pessimistic group later in life. One possible implication of this study is that interpreting in an optimistic way the bad events that befall all of us may serve to buffer the stressing effects of those events. We must, of course, be cautious in drawing such conclusions until more evidence is available. It is entirely possible that some other variable influences both explanatory style and health later in life.

One final potential buffer of the stress-illness relationship that has been investigated is **expressive style** (Labott & Martin, 1987). These investigators found that the use of hu-

mor as a way of coping moderated the stressing effects of negative life events, whereas emotional weeping (often thought to be cathartic) did not. In fact, their study reported that subjects who engaged in frequent weeping showed increased levels of mood disturbance when negative life events were frequent.

Perhaps explanatory style (pessimistic-optimistic) and expressive style (weeping-humor) interact in their buffering effects. One might predict the least buffering when the explanatory style of pessimism is linked to the expressive style of frequent weeping. The same logic suggests that the greatest buffering would result from a combination of optimistic explanatory style and humorous expressive style. Future research may shed some light on such interactive buffering effects.

Several techniques for consciously dealing with stress have also been proposed. We will close this section by mentioning a few of them.

Selye (1956) believed that **knowledge is a curative**. If we remove some of the mystery from a process, it becomes less frightening. This suggests that knowing something about our reactions to stress ought to help us deal with stress. Indeed, just realizing we are tense can often help us reduce the tension.

Hinkle's studies over many years show that some people tolerate stress better than others. He has noted that those who tolerate stress well and remain healthy seem able to **emotionally insulate** themselves from the events around them. Perhaps an ability to be objective and to accept situations that cannot be changed helps these people tolerate stress.

George Ruff and Sheldon Korchin (1967) studied the ways in which the Mercury astronauts dealt with stress. The astronauts, they found, had strong drives toward mastery and achievement, which were often frustrated by unavoidable program delays and equipment problems. Nevertheless, the astronauts were able to tolerate stress well, primarily by looking beyond the momentary frustrations to the future. Additionally, the astronauts tended to describe themselves in emotionally positive terms, and anticipatory anxiety (e.g., before a flight) seemed to facilitate their performance rather than interfere with it. For example, when they became anxious about something going wrong, they immediately went over the contingency plans for that emergency. Mandler (1967), in an invited commentary on Ruff and Korchin's research, noted that one of the most adaptive responses to stressors is to have alternate plans ready for the occasion. Perhaps we can all learn something from the astronauts and deal with our own stress situations by formulating plans in advance.

Many people have become interested in various types of meditation as a way of reducing the stress in their lives. Herbert Benson has written a very interesting book, *The Relaxation Response* (1975), that analyzes many types of meditative techniques and distills them into four steps that are common to all. According to Benson, all types of meditation promote relaxation. He believed that meditation reduces stress because it counteracts overactivity of the sympathetic nervous system at the level of the hypothalamus (Benson, 1975; Benson et al., 1977; Hoffman et al., 1982). Thus meditative techniques may result in reduced stress by activating neural mechanisms that oppose or inhibit the sympathetic nervous system and the stress responses of the body. However, more work on meditation's physiological effects on stress is needed before we can draw any meaningful conclusions.

SEXUAL AROUSAL

For practical purposes, sexual motivation may be equivalent to sexual arousal. It is useful, therefore, to examine research on sexual arousal. Most of the work on sexual arousal is from the pioneering research of Masters and Johnson (1966, 1970, 1974; see also Luria, Friedman, & Rose, 1987, for an overview).

The initial research of Masters and Johnson involved a study of the sexual responses of 694 people, 382 women and 312 men. During the 12 years covered by this research over 10,000 orgasms were directly observed. Based on these data, Masters and Johnson report that human sexual responses can conveniently be described as consisting of four stages. Both men and women go through these four stages but in slightly different ways.

Stages of the Human Sexual Response Cycle

Two basic physiological responses occur during sexual behavior that are similar in both men and women. These two responses are vasocongestion and myotonia. **Vasocongestion** is the concentration of blood in certain portions of the body. In the male, vasocongestion produces penile enlargement and erection; in the female, vasocongestion produces clitoral enlargement. **Myotonia** is an increase in muscle tone throughout the body. In both men and women sexual behavior leads to increases in bodily muscle tone that are maintained until orgasm.

Excitement The first stage of the sexual response cycle is excitement. Sexual excitement may be induced by physical stimuli such as a touch or a caress or by psychological stimuli such as erotic pictures or fantasies. During the excitement phase the penis of the male becomes erect due to vasocongestion, and the vagina of the female lubricates and lengthens. This phase, and the last (resolution), compose the greatest amount of time spent in the sexual response cycle.

Plateau During this second phase of the sexual response cycle identified by Masters and Johnson many of the changes that have already occurred during the excitement phase continue. Sexual arousal is intensified during plateau, perhaps in preparation for the climax of orgasm which follows this phase.

Orgasm Orgasm is a sexual climax during which the building sexual tension is dramatically reduced. In the male only one orgasm typically occurs per cycle, during which ejaculation takes place, whereas in the female, orgasm may occur once, several times, or not at all.

Resolution Immediately following orgasm there is a **refractory period** in men during which further sexual behavior does not occur. In young men this refractory period usually lasts 10–30 minutes. In older men the refractory period is longer. Following orgasm women do not have a definable refractory period and are capable of continued sexual activity and multiple orgasms. During the resolution phase the body returns to its prearoused state in reverse order through the stages.

Other Bodily Changes During Sexual Behavior

Female Bodily Changes During the sexual response cycle several bodily changes occur in women. In addition to myotonia, respiration typically increases from 12 to as many as 40 breaths per minute. Heart rate also increases from around 60 beats per minute to as many as 100–180 beats per minute. Blood pressure rises and reaches a peak during the late plateau stage just prior to orgasm. Sometimes involuntary contractions of the hands and feet occur (called **carpopedal spasm**), causing the toes to curl up or the hands to close.

The breasts and nipples change in both size and color; nipples become erect, and the size of the breasts increases as a result of blood flow to the breasts. An increased blood flow to the skin causes a reddening of the skin (called the **sex flush**) that may cover the upper abdomen and breasts and spread to other parts of the body including the face, thighs, buttocks,

and back. The uterus increases in size and rises up and away from the vagina. This elevation increases the length of the vagina. The vagina also expands. During the sexual response cycle the clitoris initially swells and lengthens due to vasocongestion. Later in the cycle but before orgasm, it retracts out of sight under the clitoral hood. The inner lips of the vagina (labia minora) turn bright red in some women just prior to orgasm as a result of increased blood flow to the area.

During orgasm the vagina contracts rhythmically (at about .8-second intervals) for up to 15 contractions. The more intense the orgasm the greater the number of contractions; however, the intensity of the orgasm does not appear to depend on these contractions (Luria et al., 1987). The uterus also rhythmically contracts during orgasm, and the anal sphincter may also sometimes contract.

Male Bodily Changes Myotonia occurs during the late excitement and plateau phases. As is true of women, men also show increases in respiration and heart rate and may also experience the sex flush, nipple erection, and carpopedal spasms of the hands and feet. Male sexual arousal is first evidenced by penile erection, although erection of the penis can occur for other reasons as well (e.g., during dream sleep, and in fear- or anxiety-producing situations: Luria et al., 1987).

During the excitement phase the testes elevate and rotate. The testes also increase in size, and the scrotum increases in thickness and contracts. When the testes are fully elevated, orgasm occurs. During the plateau phase the skin of the penis may become deep red or purple as a result of vasocongestion. Fluid from the Cowper's gland (sometimes containing sperm) may also seep from the penis during the plateau phase. A woman could thus become pregnant even though the male did not ejaculate while in her vagina.

Men report that orgasm is sometimes felt

even before the contractions associated with ejaculation occur. They also report that orgasm is experienced as a two-stage process. In the first stage the orgasm is felt as imminent and unstoppable. In the second stage semen is ejaculated. During the second stage the prostate, seminal vesicles, and vas deferens contract rhythmically and involuntarily. The urethra also contracts, expelling the semen containing the sperm. Contractions, as in the female, occur at about .8-second intervals initially, but then lengthen to as much as several seconds apart. The force and volume of the ejaculation depend on how long it has been since a previous ejaculation (Luria et al., 1987).

Sexual motivation would seem to be the clearest example of the close relationship between changes in arousal and motivated behavior. For all practical purposes, it would seem that sexual behavior results from changes in sexual arousal. Some researchers, however, have suggested that prior to sexual arousal (as outlined above) sexual desire is necessary (Kaplan, 1978). Sexual desire may be likened to appetite; that is, one must first want to be sexually aroused before arousal can occur. Kaplan has noted that some people lose their sexual appetites, a condition she terms **hypoactive sexual desire**, and as a result become uninterested in sexual behavior.

Furthermore, a distinction can be made between reaching orgasm and satisfaction as a result. Some individuals report reaching orgasm but do not find it satisfying (see, e.g., Zilbergeld & Ellison, 1980). Luria and associates (1987) have suggested that a more complete description of the human sexual response cycle ought to include both desire and satisfaction. Their model suggests that the human sexual response cycle occurs in the following order: desire, excitement, plateau, orgasm, resolution, satisfaction, refractory period.

Certainly there remains much to be understood about human sexuality. Although we have learned a great deal about the physiolog-

ical changes that occur during sexual behavior, we still know very little about the psychological components. Arousal theory has proven useful in understanding many of the physical changes that occur during sexual behavior; future research on the psychological aspects of sexual behavior may or may not make sense from an arousal perspective.

SUMMARY

In this chapter we have examined theories and research suggesting that motivation and emotion can be understood in terms of arousal. Arousal theory was strengthened by the discovery of brain mechanisms that serve to activate the cortex (i.e., the reticular activating system of the midbrain), and this led to the development of theories proposing that arousal is motivation. It soon became clear, however, that arousal is not a unitary process but consists of several types of arousal (e.g., cortical, autonomic, behavioral). Arousal theory has far to go in regard to motivation. If we grant that an aroused organism is motivated, what determines whether it eats, drinks, copulates, or falls asleep? Arousal theory has little to say about the activation of specific motives or the direction that behavior will take.

Sleep was originally thought to involve little arousal. We now know that this too is an oversimplification. Recordings of the electrical activity of the brain show definite changes at different levels of sleep and also show similarities between cortical activity during REM sleep and during waking. Physiological studies have begun to trace the systems involved in sleep and show that brainstem mechanisms apparently play a major role in both sleeping and dreaming. Although the role of other brain structures is still unclear, they too appear to be actively involved in the process of sleep.

Large deviations from our normal level of functioning may lead to an aroused state called stress. Stress is conceived as being the body's attempt to cope with or adapt to a changed environment. Stress can occur from both physical and psychological causes and leads to a generalized reaction called the general adaptation syndrome. Much of the stress reaction involves the pituitary and adrenal glands of the endocrine system. Activation of the pituitary-adrenal axis is triggered by the perception of a stressor, resulting in mobilization of the body to cope with the stress.

Considerable research conducted on the relationship of life change and illness indicates an association between the two. The major problem with life-change research has been that individuals vary greatly in their ability to withstand stress. These individual differences in the effects of life change and illness now appear to result from buffering agents that reduce the effects of the stress. The personality style of hardiness, physical exercise, and controllability have all been implicated as factors reducing the association between life change and illness.

Most people would like to be able to reduce the amount of stress they experience. Research indicates that knowledge of the body's reactions to stress and the preparation of alternate plans to combat frustration leading to stress are effective means of reducing stress. Some people may also be more immune to stress because they can emotionally insulate themselves from the life changes they experience. Meditative techniques may be effective in reducing stress because the meditative experience triggers mechanisms within the hypothalamus that inhibit overactivity in the sympathetic nervous system. Much work, however, remains before we can fully understand the processes involved.

SUGGESTIONS FOR FURTHER READING

House, J. S., Landis, K. R., & Umberson, D. (1988). Social relationships and health. *Science*, *241*, 540–544. This article provides a good overview of recent studies on social relationships and health.

Long, M. E. (1987). What is this thing called sleep? *National Geographic*, *172* (6), 787–821. This article provides a very readable summary of many different topics on sleep. The relation of sleep to body rhythms is particularly well covered.

Luria, Z., Friedman, S., & Rose, M. D. (1987). *Human sexuality*. New York: Wiley. Luria et al. provide an excellent overview of the literature on human sexuality.

Chapter Four

Physiological Mechanisms of Regulation

CHAPTER PREVIEW

This chapter is concerned with the following questions:

1. Which brain structures appear to control hunger, thirst, and sexual motivation?

2. What do anorexia and bulimia suggest about the homeostatic control of eating?

3. What factors have been proposed as important in the development of obesity?

LOCAL THEORIES

As I sit in front of my word processor, munching on a sandwich and contemplating how to begin this discussion of the physiological mechanisms of regulation, it occurs to me that the topics of hunger, thirst, and sexual motivation are terribly complex. The bulk of the research that has been conducted on hunger and thirst has taken the view that homeostasis is the primary mechanism controlling ingestion of food or water. That is, it has generally been assumed that we eat food to maintain our energy balance and drink water to maintain our fluid balance. Early approaches suggested that changes

in stomach contractions or a dry mouth are the signals that initiate eating and drinking, respectively. For example, Cannon and Washburn (1912) reported that stomach contractions are associated with hunger in humans. Washburn swallowed a balloon that was inflated and then attached to a marking pen that recorded Washburn's stomach contractions on a moving piece of paper (see Figure 4.1). Washburn was also instructed to indicate when he felt subjectively hungry. His hunger pangs tended to line up with his stomach contractions, leading Cannon and Washburn to assume that stomach contractions are the basis of hunger signals and, as a result, of eating.

The Cannon and Washburn theory was known as the **local theory of motivation** because it assumed that the signals that control motives such as hunger and thirst are produced in the peripheral organs of the body (as opposed to the brain). The local theory of motivation, however, turned out to be inadequate. For example, severing the nerve that carries information between the central nervous system and the stomach does not eliminate the experience of hunger. The **vagus** nerve is the major source of this information;

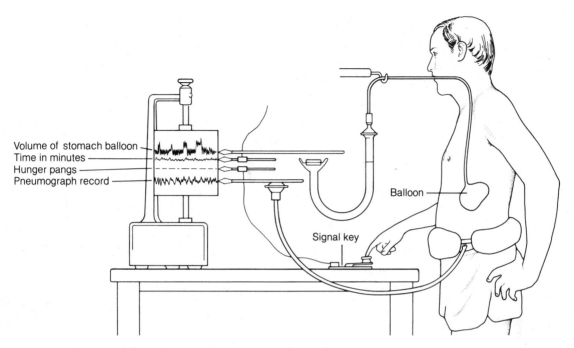

Volume of stomach balloon
Time in minutes
Hunger pangs
Pneumograph record

Balloon

Signal key

Figure 4.1 *Experimental setup used by Cannon to measure stomach activity and the subjective experience of hunger. (Adapted from W. B. Cannon, 1934. Used by permission.)*

when severed it causes stomach contractions to cease but not the experience of hunger in humans (see, e.g., Grossman & Stein, 1948). Morgan and Morgan (1940) had earlier shown that severing the vagus does not eliminate food intake in rats given insulin, so it appeared to researchers that changes in the periphery of the body are unnecessary for the experience of hunger (see Cofer & Appley, 1964, for a more complete discussion of this research). Because the early peripheral explanations appeared unable to account for motivated states such as hunger and thirst, it was natural for researchers to begin looking to the brain as the possible site of control.

CENTRAL THEORIES

Central theories of motivation emphasize the idea that specialized cells in the brain detect changes in the body's state and trigger appropriate motivation. Such models de-emphasize the role of the periphery in the regulation of eating and drinking. Several areas of the brain have been implicated in the homeostatic control of motivated behavior, but the greatest amount of research has focused on a small structure, buried deep within the brain, called the **hypothalamus**. As its name implies, it is located below the thalamus. Figure 4.2 shows the location of the hypothalamus in relation to other brain structures.

Although the hypothalamus represents only a very small portion of the entire brain, cells lying within this area and fibers coursing through it are involved with many important functions. For example, the hypothalamus controls the activation of both the sympathetic and parasympathetic portions of the autonomic nervous system as well as the pituitary

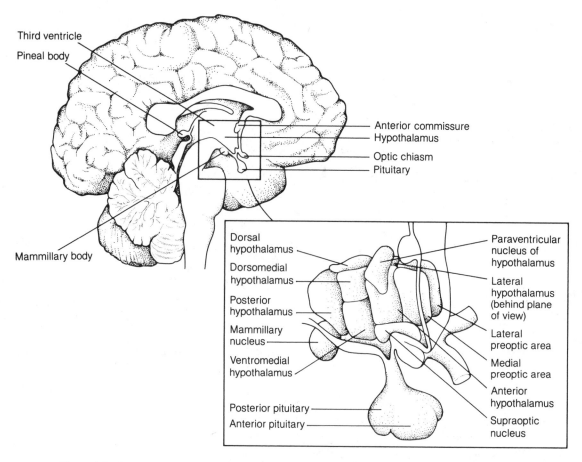

Figure 4.2 Relation of the hypothalamus to other brain structures and its major cell groups. (Adapted from Kalat, 1984. Used by permission.)

gland and, as a result, the rest of the endocrine system (Carlson, 1977; Guillemin & Burgus, 1976). Changes in feeding, drinking, sexual behavior, aggressiveness, and fear have all been reported as a result of experimental damage to or stimulation of this area. The hypothalamus is also richly endowed with blood vessels, which makes it well suited to sample changes in blood components (e.g., blood glucose, water content, hormone levels, and so on).

HOMEOSTATIC REGULATION

The homeostatic model assumes that regulatory mechanisms exist within the body that *sample* the internal environment; when changes move the body away from some optimal value, these mechanisms trigger circuits that generate motivation to return the organism to a balanced state. Figure 4.3 outlines a simple version of how such mechanisms might work. Much of the research directed at under-

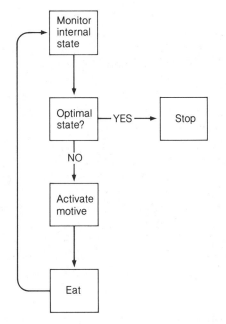

Figure 4.3 *Flowchart of a hypothetical mechanism to maintain energy homeostasis.*

standing the regulation of motivational states has concentrated on the hunger motive and, in particular, on the role of the hypothalamus in hunger.

REGULATION OF HUNGER

Hunger motivation has been generally assumed to be homeostatic in nature. When an imbalance exists, say, in the levels of sugar in the blood (**blood glucose**), this change is detected by specialized cells called **glucoreceptors** that trigger the motive to eat. As blood glucose levels rise, these (or perhaps other) glucoreceptors inhibit further eating because energy levels are now adequate. Some homeostatic mechanism like the one outlined above has usually been assumed to control **short-term regulation** of energy intake, that is, when we eat a meal (intermeal interval) and how much we eat (meal size). Generally, a

second homeostatic mechanism, which controls **long-term regulation** of energy reserves, has also been assumed. The mechanism controlling long-term regulation is involved with maintaining adequate energy stores so that if short-term energy intake proves inadequate, these stores can be called upon to maintain normal functioning. This long-term regulation is usually thought to involve the detection of changes in the amount of fat stored within the adipose tissue and the activation of hunger if stores fall below some optimal amount. We will now examine the concepts of short- and long-term regulation of hunger motivation.

Short-Term Regulation

Short-term regulation involves the control of eating over periods of time, such as from one day to the next or from one meal to another. Because short-term regulation was thought to function primarily to balance energy intake with energy expenditure, it was assumed that this system monitored some aspect of energy availability and triggered eating when available energy began to drop. The question of interest, of course, is: Where is this short-term system and how does it work?

A clue to the possible location of the system was provided in a study by Hetherington and Ranson (1940), who found that lesions of the hypothalamus produced obesity in animals. Later research localized the obesity effect to damage in the region of the **ventromedial hypothalamus (VMH)**. When this area of the hypothalamus was damaged, the affected animal would begin eating large quantities of food, a condition known as **hyperphagia**. Figure 4.4 pictures a rat made obese by damage to this area. Hyperphagic animals can eat enormous amounts of food, sometimes increasing their body weight to twice that of normal (Stevenson, 1969); however, they do not eat until they burst. Eventually these extremely obese animals stabilize

Figure 4.4 An obese (hyperphagic) rat. The dramatic weight increase is due to a lesion in the ventromedial hypothalamus. The rat actually weighs more than 1,000 grams because the dial has gone beyond the capacity of the scale. (Photo courtesy of Neal Miller.)

their weight at this elevated level and maintain themselves around this new weight.

A second clue concerning the operation of this system was provided by Anand and Brobeck (1951), who found that lesions in a second region, called the **lateral hypothalamus (LH)**, caused animals to stop eating. Figure 4.2 shows the location of the lateral hypothalamus. These LH-damaged animals would neither eat nor drink (conditions called **aphagia** and **adipsia**, respectively) and would die unless the experimenter intervened. If the animals were kept alive by the experimenter, however, they would eventually recover (Teitelbaum & Stellar, 1954) and maintain themselves, though at a weight considerably below normal.

The discovery of areas within the hypothalamus that have specific and opposite effects on the eating behavior of animals led to the concept of **centers** that work together to regulate hunger (e.g., Stellar, 1954). The VMH was considered to be a **satiety center** that "turns off" eating when energy intake is sufficient. If this center was damaged, then the animal could not inhibit its eating and thus became obese. Conversely, the LH was thought to be an **excitatory center** that "turns on" eating when new sources of energy are needed. According to the center hypothesis, damage to the LH should lead to a lack of eating because the cells that would normally initiate eating are damaged. The concept of excitatory and inhibitory centers within the hypothalamus that regulate food intake generated a tremendous amount of research. A major thrust of this research was an attempt to determine what changing conditions within the body signal the LH to initiate eating and, conversely, what conditions signal the VMH to inhibit eating. Changes in blood glucose provided a likely candidate.

The Glucostatic Theory of Hunger   In 1955 Mayer proposed that receptors in the hypothalamus are sensitive to changes in the ratio of blood glucose in the arteries to that in the veins. A decrease in blood glucose detected by glucoreceptors in the LH was thought to trigger eating, while an increase in blood glucose detected by glucoreceptors in the VMH was thought to inhibit further food intake. Mayer's theory was based in part on a report by Brecher and Waxler (1949) showing that injections of a chemical called gold thioglucose killed cells in the VMH. It was presumed that these cells were killed because they absorbed the chemical as a result of its similarity to glucose.

The glucostatic theory has enjoyed considerable popularity, but its credibility has recently come upon hard times. Several lines of research suggest that although glucoreceptors may exist in the VMH and LH, they are not the primary mechanisms responsible for normal short-term regulation. For example, it has now been shown that gold thioglucose damages the VMH because it destroys the capillaries feeding the VMH rather than being absorbed by the cells because of its similarity to glucose. Other chemicals that destroy capillaries also damage the VMH even though they do not contain glucose as part of their makeup (Carlson, 1977; Mogenson, 1976). The destructive action of gold thioglucose on capillaries rather than on the VMH cells casts doubt on the presence of glucoreceptors in the VMH. Further doubt was created by Gold's (1973) study showing that lesions that are restricted entirely to the VMH and do not damage adjacent fiber bundles do *not* result in obesity. When the adjacent bundles are damaged, however, the VMH obesity effect is found. Gold's results question the role of the VMH in the "turning off" of food-motivated behavior and suggest that fibers passing near the VMH may be responsible for the obesity, because these fibers are often damaged when VMH lesions are made.

The role of the LH in the activation of eating behavior is also not as certain as the early research seemed to indicate. Evidence for glucoreceptors in the LH does exist (Oomura, 1976), and the area does seem to be involved with eating as a result of changes in glucose (Epstein & Teitelbaum, 1967); however, the role of the LH in normal eating seems doubtful (Grossman, 1976; Zeliger & Karten, 1974; Blass & Kraly, 1974; Kraly & Blass, 1974). For example, Blass and Kraly noted that depriving LH cells of glucose must be extreme before feeding is induced in normal rats. As a result, they suggested that the LH may be part of an emergency system that is triggered only under extreme conditions.

The most damaging evidence to the idea that the LH normally initiates eating is a group of studies showing that LH lesions result in a general motivational deficit of which eating is only a small part (Marshall & Teitelbaum, 1974; Stricker, Friedman, & Zigmond, 1975; Stricker & Zigmond, 1976; Wolgin, Cytawa, & Teitelbaum, 1976). Stricker and his associates have shown that LH-damaged animals do not react appropriately to highly stressful situations. Similarly, Teitelbaum and his colleagues have found that LH-damaged animals do not react to stimuli normally associated with motivated behaviors and also show large deficits in normal arousal levels. The LH-damaged animal is therefore handicapped in many ways unrelated to hunger motivation. Lack of eating in such an animal probably reflects these more general deficits rather than damage to a glucose-sensitive, short-term regulatory system.

Where does all this research leave us with respect to the theory that the hypothalamus contains glucose-sensitive receptors that control feeding and satiety? It seems clear that the VMH and LH are involved in hunger motivation in some fashion. There is evidence that glucoreceptors exist in the brain; injection of glucose into it suppresses feeding, and intense glucose deprivation will initiate feeding. But glucoreceptors in the brain are probably part of an emergency system that comes into play only when glucose levels drop drastically. It is also known that both the VMH and LH are involved in various behaviors in addition to eating; damage to either, therefore, results in complex behavioral changes of which eating (or lack of eating) is only a part. Consequently, the concept of a dual system of excitatory and inhibitory centers within the hypothalamus that monitor glucose levels and that turn hunger on or off seems incorrect. The conclusion that glucoreceptors in the brain do not control normal feeding behavior has led some researchers to look again to the periphery of the body for the signals that initiate and inhibit eating.

Peripheral Detectors for Short-Term Regulation What peripheral mechanisms trigger feeding behavior and what mechanisms stop feeding? Though a single mechanism could both start and stop eating, several systems are probably involved. If we think of the body as similar to a NASA rocket, in which several "backup" systems become active as conditions change, we should not be surprised to discover that the triggering and interruption of feeding result from more than one type of signal. Indeed researchers have found evidence for more than one signaling system.

When we eat, enzymes in the saliva begin to break down the food into its components. This process is continued by the stomach, which then empties its contents into the upper small intestine, called the **duodenum**. The products of digestion, such as simple sugars and amino acids, are absorbed by the duodenum and enter the bloodstream, where they travel immediately to the liver; fats take a different route (Carlson, 1977). Several mechanisms in the stomach may act as satiety signals to turn off eating. Two such mechanisms are stretch receptors in the stomach wall, which serve to limit intake, and nutrient detectors, which inform the brain of the presence of specific nutrients (Carlson, 1977). Apparently a feedback loop also exists between the stomach and the brain because stomach activity is modified by its contents. The stomach does not appear to regulate by itself, however, because individuals whose stomachs have been removed still report hunger and still regulate.

The duodenum is a likely site of the elusive glucoreceptor because injections of glucose directly into the duodenum suppress eating in free-feeding rabbits (Novin, 1976). The duodenum also secretes a hormone called **enterogastrone** that has the effect of reducing stomach activity. Injections of enterogastrone also suppress feeding for as long as 17 hours in mice, so some component of enterogastrone seems to serve as a satiety signal. That component is a chemical called **cholecystokinin (CCK)**.

Numerous studies have provided evidence that CCK, secreted by the upper intestine in response to food, signals the brain to halt eating (Gibbs, Young, & Smith, 1973; Houpt, Anika, & Wolff, 1978; Kraly, 1981b; Kraly et al., 1978; Saito et al., 1982; Schallert, Pendergrass, & Farrar, 1982; Straus & Yalow, 1979). One line of research involved a comparison of CCK concentrations found in the brains of obese and nonobese mice. This study, conducted by Straus and Yalow (1979), showed that genetically obese mice have only about 25% the amount of CCK present in their brains as normal mice have and suggests that overeating by these obese mice may result from a lowered concentration of CCK. Saito and associates (1982) have demonstrated an association between CCK receptor sites in the brain and obesity, but it is not clear how their results relate to those of Straus and Yalow (1979). Though the data seem to clearly show that CCK serves as a satiety signal in some circumstances, the importance of CCK as a major hormonal satiety signal is a matter of some debate (see, e.g., Kraly, 1981a, 1981b).

The liver now appears to be a source of both hunger and satiety signals (Novin, 1976; Vanderweele & Sanderson, 1976). Injections of glucose into the hepatic portal vein (which passes through the liver) suppress feeding, while injections of glucose in the jugular vein (which supplies the brain) have no effect. The satiating effect of portal glucose injections is eliminated, however, if the vagus nerve is cut. This suggests that glucoreceptors may exist in the liver that transmit their information to the hypothalamus along the vagus nerve. In support of this liver-hypothalamic relationship, Schmitt (1973) has shown that portal infusion of glucose changes the rate of neuron firing in the hypothalamus. It thus appears that the liver may be one source of satiety signals sent to the brain to suppress feeding.

On the other hand, evidence also exists that the liver may initiate feeding. For example, Novin (1976) reported experiments in which 2-DG was infused into the hepatic portal vein. Because 2-DG blocks glucose utilization, this should "fool" the liver receptors into functioning as if blood glucose was low and thus initiate eating. That is precisely what happened, with the onset of feeding being very rapid. Novin's results suggest that the liver monitors glucose availability and sends this information to the hypothalamus, which either initiates or suppresses feeding. Novin further believed that glucose detectors exist in both the duodenum and the liver. He proposed that receptors in the duodenum act as the feeding suppressor if hunger is only minimal but are overridden if the animal has been deprived. Under conditions of deprivation, the liver receptors determine when feeding will be suppressed. Novin also suggested that these detectors relay their information to the LH and that the information is specific to glucose.

It seems possible, therefore, that short-term regulation of feeding is accomplished by a glucose-sensitive system, but the receptors of this system reside in the duodenum, the liver, or both.

Long-Term Regulation

Studies in long-term regulation of feeding behavior examine the mechanisms that control feeding so as to keep body weight stable. Though many of us complain about being overweight, our body weight appears to be relatively well regulated; that is, although our weight may not be what we would prefer, we do maintain a particular weight quite consistently, varying only a pound or two over long periods of time.

What are the mechanisms that allow an organism to regulate its body weight? Most theories of long-term regulation assume that some receptor system (or systems) acts to monitor body fats and then regulate food intake to keep body fats fairly constant. Such theories are called **lipostatic** (fats are lipids).

Set-Point Theory: A Lipostatic Theory of Hunger Richard Keesey and his colleagues (Keesey et al., 1976; Keesey & Powley, 1975; Powley & Keesey, 1970) argued that each of us has a "normal" level of body weight that is rather consistently maintained. They viewed the LH as concerned with proper regulation of the body's normal weight or **set-point**. If the LH is damaged, the lack of eating and drinking observed in such cases is not a deficit in the ability to eat but rather a change in the body's set-point to a new, lower level. Lack of eating, then, is the way in which the organism reduces its body weight to the new set-point.

Keesey and Powley noted results that support this kind of interpretation. When LH-damaged animals recover, they begin eating again in an apparently normal manner, except that they maintain themselves at a lowered body weight. Recovered animals also maintain this weight against various dietary challenges. For example, if they are given a concentrated diet, they eat less to maintain the new set-point while dilution of their diet leads to increased eating in order to maintain their weight.

If the alteration of feeding behavior evidenced by such animals is their way to reduce body weight to a new set-point, then depriving these animals prior to lesioning the LH ought to eliminate their typically observed lack of eating and drinking. Indeed Keesey found that previously deprived, LH-lesioned animals began to eat almost immediately, supporting the idea that the LH is involved with the determination of a body weight set-point.

Keesey and Powley noted that the VMH may also control the body's set-point. (Damage to the VMH, you will recall, causes overeating and obesity.) It is possible, they argued, that lesions of the VMH lead to a raising of the body weight set-point to a new, higher level. They noted that VMH-damaged animals defend their new, higher body weights against dietary challenges in much the same way, though not as completely, as LH-damaged animals defend their lowered body weights. Further, VMH-damaged animals tend to be finicky eaters.

The most likely stimulus for regulation around a set-point is body fat. Keesey and associates proposed that the LH and the VMH work in a reciprocal fashion to determine a set-point for adipose (i.e., fatty) tissue. What then is the stimulus to which the set-point is sensitive? One way in which the set-point might work is to monitor some aspect of the fat cells. Some monitoring of fat cells does occur; Faust, Johnson, and Hirsch (1977a) found that adipose tissue surgically removed from 3-week-old rats was replaced very precisely. Results of this research indicated some type of developmental regulation of the number of fat cells within the body. Regeneration of fat cells occurred only during a very limited developmental span, however, for the researchers found that by 15 weeks of age, regeneration no longer occurred. These researchers noted, too, that diets high in fat content led to greater regeneration of fat cells than diets low in fat, suggesting that dietary content may also play a role in the development of fat cells in young organisms. The study by Faust and associates is important because it shows that fat cell number is genetically regulated but can also be influenced by diet in young organisms.

More importantly, Faust, Johnson, and Hirsch (1977b) found in a second study that surgical removal of adipose tissue (without regeneration) led to an increase in size of individual fat cells. The amount that these enlarged cells could increase was clearly limited, however, indicating some sort of regulatory mechanism.

How might fat cell size be regulated? Wirtshafter and Davis (1977) obtained data indicating that a substance in the blood might provide the brain with the necessary information about the body's stores of fat. The substance involved is blood glycerol. Wirtshafter and Davis noted that the glycerol content of the blood is related to the size of the fat cells. Since the size of the fat cells would indicate something about the amount of stored fats, increases in blood glycerol should indicate increases in body weight.

Wirtshafter and Davis guessed that if blood glycerol is indicative of body weight, injections of glycerol ought to "fool" the regulatory mechanism into functioning as if the organism were heavier than its actual weight, thus causing the animal to stop feeding and ultimately to lose weight. To test this idea, one group of rats was given daily injections of glycerol; a second group was given glucose injections as a control condition. The glucose injections resulted in an increased body weight, while the glycerol injections led to a reduction in body weight.

If a new set-point for body weight had been established by the glycerol injections, the researchers expected that the glycerol-treated animals should return to this new set-point if deprived rather than to their previous body weight. This hypothesis was tested and confirmed in a second experiment. Wirtshafter and Davis concluded that glycerol controls body weight directly rather than first being converted to glucose before it is detected (as a glucostatic theory might predict). They reached this conclusion because their glucose control group did not lose weight and because glycerol injected directly into the brain causes a suppression of feeding. This suppression suggests that some area in the brain (probably the hypothalamus) may be sensitive to glycerol levels.

If glycerol levels are important for long-term regulation, then injections of glycerol ought to cause obese humans to lose weight like the rats in the Wirtshafter and Davis (1977) experiments. Unfortunately, such a procedure has been tried (see Kolata, 1985) and it did not work to reduce weight in humans. Perhaps some other signal is monitored for long-term regulation. One possibility is adipsin.

Cook and associates (1987) have discovered a molecule that may signal the state of fat stores. These researchers found that the **adipsin** molecule is produced by fat cells and is abundant in the blood. Changes in adipsin levels were found to vary with the metabolic state of rats: adipsin levels increased in fasting rats and decreased in rats infused with glucose (Flier, Cook, Usher, & Spiegelman, 1987). Although more research is needed, it is possible that adipsin levels could provide the necessary signal concerning the energy balance of the fat stores at least in some types of genetically determined obesity.

Keesey and Powley thought that insulin might be another possible regulatory candidate because it is involved in the storage of energy in the fat cells. They suggested that the VMH may control insulin release because cutting the vagus nerve (which also stimulates the pancreas to release insulin) eliminates the obesity of VMH-damaged rats. In support of the insulin hypothesis, Oomura (1976) has reported that cells in the LH and VMH are sensitive to glucose, insulin, and free fatty acids, which indicates that a system such as that proposed by Keesey and Powley could exist. Woods, Decke, and Vaselli (1974) have proposed that two hormones, insulin and somatotrophin (i.e., growth hormone), are involved in the long-term regulation of body weight. Several lines of research, therefore, suggest that eating behavior, viewed from the perspective of long-term regulation, involves some system capable of detecting changes in the body's fat stores and altering intake to adjust these stores.

Most theorists interested in the study of hunger have viewed feeding behavior as a two-process system—a short-term process that

monitors glucose and a long-term process that monitors lipids. Friedman and Stricker (1976) have proposed an exception to this general approach. Briefly, they have suggested that hunger is best understood as a single mechanism that monitors the availability of all fuels, both external (food) and internal (fats). Hunger signals, according to this model, are sent to the brain from the liver when fuel from the intestines *and* adipose tissue "is inadequate for maintenance of bodily functions without significant hepatic contributions" (Friedman & Stricker, 1976, p. 423). Friedman and Stricker suggest that the stimulus for hunger may be a shift in liver metabolism, which would later be reversed when food is eaten. This model does not need to make distinctions between short-term and long-term regulation or between glucostatic and lipostatic mechanisms. Additionally, it does not require the concept of set-point because it assumes that hunger "appears and disappears according to normally occurring fluctuations in the availability of utilizable metabolic fuels, regardless of which fuels they are and how full the storage reserves" (p. 424). These researchers further concluded that the central control of feeding behavior by the hypothalamus is incorrect as it stands; their evidence suggests that LH lesions influence all motivated behaviors rather than just eating and that VMH lesions cause changes that make it difficult for animals to use stored fuels, and as a result, they must overeat.

Powley (1977) has also noted several problems with previous explanations of the role of the VMH in eating. He has proposed that VMH lesions exaggerate autonomic and endocrine responses to food, responses that he calls **cephalic reflexes of digestion**. According to Powley, these reflexes, such as increases in saliva and insulin release as a result of the taste or smell of food, lead to overeating and other symptoms observed in VMH-damaged animals.

Ideas concerning the roles of the LH and

VMH in the regulation of hunger are clearly changing. A major problem with all of the hunger theories that have been offered to date is that they do not explain why organisms begin eating *before* homeostasis has been disrupted. In humans eating often occurs before changes in energy balance are great enough to trigger such behavior. In fact we often seem to eat in order to avoid the loss of homeostasis. Such behavioral strategies suggest that homeostatic regulation of feeding can be easily overridden and that factors in addition to homeostasis must be at work in normal eating behavior. Three examples of nonhomeostatic eating in humans are discussed in the next section.

FAILURE OF REGULATION

Anorexia Nervosa

Anorexia nervosa is a condition in which an individual severely restricts food intake, in some extreme cases to the point of starvation and death. The condition is most common in adolescent or young adult women, with an estimated occurrence of between .24 and 1.6 per 100,000 individuals annually (Bemis, 1978), but appears to be on the rise in the elderly too (see Hsu & Zimmer, 1988). Examples of male anorexia nervosa are also known but are extremely rare (see, e.g., Bruch, 1973, chapter 15). In women symptoms typically become apparent by age 25 or 30, although the onset of the condition is thought to begin earlier. Examples of anorexia nervosa were clearly described in the medical literature more than 100 years ago by Gull in England and Laségue in France (Gull, 1874; Laségue, 1873; both as reported by Bruch, 1973) and though the condition was once thought to be extremely rare, the incidence of anorexia has doubled in the last 20 years (Bemis, 1978; Herzog & Copeland, 1985).

The primary symptom of anorexia is a large reduction in weight as a result of the individual's restriction of food intake. Often a reduction of 25% of original weight is considered a minimum value for diagnosis of anorexia nervosa (Feighner et al., 1972; but see the American Psychiatric Association, *Diagnostic and Statistical Manual of Mental Disorders, Third Edition—Revised*: 15% reduction). A second major symptom in women is amenorrhea (absence of menstruation), which often occurs before the loss of weight. A third symptom is a distorted attitude toward eating that often includes denial of the need to eat, enjoyment in losing weight, and a desired body image of extreme thinness. Some researchers have emphasized this last symptom particularly, noting that patients suffering from anorexia nervosa often insist that they are fat even when severely underweight (Bemis, 1978). Here is a list of the criteria developed by the American Psychiatric Association and excerpted from the *Diagnostic and Statistical Manual of Mental Disorders, Third Edition—Revised* (DSM III-R) (1987), for the diagnosis of anorexia nervosa. (Used by permission.)

1. Refusal to maintain body weight over a minimal normal weight for age and height, e.g., weight loss leading to maintenance of body weight 15% below that expected; or failure to make expected weight gain during period of growth, leading to body weight 15% below that expected.

2. Intense fear of gaining weight or becoming fat, even though underweight.

3. Disturbance in the way one's body weight, size, or shape is experienced, e.g., the person claims to "feel fat" even when emaciated, believes that one area of the body is "too fat" even when obviously underweight.

4. In females, absence of at least three con-

secutive menstrual cycles when otherwise expected to occur (primary or secondary amenorrhea). (A woman is considered to have amenorrhea if her periods occur only following hormone, e.g., estrogen, administration.)

Clearly the anorexic patient is no longer maintaining a homeostatic energy balance, and as energy reserves in the body are depleted, body weight drops. The question of interest here is *why* anorexic patients no longer maintain energy homeostasis. Historically, opinion concerning the reasons for this lack of homeostasis has alternated between physical and psychological explanations. The term **anorexia** implies that the individual does not experience hunger (anorexia—lack or loss of the appetite for food; *Dorland's Illustrated Medical Dictionary*, 1965); however, it is not clear that anorexic patients have a true loss of appetite because these individuals often demonstrate bizarre eating habits as well as refusal to eat. For example, anorexics will sometimes binge-eat, hoard food, and show a preoccupation with food or cooking. As noted by Bemis (1978, p. 595), "Most accounts emphasize that the curtailment of intake is more often motivated by the desire for an extremely thin appearance than by genuine 'anorexia' or lack of hunger."

As originally described by Gull and Lasègue, anorexia was thought to be psychological in origin; however, considerable doubt was cast on this analysis when Simmonds (1914, as noted by Bruch, 1973) described a case of an emaciated woman who at autopsy was discovered to have lesions of the pituitary gland. This led many researchers to assume that anorexia involved a malfunction of the endocrine system. In the 1930s the emphasis began to swing back toward psychological causes of anorexia, an emphasis that has remained to the present (Bruch, 1973). The debate concerning the causes of anorexia is far from resolved, however, because several cases initially diagnosed as anorexia nervosa have later been shown to result from brain tumors of various sorts (Ahsanuddin & Nyeem, 1983; Heron & Johnson, 1976; Kagan, 1951; Swan, 1977), although in the larger number of cases, no pathology is detected (Bemis, 1978).

Ploog and Pirke (1987) have described some of the physiological changes that occur during anorexia. Metabolic and somatic changes are often first indicated by amenorrhea. During bouts of anorexia blood pressure can drop to dangerously low levels, and heart rate may decrease to as few as 30 beats per minute. CT scans of the brains of anorexics reveal evidence of brain atrophy and an enlargement of both external (e.g., widening of the sulci) and internal (e.g., enlargement of the lateral ventricles) cerebrospinal fluid–filled spaces. In other words, the brain seems to shrink. Ploog and Pirke found morphological changes in the brains of about 82% of the anorexics studied. After weight gain, about 42% of those showing initial enlargement of the external cerebrospinal fluid spaces showed a return to normal or markedly reduced widening. Witt, Ryan, and Hsu (1985) have found that anorexic patients show learning deficits on a difficult paired-associated learning task. These researchers also found that the longer the patients had been anorexic the poorer they performed on the task. Considering the findings of Ploog and Pirke noted earlier, it is possible that the learning deficit is in some way associated with the morphological changes in the brain that occur during anorexia.

Impairment of the sympathetic nervous system occurs in anorexia, as do endocrine malfunctions. Most prominently, cortisol levels are elevated during anorexia and appear to be an adaptation to starvation. Gonadal function is also impaired. The endocrine changes noted above appear to result from hypothalamic dysfunction occurring during the acute phase of anorexia. Finally, Ploog and Pirke argue that anorexia results in changes in the hunger drive. Specifically they view the hunger drive as being perverted by the anorexic condition to the point that the consequences of hunger, such as weight loss, are pleasurable to the individual. This creates an ambivalent situation for the anorexic in which hunger motivation creates an obsession with food but the weight loss from not eating is strongly rewarding. They suggest that this ambivalence may account for the bulimic behavior that often occurs in anorexics, and for the commonly observed obsession with food, while not eating.

Ploog and Pirke point out that the metabolic, endocrine, and CNS changes help to account for some of the symptoms commonly associated with anorexia; however, they believe that anorexia is best understood as a type of addictive behavior and needs to be treated as such.

Regina Casper (1983), in a review of bulimia nervosa, concluded that it is likely that "there are biological factors in anorexia nervosa . . . which promote and sustain the progressive weight loss" (p. 10). At this juncture in our understanding, it is best to keep open the possibility that *both* physiological and psychological factors play a role in anorexia nervosa. These factors override the basic homeostatic mechanisms of hunger and lead to severe emaciation and sometimes even death.

Bulimia Nervosa

Anorexia nervosa patients are unwilling to eat, even to the point of self-starvation. People suffering from bulimia nervosa, on the other hand, binge-eat large quantities of food in a very short amount of time. During these binges the person can consume an enormous number of calories, in one study ranging from 1,000 to 55,000 calories per episode (Johnson et al., 1982). Two studies found the incidence

of bulimia in college populations to range between 3.8% and 13% (Halmi, Falk, & Schwartz, 1981; Stangler & Printz, 1980).

The bulimic individual cannot stop eating once the binge begins and feels guilt, depression, and panic after the binge. Persons suffering from bulimia report a great sense of loss of control after a binge-eating episode and as a result induce vomiting, abuse laxatives, or go on severely restrictive diets to regain a sense of control and maintain their weight.

Johnson and associates (1982) surveyed 316 cases that met the diagnostic criteria for bulimia established by the American Psychiatric Association's *Diagnostic and Statistical Manual of Mental Disorders, Third Edition* (1980). See the list below for characteristics of bulimia for DSM III-R (used by permission).

1. Recurrent episodes of binge eating (rapid consumption of a large amount of food in a discrete period of time).

2. A feeling of lack of control over eating behavior during the eating binges.

3. The person regularly engages in either self-induced vomiting, use of laxatives or diuretics, strict dieting or fasting, or vigorous exercise in order to prevent weight gain.

4. A minimum average of two binge eating episodes a week for at least three months.

5. Persistent overconcern with body shape and weight.

They found that the "typical" bulimic was female, white, college educated, and in her early twenties. Further, these women tended to come from middle- and upper-class families that had more than one child. Although bulimia has been shown to be related to anorexia—40% to 50% of women diagnosed as anorexic will develop bulimia at some time during their time of disordered eating (Johnson & Larson, 1982)—in the bulimic women sampled by Johnson and associates, the majority were of normal weight. Purging behavior to control weight gain from the binge-eating episodes was very common in the sample. As reported by Johnson and associates the most common purging method was self-induced vomiting; the second most common method was the use of laxatives.

Table 4.1 presents the most commonly reported factors that led to the binge-eating episodes by these women. As can be seen in the table, the two most frequently mentioned factors were difficulty in handling emotions and restrictive dieting.

A study by Johnson and Larson (1982) examined the emotion factor by having bulimic women and a sample of normal women wear electronic pagers that signaled them to fill out a questionnaire concerning their emotional state and what they were doing at the time of the signal. The signals were sent out randomly, one signal per two-hour period, between the hours of 8:00 a.m. and 10:00 p.m. Bulimic women reported significantly more negative states than did the normal women on six of the eight mood items. Women in the bulimic group were sadder, lonelier, weaker, more irritable, more passive, and more constrained than those in the normal group. The bulimic sample also reported more fluctuations in mood and wider oscillations, indicating that their emotional state was less stable than that of the normal sample.

Table 4.1 Precipitating Factors

N = 316	Percentage
Difficulty handling emotions	40%
Restrictive dieting	34
Interpersonal conflict	7
Loss or separation	6
Other	8
Uncertain about onset	5

(Adapted from Johnson, et al. 1982. Used by permission.)

It has been suggested that anorexia and bulimia are variants of the DSM III category of major affective disorder (see, e.g., Cantwell, Sturzenberger, Borroughs, Salkin, & Green, 1977). In particular, depression is associated with both anorexia and bulimia. Laessle, Kittl, Fichter, Wittchen, and Pirke (1987) sought to determine whether anorexia and bulimia were best conceived as variants of major affective disorder. They interviewed 52 patients with a history of anorexia or bulimia, using a standardized interview technique. These researchers found that 44.2% of their sample were diagnosed as having the DSM III characteristics of major affective disorder (depression); however, in the majority of these cases the affective disorder developed *after* the onset of the eating disorder. The study by Laessle and associates therefore implies that the depressive symptoms commonly seen in anorexia and bulimia are secondary to the eating disorder and would seem to provide evidence contrary to the idea that anorexia and bulimia are variants of major affective disorder. Indeed Laessle and associates suggest that changed patterns of eating in anorexia and bulimia could produce depressive symptoms by causing changes in neurotransmitter systems involved with depression.

Theories of Bulimia Three general categories of explanation have been proposed for understanding bulimia. They are the sociocultural approach, the clinical/psychiatric approach, and the epidemiological/risk factors approach (Crandall, 1988).

The **sociocultural approach** suggests that changing societal norms have put an increasing emphasis on thinness for women at the same time that such norms are almost unattainable. The biological necessity to eat is put into conflict with unrealistic social norms of body shape and appearance and as a result abnormal eating patterns (binge-purge) may develop.

The **clinical/psychiatric approach** suggests that bulimia is associated with clinical symptoms such as impulsiveness, low self-esteem, parental psychological health, or major affective disorder (e.g., Hudson, Pope, Jonas, Yurgelun-Todd, & Frankenburg, 1987; but see Hinz & Williamson, 1987, for a different point of view). Disordered eating, then, is often viewed from this perspective as symptomatic of psychological distress.

Unlike the first two approaches, the **epidemiological/risk factors approach** makes no underlying assumptions about the causes of bulimia (e.g., unrealistic cultural norms; psychological distress) but rather attempts to determine what factors put an individual at risk for developing bulimia. A number of factors have been identified such as body image, emotional lability, family relationships, hormonal changes, sex roles, stress, genetic predispositions, and so forth (see Striegel-Moore, Silberstein, & Rodin, 1986, for a review).

Crandall has combined several aspects of the approaches mentioned above in a **social contagion** theory of binge-eating, which proposes that norms provided by social groups (the sociocultural approach) will be especially contagious to an individual experiencing psychological distress (the clinical/psychiatric approach). The symptoms identified by the epidemiological/risk factors approach are also relevant: some risk factors may increase the likelihood of social influence (genetic predispositions, stress), while other risk factors may be understood as resulting from social learning (body image, sex roles).

Crandall's (1988) ideas are based on a study of the social aspects of binge-eating. In an ingenious study Crandall measured the eating behavior and friendship patterns of women belonging to two separate sororities at a large state university. The results of her study showed that binge-eating was subject to social pressures. In one sorority the more a woman reported binging, the more popular she was

judged to be by her sorority sisters. In the second sorority, popularity depended on binging "the right amount" (p. 588). That is, women who binged near the mean amount for the group as a whole were judged to be the most popular. Furthermore, Crandall found that individuals became more like their friends over time. The binging behavior of an individual could be predicted from the binging behavior of her friends. This result did not appear to be attributable to similar individuals gathering together (assortative grouping), because the binging behavior of an individual changed across time, becoming more similar to the binging behavior of the group.

Even though binge-eating is quite common on college campuses, most individuals do not binge. How can one explain the fact that persons are not equally susceptible to social contagion effects? Crandall proposes that women who experience distress (e.g., feelings of low self-esteem) are more open to social influence than those not distressed. If the norm within a group is to binge-eat and a woman receives support and approval from that group, she is more likely to adopt the norms of that group and binge-eat also. Crandall suggests, therefore, that binge-eating is an acquired behavior pattern that may be adopted through modeling and social control processes.

Johnson and Larson suggested that bulimic individuals actually become addicted to eating because eating serves to moderate the mood swings. However, because the binges lead to huge increases in caloric intake, these individuals develop purging as a mechanism that allows them to binge-eat without becoming fat. Johnson and Larson further suggested that a combination of factors, both physical and psychological, leads some individuals to use food as a means of tension regulation, as contrasted to such other means as alcohol or drug abuse.

In a manner somewhat similar to the anorexic, the bulimic seems able to override the normal homeostatic control of eating. For the anorexic the normal cues for initiating eating are in some unknown manner either ignored or unfelt, while for the bulimic the cues associated with the end of an eating episode are ignored or unfelt. In both cases the homeostatic control of energy balance is disrupted. For the bulimic, however, an approximate balance is achieved through purging behaviors. The research on the eating disorders of anorexia nervosa and bulimia nervosa shows that the homeostatic control of hunger can be overridden; research on obesity also suggests that it is not difficult to override these controls.

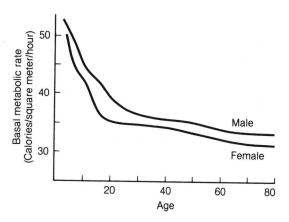

Figure 4.5 *Decrease in basal metabolic rate with increasing age. From R. B. Stuart & B. Davis,* Slim Chance in a Fat World. *Copyright 1972 by the Research Press Company, Champaign, Illinois. Used by permission.)*

Obesity

Obesity involves the long-term imbalance between energy intake and energy usage. Whenever intake exceeds usage, the excess energy is stored away in the form of fat. Obesity is a major problem in America. Though definitions vary somewhat, obesity is usually defined to be weight 20% above the tabled values for the person's height and build (e.g., The Metropolitan Life Insurance Co. tables). Using this definition, it has been estimated that 25%–45% of American adults are overweight (Grinker, 1982).

Information collected since the early 1900s shows that for both men and women, weight (for a given height) has increased since the early part of the century. Some of this increase is probably due to changing work patterns that now require less physical activity. This is suggested by the fact that the average daily caloric intake has remained relatively constant over this same period of time (Grinker, 1982). In some individuals body weight tends to increase with age, although body weight is remarkably stable for many others (see Grinker, 1982, for a review of studies).

Even though body weight may remain stable, people do get fatter with age. Two factors contribute to the increase in body fat. The first is a reduction in basal metabolic rate with age. **Basal metabolism** is the energy we consume just to maintain bodily functions at rest. Approximately two thirds of the energy we expend is consumed by basal metabolic processes; the remaining one third is expended as a result of exercise (Franken, 1982; Rodin, 1981). As we get older our basal metabolism slows down; we need less energy to maintain bodily processes. Figure 4.5 shows the decrease in metabolic rate that occurs with age. If we continue to take in the same amount of calories daily as we did earlier in life and do not change our pattern of exercise, then we can gain weight simply because we expend less energy to maintain our basal metabolism.

A second factor that contributes to increased fat is a change in the composition of the body with age. Lean body mass (LBM)— the weight of muscle and bone and so on— decreases with age, while body fat increases with age (Grinker, 1982). (Approximately 15% of the body weight of an individual of normal weight is stored fat; this fat storage is equivalent to about one month's supply of calories.) As a result, even if our weight remains constant, our percentage of body fat will increase and we will be fatter. Thus, even in the individual of normal weight, physical changes associated with aging lead to an increased percentage of body fat. It seems from the information noted above that everyone, whether overweight or not, is predisposed toward increasing stores of body fat. The question of interest to us here is which additional factors might lead to and maintain obesity in some individuals.

Adaptiveness Gone Wrong   Certainly our ability to store energy in the form of fat for future use has been adaptive. For most of our evolutionary history, food resources have been unreliable. Because the individual of normal weight already has approximately a one month's supply of stored energy, some researchers have viewed obesity as the continued storage of energy, beyond the normal reserves, for famines that are no longer frequent (Margules, 1979). Because the energy reserves are not drawn down by lack of adequate food, the storage system continues to add to already adequate reserves. In the past the control of obesity may have been primarily environmental. When times were hard and food was scarce, the reserves were called upon to maintain life; when conditions improved, energy was again stored away. If this line of reasoning is correct, then humans may not have well-developed mechanisms for limiting fat storage beyond some minimum level, because nature usually limited the storage through periods of famine. Though such a hypothesis is logical, it is difficult to prove and does not explain why so many individuals who have easy access to food do maintain normal weight. Margules (1979) has suggested that the reason some people become obese while others do not results from genetic differences in

the production of beta-endorphin (a chemical found in the brain). For example, Margules and associates (1978) found elevated levels of beta-endorphin in genetically obese rats and mice. Beta-endorphin has several effects, one of which is the reduction of the arousing properties of stimuli, which in turn results in lowered activity and consequently conservation of energy.

Genetic Predisposition   Evidence also exists that some people are genetically programmed to carry more fat than others. Hirsch and Knittle (1970) found that severely obese individuals had more than twice as many fat cells as normal weight individuals and that the fat cells of the obese were larger than those of normal weight individuals. Because dieting does not reduce the number of fat cells (but reduces individual fat cell size), persons with a large number of fat cells may be genetically programmed to carry more weight than the normal individual (Grinker, 1982). Because several strains of genetically obese animals exist (e.g., the Zucker rat and the ob/ob mouse), it seems likely that genetic differences in fat cell numbers would also exist within humans.

One particularly interesting finding by Jones and Friedman (1982) suggests that undernourishment of female rats during their first two trimesters of pregnancy leads to obesity and enlargement of fat cells in male offspring (female offspring did not become obese but did show some fat cell abnormalities). Their research was prompted by a report by Ravelli, Stein, and Susser (1976), who analyzed the body weights of 300,000 Dutch army draftees whose mothers had been subjected to undernourishment during World War II. Ravelli and associates reported that men whose mothers had been exposed to famine conditions during the first two trimesters of their pregnancy had a higher incidence of obesity than the population in general. It is possible, therefore, that intrauterine conditions during the development of the individual, as well as genetic predispositions, may play a part in obesity.

Brown Fat Research with rodents has suggested that a metabolic defect may lead to obesity. When excess foodstuffs are taken in, some of the incorporated energy is burned off as heat. Brown fat deposits are the primary source of this heat (Glick, 1982). Several research reports show that a malfunction in brown fat heat production is the basis for the obesity in genetically obese rodents (Himms-Hagen, 1979; Trayburn et al., 1982). Thus, the argument goes, malfunctioning brown fat heat production does not burn off enough excess energy, so fat gets stored away and leads to obesity. Although this research is very exciting and has even been picked up by the media, a fundamental problem remains to be resolved if the analysis is to be applied to human obesity. The problem is that humans have only a small amount of brown fat deposits (Grinker, 1982), so malfunctioning of this system is less likely to have a large effect on body weight. The role of brown fat in human obesity remains to be shown.

Obesity as Maintaining Obesity Judith Rodin (1981) of Yale University has pointed out that one consequence of being obese is that it is harder to lose weight. Several factors contribute to this sorry state of affairs. First of all, the fatter an individual is, the fatter he or she can become. Obese persons usually have higher levels of insulin than persons of normal weight. This situation, called **hyperinsulinemia**, increases the amount of energy stored away as fat because insulin is involved in the storage process. But hyperinsulinemia seems to induce hunger, so the obese individual is hungrier and stores away more of this energy as fat than does the normal weight individual.

Obesity also has an impact on activity levels. Obese persons are usually less active than

slender persons (Bullen, Reed, & Mayer, 1964), so they burn fewer calories, thus maintaining the obese state through lowered activity. In addition to lowered activity levels, energy consumption is influenced in another way by obesity. Fat tissue is metabolically less active than lean tissue (Rodin, 1981). Because a larger percentage of body weight is fat in obese individuals, they need fewer calories to maintain their weight as a result of this lowered metabolism.

Finally, dieting may help to promote obesity. Metabolic rate is reduced during food deprivation, which in turn makes losing weight more difficult; to add insult to injury, each successive dieting episode leads to a larger reduction in metabolic rate, making weight loss ever more difficult (Rodin, 1981). Thus, once it has developed, obesity appears to be a major factor in its own maintenance. With these cheerful thoughts in mind, let's look at psychological factors that might help us understand the development of obesity.

Externality In 1971 Stanley Schachter presented a theory of eating behavior proposing that obese individuals are more influenced by **external environmental cues** than by internal homeostatic cues in regard to eating. External environmental cues include such things as time of day, taste of food, quantity of food, and effort. In contrast, persons of normal weight were thought to eat more in response to internal cues such as stomach contractions and blood sugar level.

Schachter proposed the idea of externality as a result of several studies indicating that overweight subjects are more responsive to external cues associated with eating. For example, in one study by Schachter and Gross (1968), the speed of two clocks was altered so that one ran twice as fast as normal and the other ran half as fast as normal. In the experiment, which began just before dinner time, subjects were left alone for 30 minutes, while the clocks in their rooms indicated that either one hour or 15 minutes had passed. Subjects who had the "fast" clock thought it was after 6:00 p.m. when the experimenter returned to the room, while subjects with the "slow" clock thought it was 5:20 p.m.

The experimenter, upon entering the room, nonchalantly offered the subject some crackers to snack on while the subject filled out some additional questionnaires. Both obese and normal weight subjects were tested, half of each group in the fast-clock situation and half in the slow-clock situation. The question of interest was how many crackers obese versus normal subjects would eat as a result of the apparent time. If obese people are sensitive to external cues associated with eating, then obese subjects in the fast-clock situation should eat more crackers than those in the slow-clock situation because they would believe that it was dinner time. Normal weight subjects, on the other hand, should not be especially influenced by the doctored clocks because they were presumed to be influenced by internal cues independent of the apparent time.

The results of the experiment showed that obese subjects in the fast-clock situation ate almost twice as many crackers as those in the slow-clock situation. (It is interesting to note, however, that this difference between the groups was only marginally significant, $p < 0.07$.) Surprisingly, the normal subjects in the slow-clock condition ate more than those in the fast-clock condition. This unexpected result probably occurred because subjects in the fast-clock condition did not want to spoil their dinner by eating the crackers. Several of the normal subjects in the fast-clock condition gave this reason for declining to eat any crackers. The results, then, although not as statistically significant as one would like, were nevertheless in the predicted direction—obese subjects were influenced to eat more when the clock indicated that it was close to mealtime.

A second external cue that might be expected to influence eating behavior in the obese is taste. Nisbett (1968) examined the effects of taste on the amount eaten of either a good- or a bad-tasting ice cream. Overweight, normal, and underweight subjects were used in the experiment. The results of the experiment showed that overweight subjects ate more of the good-tasting ice cream than normal or underweight subjects, just as the externality hypothesis predicted. According to the hypothesis, normal and underweight subjects should eat more of the bad-tasting ice cream than the overweight subjects, who should be more sensitive to the taste. Though Nisbett did find that underweight subjects ate more of the bad-tasting ice cream than normal weight subjects, the overweight subjects also ate more. Schachter (1971b) attributed this discrepancy in the results to the fact that all three groups ate very little of the bad-tasting ice cream; though differences between the groups were found, they were small.

A study by Hashim and Van Itallie (1965) supports Schachter's contention. These researchers restricted obese and normal weight subjects to a bland, liquid diet that they could eat as much or as little of as they wanted. Obese subjects immediately reduced their food intake and lost weight, while normal weight subjects maintained their daily caloric intake (and weight) despite the bland food. In the Nisbett study quinine was used to make the bad ice cream taste bitter, probably bitter enough to cause all three groups to eat very little. In the Hashim and Van Itallie study, on the other hand, the liquid diet was not aversive, and obese and normal weight subjects consumed very different amounts. The results of Nisbett's good-tasting ice cream condition together with the results from Hashim and Van Itallie's study support the notion that obese individuals are more reactive than normal weight individuals to the taste of food.

Obese subjects also appear less willing than subjects of normal weight to expend effort to obtain food. In an ingenious experiment Schachter (1971a) asked overweight and normal weight subjects to fill out some personality tests at a table on which a bag of almonds and a nutcracker were placed. The experimenter told the subjects to help themselves to the nuts. For half the subjects the almonds were already shelled, while for the other half the shells had to be removed before the almonds could be eaten. Approximately half the normal weight subjects ate some nuts whether or not they had to be shelled. However, only 1 of 20 overweight subjects was willing to expend the effort to shell an almond, though 19 of 20 ate the nuts if they were already shelled. Schachter (1971a) also found that Americans of normal weight are more than five times as likely as those who are overweight to use chopsticks when eating Oriental food. The obvious conclusion is that for Americans, eating with chopsticks requires more effort than eating with a knife, fork, and spoon and that obese individuals are unwilling to expend the extra effort. The results of these studies, therefore, indicate a difference in the willingness of obese and normal weight subjects to work for food.

Finally, Schachter and Rodin (1974) have noted an interesting parallel between the behaviors of VMH-lesioned animals and obese humans. As you recall, VMH-lesioned animals become hyperphagic, eating large quantities of food and rapidly gaining weight. Eventually the animals reach a new, much higher weight, which they then maintain. Schachter and Rodin compared the behavior of the obese, VMH-damaged animal during this second, static phase to the behavior of the obese human. First of all, the VMH-damaged animal is finicky. If quinine is added to its food, it reduces intake below that of normal animals eating quinine-adulterated food. Additionally, if elements are added to the food of a VMH-damaged animal that it particularly likes, it increases intake beyond what is usual and

beyond that of a normal animal with the same additives in food. Obese humans, as we have already seen, also eat smaller amounts of bland food and larger amounts of good-tasting food, a pattern that could be described as finicky.

Schachter has noted other similarities between VMH-damaged animals and obese humans. For example, rats made obese by VMH damage eat only a little more than their normal counterparts in order to maintain their elevated weight (approximately 26% more daily). Similarly, obese humans in studies cited by Schachter and Rodin (1974) were found to eat only slightly more than normal weight humans. VMH-damaged rats eat fewer meals per day but consume more at each meal; obese humans behave similarly (Schachter & Rodin, 1974). Finally, research has shown that both obese, VMH-damaged rats and obese humans eat faster than normal weight subjects. The relationship noted by Schachter suggests that changes within the VMH could be a factor in human obesity; however, we should be very careful about drawing such a conclusion because the observed relationship is correlative. Several factors may contribute to similar behavioral changes in both VMH-damaged animals and humans that have nothing to do with malfunctioning of the VMH in humans. It remains to be shown that obesity in humans is typically associated with abnormal changes in VMH activity.

Problems with the Obesity-Externality Concept The proposed relationship between obesity and sensitivity to external cues has been enormously popular, and Schachter's research has been widely cited. But there is now a substantial body of research showing that the obesity-externality relationship is too simple (see Rodin, 1981, for a review). First of all, Rodin has noted that many studies have been unable to show that obese individuals are more responsive than normal weight persons to external food (or nonfood) cues. Additionally, it is clear that within every weight category there are persons who are externally responsive and others who are internally responsive. Being overweight is therefore not exclusively associated with externality. Similarly, sensitivity to internal cues does not lead to very good regulation, even in normal weight persons, if these cues are all that is available. Thus it would appear that individuals of normal weight are not especially sensitive to changes in their internal state.

A further problem with the obesity-externality hypothesis is that external cues can trigger internal physiological states. Put simply, external cues interact with and may create internal states, which in turn influence eating. For example, both saliva and insulin secretion increase in the presence of external cues that reliably predict the availability of food (several studies noted by Rodin, 1981).

Just as external cues may influence internal states, so too may internal states alter responsiveness to external cues. Data on stress-induced eating in animals suggest that increased arousal levels lead to an increased awareness of and responsiveness to external cues (e.g., Rowland & Antelman, 1976). In the Rowland and Antelman (1976) study, mild tail pinch (the arousal manipulation) administered to rats in the presence of sweetened milk led to hyperphagia and weight gain. Thus internal states probably influence receptivity to external cues associated with eating. The data noted here pose a problem for the obesity-externality hypothesis because internal and external states interact in complex and as yet poorly understood ways. What is clear at this point is that obesity involves more than increased responsiveness to external cues.

Homeostatic Regulation Reconsidered

The three examples of failure of homeostatic regulation—anorexia nervosa, bulimia ner-

vosa, and obesity—tell us that hunger motivation is more complex than previously thought. If homeostatic mechanisms of eating behavior do exist, we can override them rather easily. In particular, external cues associated with food (taste, smell, texture, and so forth) can often seem to stimulate eating behavior in the absence of any real need. Americans' preference for junk food is probably a good example of how such cues can lead to eating behavior in the absence of any homeostatic imbalance. Hunger studies during the past several decades have searched for the physiological changes that trigger eating. Glucose, insulin, and lipid receptors, as well as several other mechanisms, have been suggested as the monitoring devices for starting feeding behavior. To date this research has proven less useful in expanding our understanding of hunger motivation than hoped. As a result, some researchers are now calling for new approaches. Smith (1982), for example, suggested that we study the satiety signals that bring eating to a halt rather than continue to search for the elusive triggers of eating.

It is theoretically possible that eating behavior is not completely regulated. In our evolutionary past, food resources were considerably more unstable than at present. The sight, smell, taste, and other external cues associated with food might lead to eating, even in a nonhungry person, because the next opportunity to eat might not occur for several days. It would be adaptive, therefore, to be responsive to external, food-related cues and to *eat when food is available* even if homeostasis is currently being maintained. A good deal of research suggests that humans eat in response to various cues other than those associated with homeostasis; as noted before, regulation is poor when only internal cues are available (Rodin, 1981). So it is possible that specific homeostatic mechanisms are less important to the initiation of eating than the cues associated with the availability of food. Perhaps, given the availability of food and the relative lack of other strong motivation, we eat. Eating, like grooming behavior in the rat, may have a very high probability of occurrence, and as a result, specific internal mechanisms triggering eating may be of secondary importance.

For the present it seems best to leave open the possibility that hunger motivation can be homeostatically triggered under certain emergency conditions, but apparently humans usually eat *before* homeostasis is disrupted; that is, our eating does not typically seem to be triggered by homeostatic imbalance. External, food-related cues and learned patterns of behavior are likely to play an important role in this nonhomeostatic eating.

REGULATION OF THIRST

We have just seen that evidence for the homeostatic regulation of hunger is less clear than might have been expected. We will now examine research concerning the homeostatic regulation of thirst. Our examination of these data will reveal that homeostatic regulation of water balance does occur, but that once again, nonhomeostatic mechanisms also play a role in drinking.

Early theorists regarded thirst to be the result of peripheral changes such as a dry mouth, because it was known that dehydration reduces the flow of saliva (Cannon, 1929). Dryness of the mouth, however, cannot account for the regulation of water balance (Fitzsimons, 1973), although it may be involved in special circumstances associated with eating dry foods (Kissileff & Epstein, 1969; Kissileff, 1973).

Extracellular and Intracellular Mechanisms

Water is not evenly distributed throughout the body. The largest amount of water, approximately 67%, resides within the body cells.

About 26% is found in the spaces between the cells, and roughly 7% of body water is contained in the blood (see Figure 4.6). Research indicates that separate mechanisms are activated by change in the water content of the cells (termed **intracellular mechanisms**) and in the water content of the fluid surrounding the cells (termed **extracellular mechanisms**). For example, it is known that extracellular fluid is lost as a result of diarrhea or loss of blood, yet cellular water changes do not occur. Because this loss of extracellular fluid leads to thirst, any strictly intracellular explanation of thirst must be incomplete. (Incidentally, thirst resulting from the extracellular fluid loss of bleeding explains why a common cry of the wounded on the battlefield is for water.) Extracellular thirst occurs when fluids are lost from the extracellular spaces, while intracellular thirst results from fluid loss from within the cells.

Evidence for these two systems can be seen in a study by Eliot Blass (1968). Blass showed that damage to the frontal area of the brain in rats leads to a deficiency in the maintenance of proper water balance when the cells of the body are dehydrated (i.e., lack water) but not when the extracellular fluid is reduced. The control mechanisms for maintaining intracellular fluids, therefore, are probably independent of those that control extracellular fluids. Two motivational mechanisms have been proposed: the first, associated with intracellular fluid balance, is known as osmometric thirst; the second, associated with extracellular fluid balance, is known as volumetric thirst. To understand the research on thirst, we must briefly examine the action of the kidneys in the retention of fluid.

The Kidney

Normally we drink more water than we need, and the excess is excreted by the kidneys. The kidneys function to absorb sodium dissolved in the fluids of the body and to remove waste

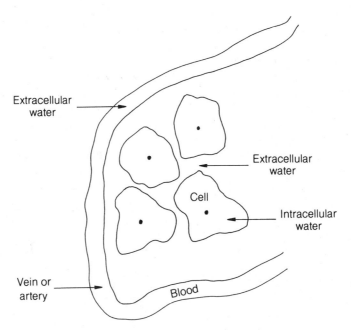

Figure 4.6 *Intracellular and extracellular spaces.*

products of metabolism. In the process of absorbing sodium, about 99% of the water filtered by the kidneys is reabsorbed. Because control of water balance is intimately tied to proper sodium balance, it has been suggested that thirst is controlled by sodium detectors (Andersson, 1971).

The kidney's ability to reabsorb both sodium and water can be altered. For example, when the flow of blood through the kidney drops, a substance called **renin** is secreted. (Renin can also be secreted when the kidney is activated by the sympathetic nervous system.) Renin interacts with a chemical produced by the liver called **angiotensinogen** and converts it to angiotensin II (which I will refer to as simply angiotensin). Angiotensin stimulates the adrenal cortex (see Chapter Three for an explanation of the adrenal gland) to secrete **aldosterone**, which in turn causes the kidney to increase its reabsorption of sodium and, as a result, water (Carlson, 1977). Thus a drop in

blood volume detected by the kidney or a command from the sympathetic nervous system causes an increase in the amount of water retained through reabsorption.

The ability of the kidney's collecting ducts to absorb water can also be altered by a pituitary hormone called **antidiuretic hormone (ADH)**. Lack of this hormone leads to a disease known as **diabetes insipidis,** where an individual passes great quantities of water and must therefore drink large amounts to avoid dehydration. Although the pituitary gland releases ADH in order to increase reabsorption, ADH is actually manufactured in the hypothalamus (Carlson, 1977). It is reasonable to expect, therefore, that the hypothalamus or regions near it are connected with the regulation of water intake. Indeed research suggests that receptors in the general area of the hypothalamus are sensitive to changes in the relative concentrations of the intracellular and extracellular fluids.

Osmometric Thirst

Although sodium is a necessary ingredient for life, it cannot easily pass into the cell body. As a result, any buildup of sodium outside of cells would create a condition in which water would be pulled from the cells by a process called **osmosis** (the tendency of fluid to travel through a semipermeable membrane in order to equalize the concentrations of the fluids on either side of the membrane). One possible mechanism of water regulation, therefore, would be specialized cells that could detect a change in their own volume as a result of cellular water loss due to osmosis. These **osmoreceptors** could trigger drinking behavior when cell volume decreased so that cell fluid balance could be returned to normal.

Indeed indirect evidence for such a mechanism has been known for some time. For example, Verney (1947) found that injections of salt solution into the blood supply of the brain lead to the secretion of ADH and, as a result, increased water retention by the kidney. Similarly, Andersson (1971) showed that salt solutions injected directly into the LH produce drinking behavior. The injections of salt solution into the brain presumably "fool" the osmoreceptors into functioning as if the body cells are dehydrated. Actually the osmoreceptors alone were dehydrated by the increased concentration of sodium that drew the water from them. Normally this would occur only if the other body cells were also dehydrated.

The research noted earlier by Blass (1968) indicated that the osmoreceptors must lie somewhere in the vicinity of the brain's frontal area, because destruction of this region leads to deficits in the control of cellular water balance. Blass and Epstein (1971) were able to further limit these receptors to the region of the lateral preoptic area, located in the front of the hypothalamus in the rat brain. In their study Blass and Epstein showed that destruction of the lateral preoptic area abolishes or

greatly reduces drinking in response to cellular dehydration. They also showed that local dehydration of the preoptic region activates drinking, while hydration of the same area suppresses drinking in rats whose preoptic area is intact. Peck and Novin (1971) simultaneously reported that the same area contained osmoreceptors in the rabbit. Thus a regulatory mechanism in the lateral preoptic region apparently monitors cellular fluid balance and either initiates or suppresses drinking in response to osmotic changes. Such a mechanism can account for the regulation of osmometric thirst but cannot explain drinking that results from changes in extracellular fluid balance. Because these latter changes also trigger thirst, it is important to examine what is known about these mechanisms.

Volumetric Thirst

A reduction in the fluid balance of the extracellular space results in a situation known as **hypovolemia,** a condition that activates compensatory mechanisms to restore proper fluid balance (Carlson, 1977). Hypovolemia may occur for a variety of reasons. For example, loss of large amounts of blood reduces extracellular fluid and initiates thirst. Similarly, diarrhea and even vomiting can lead to hypovolemia and accompanying thirst. Loss of fluid from the extracellular body compartments does not change the osmotic balance between the cells and those compartments, so any mechanism that monitors cell volume will detect no change. Therefore a second mechanism must monitor the extracellular fluid and trigger thirst when that volume is reduced.

At least two detectors of extracellular fluid volume have been identified. The atrium of the heart contains stretch receptors that detect changes in venous blood pressure (the pressure of the blood returning to the heart). If this pressure drops, these receptors stimulate the pituitary to release ADH and the kidney to release renin. As we have seen, these two chemicals increase the amount of water retained by the kidneys, which in turn increase blood volume.

The second system involves detection of angiotensin. The activation of thirst and subsequent water intake to compensate for reduced extracellular fluid is thought by several researchers to result from the brain's sensitivity to this chemical. Angiotensin has been shown to be a powerful stimulus for drinking in several species, including monkeys, dogs, cats, goats, rabbits, and pigeons (Fitzsimons, 1973). For example, Fitzsimons and Simons (1969) found that infusion of angiotensin into the blood supply of rats with a normal water balance leads to drinking. Additionally, Epstein, Fitzsimons, and Rolls (1970) showed that injection of angiotensin directly into the brain elicits drinking, while Malvin, Mouw, and Vander (1977) found that agents that block uptake of angiotensin by the brain also block drinking.

The data noted above are consistent with the idea that angiotensin manufactured in the periphery of the body travels to the brain and stimulates cells responsible for thirst motivation. As might be expected, researchers initially looked for these detectors near or in the hypothalamus, the brain region so intimately involved with basic motivational states. Some research seemed to indicate that the medial preoptic area was the site of angiotensin detection (Epstein, Fitzsimons, and Rolls, 1970), but this site was questionable because angiotensin passes through the blood-brain barrier very slowly (Volicer & Lowe, 1971). (The blood-brain barrier allows some substances to pass from the blood to the brain cells while restricting others.) The site of action of angiotensin was eventually determined to be a structure called the **subfornical organ (SFO)** (Simpson & Routtenberg, 1973; Volicer & Lowe, 1971). The SFO is of particular interest because it lies outside the blood-brain barrier on the surface

of the fluid compartments of the brain (i.e., ventricles). As a result, it can detect changes in angiotensin transported to the brain and send this information to other brain structures involved with fluid regulation (Epstein, 1982). Simpson and Routtenberg (1973) had shown that the SFO is very sensitive to angiotensin; activation of drinking occurs in less than three seconds when angiotensin is delivered to it. When Simpson and Routtenberg destroyed the SFO, they found that drinking in response to angiotensin was abolished. Based on these findings, they suggested that the SFO is the site of receptors sensitive to changes in extracellular body fluids. Subsequent research has confirmed the SFO to be the critical structure (see Epstein, 1982, for a review of this literature).

Inhibitory Control of Drinking

We have examined research concerned with the initiation of drinking as a result of both intracellular and extracellular changes. But we have not examined mechanisms that "turn off" drinking. Inhibition of water intake poses a smaller problem for the body than inhibition of food intake because excess water can be controlled relatively simply by increased excretion through the kidneys. Because water balance can be controlled by changes in excretion, it would not be surprising if inhibitory mechanisms are less developed than mechanisms that initiate drinking. Like hunger motivation, mechanisms appear to trigger drinking behavior when homeostatic balance is disrupted; however, also like hunger motivation, this homeostatic balance appears to be easily overridden. Drinking behavior usually occurs *before* homeostatic balance is disrupted. In this regard Kraly (1984) has suggested that researchers need to study normal drinking behavior, that is, drinking that occurs before either intracellular or extracellular fluid balances are disturbed. Kraly noted, for example, that normal drinking occurs around meals for most mammals. In the rat 70% to 90% of daily water intake occurs within a time interval ranging from 10 minutes before meals to 30 minutes after meals (Fitzsimons & LaMagnen, 1969; Kissileff, 1969) and does not appear to be a response to any homeostatic imbalance (Kraly, 1984). These data, together with other considerations noted by Kraly, suggest that drinking behavior is closely tied to eating, and, in fact, eating appears to be a potent stimulus for drinking. It would therefore seem that drinking, like eating, often occurs when no apparent homeostatic imbalance is evident. Further, because eating and drinking interact, the role of food ingestion on drinking behavior needs to be explored. As suggested by Kraly, gastrointestinal tract changes that result from food ingestion probably stimulate drinking behavior that is nonhomeostatic in nature. Thus, although organisms certainly do drink in order to protect both intracellular and extracellular fluid balance, they also drink when these balances are not in jeopardy. Further study of nonhomeostatic drinking, such as often occurs at mealtimes, could go a long way in helping us understand thirst motivation.

REGULATION OF SEXUAL MOTIVATION

Hunger and thirst are two motivated states regulated in part by the hypothalamus. Other motivated states are also partially regulated by the hypothalamus; among them are sexual and maternal behaviors, temperature regulation, fear, and aggression. Though much remains to be understood about the mechanisms of regulation for each of these motives, we will briefly examine some of the research on regulation of sexual motivation.

The brains of males and females are set up differently as a result of the presence or absence of sex hormones (see Feder, 1984, for a review). Research has shown that the mammalian brain is essentially female unless altered by the presence of male sex hormones (e.g., testosterone). Male brains are created by the presence of testosterone during a critical period in their development.

Seymour Levine (1966) has conducted considerable research on the relationship between sex hormones and male and female sexual behaviors. For example, Levine injected female rats that were less than four days old with the male sex hormone testosterone. The injected females did not develop normal female physiology; the ovaries were severely reduced in size, they did not produce egg cells, and the ovulation cycle was disrupted. Levine also castrated male rats at a similar age in order to eliminate testosterone in them. The castrated males showed some signs of female physiology; if an ovary was surgically implanted in one of these males at maturity, the ovary produced egg cells. Similar results have been obtained with both guinea pigs and monkeys.

Levine has suggested that the administration of testosterone during a critical period of an animal's life permanently alters the brain so that the female pituitary cycle is lost and the brain becomes insensitive to both estrogen and progesterone (female sex hormones), regardless of the genetic sex of the animal. This critical period appears to be the first few days of life in rats but occurs before birth in both guinea pigs and monkeys, so injections of testosterone in these latter two species must be given before birth for masculinizing effects to be apparent. In the genetic male minute amounts of testosterone are secreted during development in the uterus, and these minute amounts are enough to masculinize the brain. In the genetic female or in males where testosterone is absent, the brain develops feminine circuitry.

More interesting from a psychological viewpoint are the long-term effects of early administration of testosterone to females. Levine injected testosterone into young female rats to masculinize them and then tested these animals in adulthood for normal female sexual behavior (e.g., normal female rats exhibit a behavior pattern known as **lordosis**, which consists of arching the back and elevating the pelvis in order to permit mounting by the male). These masculinized female rats did not show normal female sexual behavior even when given injections of estrogen and progesterone, hormones necessary for sexual behavior in the normal female rat. On the other hand, if these masculinized females were given additional injections of testosterone as adults, they displayed the complete copulatory pattern of male sexual behavior, including the movements associated with ejaculation. Apparently the early administration of testosterone either inhibited the development of normal female sexual behavior or blocked its expression. Similarly, when male rats castrated at an early age were given estrogen and progesterone, they behaved precisely like normal females. The lack of early testosterone in these male rats either led to the failure of the male sexual pattern to develop or blocked the expression of the pattern.

Evidence concerning the importance of sex hormones in brain development has also begun to surface in human studies. Geschwind (cited by Marx, 1982) has proposed that an excess of or unusual sensitivity to testosterone during pregnancy alters brain circuitry so that the individual is more likely to have the right half of the brain dominate functions such as speech and handedness (right-brain dominance is associated with left-handedness). Geschwind has further proposed that the amount of testosterone present during development is crucial: if the excess testosterone is of the right amount, giftedness in such areas as

art, music, or mathematics may result, but if the excess is too great, serious abnormalities such as autism, dyslexia, and immune system disorders may result (Kolata, 1983). In a startling confirmation of Geschwind's proposals, Benbow and Stanley (noted by Kolata, 1983) found that the mathematically gifted males in their national sample were more than twice as likely to be left-handed as the national average. Furthermore, 60% of these left-handed males had immune system disorders (typically allergies and asthma), which was five times greater than the national average.

Further research on the relationship between sex hormones and brain development may lead us to a better understanding of both creativity and abnormality; fetal testosterone currently appears to play a critical role in both. How sex hormones alter the developing circuitry within the brain is unknown; however, as was the case with both feeding and drinking behavior, sexual behavior appears to be regulated by mechanisms in or near the hypothalamus.

Hypothalamic Regulation

Much more is known about the role of the hypothalamus in the control of hunger and thirst than is known about its role in sexual behavior. Though other structures are also involved in the regulation of sexual behavior, the hypothalamus is of major importance (Sawyer, 1969).

Tumors or other pathologies of the hypothalamus can modify the development or maintenance of sexual behavior in humans. Tumors of the hypothalamus may lead to early sexual development with gonadal enlargement and the appearance of secondary sexual characteristics (e.g., pubic hair) in children as young as eight. For reasons that are still unclear, this early development seems more common in boys than in girls. Damage to the hypothalamus may also produce the opposite effect, leading to **hypogonadal** conditions, including a lack of sexual motivation, under-development of the genitals, and a lack of secondary sexual characteristics.

In many animals sexual behavior can be accomplished reflexively at the level of the spinal cord. For example, erection, thrusting movements, and ejaculation in the male have all been shown to occur after the spinal cord has been cut to eliminate brain influence. Lordosis can also be accomplished at the spinal level (Beach, 1967; Hart, 1967). Human males with spinal cord damage have been known to accomplish erection and ejaculation, but they do not experience orgasm as a result (Carlson, 1977).

Much of the research on the physiological mechanisms of sexual behavior has been conducted on the rabbit and the rat. Rabbits are particularly useful subjects because females ovulate as a result of intercourse. They therefore enable the researcher to test which brain structures are involved in sexual activity by checking for ovulation after different brain areas have been stimulated or removed. The phenomenon of intercourse-induced ovulation also helps explain why rabbits are so numerous.

Lesion Studies   Several studies (see Sawyer, 1969) have shown that lesions in the anterior hypothalamus abolish the estrous cycle in female mammals. Replacement therapy with estrogen fails to reestablish the cycle, suggesting that this part of the hypothalamus may contain cells sensitive to circulating female sex hormones. Lesions in the preoptic region, particularly the medial preoptic area, abolish or reduce sexual behavior in male rats (Heimer & Larsson, 1966/1967), and testosterone therapy is ineffective in reestablishing the behavior. Thus this region in the male rat may contain receptors sensitive to the male sex

hormones. Lesions in the VMH also abolish estrus in females, but estrogen replacement therapy successfully restores sexual behavior. Similar results have been obtained with males lesioned in the VMH (Buck, 1976; Sawyer, 1969). Because hormone replacement therapy successfully restores sexual behavior in VMH-lesioned animals, the role the VMH plays in sexual behavior is probably different than the roles played by the anterior hypothalamus and preoptic areas. It is likely that these two areas detect changes in the levels of circulating sex hormones, while the VMH is probably involved with the expression of sexual behaviors. Clearly these several areas interact in order to produce sexual activity.

Electrical and Hormonal Stimulation Studies   Increases in male sexual behavior have been reported as a result of electrical stimulation of the preoptic region. Electrical stimulation in both the anterior hypothalamus and the preoptic area has also produced ovulation in female rabbits (Carlson, 1977; Sawyer, 1969). Herberg (1963) produced slow emission of semen in rats by electrically stimulating fibers (the medial forebrain bundle) that pass through the hypothalamus, and Sawyer (1969) has reported that electrical activity in these same fibers, as well as in the anterior hypothalamus, occurs as a result of vaginal stimulation in cats.

Stimulation of the hypothalamus by sex hormone injection also leads to changes in sexual behavior. Fisher (1964) found that male rats display sexual behavior when testosterone is injected directly into the lateral preoptic area. Unexpectedly, he also found that testosterone injected into the medial preoptic area leads to maternal behavior in male rats. This novel result implies that the neural circuits for both masculine and feminine behavior are present in both male and female but are usually activated only by their respective hormones. In Fisher's "maternal" males the maternal behavior was probably triggered artificially. Estrous behavior in female cats can also be triggered by hormone implants even though the ovaries have been removed. Placements that produce estrus include the anterior hypothalamus and the medial preoptic area (Sawyer, 1969).

The hypothalamus would seem to regulate sexual motivation, at least in part, by blocking the spinal reflex aspects of sexual behavior until conditions are appropriate for their occurrence. For example, Barfield, Wilson, and McDonald (1975) and Clark and associates (1975) found that lesions between the hypothalamus and the midbrain *increase* sexual behavior in male rats. The increased sexual behavior is the result of a decrease in the amount of time between ejaculations. Male rats normally go through a refractory period after ejaculation during which they are uninterested in sexual activity and show sleeplike EEGs. Lesions that disconnect the hypothalamus from the midbrain reduce this refractory period from approximately 5 to 2½ minutes, suggesting that the hypothalamus may normally inhibit sexual activity.

The information briefly reviewed in this section suggests that the hypothalamus (or structures near it) is sensitive to and responsible for the proper regulation of both sex hormones and sexual behavior. The anterior hypothalamus and the preoptic areas seem particularly sensitive to the circulating sex hormones and may contain sex hormone detectors that in turn regulate hormonal output and also influence other areas, such as the VMH, leading to the expression of sexual behavior. The influence of sex hormones on behavior is complex: on the one hand, they appear important for the organization of brain circuitry during fetal development; on the other, they regulate and make possible sexual behavior. Much additional research remains to be conducted before we fully understand the manner in which sexual behavior is regulated.

REGULATION OF AGGRESSIVE MOTIVATION

To conclude this chapter we will briefly consider evidence for neural circuitry underlying aggression. In particular we will examine research on animal aggression, a topic with some relevance for studies of anger in humans.

Early work by Cannon (1929) showed that the cortex of the brain is unnecessary for the expression of anger. In fact decorticate cats showed what Cannon called *sham rage*, a term used because true emotional behavior, it was assumed, could not occur without the cortex. But the rage observed included the typical behaviors seen in angry cats, such as the lashing tail and arched back, as well as snarling, clawing, and biting. The cats also showed autonomic arousal with dilation of the pupils, piloerection (i.e., erection of the fur), rapid heartbeat, and increases in adrenalin and blood sugar. The sham rage response was therefore very similar to the normal expression of rage except that it was not directed toward the provoking stimulus (Bard & Mountcastle, 1964). Bard (1928) determined that this rage response depended upon the hypothalamus being intact, particularly the posterior portion. These early studies led to the idea that the cortex of the brain acts to suppress aggressive emotional behavior directed by the hypothalamus. Although recent theory is more complex, the assumption that cortical areas serve to inhibit aggressive behavior still appears valid.

The Limbic System

As early as 1937 James Papez proposed that the hypothalamus, along with several other structures, forms part of a circuit that participates in emotional expression. Papez identified the hypothalamus, anterior thalamic nuclei, the cingulate gyrus, and the hippocampus. Today these structures, along with the amygdala, are known as the **limbic system**, which is shown in Figure 4.7.

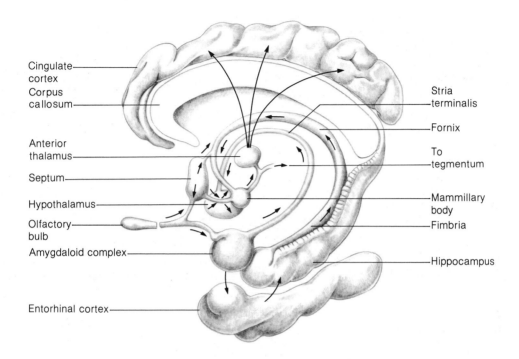

Cingulate cortex
Corpus callosum
Anterior thalamus
Septum
Hypothalamus
Olfactory bulb
Amygdaloid complex
Entorhinal cortex

Stria terminalis
Fornix
To tegmentum
Mammillary body
Fimbria
Hippocampus

Figure 4.7 Structures and connections of the limbic system. *(From Carlson, 1977. Copyright © 1977 by Allyn & Bacon, Inc., Boston. Used by permission.)*

The involvement of the limbic system in emotion was further supported by the experiments of Kluver and Bucy (1939), who surgically removed the temporal lobes of monkeys. Bilateral (i.e., both sides) destruction of the temporal lobes resulted in a set of symptoms that included changes in emotionality. These formerly wild, aggressive monkeys became very "tame" after the operation and exhibited little emotionality. In some cases anger and fear were permanently lost, while in others it returned after the operation but in much subdued form. Because these temporal lobe lesions seriously damaged the underlying amygdala and hippocampus of the limbic system, Kluver and Bucy's research provided striking confirmation of Papez's theory.

Rosvold, Mirsky, and Pribram (1954) further showed that damage to the amygdala leads to profound losses of social dominance behavior in monkeys. Because the dominance order of monkeys is maintained largely through aggression or threats of aggression, such losses indicate that the amygdala is important for the normal expression of aggressive behavior. In some monkeys, interestingly, while damage to the amygdala severely reduced aggressiveness in social interactions, it increased aggression (e.g., threatening behavior toward the experimenter) if the animals were isolated. This latter result suggests that the amygdala has different effects on different kinds of aggression, a point to which we will return.

Earlier in this chapter we noted some research suggesting the importance of two areas within the hypothalamus in the regulation of hunger, thirst, and sexual behavior. Those two areas, the lateral hypothalamus (LH) and the ventromedial hypothalamus (VMH), also seem to be involved in aggressive behavior (Moyer, 1971; Smith, King, & Hoebel, 1970). Flynn and his co-workers (Flynn et al., 1970) have distinguished two types of aggression known as **affective attack** and **quiet biting attack**.

Affective attack appears very similar to the rage behavior seen in the decorticate cats mentioned previously. There is significant sympathetic arousal evidenced by pupil dilation and piloerection. A cat displaying this type of aggression hisses and snarls, with its back arched, and it attacks, screaming, with claws bared and teeth ready to bite. This rather extreme set of emotionally laden behaviors can be elicited simply by electrically stimulating the VMH.

Quiet biting attack is aggression of quite a different sort. Emotionality is minimal, and no screaming or growling is observed. The cat stalks its prey and pounces upon it, biting it in the neck region. It uses its claws not to slash but to roll over the prey so that a killing bite can be made. Such behavior looks very much like the typical predatory behavior of cats and can be obtained by electrically stimulating the LH. Bandler and Flynn (1974) also found areas within the thalamus that elicited quiet biting attack when stimulated. They lesioned this area and then traced the degenerating fibers to the midbrain. When the appropriate area of the midbrain was lesioned in another group of cats, stimulation of the thalamus had no effect; however, stimulation of the LH still elicited quiet biting attack. Thus predatory aggression appears to be complexly controlled.

The periaqueductal gray area of the midbrain is known to be involved in aggressive behavior because, even after destruction of the hypothalamus, partial aggressive responses such as spitting and snarling can still be obtained from this area (Bailey & Davis, 1969; Bard & Mountcastle, 1964). These findings suggest that the motor patterns of aggressive behavior are mediated at the level of the midbrain, while the hypothalamus may be involved in the spontaneity of aggressive behavior (Flynn et al., 1970).

The hypothalamus may in turn be regulated by the amygdala. Gray (1971) has proposed that the amygdala inhibits the hypothalamus, which in turn inhibits the midbrain aggressive patterns of behavior. Gray further proposed that just one neural system controls both fight (i.e., affective attack) and flight behavior. If the environment is conducive to escape, flight will occur; if escape is impossible, attack occurs. Gray argued that the decision to attack or flee is made by the ventromedial hypothalamus (VMH).

Other theorists, notably Flynn, have argued that the thalamus contains separate neural systems for attack and flight. For example, Flynn and his associates lesioned an area of the thalamus that resulted in the elimination of flight behavior when painfully stimulated. Although this lesion abolished flight as a response to hypothalamic stimulation, it did not eliminate hypothalamic stimulation–induced attack. The proposals of Gray and Flynn are not directly comparable, however, because Gray's concerns affective attack, while Flynn's concerns quiet biting attack. So the issue of whether attack and flight behaviors are regulated by independent neural systems or by one system cannot be definitely answered. However, it is generally agreed that the organization of aggressive behavior requires the amygdala, the hypothalamus, and the midbrain regions. Although the amygdala is often considered to exert an inhibitory influence on the hypothalamus, this is probably too simple an assumption because the amygdala is composed of several groups of nuclei (clumps of neurons) that serve different functions.

For example, Miczek, Brykczynski, and Grossman (1974) showed that lesions of different parts of the amygdala produce different effects on aggressiveness: lesions in one part eliminated both attack behavior and dominance in male rats that had been dominant before surgery, while lesions in a different part had no effect on this type of aggressiveness. Similarly, aggression following footshock was only slightly reduced by some lesions, while other lesions greatly reduced it. Several types of aggression are thus apparently controlled by different systems within the amygdala.

Sensory information is also important to the expression of aggressive behavior. In fact the same electrical stimulation of hypothalamic areas that elicits attack also sets up sensory fields used during the attack (Flynn, 1969). During stimulation, for example, touching the head of a cat near the mouth causes the head to move so that the stimulus comes into contact with the lips; when the lips are touched by the stimulus, the jaw snaps open to bite. Figure 4.8 shows the sensory fields set up by electrical stimulation of the hypothalamus. Flynn's data suggest that during attack behavior, sensory fields originate and guide the attack.

Types of Aggression

The research by Flynn and his colleagues suggests that more than one type of aggression may exist and that each type may be served by its own neural system. This notion has been argued most persuasively by Kenneth Moyer (1971), who has presented evidence for at least seven types of aggressive activity, as follows:

1. predatory aggression: aggression elicited by a natural object of prey

2. intermale aggression: aggression typically released by the presence of another male; the attack is usually without provocation

3. fear-induced aggression: aggression that occurs when escape is blocked

4. irritable aggression: aggression usually described as either anger or rage; attack occurs in response to a broad range of stimuli, either animate or inanimate

5. territorial defense: aggression in defense of a territory; the aggression is usually against a member of the animal's own species

6. maternal aggression: aggression involving defense of the young, typically performed by the female in mammals

7. instrumental aggression: aggressive be-

A   B

Figure 4.8 Sensory fields set up by electrical stimulation of the brain. *A*, shaded area indicates area that elicits head movement when touched, bringing stimulus into contact with the lips; *B*, sensory field along the lips that causes mouth to open when contacted by the stimulus. (From Flynn, 1969. Used by permission.)

havior that is a learned response and is performed when that response is reinforced

Though little is known about the neural systems underlying most of the aggressive behaviors that Moyer has proposed, predatory aggression appears very similiar to the quiet biting attack noted by Flynn, and the LH appears to be important in its regulation. Irritable aggression also seems to correspond closely with Flynn's affective attack, and the VMH has been implicated in its performance. Moyer has also provided evidence that the amygdala affects different types of aggression in more than one way. He noted, for example, that stimulation of the basal nucleus of the amygdala facilitates fear-induced aggression but inhibits predatory attack and irritable aggression, while destruction of the entire amygdala reduces all three types of aggressive behavior.

Allergic Aggression An interesting idea suggested by Moyer is that aggression in humans may sometimes by triggered by allergies. Many people have allergies, usually evidenced by such typical symptoms as nasal congestion, fatigue, and so on. But evidence is accumulating that specific allergic reactions may sometimes lead to violent behavior (Moyer, 1975), which can vary from mild irritability to temper tantrums and wild fury. Moyer reported a case, for example, in which a boy was allergic to most sugars. The boy, who could eat only maple sugar, would react aggressively if he ate any other type. Within 20 minutes of eating a banana, for example, his violent tantrums would become almost uncontrollable.

Moyer proposed that allergic aggression results from a temporary swelling of the brain areas that normally control aggressive behavior. The allergic reaction may trigger aggressive circuits within the brain or disturb other circuits that normally hold aggression in check. In either case the result is violent behavior.

Though allergic aggression is uncommon, it has been relatively well documented. Various offending allergens may trigger an aggressive episode. The most common of these include pollen, various drugs, and many foods—among them, milk, chocolate, cola, corn, and eggs. The only way to identify the allergen is to remove various substances from the personal diet or environment and watch for an improvement in behavior. If the removed substance is the culprit, reinstating it will reintroduce the aggressive behavior. If Moyer's analysis is correct, some aggression might be controllable by simple changes such as altering a person's diet or getting rid of the cat.

Much remains to be worked out before we fully understand the neural systems that regulate aggressive behavior. The limbic system seems to be involved in emotionality, but how it regulates the expression of particular emotions is still largely a mystery. Of the emotions studied, anger or rage (as evidenced by aggression) has received the most attention in regard to physiological mechanisms of control. Models such as Moyer's are important because they point out that aggression is probably not a single behavior but several that are elicited by different conditions. These different types of aggression also probably depend upon different neural systems.

SUMMARY

In this chapter we have analyzed theory and research concerning the physiological regulation of four motivated states. These approaches emphasize homeostasis, the view that motivation is triggered when bodily conditions move too far away from some optimal level.

Considerable evidence exists for homeostatic regulation of hunger, thirst, and sexual motivation; however, these homeostatic mechanisms can be easily overridden by other factors. These overriding factors are most easily observed in the eating behavior of humans, who may become anorexic, bulimic, or obese. In each of these cases homeostasis is violated. Similarly, drinking behavior, though homeostatically regulated under some circumstances, more often occurs before such regulation is disrupted. The reasons for this "preventive drinking" remain obscure but probably result, at least in part, from an interaction between eating and drinking. Sexual behavior in animals other than humans may be the most highly regulated of the three motives discussed, because such behavior usually occurs only under appropriate hormonal conditions. Though hormonal conditions play a part in human sexual behavior, human sexuality is more often controlled by learned social and cultural factors that we are presently only beginning to understand. The effect of sex hormones on human behavior, in fact, appears to be most potent during prenatal development. Prenatal testosterone has organizational effects on the developing brain that may be responsible for creativity and giftedness on the one hand and dyslexia and immune system disorders on the other. Fetal hormone contributions to adult behaviors represent a most exciting area of current research; these same hormones probably influence motivation in as yet unspecified ways.

Limbic system structures are involved with the regulation of emotional behavior. Damage to various parts of the limbic system leads to changes in emotionality. Because anger and rage are the easiest identified emotions in animals, most physiological research on emotion has focused on the regulatory mechanisms involved in aggressive attack.

Early work showed that the cortex is not necessary for rage behavior, and subsequent research showed that the LH and VMH are important. The motor patterns of attack are apparently integrated by midbrain mechanisms that are normally held in check by the hypothalamus. The hypothalamus, in turn, is probably controlled by the amygdala. Several types of aggressive behavior have been identified, but only a few (e.g., predatory and irritable aggression) have been associated with particular brain structures.

It is worth emphasizing that the same structures (e.g., the LH and VMH) have been implicated in several different motive states, including hunger, thirst, sex, and aggression. Many fiber tracts course through the hypothalamus, and damage to the various areas, causing changes in motivated behavior, may consist of interruption of these fiber systems. In addition, changes in behavior may result from damage to a general arousal system that is independent of the particular motive being tested. Early proposals that suggested the presence of "centers" within the hypothalamus for various motive states have not generally been supported by research. Clearly much work remains before we can say with any confidence how the brain regulates motivated behavior.

SUGGESTIONS FOR FURTHER READING

Crandall, C. S. (1988). Social contagion of binge eating. *Journal of Personality and Social Psychology, 55,* 588–598. This article provides an excellent introduction to theories of binge-eating as well as relevant research on the social aspects of binge-eating.

Herzog, D. B., & Copeland, P. M. (1985). Eating disorders. *New England Journal of Medicine, 313,* 295–303. This article provides a good overview of current views of anorexia and bulimia.

Kolata, G. (1985). Why do people get fat? *Science, 227,* 1327–1328. This short summary article provides insight into why obesity is so hard to overcome.

III

DRIVES, INCENTIVES, AND LEARNING

Chapter Five

Drive Theory

CHAPTER PREVIEW

This chapter is concerned with the following questions:

1. What is drive and how did it become a dominant theory in motivation?

2. What are the principal constructs of the drive theory of Clark Hull?

3. Can drive theory "explain" the activation and direction of behavior?

It had been a hard year. The raccoon awoke from a fitful sleep and yawned. The rumbling in his stomach reminded him of last night's meager offerings—a few crickets, some small plants that grew along the edge of the lake, and little else. He yearned for a nice plump fish, but the long hot spell had baked the earth, and the lake had receded, leaving long mud flats. The fish had receded with the water, preferring to stay at the bottom of the deep lake during the relentless August heat.

The raccoon had in fact been hungry for a long time. The previous winter had been bitterly cold with deep snows that had covered most of the edible plants. Spring's promise had been shattered as the dry, hot summer had

quickly followed the winter's snows. Each night he foraged for what little food was available in the general vicinity of the lake, but competition for the limited resources was fierce, and few inhabitants of the lake watershed were getting enough to eat.

At sunset he started off. The grumbling of his stomach prompted the raccoon to search further to the east than he usually ventured. Soon he discovered something new to his experience—railroad tracks. The tracks ran north-south, and because traveling along them was easier than through the heavy underbrush, he began following the tracks to the north.

Soon he came to another new set of perceptions, strange smells and light that came from neither sun nor moon. His aching gut demanded that he explore the possibility of food in these new surroundings, so he left the tracks and approached the dimly lit houses cautiously.

Off to his left the smell of food wafted toward him on a gentle breeze. He crept closer. Light from an unshuttered window revealed a circular metallic object from which the smell seemed to be rising. He sprang to the top of the garbage can, where his nose was

129

immediately assailed by a mixture of strong odors. He scratched at the top, but the galvanized steel was too strong for his claws. Standing on the lid, he worked his way around the edge of the top until he found a small crack between the lid and the container. The weight of his body on the far side plus an upward thrust with his forepaws levered off the lid and deposited him into a pile of wood next to the can. In attempting to break his fall, he had lashed out with his hind feet and knocked the can over, spilling its contents onto the driveway. Scrambling to his feet, he greedily began to rummage through the contents.

The raccoon dined well that night and the night following and the night after that. He became adept at popping off garbage can lids and knocking over the cans. Each night he trekked from his old hollow oak tree overlooking the lake to the railroad tracks and from there to the house.

Life was good now and he became sleek and fat; his coat shined. He no longer searched randomly for food but marched purposefully to the group of houses north of the lake. He discovered other houses and other garbage cans. He became finicky, choosing only the best remains and leaving the rest. Yes, life was good. Maybe next year he would move from the old oak to something a little closer to his work.

This only partially fictional account of a raccoon points out some of the important concepts in this chapter. The concept of drive has assumed that the motivation of behavior depends upon some physiological need such as hunger. When a need state exists, the organism becomes motivated to reduce the need in whatever way it can. An organism becomes aware of a specific need state by specific stimuli (e.g., hunger pangs), which direct the organism to search for appropriate objects to reduce the need. If no response is immediately available for resolving the situation, the motivation is channeled into a general increase in

activity, which serves to bring the organism into contact with more and more objects that might satisfy the need. The raccoon's travel north along the railroad tracks resulted from this increase in general activity, which eventually led him to my yard. By the way, he still stops by when I forget to close the garage door and ransacks my garbage, even though the lake level is high again.

Responses leading to reduction of the need state or stimuli that accompany that state are learned and repeated whenever necessary. Learning, then, is seen as dependent upon the reduction of motivation (i.e., the reduction of drive).

In the rest of the chapter we will examine the evidence for drive as the motivator of behavior. We will first look at why the drive concept became a popular explanation for motivated behavior, then proceed to a review of Clark Hull's drive theory, which dominated all others. We will note the major assumptions of this theory and how well it fared. One alternative to the drive reduction explanation of behavior will be introduced through the work of Sheffield on drive induction.

EARLY FORMULATIONS OF DRIVE

Although the term **drive** was first coined by Woodworth in 1918, the idea that forces *within* the individual activate behavior was suggested earlier by Freud (1915). Freud in fact used the German word *trieb*, which means *moving force*. When Freud's work was translated into English, *trieb* was translated as *instinct* (Cofer & Appley, 1964). This choice probably occurred because the term *drive* did not yet exist and because motivational theories in the early 1900s were typically couched in terms of instincts. (See Chapter Two for information on these early instinct theories.) It seems clear that had the term *drive* existed at the time the translation was made, it would have more accurately reflected Freud's concept of moving force. Freud, then, was in many respects the first drive theorist, which is why his ideas are included here.

Freud's Moving Force

Sigmund Freud was one of the first theorists to use the concept of energy in his explanation of motivation. Freud's description of motivation used the concept of **psychic energy**, which unfortunately he never clearly defined. Sometimes he likened it to stimulation or excitation of the nervous system; at other times he likened it to a hydraulic system of storage and flow of energy (Cofer & Appley, 1964).

Nevertheless, Freud believed that psychic energy accumulates in the personality structure called the **id**. These forces operate on the individual with a constant pressure that, unlike external pressures, cannot be escaped (Freud, 1957). Psychic energy builds up when some **need** exists. By using the concept of need, Freud was apparently connecting moving force to changes in bodily functions. We satisfy a need by channeling psychic energy into behaviors (such as eating an orange when hungry) that reduce the need. Thus, when the body needs food, psychic energy will build up for "food getting." We will use this energy to generate behavior intended to obtain food, and the need will no longer exist.

Generally, increases in energy, whether external or internal, were seen as aversive (i.e., painful and to be avoided). In his **principle of constancy** Freud argued that the nervous system functions to eliminate or reduce stimuli that impinge on it. Reduction of stimulation was seen as pleasurable, while increases in stimulation were unpleasurable. Being hungry increases psychic energy and is unpleasurable; eating well is pleasurable because it reduces the psychic energy.

Freud believed that moving force possesses four characteristics: **pressure, aim,**
object, and source. *Pressure* (also called **impetus**) is the strength of the force; the stronger the force, the more motivated the behavior. The *aim* of moving force is satisfaction, which is obtained by removing or reducing stimulation. If reduction of the stimulation is incomplete, the force will be only partially satisfied. The *object* of moving force, which may be either internal or external to the individual, is the means through which the force is satisfied. The object may change in the course of an individual's life. Freud believed that we find ways of satisfying moving force as we learn new things; objects that satisfy can also become limited, however, through the process of **fixation** (i.e., the close attachment of an object to its moving force). The bodily processes that activate moving force are its *source*. Thus the source is equivalent to the earlier mentioned need.

Let's take an example and work through it using Freud's concept of moving force. Suppose we are thirsty. A need state exists because we need water, and this need is the source of stimulation of the "drinking force." If we have had nothing to drink for 36 hours, the **pressure** to drink will be greater than if we had drunk water an hour ago. Now the **aim** of the force is to satisfy the need that exists, so the drinking of water (i.e., the **object**) will be pleasurable and will reduce both the need and the energy causing us to drink. However, most of us discover as we grow older that other fluids will satisfy our needs, so the object of the force may change from only water to other beverages such as coffee, tea, soft drinks, or beer. Now as often happens in adults, we may satisfy our need for water by using a very restricted object, say, coffee. In Freud's terms, then, we could say that heavy coffee drinking results from a fixation of an object through which the drinking force is satisfied. The diagram in Figure 5.1 may help clarify Freud's concepts concerning moving force.

Freud proposed two major classes of mov-

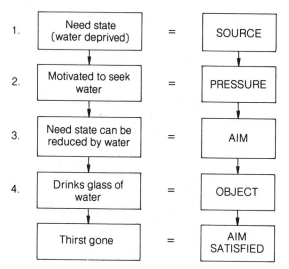

1.	Need state (water deprived)	=	SOURCE
2.	Motivated to seek water	=	PRESSURE
3.	Need state can be reduced by water	=	AIM
4.	Drinks glass of water	=	OBJECT
	Thirst gone	=	AIM SATISFIED

Figure 5.1   Freud's four characteristics of moving force and how they relate to behavior.

ing force: the **life force** and the **death force**. He called the psychic energy that powers the life force **eros**. Life force consists of the reproductive or sexual force and the life maintenance force. Freud called the energy that powers the reproductive force **libido**. Before puberty the reproductive force exists as separate forces associated with the various erogenous zones of the body, but at puberty, these separate forces fuse into one, whose primary function is to maintain the species. Freud believed that trauma during development or inappropriate rearing could lead to the **displacement** of sexual energy onto inappropriate objects. He considered displacement as a channeling of energy into behaviors not typically associated with a particular moving force. For example, one's sexual energies might get displaced into viewing photographs of nudes if opposite-sexed partners are unavailable. The life maintenance force controls the behaviors involved with preserving the individual, such as hunger and thirst. While noting their existence, Freud did not describe them in any detail.

Freud believed that motivated behavior acts to bring stimulation to some optimal level. For Freud, this optimal level was as low as possible; in fact he believed the lowest level (i.e., death) to be the optimal level. The death force and its associated energy, **thanatos**, then, directly oppose the life force. Generally, however, the death force is not directly observable in behavior (although suicide is sometimes analyzed as a direct expression of the death force) except in the case of aggression, which Freud believed to be the result of displacing the death force outward onto others. As such, aggression represents a compromise satisfactory to both the life and death forces; the energy of the death force is reduced by the aggressive behavior, but the individual's life is also maintained.

The moving forces can undergo various alterations or modifications during a person's lifetime. The force itself would not change, but its behavioral manifestations might. For example, a force can become reversed into its opposite. In **reversal** the active (or passive) aspect of the force's aim is altered. Freud discussed masochism as an example of reversal. According to Freud, the active aim of torture is reversed into the passive aim of being tortured, although both lead to a reduction of energy and thus to satisfaction. A second alteration discussed by Freud is the **turning round** of force. The change here occurs in the force's object. Reversal and turning round often go together. In masochism, for instance, the masochistic individual turns the object of the assault away from others and onto the self (i.e., turning round), as well as reversing the aim from active to passive. Freud also noted, however, that reversal and turning round are never complete and that some active outward manifestations of the force can still be observed (as would occur in the masochist who is sadistic in some situations).

Other modifications of moving force include **repression** and sublimation, but only repression will be discussed here because of its central importance to the Freudian model of behavior. In repression the individual resists the force to the point that it becomes unrecognized. Freud argued that we will repress a moving force if activity related to it would cause us more pain than pleasure. However, repression does not eliminate the energy behind the moving force; in fact Freud regarded neurotic behavior as a distorted attempt to rid oneself of accumulated energy.

The concept of repression raises an important point in the Freudian model of motivated behavior: a great deal of motivation is **unconscious**. Because of the mechanisms of repression and displacement, we cannot necessarily assume that a certain behavior represents the motive it appears to represent. This can be seen in the example of masochism—Freud believed that the motive is actively to aggress. Whether or not one accepts Freudian theory, it is important to realize that in the complexity of human experience, behaviors do not always correspond in a one-to-one fashion with their underlying motives.

Criticisms of the Freudian Model

Freudian motivational theory has been criticized on several grounds (see, e.g., Bolles, 1975). First, the theory is empirically weak; it needs verification from research outside the clinical setting. Second, it is unclear how Freud's theoretical terms relate to one another and to observable events. As Bolles has noted, the theory makes possible a number of different interpretations for the same phenomenon, and opposing interpretations are also possible. Finally, and perhaps most damaging, the theory cannot predict behavior. Although the theory can "explain" any behavior "after the fact," it does not reliably predict how certain experiences will influence future behavior. For example, the repression of sexual energy

may lead to any number of different behaviors, ranging from displacement into fantasies or fetishes (e.g., boots as sexual objects) to displacement into scientific or creative endeavors. Unfortunately, there is no way to predict how the accumulated energy will be released. Even though Freud's psychoanalytic theory was the first drive theory, it remained for American psychology to develop the drive concept more fully. Let's examine, then, the drive concept as it was developed in the early part of the twentieth century.

DRIVE

Drive, as a motivational construct, was usually associated with maintenance of the homeostatic balance of the organism. **Homeostasis** is a process in which bodily mechanisms attempt to keep the body at some optimal level. Thus, if one had nothing to drink for several hours, a thirst drive, whose purpose was to return the fluid balance to its proper state, was said to become activated. Much of the work discussed in Chapter Four was based on the assumption (sometimes implicit) that a drive state was triggered by homeostatic mechanisms within the body. Drive was seen as intimately tied to the needs of the organism. If a condition of organic deficiency or excess existed, a drive to bring the body back into proper balance was thought to be activated (Woodworth, 1958; Woodworth & Schlosberg, 1954).

Perhaps you are wondering why theorists felt it necessary to assume a drive state independent of the needs that generated it. It would seem much simpler to assume that when a need state exists, behavior is activated directly by that need, without postulating an intervening process such as drive. The usual answer given was that some needs exist that do not result in behavior. For example, reducing the amount of oxygen in the air we breathe leads to no discomfort (in fact it often leads to feelings of euphoria), even though the need is desperate. It is also true that drives leading to the activation of behavior exist when no needs can be demonstrated. The sexual drive is among the strongest, yet applying the idea of need to it does not work very well because the individual's survival does not depend on it. Thus a drive concept appeared necessary because some real needs exist that do not activate behavior and because behavior is sometimes activated when no life-preserving needs seem to exist. The concept of drive, then, was an inferred construct: drive is usually activated by a need but can, under some circumstances, be activated independent of need.

Different theorists have ascribed somewhat different characteristics to drive—but all drive theorists have assumed that one basic characteristic of drive is that it energizes behavior. The presence of a drive, then, is seen as causing the organism to begin making responses. A second, often assumed characteristic is that behaviors that reduce the need state also reduce the drive state.

With this background on some of the general characteristics of drive, we will now look at why the drive concept developed.

The Rise of the Drive Concept

Robert Bolles (1967, 1975) has noted several factors that led to acceptance of the drive concept. For example, the drive concept came along just when the early instinct approaches of James and McDougall had been quite thoroughly discredited. The demise of the instinct concept left a conceptual vacuum that drive neatly filled. Drive theory was not a large departure from the instinct concept because both were thought to be biologically based; both were regarded as motivators of behavior; and both explained the subjective aspects of motivated behavior. Thus, from a drive viewpoint, the feelings of "being hungry" could now be regarded as the result of a hunger drive rather than of a food-seeking instinct.

A clear advantage that the drive concept had over the instinct concept was that drive was believed to have a readily identifiable physiological basis. Though instincts were also supposed to have such a basis, little success had been achieved in locating neural systems involved in instinctive behavior.

As noted by Bolles, the drive concept was also presented at a time when the local motivation theories were being shown inadequate. Cannon (1929) believed that hunger results from peripheral (i.e., local) cues such as stomach movement, while thirst could be understood in terms of peripheral cues such as a dry mouth from a reduced flow of saliva. However, several researchers (e.g., Adolph, 1939; Wangensteen & Carlson, 1931) had shown that the stomach could be removed without any apparent loss in hunger sensations; and dogs that were allowed to sham-drink water (i.e., the water entered the mouth but never reached the stomach because the esophagus had been cut, allowing the water to drain out) kept their mouths wet, but their thirst was not reduced. The drive concept, in contrast to the peripheral theories, assumed that more central brain structures monitored the state of the body. Thus drive theory meshed nicely with the physiological research beginning to show the involvement of the hypothalamus in motivated behavior.

Other research on activity suggested that organisms become more active when motivated. Work from Curt Richter's laboratory (Richter, 1927; Wang, 1923) showed that increases in activity are correlated with the estrous cycle in female rats and that hungry animals are also more active. Because drives were conceived as energizing behavior, the research on activity fit nicely with the developing drive concept. Richter's work was regarded as strong support for drive theory, showing that increases in activity are in fact correlated with various motivated states. Richter's work also made sense from an evolutionary perspective. Organisms in a state of need would be more likely to have that need satisfied if they were more active because increased activity would increase their chances of finding something to reduce the need. At the time it seemed to many researchers that drive theory was the key to unlock the secrets of behavior.

At approximately the same time as the research on activity was being published, Warden (1931) and others were attempting to measure the strength of various drive conditions and thus make comparisons between various motivational states. Warden used what is known as the **Columbia obstruction box** to measure the strength of motives such as hunger, thirst, sex, exploration, and maternal behavior. The basic procedure involved putting the animal in the start compartment and observing how many times it crossed an electrified grid floor in order to reach the goal section, where a reward relevant to the motive

was placed. Thus, if the rat was hungry, food was placed on the other side of the shock grid; if thirsty, water, and so on. Warden's results are shown in Figure 5.2 for a number of different motives as a function of the length of time the animals had been deprived. These results reveal something about the course of motive change as deprivation becomes more severe. For example, hunger motivation (as measured by number of grid crossings) seems to peak at about three days, then begins to drop off. Motivation to obtain water peaks much earlier, approximately one day, then drops off rapidly. Both of these findings make sense; we can exist longer without food than without water, so water deprivation should lead to maximal motivation more quickly than food deprivation. The drop-off of motivation in both cases can be understood as resulting from a general weakening of the organism because of water or food lack. Again, because we can exist longer without food than without water, we

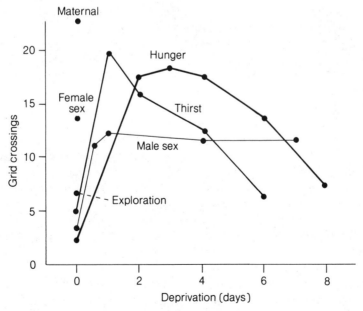

Figure 5.2 *Number of grid crossings for several different motive states in rats. (From Warden, 1931. Used by permission.)*

would expect this weakening (called **inanition**) to occur sooner in water-deprived conditions.

Warden, however, wanted to do more than just trace the course of drive for the various motives singly. He wanted to compare various motives in order to conclude, for example, that thirst at its peak is more motivating than hunger at its peak. This attempt to make comparisons across drives is where the obstruction box method ran into considerable difficulty (Bolles, 1967, 1975).

First, it was not clear how much of the drive strength, as measured by grid crossings, resulted from the deprivation conditions and how much resulted from the particular goal object chosen. For example, the choice of a particular type of food used to assess hunger motivation would influence the number of grid crossings. Yet different incentives were not studied, so one cannot assess the relative contribution of this factor in the grid-crossing data. We also do not know that the goal objects used in the different motive conditions were equal. Thus more grid crossings might have occurred because the water "tasted" better than the food rather than because different strengths of drive were induced by water and food deprivation. Therefore the number of times an animal crossed the electrified grid probably measured a drive state produced by the deprivation conditions plus the desirability (termed **incentive** or **incentive value**) of the object chosen to reduce the need.

Second, Warden's method did not rule out the effects of learning. Warden typically used a 20-minute test session, which was certainly long enough for his animals to learn something about the conditions of the experimental situation. Within any session, grid crossings occurred more frequently early in the session, suggesting that the animals might have learned to stop crossing the "hot" floor rather than continue to endure this painful stimulus to get something they needed. War-

den's results, then, probably included a learning component (which, in this case, probably reduced the apparent drive strength), the extent of which is unknown, so we cannot conclude how strong the various drives really were.

We have considered Warden's research in some detail because it points out a central problem in the study of motivation: How can we accurately measure the strength of various motives? One of the most difficult problems confronting motivation researchers is how to equate the deprivation, incentive, and learning conditions of motives so that the strengths of various motives can be compared. No totally satisfactory method has yet been devised. Regardless of the criticisms that can be made of Warden's work, it was very important at the time it was conducted because it seemed that he had succeeded in measuring various drives. Thus his research gave a big boost to the drive concept.

In order to understand the concept of drive more fully, we will now examine the drive theories of Woodworth and Hull.

Woodworth's Drive Theory

As mentioned earlier, Woodworth first coined the term *drive*. Woodworth (1918) was also one of the earliest theorists to make a clear distinction between the **mechanisms** of behavior and the **forces** (i.e., drives) that propel those mechanisms. The question of mechanism involves a concern with *how* we perform a set of responses; the question of force involves a concern with *why* we perform a particular behavior. This latter concern is the province of motivation, and *drive* was the term Woodworth chose to describe the forces. Woodworth argued that different drives underlie different behaviors. Thus a hunger drive motivates food getting, a thirst drive motivates drinking, and so on.

Woodworth (1958) believed that all

behavior (other than reflexes) is motivated. Without drive there is no power directed to the mechanism to make it perform behavior. Drive is necessary for behavior to occur. Drives are activated by needs that result from some organic state of deficiency or excess. One example of a drive resulting from an organic excess is the state that exists when the bladder is full and it's 20 miles to the nearest rest stop. Thus needs activate drives, and drives, in turn, activate behavior. As noted earlier, drives were a necessary construct for Woodworth because not all needs lead to behavior. Furthermore, not all behaviors are the result of bodily needs. Woodworth assumed, in fact, that incentives can also arouse drive (as often happens when the first few bites of food make us hungry). Drive, according to Woodworth, has three characteristics: **intensity, direction**, and **persistence**.

Intensity The intensity characteristic of drive refers to the fact that drive has activating properties. Activation of behavior by drive can vary from low levels, as in dreaming, to high levels associated with anger or fear. Woodworth believed that high levels of drive are in fact accompanied by emotion. We do not normally think of intense hunger or thirst as emotional, though they often do have an emotional component. For example, an individual who had received a kidney transplant could drink only small quantities of water and, as a result, was constantly thirsty. Drinking water was a very special event for this individual—in fact it was an extremely emotional one.

One characteristic of drive implied by the intensity dimension is that when drive exists, the organism either becomes sensitized so that it responds to previously unnoticed stimuli, or the presence of drive leads to a general activation of diffuse, random muscle activity. Though Woodworth (1958) kept both possibilities open, he favored the idea of sensitization as more likely.

Direction Woodworth also believed that drive has directionality. Drives were seen as leading to either approach or avoidance behavior. Drive sensitizes the organism to the particular stimuli important for the motive, as just noted, and determines selectivity; for example, when hungry, we approach food but not sexual stimuli. Remember that Woodworth preferred the idea of several different types of drive, one for each motive. This makes the idea of directionality more plausible, because only the hunger drive then motivates the organism to perform behaviors associated with food getting, only the sex drive activates sexual behaviors, and so on. Woodworth agreed with other theorists that the specific directions taken by behaviors are learned; the tendency to approach or avoid, however, was seen as characteristic of the drive state.

Persistence The third characteristic of drive for Woodworth is persistence. Drive acts not only to channel behavior along particular lines (i.e., to approach or avoid) but also to continue the behavior until the difference between the existing and preferred situations is reduced. Drive in this sense keeps the person "on task" until the conditions leading to the drive state are eliminated. It is in fact the persistence of behavior that causes us to theorize the existence of motives; the fact that behavior persists implies that something is keeping it active. That thing, according to Woodworth, is drive.

Hull's Drive Theory

Of all the conceptions of drive, none was more influential than that of Clark Hull. Hull's theory was detailed in three books (1943, 1951, 1952) that generated a tremendous amount of research over more than 20 years. Because of the importance of Hull's theory in the development of the drive concept, we will examine it in detail.

Hull's theory so dominated both learning and motivational thought that for many years, it was the central core of most research. Even as late as 1967, Hull's motivational theory was influential enough to require six chapters in Bolles's text *Theory of Motivation* (1967). Though today we recognize that Hull's theory cannot explain everything we know about motivated behavior, it is nevertheless important—both because it exemplifies one type of motivational theorizing and because it generated other, less comprehensive approaches that are still important today.

Hull's model for behavior was basically a survival model (Weiner, 1972). He was influenced by a number of early theorists, particularly Darwin. Hull's approach assumed that motivation develops to meet the organic needs of the organism because such a system gives the animal an advantage in the struggle to survive, ideas based firmly on the theory of evolution. Hull was also influenced by Cannon's research (discussed in Chapters Three and Four) and incorporated Cannon's concept of homeostasis into his own behavioral system. Thus organic needs were seen as giving rise to a drive that brings the body back into a state of balance by activating appropriate behaviors.

Hull also incorporated many of the ideas of Watson, Pavlov, and Thorndike into his system. For example, Hull's behavioral analysis, like that of Watson, was very mechanistic; he gave no importance to concepts such as expectancy, purpose, or cognition. Hull was also greatly influenced by Thorndike's (1913) **law of effect**, which was the forerunner of our modern concepts of reinforcement. Thorndike believed that learning involves the connection of stimuli and responses. The connection of a stimulus and response becomes stronger each time the pairing of these two is followed by a satisfying (i.e., reinforcing) state of affairs. Hull incorporated reinforcement into his behavioral system in two ways. First, in

agreement with Thorndike, **habits** (Hull's term for learning) become stronger as a function of how often the pairing of a stimulus and response is followed by reinforcement. Second and more important to a discussion of motivation, Hull believed that reinforcement occurs when drive is reduced. Hull's basic position, then, was that learning occurs because the motivational conditions of the organism change.

Hull also felt that psychological principles, like mathematical ones, should be derived from a basic system of postulates (i.e., assumptions). For this reason, much of his theorizing involved the development of formulas that mathematically described the various components of his system. We will not concern ourselves with these equations except in relation to the way that he thought the components of behavior interact.

Hull's behavioral system concerned three major problems (Cofer & Appley, 1964). His first question was, what constitutes drive and what are its characteristics? Secondly, Hull asked how drive influences behavior—what is the relationship between drive and learning in determining when behavior occurs? Finally, Hull was interested in discovering which nonmotivational factors (e.g., learning) influence behavior.

Reaction Potential, Habit Strength, and Drive   Hull developed a formula that expressed how the strength of a behavior is related to learning and motivation. The formula was:

$$_sE_r = {_sH_r} \times D$$

In words the formula says that the strength of behavior ($_sE_r$) depends upon (=) both the strength of the learned response ($_sH_r$) in the situation and the strength of drive (D). Notice that the relationship between $_sH_r$ and D is multiplicative. The multiplication of habit by drive is an important assumption because it indicates that if either drive or learning is zero, no behavior will occur. For example, suppose a rat is taught to press a bar in order to obtain food. If the rat has learned this response well, $_sH_r$ will be strong. If the rat is also hungry, drive will be high, and because D multiplies $_sH_r$, the probability of the rat's performance of the response will be high. Now suppose that we prefeed the rat so that it is not hungry. Even though the bar-press habit will be strong, D will be close to zero (assuming that other sources of drive are also low), and the probability of the bar-press response will be low. Conversely, if the rat has not learned to press the bar, $_sH_r$ will be close to zero, and the probability of the bar-press response will be low, even though the rat may be very hungry and thus have a high drive level.

Hull's formula indicates that behavior is a function of three variables: the strength of the response that we expect the organism to make, the strength of the drive of the organism, and the multiplicative relationship between the two.

Because Hull believed that learning involves the connection of stimuli and responses as the result of reinforcement—and because each reinforced pairing of a stimulus and response was believed to increase habit strength by a small amount—it is important to understand what constitutes reinforcement. Hull believed that reinforcement occurs when drive is reduced. Thus an object (e.g., food) is reinforcing because it reduces the motivational level of the organism. In a sense, then, learning depends upon adequate motivation. If there is no drive, a response will not occur and thus cannot be reinforced. Hull's emphasis on reinforcement resulting from a lowering of drive is known as a **drive reduction model** of learning. Hull saw drive as possessing particular characteristics that were somewhat differ-

ent from those proposed by Woodworth. One major source of difference between the two theorists was Hull's concept of **generalized drive**.

Generalized Drive Drive was conceived to be a **general pool** of energy that can activate either instinctive or learned behaviors. Unlike Woodworth, who suggested different drives for each motive state, Hull believed that only one generalized drive state exists, to which several different motivating conditions can contribute. Thus an animal that is both hungry and thirsty should have a higher drive level than one that is only hungry or only thirsty. Drive was considered to be the sum of all need sources of the organism acting at a given point in time. Thus, while the sources of drive are plural (e.g., hunger, thirst, sex, and so on), drive itself is singular and nonspecific.

The concept of a nonspecific drive means that drive must also be nondirective. For Hull drive was conceived as activating behavior but not directing it toward any particular goal. Thus its major characteristic is that it energizes behavior.

But if drive is simply the power that runs the processes involved in behavior, the question that should now occur to you is, what determines the response, out of the many possible ones, that actually does occur? The answer, according to Hull, is that the need states that trigger drive also activate receptor mechanisms that give rise to characteristic stimuli. Thus, when we are hungry, drive is triggered and **drive stimuli** (symbolized as S_d) are felt. Such drive stimuli might consist of stomach contractions or that "empty" feeling we sometimes experience.

These drive stimuli were thought to be identical to any other stimuli. They connect to responses that are followed by reinforcement. Thus, if we follow that empty feeling with opening the refrigerator door and getting an apple, the reduction in drive will lead to strengthening the "refrigerator door-opening" response. The next time we experience the S_d associated with hunger, we will be more likely to open the refrigerator door again.

Drive stimuli, then, provide the directionality to behavior. According to Hull, organisms can discriminate the various S_d's for hunger, thirst, sex, and so on and will respond to them by behaving in ways that have been reinforced in the past. Generalized drive, then, acts as the force underlying behavior, and drive stimuli serve as the steering mechanism.

Drive, therefore, is important for the development of behavior in three ways (Hilgard & Bower, 1975). First, without drive, no drive reduction can occur; because reinforcement (and therefore learning) depends upon the reduction of drive, no learning can occur without drive. Second, drive is an energizer of behavior; without drive no behavior will occur. Third, the drive stimuli that provide the directionality to behavior depend upon the existence of the drive state. Without drive, no S_d's exist that can become connected to

responses leading to adaptive behavior. The functions of drive and the relationships between needs, drive, drive stimuli, and learning are shown in Figure 5.3.

How did Hull come to the conclusion that reaction potential is the result of a multiplicative relationship between learning and drive? Hull based his behavioral formula on the experiments of two of his students, Williams (1938) and Perin (1942).

Both Williams and Perin taught groups of rats to press a bar in order to get a food reinforcement. The drive level during training for both rat groups was an identical 23 hours of food deprivation. Several groups were used in each experiment, each receiving different amounts of training (Perin, for example, trained rats with 5, 8, 16, 30, or 70 reinforced trials). After the groups had been trained on the bar-press response, they were extinguished. Extinction is an experimental procedure whereby the organism is allowed to make the previously reinforced response, but reinforcement no longer follows the response. The extinction procedure is commonly used in psychology to measure the strength of a

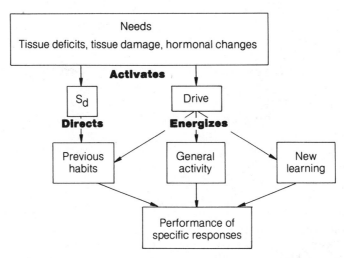

Figure 5.3 *Diagram of the relationship between needs, drive, drive stimuli, and learning in the performance of behavior.*

learned response; the longer the animal continues to respond, the stronger the response.

It was in the extinction conditions that Williams's and Perin's experiments differed. Williams extinguished his rats under a hunger motivation of 22 hours, while Perin extinguished his under a hunger motivation of only 3 hours. These experiments, then, concerned the effects of both the amount of initial training ($_sH_r$) and the drive level during extinction (D) on the strength of bar pressing ($_sE_r$). Figure 5.4 shows the results of these two experiments.

Several things are worth examining in these results. First, note that as the number of training trials increased, so did the number of bar presses in extinction. This was true regardless of whether the animals were extinguished under 3 hours or 22 hours of hunger. This result also fits with Hull's idea that habit strength increases with the number of reinforced responses. Second, note that the number of responses given by Williams's rats was much greater than the number given by Perin's rats. Because the training procedures were the same, this difference must be due to the drive levels produced by 3 and 22 hours of hunger. This result also fits with Hull's assumption that drive activates learned responses; the stronger the drive, the stronger the behavior when learning is held constant. Compare, for example, the number of responses given by animals trained for 30 trials in both Williams's and Perin's experiments. Williams's 22-hour hungry rats gave many more responses. Finally, the strong similarity in the shapes of the two curves fitted to Williams's and Perin's data should be noted; the curve shapes are practically identical. To generate Williams's curve from Perin's, one need only multiply the formula for Perin's curve by the appropriate number. This last result led

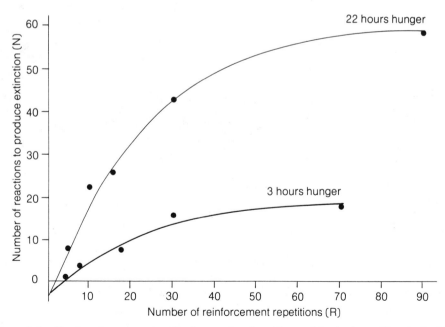

Figure 5.4 *Number of responses in extinction as a function of hours of deprivation and length of training. Williams's data are represented by the 22-hour curve and Perin's by the 3-hour curve. (Adapted from Perin, 1942.)*

Hull to the conclusion that reaction potential is determined by the multiplication of habit strength by drive.

If you find this conclusion somewhat unclear, consider the following: Perin's rats were extinguished under 3 hours of food deprivation. The curve for the number of responses given in extinction changed as training trials increased. Williams's rats were trained just like Perin's but were 22 hours hungry. Thus we could take Perin's curve, multiply it by the appropriate number indicating a drive level of 22 hours, and arrive at the curve shown for Williams's data.

Perin conducted a second experiment using four groups of rats, all given 16 training trials while in a drive state of 23 hours of food deprivation. In extinction the drive level was manipulated so that one group was extinguished after 1 hour of deprivation, while other groups were extinguished after 3, 16, or 23 hours of deprivation. The results of this experiment are shown in Figure 5.5. As can be

seen, the strength of the behavior, as measured by responses in extinction, rose as the deprivation level increased. Therefore, with learning held constant at 16 trials, behavior increased with increased drive level. Note also that the curve was not zero when number of hours of hunger was zero (i.e., satiation). Hull interpreted this occurrence of behavior in the absence of the hunger drive to mean that other irrelevant drives were activating the tested habit. Thus he saw this as evidence for his belief that drive is a general pool of energy accumulated from many sources and capable of activating whatever habit is dominant in the situation.

The Perin and Williams studies provided almost the sole basis for Hull's theorizing about the relationship of learning and drive to behavior performance. These studies indicated that habit strength and drive are independent of each other but combine in a multiplicative fashion to determine the performance of behavior.

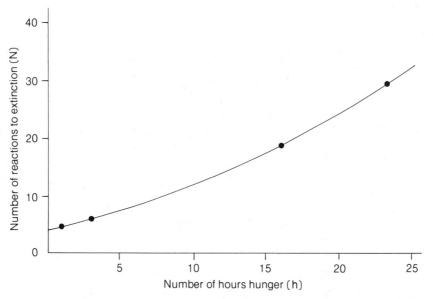

Figure 5.5   *Number of responses in extinction for varying hours of hunger. Training was held constant at 16 trials for all deprivation conditions. (Adapted from Perin, 1942.)*

Incentive In 1951 and 1952 Hull included yet another motivational construct. Originally he had thought that factors such as the quantity or quality of reinforcement influence the buildup of habit strength. However, several experiments (see Chapter Seven for details) had shown that the influence of reinforcement quantity and quality is on performance rather than learning. Thus we may perform more strongly for a large rather than a small reward, but we apparently do not learn any faster with large rewards.

These experiments led Hull to the conclusion that the characteristics of the goal object influence the organism's motivation. To account for this, Hull included the construct of **incentive motivation**, symbolized as **K**. (Much work on the influence of incentives was conducted by Kenneth Spence, a former student of Hull, and psychological lore insists that the symbol K stands for Kenneth as a recognition of Spence's contribution to the theory.)

Hull assumed that the incentive value of a goal alters behavior in the same manner as drive; that is, the strength of a response was now regarded as the result of the multiplication of habit, drive, and incentive. Thus the formula becomes:

$$_sE_r = {}_sH_r \times D \times K$$

Hull's early theory (1943) was based primarily on the idea of motivation as an internal energizer of behavior. By 1952 he realized that this was inadequate. Characteristics of the goal also influence the performance of behavior, and incentive motivation was his attempt to deal with this fact.

If you are having difficulty conceptualizing just what K is, perhaps the following example will help. Suppose that you are hungry, so that drive is at some nonzero level. Suppose further that for the same price you can have a hamburger that tastes like the cardboard plate it is served on at the local fast-food shops, or

you can walk ten minutes off campus and get a delicious steak and cheese sub (if you don't like this choice of foods, fill in your own favorites). All other things being equal, you would probably take the ten-minute walk for the sub, but you wouldn't walk that far for the tasteless hamburger. Thus the incentive values of the two goals (i.e., hamburger and sub) are different and will activate behavior in different amounts. In a very loose sort of way, you can think of incentive motivation as describing the desirability of various goals toward which your behavior might be directed.

Though drives are supposedly tied to needs, incentives are learned. Originally you had no preference for steak and cheese subs over hamburgers, but through experience your preference developed for subs. Basically Hull believed that incentives are learned via the process of classical conditioning. Stimuli associated with the reduction in drive will, on their next occurrence, stimulate some fraction of the final goal response (e.g., chewing). Because Hull's analysis of incentive development is somewhat complex, a fuller explanation is given in Chapter Seven, which deals exclusively with incentive motivation.

By the early 1950s Hull had also made some other changes to his theory. He realized that an explanation of reinforcement in terms of need reduction was inadequate. Motivated behavior sometimes occurs even though no needs are reduced or before reinforcement has had time to physically change the organism. For these reasons Hull modified his stand on reinforcement by suggesting that it occurs when drive stimuli are reduced. For example, eating food was now seen as reinforcing because it reduced the drive stimuli (e.g., stomach contractions) associated with the hunger drive state, not because it reduced drive. The formula noted above was not the final statement of Hull's model for behavior. Hull incorporated two additional constructs, **stimulus intensity dynamism (V)** and **inhibition** (of which there were two types, **reactive** and **conditioned**). Hull never developed the concept of stimulus intensity dynamism to any great degree, so it has not assumed much importance in his model. The two types of inhibition, although important concepts, were developed primarily to account for the extinction of learned behaviors and need not be examined here (see Petri, 1981, for a fuller discussion of these components of Hull's theory).

Some Thoughts About Hull's Drive Theory
Though Hull liked to express his ideas mathematically, an understanding of his approach does not require mathematics. Put simply, Hull said that behavior results from what has been learned, from the currently active drive level, and from the characteristics of the goal.

Now that you have a basic idea of drive approaches to motivation and considerable details about the most prominent approach, let's see how the drive concept has fared with respect to research conducted to test its various concepts.

Problems with Drive Theory

As the title of this section implies, drive theory has not turned out to be the final answer in our search to understand motivated behavior. Bolles (1967, 1975) has provided an excellent and exhaustive review of research concerned with the adequacy of Hull's drive theory. Instead of detailing a summary of his drive theory's shortcomings, we will discuss only a few general areas in which his theory has proven unable to handle the data (consult Bolles for a detailed analysis).

Need and Drive Reduction   One basic tenet of Hull's drive theory was that a reduction in needs is necessary for reinforcement to occur. Later Hull altered this idea and maintained that reinforcement occurs when drive stimuli are reduced. Nevertheless, his theory still assumed an intimate relationship between the existence of need states and drive states. This anchoring of the drive construct to the bodily conditions of need was one reason why drive theory became popular when the early instinct approaches were shown to be inadequate. Therefore research that demonstrated the occurrence of reinforced learning without any reduction in need was a strong argument against drive theories such as Hull's, which assumed need or drive reduction.

Some of the more ingenious experiments were done by Fred Sheffield. In one experiment Sheffield, Wulff, and Backer (1951) showed that male rats will learn a response that leads to initiation of a consummatory response even though no needs are reduced. Their male rats learned to make a response in order to get the chance to mount (i.e., copulate with) receptive female rats. Before the rats' ardor could be consummated, however, the experimenters pulled the males away from the females. Because ejaculation was not permitted, no drive was reduced nor was any need state changed (one wonders whether any drive stimulus could be said to be reduced, either). A strict Hullian approach would have to say that this was not a reinforcing situation and therefore that the male rats should not have learned how to approach the receptive females. But apparently Sheffields's rats were unaware of Hull's theory because they learned how to approach the females quite readily.

In another experiment Sheffield and Roby (1950) showed that hungry rats will learn to make a response in order to get a sweet-tasting solution of saccharine water. Because saccharine has no caloric value, no drive can be said to be reduced. Additionally, Sheffield, Roby, and Campbell (1954) showed that solutions of saccharine and dextrose (a type of sugar) that elicit equal drinking rates are equivalent as rewards for behavior.

Sheffield's work indicated that neither drives nor needs must be reduced in order for reinforcement to initiate learning. Instead he proposed what is called a drive induction theory of motivation.

Drive Induction Sheffield (1966a, 1966b) proposed that animals will learn to make responses that lead to an increase in motivation rather than to a reduction of it. Rewards were viewed as objects that increase the excitement of the organism. Thus the stimulus properties of a goal object can be drive inducing. Sheffield noted that dangling a carrot in front of a hungry rabbit does not relax the rabbit; the carrot excites it.

A consummatory response (e.g., chewing and swallowing food, lapping water, or mounting behavior) was believed important in the induction of drive. If the goal stimuli associated with the consummatory response do not lead directly to a consummatory response, excitement is generated. This excitement from cues associated with the consummatory response is what Sheffield meant by the term **drive induction**. For example, he noted that placing a rat pup under a wire cage so that the mother can see, smell, and hear it but not retrieve it (i.e., the consummatory response) leads to quite agitated behavior from the mother rat.

In a more experimentally controlled situation, Sheffield and Campbell (1954) were able to show the energizing effects of cues associated with the consummatory response of feeding. Rats were placed in individual activity cages (that measured the amount of movement) inside a soundproofed cabinet and soundproofed room. These rats were fed only once daily when their food automatically dropped into the cage. For the experimental group of animals, a change occurred in their environment starting five minutes before delivery of the food, while for the control group, the environmental change was unrelated to the food arrival. The environmental change involved both auditory and visual cues consisting of the turning off of the exhaust fan and a shift from dark to light (or, for some animals, light to dark). Figure 5.6 presents the results of this manipulation. As can be seen, the experimental animals that had environmental cues correlated with the arrival of food became much more active, while the control animals gradually adapted to the changing environmental condition unrelated to the arrival of food. This experiment seems to present clear evidence that cues associated with the arrival of food, and thus the consummatory response, can activate or induce motivation.

Sheffield's experiments on activity changes as a result of environmental cues have sometimes been called the "caretaker" experiments. Anyone who has cared for rats kept on a deprivation schedule is familiar with the phenomenon, and perhaps you have observed the phenomenon yourself. As you prepare your pet's dinner (e.g., cleaning the bowl, opening a can), the pet becomes more and more agitated. The increase in the activity of your pet is clearly related to the cues you provide that dinner will arrive momentarily.

The important points for our purposes are that reinforcers can lead to learning without reduction of any drive and that cues associated with reinforcement may also have the effect of increasing motivation when they are presented before the consummatory response can occur. Thus drive reduction theories of motivation such as Hull's cannot account for situations in which behaviors occur even though no drives are reduced. They also cannot account for situations in which drive is induced by factors other than need.

It is worth pointing out that in the "real world" outside the laboratory, both effects generally occur. The sight and smell of food lead to the activation of behaviors to obtain

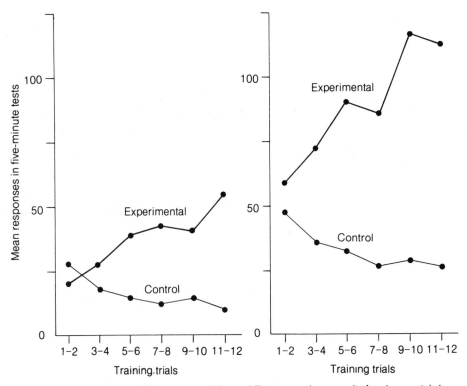

Figure 5.6 *Mean increase in activity (measured in a stabilimeter cage) as a result of environmental change. The environmental change in the left panel was the turning off of an exhaust fan and a shift from dark to light. In the right panel, the change was turning off of the exhaust fan and a shift from light to dark. For experimental animals, the environmental change preceded the arrival of food by five minutes, while for the control group, the environmental change was uncorrelated with the arrival of food. (From Sheffield and Campbell, 1954.)*

the food, and its consumption does eventually reduce need.

Drive as a General Activator   A second major component of Hull's drive theory was the assumption that drive is a general activator of behavior and that drive stimuli provide the steering mechanism for directing that activation. Because drive is a general pool of energy, other drives not relevant to the task at hand (e.g., sexual motivation in a hungry rat) should add to the general motivational level D. Numerous experiments have been conducted to ascertain whether irrelevant drives "add to" the overall level of drive and whether one

drive can substitute for another (e.g., training a response under thirst motivation and then testing it under hunger motivation). The results of these studies provide no clear, general indication that different sources of drive summate or that one drive can be substituted for another (Bolles, 1975).

What then of the most hallowed assumption in drive theory, that drives energize behavior? As mentioned earlier, this assumption was based on work by Richter and others and seemed to show that activity increased as deprivation time increased. Sheffield and Campbell's data, mentioned a moment ago, suggest another interpretation. Recall that these researchers also measured activity and found that it increased in hungry rats if environmental cues preceded the arrival of food. If you glance back at Figure 5.6, you will notice that a gradual increase in measured activity occurred over several days of testing. This finding suggests that the activity increase is a learned rather than an innate response to deprivation and that the activity increase results from external rather than the internal stimuli assumed by Hull's theory. Additionally, Campbell and Sheffield (1953) found that food deprivation lasting up to 72 hours caused only slight increases in activity, as measured by a stabilimeter cage, if external stimuli were held constant. Thus the work of Sheffield and Campbell suggests that a large portion of the activity observed in deprivation situations results from the association of external cues with food arrival rather than from some internal drive state. Several additional studies (see Baumeister, Hawkins, & Cromwell, 1964, for a review) have also found that activity levels change little if environmental conditions are held constant.

Most of the early research upon which Hull based his concept of behavior activation by drive was conducted on rats, which were tested in the running wheel. As studies accumulate, it becomes increasingly apparent that the results of testing activity increases depend upon both the type of measuring device used (e.g., running wheel, stabilimeter, squares crossed in an open field, and so on) and the species studied. Moreover, the correlations between the various measures of activity are low, which indicates that the measures are not easily comparable (Baumeister, Hawkins, & Cromwell, 1964). The lack of agreement across both methods and species suggests that activity changes are not the very general response to need states (and thus indicative of the presence of drive) that Hull supposed them to be. Whether activity increases or decreases as a result of deprivation conditions apparently depends upon the need state studied, the method of study, and the species stud-

ied. Because no clear relationship between needs and activity can be used as an index, the drive state must be severely hedged. Indeed it may be simpler to dispense with the concept of generalized drive altogether.

Sexual Motivation as Drive

One of the major tenets of drive theory has been that internal bodily changes are detected by appropriate monitoring systems which, in turn, activate drive. As we saw in Chapter Four there appear to be mechanisms in the area of the hypothalamus that do indeed monitor changes in sex hormone levels. Other areas close by also appear to be concerned with the expression of sexual behavior. Let us look for a moment, then, at the concept of a sex drive.

Freud, of course, viewed sex as having drive properties. Sexual tension was seen as building up in the id, creating an uncomfortable state that could be relieved by sexual behavior or by reduction of the sexual energy (**libido**) through displacement by the ego. Subjectively, something like a sex drive does seem to exist. Men and adolescent boys in particular often speak of being "horny," and there is associated with this feeling a sense of tension. Luria and associates (1987) quote a 21-year-old male who indicated that he got so horny he couldn't think of anything else; this state of tension interfered with his classwork, and the feeling was sometimes so strong that it was aversive. Both Freud and drive theorists would analyze this example as having the qualities associated with a drive state. Women also seem to have similar episodes but perhaps not so debilitatingly.

Other evidence suggests that the drive concept may make sense in regard to sexual behavior. For example, Beach and Jordan (1956) found that the longer the sexual deprivation in male rats, the shorter the latency for both mounting and intromission when given access to a female rat. Similarly, as noted in Chapter Three, the force of ejaculation and the volume of ejaculate in human males increases with time since last orgasm. Both of these findings are supportive of the sex drive concept. Given that something similar to a sex drive does seem to exist in humans, the next logical step is to try to determine what internal changes might trigger this drivelike state. The research to date suggests that changes in certain hormones are probably responsible.

The hypothalamus directs the pituitary to secrete a series of hormones called gonadotropins. The gonadotropins **follicle stimulating hormone** (FSH) and **luteinizing hormone** (LH) stimulate the gonads (testes in males, ovaries in females) to secrete gonadal hormones (Hoyenga & Hoyenga, 1979). Three major gonadal hormones appear to be important for male and female sexual behavior: androgens, estrogens, and progesterone. The **androgens** are often called the male sex hormones, although they are also produced in a smaller degree in women. The major androgen is **testosterone**, which is manufactured primarily by the testes in the male but is also produced in smaller quantities by the adrenal glands in both males and females and by the ovaries in females. Female levels of testosterone vary between 6% and 20% of the levels found in males (Money, 1980). The **estrogens** are sometimes called the female sex hormones; however, as was the case with the androgens, estrogens are also produced in both males and females, although to a smaller degree in the male. Male estrogen levels are 2%–30% of female levels. The major estrogen of interest is **estradiol**. Women also produce **progesterone**.

There is considerable evidence that testosterone is needed for sexual behavior in males. For example, a minimal level (2 nanograms per milliliter) of testosterone must be present for human male sexual interest and also for maintaining an erection (Luria et al., 1987). Sometimes, as a result of cancer or other disease, castration is necessary. Sexually inexperienced men do not behave sexually after castration, but loss of testosterone through cas-

tration does not immediately reduce sexual behavior in sexually experienced men, whose sexual behavior may continue for more than a year after surgery. This latter finding indicates that male sexual motivation is not entirely controlled by hormonal levels and that experience plays an important role. Similar results have been found in animal studies (Hart, 1974).

Studies of the hormonal influence of estradiol on human female sexual behavior are inconclusive. Removal of the ovaries or menopause (and thus reduction of estrogens) has no discernible effect on sexual motivation in women (Money, 1980). Furthermore, estrogen and progesterone levels change dramatically during the menstrual cycle, but no consistent patterns in sexual interest have been shown (Luria et al., 1987). In rodents estrogen and progesterone levels do appear to be important for normal sexual activity. Female rats show the highest levels of sexual receptivity when sex hormones are at their peak. In primates sexual interest in the female appears to peak at about the time of ovulation, when estrogen levels are highest (Hoyenga & Hoyenga, 1984). The data from animal research, therefore, are not consistent with the data from human research.

Interestingly, androgen levels may also be important to sexual behavior in women as well as in men. As noted above, removal of the ovaries has no obvious effect on a woman's sexual behavior; however, if the adrenal glands are removed, sexual interest decreases dramatically (Gray & Gorzalka, 1980). Since the adrenal glands are a major source of androgens in women, it seems possible that sexual interest is promoted by androgen in females as it is in males.

Problems with the Sex Drive Concept

Although sexual motivation may represent the drive concept more clearly than other motives, the sex drive concept is not free of problems. As you will recall from earlier in the chapter,

Hull's drive concept requires that learning not occur unless either a drive or drive stimuli are reduced. You should also recall that Sheffield, Wulff, and Backer (1951) showed that male rats would increase their running speed in an alleyway for the chance to mount a receptive female even when they were not allowed to ejaculate and thus reduce their sexual drive state. The research of Sheffield and associates shows that learning can occur without any reduction in the sex drive and poses a problem for the sex drive concept.

Additionally, the concept of drive traditionally has been closely tied to the concept of homeostasis. However, it is not clear how any homeostatic imbalance is imposed by sexual deprivation. Certainly sexual behavior is neither necessary for the survival of the individual nor debilitating if not performed. The principle of homeostasis, therefore, would not seem to apply to sexual motivation in the same way that it applies to hunger or thirst motivation.

Although the above considerations indicate that under some circumstances sexual behavior does not occur in the way that Hull's drive theory predicts, it should be remembered that contradiction of Hull's theory does not necessarily invalidate the drive concept in general. Perhaps the sex drive concept could be retained if the assumptions about how drive influences behavior were modified.

Some Thoughts About Drive Theory's Problems Where does all this information leave us in regard to drive theory? The Hullian formula expressing behavior as a function of learning, drive, and incentive had great intuitive appeal and generated a tremendous amount of research. As a result we have learned a great deal about the variables that influence behavior. For example, much of the work conducted on the physiological mechanisms of regulation was generated in the search for the neural substrate of drive. The results of these studies, as we have seen, can stand in their own right, independent of the

drive concept.

Hull's model for behavior was also useful as an example of theory building in psychology. Hull presented his ideas in specific detail and provided a network of relationships between his concepts that could be experimentally tested. He was also not afraid to modify his theory as new information became available. Hull's inclusion of incentive motivation was largely based, in fact, on research conducted by theorists opposed to his point of view.

But Hull's drive theory has not withstood the concerted experimental examination of its basic assumptions. Drive reduction cannot be the only basis for reinforcement, nor does drive show the characteristics that he believed it did. Drive stimuli have proven elusive and apparently do not account for very much of the direction of behavior.

Furthermore, as noted in Chapter Four, animals often eat and drink when no apparent homeostatic imbalance is present. Additionally, it is not clear how other behaviors involving sexual motivation or avoidance of pain would result from a homeostatic imbalance. Satinoff (1987) summarizes the problem well when she states:

The question is, how well do feeding and drinking conform to homeostatic principles? In other words, what proportion of these behaviors is motivated by nutrient or fluid depletion? In the real world, the answer seems to be very little. (p. 343)

In the next two chapters we will examine motivational concepts that are related to what organisms learn. We shall discover that learning about goals and the behaviors necessary to reach those goals can have a large influence on motivation. Although loss of homeostasis can undoubtedly trigger motivation to seek out conditions that will restore the homeostatic balance of the organism, homeostatic regulation does not appear to be the major determinant of motivation as was once thought.

As more and more is learned about the variables involved in motivated behavior, drive slips further and further into the background. At this point the consensus among those who study motivated behavior is that the drive concept is unnecessary. Today research emphasis is directed toward understanding specific types of motivated behavior rather than attempting to incorporate all information into one grand theory. Much of the theory and research examined in this book has resulted either directly or indirectly from researchers' attempts to formulate smaller, more specific theories owing to the failure of Hull's theory.

SUMMARY

In this chapter we have examined the concept of drive. The historical reasons for drive theory's rise to prominence included the inadequacies of the early instinct and local theories of motivation, as well as research indicating that conditions of need led to changes in activity. Freud was perhaps the first drive theorist. Woodworth's development of the drive concept led to the behavioral theory of Clark Hull. Hull's highly formalized theory generated a tremendous amount of research but, in the end, was unable to account for all that was known about motivated behavior.

Specifically, generalized drive does not always lead to activation of behavior; motivation was shown to exist in the absence of any need state; and reinforcement results in learning even though drive reduction does not occur. Sheffield's experiments indicated that conceptualizing reinforcement as leading to an induction of drive, rather than to a reduction of it, might prove more useful. After many years and much research, the drive concept has gone the way of its predecessors.

Despite the overall inability of drive theory to "explain" behavior, much has been gained from the studies generated by it. The research on incentive motivation and acquired drives that is detailed in the next few chapters—as well as the work on physiological mechanisms of regulation discussed in Chapter Four—was generated largely as a result of drive theory. The information gained in all these areas is useful to our understanding of the factors that control behavior, whether tied to a drive construct or not.

Perhaps the most important contribution that drive theory made to the study of motivation was Hull's emphasis on a specifically defined, carefully constructed network of testable relationships. It provided (and still provides) a demonstration of how theory ought to develop. As new information became available, the theory evolved; and if Hull had lived, the theory may have continued to change. Drive theory was perhaps also useful in making apparent to most researchers that a single theory could not hope to explain all motivated behavior. Increasingly it appears that motivation is multiply determined; some behaviors are programmed into the organism, while others are learned or depend upon social interactions or environmental conditions. Toward the end of his life, Hull began to emphasize the properties of the goal as important to determining behavior via the concept of incentive motivation. Incentive motivation as a concept is still very much with us. In Chapter Seven we will examine it in detail.

SUGGESTIONS FOR FURTHER READING

Bolles, R. C. (1967). *Theory of motivation.* New York: Harper & Row. This first edition of Bolles's motivation text provides an excellent review of Hull's drive theory. Although very technical in parts, this book provides the best overall review of the pros and cons of drive theory.

Hull, C. L. (1943). *Principles of behavior: An introduction to behavior theory.* New York: Appleton-Century-Crofts. This text represents Hull's most vigorous attempt to develop a model of behavior. Although sometimes rather difficult reading, the concepts underlying generalized drive are spelled out here. Recommended for the advanced student.

Satinoff, E. (1987). Biology of drives. In G. Adelman (Ed.), *Encyclopedia of Neuroscience*, Vol. I, pp. 342–345. Cambridge: Birkhauser Boston. This short article provides a good introduction for the beginning student to the major factors associated with the drive concept.

Chapter Six

The Development and Direction of Motivation by Learning

CHAPTER PREVIEW

This chapter is concerned with the following questions:

1. How are motives acquired?

2. How does classical conditioning contribute to the motivation of behavior?

3. How does operant conditioning contribute to the motivation of behavior?

4. How is observational learning involved in the development of motives?

5. How does the phenomenon of learned helplessness influence motivation?

Johnny likes to watch television. His favorite shows involve lots of action and violence. In one show he observed a boy about his own age set a fire because the boy was angry with his parents. Johnny's observation of the fire-setting sequence had no immediately observable effect on his behavior; however, about a week later, after an argument with his parents, Johnny attempted to start a fire under the coffee table.

What motivated Johnny to behave this way? Several theorists have argued that our motives can be developed and directed simply through observation of appropriate models. They have further suggested that behaviors may often be learned but not performed until some time later when conditions are favorable for their occurrence. The example of Johnny's behavior suggests that learning can play a prominent role in the development and direction of motivation. Research has shown that several types of learning can influence both the development of motives and the way in which motives are expressed in behavior. This chapter, then, concerns the research and theory surrounding the idea that many motivated behaviors are acquired or directed by learning.

The concept of acquired motivation is necessary for any complete understanding of motivated behavior because much behavioral diversity clearly depends upon motives that are acquired or altered during the life of the organism. Though motives appear to be learned in both animals and humans, most theorists believe that acquired motives account for a larger proportion of behavior in humans.

Several kinds of learning have been implicated in the development or modification of motivated behavior. Among them are Pavlovian classical conditioning, operant conditioning, observational learning, and learned helplessness. We will examine each in turn.

PAVLOVIAN CLASSICAL CONDITIONING

In the process of classical conditioning, a formerly neutral stimulus gains the ability to elicit a response from an organism because it has been paired with some other stimulus that reliably (and usually rather automatically) elicited that response in the past.

Pavlov (1960) was originally interested in studying the digestive process, particularly the role of salivation in digestion. He chose the dog as his experimental subject because of its ability to generate copious amounts of saliva. He perfected an operation that allowed him to free the salivary gland from the inside cheek of the dog and suture it to the outside of the cheek. In this way he could connect the gland to a tube and accurately measure the amount of saliva secreted under various conditions.

Pavlov knew that a dog would begin salivating if given meat powder (or even a weak acid solution), so when he wanted his dogs to salivate, he would present meat powder to them. He noticed, however, that some of his dogs began salivating as soon as he brought them into the experimental room. Many theorists would have considered this an irritating interference to what they wanted to study. Pavlov, however, recognized that he was witnessing an interesting phenomenon, and he determined to study it in detail.

He therefore set up the situation shown in Figure 6.1. A dog was put into a harness and the salivary gland was connected so that the amount of salivation could be measured. Then he presented meat powder and some neutral stimulus (e.g., a ringing bell) together to the dog. The meat powder of course elicited salivation in the dog; but after a few pairings of the bell and meat powder, the bell alone would also elicit salivation. The bell, because of its association with the meat powder, had come to have similar effects on the dog's behavior.

Pavlov called the meat powder an **unconditioned stimulus (UCS)** to indicate that its effect on behavior was unlearned or automatic. He called the salivation response to the meat powder an **unconditioned response (UCR)**, again to indicate the unlearned nature of this response to the UCS. The bell was termed a **conditioned stimulus (CS)** because, though originally neutral, it developed (by association with the UCS) the ability to elicit a response that Pavlov called the **conditioned response (CR)**. The term *conditioned* was chosen to indicate that learning was involved in eliciting the CR by the CS.

It is important to realize that the CR and UCR are both salivation in this example, but they are considered as different responses. This is because the UCR occurs automatically to the presentation of the UCS, while the CR only develops after several pairings of the UCS and CS. The CR is thus something new, a learned response to a formerly neutral stimulus.

If we now remove the UCS and present the CS alone, CRs will continue to occur for a while. Continued presentation of the CS without the UCS, however, eventually leads to extinction (i.e., a process in which the CS no longer reliably elicits a response).

From a motivational viewpoint, some of the motivating properties of the UCS (in terms of its ability to generate a response) are apparently acquired by the CS through association of the two stimuli. This means that neutral stimuli in our environment can come to have motivational influences on our behavior if they are paired with UCSs that are strongly motivational. For example, suppose that your instructor in this course announces on the first day of class that pop quizzes will constitute

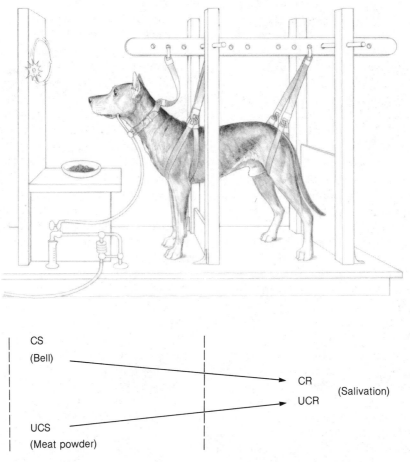

Figure 6.1 A typical Pavlovian setup. CS = conditioned stimulus; UCS = unconditioned stimulus; CR = conditioned response; UCR = unconditioned response.

50% of your final grade. Further, suppose that pop quizzes are highly anxiety producing for you, as for many students. Your anxiety concerning whether there will be a quiz during class will lead rather automatically to autonomic changes associated with your aroused state—what are commonly called "butterflies in the stomach." Each day when you walk into class, you are anxious and have "butterflies." The stimuli of the classroom, such as the greenish walls and cracks in the ceiling, will always be associated with your anxiety and will

become capable of eliciting "butterflies" even on days when your instructor is absent or has announced that there will be no quiz. The formerly neutral cues of the room have now taken on motivational and emotional properties for you and call forth the anxiety response.

Another important aspect of the classical conditioning of motivated states is that for all practical purposes, the organism is passive in the learning process. If conditions are right, the learning will occur whether we want it to or not. This suggests that some maladaptive behaviors (e.g., phobias) may be learned via accidental pairings of neutral stimuli and negative emotional or motivational states.

There is in fact considerable evidence that some maladaptive behaviors do result from classical conditioning situations. Pavlov again was one of the first to demonstrate what is called experimental neurosis.

Experimental Neurosis

Pavlov (1960) was conducting an experiment to determine the ability of dogs to discriminate between the shapes of different objects. Projected on a screen in front of the animal was either a luminous circle or a luminous ellipse. The circle (CS) was accompanied by feeding (UCS), and salivation (CR and UCR) was measured. The dog quickly learned to salivate at the sight of the circle. Once the conditioned response to the circle was well established, an ellipse was introduced with the axis ratio 2:1, as shown in Figure 6.2B. The ellipse was never paired with food, and the dog again quickly

learned to salivate when the circle was presented but not when the ellipse was presented. Pavlov then began to change the axes of the ellipse so that it more closely approximated a circle (Figure 6.2A). Each time the ellipse was changed, the dog showed that it could discriminate between the circle and the ellipse by salivating to the one but not the other. Eventually the axes were changed to a 9:8 ratio (Figure 6.2C), and discrimination was incomplete. After three weeks of testing discrimination between the circle and the 9:8 ellipse, the dog's behavior began to worsen, and the conditioned response finally disappeared altogether. The dog, formerly quiet, now began moving around in the harness, bit the apparatus, and barked violently when led to the experiment room. When tested on the original discrimination between the circle and the 2:1 ellipse, there was no evidence of discrimination. Pavlov noted that much of the behavior of the dog appeared similar to neurotic behavior seen in humans.

The experimental neurosis generated by

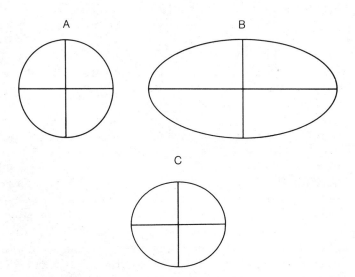

Figure 6.2 *Stimuli in differentiation experiment that led to experimental neurosis. A = circle (axis ratio 1:1); B = ellipse (2:1); C = ellipse (9:8).*

Pavlov's discrimination experiment was apparently the result of the increasingly difficult discrimination. It began to interfere with behavior when the dog could no longer clearly discriminate. The task became very aversive for the dog, as evidenced by its restlessness and attack on the apparatus. The dog's reluctance to enter the discrimination room also indicated a strong motivation to avoid the frustrating situation. Of some theoretical interest is a point made by Mineka and Kihlstrom (1978). They argued that experimental neurosis is not generated by the classical conditioning procedure per se but by the organism's lack of predictability or controllability. As we shall see in Chapter Twelve, one's ability to control one's environment may have important motivational properties.

Classical conditioning, then, is apparently associated with the acquisition of certain motivational states; however, it remained for Watson to show in a straightforward manner that classical conditioning can lead to the development of motivation and emotion.

John Watson and Rosalie Rayner (1920) classically conditioned a small boy to fear a white rat. Albert, the infant in the experiment, was nine months old at the start of the experiment. Watson and Rayner tested Albert to determine what stimuli would be frightening to him. They quickly discovered that Albert was a very placid baby, showing no fear to a variety of objects (e.g., a white rat, a rabbit, a dog, a monkey, masks with and without hair, cotton wool, and even burning newspapers). The only stimulus that would reliably elicit any emotionality in Albert was the sound made when a 3/4-inch-thick steel bar was struck with a hammer. Albert would start violently at the sound, check his breathing, raise his arms, tremble, and start to cry. The sound made by striking the bar was thus a UCS for the emotional response (UCR) of fear that Albert demonstrated.

When Albert was 11 months old, the experiment proper was begun. A white rat (CS) was presented to Albert. Just as he touched the rat, the bar was struck and he would start violently. After only two pairings of the rat and the sound, Albert became wary of the rat, no longer immediately reaching out for it. After a total of only seven pairings, Albert would begin to cry immediately upon presentation of the rat and start to crawl away so quickly that he had to be kept from falling off the examination table. It seems clear that at this point, the formerly neutral stimulus of the white rat had become an aversive stimulus that produced both emotionality and motivated behavior (as evidenced by Albert's attempts to crawl away).

Five days after the initial pairing of the rat with the sound, Watson and Rayner ran generalization tests. They were interested in determining if Albert was now only afraid of white rats or whether other similar objects might also elicit fear from him. They presented Albert with a rabbit, a dog, and a fur coat. For all three he began crying and attempted to crawl away. Albert was also wary of cotton wool (which has a furry appearance) but did not cry and eventually began to play with it. He also showed negative reactions to Watson's hair and to a Santa Claus mask. The emotionality had clearly generalized to other furry objects. A second set of generalization tests was conducted 31 days later. Albert still showed withdrawal behavior to the furry stimuli, but the reactions were much less intense than formerly. Classically conditioned emotional responses, then, can be relatively permanent.

Watson and Rayner's generalization tests were not correctly conducted, because they reconditioned little Albert several times between the initial conditioning procedure and the subsequent generalization tests (Harris, 1979). Nevertheless, their research was widely read, and subsequent research has confirmed that classically conditioned responses do generalize (Schneiderman, 1973), though the replicability of Watson and Rayner's experiment is less certain (Harris, 1979).

The search for the relationship between neurotic, maladaptive behaviors and the stimuli that trigger those behaviors has continued. Liddell (1954) used classical conditioning procedures to study emotionality in sheep and goats. He found that if the UCS produced an emotional UCR, then a CS paired with the UCS would also produce an emotional response. Liddell found that experimental neuroses developed in his sheep when electric shock was used to condition leg flexion and the animal's task was made difficult. The neuroses, once developed, generalized from the experimental situation to the barn and pasture as well. Neurotic sheep displayed fast, irregular heartbeats during sleep and were very sensitive to external stimuli of any kind. When under attack by roaming dogs, the neurotic sheep were invariably the ones killed; when threatened, they ran off by themselves rather than following the flock and were thus easily attacked. Interestingly, Liddell found that young lambs could be "protected" from experimental neuroses simply by having their mothers present in the experiment room during the classical conditioning sessions. Under these conditions the lambs showed no neurotic behavior.

Elimination of Motivated Behaviors Through Conditioning

Just as motivation may result from the pairing of a neutral stimulus with an emotion-arousing unconditioned stimulus, so may reactions be eliminated in a similar manner. Rachlin (1976) noted that maladaptive reactions may be eliminated either through extinction procedures or

through a process called "counterconditioning," in which the negative CS is paired with a strongly positive UCS. Counterconditioning is generally preferred over extinction procedures because it provides a specific response to replace the negative conditioned response.

Wolpe (1958, 1973) has developed a therapeutic technique termed **systematic desensitization** that employs counterconditioning as part of its procedure. In systematic desensitization the patient is first taught to relax deeply. Once the person can relax on command, a list of anxiety-producing situations that involve the CS is made. The list (called an **anxiety hierarchy**) is arranged from least anxiety producing to most anxiety producing. The patient is told to think about the first (i.e., least) anxiety-provoking situation on the list and to relax. Once the individual can relax at the same time that he or she is thinking about this situation, the individual is asked to think about the second situation on the list and to relax. This continues until the individual can think about the most anxiety-arousing situation and at the same time relax. When this has been achieved, the person is said to be desensitized. Thus, through the pairing of a negative CS (e.g., some anxiety-arousing thought) with a positive UCS (i.e., relaxation), the negative state loses its aversiveness. The situation is diagrammed as follows:

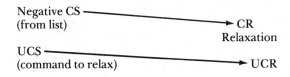

It seems clear that motivational states can be acquired and eliminated through the process of classical conditioning. An additional line of evidence supporting the importance of classical conditioning of motivated behavior comes from Russian research on the conditioning of internal states, a procedure termed **interoceptive conditioning**.

Interoceptive Conditioning

Interoceptive conditioning is defined by Razran (1961) as classical conditioning in which either the CS, UCS, or both are applied directly to the internal organs or the mucosa.

Three types of interoceptive conditioning have been demonstrated. In **intero-exteroceptive conditioning** the CS is applied internally, while the UCS is applied externally. Razran reported a Russian experiment that conforms to this design. A female dog had a rubber balloon, through which cool water could be irrigated, inserted into the uterus. Paired with the CS of cool water was the presentation of food, which of course elicited salivation as the UCR. In just 6 to 9 trials the cool water began eliciting salivation and became a stable response after only 25 pairings. That the cool water was indeed the stimulus controlling the CR was shown by the fact that the dog could learn to discriminate water temperature, salivating when cool water (8°–12°C) was irrigated through the balloon but not salivating when warm water (44°–48°C) was irrigated.

Intero-interoceptive conditioning occurs when both the CS and the UCS are applied internally. Again the Soviet literature demonstrates such conditioning (Razran, 1961). Loops were formed in the intestines of several dogs and could then be manually distended. Distensions of the intestinal loops served as a CS, which was paired with the delivery of carbon dioxide (CO_2) to the lungs (UCS). Inhalation of CO_2 leads to changes in the respiration rate, described as **defensive breathing**. Conditioning occurred after only 3 to 6 pairings of intestinal distension with CO_2 inhalation and became stable after 5 to 16 trials. Thus intestinal distension acquired the ability to produce defensive breathing in dogs.

Extero-interoceptive conditioning occurs when an external CS is paired with an internal UCS. A human conditioning experiment reported by Razran (1961) can serve as an example of this type of conditioning. Human subjects hospitalized because of urinary complications volunteered to have balloons inserted into their bladders. A series of dials was connected to the balloons so that the patient could see whether the balloon was being inflated or not. Thus the dials served as an external CS, which was paired with an internal UCS of bladder distension.

Inflation of the balloon led to reports of a strong urge to urinate, as would normally occur if the bladder were filling with urine. After several pairings of the dial readings with balloon inflation, the experimenters disconnected the dials, so that inflation of the balloons was not gauged, and manipulated the CS and UCS independently. The patients reported strong urges to urinate when the dial readings were high, even though balloon inflation was absent. This of course indicates that the dial readings had become conditioned stimuli that elicited the internal response of the urge to urinate. Low dial readings failed to produce the urge to urinate, even when the inflow of air was considerably higher than the amount that normally produced the urge. Clearly internal changes can become associated with external stimuli.

A real-life situation that appears comparable to this experiment is when the physician asks you for a urine sample as part of a physical examination. The physician will usually lead you to the bathroom and turn on a water faucet before he or she leaves. The sound of running water is an external stimulus that is always associated with urination and has become a CS for urination. This sound almost always helps even the most reluctant person to provide the necessary sample.

Implications of Interoceptive Conditioning
Razran (1961) reported a total of 14 experi-

ments involving interoceptive conditioning of one or another of the three types mentioned. These 14 experiments represent hundreds of experiments that the Soviets have carried out on this type of conditioning in both animals and humans. Razran pointed out that these experiments have some important implications for our understanding of behavior.

First, we are usually unaware of interoceptive conditioning when it occurs. Thus some of our behavior will be unconscious to the extent that it is the result of interoceptive conditioning. Second, interoceptive conditioning cannot really be avoided. We carry the stimuli with us no matter where we go. It is reasonable to expect that some behaviors will result from the pairing of internal or external changes with bodily changes that happen to be occurring at the same time. Third, the research examined by Razran indicates that interoceptive conditioning is more permanent (i.e., more resistant to extinction) than typical external classical conditioning. Thus interoceptive conditioning can have long-term effects on our behavior. Finally, interoceptive conditioning has important implications for psychosomatic medicine (see also Buck, 1976; Tarpy & Mayer, 1978). For example, an anxiety-producing UCS that causes vasoconstriction (resulting in increased blood pressure) could become associated with tests (i.e., an external CS) so that a student becomes hypertensive in school situations. It is also important to keep in mind that conditioning may generalize to other similar situations so that test anxiety could lead to hypertension in other competitive situations.

The studies noted by Razran suggest both that motivated behavior may develop as a result of interoceptive conditioning and that we are often largely unaware of the reasons for our behavior because we are not conscious of the conditioning process when it occurs. Interoceptive conditioning can potentially play an important role in the motivation of

behaviors over which we have little voluntary control; some maladaptive behaviors are probably developed in just this way.

Another area of study in which it has become apparent that classical conditioning influences motivation is taste-aversion learning. Originally it was felt that this type of learning situation was fundamentally different from classical conditioning of other behaviors (see, e.g., Rozin & Kalat, 1971); however, as noted by Domjan and Burkhard (1982), the learning process does appear to be one of classical conditioning. As we shall discover, however, the CS-UCS relationships in taste-aversion learning are rather different from the typical arrangements of these stimuli in standard classical conditioning.

Learned Aversions

Research associated with the topic of learned aversions has appeared under a variety of headings. Sometimes it is termed **long-delay learning** or **taste-aversion learning**, both of which describe some characteristics of the early research. "Learned aversions," however, seems the more appropriate heading for our purposes because it emphasizes the motivational nature of the learned behaviors.

People have long known that it is very difficult to poison rats because, once poisoned, rats will avoid the bait that made them ill. Several learned aversion studies provide some insight into why rats are so difficult to poison. A study by Garcia and Koelling (1966) provides us with our first clues. Garcia and Koelling presented one group of rats with the opportunity to drink water. At the time of drinking, an audiovisual display occurred that consisted of a flashing light and a clicking sound. To use the researchers' terminology, the rats were exposed to "bright-noisy water." Another group of rats was also given the opportunity to drink water, but rather than an audiovisual display, the water they were given was distinctly flavored (either sweet or salty) and thus could be labeled "tasty water."

After drinking their solutions, the groups were bombarded with X-rays, which produced nausea and gastrointestinal disturbance. Two additional groups received footshock rather than the illness-inducing X-rays. The results of the study showed that the animals who had the "tasty water" and X-rays later avoided the flavored solution; they had formed a learned aversion to the taste of the water as a result of the illness. Of particular interest, however, was the finding that the animals with "bright-noisy" water did not develop an aversion to the water as a result of the X-rays. The two

footshock groups showed just the opposite effects; the taste of the water did not become associated with the shock, but the audiovisual display did. Figure 6.3 shows the results of these tests.

The important point of the experiment was that the taste cues were associated very easily with illness but not with the footshock. The audiovisual cues, on the other hand, were readily associated with shock but not with illness. What the rats learned was constrained by their biological heritage. It would be adaptive to associate tastes and illness quickly, while little advantage (for rats) would occur in associating taste with some external painful agent.

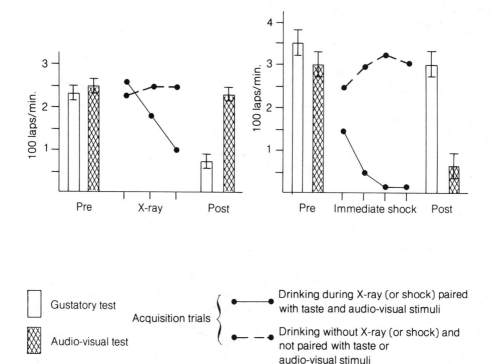

Figure 6.3 Water intake (measured in hundreds of laps per minute) before (Pre), during, and after (Post) learned aversion acquisition. As can be seen, nausea produced by X-rays reduced water intake associated with taste cues, both during and after acquisition, while intake was unaffected by the audiovisual display. The graph on the right shows that although shock was not associated with the taste of water, it became associated with the audiovisual stimulation. (Adapted from Garcia & Koelling, 1966. Used by permission.)

On the other hand, stimulation of the distance receptors (e.g., vision and hearing) would provide information about the external environment that would be useful if easily associated with externally harmful events.

In a second experiment Garcia, Ervin, and Koelling (1966) showed that the taste-illness connection can be made even when the interval between tasting and illness is as long as 75 minutes. Thus rats are apparently programmed in such a way that they can associate illness with specific tastes, even though the illness may not occur for a considerable time after a substance has been ingested. It is not hard to see the adaptiveness of a mechanism that allows associations to be made across long periods of time. This, in conjunction with the rat's sensitivity in associating illness with taste, points out why they are so difficult to poison. If the poison doesn't kill them the first time, the battle is lost because the taste-illness association formed will strongly motivate the rats to avoid that substance in the future.

Seligman (1970) has proposed that the associability of events in the environment can be described as consisting of a continuum. At one end of the continuum are events that can be easily and quickly associated; these are said to be **prepared associations**. At the other extreme are associations that an organism apparently cannot learn; these are called **contraprepared associations**. Between the two extremes are said to be **unprepared associations** because, though they can be learned, numerous experiences with the events are necessary for an association to be formed. The preparedness hypothesis argues that different species will have evolved different prepared, unprepared, and contraprepared associations as a result of the selective pressures of evolution. Thus a species may quickly learn a response to one set of environmental circumstances but not to another set because evolution has prepared one type of association to be easily formed—while at the same time making other associations difficult or impossi-

ble. Thus biological constraints on learning exist and must be considered if we are to understand motivation.

Learned aversions with strong motivational properties for future behavior can be formed in several species in addition to rats and using stimuli other than taste. For example, quail learn to avoid water after having been made ill, and they can associate the illness to both taste and visual cues. In fact for quail the visual cue appears to be more important (Wilcoxon, Dragoin, & Kral, 1971). Domjan, Miller, and Gemberling (1982) developed an aversion to the shape of cookies in vervet and grivet monkeys. The monkeys in this study were made ill after eating circular cookies but not bar-shaped cookies and were tested in total darkness so that visual cues could not be used. The monkeys developed an aversion to the circular cookies but continued to eat the bar-shaped cookies even when the illness-inducing injection was delayed for up to 30 minutes. It seems clear that aversion to cues associated with illness can occur with sensory modalities other than taste and is a general phenomenon seen in numerous species. Learned taste aversions have also been demonstrated in humans, as we will see in the following section.

Learned Taste Aversions in Cancer Patients

Several drugs used in the treatment of cancer produce side effects of nausea and vomiting. It is also well known that cancer patients frequently suffer loss of appetite (termed **anorexia**). Ilene Bernstein (1978) designed a study to determine if this loss of appetite might be a learned aversion that develops as the result of associating the taste of food eaten before the nausea-inducing chemotherapy.

Bernstein chose as subjects 41 children (ages ranged from 2 to 16 years) who were receiving chemotherapy on an outpatient basis. One group of patients received an unusual-tasting ice cream shortly before the drug treatment. A second control group was given no ice cream prior to the drug therapy. A third group, also serving as a control, was given ice cream but received a drug that did not produce nausea and vomiting.

The group that received the ice cream before becoming nauseated from the chemotherapy showed an aversion to the ice cream when offered it two to four weeks later. Neither of the two control groups showed any aversion to the ice cream. A retest conducted four and one half months after the first test and using a new ice cream revealed that the aversion for the initial ice cream was still present.

Of particular interest was that most of the children knew that the nausea and vomiting were results of their drug therapy, not of the ice cream; yet their aversion to the ice cream still developed. Humans, like rats, appear prepared to associate illness with the taste of previously ingested foods. Probably at least part of the appetite loss experienced by patients undergoing chemotherapy results from a learned aversion that develops from associating previously eaten foods with side effects of the drug treatment.

As we have just seen, conditioned aversions may partially account for changes in the eating patterns of cancer patients undergoing chemotherapy treatments. There is also evidence that the nausea and vomiting often associated with chemotherapy can become conditioned to stimuli in the environment (Burish & Carey, 1986). Thus the stimuli of the doctor's office, smells, tastes, or even thoughts concerning the chemotherapy can come to elicit nausea and vomiting independent of the actual physical effects of the therapy.

Burish, Carey, Krozely, and Greco (1987) sought to determine whether **progressive muscle relaxation therapy** (**PMRT**) and **guided relaxation imagery** (**GI**) could be used to prevent the development of conditioned nausea and

vomiting. Two groups of patients undergoing chemotherapy were used in the experiment. One group was trained in PMRT and GI prior to the first chemotherapy injection and used these techniques later to relax before scheduled injections. The second group, which received no PMRT or GI training, acted as a control group and simply rested quietly before injections were given.

The results of the study showed that PMRT and GI training reduced the feelings of nausea during the chemotherapy sessions in the trained group relative to the control group as measured by both self-reports and nurse reports. Although no significant differences between the two groups were found during the first three chemotherapy sessions, sessions four and five produced significantly more nausea in the control group. This finding is especially important because conditioned nausea and vomiting generally take three or more sessions to develop. Apparently the relaxation training reduced the severity, and perhaps prevented the development, of conditioned nausea in the trained group.

The amount of anxiety, nausea, and vomiting was also monitored at home during the 72 hours following chemotherapy. Once again, the relaxation-trained group reported lower levels of anxiety, nausea, and vomiting. As Figure 6.4 clearly shows, the relaxation-trained group was considerably below the control group on all three measures.

The nausea and vomiting produced by chemotherapy agents can be very aversive and in some cases sever enough to lead the patient to refuse treatment (Wilcox, Fetting, Nettesheim, & Abeloff, 1982). Some part of the aversiveness of chemotherapy is potentially the result of a conditioned aversion to the stimuli associated with the treatment. The relaxation procedure of Burish and associates (1987) is important because it seems to be capable of reducing the severity of the conditioned nausea and vomiting linked with such treatments.

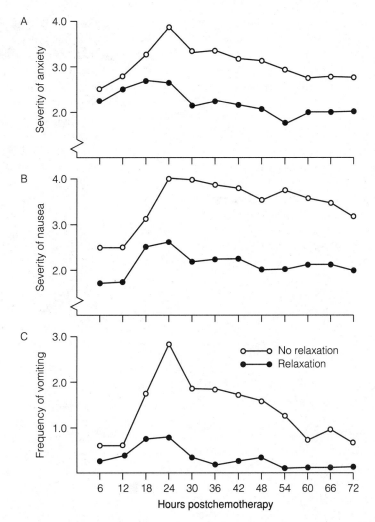

Figure 6.4 *Mean patient ratings of A, anxiety; B, nausea; and C, vomiting during the first 72 hours after chemotherapy. (From Burish et al., 1987; Copyright © 1987 by the American Psychological Association. Used by permission.)*

Burish and his associates propose that PMRT and GI interfere with the development of conditioned nausea and vomiting by diverting attention from the chemotherapy context and thus blocking conditioning to those contextual cues. A second mechanism noted by these researchers that may limit the conditioned nausea and vomiting is the reduction of muscle contractions along the gastrointestinal tract. PMRT and GI may reduce these contractions and thus reduce feelings of nausea and vomiting. Finally, Burish and associates suggest that PMRT and GI may interrupt conditioning of nausea and vomiting because these procedures reduce anxiety. When PMRT and GI are not used the anxiety experienced may provide cues that can elicit nausea and vomiting through conditioning.

The work of Burish and his colleagues is an important first step in reducing the strong negative motivation that often develops with chemotherapy treatment. Their work is also significant in showing how easily aversive motives can be learned through classical conditioning.

As the studies discussed in this section show, classical conditioning can lead to the development of motivated behavior in several different kinds of experimental situations. It therefore seems reasonable that some behaviors are motivated by cues that originally gained the power to activate responses through the process of classical conditioning. Operant conditioning also seems to be a factor in the motivation of behavior. In the next section we will examine some of the variables that seem to influence the motivation of operantly conditioned behavior.

OPERANT CONDITIONING

If we are to understand the motives underlying the behaviors we observe, we must first understand how these motives are acquired. One way is through the process of classical conditioning; another way is through the reinforcement of appropriate responses, called **operant conditioning**.

Whether classical and operant conditioning are really different processes has been the subject of considerable debate (e.g., see Davis & Hurwitz, 1977), but the situations under which one or the other occurs are different. Classical conditioning results from the association of stimuli, while operant conditioning occurs as a consequence of a response. Whether underlying processes involved in the two situations are different or not is certainly debatable. However, we will treat them here as if they are separate processes.

Modern ideas on operant conditioning have evolved from the early work of Thorndike (1913), who argued that the consequences of a response strengthen the connec-

tion between that response and some stimulus in the environment. The strengthening of this connection was termed the **law of effect**, clearly the forerunner of our present concept of reinforcement. Skinner (1938) emphasized the idea that reinforcement serves not so much to strengthen a connection between a stimulus and a response but rather to strengthen the response itself, making its occurrence more probable. Though one can analyze the situation as one in which the response is strengthened by reinforcement, one can just as logically argue that the effect of reinforcement is to motivate behavior. (Skinner, however, preferred to analyze behavior without any reference to motivational constructs.)

The motivational properties of reinforcement have led some theorists, such as Bindra (1969), to propose that reinforcement and incentive motivation are two labels for the same phenomenon. Thus, depending upon one's theoretical point of view, much of the literature on reinforcement can be interpreted as evidence of incentive motivation; similarly, much of the data on incentive motivation can be analyzed from a reinforcement point of view. The important point for us is that operant procedures lead to the acquisition of new behaviors, which are motivated by the consequences of those behaviors.

Consider a hypothetical example. Suppose that a child in school discovers that hard work and good grades are consistently followed by strong praise from his or her parents. If the praise is a strong reinforcer, the child will become motivated to work hard in order to obtain more praise from the parents. Now imagine another child whose parents do not value good grades and therefore do not reinforce academic performance but do reinforce their child's athletic ability. It is not hard to imagine that schoolwork for the second child will be relatively unimportant and perhaps only minimally tolerated because it allows him or her to play sports. We can generalize the example a little further and note that society rewards and punishes us for certain behaviors but not for others. Different societies have different ideas of what behaviors are acceptable and will, therefore, shape our behavior. To the extent that different groups within a society also reinforce different behaviors, persons exposed to those groups will be motivated to respond in different ways. To a boy growing up in the ghetto, aggressiveness and being "streetwise" may be strongly reinforced, while a boy growing up in the farm belt may learn that hard work and patience are rewarded.

We can manipulate reinforcement in several ways that subsequently alter behavior. For example, we can alter the quantity of reinforcement and determine if large versus small rewards motivate behavior in different ways. Similarly, we can vary the quality of reinforcement and note the effect of this manipulation on behavior. We can even impose different time delays between the response and subsequent reinforcement and note behavioral changes that take place as a result. Finally, we can change a reinforcer after behavior has been established and see how contrasts between differing reinforcers influence responding. Considerable research exists on the effects of these various manipulations. Though it is beyond the scope of this text to examine this experimentation in all its complexity, we will look briefly at some general findings in each of these areas and caution the reader that many conflicting data also exist. (The interested reader should consult Bolles, 1975, for a comprehensive review of this literature.)

Quantity, Quality, and Contrasts of Reinforcement

In 1942 Crespi conducted an experiment in which different groups of rats received different amounts of reinforcement for running down an alleyway. Rats that received larger rewards ran faster than rats that received

smaller rewards; thus the amount of reward led to differing levels of performance. Crespi's experiment, as we will see in the next chapter, was used as evidence for the incentive motivational effects of reinforcement, because when he later switched the rats to a common amount of reinforcement, the behavior of all groups quickly approached the same level of performance. The initial differences in performance, however, typify the basic findings when amount of reinforcement is studied; **the greater the quantity, the better the performance**. This positive correlation between amount of reinforcement and performance has been dubbed the **amount of reinforcement (AOR) effect** by Bolles (1975).

The general results of Crespi's study have been replicated several times (see, e.g., Zeaman, 1949; Metzger, Cotton, & Lewis, 1957), and the AOR effect has been found in various situations. Based on these studies, we may conclude that increasing amounts of reinforcement usually lead to more intense or vigorous behavior. Amount of reinforcement, however, does not seem to lead to greater persistence of behavior; in fact large reinforcements lead animals to stop responding more quickly when reinforcement is withdrawn in extinction (Hulse, 1958; Wagner, 1961). This somewhat surprising finding suggests that the motivational effect of amount of reinforcement is short lived; it increases performance as long as it is present, but behavior is quickly reduced in its absence.

Like quantity of reinforcement, quality of reinforcement also has motivational effects. For example, Simmons (1924) reinforced different groups of rats with different kinds of food for finding their way through a complex maze. The group rewarded with bread and milk performed better than a second group given sunflower seeds, which in turn performed better than a third group given nothing. Likewise, Elliot (1928) found that rats perform better for wet bran than for sunflower seeds. Thus a general **quality of rein-**

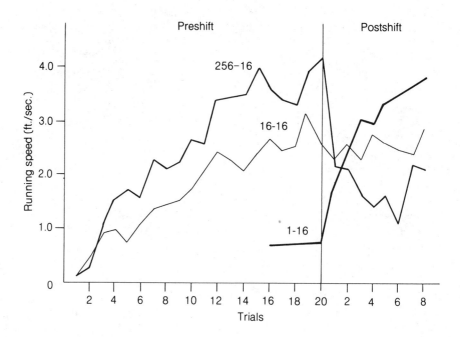

Figure 6.5 *Crespi's (1942) incentive motivation experiment. Groups were given 1, 16, or 256 pellets of food. On trial 20 all groups were switched to 16 pellets. Note how running speed shifts rapidly when the conditions of reinforcement change. (Adapted from Crespi, 1942. Used by permission.)*

forcement effect alters performance in much the same way as amount of reinforcement. This quality of reinforcement effect has been found in numerous experimental situations, including complex mazes, T-mazes, runways, and operant chambers. (Bolles, 1975, has provided a comprehensive review of this literature.)

A most interesting effect of manipulating reinforcement variables is the behavioral change one finds if the amount or quality of reinforcement is altered within an experiment. In Crespi's experiment rats receiving both large and small amounts of reinforcement were switched to a medium amount. Before the switch to a common amount of reinforcement, the groups were performing quite differently, with the animals receiving

the large reward running the fastest, followed by the medium-reward group, and finally the small-reward group. After the switch to the medium amount of reinforcement, the group that had been receiving the large amount performed *worse* than the control group, which had been receiving this amount all along. This effect has been termed **negative contrast**. In opposite fashion, the small-reward group performed *better* than the controls when switched to the medium amount of reinforcement. This effect has been called **positive contrast**. The results of Crespi's experiment are shown in Figure 6.5.

Positive and negative contrast effects have important implications for the motivation of behavior because they show that the past history of reinforcement influences responding on current conditions of reinforcement. For rats in the small-reward group in Crespi's experiment, a switch from 1 to 16 pellets was a large change, which they reflected by overshooting the performance of the group that had received 16 pellets from the beginning. On the other hand, rats in the large-reward group, switched from 256 to 16 pellets, experienced a huge change downward from what they had formerly received, and their performance dropped drastically to a level below that of the group that had continuously received 16 pellets. Because all groups were receiving the same amount of reward after the switch, the behavioral differences must have resulted from the differing past histories of reinforcement that the groups had experienced.

Research conducted after Crespi's usually found negative contrast but often had difficulty demonstrating positive contrast. Dunham (1968), in a review of the literature at that time, concluded that positive contrast does not exist and that when it does appear in experiments, it is due to comparisons against an inappropriate control group. More recently, however, Flaherty (1982) has reviewed contrast effects and finds that positive contrast is a reliable phenomenon.

Contrast effects also occur when quality of reinforcement is changed in an experiment. Typically, shifts in the quality of reward lead to shifts in performance that are similar to those seen when amount of reinforcement is changed (e.g., Panksepp & Trowill, 1971).

One final contrast situation should be mentioned. This situation is particularly interesting because it involves changes in both amount and quality, although the research has not typically been analyzed from a contrast point of view. The research concerns **latent learning**, that is, learning in the absence of any reinforcement. Blodgett (1929) conducted an experiment in which one group of rats was reinforced with food for learning to traverse a maze, while a second group received nothing. The nonreinforced group appeared to learn little. When food was later provided at the end of the maze, however, the performance of the nonreinforced group quickly matched that of the group that had been rewarded throughout, indicating that the nonreinforced rats had indeed learned the maze but were not inclined to demonstrate this learning until there was some motivation to do so. The introduction of food for the nonreinforced group represents a contrast between nothing and something. Presumably the introduction of food is an increase not only in amount but also in quality, and a strong change in performance occurs.

The importance of the latent learning experiment and others related to it (see, e.g., Buxton, 1940; Seward, 1949) was to argue that the effect of reinforcement is on performance (i.e., motivation) rather than on learning. Although this issue was hotly debated at the time and has never been completely resolved, it seems clear that one major effect of reinforcement is to alter the motivation of the organism. Changes in quantity, quality, and particularly contrasts between different levels of quantity and quality have large effects on motivation. Whether these variables also affect learning is less clear.

Primary and Secondary Reinforcement

So far we have not distinguished between various types of reinforcement. This has been intentional because the principal characteristic of a reinforcer is that it increases the probability of the response that it follows. Nevertheless, we commonly make a distinction between **primary reinforcers**, which increase a response because of their very nature (i.e., unlearned reinforcers such as food, water, avoidance of pain, and so on), and **secondary reinforcers**, which come to control responding because they have been associated with primary reinforcers in the past.

Generalized Conditioned Reinforcers

Suppose a stimulus is paired with not just one primary reinforcer but with several, perhaps in many different situations. What would be the effect of such multiple pairings? The stimulus would become what is called a generalized conditioned reinforcer (Reynolds, 1975). A generalized conditioned reinforcer gains its reinforcing properties from the several primary reinforcements with which it has been paired.

As a result, a generalized conditioned reinforcer can become somewhat independent of any individual primary reinforcer and strengthen or maintain behavior for a relatively long period of time even though not often paired with primary reinforcement. Perhaps the best example of a generalized conditioned reinforcer is money. Because money has been paired with so many reinforcers in the past it becomes a strong generalized conditioned reinforcer and will maintain behavior for long periods without recourse to primary reinforcement. Indeed some individuals appear to be so reinforced by money that increasing their supply of it becomes an end unto itself.

Tokens and Token Economies
Money is not only a generalized conditioned reinforcer that can be used to maintain a variety of behaviors, it is also a *token* that serves as a reminder of the other reinforcers it will buy. Interestingly, humans are not the only animals capable of using conditioned reinforcers as tokens. For example, chimpanzees have often been used in research on token rewards. Early studies by Cowles (1937) and Wolfe (1936) showed that chimpanzees would learn a new response for token reinforcement (in these experiments poker chips could be traded for grapes) as quickly as for the grapes themselves and would learn new responses even when a delay of as much as one hour was instituted between the arrival of the token and its exchange for primary reinforcement. Chimps were also ob-

served to beg and steal tokens from one another. Thus the tokens seemed to share many of the characteristics of money in human society.

Tokens other than money have also been used in several human applications. In a **token economy** tokens are used as reinforcers for appropriate behavior and can later be exchanged for various reinforcers such as candy, cigarettes, television privileges, or other commodities and opportunities. Since the early work of Ayllon and Azrin (1968) with psychiatric patients, token economies have been used in a variety of settings such as schools, mental institutions, and prisons.

Token economies have become a viable alternative to other methods of controlling unruly and inappropriate behavior and indeed as noted below have been used to alter a number of widely divergent behaviors. For example, Padgett, Garcia, and Pernice (1984) used tokens to help a severely retarded 25-year-old woman learn to stay on the pathways from one building to another at the institution where she lived. This woman had a 6-year history of wandering off the pathways and getting lost on the institutional grounds. The researchers paid the woman tokens for staying on the paths and "charged" her tokens for wandering. After only two days of this treatment, wandering was reduced to zero and remained near zero during the period in which tokens were given. A follow-up six months after treatment found that wandering was no longer a problem.

A rather innovative application of token reinforcement was made by Jenson, Paoletti, and Peterson (1984). These researchers used tokens to reduce a behaviorally disturbed 10-year-old boy's chronic throat clearings. Prior to the use of tokens, the boy would clear his throat as many as 390 times in a five-hour period. After 23 days in which he received tokens for reduced throat clearings, this behavior had dropped to as few as 3 throat clearings in a five-hour period. In an educational setting

Udwin and Yule (1984) report some success with using tokens in teaching spelling words to an 11-year-old boy who had a spelling age of approximately 6 years.

One of the clearest examples of how a token economy can alter behavior is provided by Fox, Hopkins, and Anger (1987). These researchers conducted a long-term study of the effects of a token economy on accident and injury rates in two separate, dangerous, open-pit mines. As you are probably aware, mining is a hazardous occupation: in 1985, 500 people were killed in mining accidents and over 40,000 work-related injuries were reported (National Safety Council, 1986). Therefore any strategy that is useful in reducing these rates has important, and real, consequences.

Fox and his colleagues devised a token economy in which trading stamps were given to mine employees for working without accidents or injuries. These stamps could then be redeemed for various items at redemption stores. The stamps were awarded for several different categories of safety-related behavior. Employees were given stamps at the end of each month if they had not suffered a lost-time injury. Additionally, workers received extra stamps each month if all members of their work group had no lost-time injuries. Safety suggestions submitted by the workers and adopted by the mine were also rewarded with additional stamps.

Workers who missed work because of job-related accidents or injuries forfeited their monthly stamp award and monthly group award for one to six months depending on the number of days missed. Additionally, all members of an injured worker's group lost their monthly group award until the injured worker returned to work. Workers also lost the individual stamp award for one month for each $2,000 worth of accident-related damage to mining equipment. Finally, failure to report an accident also resulted in loss of a month's stamp award for both the individual and the group.

The token economy thus promoted safe behavior (by awarding stamps) and punished accidents and injuries (by withholding stamps). The approach is especially ingenious for its use of social pressure to promote safety. The group stamp awards created a situation where an accident or injury to any member of the group caused the group stamp award to be lost for all the members of that group. Thus there should have been social pressure on individuals to behave in a safe manner.

This token economy was initiated in the Shirley Basin mine in 1972 and continued for 12 years; in the Navajo mine the token economy was begun in 1975 and was still in use at the time of the article's publication (1987). When these economies were instituted both mines had yearly averages of lost work days due to injuries that were three to eight times higher than the national average for all mines.

The token economies had a dramatic effect on work-related injuries and accidents. As Figure 6.6 shows, the number of lost-time injuries dropped at both mines. By the end of the second year of the economies, work-related injuries at the Shirley Basin mine had dropped to about 15% of the baseline period and for the Navajo mine to about 32% of the baseline period. Cost of injuries dropped from $294,000 a year during baseline to $29,000 a year average during the token economy at the Shirley Basin mine; at the Navajo mine they dropped from $367,696 to $38,972 a year. (The cost of the stamps during the period of the study varied between $9,288 and $12,522 a year at the Shirley Basin mine and $11,359–$13,415 at the Navajo mine.) During the last 10 years of the token economy program the number of days lost to work injuries was about ¼ the national average at the Shirley Basin mine and ¹⁄₁₂ the national average at the Navajo mine. Clearly the token economy had a large effect on behaviors associated with accidents and injuries.

Receiving the stamps appeared to be highly motivating. At one of the mines the union representative asked that the token pro-

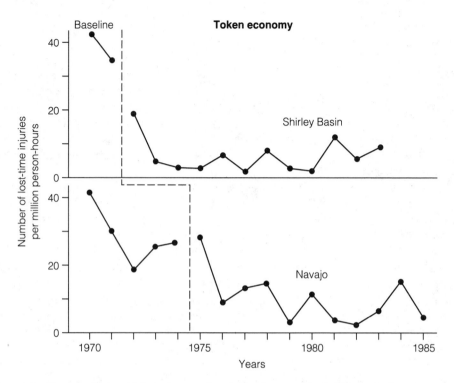

Figure 6.6 *Number of related injuries by year (per million hours worked) that required one or more days lost from work. (From Fox, et al. Used by permission.)*

gram be written into the contract between the union and the company. Additionally, as an informal check, stamps were purposely omitted from eight workers' pay envelopes. The spouse of one of the workers called the mine demanding that the stamps be issued, and a second worker's spouse drove over 50 miles to pick up the missing stamps. If these two instances are representative of the general attitude of the workers and their families, then it seems clear that the stamps had motivational effects.

As these examples show, token economies can be used in a variety of settings to modify behaviors that have proven difficult to alter with more conventional techniques. Token economies may be particularly effective in sit-uations where verbal methods are ineffective or difficult.

The modification and development of behaviors through the use of reinforcement, provide flexibility and variability to behavior. As reinforcement is extended or withdrawn, we will be motivated to behave in those ways that provide consistent reinforcement.

Many learning situations are actually composed of a combination of classical and operant conditioning. Several lines of research suggest that interactions between classical and operant conditioning have important motiva-tional consequences. In the next section we will examine research concerned with these interactions.

CLASSICAL-OPERANT INTERACTIONS IN MOTIVATION

Acquired Fear

We generally consider a stimulus motivating if an organism will learn a new operant response in order to either remain in the presence of that stimulus or remove itself from its vicinity. In a now classic study, Miller (1948) showed that fear can be acquired and that its reduction will motivate new learning.

Miller used a two-compartment box like that shown in Figure 6.7. One compartment was painted white, and the other was painted black. The white side had a grid floor through which the animal could be shocked, while the black side was "safe." The two compartments were separated by a door with horizontal black and white stripes. This door could either be opened by the experimenter or by the animal turning a wheel or a lever. Six-month-old male albino rats were given ten shock trials in the white compartment after determination that the rats preferred neither the white nor black side. On each trial the experimenter dropped the door so that the rat could escape from shock in the white compartment into the safe black compartment.

Starting with the eleventh trial and continuing for five trials, each rat was placed in the white compartment and allowed to escape through the open door, though no shock was now being delivered. The rats readily performed the escape response from the white side even though shock was absent.

Following the 5 nonshock escape trials, 16 trials were run in which the rats had to turn the wheel slightly in order to cause the door to drop so that they could escape into the black side. Again during these trials, no shock occurred. In order to escape the white compartment, 13 of the 25 rats learned to turn the

wheel. The 12 rats that failed to learn the response appeared to develop habits (e.g., freezing) that interfered with learning of the wheel-turning response. The 13 rats that did learn the wheel-turning response made the response more and more rapidly across the training trials, indicating that they understood the relationship between their behavior and the dropping of the door. Figure 6.8 shows the data from these animals.

After the sixteenth trial, the wheel-turning response was made inoperable, but pressing the lever would now cause the door to drop. Of the rats that had learned the wheel-turning response, 12 also learned to press the lever in order to drop the door, and again responding improved across trials.

Miller's experiment suggests that the cues of the white compartment became associated with the shock and developed the capability of motivating escape from the compartment. This motivation to avoid the cues of the white compartment could then be used to generate new, arbitrary responses such as wheel turning and lever pressing. These responses were presumably reinforced by the reduction of the white compartment cues that occurred when the rats succeeded in reaching the safe black compartment.

Incidentally, the motivation to avoid the white compartment was acquired through the pairing of the white compartment cues and shock, which is, of course, a classical conditioning situation. The motivation, once acquired, then generated operant behaviors that were reinforced by the reduction of the white compartment cues that occurred when the rats reached the black side. This has led some theorists (e.g., Mowrer, 1947) to argue that two factors are involved in avoidance behavior, a classically conditioned fear response and an operant response reinforced by a reduction in the acquired fear. Miller (1948) has suggested that neurotic symptoms might exem-

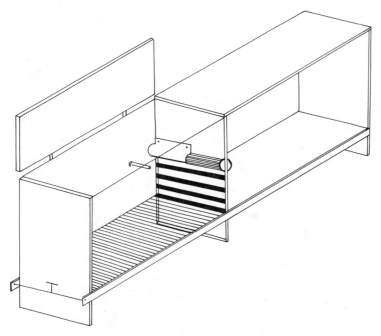

Figure 6.7 *Miller's 1948 acquired-drive apparatus. Shock is delivered through the grid floor on the left side of the box. Turning the wheel or pressing the lever causes the center door to drop so that the rat can enter the safe compartment on the right.*

plify just this sort of situation; cues associated with fear motivate neurotic behavior, which is then reinforced by a temporary reduction in the anxiety.

The acquisition and subsequent motivating properties of aversive stimuli seem fairly well established. Brown, Kalish, and Farber (1951) showed that an acquired fear would energize other behaviors that are independent of the original fear-producing situation. For example, rats that had acquired a fear response showed a heightened startle reaction to the sound made by a toy "popgun."

Conditioned Emotional Responses (CERs)

In a procedure termed **conditioned emotional response training**, an organism such as a rat is taught to press a lever in order to obtain food according to some schedule of reinforce-

ment (e.g., a fixed-interval, four-minute schedule). On such a schedule the rat can receive a pellet of food once every four minutes if the bar is pressed, but responses that occur prior to the scheduled interval go unreinforced. After behavior to the schedule has become consistent, the rat is subjected to pairings of a tone and shock, which are independent of the bar-pressing response using classical conditioning. If the tone is now presented alone (without shock), it will suppress the lever pressing for food. The disruption of the bar-press response is theorized to occur because the tone has become fear producing as a result of being paired with the shock. Thus, when the tone is sounded, a conditioned fear is generated in the animal that has the effect of suppressing ongoing behavior (i.e., lever pressing).

Thus once again we see that a neutral stimulus can acquire emotional or motiva-

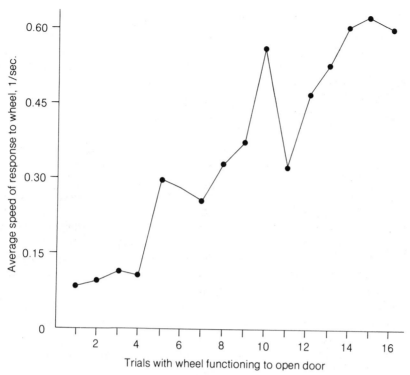

Figure 6.8 *Average speed of wheel turning across the 16 trials in which wheel turning allowed access to the safe compartment. (From Miller, 1948.)*

tional properties that lead to changes in behavior. One would expect that stimuli associated with positive emotional or motivational states ought to become conditioned motivators as well. While logically this should be true, the evidence for acquired motives based on positive states is not very convincing (Cofer & Appley, 1964). This asymmetry of effects possibly arises because of biological constraints on learning. Perhaps it is more adaptive to associate environmental stimuli with negative events, so as to avoid these events in the future, than to associate particular stimuli with positive events. Mineka (1975) has argued a similar point of view, suggesting that it would not be particularly adaptive for homeostatically controlled motives to be easily conditionable to external cues.

Learned Helplessness

We conclude this section with an examination of special learning conditions that seem to result in demotivation of behavior. This phenomenon has been termed **learned helplessness**.

Martin Seligman (1975, 1976) believed that learned helplessness is the laboratory analogue of reactive depression in humans. Learned helplessness can be defined as a psychological state involving a disturbance of motivation, cognitive processes, and emotionality as a result of previously experienced uncontrollability on the part of the organism. The learned helplessness phenomenon developed from studies on the interaction of Pavlovian and operant conditioning in avoidance learning (Maier, 1970; Overmier, 1968; Overmier & Seligman, 1967; Seligman & Maier, 1967; Weiss, Krieckhaus, & Conte, 1968). Seligman, for example, found that dogs given inescapable shock before being placed in a shuttlebox, where they can avoid the shock by jumping a hurdle, fail to learn the response. After initially struggling at the onset of shock in the shuttlebox, the dogs seem to "give up" and passively endure the shock.

How can we know if the results obtained in these experiments are caused by the uncontrollability of the situation or by the effects of the shock? To answer this question, researchers use what is called a **triadic design** (Seligman, 1975). In this design three groups are employed. One group is placed into a situation in which it can control its environment by making some response. For example, dogs might be trained to turn off shock by pressing a panel with their noses. A second group receives exactly the same conditions as the first group (e.g., shock), but no response they make has any effect in controlling the environment. The third group receives no treatment.

After this initial part of the experiment, all three groups are put into a new situation such as learning to jump a hurdle to escape or avoid shock. Results from experiments using the triadic design (e.g., Seligman & Maier, 1967) showed that the first group, which could control its environment, and the third group, which received no training, both learned the new response. The subjects of the second group, which had no control over its environment, initially were significantly slower to learn the new response and often did not learn it at all. Since Groups 1 and 2 both received exactly the same number of shocks, the differences in the second phase of the experiment must result from the fact that Group 1 could control its environment, while Group 2 could not. Also, the fact that Groups 1 and 3 both learned the new response showed that the aversiveness of the shock itself was not impor-

tant to the effect. Thus we are forced to conclude that the helplessness effect results from the inescapability, not from the characteristics, of the shock (but see Lubow, Rosenblatt, & Weiner, 1981, for another view). Also worth noting is the point that the helplessness effect (i.e., the inability to learn to control one's environment as a result of previous experience of no control) is not the same as the theory of learned helplessness, which attempts to explain these effects.

The failure of the dogs to learn the avoidance response of jumping over the hurdle apparently resulted from the previously experienced inescapable shock. The dogs had learned that they were helpless to prevent shock earlier and therefore, when later transferred to the shuttlebox, failed to recognize that their behavior could now be effective in reducing the shock—and so they continued to be helpless. Dogs subjected to helplessness training are also different outside the experimental situation. When an experimenter attempts to remove them from their home cage, they do not resist, as normal dogs do, but sink to the bottom of the cage and adopt a submissive posture.

Although helplessness was originally demonstrated in dogs, it has also been shown in other species, including cats, fish, monkeys, rats, and even humans (Seligman, 1975). Surprisingly, rats have proven to be the most difficult organism with which to demonstrate helplessness—but if the response is difficult or unnatural (e.g., requiring three bar presses rather than one to turn off shock), helplessness also occurs in rats.

Symptoms of Helplessness

Passivity (Motivational Deficit) Seligman (1976) believed that four primary symptoms of helplessness exist, the first of which is passivity. An example of passivity is provided in an experiment by Hiroto (1974). College students were put into an experimental situation where they were subjected to inescapable noise. Later these subjects were transferred to a second situation in which they could escape noise by moving their hands in a finger shuttlebox. Most of the subjects sat passively, enduring the noise much as Seligman's dogs had taken shock. Subjects in a control group that had initially learned to turn off the noise by pressing a button quickly learned to move their hands in order to silence the noise.

The passive aspects of learned helplessness can apparently develop even if the situation is a positive one, such as in uncontrolled reward. Engberg and associates (1972) taught one group of pigeons to jump on a treadle to receive grain. A second group also received grain, but its delivery was unrelated to their responding. A third group received no grain. All three groups were then transferred to a situation in which they had to learn to peck a lighted key in order to obtain grain. The group that had originally learned to jump on the treadle learned the key-peck response fastest. The pigeons that had received nothing earlier were second fastest. And the group that had received "free" grain learned very slowly. Engberg and associates termed this effect **learned laziness**. Their data suggest that uncontrolled reward also makes animals less able to behave in order to receive reinforcement in the future. Seligman believed that the passivity shown by animals in helpless situations is the result of a motivational deficit produced by the uncontrollability of events.

Retardation of Learning (Associative Retardation) Seligman noted that animals exposed to helplessness situations also develop a learning deficit. Dogs that eventually do learn to avoid shock after exposure to inescapable shock learn very slowly and often revert back to their earlier behaviors of passively enduring the shock. Seligman suggested that the helpless animal has learned that the consequences

of a situation cannot be altered by its behavior, which in turn makes it more difficult later for the animal to see that it can now influence what happens. Miller and Seligman (1975) have also found evidence for retardation of learning in humans subjected to helplessness situations.

Somatic Effects Seligman (1976) has reported that helpless dogs and rats are much less aggressive in aversive or competitive situations than normal nonhelpless animals. For example, if two rats are placed in a box in which the floor can be electrified and there is a "safe" pedestal large enough for only one rat, the rat that was earlier subjected to a learned helplessness situation invariably loses. Similarly, dogs subjected to inescapable shock as puppies always lose when competing for food with dogs that have had experience with controllable shock (Seligman, 1976). Maier, Anderson, and Lieberman (1972) obtained similar results with rats.

Reduction of Helplessness with Time Finally, Seligman noted that learned helplessness seems to decrease with time. In the Overmier and Seligman (1967) study, dogs were helpless if tested a day after only one training session with inescapable shock. However, if a week lapsed before testing, helplessness had somewhat dissipated. Multiple training sessions with inescapable shock, however, lead to relatively permanent helplessness.

Causes and Prevention of Helplessness The key to understanding the phenomenon of learned helplessness is the concept of **control**. Trauma (e.g., electric shock) by itself is not sufficient to produce learned helplessness as long as the organism can come to control the trauma in some manner. Learned helplessness apparently results from the organism's act of learning that it cannot control what happens to it. Thus the expectation that behavior will be ineffective in changing a particular environment leads to a drastic reduction in attempts to control the environment in other situations. The helpless organism, in essence, "gives up."

If control of the environment is actually the crucial component that determines the development of learned helplessness, teaching an organism that it can control its environment should reduce learned helplessness. Seligman, Maier, and Geer (1968) found that forcibly dragging helpless dogs from the shock side to the safe side of a shuttlebox eventually eliminated learned helplessness. Only by forcing the correct response from the animals could helplessness be overcome. Presumably the forced responding caused the animals to "see" that shock could be alleviated by responding. Other procedures (including tempting the dogs with Hebrew National Salami!) were ineffective (Seligman, 1976).

The concept of control also suggests that one might prevent the development of learned helplessness by first teaching animals to control their environments *before* subjecting them to helplessness situations and thus "inoculate" them against helplessness in this manner. Indeed prior training in controlling shock prevents the development of learned helplessness in dogs that are later subjected to inescapable shock (Seligman & Maier, 1967).

Seligman's data on learned helplessness are very important for understanding the motivation of behavior. His analysis suggests that motivation in the present depends upon past experience with controlling one's environment. Lack of success in the past will tend to have a demotivating effect upon future behavior. When the lack of success (i.e., control) is extreme, the organism may stop responding altogether.

Seligman (1975, 1976) has pointed out the similarity between the laboratory phenomenon of learned helplessness and the real-world phenomenon of depression. He believed that

learned helplessness is an animal model for certain types of depression in humans. He proposed in particular that the symptoms of learned helplessness are similar to those of reactive depression, which seems to be triggered by some external event such as the loss of a job, death of a loved one, rejection, financial problems, physical disability, and even old age. For example, depressed individuals tend to be passive, tend to have a negative cognitive set (i.e., they believe that their behavior will be ineffective), are usually less aggressive and less competitive than nondepressed persons, and usually improve with time. Depression, like learned helplessness, may be caused by the belief that responding will be useless in providing relief from aversive situations. Work on learned helplessness suggests that individuals suffering from reactive depressions might be helped by therapies that show them how their behavior can be effective in changing their environment.

The proposed similarity between learned helplessness in animals and depression in humans has generated great debate among theorists. Several criticisms of Seligman's approach include those of Costello (1978) and Wortman and Brehm (1975). Costello, for example, argued that data collected on depressed individuals by Seligman and his colleagues (e.g., Miller & Seligman, 1975) do not necessarily support the idea that the depressed individual believes that his or her behavior is ineffective but may indicate a general lowering of motivation in depressed persons.

A second, more damaging criticism of the learned helplessness model of depression is the fact that depressed persons usually feel guilty and blame their failures on their own inadequacies. It is hard to see how belief in a lack of control would lead to self-blame; rather the self-blame and guilt manifested by depressed individuals suggest that depressed persons believe that they *do* have control but that events still turn out wrong (Costello, 1978).

The learned helplessness model of depression, then, does not predict the loss of self-esteem that is prevalent in cases of depression.

Criticisms leveled against the theory have caused Seligman and his colleagues to reevaluate and reformulate the learned helplessness model of depression (Abramson, Seligman, & Teasdale, 1978). The reformulated theory emphasizes the importance of the individual's attribution of the reasons for lack of control. For example, the lack of control might result from some personal inability or simply uncontrollable factors. The amount of helplessness shown and its time course should be influenced by the attributions that one makes about why one has no control over events. The reformulated theory applies to human behavior, particularly to depression; however, an attributional analysis of helplessness does not appear necessary to explain the animal research. We will examine Seligman's reformulated theory in detail in Chapter Eleven, along with other attribution models of motivation.

The importance of Seligman's research as it relates to this chapter is that it points out, once again, the interaction of classical and operant conditioning in the motivation of behavior. Learned helplessness situations can lead to deficits in motivation, which then influence later behaviors in various situations. How far the learned helplessness model can be generalized (and also whether Seligman's analysis explains the learned helplessness data better than other, competing approaches) is still hotly debated; however, the results of helplessness studies point out the importance of past experience, formed in classical and operant conditioning situations, to alter the motivation for future behavior.

OBSERVATIONAL LEARNING (MODELING)

We will continue this discussion by examining a third type of learning that has also been implicated in the acquisition and direction of motivated behavior.

Studies of observational learning are based on the idea that a large part of human behavior results from vicarious learning; that is, we all learn a great deal simply by observing others. This approach, called **social learning theory**, emphasizes the idea that social conditions are important determiners of behavior (Bandura, 1971). Social learning theory was first recognized as influential for behavior by Miller and Dollard (1941); however, Albert Bandura and his associates have developed the concepts of social learning theory to the greatest extent (Bandura, 1969, 1971, 1977).

Bandura argued that humans are neither compelled by inner forces, such as the Freudian model suggests, nor totally controlled by the environment, as held by the strict behaviorist model. Rather, human functioning is best understood as the result of interactions between particular behaviors and the conditions that control them. Considerable emphasis is placed on vicarious, symbolic, and self-regulatory processes as determiners of behavior.

The social learning analysis of behavior argues that our ability to learn through observation (termed **modeling**) is large and allows us to build patterns of behavior without having to resort to trial and error. We learn to be motivated by particular objects in our environment, and we learn emotional responses to particular situations through modeling. Observed behaviors are stored symbolically and retrieved at some later time to guide behavior. Our ability to represent events symbolically also allows us to foresee the probable consequences of a behavior and thus alter our behavior accordingly.

Finally, humans can regulate their own behaviors internally. We reinforce ourselves for appropriate behavior and punish ourselves for inappropriate behavior. Self-reinforcement increases performance primarily through its motivational effects. In determining whether to reinforce ourselves, we compare our present behavior against that of others and our own past performances. We also evaluate our behaviors by noting how other people react to them. Finally, we will tend to adopt as standards of performance the standards that we observe in others (Bandura, 1977). As seen by social learning theory, then, we are active, observing organisms who profit from the experiences of others and can store these observations symbolically for future use and regulate our behavior through self-administered rewards and punishment.

An important point is that observational learning occurs without either the practicing of a response or reinforcement. Consider the various ways in which we could murder someone, as modeled for us by television. Most people can think of at least several ways in which the deed could be done, though few of these behaviors (one hopes) have actually been performed or rewarded. The point is that the potential behaviors have been learned, even though they have not been performed.

The primary functions of reinforcement, according to Bandura, are informational (i.e., telling us what effects our behavior has on the environment) and motivational. Rewards and punishers serve as motivators because they lead to the development of expectancies that particular responses will cause particular outcomes. Bandura argued that our cognitive abilities allow us to convert these expectancies into current motivators.

Modeling Processes: Attention, Retention, Reproduction

Before we can profit from the modeled behavior of others, we must first *attend* to their behavior. Accordingly, we will observe and imitate models with whom we are in frequent contact more than those we see less frequently.

The characteristics of the model also influence our attention processes. Some models attract us so strongly that we cannot seem to avoid being influenced by the behaviors they depict. Television can sometimes serve as this sort of model.

Once we have observed a behavior, we must still incorporate it into memory in some form. Bandura argued that modeled behavior is stored in both a **verbal code** and an **imaginal code**. When trying to remember an observed behavior, we remember both a series of verbal instructions (e.g., turn the nut to the left) and an image of the behavior (e.g., imagining a wrench turning the nut to the left). The verbal and imaginal memory codes serve as a guide for reproducing the observed behavior (i.e., we pick up the wrench and turn the nut to the left). Rehearsal of the behavior, either actual or mental, improves the performance of the behavior. Interestingly, Bandura sees rehearsal as primarily aiding in the recall of the observed behaviors rather than in the strengthening of correct responses.

Even though we have observed and symbolically stored a behavior, we can only imitate it if we can string together the correct pattern of responses. Normally our responses are rough approximations of the observed behavior. We then refine these approximations as a result of the information feedback we receive about the consequences of the behavior. Thus, in teaching someone to serve in tennis, one first demonstrates the motions required to get the serve into the opposite court. The observer then approximates the serve (usually very roughly) and alters the next attempt based on the results of the first (e.g., hitting the ball in a more downward fashion if the first attempt was long).

Modeling Processes: Vicarious Reinforcement

While behavior is influenced by the direct

reinforcement of responses, it is also influenced through observing the effects of a model's behavior. If we see a model being reinforced for a particular behavior, we too are likely to perform that behavior. On the other hand, if we observe the model being punished for a particular behavior, we will be less likely to perform that response ourselves. Such patterns are called "vicarious reinforcement situations" because we alter our behavior as a result of observing the consequences of others' behaviors.

Vicarious reinforcement can be distinguished from observational learning by noting that we may learn particular behaviors simply by observation without necessarily noting the consequences of those behaviors. However, observing the effects (e.g., reward or punishment) of a particular behavior performed by a model will alter the probability that we will perform the modeled behavior. Thus observation of reinforcement or punishment, though unnecessary for the occurrence of observational learning, does alter the likelihood that we will engage in the behaviors we have observed.

Vicarious reinforcement is important for our understanding of motivated behavior. If, for example, we observe someone cheating on a test and, as a result, getting a good grade, we may be less reluctant (i.e., more motivated) to cheat also. Bandura (1971, 1977) pointed out that one main effect of observing modeled behavior is to strengthen or weaken inhibitions related to particular behaviors. Thus vicarious reinforcement is important because it may disinhibit motivated behaviors normally kept in check. In a similar fashion, observation of modeled behavior may also serve to check behaviors that an individual would be inclined to perform otherwise. In this regard it seems likely that one aspect of socialization involves learning to inhibit impulses (via observation) that are not for the common good.

Bandura (1977) also pointed out that

vicarious reinforcement serves as a **reference standard** against which we compare the rewards that we receive. The observation of another person being highly rewarded for performing a behavior for which we have received only a little reduces the effectiveness of our reward. Vicarious reinforcement, then, can obviously work either to motivate or demotivate behavior, depending upon what we observe.

LEARNING AND AGGRESSION

Consider the following. On December 13, 1966, NBC aired a drama written by Rod Serling titled *The Doomsday Flight* (R. N. Johnson, 1972). The storyline concerned a bomb threat to an airline in order to extort a large sum of money. The airline is led to believe that a barometric bomb had been placed on the plane before takeoff. If the airline did not meet the extortionist's demands, the bomb would go off automatically when the plane descended below an altitude of 5,000 feet. Of course if the airline paid the ransom, then the caller promised to tell them where the bomb was hidden and everyone would be safe.

Before the show was even over a bomb threat was made against an airline that was very similar to the particulars of the television show. Within 24 hours of the broadcast four more extortion demands were made to various airlines.

On July 26, 1971, *The Doomsday Flight* was rerun by a television station in Montreal. A few days later a caller threatened a 747 with 379 persons aboard shortly after the plane had taken off. The caller insisted that a barometric bomb had been placed on the plane and would go off if the plane descended below an altitude of 5,000 feet (not even the altitude was changed!). The airline, by now aware of the scriptwriter's solution, diverted the plane to Denver, whose airport's altitude is 5,339 feet. It would seem that both extortionists and airline officials are capable of modeling their behavior after that observed on television.

The modeling of potentially violent and aggressive behavior after the scripts of television shows occurs from time to time; the aggressive behaviors seen after *The Doomsday Flight* are not peculiar to that particular script (see Geen, 1972, and the *Baltimore Sun*, 1990, for other examples). The point of this example, and others that could be mentioned, is that they suggest some aggressive behaviors may be learned.

As we have seen earlier in this chapter, motives can be learned as a result of classical conditioning, operant conditioning, and observational learning. Let us see how these three types of learning may also contribute to aggressive motivation.

Classical Conditioning and Aggression

Ulrich and Azrin (1962) developed what they termed a **pain-aggression model** of some types of agonistic behavior. For instance, if two rats are placed in a cage with a grid floor through which electric shock can be administered, the rats will rear up on their hind feet and box at each other. If an animal has only inanimate objects against which it may aggress, it may nevertheless attack such objects (Azrin, Hutchinson, & Sallery, 1964). If painful stimulation elicits aggressive behavior reflexively, as they suggest, then it ought to be possible, using classical conditioning, to pair a neutral stimulus with pain so that the conditioned stimulus also elicits aggression. Vernon and Ulrich (1966) demonstrated the classical conditioning of aggressive behavior, although in their study the conditioned response was not very strong and took many trials to develop. Additionally, Adler and Hogan (1963) were able to cause Siamese fighting fish to emit threat displays to a formerly neutral stimulus by using classical conditioning procedures.

Some evidence for classical conditioning of aggressive behavior in humans also exists. Berkowitz and LePage (1967) conducted an experiment in which subjects were directed to deliver electric shock to another person when that person made mistakes on a learning task. In one condition, a gun was present in the same room as the subject, in a second condition it was absent. Berkowitz and LePage found that more intense shocks were given in the presence of the gun than in its absence. They argue that the gun served as a situational cue that elicited more aggression because guns have been paired with aggression in the past. Although not a direct test of the classical conditioning of aggression, their results can be interpreted as deriving from the former pairing of guns and stimuli that elicit aggression.

Apparently aggression-eliciting stimuli can be quickly learned. Berkowitz and Geen (1966) conducted an experiment in which individuals were subjected to shock by a person who was supposedly evaluating their performance on a task. Following this part of the experiment, some subjects saw parts of the film *Champion* in which Kirk Douglas takes a terrible beating during a boxing match. Other subjects saw a film of a footrace. After viewing the films, the subjects were given the opportunity to evaluate the performance of the individual who had shocked them earlier by now shocking him. Some subjects were told that the name of the person they were evaluating was Bob, while others were told his name was Kirk (i.e., the same as in the boxing movie). Subjects who had been shocked, seen the boxing movie, and were shocking a person named Kirk were more punitive than those who had been shocked, seen the boxing movie, but were shocking a person named Bob. Apparently the association of the name Kirk with aggression in the movie led to the name eliciting more aggression later.

Such seemingly simple and subtle associations may have an influence on how we behave toward other people. Changes in aggressive behavior may then occur as a result of prior associations formed through the process of classical conditioning. In 1970 Berkowitz reviewed the available literature on the learning of aggressive behavior and concluded that some human aggression could be understood as resulting from classical conditioning. Impulsive aggression, where an individual may react aggressively almost without thinking, seemed especially open to classical conditioning procedures. Berkowitz also concluded, however, that classical conditioning could not account for all types of violence that humans commit.

Operant Conditioning and Aggression

As we have seen earlier, operant conditioning procedures can also lead to learned motives. It seems likely, therefore, that operant conditioning principles would be involved with learned aggressive behaviors. As you will recall, in this type of learning a response leads to some consequence. If the consequence is reinforcing, the probability of the behavior that produced it will increase in the future. Thus if a young child hits a playmate and as a result gains access to a desired toy, it is reasonable to expect that the child will resort to hitting playmates in the future when he or she wants something they have.

Laboratory studies of operant aggression have sometimes used verbal reinforcement such as praise to alter aggressive behavior in humans. For example, Geen and Pigg (1970) conducted an experiment in which college students were told to deliver shock to another person when that person made mistakes in a learning task. The experimental group of subjects was praised for their aggressive behavior; the control group was not. The praised group delivered more shocks than the control group and, in addition, also used higher intensities. Later both groups were also given a word as-

sociation test; the praised group emitted more aggressive words, suggesting that the verbal reinforcement increased not only the aggressive behavior of delivering shocks but other aggressive responses as well.

The act of aggression may itself be reinforcing. Myer (1964) found, for example, that some rats will attack and kill mice even though given no conventional reward for doing so. These killer rats were not hungry, nor were they allowed to eat the mice they killed. Nevertheless, killer rats would reliably kill again and again when given the opportunity. Not all rats are killers; however, Myer and White (1965) found that rats that did kill mice would learn to choose the arm of a T-maze where they could attack and kill a mouse, whereas nonkillers would choose the arm containing a rat pup (which they do not kill). Killer rats have also been taught to press a lever in order to be given the opportunity to kill (Van Hemel, 1972).

Whether humans find aggression rewarding is not clear, but aggressive behavior in humans may be reinforced and maintained by secondary reinforcement: social approval by peers, increased attention, and so forth. Brownmiller (1975), for example, notes that social approval can become a powerful reinforcer of aggressive behavior in gangs.

In summary, it seems evident that aggressive responses are subject to the same rules of reinforcement as other behaviors. If aggressive behavior is followed by consequences that are positive for the individual, those aggressive responses will become more probable.

Modeled Aggression

We began this discussion of aggression with the example of individuals using behaviors they had seen demonstrated on television to attempt to extort money from airlines. Such behavior is termed observational learning or modeling.

The classic experiment of modeling of aggressive behavior was conducted by Bandura, Ross, and Ross (1961, 1963) and has been briefly mentioned at several points earlier in this book. Let us now look more closely at how these researchers demonstrated observational learning of aggressive behavior.

In their 1963 experiment they matched nursery school children on aggressiveness before the experiment began and assigned them to one of five groups. Group 1 observed adult models behaving in an aggressive way against a Bobo doll. Group 2 saw a filmed version of the same behavior. A third group watched a model in a cat suit performing the aggressive behaviors on a television. Two control groups were also run. The first control group (group 4) was not exposed to any modeled aggressive behavior; the second control group (group 5) saw an adult model behave in a calm, nonaggressive manner. Children in all five groups were then mildly frustrated and put into a new situation with a room containing toys, some of which were the same toys that the aggressive groups had seen used earlier by the models.

The models in this experiment had been instructed to use nontypical kinds of aggressive responses. In addition, the models used particular words such as *socko, pow*, and so forth while behaving aggressively. These nonstandard aggressive behaviors and the verbalizations were used to more easily determine when the children were modeling the behavior they had seen earlier. The results were clear. In all three of the groups that saw a model behave aggressively, imitative aggression was initiated. The children tended to use the same novel aggressive behaviors they had seen and also tended to use the verbalizations they had heard. These same responses were almost nonexistent in the two control groups, so it seems clear that these behaviors were modeled on the behavior the children had observed. Although the greatest degree of modeling occurred with the live model, statistical analyses showed that the filmed model was just as effective in producing the modeled aggressive behaviors. The children were less inclined to imitate the cartoon character, although the imitative behavior of this group was still considerably above that of the two control groups.

Of some theoretical interest was the additional finding that total aggressive responses of the three groups of children who had seen modeled aggression were also increased. That is, observing someone else behaving aggressively seemed to not only provide a model for novel aggressive responses but also had the effect of disinhibiting the typical aggressive behaviors of these children.

Although the studies of Bandura and his associates have been criticized as being unrealistic and perhaps biased toward the production of aggressive behavior (e.g., Bobo dolls are *designed* to be hit), the number of studies that have now accumulated (see, e.g., Bandura, 1973; Eron & Huesmann, 1984) makes it difficult to deny that aggressive behaviors can be learned through modeling.

From the brief summary of studies noted in this section, it is apparent that aggressive behavior can be learned. This learning may sometimes result from association of stimuli that are present at the time aggressive responses are triggered (classical conditioning). It may also occur because aggressive behavior is rewarded (operant conditioning). Finally, aggressive behavior may occur because it is observed in others, seen on television, or read about in the media (modeling). Although our nervous systems are surely programmed to allow aggressive behaviors to occur, many, if not most, of the circumstances in which these aggressive behaviors occur are learned. And just as we can learn when to aggress, we just as surely can learn to inhibit aggressive behaviors through these same learning processes.

SEXUAL MOTIVATION AND LEARNING

As we noted in Chapter Five, sexual motivation has some of the characteristics of drive. On the other hand, almost all researchers agree that in humans a large component of our sexual behavior is learned. Our culture teaches us rules of sexual conduct that are called **sexual values** (Luria et al., 1987). For example, societies decree what sexual behaviors are "normal" and under what conditions these behaviors should occur. They also teach us with whom we may have sex and with whom we may not.

We learn how to behave sexually by learning the rules of the society in which we live. The agents of this learning are parents and other relatives, religious and political leaders, books, movies, and television programs, sex education classes in schools, and even advertising. Although the learning is often incidental, we learn nevertheless.

Although we tend to think that the rules of our society are "correct," differing cultures also differ widely in what is acceptable. Extreme obesity was considered erotic in early Hawaiian society. In Polynesia the exchange of betel nuts and pepper was a sexual act between an unrelated man and a woman; eating together was forbidden of an adult brother and sister in one society because it was considered incestuous (Davenport, 1976). It is useful to remember that sexual values and behaviors considered appropriate or inappropriate can vary widely across cultures and thus must result from learning.

According to Luria and associates (1987), most people learn the rules of sexual behavior during adolescence. These writers indicate that in the United States sexual intercourse is approached through a series of increasingly intimate interactions, beginning with the most public and progressing to the most private parts of the body.

Sexual behavior usually begins with kissing. Initial kisses often are followed by "French" kisses, where the tongue is put into the partner's mouth. The next progression in this shared intimacy is usually exploration and fondling of the girl's breasts, first over clothes and later under the clothes by the boy. Next, the girl's genitals are fondled over clothes and then under clothes. At this point the girl often fondles the boy's genitals over clothes and, somewhat later, under clothes. By this time mutual manipulation of the genitals is common and may continue to orgasm or may be followed by intercourse. What is especially surprising and suggestive of the strong role of learning is the close agreement between males and females surveyed about the hierarchy of the sexual progression noted above (Bentler, 1968a, 1968b).

Obviously adolescents have learned what behaviors to engage in and in what order. It seems likely that much of this learning is a combination of information gained from same-sex friends, sexual exploration with a partner, and masturbation (Luria et al., 1987).

Research with animals also points out the importance of learning. Fillion and Blass (1986) exposed male rat pups to a specific odor (citral, a lemonlike scent) during suckling. When exposed in adulthood to receptive females scented with citral, these male rats ejaculated more quickly than when exposed to females not scented. Thus the early odor experience had an effect on later adult sexual behavior. Lorenz (1970) has argued that the early experience of imprinting (see Chapter Two) can create an irreversible bond that influences sexual behavior at maturity. As we saw in Chapter Two, however, the lasting effects of imprinting on later sexual behavior do not occur for all species (Mortenson, 1975).

As noted in Chapter Five, castrated male animals with prior sexual experience maintain sexual behavior longer when compared to sexually inexperienced males who have been castrated (Hart, 1974). This maintenance must be the result of learning. Additionally, Harlow and Harlow (1962, 1966) have shown that social isolation impairs the development of skills necessary for normal sexual behavior in monkeys. Although their monkeys appeared to have adequate sexual motivation, the monkeys had apparently not learned how to behave appropriately. The Harlows' results support the notion that learning is a crucial component in the expression of normal sexual behavior.

Many researchers believe that most variations in sexual behavior (fetishes, sadism, voyeurism, exhibitionism, and so forth) are also the result of learning processes. What is not clear, however, is how these particular sexual variations are learned. One example of a learned sexual variation is an experiment by Rachman (1966; see also Rachman & Hodgson, 1968), who was able to produce a boot fetish in three male subjects by pairing slides of boots with slides of nude women. For the three subjects, who were young, unmarried psychologists, penis volume changes were obtained to the boots after 24–65 pairings of the boot-nude slides. The artificial fetish was extinguished at the conclusion of the experiment. This particular learned sexual behavior can be understood as an example of classical conditioning. Although it seems evident that learning plays a major role in the sexual behavior of humans, the conditions that exist at the time sexual behaviors are learned are usually not known. Future research may provide some insight into how various sexual behaviors are learned.

SUMMARY

In this chapter we have examined the role of learning in the development and direction of motivation. As we have seen, three separate learning processes—classical conditioning, operant conditioning, and modeling—are capable of developing motivational states.

Classical conditioning has been shown to be involved in the generation of experimental neuroses, the development and elimination of emotionally motivated states, and learned aversions. Additionally, appropriate situations can lead to the classical conditioning of interoceptive states, which can in turn contribute to psychosomatic illness.

Operant conditioning techniques can also generate motivation. Parameters of reinforcement such as quantity and quality of reward influence motivation; in general, more and better quality rewards generate more motivation. Contrasts between differing amounts of reinforcement are also important for motivation; the past history of reinforcement influences the motivational value of current reinforcers. The interaction of classical and operant conditioning is also an important factor in learned motives. Acquired fears, conditioned emotional responses, and learned helplessness are all examples of motivation generated as the result of this interaction.

Human motivation can also be generated through the simple observation of others. When we see others rewarded for behaving in particular ways, we not only learn those behaviors through observation but are also motivated by their successes to behave in a like manner. If we wish to understand motivated behavior, we clearly must examine how learning contributes to its development.

SUGGESTIONS FOR FURTHER READING

Bandura, A. (1973). *Aggression: A social learning analysis*. Englewood Cliffs, N.J.: Prentice-Hall. Bandura presents a large body of research concerned with the learning of aggression through the observation of models.

Seligman, M. E. P. (1975). *Helplessness: On depression, development, and death*. San Francisco: Freeman. This book provides a good introduction to the concept of helplessness.

Chapter Seven

Incentive Motivation

CHAPTER PREVIEW

This chapter is concerned with the following questions:

1. What is incentive motivation?

2. How has incentive motivation been explained theoretically?

3. How have the concepts of expectancy and meaningfulness been incorporated into the incentive concept?

Bob drove down the highway looking both right and left at the restaurant signs. It was almost noon and he had not had anything except coffee since lunch yesterday. He had worked all night on a new advertising promotion for the bank and had, just moments before, finished it. The position of senior advertising analyst had recently opened up, and he thought he had a good chance for the position if his current campaign was successful. It was something he had worked toward for the past three years, and his promotion now hinged on this one project.

As Bob drove along, stopping frequently because of red lights, he mused about where to eat. The familiar fast-food stores crossed his vision, but he was unmoved by them. What he really wanted was a big steak and a baked potato and salad, not a greasy hamburger and cold French fries. The thought of the steak made his mouth water, and he increased the speed of his car. . . .

This short vignette of a few moments in the life of a fictitious individual illustrates several ideas concerning the concept of incentive motivation. Just what do we mean by **incentives** and **incentive motivation**?

First, it is important to note that the term *incentive* usually describes some goal object that motivates us (e.g., a big steak was an incentive for Bob). Incentives, then, are generally important for us to either reach or avoid. Like Bob, we may value the sensations associated with a good meal (a positive incentive) and avoid tasteless ones (a negative incentive). Incentives differ in value for us from moment to moment, in fact, and from one time to another. While Bob was working on his project, steak was not an incentive and did not influence his behavior; but after the project was completed, a good meal was an incentive that caused him to drive down a crowded highway in order to obtain it. We may also assume that after he eats the meal, another similar meal would hold little value for him, although other incentives may now influence his behavior.

Incentives, then, motivate behavior. This can be seen in yet another way in the story of Bob. A strong motivation existed in him to gain the promotion to senior advertising analyst and had in fact influenced his behavior for several years. The incentive of promotion was strong enough to override temporarily his physiological needs for food and sleep. Another point to observe in the episode is that incentives are not wired in but are learned. Bob was not born with a need to become senior advertising analyst; somewhere along the way he learned something that made this an important goal for him. Finally, the story of Bob illustrates the idea that thoughts can serve as incentive motivators. We will explore this approach later in this chapter and more fully in Part IV of this book.

The concept of incentives as motivators of behavior has been a useful tool in attempting to explain why people (and animals) do the things they do. Its use in theory recognizes that objects or events can modify and influence our behavior over and above physical needs.

Incentive motivation may be thought of as a mediator (M) that comes between the stimulus characteristics (S) of some goal object and the responses (R) that are directed toward that object. We can view this relationship between stimulus, mediator, and response as S → M → R. Further, Overmier and Lawry (1979) have provided considerable evidence that this linkage actually consists of two separate links, one between the stimulus and the mediator (S → M) and a second between the mediator and the response (M → R), so that the relationship should be analyzed as S → M, M → R. Each link may be separately influenced by the conditions in situations where incentives are present, so

the possible outcomes of manipulating incentive motivation can be rather complex.

Incentive theorists have been concerned with how M is established and what properties of M cause it to alter behavior. As we shall discover, most theorists have emphasized classical conditioning as the way in which M is established, but they disagree on its properties. One approach has emphasized the energizing properties of M, a second has suggested that emotionality is important, while a third has emphasized the informational aspects of the mediator. We shall examine each of these approaches in the following sections.

INCENTIVES AS ENERGIZERS

As noted in Chapter Five, the concept of drive was once the primary device used to account for the motivation of behavior. Several experiments, however, showed that external objects (i.e., goals) also motivate behavior, thus forcing a modification of this system. As representative of this work, we will reexamine the classic experiment of Crespi (1942) discussed in Chapter Six.

Recall that Crespi trained rats to run down an alleyway to get pellets of food. One group of rats got a large reward (256 pellets), while a second group got a small reward (1 pellet) for the same behavior. A third group served as a control, receiving 16 pellets throughout the experiment. On the twentieth trial, Crespi switched the large- and small-reward groups to 16 pellets so that all three groups received the same number of pellets per trial. The large-reward group, now getting smaller rewards, abruptly slowed down in relation to the control group; the small-reward group, now receiving a larger reward, quickly began running much faster in relation to the controls. Figure 7.1 shows the results of his study. Zeaman (1949) obtained similar results under similar conditions.

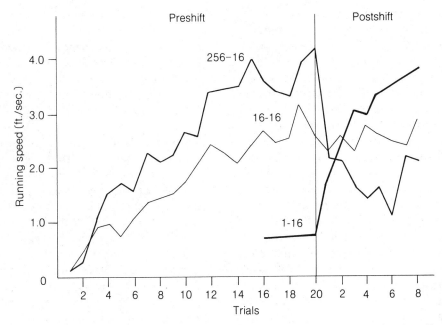

Figure 7.1 *Crespi's (1942) incentive motivation experiment. Groups were given 1, 16, or 256 pellets of food. On trial 20 all groups were switched to 16 pellets. Note how running speed shifts rapidly when the conditions of reinforcement change. (Adapted from Crespi, 1942. Used by permission.)*

The important point for our present discussion of Crespi's experiment is that the behavior (of running down the alleyway) changed drastically and quickly when the incentives were changed. Hull's drive theory could not explain the immediate changes in behavior observed when the incentives were shifted; these changes were too abrupt to result from changes in habit strength (i.e., sHr) or drive (D). Up to the time of Crespi's experiment, theorists such as Hull had assumed that different amounts or sizes of reward influence the rate of learning but do not alter the motivation of the organism. Crespi's study showed that just the opposite is true; different incentive objects influence how hard the organism is willing to perform but not what is learned. The term *incentive* was chosen to represent this type of motivation.

Incentive Motivation K

In the early 1950s theorists began to incorporate the concept of incentive into their explanations of behavior (e.g., Hull, 1951, 1952; Spence, 1956). For Hull reaction potential (i.e., behavior) was now seen as a joint function of learning (i.e., habit strength), drive (D), stimulus intensity (V), and incentive motivation (K). If the anticipation of a goal influences the motivation of an organism, then the next question becomes: How do incentives develop?

Hull-Spence and r_g-s_g Because of the general similarity of their approaches, we will consider Hull and Spence together. Both used the symbol *K* for incentive motivation in their formulas for behavior, and both assumed that the incentive value of a goal object could be indexed by the vigor of the **consummatory response** it elicited. Thus a large reward should lead to more vigorous chewing and swallowing, in the case of food, than a small reward. The consummatory response (symbolized as R_g), however, does not occur in a vacuum; for rats the stimuli of the goal box are present during its occurrence (e.g., visual sensations of the food cup, texture of the floor, brightness of the walls, and so on). Stimuli present when R_g occurs will become associated with it (via classical conditioning) and will tend, after a few trials, to elicit R_g directly. To the extent that these stimuli (e.g., the same floor texture and wall brightness in the start box of a maze) also occur before the organism reaches the goal box, they will tend to elicit R_g before the goal. Now it would be rather disruptive (and maladaptive) if a rat sitting in the start box of a maze responded with a full-blown R_g, chewing and swallowing nonexistent food. At the very least it would interfere with the necessary responses of getting from the start box to the goal box, where the food could actually be obtained. For this reason it was assumed that stimuli similar to those present in the goal box would elicit only a **partial consummatory response** (symbolized as r_g), which would not interfere with the instrumental responses (e.g., running) required in order to reach the food. Thus a rat might salivate or make small chewing movements in the start box but would not express the full-blown R_g.

This approach further assumed that the organism could sense that it was making these r_g's. For example, close your eyes and hold your right arm out straight. Now with your eyes still closed, bend your elbow 90 degrees. Even with your eyes closed, you know that your arm is bent because of sensory feedback from your arm muscles and joints. The logic for sensing the r_g's is the same; sensory feedback in the form of stimuli (symbolized as s_g) inform the organism that it is making r_g's.

The occurrence of these partial responses and their stimuli, commonly called the **r_g-s_g mechanism**, serves to motivate the instrumental responses that must be made in order to get to the goal box and engage in the R_g. This explanation, we should emphasize, is entirely a mechanical one. Through the process of classical conditioning, the stimuli in the environment come to elicit small parts of the final R_g, and the feedback from these responses serves to motivate ongoing behavior. Though the sight of a rat frantically pushing at the door of the start box might appear to express the rat's anticipation of an expected reward at the end of the maze, the model assumes no thinking on the part of the rat. We could in fact program a computer to behave similarly. Hull (1930, 1931) originally proposed the r_g-s_g mechanism to explain the apparent purposiveness of behavior and the anticipation of goals. Spence (1956) applied the mechanism to incentive motivation, proposing that incentive motivation is the result of these r_g's and their feedback s_g.

Incidentally, r_g-s_g occurs throughout the path from start box to goal box, to the extent that stimuli are similar along the way. As the organism approaches the goal area, more and more stimuli should occur that have been associated with R_g; thus r_g-s_g should increase and increasingly motivate ongoing behavior. This accounts for the often observed phenomenon that organisms appear more motivated (e.g., by running faster) near the goal. Figure 7.2 provides a schematic representation of the process.

But what if the stimuli are different in the beginning than at the goal? The answer is that the stimuli that become associated with R_g and thus develop r_g-s_g do not have to be external to the organism. The sensations we feel when hungry, for example, are with us all the way from start to goal; and because they are present when R_g occurs, they should also elicit a fractional anticipatory response (r_g). These

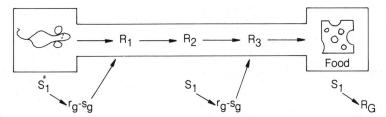

Figure 7.2 The r_g-s_g mechanism. Food at the end of the runway leads to the consummatory response R_g. Any stimuli present at the time R_g occurs will tend to elicit a fraction of that response (r_g). When these stimuli (S_1) appear earlier in the maze, they will call forth r_g and its feedback stimulus s_g. The r_g-s_g complex then serves to energize the instrumental responses (R_1, R_2, and so on) that lead to the goal.

stimuli are of course Hull's drive stimuli (S_d), which were discussed in Chapter Five.

One final point should be mentioned concerning the **fractional anticipatory response mechanism**, as r_g-s_g has come to be called. As originally formulated, it was a peripheral explanation of incentive motivation, and r_g was thought to consist of minute muscular responses and the associated sensory feedback from these muscle contractions. Attempts to locate and measure r_g's have not proven very successful (see Bolles, 1975, for a thorough review; also Beck, 1978; Black, 1969; Logan, 1968). Today many theorists postulate some sort of central mechanism that acts like the peripheral r_g-s_g mechanism. For example, sensing of stimuli associated with a past R_g may activate memories of the R_g that act as triggers for motivated responding.

Even though little direct evidence for the r_g-s_g mechanism exists, it still influences our theories as a conceptual model. As long as we maintain an ever critical eye and realize that the relationships between our model and reality may not be one to one, it may continue to prove useful.

The Persistence of Behavior

One area in which the fractional anticipatory response explanation of behavior is still very much alive is the study of behavior persistence.

Surely one of the most fundamental aspects of people's behavior is that it persists even in the face of difficulty. The question is, why? Amsel has been studying this question for many years (Amsel, 1972; Amsel & Roussel, 1952), and his answers suggest that a mechanism very much like the r_g-s_g mechanism may be involved.

Amsel and r_f-s_f Amsel has been primarily interested in the question of what happens when a rat reaches a goal where it has been rewarded in the past and now finds nothing. If the rat has been in the situation several times and has been rewarded, incentive motivation will have developed (following the Hull-Spence approach) via r_g-s_g. But if the rat now discovers that its efforts are for naught, according to Amsel, an unlearned **frustration response** occurs (symbolized as R_F). Any stimuli present at the time R_F occurs will tend to become associated with it; if stimuli also occur earlier in the sequence of events, they will tend to elicit **partial frustration responses (r_f)**. As with r_g-s_g, the organism knows it is making these responses because of feedback stimuli (s_f). These partial frustration responses typically cause the animal to stop its present behavior and engage in some other behavior (e.g., biting the experimenter). Frustration from nonreward, then, normally leads to competing responses that take the organism off in new and perhaps more adaptive directions.

Suppose, however, that we design our situation so that competing responses are difficult to make and also arrange that whatever original responses *can* be made have been followed by reward in the past. What would happen?

Amsel proposed that the partial frustration responses (r_f) and their associated stimulus feedback (s_f) become **counterconditioned** to the responses the organism is making. By using the term *counterconditioning*, Amsel suggested that the motivation generated by the frustration of nonreward is channeled into the very response that causes frustration. The competing responses that would normally develop as a result of this frustration are countered by the situation, and the motivation becomes conditioned to the only responses that can easily occur: the responses leading to the sometimes reward-filled goal box. In other words, the r_f-s_f mechanism serves as a motivator for ongoing behavior, just as r_g-s_g would under other circumstances.

When might such circumstances as just described occur? The answer is: when an animal is put on a partial reinforcement schedule. On such a schedule some responses are rewarded with a bit of food or a lick of water, while at other times the same responses go unrewarded. One of the best-established phenomena in psychology is that organisms reinforced on a partial reinforcement schedule persist in their responding longer when food is taken away (i.e., extinction) than others that have been reinforced for every response (i.e., a continuous reinforcement schedule, or CRF).

How might frustration theory account for this persistence? During training the continuous reinforcement group is rewarded on every trial. Thus r_g-s_g should build up and motivate the necessary responses for reaching the goal. For the partial reinforcement group, r_g-s_g would build up too, although more slowly, on those training trials that are rewarded. In addition, however, r_f-s_f would build up on

trials that went unrewarded. Initially this would lead to competing responses (resulting in less or slower behavior). These competing responses would eventually die out because they always went unreinforced (i.e., extinguish), and r_f-s_f would become counterconditioned to the same response that r_g-s_g is activating. For the partial reinforcement group, then, we have two sources of incentive motivation on every trial, r_g-s_g (built up on rewarded trials) and r_f-s_f (built up on nonrewarded trials). Because the competing responses generated by r_f-s_f have extinguished, the incentive motivation generated by r_f-s_f will become channeled into whatever responses are occurring (i.e., the responses leading to the goal because they are sustained by r_g-s_g).

Now for the crucial part. In extinction the CRF group responds and goes unrewarded. This leads to R_F and thus to r_f-s_f and the development of competing responses. If the reward has been permanently removed, the incentive effects of r_g-s_g will die out rather quickly and become replaced by r_f-s_f and competing responses. Because r_f-s_f has never been counterconditioned in CRF animals, its occurrence will not cause the running responses to continue but will lead to a quick cessation of responding—because r_g-s_g is no longer present to sustain the correct responses—and r_f-s_f will elicit competing responses. Continuously reinforced animals consequently stop responding rather quickly. The partially reinforced group, on the other hand, has two sources of motivation that have been connected to the responses no longer being rewarded. The r_g-s_g part will die out, but the responding will continue longer in this group because it is sustained by the motivation generated by r_f-s_f. Amsel's approach therefore provides a neat explanation of the well-known fact that partially reinforced responses are more persistent than continuously reinforced responses. This effect is called the **partial reinforcement extinction effect (PREE)** and is quite reliable.

If one stops and considers the "real" world, one soon discovers that partial reinforcement is the rule rather than the exception. Perhaps only in the laboratory can we constrain the environment in such a way as to make continuous reinforcement possible. We make many hundreds of responses every day, most of which are not immediately, if ever, rewarded; yet we persist. Why? Perhaps for the same reason the rat does—because sometimes it pays off, and nothing else seems to work.

The frustration of doing badly on a test may motivate us to study harder for the next one (if we have been rewarded in the past by studying hard). On the other hand, doing poorly on a test may lead to competing behavior (e.g., listening to our favorite record albums). The important point is that frustration will channel into ongoing behavior and make it more persistent if that behavior has been rewarded at some time in the past; otherwise it will lead to competing behavior that will reduce persistence. Thus the type of behavior activated depends upon our past experiences with reward and nonreward.

What sort of evidence did Amsel provide in support of his ideas? Actually quite a bit.

In a now classic experiment, Amsel and Roussel (1952) ran rats in the situation depicted in Figure 7.3. Rats ran from the start box to Goal Box 1, where they were fed; then ran Alley 2 to Goal Box 2 to get additional food. After training the rats on this procedure, food was sometimes withdrawn from Goal Box 1. Amsel surmised that this should lead to

R_f, which would show up as faster running in Alley 2 on nonreinforced trials. He compared the speed of traversing Alley 2 on reinforced versus nonreinforced trials and found that, indeed, rats ran faster after nonreinforced trials. While the results of this experiment were open to several alternative explanations, further research has tended to support Amsel's approach. Nonreward following a response that has been regularly reinforced in the past apparently does energize behavior, as Amsel claimed it should.

Does frustrative nonreward lead to competing behavior? Again research seems to bear Amsel out. In a study by Adelman and Maatsch (1955), two groups of rats were taught to run to a goal box to obtain food. Later the food was withheld (i.e., extinction was introduced). One group of rats was allowed to retrace its path from the goal box to the start box, while the second group was allowed to escape from the situation by jumping completely out of the goal box. The rats allowed to retrace their path quickly extinguished, while the rats allowed to jump out of the goal box continued to run to the goal box for many trials. For both groups, the frustration of nonreward led to new responses, as Amsel predicted. The rats allowed to retrace developed a new response that competed with the old running response, and they extinguished quickly. For the rats allowed to jump out, competition between this response and the running response did not occur, and they extinguished much more slowly. Thus frustrative nonreward does seem

Figure 7.3 Diagram of the experimental situation in Amsel and Roussel's 1952 frustration experiment. See text for explanation.

to produce new responses that can compete with previously learned responses.

A study by Ross (1964) provides strong support for both the energizing effects of frustration and the incorporation of this energy into behaviors present at the time frustration occurs. In the first phase of the experiment, six groups of rats were trained to make one of three responses in order to get food. Three of the groups received continuous (100%) reinforcement and served as controls against which the others, receiving partial (50%) reinforcement, could be compared. For two of the groups, the required response was to run to the food well; for two other groups, the correct response was to jump a gap in the floor to get to the food; and for the last two groups, the correct response was to climb a wire mesh wall in order to reach the food. (One group in each pair was continuously reinforced for making the correct response, while the other group was partially reinforced.) All three responses were about equal in difficulty and were in fact learned at approximately the same rate. Amsel's frustration theory predicts that the animals in the three partially reinforced groups should experience frustration on the nonreinforced trials and that the resulting r_f-s_f should become conditioned to whatever response the rats had to learn to get to the goal (i.e., running, jumping, or climbing).

In a second phase of the experiment, all six groups were taught to run for water in an experimental chamber different from that used in phase 1 and were reinforced 100% of the time. In the crucial final phase of the experiment, the running response to water was extinguished. The extinction process should reinstate frustration, and Amsel's theory predicts that the responses conditioned to frustration during phase 1 should lead to differing rates of extinction in the final phase of the experiment as a function of whether the response initially associated with r_f-s_f facili-

tated or hindered the running response learned in phase 2. For the animals taught to run in phase 1, the frustration reinstated during extinction should lead to increased persistence, because running was the correct response in phase 2, and r_f-s_f should channel into the ongoing response. For rats taught to jump in phase 1, reinstitution of frustration by extinction should interfere somewhat with running and reduce resistance to extinction. For the climbing group, reinstitution of frustration should call up the climbing response, which should seriously interfere with the running response, and extinction should occur quickly. The three partial reinforcement groups, when compared against their respective continuous reinforcement controls, behaved as predicted by frustration theory.

Ross's data provide confirmation of both the energizing effects of frustration and the channeling of this energization into ongoing behavior. Further, the effects of this channeling on behavioral persistence were shown to depend upon the relationship of the energized response to the response being extinguished. The energized response may lead to either greater or reduced resistance depending upon whether it facilitates or hinders the response undergoing extinction.

Amsel's frustration theory appears able to handle many of the phenomena known in learning and motivation research. It is an incentive theory because the presence or absence of the goal influences the motivation of the organism. Anticipatory frustration responses and their stimulus feedback (i.e., r_f-s_f) may lead to the energizing of competing behavior or to the activation of instrumental behavior, depending upon the circumstances. The persistence of behavior, then, is established according to the organism's past history with the incentive.

Amsel (1972) in fact saw frustration theory as part of a more general theory of persistence. Persistence develops whenever organisms learn to approach or to continue responding despite stimuli that would normally disrupt that behavior. This occurs because the disruptive stimuli become counterconditioned to the ongoing responses in the situation. Amsel noted that emotional responses and their consequent feedback stimuli are often disruptive, but they often eventually become counterconditioned to ongoing behavior.

Consider the emotional arousal you feel when the deadline for a paper approaches. The unpleasant emotional state may initially lead to all sorts of competing behaviors that "put off" the work necessary for completion of the paper. If, however, you begin to work on the paper as a result of the emotion produced by the approaching deadline, you may discover that these feelings will generate the responses needed to complete the task. One might argue in fact that one aspect of a "good" student's behavior is that he or she has learned to channel (i.e., countercondition) the emotionality and frustrations of college life into constructive behavior. Academically poorer students, on the other hand, may not have learned to countercondition their emotions and frustrations in appropriate ways.

The concept of counterconditioning implies that emotional responses will not lose their "emotional quality" until they become attached to ongoing behavior. If for some reason they do not become attached, these emotion-producing stimuli will continue to disrupt behavior.

Amsel's frustration theory has proven enormously successful; however, it is only one of several theories that attempt to describe how incentive motivation may alter behavior. And it has been criticized on a number of points (e.g., Bolles & Moot, 1972; Staddon, 1970). Also, Amsel's theory describes the motivating properties of the removal of an expected incentive; it does not deal directly with the positively motivating properties of incentive availability, which is assumed to be covered by the r_g-s_g mechanism.

INCENTIVES AS GENERATORS OF EMOTION

The research of Amsel and his colleagues provides support for the notion that the mediating effect of an incentive is motivational; other theorists, such as Neal Miller, Frank Logan, and O. Hobart Mowrer, have taken somewhat different approaches. We will examine Mowrer's theory as one alternative to the r_g-s_g approach because he proposes that incentive motivation mediates between stimulus and response by creating emotional states.

Mowrer: Fear, Hope, Relief, and Disappointment

Mowrer (1960) argued that incentive motivation is the primary instigator of behavior. For Mowrer incentive motivation is closely tied to the learning of emotional responses. He proposed four primary emotions: fear, hope, relief, and disappointment.

According to Mowrer, any increase in drive (e.g., from electric shock or food deprivation) leads to the emotion of fear. The emotional responses associated with the state of fear will become connected to any stimuli that are present at the time the emotion occurs. After several such pairings, the stimuli become cues that signal the approach of an increase in drive and create a state of fear before the actual arrival of the increased drive state. This conditioned fear then motivates the organism to make whatever responses it can to remove itself from the situation containing the fear cues. The role of reinforcement in Mowrer's system is to activate one of the four emotions rather than to influence instrumental responses directly. For Mowrer, then, learning alters what the organism wants to do (i.e., incentive) rather than what the organism can do.

In an analysis similar to that of fear, Mowrer proposed that a decrease in drive (e.g., from a full stomach) is accompanied by the emotion of hope. Any cues present at the time hope occurs will become associated with the emotion and eventually begin to serve as signals that a decrease in drive (and thus hope) is imminent. Thus again Mowrer saw behavior as being activated by an emotional incentive. Stimuli that produce the emotion of hope will activate behaviors that keep the organism in their presence, while stimuli associated with fear will activate avoidance behaviors.

Mowrer proceeded a step further to analyze the situation in which hope is expected (because the cues for it are present) but not forthcoming. Such a situation leads to the third emotional construct of incentive motivation—disappointment. Disappointment occurs when hope cues that predict a decrease in drive do not lead to an actual drive reduction. Disappointment, like fear, is a negative state for the organism and motivates behavior that will have the effect of removing the cues that signal disappointment.

Finally, in a symmetrical fashion to his analysis of disappointment, Mowrer proposed the emotion of relief. Relief occurs when a cue that signals an increase in drive is taken away. Stimuli present at the time the fear cues are removed will become relief signals. Thus a bell ending a difficult laboratory class could become a relief cue if the stimuli associated with the class have become fear cues. As with hope, organisms attempt to maintain situations that predict relief.

Let's look at an example. A rat is taught to press a lever in order to obtain pellets of food. Food in the stomach reduces drive and thus produces hope. A light above the bar is always on when food arrives. After several trials in which the rat obtains food in the presence of the light, the light becomes a cue that food (and therefore a decrease in drive) is about to occur. At this point the light will activate behaviors that keep the rat in its presence, and it becomes an activator of hope even before the food arrives. If we carry our imaginary experiment a step further, we can see how Mowrer's concept of disappointment might work. Suppose we sound a tone for five seconds, after which we turn off the light and remove the lever from the chamber. After a few pairings of tone and light, the tone will become a cue signaling the removal of hope. The tone will activate the emotion of disappointment as well as behaviors designed to remove the rat from this aversive situation.

Mowrer's approach to incentive motivation emphasized the importance of emotion as a mediator between the stimulus characteristics of incentive objects and instrumental behavior; thus, **rewards and punishers generate emotion.** Cues associated with the triggering of emotion eventually become capable of triggering the emotion before the emotion-producing event. The activation of this anticipatory emotion then directs instrumental behavior toward or away from objects in the environment.

Mowrer's position is unique in its recognition of both drive induction and drive reduction as contributors to behavior. Fear and disappointment cues signal drive induction situations, while hope and relief cues signal drive reduction situations. We should keep in mind, however, that the motivators of behavior are the emotions, not the drive conditions directly. Changes in drive serve to establish the various emotions (Bolles, 1967).

Bolles (1967) and Miller (1963) have pointed out several conceptual difficulties with Mowrer's approach. Miller noted that although the system can account for much behavior once behaviors start occurring, it does not explain how behavior is triggered the first time. For example, once a rat has learned that cues in the start box of a maze are associated with hope because food is in the goal box, behavior will continue; but what causes the rat to traverse the maze the first time? Mowrer provided no ready answer, and Miller considered this problem a fatal flaw in the theory.

INCENTIVES AS CARRIERS OF INFORMATION

Mowrer's approach suggests that informational stimuli generate emotions that in turn lead to approach or withdrawal behavior in the situation. Other theorists have also emphasized the importance of the informational aspects of cues for incentive motivation. Their theories emphasize the idea that incentive motivation serves to mediate between stimulus and response because predictive stimuli generate incentive motivation, which in turn directs appropriate responding. Although these approaches are in many respects similar to Mowrer's, they differ in emphasis; emotions are seen not as the instigators of behavior but as cues that predict (i.e., provide information about) the goal and direct behaviors toward that goal. The concept of predictability as an explanation for incentive effects owes much to the theoretical concepts of Tolman. Let us turn, then, to Tolman's ideas before we examine the concept of predictability.

Tolman: Cognitive Formulations

The approaches we have examined so far have emphasized mechanical explanations of incentive effects on behavior, but not all theorists have chosen to view incentives in that way. Most notable among this latter group was Tolman, who argued that incentive motivation results from the development of expectancies. Let us briefly examine his point of view.

Edward Chase Tolman (1959, 1967) provides a good counterpoint to the theories of Hull and Spence. While those researchers attempted to reduce behavior to the smallest possible unit (an approach termed **reductionism**), Tolman took a much more wholistic view. Tolman was much less concerned with the particular muscular responses made on the way to the goal than with the fact that organisms worked to obtain goals. He viewed behavior as purposive; rats as well as humans, he thought, develop expectations that particular behaviors will lead to particular goals.

Tolman (1967) pointed out that different goals have different values for an organism. For example, Simmons (1924) trained rats to find their way through a complex maze, and different groups received different rewards at the end. She found that a group given bread and milk performed better than a second group given sunflower seeds as a reward, and the second group, in turn, performed better than a group given nothing. In a similar experiment Elliott (1928) found that wet bran led to better performance in a complex maze than sunflower seeds.

Following the earlier work of Blodgett (1929), Tolman and his students continued work on **latent learning**. These studies attempted to show that reinforcement is not necessary for learning to occur. Additionally, they showed the importance of appropriate incentives for the performance of learning. In these experiments groups of rats were trained to traverse a complex maze. One group received food at the end of the maze and learned to run quickly and reduce errors to receive the reward. A second group received nothing at the end of the maze; its performance showed little indication of having learned how to get through the maze efficiently. A third group received nothing in the maze until the eleventh trial, when it began to receive food rewards. During the first ten trials, this third group, like group 2, showed little evidence of any learning. When reward was introduced, however, the third group's performance rapidly improved to the level of group 1. This change in performance was quite rapid and indicated to Tolman that learning had in fact occurred during the first ten trials but was not apparent in performance until the food incentive was introduced (Tolman & Honzik, 1930a).

These experiments led Tolman to conclude that goal objects exert different amounts of demand on performance, or, in simpler terms, that incentives differ in value. Incentives, then, come to have control over behavior, their effects depending upon the value of the particular incentive for the organism.

Expectancy An important aspect of Tolman's view was that incentive objects influence behavior only if they are experienced enough times so that a **cognitive expectation** is built up. By cognitive expectation, Tolman meant that the organism, after several experiences with a goal, comes to expect that particular behaviors will lead to that goal in the future. Thus the rat that has received wet bran mash ten times in a row for traversing a maze will come to expect that traversing the maze *this time* will lead to wet bran mash.

What would happen if, as devious experimenters, we sneakily changed the rules of the game? Tolman said that changing incentives after an expectation has been acquired leads to a disruption of behavior, particularly if the change is from a more demanded to a less demanded incentive. Tolman noted in fact that just such a change provides evidence for the existence of cognitive expectancies. As an example of such an experiment, he cited a classic study by Tinklepaugh (1928) in which monkeys observed an experimenter place food under one of two containers; then after a short delay, they were required to choose the correct container. On some trials Tinklepaugh changed the reward from a more preferred substance, such as banana, to a less preferred

substance, such as lettuce. The monkeys, upon discovering the lettuce, did not eat it but searched for the "lost" banana and sometimes shrieked at the experimenter as if angry (apparently the monkeys also had some expectation of where the devious change originated). For Tolman disruption of the normal, learned behavior of choosing the container under which the monkey had seen food placed indicated that a cognitive expectation of obtaining a bit of banana had developed.

Tolman also recognized the interaction of the physiological state with the incentive value of the goal. Tolman cited an experiment by Szymanski in which a female rat was taught to run a maze in order to get to her litter. As the litter became older and no longer nursed, the speed and accuracy of the female rat declined, presumably because the litter was no longer a strongly valued incentive. Thus the changed physiological state reduced the incentive value of the litter.

Tolman, then, presented a model of incentive that emphasized the buildup of expectancies concerning the behaviors that will lead to certain goals. These expectancies both energize and guide behavior. Positive incentives are approached and negative incentives are avoided; more highly valued incentives energize behavior more than less valued incentives. When an expectancy is disconfirmed, as in the Tinklepaugh experiment, behavior is disrupted. Unlike the Hull-Spence approach, which explains incentives in terms of minute, partial, consummatory responses, Tolman conceived incentives as central representations (i.e., thoughts) of the relationship between particular behaviors and the goals to which they lead.

The theories of both Mowrer and Tolman emphasize the idea that predictive cues (expectancies) are important in the development of incentive motivation. Perhaps the mediating effect of an incentive depends upon its ability to predict goals in just this way. Several theories that stress the importance of predictability in the development of incentive motivation have been proposed; we will examine only two, the ideas of Overmier and Lawry and those of Bindra.

Predictability

Bolles and Moot (1972), in a review of the incentive concept, suggested that cues become incentive motivators to the extent that they predict the arrival or withdrawal of some goal object. In their view, whether a cue takes on motivational control (i.e., incentive) or not depends upon whether it predicts some future event. Predictive cues are thought to motivate ongoing behavior and reinforce completed responses (i.e., act as secondary reinforcers).

One way to make a cue predictive is to pair it with a reinforcer such as food in a classical conditioning procedure. Each time the stimulus is presented, so is the food. Once the stimulus has been paired with a reinforcer for several trials, we can then change the situation so that a bar-press response is required in order to obtain food. The question of interest is whether presentation of the cue associated with food in the classical conditioning situation will influence the learning of the bar-press response. If bar pressing is facilitated by the presence of the cue, we have evidence for an incentive effect of the cue (appropriate control groups are necessary, however, in order to say that the cue previously associated with food facilitates the instrumental response).

Experiments involving this transfer-of-control design have often obtained facilitation (see Bolles & Moot, 1972; Trapold & Overmier, 1972). Bolles and Moot noted, for example, that cues associated with food facilitate performance of an operant response, while cues predicting the withdrawal of food have a demotivating effect. This suggests the interesting possibility that we may find ourselves unmotivated to perform certain be-

haviors because the cues associated with the task predict lack of success. Perhaps the child who has little motivation for schoolwork is immersed in a school or home environment that contains cues paired with a lack of success in the past. These cues would have a demotivating effect on the child's performance, and because the pairing process requires nothing of the child other than exposure to the cues, the child will probably not even be aware of why school is a bore. Clearly it is important, both theoretically and practically, to understand how predictive cues may influence the motivation of organisms.

As noted at the beginning of this chapter, incentive motivation can be conceptualized as acting like a mediator between environmental stimuli and responses to those stimuli. Further, Overmier and Lawry (1979) regard the mediational aspect of incentives as composed of two separate links: there is one link between the stimulus and mediator (S → M) and a second independent link between the mediator and response (M → R). Considerable evidence has now accumulated (see Overmier & Lawry, 1979, for an extensive review) that one way in which incentives mediate behavior is through their informational properties; incentives, according to this point of view, serve as cues that aid in response selection. Overmier and Lawry have noted, however, that an informational explanation cannot account for all that is known about mediation effects in transfer-of-control experiments, and they have further suggested that incentives have both an energizing *and* a cueing function. Thus when cues associated with a goal reappear at a later time or in a different situation, they are thought to both energize behavior and direct responding according to associations they have gained earlier. Though both energizing and informational aspects of mediators play a role in altering learning and performance, Overmier and Lawry have provided evidence that the informational aspects are more important, at least in situations where these two aspects of an incentive compete for the control of behavior. The data presented by Overmier and Lawry (1979) for their dual-link, mediation explanation of incentive effects are based on a series of complex and subtle experiments that are beyond the scope of this discussion; however, the studies reported by them support the view that incentives alter performance because they provide information about goals.

Stimuli that are consistently associated with reinforcement become reinforcers in their own right and are called **secondary** (or **conditioned**) **reinforcers**. Many theorists now believe that reinforcement serves to develop incentive motivation rather than to strengthen stimulus-response connections (Bindra, 1969; Klinger, 1977; Trapold & Overmier, 1972). This means that secondary reinforcers are also incentive motivators and should have both energizing and response selection properties.

Most of us have probably never considered why money is worth working to obtain. It is, after all, just paper and ink or small circular globs of metal. Why then do we value it? We value money because we associate it with rewards that have value for us. These may be either physiological (e.g., money buys food, water, and even sex) or learned (e.g., money buys status, a new car, or a house in suburbia). For humans, then, money serves as a strong secondary reinforcer. Because secondary reinforcers are also incentive motivators, money activates and directs our behavior because it predicts the availability of items of importance to us; if we could not buy items with money, having it would not be motivating. In periods of inflation any given amount of money (e.g., a dollar) does become less motivating. Many years ago a dollar would get us into a movie and buy us a bag of popcorn too. Today parking in the lot next to the movie theater in most large cities will cost at least a dollar. A dollar obviously does not have the same incentive value it once had because it predicts less (in terms of what it represents or can be exchanged for) than it did formerly.

It is important to recognize that incentives are relative rather than absolute. How motivating a particular incentive will be depends upon the background of events against which it is compared. Because the background changes over time, so too will the value of incentives.

The work of Trapold and Overmier (1972), Bolles and Moot (1972), and Overmier and Lawry (1979), as well as others, has contributed a great deal to our understanding of the manner in which a stimulus associated with a goal can become an incentive motivator. Dalbir Bindra at McGill University developed a motivational model that incorporates not only predictive cues but also organismic states (i.e., drive) and goals. Let us turn now to a brief overview of his thinking. (For a fuller understanding of Bindra's approach, see Bindra, 1968, 1969, 1972, 1974.)

The Bindra Model   Bindra has proposed a model of behavior that emphasizes the production of a central motive state (first proposed by Morgan, 1943) that activates goal-directed behaviors toward incentive objects. According to Bindra, motivational state and emotional state are identical, so his model is also a model of emotional behavior.

Bindra argued that a central motive state is generated whenever certain organismic conditions exist (e.g., changes in hormonal conditions, blood sugar, and so on) and the organism is stimulated by the properties of an incentive object (e.g., odor, taste, visual or auditory stimuli). Thus the organismic state (i.e., drive) and the stimuli from the goal object (i.e., incentive) combine to produce a central motive state.

The activation of this central motive state triggers innate sensory-motor coordinations (generally autonomic) such as salivation or heart rate changes that prepare the organism for contact with (or escape from) the incentive object. In addition, activation of the central motive state triggers sensory-motor coordinations previously established by either learning or maturation. For example, the central representation (i.e., memory) of the stimulus properties of food activates instrumental approach behaviors and, upon contact with food, consummatory behaviors such as chewing and swallowing.

Bindra's system assumes that incentive stimuli serve both energizing and direction functions. The steering of behavior is accomplished by the stimuli associated with the goal object (e.g., food) and serves to select the proper behaviors (e.g., approach, chewing, swallowing) rather than other possible responses. Neutral stimuli can become incentives through simple pairing with other incentives that already arouse the central motive state. Through this contingency learning process, a stimulus (e.g., the sound of a can being opened heard by your dog) can become a predictor of future stimuli (e.g., the odor, taste, and texture of the dog food) and serve to motivate behavior.

Our previous example illustrates how a stimulus can gain incentive properties, but let's also see how a stimulus can demotivate behavior. Suppose that a certain stimulus (S_1) always predicts the absence of a second stimulus (S_2). Suppose further that S_2 is a stimulus characteristic of some highly preferred goal object. Because S_1 predicts the absence of S_2, S_1 will suppress the central motive state. Unless the central motive state is present, behavior will not occur.

This brings us to a point that is probably obvious but is still worth mentioning. Incentive objects may be either positive or negative. Positive incentives elicit approach behavior, while negative incentives generate withdrawal. Because neutral cues can become attached to incentives, such formerly neutral cues can come to predict three relationships. A positive relationship (in which S_1 leads to S_2) predicts the imminent presentation of an incentive object. A negative relationship (in which presentation of S_1 is followed by the absence of S_2) predicts that the incentive, either good or bad, will not be forthcoming. Finally, a neutral relationship exists when a stimulus has no consistent relationship with the incentive and thus provides no information about its occurrence (i.e., S_1 predicts nothing about the occurrence of S_2). The particular behavior that one observes, then, will depend upon whether the incentive itself is positive or negative (e.g., food versus shock) plus the relationship between the stimuli that provide information about the incentive and incentive object. For example, a stimulus always associated with the absence of shock would be expected to elicit approach, while another stimulus associated with the absence of food would elicit withdrawal.

Bindra's system is particularly interesting because it attempts to provide in one coherent framework a model that includes the state of the organism (i.e., drive), the influence of the goal properties (i.e., incentive), and the association of cues with the incentive (i.e., predictability). More research is needed, however, before we can determine the usefulness of Bindra's motivation model.

Before ending our discussion of incentive motivation, we must examine one more theoretical approach. The approach proposed by Eric Klinger (1975, 1977) is important because it stresses cognitive factors (in a fashion similar to Tolman) and because it is an incentive theory derived from work with humans. As we will see, incentives in Klinger's system serve as mediators between stimulus and response to the extent that they are emotionally meaningful.

Klinger: Meaningfulness

Klinger's basic idea is the importance of meaningfulness for people's lives. Meaningfulness, in turn, is provided by incentives toward which people work. He believed that people pursue those objects, events, and experiences that are emotionally important for them. Thus emotionality is incorporated into the incentive concept for Klinger. If a person is deprived of the incentives important to him or her, life becomes less meaningful. People therefore work (i.e., behave) in order to obtain those incentives that are prized.

One interesting aspect of Klinger's approach is his demonstration that those incentives that provide meaningfulness are not extraordinary. In fact family, children, and personal relationships seem to be the most common sources of meaning for most people (Klinger, 1977). Klinger also noted that those people who are most certain that their lives are meaningful mention very concrete categories when describing what is meaningful for them.

Incentives and Goals   Klinger makes a distinction between incentives and goals in human behavior. Incentives are objects or events that are valued. However, people will not necessarily be willing to work to obtain everything that has incentive value. For example, a person might value owning a 50-foot yacht but be unwilling to behave in such a way as to obtain one (e.g., taking on a second job). While a yacht is an incentive because it is valued, it is not a goal unless the individual is willing to expend effort in order to obtain it. Thus goals are always incentives, but incentives may or may not also be goals.

Klinger noted that in a very real sense, no organism really exists separately from its goals (because goals such as food, water, and avoidance of pain are necessary for survival), although, at the human level, goals may include items unnecessary for survival (e.g.,

intimacy, understanding, religious belief, and so on). Thus goals and incentives are a part of the very fabric of life and influence behavior continually.

When a person decides to pursue a particular incentive (i.e., so that it becomes a goal), that person is said to be **committed** to that particular goal. Such a goal is termed a **current concern** by Klinger. An individual is usually committed to several current concerns at any one time, even though one's behavior is selective; that is, current concerns exist, even though behavior at any given moment may not reflect them.

Disengagement Phases   A current concern continues to influence behavior until either the goal is reached or the individual goes through the process of disengagement. Disengagement occurs when a goal that one is working toward is made unreachable. Klinger believed that available evidence from various sources suggests that disengagement from a goal involves a shifting of behavior through a cycle. This cycle can be conveniently described as consisting of five phases (though Klinger considered the cycle itself to be continuous):

1. **Invigoration**. If blocked from reaching a goal, the behavior of an individual at first becomes stronger. Klinger in fact considered Amsel's frustration effect (mentioned earlier in this chapter) as an example of invigoration. Klinger also suggested that one consequence of invigoration is that the blocked incentive becomes more attractive and other incentives become temporarily reduced in attractiveness (see Klinger, 1975, for a review of experiments leading to this conclusion). Thus the individual in the invigoration phase becomes rather single-minded in his or her attempt to reach the blocked goal.

2. **Primitivization**. If stronger, more concerted efforts do not succeed in making a goal obtainable, behavior is seen as becoming more stereotyped and primitive until it becomes destructive. For example, Barker, Dembo, and Lewin (1941) showed that children's play behavior becomes more primitive after frustration. Similarly, Hinton (1968) showed that adults respond more primitively on tests of originality and divergent thinking after frustration.

3. **Aggression**. As blocking of goal attainment continues, responding becomes more and more primitive until it becomes aggressive. Aggressive behavior as a response to blocking of goal attainments is well documented (e.g., Dollard et al., 1939; Johnson, 1972) and may be the individual's last attempt to obtain his or her goal before giving up (Klinger, 1975).

4. **Depression**. According to Klinger, when all attempts at reaching a goal fail, depression sets in. The depressive state may vary from mild disappointment to extreme depression. Typically, instrumental striving for the goal stops, and the individual expresses feelings of helplessness and hopelessness. Depressed individuals also become uninterested in the incentives that usually influence them and appear unmotivated in social interactions (Libet & Lewisohn, 1973). Klinger believed that depression is a normal part of disengaging from an unobtainable goal and that the depressive state may serve gradually to reduce the emotional value of the incentive so that other incentives may again be pursued.

5. **Recovery**. The final phase of the disengagement cycle is recovery. As Klinger noted, not much is known about what triggers recovery in the natural situation, but recovery usually does occur. Klinger suggested that successes in obtaining other goals may serve to stimulate recovery from depression. For example, Beck (1967) has shown that depressed patients are particularly sensitive to success in minor tasks.

Grief as Disengagement Anyone who has lost a close personal friend or relative through death knows the feelings associated with what is commonly called grief. Bowlby and Parkes (1970) suggested that working through the grief process involves four separate dimensions. First, there is **shock** or **numbness**, during which decision making may be difficult. During this stage the grieving individual may show panic, distress, and even anger. Phrases such as "this can't be" indicate difficulty in accepting the loss.

The second dimension of *mourning* (i.e., the working through of the grief) involves a **yearning and searching** for the lost person. Stimuli associated with the departed individual bring reactions of restlessness, anger, or ambiguity, and the grieving individual asks questions such as "What does it mean?" or "How can this be?"

The third dimension noted by Bowlby and Parkes involves **disorientation and disorganization**. This dimension often involves depression and feelings of guilt, as expressed by such thoughts as "Did I do all that I could?"

Finally, the fourth dimension involves **resolution and reorganization**. Gradually the individual begins to put the death of the loved one into perspective and begins to behave more competently. New roles may be assumed, and one's thoughts become congruent with the reality of the situation.

Bowlby and Parkes's dimensions of the mourning process bear striking resemblance to the disengagement cycle proposed by Klinger (1977). From Klinger's perspective the mourning process can be viewed as an example of disengaging from an important lost incentive (i.e., the loved one). Outbursts of panic and distress and feelings of restlessness represent the invigoration phase of the cycle, while anger and disbelief constitute the cycle's frustration-aggression aspect. Bowlby and Parkes's disorientation and disorganization dimension corresponds closely with Klinger's depression phase of the cycle, which generally precedes the final disengagement from the incentive and leads to behavior directed toward new incentives (or toward old ones temporarily overshadowed by the loss). Thus the resolution and reorganization dimension of Bowlby and Parkes corresponds well with Klinger's recovery phase.

An important point suggested by the analysis of grief is that an individual with several important incentives might be expected to deal with the loss of a loved one better than another who has few incentives other than the deceased. Perhaps with these latter individuals, we need to develop new important incentives or help them redirect their behavior toward existing incentives. We often seem to do this intuitively; at funerals people often express such advice as "You've got to live for your children now."

Incentives and Thoughts Klinger also presented evidence suggesting that incentives influence almost all of our behavior, including our thoughts and what we attend to. According to Klinger, thought (either in the form of language or images) may be divided into three categories: *blank states, respondent segments,* and *operant segments.*

1. **Blank States.** Blank states are periods of time during which no thought content is apparent. Incentives do not seem to influence blank states, but blank states may themselves be strong incentives (e.g., in

the individual who practices meditative techniques in order to obtain a blank state for a short time).

2. **Respondent Segments.** Respondent thought is thinking that occurs rather automatically and without conscious effort to mold it in particular ways. These thought sequences are not intended to solve any problem but are miscellaneous. They often include what is typically called mind wandering, daydreaming, reverie, or fantasy.

    Respondent thoughts are apparently quite frequent and intrude into other types of thinking (e.g., when trying to study). In his research on respondent thought, Klinger found that the respondent segments that people report experiencing are closely related to the incentives important to them. Klinger suggested that respondent thought segments are triggered by cues associated with one's current concerns. Thus our goals are apparently the basis for much of our respondent thought. Because respondent thought sequences are so frequent and because they appear to be closely related to the important goals in our lives, Klinger believed that respondent thought sets the "tone" of our inner lives.

3. **Operant Segments.** Operant thoughts are attempts to direct our thinking along specific avenues, usually in order to solve some problem. Operant thinking is also influenced by current concerns and cues that relate to goals. In this respect operant and respondent thought segments are alike, differing only in that operant thought imposes additional constraints upon the thought process that do not exist in respondent thought. Important elements, then, in both operant and respondent thought are the current concerns of

the individual. In operant thought the ideas may be aimed specifically at developing ways in which to obtain the goals of current concern. Klinger's work on thought processes suggests that incentives and goals strongly influence what we think about.

INCENTIVE ASPECTS OF SEXUAL MOTIVATION

In this chapter we have examined research that shows many behaviors are motivated by the characteristics of their goal objects. We have used the term *incentive motivation* to describe such situations. In Chapter Five we found that sexual behavior has some of the characteristics of a drive; does sexual motivation also have some of the characteristics of incentive motivation? Let us see.

Incentive motivation theories tell us that the characteristics of goals are often quite important in motivating behavior. If the goal is copulation, then the question becomes, What sort of stimuli possessed by an animal would reliably produce sexual arousal and sexual behavior in a potential partner? For many animals sexual odors are important stimuli for attracting a mate. Female rats in estrus (i.e., sexually receptive) produce a urinary odor that attracts male rats (Pfaff & Pfaffmann, 1969). Odors used as chemical signals (in this example the odor signals sexual readiness) are called **pheromones**. According to Money and Ehrhardt (1972), male rhesus monkeys are aroused, at least in part, by the vaginal odor of sexually receptive rhesus females.

Although there is no direct evidence that humans are sexually aroused by specific odors produced by a potential sexual partner (Luria et al., 1987), it is known that women's sensitivity to smell is altered by hormonal changes. Money and Ehrhardt (1972) report that after puberty women are more sensitive to the smell of musk and some urinary steroids. Parlee (1983) has also shown that some women have a lowered sensory threshold for scents around the middle of their menstrual cycle. It is not clear, however, whether these changes are in some way related to the likelihood of sexual behavior.

Although humans may not be directly sexually aroused by odorous signals, as is true of many other species, the size of the perfume industry and the deliberations people make about selecting a perfume or cologne suggest that odor is important in social situations. Furthermore, if one were to believe advertisements, the appropriate perfume or cologne can have members of the opposite sex groveling at one's feet. Given the lack of reasonable data, it is probably best to conclude that odor may contribute to sexual attractiveness, but probably not in the way pheromones do in other species.

Humans are predominantly visual animals and, as such, we might expect that visual stimuli provided by a potential sexual partner would have incentive value. Money and Ehrhardt (1972) argue that humans have a sexual signaling system which at a distance is visual and at closer distances involves touch. Both men and women find some potential partners more sexually arousing than others. What sort of visual signals might prove arousing? One way to try to answer this question is to ask what sorts of attributes an individual finds alluring in a member of the opposite sex. The answer seems to be **physical attractiveness** (Harmatz & Novak, 1983; Luria et al., 1987; Symons, 1979).

Research is consistent in showing that physical attractiveness is a major component of sexual attractiveness (Harmatz & Novak, 1983). Berscheid and Walster (1974), for example, found that subjects rated as attractive by trained observers reported having more dates than subjects rated as less attractive by these observers. Furthermore, Berscheid and

Walster report that people generally agree very closely on ratings of physical attractiveness and that physical attractiveness has a large influence on the formation of heterosexual relationships. It also has been noted that members of heterosexual pairs tend to be approximately equal in attractiveness (Symons, 1979).

Symons (1979) has provided a thoughtful and thought-provoking review of the characteristics that constitute physical attractiveness. He also argues that physical attractiveness is an indicator of likely reproductive success and, therefore, evolutionary pressure has been brought to bear on attractiveness and its recognition. This evolutionary pressure has led to the innate recognition of, and preference for, certain (and different) physical traits in men and women.

Female Attractiveness

According to Symons (1979), the two major attributes of female attractiveness are **health** and **age**. A healthy, young woman is more likely to successfully reproduce and raise offspring. Symons's analysis suggests that men should find attractive any characteristics that are indicators of health. He notes that Ford and Beach (1951) found that a good complexion and cleanliness were considered attractive by all the groups they studied. In primitive cultures complexion and cleanliness ought to provide some indication of health and, as a result, ought to be seen as attractive. Symons suggests that other physical characteristics such as clear eyes, firm muscle tone, good teeth, beautiful hair, and so forth might also be indicators of health and thus seen as attractive. Although there are few good data on the subject, it is interesting that many of the products advertised for women do attend to these physical characteristics (contact lenses for the eyes, health spas to increase muscle tone, toothpaste that whitens teeth, hair dyes, perms, and so on). Symons proposes that

paying close attention to the skin and being attracted by a clear complexion are probably innate.

Youth is the second physical characteristic that Symons says is important to attracting a man to a woman. Indeed G. C. Williams (1975) has argued that youth is the most important determinant of human female attractiveness. The age of the female is important because it is closely linked to her reproductive value. A woman of 17, for example, has almost all of her reproductive years in front of her, while a woman of 35 has most of her reproductive years behind her. According to this analysis, then, men ought to be strongly attracted to younger women because of their greater reproductive value. Symons (1979) provides cross-cultural data to support the idea that youth in women is a strong sexual attractor to men. He also believes that youth as a factor in sexual attractiveness is relatively innate. In other words, men are genetically programmed to find younger women sexually attractive.

Neither health nor age has been seen as an important variable by most researchers of attractiveness, however. It is somewhat ironic that most studies have been conducted in Western countries, where health is relatively good, and where most of the subjects have been of college age (i.e., young): it is no wonder, then, that health and age have been largely overlooked as major contributors to female attractiveness. Further studies of these two variables could provide important insights into physical attractiveness.

The third characteristic that Symons proposes as sexually attractive in women is **novelty**. According to Symons, in a primitive hunter-gatherer society a man could expect to produce four or five offspring with one wife during her reproductive years. If, however, he had a second wife he could double his reproductive success. Where multiple wives were not possible an extramarital affair that led to just one additional offspring would have increased his reproductive success by 20% to 25%. Since behavioral strategies that lead to the greatest number of offspring will tend to be selected, one can understand why men should be attracted to, and desire to mate with, numerous females. Thus one strong characteristic that should be attractive in women is novelty.

In herd animals the female novelty effect can be quite strong. For example, after a bull has ceased to copulate with a cow the introduction of a new cow will lead to copulation anew, and the response of the bull to the seventh cow will be almost as strong as to the first (Schein & Hale, 1965). Rams show a similar effect to the introduction of new ewes, and male rats also show this phenomenon. Even roosters copulate more when multiple partners are available (Symons, 1979).

The stimulatory effect of the introduction of a new female on male sexual behavior has been dubbed the **Coolidge effect** after a purported conversation between President Calvin Coolidge and his wife. Supposedly the president and first lady were visiting a government farm. In passing by the chicken coops Mrs. Coolidge asked her guide whether the rooster copulated more than once a day. Her guide assured her that the rooster copulated with the hens dozens of times per day. Mrs. Coolidge asked that this fact be told to the president. Later the president passed by the chicken coops and was given the information about the rooster that Mrs. Coolidge had requested. The president, upon hearing the information, asked whether the copulations were with the same hen every time. The answer was that the copulations were with a different hen each time. The president asked that that information be conveyed to Mrs. Coolidge (Bermant, 1976).

Finally, Symons argues that there is no convincing evidence for specific physical characteristics of the female that are capable of stimulating the male visually (in this regard he disagrees with Morris, 1967). The most consistently sexually arousing stimulus for males is the sight of the female's genitals; however, unlike some other primates, in which estrus produces highly visible changes in coloration or size of the female's genitals, human females experience no such obvious changes.

Research has shown that there are consistent differences in male preference (e.g., some men consistently prefer long legs, others large breasts, and so forth; Wiggins, Wiggins, & Conger, 1968); however, it is likely that these preferences are learned. Luria and associates (1987) have argued that the only innately sexually arousing stimulus is light touch, especially of the genitals, and that preferences for large breasts, long legs, or firm buttocks are learned erotic stimuli.

Male Attractiveness

If men are attracted to healthy, young women who are novel, what characteristics do women find sexually attractive in men? Compared to the male, the human female has fewer potential offspring and a much higher parental investment in those she does produce. As a result, evolutionary pressures ought to have selected for conservatism in female sexual behavior. That is, in a society where males compete for status, the female is likely to have greater reproductive success by remaining with one high-status male who can provide her and her offspring with the essentials for survival. Thus, one would predict that social dominance and status would be especially attractive to the female.

Symons suggests that in the female what is innate is a **selection rule** (e.g., be attracted to high-status males) rather than recognition of specific traits such as health and age. Thus, according to this analysis, the physical attributes of the male should be less important than characteristics indicative of status. Ford and Beach (1951) report that cross-culturally, male attractiveness is typically based on skills and abilities rather than appearance. It is of some interest in this regard that Berscheid and Walster (1975) found that the only male physical trait that was consistently considered sexually attractive was height. Tall males might be expected to have some advantage in male-male competition, and thus attraction to taller males, on the average, could be expected to confer some reproductive advantage to the female.

Symons (1979) too suggests that male sexual attractiveness depends less on handsomeness than on skills and abilities. Since skills, abilities, and status take some time to develop, one could also argue that women will often prefer older males to younger males who have yet to develop skills or status. Certainly in some primitive cultures younger men have had to compete against older dominant men for young women (Symons, 1979).

To summarize, it would appear that characteristics of the goal object (i.e., the partner) for heterosexually motivated behavior do act as incentive motivators for sexual attraction. For the male, physical attributes associated with health and youth are sexually stimulating, as is novelty. For the female, sexual attractiveness would appear to be based less on physical characteristics such as handsomeness than on dominance and status. These differences in sexual attraction appear to be understandable in terms of the differing needs of the male and the female in assuring the survival of their genes.

SUMMARY

In this chapter we examined the concept of incentive motivation. The basic idea underlying the concept of incentive motivation is that the characteristics of the goals that we work to obtain influence our behavior. Explanations of incentive motivation have ranged from highly mechanical, stimulus-response theories, such as the Hull-Spence r_g - s_g mechanism, to the more cognitive theories of Tolman and, more recently, Klinger. Amsel's analysis of the per-

sistence of behavior as resulting from the counterconditioning of fractional frustration responses is a modern extension of the Hull-Spence model.

Mowrer's emphasis on the idea that incentives generate emotion has provided an alternative proposal for how goals may generate behavior and is related to the currently popular explanations that emphasize the informational property of incentives. Tolman's emphasis on the importance of expectancies as generators of behavior was also a significant contribution to our understanding of incentive motivation and, like Mowrer's theory, pointed out the importance of informational cues.

Theories stressing the importance of the informational properties of cues associated with goals and the effects of these cues on behavior have emphasized the concept of predictability. Perhaps the most extensive analysis of incentives from this point of view has been conducted by Overmier and Lawry, who regarded incentives as mediators between stimuli in the environment and the responses of the organism. Others, such as Bolles and Moot and Trapold and Overmier, have also stressed the importance of predictability in incentive motivational situations, while Bindra has attempted to gather together the concepts of drive, incentive, and predictability in the concept of central motive state.

Finally, Klinger has analyzed human behavior from the perspective of incentive motivation and concluded that incentives are the major force underlying what we do. Klinger argued that we work to obtain the goals that are emotionally meaningful to us. In addition, incentives influence not only our actions but also our thoughts and even which environmental events influence us. Further, disengaging from a sought-after goal is difficult and involves a series of predictable phases.

Incentive motivation continues to be an important theoretical approach to understanding the motivation of behavior. As we have just seen, some aspects of sexual attractiveness appear to fit an incentive motivation approach. The goals toward which we work clearly provide a strong source of motivation. For human behavior this source of motivation often seems to outweigh other sources, including, at times, homeostatic regulation.

SUGGESTIONS FOR FURTHER READING

Klinger, E. (1977). *Meaning and void: Inner experiences and the incentives in people's lives*. Minneapolis: University of Minnesota Press. Klinger provides a very readable account of his conception of the importance of incentives for human behavior.

Symons, D. (1979). *The evolution of human sexuality*. New York: Oxford University Press. This book provides an excellent analysis of some of the factors associated with sexual attraction. See especially chapters 6 and 7.

Chapter Eight

Hedonism and Sensory Stimulation

CHAPTER PREVIEW

This chapter is concerned with the following questions:

1. Can the concept of hedonism (i.e., seeking pleasure and avoiding pain) explain some motivated behaviors?

2. Does sensory stimulation motivate behavior?

3. What effects does sensory restriction have on motivated behavior?

4. Can some behaviors be explained in terms of opponent processes in the nervous system?

"If it feels good, do it." I noticed this quotation on a bumper sticker as I drove to my office not long ago. The saying is an explanation of motivated behavior (though a modern version) that has been with us for as long as recorded history. Democritus, a contemporary of Plato in ancient Greece, argued that we behave in order to obtain the greatest amount of pleasure (Bolles, 1975). Epicurus, whose name is more commonly associated with this approach, also believed that we are motivated

to obtain pleasure. Such an approach is termed **hedonism** and can be defined as the seeking of pleasure and avoidance of pain.

Hedonic theories emphasize the idea that cues or stimuli have motivational properties because they have become associated with positive or negative experiences. In many respects this is similar to arguments concerning incentive motivation. One might argue that incentives motivate behavior because they arouse hedonic effect; that is, perhaps goal objects become incentives because they arouse pleasure or pain.

HEDONISM

Various philosophers throughout the ages have argued for hedonic explanations of behavior. Hobbes, for example, believed that all actions are motivated by the desire to obtain pleasure and avoid pain (Bolles, 1975; Woodbridge, 1958). Spencer proposed that pleasurable behaviors have survival value for an organism; that is, those behaviors perceived as pleasurable were adaptive in the past history of the species. He believed that random responses that led to pain were reduced in probability. Thus for Spencer pleasure and pain became important modifiers of behavior. Spencer's approach was clearly a forerunner of Thorndike's law of effect, which was itself a forerunner of modern reinforcement theory (Young, 1961).

Troland (1932) believed that the nervous system is especially tuned to pleasurable and aversive events. He divided stimulation into three categories: beneception, nociception, and neutroception. **Beneception** occurs when pleasant feelings are aroused by stimuli, while **nociception** occurs as the result of stimuli that arouse unpleasant feelings. The third category, **neutroception**, exists when stimuli cause neither pleasant nor unpleasant feelings. Troland believed that sensations can be classified in one of these three categories. Vision, audition, cutaneous touch, and kinesthesis were considered neutroceptive. Pain, bitter taste, intense salt, intense sour, nauseating or repugnant smells, cold, excessive heat, hunger, thirst, and some visceral responses were considered nociceptive. Beneceptive stimuli included erotic stimuli, sweet tastes, some pleasant smells, low intensities of salt and sour, and some visceral responses. Thus, according to Troland, the hedonic value of an object in the environment is closely tied to the sensory qualities it possesses and the effect those stimuli have on the nervous system in terms of beneception, nociception, or neutroception.

Beebe-Center (1932) suggested that pleasantness and unpleasantness exist as opposite extremes on a hedonic continuum (Troland also suggested this). Somewhere between the extremes of pleasant and unpleasant feelings lies a neutral zone where stimuli are neither pleasant nor unpleasant. Beebe-Center maintained that pleasant and unpleasant sensations depend upon the way in which the sense organs react to stimulation. Reactions of the sense organs in one manner (which he called **bright pressure**) produce pleasant feelings, while reactions of a different type (which

he termed **dull pressure**) produce unpleasant feelings. Thus Beebe-Center believed that pleasant and unpleasant feelings result from different types of activity in the sensory systems. Beebe-Center was also one of the first theorists to acknowledge that instructions can change the perceived pleasantness or unpleasantness of stimuli. This influence of instructional set indicates that pleasantness and unpleasantness are relative to whatever else is happening to us. Beebe-Center believed that instructions alter the pleasantness of stimuli by changing the actions of the sense organs rather than by altering perception of the stimulation at some more central (i.e., brain) level. Today we would be inclined to argue that the effects of instructions are more central in nature.

P. T. Young: Sign, Intensity, and Duration

Of the modern hedonic theorists, Paul Thomas Young is perhaps the best known. Young's extensive research on food preferences led him to agree with Beebe-Center that there exists a continuum with maximum negative affect (i.e., unpleasant or aversive stimuli) at one end and maximum positive affect (i.e., pleasant stimuli) at the other end. The affective processes represented by this continuum have three properties: sign, intensity, and duration.

Positive affect is associated with approach behavior, while negative affect is associated with avoidance. Thus we can determine the **sign** of a particular affective situation by observing whether the organism approaches (+) or avoids (−) the situation. For example, rats will approach and drink a sweet-tasting fluid but will avoid (after initial contact) a bitter-tasting solution.

Affective processes also differ in **intensity.** In order to observe affective intensity differences of various substances, researchers usually employ preference tests. In a two-choice situation the chosen substance is considered to be hedonically more intense than the nonchosen one. One might, for example, compare different solutions of sugar water. If the concentration of sugar in the water is different in the two bottles, a rat will prefer the more highly concentrated solution. Through the use of preference tests, we can chart hedonic intensity differences.

The third property of the hedonic continuum is **duration.** Some hedonic processes may last only as long as sensory stimulation lasts, while others presumably outlast the stimulation.

Young graphically represents the hedonic continuum as shown in Figure 8.1, which shows the range of the hedonic continuum from the maximum negative end (i.e., distress), through a neutral indifferent zone, to the extreme positive end (i.e., delight). Differences in intensities are represented by the arbitrary units marked off along the continuum. The arrows represent the ways in which hedonic affect can change. The arrow pointing toward the positive end represents the direction of hedonic change that organisms attempt to maintain. Young believed that the nervous system is constructed in such a way that organisms attempt to maximize positive affect and minimize negative affect. Thus organisms learn behaviors that lead to positive affective change and away from negative affective change.

Though the arrow pointing toward the positive end of the continuum is the preferred situation for an organism, changes also occur in the opposite direction, indicated by the arrow pointing toward the negative end of the continuum. When such negative changes occur, an organism will be motivated to reduce the negative affect situation (i.e., to behave in some way that will again minimize negative affect and maximize positive affect).

Sensory Stimulation and the Hedonic Continuum

Sensory stimuli provide information to an organism about the conditions of its external and internal environment. Affective processes, as represented by the hedonic continuum, convey little information other than whether something is "good" (pleasant) or "bad" (unpleasant) and, in choice situations, "better than" or "worse than." Young saw this affective information as biologically primitive and of a different order from the more sophisticated discriminations we are capable of making from sensory information. This means that the hedonic continuum is not equivalent to sensory stimulation. This difference is most apparent when one compares the relationship of changes in hedonic intensity.

If we compare increases in the concentration of sugar with increases in hedonic intensity (as measured by a choice situation with laboratory animals), we discover that as a sugar solution becomes more concentrated, it is preferred over less concentrated sugar solutions as far up the concentration scale as we care to go (Young & Greene, 1953). Based on this data alone, we might be inclined to conclude that sensory and hedonic intensity are

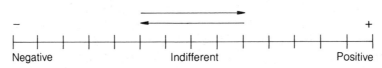

Figure 8.1   *Young's hedonic continuum. (From Young, 1959. Copyright © 1959 by the American Psychological Association.)*

closely correlated; it is quite clear, however, that this is not true. Young and Falk (1956), for example, showed that for choices between distilled water and water diluted with salt, initial preferences were for the salt solution. As concentration of the salt solution was increased, however, the distilled water was preferred. Thus preference for salt solutions increases with intensity of the solution only up to a point, after which it decreases again. For salt solutions, obviously, as sensory intensity increases, positive affect initially occurs but later turns to negative affect as the salt concentration continues to rise. Thus we cannot assume that changes in sensory intensity will initiate similar changes in hedonic affect.

The hedonic processes represented by the hedonic continuum have motivational influences on behavior. First, positive affect is closely associated with approach behavior and negative affect with withdrawal. Second, Young believed that affective processes both activate and direct behavior so that maximum positive affect and minimum negative affect are maintained. Third, affective processes lead to the development of stable motives and dispositions. For example, the sweet taste of ice cream may lead to the development of choosing ice cream over other foods.

Changes in motivation are also seen as dependent upon changes in hedonic value. If, for example, a rat is given a choice between two substances such as flour and sugar, it will prefer the sugar (Young, 1973). If, however, one of the test foods is replaced by a new food, an abrupt change occurs in the behavior exhibited toward the old substance in the choice situation. This suggests that introduction of the new substance has altered the motivation of the organism.

Young believed that the changes in motivation observed when a novel food is introduced occur because the organism has developed an expectancy of choice between two substances of different hedonic value. This expectancy is the result of **hedonic feedback** from the previous sampling of the substances; that is, the organism samples the substances it may choose between and develops a preference for one of them based on the hedonic value of each. On the first trial after a novel substance has been introduced, the expectancy that has developed is disconfirmed, and the motivation of the organism changes accordingly. Thus changes in goal objects lead to changes in expectancy, which in turn alter performance.

The Motivational Influence of Sensations
Carl Pfaffmann (1960) conducted much research on the physiological mechanisms of taste, and his work seemed to agree with Young's ideas. Pfaffmann suggested that sensory stimulation by itself is motivating and leads to approach or withdrawal behavior (without assuming something like drive reduction). He noted, for example, work done by Stellar, Hyman, and Samet (1954), which showed that animals display the typical preference-aversion function for salt (NaCl) even if the fluid passing through the mouth—and thus over the sensory receptors for taste—never reaches the stomach (because of an esophageal fistula). This research indicated that the taste sensations are sufficient to trigger approach or avoidance behavior without having to be tied to any physiological change.

In agreement with Young, Pfaffmann noted that hedonic intensity and sensory intensity are not equivalent. Recording the electrical activity of the chorda tympani (i.e., a cranial nerve sending taste information to the brain), he showed that as salt concentration in a fluid increases, so does the electrical activity of the nerve. However, hedonic value (as evidenced by choices) at first increases and then decreases as the salt concentration becomes greater. The relationship between the electrical activity of the chorda tympani and hedonic value can be seen in Figure 8.2.

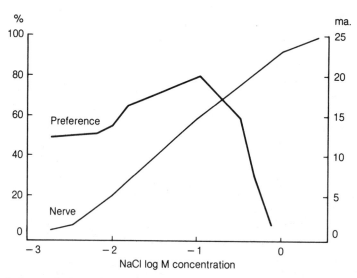

Figure 8.2 *Preference for increasing concentrations of salt and chorda tympani nerve firing in rats. Left ordinate refers to the preference function; right ordinate refers to magnitude of nerve firing. (From Pfaffmann, 1958. Used by permission.)*

Additional evidence for the importance of sensory information in motivating behavior can be seen in the fact that nonnutritive substances such as saccharine are rewarding (and thus motivate behavior designed to obtain them) because of their sweet taste (Sheffield & Roby, 1950; Sheffield, Roby, & Campbell, 1954). Pfaffmann believed that the stimulus properties of a tasted substance directly determine the hedonic value of the substance.

Hedonic Value and Contact Receptors   The stimulation of contact receptors (e.g., taste) seems much more often associated with strong emotion than is the stimulation of distance receptors (e.g., vision). Contact receptors are also much more often associated with consummatory activity (e.g., taste-eating, genital contact-intercourse, and so on).

The hedonic tone provided directly by contact receptors may have been an evolutionary adaptation. For example, distance receptors (e.g., vision) give some lead time for one to make a judgment and react, but contact receptors often involve stimuli (e.g., pain) that require a quick reaction if the organism is to survive. Hedonic value (pleasure or pain) may therefore have evolved in conjunction with stimulation of the contact receptors to quickly direct behavior. Though the relationship between stimulation of the contact receptors and hedonic value should be considered speculative, Sherrington (1947), as early as 1906, noted the existence of a relationship between contact receptors, emotion, and consummatory behavior. Additionally, those theorists who have argued most persuasively for hedonic theories of motivation have usually studied behaviors associated with the stimulation of contact receptors. Hedonic explanations of motivation may prove to be less useful when applied to behaviors associated with the stimulation of distance receptors.

We will now examine research on pain as one example of hedonistic explanations of motivation.

PAIN

Pain normally occurs when the body is injured. Pain is useful because it tells us we have been injured and often causes us to alter our behavior so that the injured part of our body has time to heal. On the other hand, pain can often seem out of proportion to the size of the injury. Small injuries can sometimes be terribly painful. Anyone who has broken a tooth can attest to the terrible pain that accompanies such a seemingly trivial injury. Or consider the phenomenon of phantom limb pain, where excruciating pain may be experienced even though the involved body part has been amputated. In these cases pain does not seem very adaptive and may, in fact, interfere with more adaptive behaviors.

One of the foremost researchers in the study of pain is Ronald Melzack, who with Patrick Wall in 1965 proposed a theory of pain that is still very influential today. Prior to their model, pain was thought to result from pain receptors sending their messages along specific pain fibers to the brain, where pain was then experienced. Melzack (1961; Melzack & Wall, 1965) realized that the perception of pain was much more variable and much more modifiable than people thought. For example, about 65% of men wounded in battle feel no pain when brought to the combat hospital (Melzack, 1961; Warga, 1987), yet approximately 80% of civilians with similar injuries typically report severe pain and ask for pain medication. Similarly, it is well known that football players, boxers, and other athletes often continue to play even though hurt, because they are unaware of the injury. Such examples led Melzack to realize that no simple and direct relationship existed between the severity of an injury and the amount of pain experienced.

Furthermore, pathological pain states such as causalgia (a severe burning pain that is sometimes caused by a partial lesion of a peripheral nerve), peripheral neuralgia (which can occur following peripheral nerve infection), and the previously mentioned phantom limb pain are often unsuccessfully treated by surgical lesions of either the peripheral or central nervous system. If the experience of pain was simply the result of the stimulation of pain receptors and the perception of those signals by the brain, then "disconnection" surgery ought to abolish the pain of causalgia, neuralgia, and phantom limbs. The fact that such surgeries are often unsuccessful suggests that the experience of pain is more than just simple perception of painful stimulation.

Additionally, Melzack (1961) pointed out that if a subject's attention is focused on the painful aspects of a procedure, pain is often experienced more intensely. Hall and Stride (as noted by Melzack, 1961), for example, showed that the word *pain* in a set of instructions caused anxious subjects to report electric shock as painful even though this shock level was not considered painful by the subjects if the word *pain* was absent. This and other experiments on the psychological aspects of pain indicate that higher brain processes can alter the experience of pain.

Based on the evidence noted above and information concerning the physiology of the peripheral nervous system, Melzack and Wall proposed a model of pain that emphasized the role of higher brain processes in controlling the experience of pain and a modulating system within the spinal cord that influenced how much pain information reached the brain. This new model was called the gate control theory of pain.

Gate Control Theory of Pain

According to the theory, stimulation reaching the spinal cord from two different fiber systems is influential in the experience of pain. Additionally, the brain exerts an effect on the spinal cord that can alter the experience of pain.

Two types of cells within the spinal cord are thought to be important. **T-cells** in the spinal cord receive input from **large-diameter A-fibers** and **small-diameter C-fibers**. When T-cells are activated by this incoming stimulation, pain may be experienced. Cells within the **substantia gelatinosa (SG cells)**, a part of the spinal cord, serve to modulate the input that arrives at the T-cells from the large- and small-diameter fibers. When large-diameter fibers are active, the SG cells are stimulated and in turn reduce the effect of large-fiber stimulation on the T-cells. Thus activity in the large fibers will initially stimulate the T-cells but will then be reduced as the SG cells close the "gate" to the T-cell. Small-fiber activation is thought to have the opposite effect. Small fibers are active much more of the time, even in the absence of any stimulation. This activity stimulates the T-cells also; however, the small fibers also inhibit the SG cell activity, which has the effect of opening the gate wider, i.e., letting more stimulation from both large and small fibers through to the T-cells. Since the SG cells serve to modulate the activity that reaches the T-cells, the amount of pain experienced will not necessarily correspond to the amount of stimulation of the large and small fibers.

Pain is thought to occur when the activity of the T-cells reaches a certain threshold. Below the threshold, pain is not experienced; above the threshold, pain is experienced. If pain were the result of just the large- and small-fiber stimulation of the SG cell gating mechanism and its effect on the large- and small-fiber stimulation of the T-cells, then pain would depend primarily on the degree and relationship of large- and small-fiber stimulation. The SG cell gate, however, also appears to be modulated by the brain through descending fibers which are capable of modifying the SG gate (and therefore the activity of the T-cells).

Such a downstream mechanism means that memories of past similar stimulation, emotions, and attention could all influence how painful the stimulation will be, by opening or closing the gate.

Melzack and Wall proposed that stimulation coming into the spinal cord was sent on to the brain, where it was analyzed and downstream modifications made to the gate *before* the slower T-cell system had much time to respond. Thus stimulation coming into the spinal cord on "fast" tracks is sent to the brain for analysis and changes are signaled downstream to the pain gate before stimulation coming across the pain fibers has had time to reach the T-cells and trigger a pain response. As a result, central modulation of the pain gates along the spinal cord could serve to suppress stimulation that would otherwise be very painful. Melzack and Wall's proposal has had a tremendous influence on our thinking about the experience of pain. Their model makes understandable how wounded soldiers and athletes can feel little or no pain even after severe injuries: brain mechanisms are keeping the pain gates shut.

The Melzack and Wall model also makes some sense of the fact that acupuncture and transcutaneous electrical stimulation (TENS) can serve to reduce pain. Remember that large A-fiber stimulation has the effect of closing the pain gate. If the large fibers are stimulated either as a result of acupuncture or TENS, the gate closes more and less pain is felt. Several studies have provided evidence that stimulation of large A-fibers does provide an inhibitory effect and reduce pain (see, e.g., Lewith & Kenyon, 1984; Melzack and Wall, 1983; Wall & Sweet, 1967).

Research since the original publication of the gate control theory has shown that the pain control gates are modulated by hormonal changes involving the **endogenous opiates**. For example, Pomeranz, Cheng, and Law (1977) showed that removing the pituitary of mice drastically reduced the analgesic effects of electroacupuncture. Since the pituitary was known to produce pain-killing **endorphins**, it seemed possible that the analgesic effects of acupuncture might result from the stimulation of sensory nerves which in turn triggered the pituitary to secrete endorphins.

In a further study, Peets and Pomeranz (1978) examined the analgesic effects of electroacupuncture on a strain of mice known to be deficient in opiate receptors (CXBK strain). When the analgesic effects of electroacupuncture on the opiate-deficient and normal mice were compared, the opiate-deficient mice showed little analgesic effect of the acupuncture, while the normal mice showed the standard analgesic effect. Further evidence for the role of an opioid system in the gating of pain is suggested by studies which show that naloxone, which blocks the effects of opiates, also blocks the analgesic effects of acupuncture (Peets & Pomeranz, 1978; Pomeranz, 1981). Mayer (1983) showed that there are opiate receptors in the spinal cord.

Current thinking on the gating of pain would be as follows: Pain information arriving at the substantia gelatinosa on the small C-fibers causes a neurotransmitter called **substance P** to potentiate the firing of cells responsible for the experience of pain. When the large-diameter A-fibers are stimulated by acupuncture or TENS, a competing signal is sent to the pituitary, which releases endorphins that act on the brainstem, which in turn stimulates the production of **serotonin** in the spinal cord. The serotonin inhibits the release of substance P, the pain signal is blocked, and analgesia results (Chung & Dickenson, 1980).

It seems probable that past experiences with pain, attention, and emotion could also influence the opiate system to modulate pain, so that, for example, a wounded soldier feels little or no pain during a battle. Thus the central modulation of pain, first noticed by Melzack, is probably mediated by the action of endogenous opiates. Indeed Bandura, O'Leary, Taylor, Gauthier, and Gossard (1987) have shown that cognitive control of painful stimulation results, in part, from activation of the opioid system. Further research on the cognitive control of pain will surely help us better understand the mechanisms of pain and its control.

Whether the hedonic value of objects is limited to the stimulation of contact receptors or not, the importance of sensory stimulation per se to behavior motivation has been extensively studied. Research has ranged from an examination of curiosity and exploratory behavior to studying the effects of depriving organisms of sensory stimulation. As we will see, the importance of sensory stimulation to normal behavior has been shown in many different experimental situations.

NOVELTY, CURIOSITY, AND EXPLORATORY BEHAVIOR

A group of studies performed primarily in the 1950s indicated that external stimuli can serve to motivate behavior directly. Terms commonly used to describe the motive state generated by external stimuli included curiosity, exploratory drive, manipulation motives, stimulus hunger, and need for stimulation (Cofer & Appley, 1964). Although the information gained from these experiments was often used as evidence against need reduction or drive reduction theories of motivation, the information is of interest in itself because it indicates that changes in the sensory qualities of the environment lead to changes in motivated behavior.

In a thorough review of the literature, Cofer and Appley (1964) noted that studies on sensory stimulation and motivation could be grouped into studies indicating that behaviors are *released* by stimulation and studies indicating a *need* for stimulation. We will examine each in turn.

Behaviors Released by Stimulation

Harry Harlow at the University of Wisconsin extensively studied primate behavior. He pointed out that external stimuli are important in motivating behavior and also argued that much of human behavior is motivated by nonhomeostatic mechanisms. For example, humans learn even though they are not hungry or thirsty, and they solve problems that have no utility, such as in playing chess or bridge. These behaviors often seem motivated simply by the sensory stimulation they provide (Harlow, 1953).

In one experiment Harlow, Harlow, and Meyer (1950) gave monkeys mechanical puzzles that could be disassembled. One group was given no food reward for "solving" the puzzle, while another group was given food. Delivery of food tended to disrupt performance on the puzzles, and the rewarded group lost interest in the puzzles sooner than the nonrewarded group. For the nonrewarded group, the behavior was apparently maintained by a motive to manipulate or explore the puzzle. Though Harlow approached these studies as examples of drives, these new drives were nonhomeostatic and sensory (Levine, 1975).

Berlyne (1960, 1963) has conducted considerable research on the conditions that motivate us to attend to our environment. He argued that exploratory activity has the function of altering the stimulus field in which we are immersed. Exploratory activity seems primarily involved in altering the stimulus input that we receive rather than causing any changes in body tissues. Exploratory behavior was also thought to be a function both of the state of the organism and of external stimuli such as surprisingness, change, ambiguity, incongruity, and uncertainty.

Berlyne suggested that factors such as novelty and uncertainty have motivational properties because they increase the arousal level of the organism. He argued that we attempt to maintain an optimal level of arousal. If stimulation drops too low (e.g, in boredom), we become motivated to increase our arousal level. On the other hand, if our arousal level becomes too high, we will be motivated to lower it. Thus novel or surprising stimuli will motivate behavior directed toward themselves if they provide a small change in arousal, because small changes in arousal are pleasant. As supportive evidence, Berlyne (1951, 1958a, 1958b) found that novel stimuli, as compared to familiar stimuli, cause one to orient toward them. Human infants three to nine months old, for example, looked at figures that had the greatest amount of contour, and adults were attracted to complex or incongruous pictures presented to them. All these situations would be expected to cause small changes in arousal and thus would be pleasant.

Montgomery (1953) also studied exploratory behavior. He allowed rats to explore one of three mazes, painted black, white, and gray, respectively. Each rat was allowed to explore twice, and the amount of time spent in exploring the second time was related to the color of the first maze explored. Montgomery found that maximum exploration occurred when the second maze was maximally different from the first (e.g., black first, white second; white first, black second) and that least exploration occurred when the second maze was identical to the first (e.g, white first, white second; black first, black second). Intermediate amounts of exploration occurred when the stimulus change from first to second maze was intermediate (e.g., white to gray; black to gray). Thus the amount of exploratory behavior shown by Montgomery's rats seemed controlled by the degree of stimulus change involved. Montgomery's data fit nicely with Berlyne's in suggesting that stimulus change (i.e., novelty) motivates behaviors such as exploration.

Donald Hebb (1966) also believed that moderate changes in arousal are reinforcing.

Because we become habituated to the familiar, we will approach new stimulus situations; if the new stimulation is too arousing, however, we will withdraw from the situation. Hebb assumed that the brain as well as the body needed to be active. According to Hebb, play behavior, seen in many organisms, occurs when other needs are not active. Though often muscular, play behavior also usually has a neural component because many of the "games" that organisms play depend upon memory of past experiences (e.g., otters sliding down a mudbank into the water or a child playing "patty cake"). Play behavior often seems to occur as the result of boredom and serves to provide a higher level of arousal.

The theories of Berlyne and Hebb were developed as alternatives to Hull's drive reduction theory discussed in Chapter Five. Studies of exploratory behavior, play, novelty, and uncertainty showed that motivation can be triggered by situations that lead to increases in stimulation. These studies provided a sharp contrast to the studies of Hull and his associates, which seemed to show that motivation is triggered in order to reduce stimulation. Berlyne and Hebb proposed that motivation is activated when stimulus conditions are either too high (drive reduction) or too low (drive induction) in order to maintain an optimal level of stimulation. In essence the theories of Berlyne and Hebb are arousal theories (see Chapter Three for other views of arousal); deviations away from optimal arousal in either direction (too much or too little arousal) trigger motivation in organisms to behave in ways that bring arousal back to the optimal level. Thus exploration, play, and reactions to novelty or uncertainty can be seen as behaviors that alleviate the deprivation that occurs from no stimulus change (Fowler, 1967). Such an analysis suggests that depriving an organism of changing stimulus input (either by eliminating it or by making stimulation unchanging) should lead to motivated behavior. As we shall

see in the next section, that is precisely what happens.

The Need for Stimulation

Many different studies suggest that a need for stimulation exists. Some studies have attempted to reduce the absolute level of stimulation to very low levels, while others have examined the effects of reduction in the patterning of stimulation (usually of a visual nature). Finally, some studies have examined the roles of monotonous or unchanging environments (Kubzansky & Leiderman, 1961). These studies are collectively called **sensory deprivation experiments**.

The effects of sensory deprivation have been researched in developing organisms as well as in adults. Results of both types of studies generally indicate a disruption of normal behavior (but see Suedfeld, 1975). We will first examine research on deprivation that occurs early in development and its relationship to motivational processes; then we will analyze behavioral changes that occur in adult animals as a result of sensory deprivation.

Early Sensory Restriction   Thompson and Melzack (1956) studied the effects of sensory restriction on the development of Scottish terriers. A four-week-old group of Scotties was divided into two subgroups. One subgroup was raised normally and served as a control for the second subgroup. The members of the second subgroup were each raised in individual cages. This experimental group was maintained in relative isolation for seven to ten months.

When the experimental Scotties were let out of their "solitary confinement," they were extremely active and playful (much like puppies), quite different in this regard from the normally raised controls. The isolated dogs continued to explore their new environment long after the control subjects had grown bored with their new surroundings. Also, the isolated Scotties explored more in maze tests than the controls; even several years after release from isolation, the experimental subjects exhibited higher activity levels. Thus sensory restriction apparently altered the normal motivational behavior of the dogs.

In another part of the experiment, the two groups of Scotties were tested for their reactions to both strange and painful objects. Normal Scotties quickly learned to avoid them (e.g., an electrified toy car that delivered a shock when touched) by running away. The isolated Scotties became highly agitated by the strange object but did not avoid it, behaving as if uncertain what to do about this strange, painful object. Most of them seemed unaware that the pain they experienced was induced by an external object in their environment.

Several tests of problem-solving ability were also conducted, and the experimental Scotties were always deficient to the normals in ability. For example, experimental Scotties were unable to correctly choose the box under which they had just seen a piece of food hidden, while normals could choose correctly even after a delay of four minutes. On maze tasks the isolates made approximately 50% more errors than the normals. Finally, when normal and isolated Scotties were put together, the normals were always dominant, even when considerably younger than the restricted dogs.

Sensory restriction, then, had long-lasting (and apparently permanent) effects on the behavior of isolated Scotties. Though not appearing unmotivated, the isolates seemed hyperexcitable and unable to direct their behavior in an efficient, adaptive manner. Thompson and Melzack's research suggests that sensory restriction may alter the ways in which motivated behavior is directed (e.g., nonescape from painful objects) and opens the question of whether sensory restriction may induce emotionality (i.e., hyperexcitability)

when normal levels of stimulation are provided.

In studies of cats, monkeys, and chimpanzees, Riesen (1961) reported very similar effects. For example, he restricted the visual sensory input of kittens by raising them in dark cages. He noted that exposure of these cats to a normal lighted environment revealed perceptual deficits and violent emotionality. Riesen found that his dark-reared animals showed (1) hyperexcitability, (2) increased incidences of convulsive disorders, and (3) localized motor impairment.

In regard to hyperexcitability, Riesen found that normal levels of illumination produced extreme fear in animals that had been dark-reared. Also, when normal patterned vision was allowed, many of the cats went into convulsions. Susceptibility to convulsions seemed to relate to the absence of patterned vision during development rather than to the absence of light per se, because cats that were dark-reared but handled and tested daily (thus allowing some patterned visual experience) did not develop the seizures. In regard to the motor dysfunction, Riesen found that visual **nystagamus** (involuntary rapid movement of the eyeball) was common in both cats and monkeys deprived of patterned light.

Riesen concluded that the increases in stimulation were emotion producing for his dark-reared subjects. In this respect his work seemed to agree with that of Hebb (1949), who argued that emotional disturbance may sometimes result as a consequence of incongruent sensory input. In Riesen's experiment the lighted environment was incongruent with the rearing histories of the animals.

Like the Scotties in the Thompson and Melzack study, Riesen's animals were hyperexcitable and emotional. Also as in Thompson and Melzack's study, Riesen's animals did not cope well with new and strange stimulus situations. Riesen's study further seemed to suggest that early sensory restriction may alter the normal functioning of the brain, as evidenced by the increased susceptibility to seizure and motor dysfunction. Other evidence (Hirsch & Spinelli, 1970, 1971) has supported this conclusion, showing that the visual patterning experienced early in development influences development of the visual processing circuits.

Research on sensory restriction indicates that adequate stimulation is necessary for normal development. Though much of the effect of sensory restriction probably results from physiological and perceptual changes, the research also suggests that motivational and emotional changes occur. New sensations, to a deprived animal, lead to fear and withdrawal.

Attachment

Maternal Deprivation The parents of young organisms provide a rich source of stimuli to the developing organism (e.g., sight, smell, touch, sound, temperature, and so on). Studies of maternal deprivation have shown that the lack of adequate parent-infant interactions also produces long-lasting effects. These effects may be due in part to reduced sensory stimulation from both environment and parent. To these studies we now turn.

The term **maternal deprivation** does not always mean the loss of the mother exclusively. Maternal deprivation refers to situations in which the developing organism receives little or no consistent care from whomever is responsible for it. In most mammals this is indeed the mother, but in humans "mothering" can be provided by any number of people, including the mother, father, siblings, other relatives, or even caretakers of various sorts.

The work of Harry Harlow shed much light on the importance of maternal stimuli for the adequate development of young organisms. He used rhesus monkeys to examine attachment processes that occur between the infant and its mother. Harlow (1958) pointed

out that the old view of the mother-infant attachment process (what we would commonly call love) argued that the process is a derived (i.e., learned) motive and is based on the fact that the mother is closely associated with reduction of the infant's needs (e.g., hunger, thirst, warmth, and so on). Derived motives, however, usually extinguish quickly when association with the primary motive is cut, but the infant-mother attachment seems lifelong.

In observing infant monkeys that for various reasons had been separated from their mothers, Harlow noted that the infants developed a strong attachment to cloth pads placed in their cages and became emotional when the pads were removed for cleaning (reminding us of Linus from the "Peanuts" cartoon, who feels insecure without his blanket).

In an initial experiment baby monkeys were taken from their mothers at birth and put into individual cages. Attached to each cage was a second cage containing surrogate (i.e., substitute) mothers that were made of either wire or soft terry cloth. These surrogate mothers are shown in Figure 8.3. For half of the baby monkeys, the wire mother "provided" the nourishment. As can be seen in Figure 8.4, the monkeys spent the largest amount of time with the terry cloth mother, regardless of which mother nourished it.

The cloth mother was more than just a soft place to sit, as became evident when these baby monkeys were made anxious; they ran to the cloth mother, who served as a source of security. In a strange environment (e.g., a new room) the cloth mother served as a secure base from which exploratory forays were made by the infant monkeys. If the cloth mother was absent (or only the wire mother was present), the infant monkeys exhibited freezing behavior, vocalizing and rocking back and forth. Clearly, then, the baby monkeys developed a strong attachment to the cloth mother as a result of the contact comfort (i.e., body contact) provided.

Figure 8.3 Surrogate mothers provided by Harlow to his infant rhesus monkeys. *(From Harlow & Suomi, 1970. Copyright © 1970 by the American Psychological Association. Reprinted by permission of the publisher.)*

Harlow and Suomi (1970) examined a number of different stimuli of the surrogate mother that might have provided sensations leading to attachment behavior. They found that while contact comfort was the most important of these stimuli when held constant, lactation, temperature, and rocking movement were also involved in the attachment process. Facial design was not important; as Harlow and Suomi noted, to a baby the maternal face is beautiful regardless of how we might judge it. Sensory stimulation involving contact comfort, feeding, temperature, and movement are apparently important sources of attachment for infant monkeys. The infant monkey is motivated to remain near its mother (whether real or surrogate), and the mother serves as a source of security from which the infant explores and learns about its world.

While the infant monkeys in the experiments just described became attached to their surrogate mothers, they also showed many bizarre behaviors and were socially abnormal. Harlow and Harlow (1962) investigated the importance of both the mother and peers on normal social development of the infant. They separated infant monkeys from their mothers at birth and raised them in wire cages for varying amounts of time. Semi-isolated, the monkeys could still see and hear other monkeys but could not interact with them. Isolation from birth to three months produced effects that were later reversible, and the effects of isolation appeared minimal, but monkeys isolated from birth to six months developed strange behaviors that appeared more permanent. Monkeys isolated for longer (some from birth to two years) were extremely abnormal. They stared fixedly into space, paced their cages, rocked and clasped themselves, and developed compulsive habits such as chewing or tearing at their own bodies until they bled. They also showed abnormal fear of other monkeys and were socially unable to

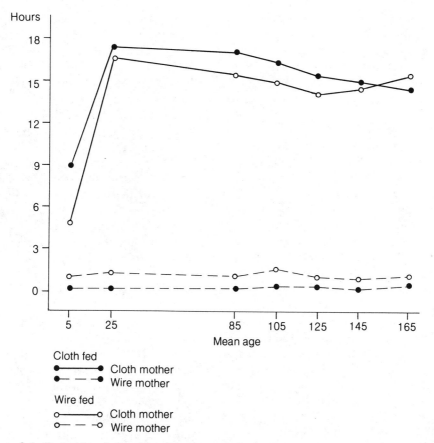

Figure 8.4 *Contact time (in hours) for cloth and wire mothers. Note that regardless of which surrogate fed the infant, most time was spent with the cloth mother. (From Harlow & Suomi, 1970. Copyright © 1970 by the American Psychological Association. Reprinted by permission of the publisher.)*

cope. For example, female isolates would fight viciously when approached by a male, and none were mated naturally. When some of these isolated females were artificially inseminated, their behavior toward their own infants ranged from indifference to outright abuse. These motherless mothers were totally inadequate.

One might be tempted to conclude that adequate maternal care is all that is necessary for normal social adjustment, but at least for monkeys we are not justified in drawing that conclusion. Monkeys raised with their mothers but not allowed social interaction with

peers do not develop normally either, nor do monkeys raised with peers but without a mother. Experience with *both* mother and peers is apparently necessary for normal development (Harlow & Harlow, 1966; Sackett, 1967).

The indifference and abuse of the monkey motherless mothers bears striking resemblance to incidents of human child abuse. Frequently in cases of child abuse, the abusing parent was also abused as a child. This suggests that proper parenting behavior depends at least partly upon having observed how parents behave. If learning about parenting while growing up is important, it is not at all surprising that Harlow's motherless mothers were inadequate. Parenting can be understood as a motivated behavior that results in part from a learning process termed *modeling*. As we saw in Chapter Six, many human motives appear to result from modeling.

Protest, Despair, Detachment, and Ambivalence   Harlow's studies provide a backdrop against which human infant behavior can be better understood. We have known for some time that children separated from their parents go through a series of behavioral changes that include protest, despair, detachment, and ambivalence. Protest and despair following separation have also been extensively studied in monkeys (Mineka & Suomi, 1978).

Bowlby (1973) reported several studies conducted during World War II that are relevant to the discussion of parent-child separation. These studies indicated that a child separated from its parents goes through a series of predictable behaviors. When a child was initially separated from its parents, there was considerable **protest** in the form of crying. The crying continued for several days and occurred sporadically for up to nine days, most commonly at bedtime and during the night. At the same time these children became uncooperative with their attendants.

Following the protest stage, **despair** set in. The children now began to accept some comfort from the attendants and sometimes became very possessive of "their" attendant. Hostility directed toward other children in the situation increased, and toilet training regressed.

When the children were returned to their parents, varying degrees of **detachment** were shown. The degree of detachment appeared to depend upon the length of time that the child had been separated from the parents. In some cases the detached behavior persisted for

several days following reunion with the parents.

The detachment phase was followed by a phase of **ambivalence** in which the child showed hostility, rejection, and defiance of the parents on the one hand, and clinging, crying, and demanding behavior of the parents on the other. The ambivalence phase sometimes lasted as long as 12 weeks.

As a general rule, familiar people (e.g., grandparents or siblings) and familiar objects (e.g., favorite toys) reduced the intensity of the separation effects. A second important factor was the "mothering" available from the parental substitute; the more mothering that was available, the less intense was the separation experience.

Let us now examine research concerning the lack of adequate mothering in which the effects, much as in Harlow's monkeys, seem permanent.

A 1915 survey by Knox (cited by Patton & Gardner, 1963) found that 90% of institutionalized infants died within a year of admission even though they received adequate physical care. Such startling statistics imply that something important for survival was missing in these infants' lives. Spitz (1946), in describing a syndrome he called **anaclitic depression**, noted that some institutionalized children show depression, a failure to respond to stimulation, and a loss of appetite and weight. A clue to the possible source of the anaclitic state was provided by a study of an institution where infants received more individual attention and did not develop the depression. Infants apparently need close interaction with an individual responsible for their care if they are to develop normally.

Deprivation Dwarfism   Gardner (1972) and Patton and Gardner (1963) have shown that lack of appropriate home conditions may result in a condition called deprivation dwarfism. (See also Money, 1977; Money & Wolff,

1974; Wolff & Money, 1973.) **Deprivation dwarfism** is a reduction of bone maturation and growth to the point that the child's physical maturation is much less than normal for its age, and these researchers found that children suffering from deprivation dwarfism were retarded in growth. Heights for age ranged from 20% to 65% of normal. The children appeared malnourished, though in most cases their diets appeared adequate. Emotionally, these children were lethargic, apathetic, and withdrawn. Their faces were sad, rarely smiling, and they typically avoided contact with other people.

This reduction in growth does not result from neural-endocrine problems or from disease but from the social environment in which these children are forced to live. Robert Patton and Lytt Gardner (1963) studied six cases of "thin dwarfs." These children were stunted both physically and psychologically. All came from disordered families in which one or both parents were emotionally disturbed and unable to cope with parenthood. Fathers were often absent from the home, and none were able to maintain steady jobs. Mothers had often come from similar family situations themselves. The relationship between the parents was also typically discordant and often violent. Maternal attitude toward the children ranged from outright hostility to indifference and annoyance. Parental care of the children could be described, at best, as passively neglectful.

When these children were removed from their hostile and deprived environment (e.g., to a hospital), they began to improve both physically and psychologically. Most of the children immediately started growing again. That these children improved in a hospital situation is in marked contrast to normal children, who often react to hospitalization with many of the symptoms of children separated from their parents.

Patton and Gardner were able to follow up two of the six children through late childhood. These children remained below average in height and weight, and skeletal growth was still behind chronological age. Residual effects of the early deprivation experience on both personality structure and intelligence also existed. Furthermore, although hospitalization produced a "catch-up" phenomenon in these children, return to the disordered environment reinstated the dwarfism symptoms (Gardner, 1972; Goodwin, 1978).

How can maternal deprivation and emotional and social disorder reduce physical development? Though the details are still sketchy, Patton and Gardner have proposed that environmental deprivation and emotional disturbance can influence endocrine functioning. The pituitary gland seems to be particularly affected.

The pituitary gland secretes a substance called growth hormone (i.e., **somatotrophin**), which stimulates growth. Quantity of growth hormone is known to be subnormal in children suffering from deprivation dwarfism, even though no pituitary malfunction is present. (The fact that these children start growing again when conditions improve also indicates that the pituitary is not malfunctioning but is being shut down by other factors.) It now appears that the mechanism suppressing the growth hormone is a disruption of the normal sleep pattern.

Children classified as deprivation dwarfs show abnormal sleep patterns. It is known that more growth hormone is secreted during the first two hours of sleep than at any other time, and if the person doesn't sleep, the hormone isn't secreted. Thus the poor social environment apparently leads to a disruption of the normal sleep patterns in these children, and the abnormal sleep pattern then alters the secretion of growth hormone, which leads to the reduction in growth.

Maternal deprivation, then, can have far-reaching effects on both physical and psychological growth. Such effects emphasize the importance of an adequate sensory environment for proper development.

Indeed Patton and Gardner (1963) have argued that a critical period exists during which external stimulation is necessary for optimal development. Without adequate stimulation, permanent deficiencies result. The disordered social environment in which these children are forced to live is a nonoptimal one. They are neglected, ignored, and abused by the parents. As a result they are stunted physically, emotionally, and psychologically. Harlow, too, from his work on monkeys, concluded that a critical period for normal development exists. The data from both animal and human research are consistent in showing that stimulation is necessary for normal development and that lack of stimulation leads to behaviors indicating motivational deficiencies such as lethargy, apathy, and withdrawal.

Mother-infant and peer-peer interactions are apparently important sources of the stimulation necessary for the normal development of an organism. Indeed one researcher who observed mother-infant interactions in free-ranging baboons (Nash, 1978) has suggested that differences in mother-infant interactions may partially account for "personality" differences observed in adulthood. The research on maternal deprivation and infant interaction is generally consistent in showing that deficiencies in mother-infant and peer-peer relationships lead to motivational deficiencies. The motivation of deprived organisms often is not only lowered but may also be inappropriate or bizarre. Changes in emotionality are also evident.

Because stimulation is apparently so important for the normal development of organisms, one might also expect that continued stimulation is a necessary condition for normal adult functioning. This does in fact appear to be true.

Sensory Deprivation in Adults Sensory deprivation studies usually deprive subjects of several sensory inputs simultaneously. Most often visual and auditory inputs are reduced or eliminated; however, tactile and other senses may also be reduced. Sensory deprivation studies may attempt an absolute reduction of sensory stimulation, a reduced patterning of sensory stimulation, or an imposed structuring (usually monotonous) of the sensory environment without any reduction in stimulation (Kubzansky & Leiderman, 1961). Most of the studies on sensory deprivation are of the reduced patterning type, because absolute reductions in stimulation are difficult to achieve.

Much of the early work on sensory deprivation was carried out at McGill University during the period 1951–54 (Heron, 1961). In the classic sensory deprivation situation, a male college student was asked to lie on a bed for 24 hours in a lighted, semisoundproofed room. Patterned vision was eliminated by the use of translucent goggles that admitted only diffused light. Cotton gloves were attached to long, cardboard cuffs that extended from beyond the fingertips to the elbow to reduce tactile stimulation. The subject's head rested on a U-shaped pillow, which reduced auditory stimulation, and an air conditioner provided monotonous background noise that masked extraneous sounds (Heron, 1957, 1961). Figure 8.5 shows the deprivation chamber and basic apparatus used.

Several behavioral tests were conducted both during and after the isolation period (e.g., IQ tests, digit span tests, associative learning tasks, and the like). A propaganda talk on the existence of psychic phenomena (e.g., telepathy, ghosts, and so on) was also given, periodically interrupting the isolation period.

Perhaps the most striking result of the experiment was that subjects could not long tolerate the isolation conditions. In the first

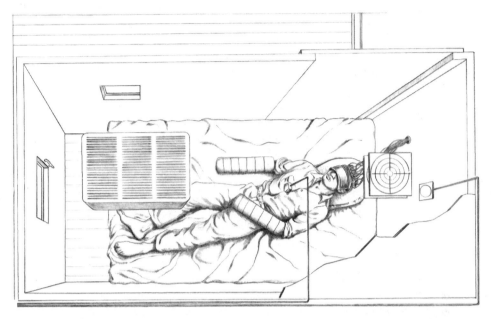

Figure 8.5   *Sensory deprivation chamber used by the McGill University group. See text for details. (Adapted from "The Pathology of Boredom," by Woodburn Heron. Copyright © 1957 by Scientific American, Inc. All rights reserved. Used by permission.)*

experiment (Bexton, Heron, & Scott, 1954) subjects usually quit the experiment after two or three days. In a later experiment the researchers used themselves as subjects and were able to tolerate the conditions for only six days (Heron, Doane, & Scott, 1956). Sensory-deprived subjects experienced boredom, restlessness, irritability, and a strong desire to terminate the experiment. Additionally, the subjects showed impaired thinking, disturbed visual perceptions (e.g., hallucinations), and changes in emotionality, as well as changes in the electrical activity of the brain as measured by the EEG. Isolated subjects were inferior to controls in six out of seven intellectual tests and also did less well than controls on tests of perceptual ability. The isolated subjects also showed a greater change in attitude than the controls after the talk on psychic phenomena,

though both groups showed a change toward belief in such events.

Visual perception was influenced by the loss of patterned vision. When the goggles were removed, plane surfaces appeared warped, and objects in the environment seemed to move when the subject moved. Surfaces such as walls often appeared to shimmer or undulate, and subjects in the experiments reported very strong afterimages. Spatial orientation was also disrupted by the sensory isolation. For example, toward the end of the isolation period, some subjects became so disoriented that they had to call for help because they "got lost" in the bathroom.

What are we to make of these results? From the point of view of motivation, sensory deprivation conditions for most people are clearly aversive. The results suggest that people need to maintain a certain level of stimulation and that they become motivated to increase it if deprived of adequate stimulation levels. Adequate stimulation also seems necessary for efficient functioning, because reduced stimulation led to decreased performance on most of the experimental tasks. Although the hallucinations reported by Heron and associates have proven more elusive to other researchers, both perceptual and intellectual functioning were clearly altered by reduced sensory input. Sensory restriction and deprivation in the form of inadequate maternal care, as previously noted, leads to permanent deficiencies. And sensory deprivation in adults apparently leads to temporary disruptions of behavior.

Jerome Bruner (1961) believed that the effects of isolation can be understood in relation to the development of adequate models or strategies for evaluating information. The deprived child lacks the rich, varied environment that will allow the proper development of these models. In this regard Bruner noted that social contact may be important because it provides a complex sensory environment. He suggested that the adult who has already developed adequate processes for dealing with incoming sensory information is constantly monitoring and correcting his or her strategies as conditions change. The effects of sensory deprivation in the adult may be to disrupt this evaluation process—which in turn may lead to a reduction in cognitive abilities and distortion in the perception of events.

A study by Bennett (1961) of jet pilots supports the idea that sensory deprivation in the adult disrupts the evaluation process. Bennett examined five cases of disorientation in fliers. In all five cases the fliers were either pilots or navigators who became disoriented when flying a straight, level course at high altitude.

Symptoms of disorientation included feelings of confusion and a loss of contact with their surroundings. In three of the five cases the illusion of turning was reported. In all five cases the disorientation occurred at altitudes above 20,000 feet when the fliers had been on a straight, level course for periods ranging from 45 minutes to 2 hours and 20 minutes. The person suffering the disorientation was in all cases isolated from the rest of the crew.

Clark and Graybiel (cited by Bennett, 1961) have reported similar findings from navy and marine pilots. These pilots reported feelings of spatial disorientation, isolation, and detachment from the earth. Three conditions were associated with the disorientation: flying alone, flying at high altitude, and a minimum of activity.

The symptoms reported by the fliers are remarkably similar to the symptoms seen in sensory deprivation experiments. Bennett noted that the lone pilot, flying at high altitude on a straight and level course, is actually quite sensory deprived, for little movement is detectable at that altitude and there is little to do. It seems reasonable to suppose, then, that the disorientation seen in these fliers resulted from the restricted sensory environment that high altitude imposes (no equipment malfunctions were found in any of these cases).

As further support for the sensory deprivation hypothesis, Bennett noted that all the disorientation symptoms were reduced or eliminated if activity was required or other people to talk with were present. Bennett's work with pilots in real-life situations also supports the ideas that changing stimulation is necessary for effective behavior and that without adequate stimulation, adaptive behaviors are reduced.

Sensory deprivation effects are probably not confined to high-altitude flying. Any situation that provides reduced or monotonous stimulation and little activity may be a candidate for disorientation effects. Driving alone at night on an arrow-straight interstate highway might produce effects similar to those produced by high-altitude flying.

Goldberger and Holt (1961) pointed out that some people tolerate sensory deprivation better than others. In one study these researchers divided individuals into two groups based on their ability to deal with primary process thought (as measured by the Rorschach test). Results showed that subjects who scored as mature handlers of primary process thought (i.e., with a minimum of anxiety) tolerated sensory deprivation better and showed less negative emotionality and more pleasant emotionality during the deprivation period.

The Goldberger and Holt study suggests that some people (i.e., those who are emotionally secure) can profit from isolation experiences if the isolation is not too protracted or severe. Suedfeld (1975) has also suggested that sensory deprivation may have beneficial effects. Suedfeld noted that some of the early studies of sensory deprivation may have been very anxiety provoking because of the experimental situation. For example, some researchers provided "panic buttons," while others used anxiety-arousing instructions or release-from-liability forms. Orne and Scheibe (cited by Suedfeld, 1975) obtained some of the typical results of deprivation studies, in fact, by using only these peripheral, anxiety-arousing conditions without any subsequent sensory deprivation.

Suedfeld noted that beneficial effects of isolation, though reported, have not been emphasized. Some subjects have reported enjoying the deprivation experience. In a series of studies (Suedfeld & Ikard, 1974; Suedfeld & Kristeller, 1982; Suedfeld, 1977, 1980) Suedfeld has shown that reduction of stimulation can be therapeutically helpful. In an environment that he calls **REST (Restricted Environmental Stimulation Technique)**, subjects have shown improvement in controlling such habits as smoking and overeating and such stress-related problems as

hypertension (Suedfeld & Kristeller, 1982). The subjects of these studies are usually asked to remain in a darkened and quiet room for 24 hours; depending upon the focus of the study, they may hear antismoking or weight control messages. Follow-up reports have indicated that the combination of REST and messages leads to significant reductions in smoking and greater weight loss in the participants of these studies. Of particular interest, foods taken into the REST situation by subjects were later reported to be less preferred and to be consumed less. Although the reasons for changes in food preference associated with REST are presently unclear, the results suggest that obese individuals might improve weight control by using procedures (like REST) that reduce the attractiveness of preferred foods (Suedfeld & Kristeller, 1982).

The consequences of restricted sensory input, therefore, may not always be negative; Suedfeld's research seems to indicate that restriction of the sensory environment may be used to modify behaviors that have proven difficult to change using other behavioral techniques. The motivational changes caused by REST are not well understood; perhaps future research will lead to the development of a theoretical framework within which changes in motivation, either positive or negative, can be explained.

OPPONENT-PROCESS THEORY: HEDONISM REVISITED

The concept of hedonism is intimately tied to sensory input because we tend to categorize sensory information as pleasant, unpleasant, or neutral. To conclude this chapter we will consider a homeostatic model of hedonic quality proposed by Richard Solomon (Solomon, 1980, 1977; Solomon & Corbit, 1974). Solomon assumes that both pleasant and aversive hedonic states are opposed by a central nervous system process that reduces their intensity. The process reduces these primary hedonic sensations by producing a hedonic state that is opposite in quality to that of the initial stimulus. Thus stimuli that give rise to pleasurable feelings will be opposed by aversive feelings generated by the process; conversely, stimuli that initially give rise to aversive feelings will be opposed by pleasant feelings generated by the process.

Let's look at how this opponent-process mechanism is presumed to work. Solomon argued that every affectively important situation has five characteristics. When a stimulus is detected, it produces a hedonic reaction that (1) quickly **peaks**; after the hedonic peak, there occurs (2) an **adaptation phase** during which the intensity of the hedonic experience declines and eventually reaches (3) a **steady level**; if the stimulus that started this chain of events now disappears, there occurs (4) a **peak-affective after-reaction** with characteristics opposite to the original hedonic state; this after-reaction slowly (5) **decays** until the intensity of the affective after-reaction returns to zero. Figure 8.6 charts these five characteristic features of an emotional reaction to a stimulus.

The opponent-process model assumes that the physiological process that triggers the initial hedonic reaction (i.e., reaction state A) will be opposed by a second physiological state, which will trigger an opposite hedonic reaction (i.e., state B). The decline in hedonic value from the peak of state A to the steady level will result from state B's effect of reducing state A. Thus the steady level of hedonic intensity in Figure 8.6 is state A minus state B. When the stimulus creating state A is no longer present, the full force of state B (i.e., the opposite hedonic reaction to state A) is felt. The state B experience then slowly decays until hedonic intensity returns to zero.

States A and B differ from each other in several ways in addition to their being of opposite hedonic quality. For example, state A develops very quickly and is closely associated with the intensity of the stimulus that produced it; when the stimulus triggering state A is removed, the hedonic state A ceases. State B, however, develops slowly, and rather than being generated by a stimulus, it is produced *as a reaction to* state A. Further, state B is slow to decrease; when state A is removed, state B continues for some time because it decays slowly. State A differs from state B in yet another way. Repeated presentations of the stimulus that produced state A have no effect on the intensity of state A; however, repeated elicitation of state B leads to a strengthening of state B. Because activation of state B has the effect of reducing the intensity of state A, as noted above, repeated presentations of the stimulus that triggered state A will actually lead to a reduction in the hedonic intensity of state A, because state B will increase in intensity as shown in Figure 8.7.

Drug Addiction

Opponent-process theory appears capable of explaining many of the behaviors associated with drug addiction. The addicting substance will initially give rise to pleasurable feelings (state A). The opponent-process, however, will gain in strength as the person continues to use the drug so that a strongly aversive state B develops. Because the pleasurable experiences of state A are reduced by the growing aversive state B, a point will be reached where the addicted individual will maintain drug use not for the pleasure it brings but rather to avoid the aversiveness of state B (withdrawal symptoms) that occurs when the drug-maintained state A is absent.

Neutral stimuli that reliably precede states A and B can become conditioned to these states. Thus any cue that consistently occurs before the "high" of a drug state A will begin to act as a secondary reinforcer for continued drug use. Similarly, neutral stimuli reliably associated with the aversive state B of

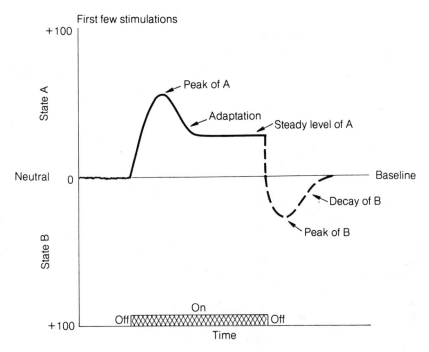

Figure 8.6 The five phases of an affective reaction to a stimulus. (Adapted from Solomon & Corbit, 1974. Copyright © 1974 by the American Psychological Association. Reprinted by permission of the publisher and author.)

drug withdrawal will negatively reinforce behaviors that reduce or eliminate these stimuli. The obvious way to avoid these negative stimuli is of course to use the drug again. The addict, then, is caught in a double bind; stimuli associated with both the pleasurable state A and the aversive state B tend to maintain drug use. Both sets of stimuli reinforce the same behavior—taking drugs. The associative effects of these stimuli are of course added to the behavioral effects of the pleasurable state A and the aversive state B, which also promote continued drug use.

Additionally, it appears that the tolerance that develops to a continually used drug can be at least partially explained as the result of conditioned A and B states. For example, Siegel (1975, 1977; Siegel, Sherman, & Mitch-

ell, 1980) has shown that rats develop a conditioned tolerance of morphine in environmental situations that signal impending drug administration. Siegel has proposed that cues signaling drug injection have become conditioned to a "compensatory process," a process that, according to Solomon (1980), apparently has many of the same characteristics as the opponent-process state B aroused by drug injection.

We have known for many years the extreme difficulty involved with breaking a drug habit. The opponent-process model provides us with a theoretical basis for understanding *why* drug habits are so difficult to break. Perhaps the model will help us develop new approaches to drug abuse that will be more effective than those currently in use.

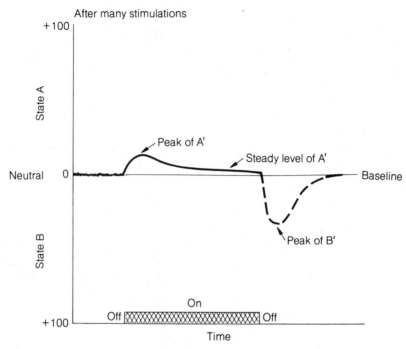

Figure 8.7 *Characteristics of the opponent process after many stimulations. Note the increase in the size of state B in comparison to state A. (Adapted from Solomon & Corbit, 1974. Copyright © 1974 by the American Psychological Association. Reprinted by permission of the publisher and author.)*

Thrill Seeking

Why do people often seek out experiences that seem dangerous, fear producing, or painful? Opponent-process theory suggests that one reason people engage in behaviors such as riding roller coasters, skydiving, racing automobiles, and playing dangerous sports is the strong state B that occurs after the initial fear-producing (or painful) state A.

One such example is parachuting. Epstein (1967, as cited by Solomon, 1980) has studied the emotional reactions of military parachutists. Prior to their first jump, chutists appear anxious. During the first free fall (i.e., before the chute opens), signs of terror are often present: eyes bulge, lips are pulled back tight against the teeth, bodies curl forward, and

involuntary urination sometimes occurs. Clearly an aversive state A seems to occur during the initial jump. Upon landing safely, the chutists initially appear stunned for several minutes and then begin to interact socially, often in quite animated ways. Solomon has suggested that this after-reaction to the jump, which may last for up to ten minutes, is a highly positive state B that is opposite in emotional quality to the fear-producing state A.

For an experienced chutist, however, the picture is quite different. With repeated jumps, the fearful state A is reduced to the point that the chutist appears not frightened but eager. According to opponent-process theory, the reduction in fear occurs because the positive state B, building up over many jumps, reduces state A. Experienced parachutists look tense or excited prior to the jump and report a thrill rather than terror during free fall. After landing, the returned chutists are very physically active, and they may jump, shout, and talk excitedly. This period of euphoria, which may last as long as two or three hours, is often described as exhilarating.

According to the opponent-process model, then, people may engage in frightening or dangerous behaviors because of the reduction in the initially aversive state A and the highly positive opposite reaction that occurs when the behavior ceases. The model presented by Solomon has potential applications for a wide variety of frightening, dangerous, or stressing situations into which people put themselves. Running marathons, skydiving, hang gliding, riding roller coasters, and watching horror movies may all have in common a strongly positive state B that follows the initial aversive state A. Further, many of these activities, in a manner similar to drug use, seem to have an addictive quality—precisely as opponent-process theory predicts.

Social Attachment

Opponent-process theory has also been applied to the attachment process (Hoffman et al., 1974; Hoffman & Solomon, 1974; Starr, 1978; Mineka, Suomi, & Delizio, 1981). Starr (1978), for example, imprinted young ducklings on a moving model of a female mallard duck. (Recall that in Chapter Two we examined the imprinting process from the point of view of instinctively motivated behavior and that imprinting appears to lead to social attachment in many species of birds.) Starr assumed that some aspect of the imprinting stimulus triggers a positive state A, because numerous studies have shown that young birds are highly motivated to approach and follow an imprinting stimulus and that such a stimulus can serve as a positive reinforcer (see, e.g., Hoffman & Ratner, 1973). Further, removal of

an imprinted stimulus typically leads to distress calling (a characteristic vocalization with a frequency that ranges between 2,000 and 5,000 Hz.), which Starr used as a measure of the negative state B. Starr's assumptions were based in part upon a study by Hoffman and associates (1974), which showed that distress calling to the withdrawal of an imprinted stimulus increased with increasing exposure to that stimulus. Thus, in the study by Hoffman and associates, distress calling appeared to index the growth of the negative state B opposing the positive state A that occurs when the imprinted stimulus is presented.

Starr not only replicated the basic findings of Hoffman and associates but found that an important factor in the development of the negative state B is the time interval between successive presentations of the imprinting stimulus. Thus, if the interval between presentations is short, say, one minute, then the negative state B grows as predicted by opponent-process theory. On the other hand, if sufficient time is allowed to elapse between presentations so that the negative state B has time to decay (five minutes in Starr's study), then state B doesn't grow stronger. This important finding, termed the **critical decay duration** by Starr, demonstrates that growth of state B (and thus subsequent reduction of state A) depends upon the time interval between activations of state A: if the time interval is short, state B will grow and reduce the emotional quality of state A; however, if the time interval is large enough so that state B decays, no reduction in the quality of state A will occur. Based on this finding, we might predict that jumping out of an airplane only once a year would lead not to exhilaration but to continued terror.

Additionally, Starr found that changes in the intensity of the imprinting stimulus (e.g., adding sound) and changes in duration (e.g., decreasing the amount of time the stimulus is present) also influence the critical decay duration. Thus a stimulus that triggers a more intense state A creates a state B that takes longer to decay; conversely, a stimulus that triggers a weak state A will lead to a state B that decays faster. Starr's work suggests that the emotional impact a stimulus will have depends upon the intensity, duration, and frequency with which we encounter that stimulus: strong stimuli of long duration or repeated frequency will generate a large state B that will oppose state A. If state A is positive, then its emotional impact will be reduced (that is, there are negative consequences of often repeated positive experiences), while a negative state A will become less aversive and even enjoyed (that is, there are positive consequences of often repeated negative experiences).

The use of opponent-process theory to explain attachment processes has generality beyond the study of imprinting in birds. Mineka, Suomi, and Delizio (1981) have found that the model also works well in describing behavioral changes in adolescent monkeys that experience multiple separation experiences. In a series of experiments these researchers found that multiple separations lead to increased social contact on reunion, that this contact declines across days, and that multiple separation experiences increase depressed and agitated behaviors. Their data suggest that for a socially attached monkey, some aspect of its source of attachment (mother, peers, and so on) produces a positive state A, which is opposed by a negative state B. Under normal conditions state B leads to reduced social contact; however, when the source of attachment is removed, the negative state B leads to self-directed behaviors such as clasping or agitated, stereotypic movements. When the monkey is reunited with its source of attachment, increased social contact occurs, presumably because state B has decayed somewhat and thus state A is heightened. More importantly, however, the researchers found that additional separations lead to a growth in state B so that self-directed maladaptive

behaviors become more pronounced and socially directed behaviors decrease. As noted by Mineka and associates (1981), the agitated, stereotypic behaviors of these monkeys appear similar to the "ceaseless activity" often seen in patients with agitated depressions (Beck, 1967, p.42).

As we have seen, opponent-process theory has been expanded to cover a host of behaviors that have often seemed quite dissimilar. Indeed, opponent-process theory has been applied to behaviors as disparate as breastfeeding (Myers & Siegel, 1985) and habitual blood donation (Piliavin, Callero, & Evans, 1982).

The concept of opponent processes that are of opposite hedonic quality and that interact to produce an affective state holds much promise. Modern hedonistic explanations clearly have much merit.

SUMMARY

In this chapter we have explored the related ideas of sensory stimulation and hedonism, and we have seen that the concept of pleasure and pain as behavior motivators has a long history. Young has suggested that there exists a hedonic continuum along which pleasurable and painful stimuli vary. Because we can move back and forth along this continuum, what is pleasurable at one point in time may be neutral or even painful at another time.

Considerable evidence suggests that sensory stimulation is important to the development and maintenance of normal motivated behavior. As a result, behaviors such as curiosity and exploration may have developed to maintain adequate levels of stimulation. Research on sensory restriction, in both young organisms and the adult, also supports the notion that stimulation has motivating properties. Thus maternal deprivation leads to various abnormalities in young monkeys, and, given the opportunity, sensory-deprived organisms will work to maintain stimulation.

Sensory isolation and abuse in children can lead to deprivation dwarfism, and sensory restriction in the adult leads to a variety of reported problems ranging from difficulties in concentration to hallucinations. Thus sensory stimulation apparently has important motivational properties, and adequate stimulation seems necessary for normal functioning.

The effect of stimuli on an individual may result from processes that occur in the brain itself. The opponent-process theory of Solomon and his associates proposes that the initial emotional state created by a stimulus will be opposed by a second emotional state that is its opposite. The reoccurrence of a stimulus leads to a growth of the second state, which reduces the emotional quality of the first state. As a result, highly positive stimuli can become less motivating over time, and, conversely, highly negative stimuli can lose much of their aversive properties with repeated exposures.

Various behaviors including drug addiction, risk taking, and attachment have been analyzed using opponent-process theory. At this point in our understanding, opponent-process theory seems to hold promise as a modified version of hedonism that may help us better understand how the stimuli we encounter in our everyday lives motivate us. Clearly hedonism is still very much with us.

SUGGESTIONS FOR FURTHER READING

Most of the research presented in this chapter comes from the primary literature found in journal articles. Although some of these articles are quite technical, two articles that the student may find of interest are the following:

Harlow, H. F. (1958). The nature of love. *American Psychologist, 13*, 673–685. In this article Harlow presents evidence for the importance of contact comfort in the social attachment process in monkeys.

Solomon, R. L. (1980). The opponent-process theory of acquired motivation: The costs of pleasure and the benefits of pain. *American Psychologist, 35*, 691–712. In this article Solomon outlines the basic concepts underlying opponent-process theory and reviews data supportive of the theory.

IV

COGNITIVE APPROACHES TO MOTIVATION

Chapter Nine

Cognitive Motivation: Expectancy-Value Approaches

CHAPTER PREVIEW

This chapter is concerned with the following questions:

1. Which early cognitive theorists helped develop the concept of expectancy-value?

2. How do expectancy-value theories explain the motivation of behavior?

3. How does the expectancy-value concept add to our understanding of achievement?

Sarah was hungry again. As a matter of fact, Sarah was always hungry. Since her heart attack, the doctor had insisted that she lose 50 pounds, and her daughter, with whom she lived, was watching her like a hawk.

Still the hunger nagged at her. She pondered the problem. If she went into the kitchen and opened the refrigerator door, her daughter Doris would certainly come running. The candy in the dish on the coffee table was also off limits; Doris would notice immediately if she reached for one.

Then Sarah was struck by an idea. Doris had bought some candy for Halloween and had stored it away in the basement cupboard. If Sarah went downstairs, Doris would assume that she was going to do some washing or ironing. She could take a small candy bar and Doris would never be the wiser.

Sarah hefted herself slowly from the chair and headed for the basement—not for the last time that week. And Doris was surprised when Halloween came.

Sarah's behavior demonstrates the idea that our actions are determined by a field of forces working together. The heart attack, the doctor's orders, and her ever present daughter limited the ways in which Sarah could deal with her perceived hunger. All these forces working together led to her devious solution of eating the Halloween candy a little at a time.

The solution to her problem that Sarah chose could exemplify a way of analyzing human motivation as suggested by Kurt Lewin. We will examine his theory later in this chapter.

The previous chapters of this book have concentrated on explanations of behavior motivation that usually do not require a thinking, purposeful organism. Certainly some types of motivated behavior are relatively fixed and mechanical in nature, but other motive states seem best explained in terms of rational, thinking organisms. Such approaches are generally termed **cognitive theories.**

As Bolles (1974) clearly pointed out, cognitive explanations of behavior are nothing new. The early Greek philosophers were cognitive in their approach to understanding the world about them. Plato, for example, argued that we do what we perceive to be right based on our *ideas* of what is right. Motivationally, Plato thought that we attempt to maximize virtue, which we determine by our thoughts. Psychologists have defined cognition a little more narrowly than the early Greek philosophers. Although definitions vary somewhat, the term **cognition** is generally used to describe those intellectual or perceptual processes occurring within us when we analyze and interpret both the world around us and our own thoughts and actions. Because of the active, interpretative nature of these processes, the term **information processing** is often used in connection with the concept of cognition. The focus of the next four chapters, then, is on theory and research describing how cognitive processes can motivate us. In this chapter, after briefly looking at two early cognitive theorists, we will focus on the cognitive approach known as expectancy-value theory.

TOLMAN'S PURPOSIVE BEHAVIOR

Tolman (1932) argued that in order to understand behavior, we must study it as a phenomenon in its own right. He argued that behavior has both descriptive and defining properties and is more than just sequences of muscle twitches. Thus Tolman advocated a wholistic study of behavior, in contrast to reductionistic approaches (e.g., Clark Hull) that attempted to understand behavior by reducing it to its smallest component parts. According to Tolman, then, behavior is molar (i.e., to be studied as a whole and not reduced to its component parts).

Characteristics of Molar Behavior

Tolman believed that molar behavior has certain defining properties. First, **behavior is always directed toward or away from some specific goal.** Thus the behavior of a hungry rat running through a maze can be characterized as an attempt to reach the goal of food at the end of the maze. Behaviors are heavily influenced by the various characteristics of the goal toward which they are directed. Behavior directed toward a goal is also **persistent,** tending to continue until the goal is obtained.

A second major characteristic of molar behavior is that behaviors leading to a goal form a **consistent pattern** of responses. Behavior is not random but represents ways in which the organism attempts to reach the goal. For example, in driving to work I make a specific pattern of responses that succeed in getting me from my doorstep to my office. This pattern of responses is relatively constant and is quite different from the pattern of responses I make when working toward other goals (e.g., going to a movie).

The third major characteristic of molar behavior is a **selectivity** to behavior, so that the shortest or easiest path to the goal will be the one taken. Several different roads will take me from my home to my office, but I usually choose the most direct one.

According to Tolman, then, we must know the goal toward which behavior is directed, the ways in which the organism behaves in order to reach the goal, and the possible routes that may be taken in order to reach the goal. Unless we know these three things, our understanding of the observed behavior will be incomplete.

Purpose and Cognition

The three characteristics of molar behavior imply that the organism has some understanding (i.e., cognition) of the goals toward which its behavior is leading. Thus behavior was seen by Tolman to be purposive. For Tolman, whether the behavior in question is that of a rat or a human, it is characterized by cognition and purpose.

Tolman was careful to define what he meant by purposiveness. First, the purposiveness of behavior is objectively defined by the behaviors observed and not by inference to anything subjective. That an organism will **learn** a series of behaviors in order to reach some goal is evidence, Tolman argued, for the purposiveness of behavior. As an example, consider my cat. As a kitten it would sometimes claw the furniture. In typical psychological fashion, I thought to break this habit by quickly following the clawing response with a period of nonreinforcement (i.e., putting the cat outside whenever it clawed the furniture). The furniture clawing decreased but did not disappear. When the cat, now an adult, desires to go outside, as you can probably guess, it gets me to let it out by perfunctorily clawing the couch, then running to the door. It seems hard to deny, at least from Tolman's point of view, that the behavior of clawing the couch has the "purpose" of reaching the goal of getting outside (it may also be instructive in pointing out that when we modify behavior, we don't always get what we expect!).

The example of my cognitive cat is perhaps an appropriate place to mention another point made by Tolman, which concerns the distinction between learning and performance. My cat did not initially learn to claw the furniture in order to be let out. It began behaving in this manner to sharpen its claws; however, because I created a contingency between this behavior and being put outside, the cat learned (and came to expect) that this

particular behavior in the future would lead to the goal of being put out. At times when the cat does not want to be outside, no evidence exists that it knows this particular relationship; it must be motivated to go out before this particular behavior is performed. Thus, as Tolman argued, learning can occur in the absence of any behavioral change; motivation is necessary for learning to be translated into performance.

In the process of learning that particular behaviors lead to particular goals, Tolman asserted, **cognitive expectancies** are established. These involve both the expectancy that a particular set of behaviors will lead to a specific goal and the expectancy that specific goals can be found in particular locations (Cofer & Appley, 1964). The Tinklepaugh (1928) experiment noted in Chapter Seven is a good example of Tolman's view of cognitive expectancy. Thus for Tolman organisms do not learn specific stimulus-response connections; they learn which behaviors lead to which goals.

Tolman's approach emphasized the idea that organisms develop a **cognitive map** of their environment. This map indicates the places in which particular goals may be found. Tolman's ideas were in sharp contrast to the strict stimulus-response approaches emphasizing the idea that learning consists of chains of responses (e.g., turn left, then right, then right again). Thus for Tolman an organism learns a general concept about the place where reinforcement can be found, not a series of responses to reach a goal.

The concept of a cognitive map suggests that organisms such as the rat acquire expectations both that behavior will be rewarded and that the reward can be found in specific locations. Tolman in fact argued that place learning is the more usual way in which animals learn. Experiments by Tolman, Ritchie, and Kalish (1946, 1947) revealed the ease with which place learning can occur. An elevated maze in the shape of a cross was used to run two groups of rats (see Figure 9.1). One group, the response-learning group, was sometimes started from start box 1 and sometimes from start box 2, but in either case the correct response was to turn right to obtain food. Thus, if the rats started from box 1, they found food in goal box 1 (as shown in Figure 9.1), while if they started from start box 2, they found food in goal box 2. A second group, the place-learning group, was also randomly started from either start box 1 or start box 2, but regardless of where these rats started, they always found food in the same place. If, for example, the food was in goal box 1, the correct response from start box 1 was a right turn, but if the rats started from start box 2, the correct response was a left turn. To efficiently solve the problem, the rats in group 2 had to learn where food was to be found rather than learning a simple turning response.

The results of the experiment showed that the place-learning group learned much more quickly than the response-learning group. This finding seems to indicate that learning *where* rewards can be found is easier than learning a specific set of responses; additionally, it supports the notion that animals develop expectations about the environment that have the characteristics of a cognitive map.

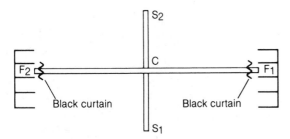

Figure 9.1 Elevated maze used by Tolman, Ritchie, and Kalish in their studies of place learning. S_1 and S_2 are starting points, while F_1 and F_2 are food boxes; C is the center choice point of the maze. (From Tolman, Ritchie, and Kalish, 1946.)

As is often the case in psychology, these results did not go unchallenged, and other experiments sometimes found that response learning was easier than place learning (see Hilgard & Bower, 1975, for a review of this work). Restle (1957) provided a possible solution to the conflicting studies by suggesting that both response and place learning can occur and that which type of learning occurs depends upon the salience of the cues in the situation. In the original study by Tolman and associates, for example, many extramaze cues were available that made place learning easy; when place cues are reduced, response learning becomes more dominant. It seems clear at this point that both response learning and place learning do occur. The important point for our purposes is that when it occurs, place learning suggests that expectations do develop concerning where rewards can be found.

One final experiment conducted by Tolman and Honzik (1930b) also substantiates the concept of expectation. In this experiment three alternate paths were available from the start box to the goal box, as shown in Figure 9.2.

During the early parts of training, rats were given experience with all three paths. If path 1 was blocked at A, rats developed a preference for route 2 over route 3, so the order of preference for the three routes was path 1, followed by path 2, and finally path 3. Later in training, path 1 was again blocked but at position B. As you can see, blocking path 1 at position B also blocks path 2 because the block is at a point common to both routes. What would a rat do upon discovering that path 1, its preferred route, is blocked at B? After retracing its steps back to the start box, would the rat now choose path 2 and again be blocked, or would it understand the relationship between paths 1 and 2 and therefore choose the least preferred but only accessible path (3) to the goal?

The rats in the Tolman and Honzik

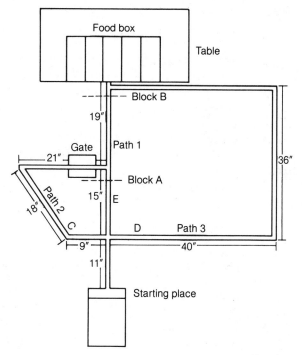

Figure 9.2 Alternate path maze used by Tolman and Honzik. See text for details. (From Tolman & Honzik, 1930. Used by permission.)

experiment typically chose path 3, demonstrating that they possessed some sort of cognitive map of the relationships between the various paths. Although this experiment was also criticized (see Hilgard & Bower, 1975, for experiments critical of the alternate path experiment), taken together with the cross maze experiment, the Tinklepaugh experiment, and numerous other studies, the conclusion seems inescapable that animals can form expectations about their environment and, further, that these expectations motivate future behavior.

Tolman realized that the physical state of the organism is important in motivating behavior. He believed that the real purpose of a behavior is to obtain a quiescent physiological state. Tolman, however, differed from theorists such as Hull in his emphasis that

physiological disturbance motivates the organism by creating a demand for certain goal objects associated with that disturbance in the past. Theorists like Hull emphasized the activation properties of physiological disturbance but not demands for specific goals.

Tolman listed what he considered to be the primary motives. These included the motives to seek food, water, and sex, to excrete wastes, to avoid pain, to rest, to experience specific types of contact, to aggress, to reduce curiosity, and to satisfy certain sensory-motor hungers. These primary motives are apparently and primarily evoked by internal changes. Tolman also noted several secondary motive states primarily evoked by external conditions. Such secondary motives included affiliation, dominance, dependence, and submission. (Interestingly, Tolman believed that both primary and secondary motives are innate.)

A third source of motivation is learned motives, which Tolman believed can be evidenced in certain aspects of personality development. For example, certain cultural goals, such as the motive to obtain wealth or business success, are learned. These tertiary motives, thought to be originally associated with the more basic motives of the individual, eventually come to control behavior relatively independently of the early motives from which they derived (Cofer & Appley, 1964).

Tolman, then, emphasized early that motivation should be understood in cognitive terms. The organism, whether rat or human, has certain classes of needs. These motives lead to a cognitive representation of the goals that will alleviate the currently active motive state and lead to the location (i.e., a cognitive map) of those goals. In addition, through learning the organism develops a cognitive expectation that certain behaviors will lead to those goals. Because of the cognitive nature of behavior, Tolman believed that studying specific responses is less important than identifying the goals toward which the behavior is leading. Although the behaviors used by an organism may vary, the goal will remain constant.

As an example of Tolman's approach, consider the route you take when driving to classes. There are usually several possible routes you might take, differing in terms of mileage, time, condition of road, and so on. You have a cognitive representation (i.e., cognitive map) of where you are located. If your normal route is blocked by a car accident or a fallen tree, you can adjust and take a different route—because you have a cognitive representation both of the school location and of the possible alternate routes you might take. If I wanted to study your motive state, I would learn less from observing the route you take than from observing where you finally go (i.e.,

to school). That is the essence of Tolman's approach.

Tolman's theory has had its detractors. Most of the strict stimulus-response theorists of his time took issue with his emphasis on the cognitive aspects of behaviors. The major criticism of Tolman's theory centers on its lack of detail (Hilgard & Bower, 1975); because of the theory's imprecise nature, definite predictions could not always be made. Nevertheless, Tolman's research proved to be particularly difficult for stimulus-response theories to explain. Perhaps more than anyone else, he brought about a reevaluation of the strict stimulus-response approach that has, in turn, led to a greatly increased emphasis on cognitive processes as explanations for behavior.

KURT LEWIN'S FORCE FIELD THEORY

Kurt Lewin (1936, 1938) described a homeostatic cognitive model of behavior motivation. His approach was a dynamic one, emphasizing that the forces acting to initiate behavior are constantly changing. He pointed out that several forces may simultaneously exert influence on behavior; thus the behavior observed is the result of the total forces acting upon the individual.

Lewin's was a cognitive approach for at least two reasons. First, his thinking was heavily influenced by the Gestalt school of psychology, with which he was closely associated. The Gestalt approach emphasized the active problem-solving and insightful nature of behavior rather than the mechanical connections emphasized by stimulus-response approaches. Second, Lewin's motivational constructs included psychological needs (which he termed **quasi-needs**) that are best understood as cognitive in nature.

To emphasize his belief that behavior can be understood only as the result of all the forces acting on an individual, Lewin described behavior in terms of **field theory**. Field theory emphasizes the idea that the reaction of an object is the result of all the forces acting upon that object within the field containing it. The field in field theory is actually a field of conflicting forces. For example, the reaction of a kite depends upon the field of forces acting upon it. Changing wind conditions, gravity, and counterforce applied by the kite flyer all serve to define the ultimate "behavior" of the kite.

Lewin argued that human behavior can be similarly understood to result from all the forces acting upon an individual at the time the behavior occurs. Lewin therefore described behavior (B) as a function (f) of the life space (L), which in turn consists of the person (P) and the psychological environment (E). Thus we can write the formulas seen in Figure 9.3a, b, and c.

The person (P), to be described in more detail shortly, is influenced by two types of needs, which create a motivational state of tension (t). Further, the psychological environment (E), which we will also detail after examination of the person, contains goals (G) that influence behavior. Behavioral force (F),

then, can be regarded as a function (f) of the internal state of tension (t) and the goals (G) that exist in the psychological environment, leading to the formulas seen in Figure 9.3d, e, and f.

Behavioral force (F), however, is also altered by the psychological distance (e) between the person and the goal; the greater the distance, the smaller the force, so that we arrive finally at the equation seen in Figure 9.3g. This last expression tells us that behavioral force will be a function of the person's tension state that results from internal needs, the characteristics of the goals that can satisfy those needs, and the psychological distance between the person and the goals.

As described by Lewin, behavioral force has the characteristics of a **vector**; that is, it has direction and magnitude. Thus Lewin drew arrows of varying lengths and pointing in various directions to describe the different forces acting on an individual at any given point in time. This field of forces acting on the person determines the resulting behavior. In order to more fully appreciate Lewin's system, we must examine the constructs of the person and the psychological environment. We will begin with his concepts of the person.

(a) $B = f(L)$

(b) $L = f(P + E)$

Therefore

(c) $B = f(P + E)$

(d) $P = f(t)$

(e) $E = f(G)$

(f) $F = f(t, G)$

(g) $F = f\left\{\dfrac{t, G}{e}\right\}$

Figure 9.3 Lewin's force field formulas. B = behavior; f = is a function of; L = life space; P = person; E = psychological environment; t = tension; G = goals; F = behavioral force; e = psychological distance. See text for details.

The Person

Figure 9.4 depicts the regions of the person. The outside ring labeled S-M represents the portion of the individual that interacts with the psychological environment. Sensory information (S) comes into the person via this region, and motor output (M) proceeds out through this region. The center portion of the individual (i.e., the inner-personal region, labeled I-P in Figure 9.4) is divided into many separate regions, each of which represents a potential need of the individual. The regions nearest the S-M area labeled p (for peripheral) are less crucial needs; that is, they are less central to the person's well-being. The interior

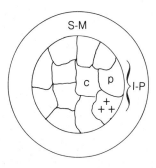

Figure 9.4 The person. S-M = sensory-motor region; I-P = inner-personal region; p = peripheral region or need; c = central region or need. Pluses symbolize an inner-personal region in a state of tension. (Adapted from Lewin, 1936. Used by permission of McGraw-Hill Book Company.)

regions labeled c (for central) represent the more crucial needs of the individual. As an example, one might think of the need for food or water as a central need and the need to cut the grass as more peripheral. The central core of the inner-personal region was seen by Lewin as having a greater influence on behavior because the core regions are in contact with many other regions. In Lewin's model this is shown by the central regions' common boundaries with many other regions. On the other hand, the central core needs were seen as less likely to be expressed directly in behavior because they are furthest from the motor regions. The boundaries of the inner-personal regions are also not fixed; core regions can sometimes become peripheral, and vice versa. Also, differentiation into more finely divided areas occurs (e.g., you're not just hungry; you're hungry for steak). Several regions may also be collapsed together into one region via restructuring. Finally, Lewin conceived the borders between regions as having differing capacities to allow tension to flow between them (termed **permeability**).

Motivational Properties of the Inner-Personal Region (Tension)   Tension is the

motivational construct that Lewin used for motivation internal to the person. Tension exists when a potential need becomes an actual need. For example, some region *within* the inner-personal area may represent the potential need for water; when the body becomes dehydrated, this particular region will be in a state of tension (indicated in Figure 9.4 by the plus signs).

When tension exists, the individual becomes motivated to reduce it; thus Lewin's model was homeostatic in character. The reduction of tension can be accomplished in one of two ways: it can be spread evenly throughout the entire inner-personal region, or it can be alleviated through a process termed **locomotion**, in which some particular region of the psychological environment dissipates the tension. Suppose that within my inner-personal region a region of tension exists because I "need" (i.e., want) a soft drink. If I am on a diet, the tension that results from this need may have to be spread evenly through my inner-personal region, raising my overall tension slightly but restoring the total region to balance. On the other hand, I might eliminate the tensions by searching through my psychological facts, which include memories that (1) there is a soft-drink machine on the third floor and that (2) I have some change with which to buy a drink. In this second instance a locomotion has occurred if I use the psychological facts to reduce the tension.

If the first avenue is chosen, the overall tension of the inner-personal region will increase slightly, but each region within the inner-personal region will be equal. It is at this point that the boundary conditions become important. If some boundaries are impermeable (i.e., do not allow passage of the tension), the increased tension cannot be spread evenly across the entire inner-personal region, and motivation will continue to exert an influence in order to equalize the tension. Also, if the region in which the tension exists has an impermeable boundary, the tension cannot be reduced either by spreading it out or by locomotion to some appropriate region in the psychological environment. This latter case appears conceptually similar to Freud's concept of repression.

Lewin postulated two types of needs that lead to the production of tension: **physiological needs** and **psychological needs** (also termed **quasi-needs**). Physiological needs include factors such as hunger and thirst, while psychological needs can be as diverse as the need to go dancing on Saturday night or the need to finish an uncompleted task. Motivation, according to Lewin, is specific rather than general. Each need creates its own motive force (i.e., energy) in the form of tension. Along with each tension state, particular classes of goal objects in the psychological environment exist that will satisfy the need and thus reduce the tension. Reaching one of these goals results in the reduction of a tension state, though the goal itself may not be a physical entity. Goals can either be specific physical objects or such cognitive acts as remembering someone's name or solving a math problem.

The Zeigarnik Effect Lewin believed that a state of tension will continue to motivate behavior until the behavior associated with the task is completed (Cofer & Appley, 1964; Sahakian, 1975). If Lewin was correct, one might expect differences to exist between completed and interrupted tasks. Bluma Zeigarnik, a Russian studying with Lewin at the University of Berlin, tested this hypothesis. Zeigarnik found that tasks interrupted before completion were more frequently recalled than tasks allowed to run to completion. The better recall was seen as evidence for Lewin's ideas concerning tension. As long as a task is incomplete, tension will remain, and the tensions will in turn keep the information concerning the task more available to memory.

A year after Zeigarnik published her results, another Russian studying with Lewin carried this research a step further. Maria Ovsiankina found that subjects given the opportunity to complete an interrupted task did so with great frequency. Ovsiankina's research provided further support for Lewin's idea that systems in tension continue to motivate behavior until a task is completed to the individual's satisfaction.

Tension from either physical or quasi-needs was regarded as motivating behavior. If a task is not completed for some reason, the tension continues to motivate the individual to complete the task, and the various aspects of the task will be more available to memory than aspects of completed tasks.

The Psychological Environment

In order to fully understand Lewin's motivational model, we must look briefly at the structure of the psychological environment, which was conceived as consisting of regions and boundaries. The psychological environment is not identical to the real world but consists of all the psychological *facts* of which one is aware. Thus psychological facts basically form the total of our knowledge as it exists in memory. For example, a fact might consist of the knowledge that food is in the refrigerator or the knowledge of a series of movements that will get us to the refrigerator.

Lewin conceptualized the satisfaction of a tension state to be the result of a locomotion from the inner-personal area, in a state of tension, to the appropriate psychological fact that satisfies the need. The border of the regions in the psychological environment, like those of the inner-personal region, have differing permeabilities so that movement is easier through some regions than others. This means that although several possible routes to a psychological fact may exist, one path will be easier because of the boundary conditions of the intervening regions (see Figure 9.5).

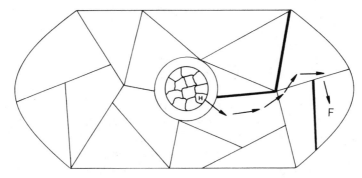

Figure 9.5   The person in the psychological environment. H = a core region in a state of tension due to hunger. The arrows indicate the direction of locomotion. Heavy black lines indicate impermeable barriers. F = food.

According to Lewin, when a need state exists in the inner-personal region, those regions in the environment that can satisfy the need acquire a value (termed **valence**) in regard to that need. This valence can be positive or negative, so that a fact can be either attractive or aversive as a way of reducing a particular need. Valence itself has no energizing properties, but it does determine which alternative psychological facts will be the most attractive as a way of satisfying a need.

The selection of the way in which a need is satisfied depends upon the construct of **force**. Force exists when an inner-personal region is in a state of tension. Force was conceived as having two properties: **magnitude** and **direction**. Thus not only are some forces stronger than others, but different forces can also exert different directions to behavior. Because several forces can simultaneously exert their influence on the individual at any given point in time, the final behavior path chosen by an individual will be a result of the magnitude and direction of all forces acting on the person. Behavior, then, was conceived as existing in a force field that ultimately determines the direction that behavior takes. Figure 9.6 represents such a force field.

Let's return to our example of Sarah and Doris at the beginning of this chapter. Figure

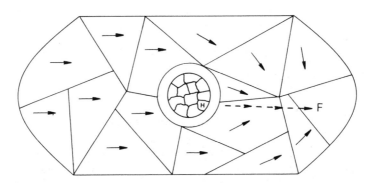

Figure 9.6   The field of forces acting to direct the locomotion of the person. H = hunger; F = food; solid arrows = field forces; dotted arrows = direction of locomotion resulting from the field of forces.

9.7 diagrams the situation. Sarah's hunger creates a tension in her inner-personal region that motivates her to get something to eat. Her recent heart attack, her daughter Doris, and the doctor's orders to reduce weight place barriers on her desire to eat. She solves the problem by eating the Halloween candy hidden in the basement because her daughter will not suspect that she is going there to eat. Sarah's behavior can be seen as a result of all the forces acting upon her, and it fits Lewin's concept of motivation rather well.

One way of summarizing Lewin's approach is to note that if one is to understand behavior, one must understand all the forces that are related to that behavior (Korman, 1974). For Lewin as for Tolman, this meant that behavior must be understood as a whole rather than from small behavioral components.

Though Lewin's analysis of behavior is unique, it is far from satisfactory. First, his terms are not clearly defined and are therefore open to differing interpretations. For example, psychological facts are in some cases like voluntary behavior (e.g., opening a door), while at other times they are subjective thoughts (e.g., remembering your fifth birthday). The differing types of psychological facts are not clearly defined, so the concept remains unclear. Second, psychological facts can change from moment to moment, but Lewin does not inform us of the conditions that cause their change. Third, several theorists have pointed out that Lewin's analyses are post hoc (i.e., after the fact). He inferred what the conditions were after the behavior had occurred (Arkes & Garske, 1977; Weiner, 1972). Finally, because of the vague nature of his concepts, we cannot make predictions about behavior from his model. Though he conducted experiments in order to test his ideas, Lewin's experiments often lacked proper control groups, thus making the data base for his ideas rather weak (Arkes & Garske, 1977; Weiner, 1972).

Although Lewin's theory suffers from some serious flaws, it is important because, like Tolman, Lewin emphasized the cognitive nature of motivation. Of particular importance, his psychological (quasi-)needs were often equivalent to thoughts and were just as important as physical needs in motivating behavior.

EXPECTANCY-VALUE THEORY

We turn now to an examination of a more modern cognitive approach to the understanding of motivation, known as **expectancy-value theory**. Expectancy-value approaches can be traced back to the theories of Tolman

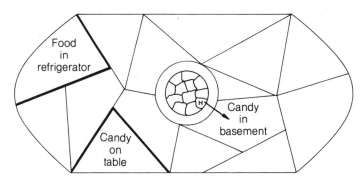

Figure 9.7 Sarah's life space.

(1932) and Lewin (1938). The basic idea underlying expectancy-value theory is that motivated behavior results from the combination of individual needs and the value of goals available in the environment. Expectancy-value theories also stress the idea that the probability of behavior depends not only upon the *value* of the goal for the individual but also upon the person's *expectancy* of obtaining the goal.

The general expectancy-value model provides an alternative to the more strict stimulus-response explanations of incentive motivation noted in Chapter Seven. Thus, instead of analyzing the effects of goal objects in terms of fractional consummatory responses and their feedback, expectancy-value theory argues for a cognitive representation of goal objects. This cognitive representation includes both an expectation that certain behaviors will lead to certain goals and the value of those goals for the organism.

The concept of expectancy is important because it assumes that behavior is a function of one's estimation of obtaining the valued goal. Thus even a highly valued goal may not generate much behavior if the expectancy of successfully reaching the goal is very small. Expectancies are generally regarded as being built up through past experience. The motives that expectancy-value theories generally attempt to explain are usually psychological in nature rather than physiological (Korman, 1974) and include such motives as achievement, dominance, power, and affiliation.

Expectancy-value theory has been applied to a number of psychological fields, including social learning theory, achievement, and work motivation. We will examine the expectancy-value approach to achievement momentarily; see Petri (1986, chapter fourteen) for a fuller discussion of expectancy-value approaches to work. Here we will examine expectancy-value concepts inherent in social learning theory.

Social learning theory examines and attempts to explain the internal and external (social) factors that influence the acquisition and regulation of behavior. Internal factors of importance include cognitive expectancies and subjective values that we place on goals, while external factors include the particular social situations that we experience. Both internal and external factors contribute to how we behave. Social learning theory also proposes that learning can occur directly through interaction with the environment or indirectly through observation of the actions of others and the consequences resulting from those actions.

Rotter (1954), for example, has noted four basic concepts of expectancy-value theory present in his social learning analysis of behavior. First, according to Rotter, our preference for an event is determined by that event's **reinforcement value**. The value of an event, however, is relative; we compare one situation against another to arrive at the value for any particular one. Second, we make **subjective estimates** of our chances of obtaining particular reinforcers, or, to put it in expectancy-value terms, we develop expectations about obtaining goals. Third, our expectations are determined by **situational factors**. Our expectations about a particular situation will be based on similar situations that we have encountered in the past. Fourth, our reactions in new situations will be based on **generalized expectations** from the past. Even though we may never have been in such a situation before, these generalized expectations will guide behavior. For example, suppose we have learned through past encounters that we can bluff others in order to get out of difficult social situations. As a result of the generalized expectancy that bluffing will work, we will probably try to bluff in a new difficult situation. Finally, Rotter has suggested that behavior depends upon the multiplication of expectancy and value so that we may write the following formula:

$$B = E \times V,$$

where B stands for behavior, E stands for expectancy, and V stands for value. Thus, according to Rotter, behavior occurs as the result of our expectations of achieving goals and the value those goals have for us.

Expectancy-value theory predicts that in situations where more than one behavior is possible, we will choose the behavior with the largest combination of expected success and value. Suppose, for example, that you are trying to decide between spending five dollars on a new movie that you want to see or on a new record by your favorite group. How will you spend your money? According to expectancy-value theory, you will choose the alternative that provides the larger combination of expected success and value. Let us suppose that the chance of getting a ticket to the new movie is only .75 because so many others want to see it and the small movie house is often sold out. Further, the movie's value to you on a scale from 1 to 10 (10 being largest) is about 7. The behavior potential for spending the money on the movie is therefore .75 times 7, or 5.25. The expected success at getting the record is 1.00 (100%) because you saw several copies of it in the record store yesterday, but the value to you is only a 6 on your 10-point scale. The expectancy of 1.00 times the value of 6 equals 6.00, so the theory predicts that you should decide to spend the money on the record, because 6.00 is greater than 5.25.

We face such choices daily, and expectancy-value theory predicts that we attempt to maximize their expected value. Unfortunately, we are often not as rational as this theory would suggest. Though we sometimes weigh the pros and cons of making particular choices, we often behave impulsively, without

considering the potential costs and chances of success that our behavior entails. Store managers use this human behavioral trait to their advantage by running sales on items (that may actually lose them money) in order to get us into the store, where we then buy other, prominently displayed items at higher prices.

Rotter has taken the concept of expectation a step beyond that discussed so far. He has argued that we differ in our expectations about the control of reinforcement. Some people feel that their behavior is responsible for the reinforcements they receive, while others believe that the reinforcements are controlled by forces outside themselves.

Rotter (1966, 1975) argued that individuals can be placed along a continuum of internality-externality in regard to how they perceive behavior as being reinforced. **Internal individuals** perceive rewards and punishments as resulting from their own behavior; that is, they believe themselves to be in control of their own behavior. **External individuals** perceive the rewards or punishments they receive as being beyond their control. For external individuals, both good and bad events are attributed to luck, fate, powerful others, or conditions over which they have no power.

Rotter developed a 29-item, forced-choice test that assessed a person's internality-externality. The questionnaire has been widely used, and internal versus external perception of control has been found to be related to a number of other variables (Lefcourt, 1966). For example, subjects who score high in the external direction have been found to be more conforming (Odell, 1959, cited by Lefcourt, 1966) and to perform less well on achievement-oriented tasks (Nowicki & Barnes, 1973). Duke and Lancaster (1976) have found that children raised in homes from which the father is absent are more external than those raised in homes where the father is present.

Rotter's internal-external locus-of-control construct is not strictly motivational (Lefcourt, 1966). Locus of control is conceived to be a generalized expectancy concerning one's ability to control the reinforcements one receives.

The locus-of-control research, of which there are over 600 published reports (Rotter, 1975), emphasizes the importance of one's perception of who controls the reinforcement one receives. Internals perceive that they control their own reinforcements, while externals see others as in control of the reinforcements they receive. The importance of the origin of reinforcement has also been noted by researchers and theorists who have examined the concept of intrinsic versus extrinsic motivation, as discussed in Chapter Twelve.

Albert Bandura, also well known for his contributions to social learning theory, expressed the importance of cognitive processes in social learning theory as follows (1977, p.10): "A theory that denies that thoughts can regulate actions does not lend itself readily to the explanation of complex behavior." Bandura clearly believes that cognitive explanations are necessary for understanding human behavior, and he has especially emphasized the importance of expectancies in social learning.

One way in which an expectancy can develop is through the pairing of two stimuli. The young child who is given a present by a favorite uncle each time he visits comes to expect that the next time the uncle visits, a present will be obtained. Bandura (1977) has argued that cognition is necessary for this expectancy to develop because several studies have shown that when stimuli are paired together, little learning occurs unless the person is aware of the relationship between stimuli. Expectancies may also be learned by observation, and according to Bandura, this observational learning (often called *modeling*) is a major way in which learning occurs in humans. If we see someone obtain a valued goal by working hard, we may come to expect that hard work pays off. Similarly, if we see someone become extremely fearful in the presence of snakes, we too may develop expectations that snakes are to be feared. Such observational learning may be particularly potent during childhood, and as a result, the child may share with its parents many of the same motives and emotions. Bandura and his associates (see, e.g., Bandura, 1973) have presented considerable data showing that aggressive behaviors can be learned through observation. One aspect of that learning is the expectancy that valued goals can be obtained as a result of aggressiveness.

The expectancy of reaching valued goals, then, is an important aspect of social learning theory. Expectancies and valued goals have also played an important role in the development of theories of achievement motivation. We will examine this role in the next section.

Expectancy-Value Theory and the Need for Achievement

Much of the early work on psychological motives was conducted by Henry Murray (1938), who believed that motivational processes result from individual needs that can best be observed in natural settings or clinical situations. Further, Murray argued that people can be classified according to the strengths of the various needs he identified (Steers & Porter, 1983). Murray defined needs to be a recurrent concern for a goal state and believed that a need consists of two components. The first component is directional in nature and includes the object that will satisfy the need. The second component consists of the energy that drives the behavior and can be thought of as the intensity of the need.

Murray and his colleagues at Harvard studied the needs of a group of college-age men and developed a list of approximately 20 major needs (**manifest needs**) as well as several additional latent needs, inner states, and general traits. A few of Murray's manifest needs are the needs for achievement, autonomy, dominance, understanding, and the need to be nurturant. Any given individual could be regarded as possessing several needs that direct and energize his or her behavior. These needs were considered to be learned and were thought to be activated by environmental cues.

Of all the needs outlined by Murray, most research has been devoted to understanding the need to achieve. Murray (1938, p. 164) defined the need for achievement as follows: "To accomplish something difficult. To master, manipulate or organize physical objects, human beings, or ideas. To do this as rapidly, and as independently as possible. To overcome obstacles and attain a high standard. To excel one's self. To rival and surpass others. To increase self-regard by the successful exercise of talent." As you can no doubt see, Murray considered achievement motivation a rather complex need that can be fulfilled in different ways by different persons; however, as is also evident in the quote, the need for achievement concerns doing difficult tasks quickly and doing them well.

The measurement of achievement motivation began with two researchers at Wesleyan University, David McClelland and John Atkinson. McClelland adapted a technique first used by Murray (1936) that asked subjects to make up a story or describe a situation depicted in a picture. The technique, known as the **Thematic Apperception Test (TAT)**, is used clinically, but McClelland and his associates felt that it could also be used to determine an individual's motives. They felt that important motives of an individual could be assessed by analyzing the TAT story for certain themes. Such an approach is called **content analysis**.

To test the validity of their assumption, McClelland and Atkinson (1948) arranged to have men at a submarine base go without food

for varying lengths of time up to 16 hours. None of the subjects knew that they were participating in a study on the effects of hunger. Subjects were led to believe that they were being tested for visual acuity. The men were asked to look at slides of various scenes that might suggest food seeking or eating and then write stories that answered questions such as: "What is happening?" "What led up to the situation?" "What is wanted?" "What will happen?" A scoring system was devised that allowed classification of stories from food-deprived and nondeprived individuals in terms of the story contents. The results clearly showed that amount of food deprivation (i.e., 1, 4, or 16 hours) was related to the food imagery found in the stories. This study provided evidence that motive states were reflected in the fantasies that individuals gave to the TAT pictures.

McClelland and associates (1949) then developed an experimental situation in which need for achievement could be aroused and, in a fashion similar to the food deprivation study, developed a scoring system based on achievement-related images in the TAT as a measure of need for achievement.

In this experiment one group of students was given several tasks to perform under "relaxed conditions." Specifically the students were told that the tasks had been recently devised by some graduate students within the department and that the group was being asked to participate in order to evaluate these tasks. The instructions were designed to lead to minimal ego involvement on the part of the subjects because the emphasis was on testing the tasks themselves rather than the students. A second group of subjects was termed the "failure condition." Subjects in this group were given the first task to perform and, after scoring their own tasks, were given a questionnaire asking for such personal information as estimated class standing, IQ, and so on. The purpose of the questionnaire was to get the subjects ego-involved by making the test scores known to each subject in relation to other achievement-related facts asked by the questionnaire.

The experimenters then led the subjects to believe that the tasks they had just taken were actually intelligence tests, and the experimenters quoted norms that were so high that practically everyone in the group failed (i.e., scored in the lowest quarter of the norms). The rest of the tasks were then administered. Subjects worked diligently on the remaining tasks. The instructions for the ego-involved group apparently had the desired effect, because the subjects were dismayed when the unrealistically high norms were announced. Finally, the subjects in both groups were given what they thought was a test of creative imagination—but was actually the TAT pictures used to score achievement imagery (several other conditions were also run, but for our purposes we note only the results of these two groups). A scoring system for analyzing the content of the TAT stories was developed, and the results showed that need-for-achievement scores were higher for the failure condition than for the relaxed condition. For example, the failure condition produced imagery that significantly more often involved a concern for performing a task well in relation to a stated standard of excellence. Results indicating an increase in achievement imagery as a function of ego-involving or achievement-orienting conditions have been replicated many times (e.g., Veroff, Wilcox, & Atkinson, 1953).

Motive for Success, Probability of Success, and Incentive Value   Achievement motivation theory for Atkinson was an expectancy-value theory because he assumed that the tendency to engage in a particular activity is related to the strength of a **cognitive expectation** (i.e., belief) that the behavior will lead to a particular consequence. In addition, the value

of that consequence for the person is also important (Atkinson & Birch, 1978). Thus people are assumed to engage in achievement-related situations as a result of their belief that doing so will lead to particular valued goals.

In achievement theory T is used to symbolize the tendency to approach an achievement-related situation. Although this tendency is influenced by external rewards (e.g., money, approval, and so on), most research emphasis has focused on intrinsic (i.e., internal) variables such as the pride associated with achievement or the shame associated with failure.

The tendency to approach achievement situations is thought to result from three variables: the **motive for success** (M_s), the **probability of success** (P_s), and the **incentive value** (I_s) **of achieving success**. M_s is regarded as a stable personality characteristic, probably learned early in life through association with parental rewards and where achievement-related cues were present at the time reward was received. The M_s will be strong in those individuals for whom achievement cues have been paired with positive emotions in the past. M_s, then, will vary in strength from one individual to another but will be relatively permanent within an individual across different situations.

The P_s, however, is assumed to vary from situation to situation because it is the person's **subjective estimate** of succeeding (i.e., obtaining the desired goal) in the particular situation. The incentive value of success is the value of actually achieving the goal and represents the fact that some goals are "worth more" than others. For intrinsic goals it is believed that the easier the task, the less value obtaining of the goal will have, while the harder the task, the greater the value of success. This is usually stated mathematically by noting that the incentive value of success is equal to 1 minus the subjective probability of success ($I_s = 1 - P_s$).

The tendency to approach achievement-related situations (T_s) is considered to equal the motive to succeed *times* the probability of success *times* the incentive value of success; that is:

$$T_s = M_s \times P_s \times I_s$$

Because $I_s = 1 - P_s$, this equation becomes:

$$T_s = M_s \times P_s \times (1 - P_s).$$

The theory becomes a little more complicated, however, because we know that some people do not approach achievement-related situations at all but tend to avoid them. T_s cannot account for these people because it describes only those conditions in which achievement situations are approached. Achievement theorists have therefore assumed that a tendency also exists to avoid achievement situations; they call this the tendency to avoid failure and symbolize it as T_{af}. If a person's attempts at achievement have been associated with negative emotional consequences in the past, the person will come to avoid cues signaling that an achievement situation is about to occur. T_{af} is, in a parallel fashion to T_s, composed of the person's **motive to avoid failure** (M_{af}) times the **subjective probability of failure** (P_f) times the **incentive value of failure** (I_f). Thus:

$$T_{af} = M_{af} \times P_f \times I_f.$$

The incentive value of failure is negative and often thought of as the embarrassment or shame that someone might feel at failing in an achievement task. It is also assumed that the probability of success and the probability of failure total 1; that is:

$$P_s + P_f = 1.$$

Thus, if our subjective probability of success in an achievement situation is .75, our subjective probability of failure will be .25. Because the incentive value of achieving the goal is related to the subjective probability for both success and failure situations, there will be more incentive value for succeeding at hard tasks and less shame at failure. On the other hand, easy tasks (i.e., where P_s is high) will have little value when completed successfully but high negative value if failure occurs.

Suppose that your calculus instructor gave a test. Some of the questions were quite easy, while others were extremely difficult. Question 1 was very easy, because 80% of the class got it correct. We can say, therefore, that the probability of success was .80 and the probability of failure was .20. According to achievement theory, your pride at getting the easy question correct will be small, because the incentive value of success depends upon the probability of success ($I_s = 1 - P_s$). Thus the incentive value of solving the easy problem is 1 − .80 = .20, indicating that one ought to feel little pride in solving the easy question. If you missed the easy question, on the other hand, your embarrassment would be considerable (.80) because $I_s + I_f = 1$.

Question 7 was extremely difficult; only 10% of the class solved it correctly. We can say, therefore, that the probability of success was .10, and the probability of failure was .90. The incentive value of solving the difficult problem correctly will be high (1 − .10 = .90), while the shame associated with failure to solve the problem will be low (.10). Achievement theory predicts that you ought to be quite pleased with yourself for having solved question 7 correctly but should feel little embarrassment if you got it wrong.

Because $P_s + P_f = 1$, mathematically $P_f = 1 - P_s$; that is, both formulas can be related to the probability of success in the situation. Thus we can combine the formulas for T_s and T_{af} into one formula that will describe whether an individual will tend to avoid or approach an achievement situation. We will call this tendency T_A, which symbolizes a person's overall tendency to approach or avoid achievement-related situations. By combining the two formulas, we arrive mathematically at:

$$T_A = (M_s - M_{af})(P_s \times [1 - P_s]).$$

This formula tells us that the tendency to engage in achievement-related situations depends upon one's achievement motivation (M_s) minus one's motive to avoid failure (M_{af}) times the subjective probability of success in the situation. Because we can expect that the probability of success will be constant for a given situation, whether one approaches or avoids the situation will depend upon which is greater, M_s or M_{af}. If M_s is greater, the person will approach the situation, but if M_{af} is greater, the person will avoid the situation.

Expectancy-value theory conceptualizes all individuals as possessing both M_s and M_{af}. The two motives will possess different strengths in different people, however, because of varied past experiences (good and bad) in achievement-related situations. People high in M_s, as a rule, will approach achievement situations, while people high in M_{af} will generally avoid them.

Achievement motivation, as we have discussed it to this point, relates to intrinsic motivational factors; that is, the achievement motive and the motive to avoid failure are seen as internal spurs to behavior. But people sometimes behave in achievement situations because of external factors such as money, obtaining a scholarship, and so on (Feather, 1961). Such factors are grouped under the general heading **extrinsic motivation** and include the kinds of variables usually labeled as reinforcement or reward. Although the influence of extrinsic motives on achievement behavior has not received a large amount of study, interest in the effects of extrinsic variables is apparently increasing (Lepper & Greene, 1978). Atkinson has also added to his formula to indicate that extrinsic factors do influence behavior in achievement situations (Atkinson & Birch, 1978).

Achieving for the Future Raynor (1969, 1974) has pointed out that not all achievement situations are of equal importance. Some achievement situations have future implications, while others do not. For example, doing well as an undergraduate may determine whether an individual gets into medical school or not. This future possibility (i.e., of getting into medical school) should influence motivation on the present task (i.e., doing well in undergraduate courses).

Future goals may have either intrinsic or extrinsic aspects (or both), and these values will multiply the perceived future probability of successfully obtaining the goal. The effect that a future goal will have on present achievement behavior will thus be an intensification of the present behavior. For example, though one might be motivated to win a game of darts, the intensity of the behavior will not be the same as one would have in studying for a crucial chemistry exam, which could have a profound effect on one's chances of getting into medical school.

Raynor's extension of achievement theory suggests that the value of a present activity toward obtaining some future goal is an important variable in determining achievement behavior. Data supportive of Raynor's approach have shown that persons high in M_s and low in M_{af} received significantly higher grades in a course when the perceived importance of that course for some future goal was high than they did when it was low (Raynor, 1970). Clearly, future goals must be taken into account when we try to understand achievement behavior.

Achievement as a Behavior Stream Atkinson has modified his conception of motivation somewhat to conceive of organisms as being continually motivated (Birch, Atkinson, & Bongort, 1974). He argued that one need not be concerned with the activation of behavior (since organisms are continually active) but with the variables that cause an organism to shift from one type of activity to another. In other words, behavior is a constant stream that is altered from time to time as conditions change. Birch, Atkinson, and Bongort believed that major sources of changing the stream of behavior are cognitive processes (or, more specifically, conscious thought). Thoughts serve to instigate new behaviors or inhibit ongoing behaviors.

The theory of achievement motivation developed by Atkinson and his associates has generated a tremendous amount of research. We will not attempt to survey this vast literature but will examine a few studies that have tried to test some of the basic predictions of the theory.

Research on Achievement Motivation Although the achievement motive has historically been measured by using the TAT, newer devices such as the **Mehrabian Achieving Tendency Questionnaire** (Mehrabian, 1969) have been developed. Similarly, the motive to avoid failure has often been measured with the **Test Anxiety Questionnaire (TAQ)** devised by Sarason and Mandler (1952), but measures such as the Alpert and Haber (1960) **Achievement Anxiety Test** are now also used. Cooper (1983) contrasted the use of the Achieving Tendency Questionnaire with the TAT and TAQ measures of M_s and M_{af}. He compared these two techniques on seven predictions made by achievement theory and found that "while there were differences in their comparative ability to predict individual variables, neither emerged as a consistently better basis for predicting across the seven variables" (p. 857). Thus both TAT and more conventional questionnaire techniques apparently can be

used to assess achievement motivation. In experiments on achievement motivation, researchers normally measure M_s and M_{af}, then artificially set P_s by telling the subjects what they can expect in regard to the probability of success. Because the incentive values of both success and failure are related to P_s, the experimenters are, in essence, setting these also.

Achievement theory predicts that the tendency to approach achievement situations will be maximal for people high in M_s for tasks they perceive as being intermediate in difficulty. Intuitively we might expect that an achievement-oriented person would attempt tasks that are hard enough to award a sense of accomplishment when successful but not so difficult as to eliminate success nor so easy as to make success worthless. The formula for the tendency to approach achievement situations also predicts this result. For example, suppose that $M_s = 3$, $M_{af} = 0$, and $P_s = .1$, then:

$$T_A = (3 - 0)(.1 \times [1 - .1]) = .27.$$

From the results of the formula, we can predict that when the probability of success is low (.1), the tendency to engage in achievement-related behavior is also low (.27). If, however, we change the situation so that $P_s = .5$ (i.e., a task of intermediate difficulty), note what happens:

$$T_A = (3 - 0)(.5 \times [1 - .5]) = .75,$$

indicating that the approach tendency will be stronger for tasks of intermediate difficulty. Finally, if we change the situation so that $P_s = .9$ (i.e., an easy task) and keep each of the other factors constant, we find that:

$$T_A = (3 - 0)(.9 \times [1 - .9]) = .27,$$

which again predicts that the tendency to approach easy tasks is low.

In a parallel fashion, we can argue that people with a strong motive to avoid failure will be inclined to choose tasks that are very easy or very hard. The very easy task assures success, while the very hard task essentially gives the individual an excuse for failure—the task was so difficult that no one could be expected to succeed. Again our intuition is supported by the achievement formula. Thus, if $M_s = 0$, $M_{af} = 3$, and $P_s = .1$ (i.e., a very hard task), then:

$$T_A = (0 - 3)(.1 \times [1 - .1]) = -.27,$$

showing that the tendency to avoid failure will be low. If we change the situation, however, so that $P_s = .5$ and M_s and M_{af} remain constant, the tendency to avoid failure becomes stronger:

$$T_A = (0 - 3)(.5 \times [1 - .5]) = -.75.$$

Finally, if the task is very easy (e.g., $P_s = .9$), the tendency to avoid failure will again be low:

$$T_A = (0 - 3)(.9 \times [1 - .9] = -.27.$$

These predictions suggest that people high in M_s will tend to select tasks that are intermediate in difficulty, while persons high in M_{af} will tend to choose tasks that are either very easy or very difficult.

Atkinson and Litwin (1960) tested these predictions by assessing M_s and M_{af} in college men. These men were then asked to participate in a ring-toss game and could select the distance to the peg anywhere from 1 to 15 feet. As expected, men whose $M_s > M_{af}$ chose distances that were intermediate (the symbol > is to be read "greater than"). However, men whose $M_{af} > M_s$ did not choose extreme distances (e.g., 1 or 15 feet) more often than intermediate distances, though there was a secondary preference at 1 to 2 feet. Clearer evidence was obtained by Isaacson (1964), who

found that men higher in M_s than M_{af} chose college majors of intermediate difficulty more often than men who were higher in M_{af} than M_s.

Feather (1961) also attempted to test the hypothesized differences between subjects differing in M_s and M_{af}. In Feather's study M_s and M_{af} were determined for 89 male subjects who were then given an impossible task to perform. The task required the subject to trace a diagram without lifting the pencil from the line or retracing. Because this was impossible for the task of concern, Feather was obtaining a measure of persistence on an insolvable task.

Feather hypothesized that subjects for whom $M_s > M_{af}$ would persist at the task longer when told that the probability of success is high ($P_s = .7$) than when told it is very low ($P_s = .05$). Subjects for whom $M_{af} > M_s$ should behave in an opposite fashion, quickly quitting the task when unsuccessful and told that $P_s = .7$; but they should continue longer if told that the probability of success is slight ($P_s = .05$). Feather made these predictions based on the assumptions that repeated failure at the task would lead to a lowering of the individual's subjective estimate of the probability of success. For $M_s > M_{af}$ subjects, the lowered probability of success (when $P_s = .7$) due to failure would reduce P_s into the intermediate range where these subjects should be most persistent, according to achievement theory. For $M_{af} > M_s$ subjects, on the other hand, failure at the task when $P_s = .7$ would lower their expectations of success into the range of difficulty most aversive for them (i.e., P_s near .5), and they would stop quickly. When $P_s = .05$, however, failure should produce even smaller expectation of success for subjects in both groups. However, this would be aversive only for subjects whose $M_s > M_{af}$; thus they should stop quickly, while $M_{af} > M_s$ subjects should continue longer. The results of Feather's study were as predicted and provided support for the concepts of the motive for success and the motive to avoid failure.

Several experiments have called into question the finding that persons high in M_s prefer tasks of intermediate difficulty. Weinstein (1969), for example, found no consistent relationship between several measures of achievement motivation and risk taking. Ray (1982), using somewhat different measures than those examined by Weinstein, also found no relationship between achievement motivation and preferred task difficulty. Cooper (1983), in a complex study examining seven predictions of achievement theory, found that level of task difficulty was one of two predictions not supported by his data. So the basic prediction that persons high in M_s will choose tasks of intermediate difficulty should apparently be viewed with some caution. However, as Cooper also noted, five of the seven predictions made by achievement theory were supported, and we can thus place some confidence in the theory as a whole.

Achievement and Society A second line of research that has evolved from achievement theory concerns the relationship of achievement motivation to societal change. McClelland (1961), in *The Achieving Society*, has outlined some of the relationships that exist between individuals' need for achievement and the economic conditions of the nations in which these individuals live. For example, McClelland (1965) showed that young men high in need for achievement tended to select entrepreneurial occupations (an entrepreneur takes the risks involved in organizing and managing a business in order to receive the profits from that business). If a nation contains a large enough number of persons high in need for achievement and they enter entrepreneurial business situations, then one should expect fairly rapid economic growth in that nation.

As a way of trying to test this idea, McClel-land (1961) collected myths, folklore, and children's stories from a number of countries and applied the methods of content analysis to determine the levels of achievement motivation present in the stories. In one study of preliterate cultures, oral folktales were analyzed for need for achievement imagery. Twenty-two of these cultures were determined to have high need for achievement imagery in their stories. Of these 22 cultures, approximately 75% had individuals who could be classified as entrepreneurs. Twenty-three other cultures were judged to be low in need for achievement (based on the imagery in their folktales), and only about 33% of these cultures contained persons who could be classified as entrepreneurs. Thus cultural attitudes about achievement, at least as measured by that culture's myths and folktales, are apparently correlated with the number of individuals willing to take the risks of managing a business that may increase the economic well-being of that culture. Cultures with high need for achievement imagery in their stories have many such individuals, while cultures low in need for achievement imagery have few.

Fyans and associates (1983) found a good deal of agreement across cultures on the meaning of achievement. They noted (p. 1010) that "there appears to be something like an achievement ethic that is universally recognized as an identifiable behavioral category." That ethic stresses work, knowledge, and freedom while devaluing the importance of family, tradition, and interpersonal concerns.

In another study McClelland collected stories in children's beginning readers that were in use in 1925 in several different countries. He then content analyzed these stories for need for achievement. As a measure of economic growth within these same countries, McClelland used electric power consumption figures from 1925 through 1950. He found that for 78% of the countries ranked above the mean in need for achievement, there were large gains in the electric power consumed during the interval 1925–50. For those countries ranked below the mean in need for achievement, only 25% showed comparable changes. Interestingly, there was no relationship between stories collected from readers in 1950 and this earlier economic growth. Therefore, achievement imagery in the children's literature of a nation apparently can be used to predict future economic changes in that nation.

Bradburn and Berlew (1961) examined English literature for achievement content at 50-year intervals for the period 1400 to 1830. These researchers used coal imports as their measure of economic growth and discovered that economic changes lagged behind changes in achievement imagery by about 50 years. When such imagery was high, coal imports were up 50 years later; when this imagery was down, coal imports were lower 50 years later. These data, although correlational, are tantalizing: they suggest that achievement attitudes, as reflected in the popular literature of a country, precede economic changes. This relationship may exist because prevailing attitudes about achievement influence the entrepreneurial behavior of large numbers of persons, and, consequently, economic growth or stagnation follows.

Similar content analyses of achievement imagery have been conducted for cultures that were once prominent and then declined. Achievement concerns generally appeared highest before a particular civilization's economic growth had peaked. Achievement imagery present at the time of peak economic growth, however, had usually declined, foretelling the decline of that civilization.

DeCharms and Moeller (1962) analyzed children's readers in the United States during the period 1800–1950 and found that achievement imagery in this country peaked around 1890. Given the 50-year lag between achievement imagery and economic change, peak eco-

nomic growth in the United States should have occurred around 1940. The continued decline in achievement imagery from 1890 through 1950 suggests that economic growth in America is now on a downward trend.

This relationship between achievement motivation and economic growth is provocative and a little frightening; however, we must keep in mind that the data upon which these findings are based are correlational (and therefore do not necessarily imply a cause-and-effect relationship) and that the relationship is not perfect: some nations scoring low on achievement imagery nevertheless showed rapid economic growth (and vice versa). More research on the relationship between achievement motivation and economic growth is clearly necessary before we can draw any firm conclusions. One aspect of this relationship that has received further study is achievement training.

Achievement Training David McClelland (1978) has taken the concept of need achievement and given it practical application. Concerned with individual differences in the need to achieve, he has found that achievement behavior can be taught. For example, in one project McClelland and his associates (McClelland & Winter, 1971) trained businessmen in Hyderabad, India, to think, talk, and act like people high in need for achievement. The businessmen were taught these traits because McClelland (1961) had previously found a strong relationship between high need for achievement and entrepreneurial behavior.

Approximately 50 men were trained to be high in need achievement, and their business activities were followed for two years after the training. McClelland found that the businessmen who had received achievement training were much more active than those not trained. The achievement-trained men had started more new businesses, had invested more money in their businesses, and had employed over twice as many new employees during the follow-up period than had the untrained group. McClelland calculated that the training program (which lasted only 40 days) resulted in a permanent increase in the standard of living for 4,000 to 5,000 people.

Thus achievement training is apparently a potentially useful tool for improving economic conditions in underdeveloped countries or even in specific ethnic groups. Miron (1976), for example, has shown that achievement motivation training can be effectively used for increasing employment in minority groups. Several of the concepts and techniques developed in the study of achievement motivation may thus have considerable applicability.

The Development of Achievement Motivation   A question of some importance is how the need for achievement develops in an individual. McClelland (1961) originally argued that need for achievement in boys 6–10 years old is related to their mothers' stress on independence and mastery. This emphasis on doing things on your own during childhood presumably leads to the development of a need to do things well later in life. McClelland and Pilon (1983), however, have reported new data suggesting that there is a relationship between need for achievement in adulthood and certain child-rearing practices that occur before the age of 5. McClelland and Pilon relocated a sample of the children whose mothers had been interviewed by Sears, Maccoby, and Levin (1957) concerning child-rearing practices. These children (now 31–32 years old) were tested for achievement motivation, and their scores were correlated with the Sears, Maccoby, and Levin ratings of child-rearing practices reported by their mothers. Two child-rearing practices—*scheduling of feeding* and *severity of toilet training*—proved to be consistently related to adult need for achievement.

Mothers who scheduled the feeding of

their children (e.g., at birth feeding every four hours) produced children with a higher need for achievement than mothers who did not schedule feeding (e.g., feeding on demand). Additionally, mothers who were more severe in their toilet training procedures produced children with higher need for achievement than mothers who were less severe. Both correlations held across sex of the child and social class. The results, which would certainly please Freud, are surprising and, as noted by McClelland and Pilon, are not part of a general child-rearing style that emphasizes orderliness and control: the relationship is specific to these two child-rearing practices, and when considered together, they account for about 30% of the variance of the adult need for achievement scores. At present it is unclear how these results fit with McClelland's earlier findings that an emphasis on independence and mastery is important for the development of need for achievement. Perhaps, as noted by McClelland and Pilon (1983), early feeding and toilet training practices develop a need for achievement in children, which in turn causes the mother to set performance goals later that lead to independence and mastery. McClelland and Pilon's results certainly call for further study of the relationship between early experiences and the need for achievement.

Fear of Success   Sex differences represent one area of study within achievement motivation research that received serious attention during the 1970s. It had been known for some time that college men and women do not react the same to achievement cues. For example, Veroff, Wilcox, and Atkinson (1953) found no differences in TAT imagery between relaxed and achievement-oriented conditions in females. A study by Field (1951) also found no increased achievement imagery in women between relaxed and failure conditions, while men showed a large difference. Field further determined that although changes in social acceptability had no effect on male achievement imagery, such changes had pronounced effect on the achievement imagery of women. Field's results suggest that women's perception of their societal role may not normally regard achievement in competitive situations as feminine, accounting for the lack of change in achievement imagery under either success or failure conditions.

Horner (1968) extended this analysis to suggest that women have a stable personality characteristic that is motivational in nature and similar in concept to M_s and M_{af}. Horner has termed this construct **fear of success**. Fear of success was conceptualized by Horner (1972) as a internal representation of society's stereotype that competence, independence, competition, and intellectual achievement are inconsistent with femininity. Basically women high in fear of success believe that success will lead to negative consequences for them. These negative aspects of success were thought to involve feelings of social rejection or of being unfeminine. Such expected negative consequences of achievement were further assumed to inhibit achievement behavior and were suggested as an explanation for the fact that women do not react to achievement-arousing situations in the same manner as men.

To test this idea, Horner added a verbal item that indicated a high level of achievement at the end of a group of TAT pictures used to measure achievement motivation. For women the verbal item was: "After first-term finals, Anne finds herself at the top of her medical school class." For men in the experiment the name "Anne" was replaced by the name "John." The subjects were then asked to complete the story of Anne or John based on the sentence. A scoring system was developed so that the motive to avoid success was scored as present if subjects indicated: some conflict in their stories concerning the success; the anticipation or occurrence of negative consequences as a result of the success; denial of

effort or responsibility for the success; denial of the lead sentence itself; or bizarre or inappropriate responses. In the initial experiment, conducted at the University of Michigan in 1965, 90 female and 88 male subjects participated. Horner found that approximately 65% of the women wrote stories to the Anne cue indicating a loss of femininity, social rejection, or other negative consequences. Typical fear-of-success stories often had Anne deliberately lowering her academic standing, dropping out of med school, and marrying. The men in the sample, however (who were responding to the John cue), typically did not write stories indicating fear of success. Of the 88 men tested, only 8 wrote fear-of-success stories (9.1%).

This pattern of differences in fear-of-success imagery between males and females has been replicated in several other studies (cited by Horner, 1972) and appears evident in girls as early as the seventh grade. Horner also found that women high in fear of success did less well in mixed-sex, competitive situations, which suggested that fear of success was inhibiting the women's behavior.

Horner's results generated much research on the concept of fear of success. For example, Hoffman (1974) attempted to determine which aspect of the success situation led to the activation of the motive to avoid success. She tested three possibilities: that success in a masculine endeavor triggered the fear of success; that public knowledge of the success triggered it; or that competitive situations triggered it. Hoffman found that fear of success in women was not different across the three conditions. As in Horner's study, however, 65% of the women tested indicated fear of success. Hoffman's results for men, however, were very different. Unlike Horner, who found only 9.1% of the males demonstrating fear of success, Hoffman found that 77% of her males showed fear of success. In fact no significant sex differences in fear of success occurred in

Hoffman's sample. Content of the male and female stories did differ, however. In the women's stories 42% centered on an affiliative loss as a result of the success, while only 15% of the men's stories concerned affiliative needs. On the other hand, 30% of the men's stories involved a questioning of the value of success, a dominant theme being a "put-down" of academic achievement. Only 15% of the female sample involved a questioning of the value of success. Finally, as noted by Hoffman, overall achievement imagery was significantly less in both males and females in her sample than in Horner's original sample (see also Hoffman, 1977).

Other studies (e.g., Breedlove & Cicirelli, 1974) found that fear of success was greater in situations involving success in nontraditional rather than in traditional feminine roles. Of the subjects given the "Anne cue," 70% responded with fear-of-success imagery, while only 49% of subjects exposed to success in a traditional role (e.g., Anne ranked first in her class in graduate elementary education) wrote fear-of-success stories.

Brown, Jennings, and Vanik (1974) gave the Anne and John cues to both male and female high school and college students. They found that both males and females in the high school sample responded with more negative imagery to the Anne cue than to the John cue. The men of the college sample also responded with more negative imagery to the Anne cue, but the college women, contrary to Horner's results, did not. The results of this study suggest that the negative imagery associated with the Anne cue may indicate a general societal expectation of the feminine role rather than an instance of fear of success. Because the men were responding to an opposite-sex cue, fear of success would seem to be ruled out. Brown also argued that Horner's criterion for fear of success may have included fear of failure. For example, Horner scored bizarre answers as indicative of fear of success. Brown suggested

that bizarre answers are more likely to be a reaction against the test situation than fear of success. Horner also scored denial (e.g., Anne's success was due to cheating) as fear of success, but Brown contended that denial could just as logically be considered an indication of fear of failure.

Finally, Brown noted that only 17% of the college women in her study showed fear-of-success imagery, while 22% of the males showed such imagery. Perhaps fear of success has become less of a factor for college-age females because of changing attitudes about women. Men's fear of success, on the other hand, has apparently increased. Fear of success in men may be related to a fear of rejection or disapproval by family members and friends (Balkin, 1986).

Peplau (1976) has suggested that Horner's fear-of-success measure is of limited usefulness. Peplau's research suggests that the image of a woman who scores high in fear of success as intellectually disabled is unwarranted. Peplau has further suggested that fear-of-success imagery represents a sensitivity by women to the sex-role implication of achievement situations, and that sex-role attitudes are actually a more consistent determinant of women's performance than fear of success. Cook and Chandler (1984) attempted to directly test the idea that fear of success was a stable motive as proposed by Horner. Cook and Chandler's results did not support the motivational nature of fear of success but suggested instead that women react to the expectations and demands of particular situations. They suggest that female achievement behavior is influenced by a woman's beliefs about appropriate sex-typed behavior in achievement situations. The sex-role explanation of achievement differences implies that women have learned that competitiveness in achievement situations is a male stereotype. Women may therefore react negatively to achievement situations not because they fear success but because they do not perceive it as part of the feminine sex role.

In support of Peplau, Williams and King (1976) have obtained evidence suggesting that sex-role attitudes correlate better with GPA, college major, career, and marriage plans than does fear-of-success imagery. They too suggest that fear of success may no longer be useful as a variable in explaining women's achievement behavior. Karabenick (1977) and Marshall and Karabenick (1977) have also obtained results contrary to Horner's predictions.

Zuckerman and Wheeler (1975), in a review of the literature on fear of success, concluded that the concept is a good one but that data on it are inconsistent. Thus the answer to why women react differently in achievement-oriented situations compared to men remains open. Fear of success may be able to bridge the gap; on the other hand, the emphasis has swung toward sex-role attitudes as important determinants of achievement behavior in women.

Achievement Styles

In the 1980s there was a swing away from interest in concepts such as fear of success to an examination of other themes within the domain of achievement motivation. One such topic concerns the ways in which we go about our achievement behavior, a subject that has been called **achievement styles**. Lipman-Blumen, Handley-Isaksen, and Leavitt (1983) have developed a model that argues for three basic achievement styles that are learned early in life and, as a result, direct the person's behavior in achievement situations. The three basic achievement styles are **direct, instrumental**, and **relational**, each of which also has three substyles.

Direct Styles   People using the direct style confront achievement situations head-on and attempt to achieve success through their own efforts. Within this category the **intrinsic-**

direct style describes people who like the demands and challenges of a task and measure their performance against some internalized standard of excellence. People using the **competitive-direct** style compare themselves to others or their accomplishments. People using this style not only want to succeed, they want to do the task better than anyone else. For such people, competition is a necessary aspect of achievement tasks. The third subcategory within the direct style is the **power-direct** style, which involves controlling other individuals, resources, or situations in order to achieve at a task. People using this style often delegate parts of the task to others while at the same time maintaining control and managing the whole situation.

Instrumental Styles   The instrumental style is typified by people who manipulate others to achieve their goals. This manipulation is usually done consciously and with full awareness; however, some people behave this way so often that they become unaware of their manipulative behavior. Persons using this style continually evaluate the potential benefit of social contacts as well as their own accomplishments. Thus having influential friends and having accomplished tasks in the past may both be used to obtain success at new tasks. People using the **personal-instrumental** style use status, reputation, personal accomplishments, education, occupation, financial or political powers, and charisma to reach desired goals. This style is often consciously used by individuals who place a high value on external approval. The **social-instrumental** style, on the other hand, emphasizes the use of personal relationships or other persons as a means of succeeding. Relationships are evaluated for their use in obtaining desired ends. People using this style have faith in their ability to get what they want by using others and usually use people quite consciously. People using the **reliant-instrumental** style of achievement also use others, but rather than manipulating them directly, these people depend upon others to solve their problems for them. When they achieve success, they do so as a result of help from other individuals. Unlike those using the social-instrumental style, persons using the reliant-instrumental style have little faith in their own abilities to succeed and expect others to obtain their goals for them.

Relational Styles The relational style can be characterized by the individual who achieves some success through association with another's achievement. Thus a person may gain some measure of success by working with someone who is successful. The **collaborative-relational** style describes the person who likes to approach tasks as a member of a group. This style typifies the "team player" who takes his or her share of the responsibility and expects an equal share of the rewards. People using this style strive for the group's goal (i.e., make it their own) rather than striving for personal goals. The **contributory-relational** style is used by individuals who meet their own achievement needs by contributing to the success of another. These people usually play a secondary role but meet their needs by helping others. Finally, the **vicarious-relational** style is used by persons who, without actively participating in it, view the success of another as their own. A person using this style is satisfied to be associated with a successful achiever and basks in the reflected glory of that successful person.

As noted by Lipman-Blumen, Handley-Isaksen, and Leavitt (1983), it would be incorrect to assume that a given individual uses only one of these nine achievement styles. Most individuals use more than one style but show a preference for one or two styles. For example, an individual might use both personal-instrumental and social-instrumental styles to achieve his or her goals. The study of achievement styles appears to be a new direction for

achievement research, one that may eventually help us clarify the differences we see in the ways that people attack achievement tasks. Before we end our discussion of expectancy-value approaches to achievement motivation, we must examine some of the criticisms that have been leveled against it.

Criticisms of Need-Achievement Theory

Need-achievement theory itself has been criticized on a number of counts. Entwisle (1972) has reviewed the literature on achievement and noted several problems. First, Entwisle provided evidence that the reliability of the TAT pictures is low, ranging between .3 and .4. The reliability estimates are even lower for females than for males and might, in part, explain sex differences in the achievement situations previously discussed. Test-retest reliability is also low, meaning that the same pictures do not trigger the same stories from one testing session to another. There is also the problem of validity; that is, is the imagery procedure really measuring achievement motivation? Klinger (1966) has suggested that need-achievement scores do not provide an adequate measure of motivation and that this, in turn, results in low predictive validity for these scores.

Another problem of considerable importance is that achievement motivation is probably multidimensional. Jackson, Ahmed, and Heapy (1976) have identified what they believe to be six different dimensions of achievement motivation. In order to understand an individual's achievement behavior if achievement motivation is indeed multidimensional, we must understand how that individual scores on the various dimensions of achievement.

Finally, some researchers have even questioned whether the need for achievement is motivational. For example, Entwisle (1972) noted that for ninth-grade subjects, the *number* of words in a TAT story correlated better with their grades than the need-achievement scores! This is difficult to understand if need for achievement is an activator of achievement behavior that would presumably be reflected in grades. Similarly, Klinger (1966) has suggested that need-achievement scores are largely situational. Thus specific situations may lead to increased achievement imagery (as measured by the TAT) *and* to increased achievement behavior; that is, although achievement imagery is related to achievement performance, it may not be a causal relationship.

Even though many problems exist with achievement theory, as demonstrated by such criticisms, the theory has generated much research of practical value. It is perhaps also the most carefully defined example of expectancy-value approaches to motivation. Achievement research assumes that expectancy (indexed by P_s) and value (indexed by I_s) are cognitive in nature and suggests that people develop mental representations (by whatever name) of the environment with which they interact.

SUMMARY

The work of Tolman and Lewin laid the groundwork for the modern cognitive theories of motivation. Both emphasized the cognitive nature of many motives and the importance of the goals toward which the behavior was directed.

Tolman stressed the concept of the purposiveness of behavior. He pointed out that goals direct our behavior and that organisms develop cognitive representations, which he termed *cognitive maps*, of their world. His research emphasized the development of expectancies and the control of behavior by

those expectancies. His ideas contrasted sharply with the more mechanical stimulus-response formulations that were current at the time he wrote.

Lewin was influenced by the Gestalt school of psychology. He argued for the dynamic nature of behavior and suggested that observed behavior results from all the forces acting on an individual at any given moment. Many of the motives that generate behavior, according to Lewin, are cognitive in nature. These cognitive motives influence behavior in the same ways as do physiological needs.

The second major concept examined in this chapter was the expectancy-value approach, which regards motivation as the result of the expectation that one can obtain particular goals and the value or incentive provided by that goal. The research cited on achievement motivation exemplifies expectancy-value theory. Atkinson and his associates have developed a model for achievement behavior that emphasizes the stable personality characteristics of need for achievement (or the motive for success and fear of failure). In addition to these stable characteristics, achievement behavior is thought to depend upon one's expectancy of succeeding in a particular situation, indexed by the individual's subjective probability of success. Finally, the value of reaching the goal in terms of pride of accomplishment or shame of failure is also regarded as important in determining achievement behavior.

Achievement has usually been studied in terms of intrinsic variables. But Feather has pointed out the necessity of studying extrinsic or external variables in order to fully understand the factors that govern achievement behavior, and research on the relationship of extrinsic factors and achievement is beginning to appear.

One of the most perplexing findings in

the literature on achievement motivation is that women do not seem to react to achievement-oriented situations in the same manner as men. Horner has proposed that women possess a stable personality characteristic that she calls fear of success. Fear of success is seen as a negative motivational state that tends to inhibit women from engaging in competitive, achievement-oriented situations because of a fear that success will lead to negative consequences. These negative consequences are generally seen as a fear of social rejection because of success or a feeling of loss of femininity. Research on the concept of fear of success has led to mixed results. More research is needed before any degree of confidence can be placed in the fear-of-success construct.

In essence theorists are again coming back to the notion that we are thinking, rational, decision-making organisms. To understand the complex behavioral patterns of the human, we must take into account the individual's expectations, past experiences, values, attitudes, and beliefs. We must also understand how these various cognitive structures interact and the processes through which they guide behavior. Ignoring the cognitive component of motivated behavior can only lead to an incomplete understanding of the forces that shape our lives.

SUGGESTIONS FOR FURTHER READING

Atkinson, J. W., & Birch, D. (1978). *An introduction to motivation* (2nd ed.). New York: Van Nostrand. This book is a good source of information on the various aspects and related research of Atkinson's model of achievement.

McClelland, D. C. (1961). *The achieving society*. New York: Van Nostrand. This book provides a good overview of much of the early work on achievement as well as the cross-cultural research.

Spence, J. T. (Ed.). (1983). *Achievement and achievement motives: Psychological and sociological approaches*. San Francisco: Freeman. This book provides a good cross section of newer approaches to achievement.

Chapter Ten

Cognitive Motivation: Social Motivation and Consistency

CHAPTER PREVIEW

This chapter is concerned with the following questions:

1. How does the presence of others influence our behavior?

2. What has been found concerning a motive to conform or obey?

3. How do situational influences such as coming to the aid of someone in distress modify our behavior?

4. What is cognitive consistency, and how does lack of it generate motivation?

5. What is balance theory, and what is cognitive dissonance?

Tim was walking down the stairs from the fifth floor when he heard someone fall on the stairs several floors below. The woman screamed as she stumbled on a step, and there was a great clatter as books, pencils, notebooks, and purse careened down the stairs. Leaning over the railing, Tim could see her lying at the foot of the stairs and could also hear her moaning softly for help.

Tim felt a strong urge to stop at the fourth floor, even though he had intended to go all the way to the first floor. After all, he thought, there are other people on the stairs. By the time I get down there, others will have helped her. Besides, he reasoned, I don't know anything about first aid, so I couldn't be of much help anyway. At that thought, he turned from the stairs and entered the fourth floor, glad to flee the emergency that existed two floors below.

Why don't people help in emergency situations? In this chapter we will explore some of the reasons. The study of **bystander intervention**, as research on helping behavior is called, is part of a larger concern with how people are influenced by social situations.

In this chapter we will also examine the theories and research that involve the motivational effects of one person on another. In addition, we will see how some situations can create a state of inconsistency in the thoughts of a person, which in turn generates motivational states that lead the person to resolve the inconsistency. Much of what we will study in this chapter falls within the domain of social psychology; however, we will only discuss research that examines the role of social situations in the activation and direction of behavior. Although many additional topics might be included here, those presented should help the reader understand the importance of socially motivated behaviors.

A moment's reflection should convince you that we behave differently when alone than when in the presence of others; our behavior is influenced by the presence of others. We will look briefly at the energizing effects of the presence of others, then proceed to examine how the presence of others can lead to conformity and obedience to authority. Next we will examine the effect that the presence of others has on helping behavior.

COACTION AND AUDIENCE EFFECTS

Around 1900 it was discovered that the presence of others sometimes has strong effects on the behavior of individuals (Zajonc, 1972). It was found, for example, that bicycle racers perform better when competing against each other than against a clock. This **social facilitation** of behavior is probably one reason why new records are set in Olympic games or, for that matter, in any competitive situation. The presence of others energizes the behavior of the contestants to higher levels.

The energizing of behavior as a result of others competing in the same task is called the **coaction effect** and is well documented not only in humans but also in other animals. We know, for example, that satiated chickens will begin to eat if put into a cage with other chickens that are feeding. A chicken will in fact consume as much as 60% more grain when raised with another chicken as compared to its consumption when raised alone (Zajonc, 1972). This facilitation of behavior has also been observed in other animals from dogs to armadillos and occurs not only in feeding behavior but also in drinking, running, and sexual behavior.

Even the lowly cockroach is not immune to coaction effects! Zajonc, Heingartner, and Herman (1969) built a roach runway and measured the speed with which roaches would run to escape light (roaches are negatively phototropic, as anyone knows who has cockroaches and has turned on the kitchen light in the middle of the night). Roaches paired in the runway ran faster than those who had to "go it alone."

Interestingly, most of the effects observed in coacting individuals also occur if one member is behaving and others serve as an audience. This **audience effect** also occurs in the cockroach. In an experiment like the light escape runway just mentioned, Zajonc, Heingartner, and Herman (1969) ran roaches either with or without a roach audience "observing" the performing roach. Roaches that had an audience ran significantly faster than those that did not.

As is true of most things in life, however, understanding coaction and audience effects is not as simple as these examples might imply. The effect of others on our behavior is not always facilitative. Sometimes the presence of others causes our behavior to deteriorate and we do worse than we might have done if left alone. This often seems to happen in professional sports. The presence of a large crowd often causes the "old pro" to play over his head, while his upstart challenger's behavior worsens.

The psychological explanation usually given for these seemingly contradictory effects of the presence of others is that coactors and audiences will facilitate performance if the performer's correct response is highly likely (i.e., **dominant**, in psychological terminology), whereas the presence of others will lead to a worsening of behavior if the performer's correct response is low in probability. This is apparently because the presence of others arouses us, and this arousal tends to trigger whatever response is dominant. If the dominant response is correct (because of practice or overlearning), the behavior is facilitated; if the dominant response is incorrect, the behavior is degraded. Thus, to return to our old pro and upstart challenger example, the old pro could be expected to have the correct responses more available because of greater experience and so will show social facilitation, while the upstart challenger will tend to show a deterioration of behavior as a result of the presence of others. The presence of others, then, arouses us to action. Our behavior, however, may be either improved or worsened by the presence of others, depending upon how likely the correct response for that situation is available to us.

This brings up a final point. Our behavior may be facilitated by others in some situations and worsened in other situations. We may perform brilliantly on the court and miserably on a test; in both cases, our performance may result from the presence of others.

We turn now to an examination of the powerful influence that the presence of others can have on our individuality and ethical behavior. The studies within this general category involve examination of conformity behavior and obedience to authority.

CONFORMITY

Most of us have found ourselves in situations where our motivation to act in a particular way has come under group pressure. For example, we might find ourselves drinking alcohol or experimenting with drugs as a result of group pressure, even though we personally do not wish to drink or take drugs. As anyone who has ever been in this situation knows, the motivation to "go along" with the group can be terribly strong. Brown (1965) noted that the mere existence of a group seems to trigger a motivation to agree or conform to the group's wishes. All of us, whether we admit it or not,

are conformists. Of course we do not all conform to the same rules, but in group situations we are very likely to agree with the group when decisions must be made.

The strength of our conformity to group pressure has been shown in a number of studies. Sherif (1947), for example, had subjects individually judge the amount of movement they perceived of a point of light in a dark room (in fact there was no movement, but the perception of such movement in a dark room, called the **autokinetic effect**, is a very strong illusion). The subjects differed widely in their individual estimates of the amount of movement they perceived, yet each individual was internally consistent. Interestingly, when Sherif put people together in groups of two or three and asked them to judge the amount of movement, their estimates converged. Thus even though subjects were individually consistent, they changed their judgments when put into a group situation in order to agree with each other. Sherif's experiment points to the power of the group to influence judgments, even when the judgment itself is an illusion.

Perhaps the best-known studies on conformity are those of Solomon Asch (1952, 1965). Asch asked his subjects to make a simple perceptual judgment concerning the length of lines. As shown in Figure 10.1, each subject was provided with a standard line and three comparison lines, from which the subject was asked to pick the one of equal length to the standard. In the basic experiment seven to nine subjects viewed the standard and comparison lines together. Then, one after another, they were asked to provide their answer to the experimenter aloud. The line comparisons were easy to make, and a control group of subjects who wrote their answers made very few errors (7.4%). What were the results?

Imagine first that you are a subject in this experiment. Seated with the group, you are shown the first standard and comparison lines.

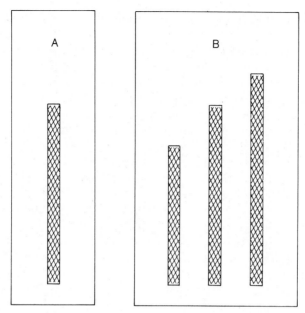

Figure 10.1 *Standard (A) and comparison (B) lines in Asch's conformity experiments. (From Asch, 1952. Used by permission.)*

Because you are next to last, you have a chance to listen to most of the others respond before you must respond yourself. On the first two trials everyone agrees, and you relax a bit and begin to wonder what could be the purpose of such an absurd experiment!

On the third trial, however, things change. When the standard and comparison lines are shown, you quickly note which is equal; but, to your surprise, everyone in front of you picks a different line from the one you thought was correct. Your turn comes, and you find yourself in a conflict situation. Do you answer as you see it, or do you conform to the answer given by the group?

Subjectively you might expect that you would stick with what you believe is the right answer. It is, after all, just a psychology experiment you're participating in because you need the cash and is of little real consequence to you. Observation of real subjects in this exper-

iment indicates that they become very uncomfortable when put in the position of going against the group decision, even when it is obviously wrong.

Asch found large individual differences in the amount of conforming behavior seen in the subjects of his experiment. Some subjects never conformed to the group decision (though generally showing much discomfort in the process), while others were completely conforming. On the whole, approximately 80% of the subjects conformed at least once during the 12 trials of the experiment.

In postexperimental interviews, subjects reported feelings of self-doubt and a desire to agree with the group. Also of some interest is that the subjects did not usually question the group judgment but sought within themselves the reasons for their unconformity with the group. Apparently an individual usually assumes that the majority is correct, even when the majority disagrees with the individual's own judgment.

Asch found that subjects who tended to yield to the group's pressure did so in one of three ways. A very small number of subjects suffered what Asch called **perceptual distortion**; that is, they indicated in the postexperimental interviews that they actually saw the group's response as correctly matching the standard. Thus these subjects, in order to conform to the group's response, distorted their own perception of the lines to resolve the motivational conflict they experienced.

A more common way in which subjects altered the situation to conform to the group's response was labeled **distortion of judgment** by Asch. In this situation subjects realized that their judgment was different from the group's but conformed because they assumed that their judgment was incorrect. Presence of the group led to a distortion of individual judgments so that they would conform to the group judgment.

Finally, some subjects conformed as a result of what Asch called **distortion of action**. For these subjects, not appearing different from the group seemed of paramount importance. They apparently lost sight of the purpose of the experiment (i.e., to judge lines) in their need to not appear different. These subjects did not necessarily assume that the group was right. That is, there was no distortion of judgment; they simply felt compelled to conform with the group's response. These subjects noted that the conflict they felt between their judgment and that of the group often triggered feelings of inferiority or of being an outsider to the group. These people, then, showed a distortion of actions but not of perceptions or judgments.

In an attempt to reduce the conformity that individuals showed to group pressure, Asch increased the disparity between the standard and the group's response (by seven inches in some cases) and still obtained an overall conformity response of 28%. For a corresponding control group, not subject to conformity pressure of the group, the error rate was only 2%. Clearly, then, the presence of others creates in us a motivational state to conform to the group's norms.

The size of the group does not seem crucial in the conformity effect when there are three or more people. In a series of experiments that varied the size of the group, Asch found that the conformity effect virtually disappeared if only one other person besides the subject was present. Apparently most people assume their judgments to be just as accurate as anyone else's in a paired situation. When two persons in addition to the subject were added, conforming responses jumped to 12.8%, and with three persons in addition to the subject, conforming responses were not significantly different from larger groups (i.e., were approximately 33%). Conforming behavior is thus apparently triggered by the presence of others at any time when more than one person is present. Amid the urban environments in which a large proportion of our population lives, the conclusion seems safe that all of us are constantly immersed in social situations that tend to activate conforming behavior in us. It would be useful, therefore, to investigate the conditions under which the pressure exerted by the group to conform can be broken. Again Asch has provided us with some of the answers.

In a modified version of the previous experiment, Asch had one of the group give the correct answer while the rest of the group conformed to the incorrect answer. The effect of only one person deviating from the group's response had a liberating effect on the subjects of this experiment. Conforming responses were reduced from 33% to about 5% to 10%. Observation of the subjects during the experiment revealed that they often looked to the deviant and seemed to gain moral support to deviate also. In this regard Asch pointed out that the nonconformer provided support to the subject (i.e., as someone else who sees it as he or she does) and also broke the unanimity of the group. The presence of one other individual who differed from the group had a substantial disinhibiting effect on the subjects so that judgments were more likely to be what the individuals actually perceived than a conforming response to the group pressure.

There seems little question that groups exert a strong influence on individuals to conform to group expectations. How do groups exert this influence? Apparently they produce their effects by subtle (and sometimes not so subtle) behaviors aimed at the deviant.

Asch tested this hypothesis by reversing the roles of subject and group in his earlier experiments. In this variation the group was naive and one subject (a male confederate of the experimenter) was instructed to give the wrong answer. As expected, the group was not swayed by the deviant but became amused at his deviancy, passing knowing glances back and forth, smiling and sometimes laughing. One suspects that these behaviors observed by the deviant in a normal situation would impel a strong desire to conform. Social ostracism is a powerful force for compliance.

The factors controlling conformity, however, are complex. As Moscovici and Faucheux (1972) pointed out, even the nonconformers in Asch's study were probably conforming but to a different set of rules, such as beliefs concerning the importance of individuality and independence. From a practical viewpoint, we can never really be sure that someone is not conforming because we do not know all the reference groups, attitudes, and beliefs that are influencing that person. Nevertheless, it is certain that groups do exert strong pressures on individuals to conform to group expectations. From the individual's point of view, groups seem to trigger a motivational state that tends to bring the individual into line with the group.

One can regard obedience to authority as a type of conformity to the rules of society and the power figures who both make and regulate the rules. Though all of us like to think of ourselves as independent and able to choose between right and wrong regardless of who tells us to do it, we are in fact much more obedient to the authority figures of our society than we generally acknowledge.

Although the concepts of conformity and obedience are functionally very similar, one can at least intuitively make a distinction between the two. First, conformity situations usually exert their influence implicitly. We "want" to conform rather than being explicitly asked to comply. Second, one can distinguish between the sources of influence. Conforming behavior is often the result of group pressure, while obedience (or compliance, as it is also called) is generally a response to the command of an individual. Finally, there is often a status or power difference between conformity and compliance situations. Conformity is typically a response resulting from the influence of peers whose status is approximately the same as that of the conforming individual. Compliance, on the other hand, typically occurs as a result of pressure exerted by someone of higher status or more power than the person asked to comply.

COMPLIANCE

In a series of studies Stanley Milgram (1963, 1965, 1975) tested subjects' willingness to obey commands that for most were unpleasant and morally unjustifiable. Milgram's basic experiment required one subject to "teach" another subject by delivering increasingly painful electric shocks for incorrect answers in a verbal memory task. In front of the teacher was a shock console with switches indicating varying voltages from 15 to 450 volts in 15-volt steps. Above the switches were labels describing the shocks' characteristics. At the low end the descriptions indicated slight and moderate shock, while at the upper end descriptions indicated extreme shock, danger: severe shock, and XXXX. Figure 10.2 shows the basic layout of the shock console.

Milgram was interested in how far subjects would be willing to go in obeying an experimenter who asked them to continue. Before Milgram ran the experiment, he asked several groups of people how far they thought they would be willing to go in delivering shock for incorrect answers. These groups (including psychiatrists, college sophomores, graduate students, adults, faculty in behavioral sciences) were all consistent in predicting that the subject serving as teacher would refuse to follow the orders of the experimenter when the shocks became very painful. The psychiatrists in particular predicted that most subjects would not go further than 150 volts, that only approximately 4% would go as high as 300 volts, and that less than one in a thousand would continue to deliver shocks all the way to 450 volts.

After obtaining these data indicating that most people believed that the majority of persons would not hurt others, even in the name of science, Milgram ran the experiment. By toss of a coin, one subject was chosen as the teacher and the other became the learner who would receive the shocks. The coin toss, how-

ever, was rigged so that the same subject was always the learner, actually a confederate of Milgram's who was an actor and faked the protestations and painfulness of the shock (no shock was in fact delivered). As the learner made mistakes in the memory task, the teacher was required by the experimenter to increase the shock. At 75 volts the learner began to make noise. By 120 volts he began to complain about the shock, and at 150 volts he started demanding to be released from the experiment. The protestation of the learner to the ever increasing shock became greater and greater as the shocks continued, until at 285 volts it became a scream of agony.

How did the teachers react to the learner's cries of pain? They were anything but relaxed. As the learner began to protest, they often turned to the experimenter, questioning whether they should continue. The experimenter firmly replied that they must continue, using prods such as "The experiment requires that you go on, it is absolutely essential that we continue," and so on. Thus the teachers were quite aware of the learner's plight and were usually distressed at having to continue delivering the painful shock.

Nevertheless, in a first experiment with Yale undergraduates, fully 60% of the teachers went all the way to 450 volts. When the experiment was over, many of the teachers

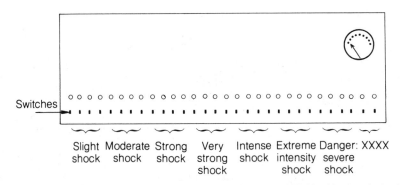

Figure 10.2   *Milgram's shock console. (Adapted from Milgram, 1965. Used by permission.)*

showed obvious relief that they no longer had to deliver the painful shocks. In a series of experiments conducted by Milgram and his associates, subjects from various occupations and social environments were tested, and the results were always the same. People obeyed the experimenter and shocked the learner much more than predicted. The basic findings have also been replicated in various parts of the world from Munich to Rome to South Africa and Australia. In some of these test situations the obedience rate ran as high as 85%.

The subjects of these experiments were not sadistic persons who got great enjoyment from the pain of others. They were persons just like you and me. But when put into a conflict situation where they had to choose between open defiance of an authority figure and obedience to a personally immoral behavior, the majority of subjects chose to obey. Milgram's research suggests that most of us have a strong motivation to obey the authority figures of our society, even when such obedience seems compromising to our own standards of conduct.

Milgram argued that the basis of obedience is one's ability to view oneself as simply an instrument carrying out someone else's wishes. In such a way we cognitively lay the blame for the learner's suffering onto someone else (viz., the experimenter). Evidence for this type of obedience analysis comes from many sources. For example, the subjects' conversations with the experimenter during the experiment often consisted of the teacher's disclaiming any responsibility for the suffering of the learner and frequent checking to see if the experimenter would accept the responsibility for whatever happened.

In one variation of the experiment the teacher was only required to read aloud the descriptive labels above the switches, not throw the switches that "delivered" shock. Under these conditions 37 of 40 subjects con-

tinued all the way to the end. When asked about the suffering of the learner, they replied that the person throwing the switches was responsible.

The concept of detached responsibility for a person's behavior suggests that increasing the subjects' feelings of responsibility should lead to a change in the obedience rate. A number of studies support this concept. For example, in one experiment (Milgram, 1975) when subjects were allowed to choose their own shock level, the average level chosen was only 60 volts.

In the original experiments the teacher was in one room while the learner was in another. When the teacher was put into the same room with the learner so that responsibility for the teacher's behavior could not easily be denied, obedience rates dropped. Zimbardo (1969) in fact has suggested that the ability to avoid responsibility for one's behavior, which he calls **deindividuation**, is an important component of much violence seen in modern society.

However, the teacher's personal responsibility in Milgram's experiments was not the only factor; characteristics of the authority figure—for example, the physical presence of the experimenter—were also important in increasing obedience. When Milgram had the experimenter deliver instructions to the teacher over a telephone, the obedience rate of the subjects who complied all the way to 450 volts dropped to about 30%. This suggests that most people find it very difficult to defy authority directly, even when their morals are compromised. It is also worth pointing out that even 30% compliance is a huge amount.

The context in which the experiment is conducted is also an important factor (Milgram, 1965). When the experiment was conducted at Yale, obedience was high; yet when the experiment was removed from the university context and conducted in a run-down section of town, obedience rates dropped. These results seem to indicate that obedience is also related to our concepts—we seem to assume that behaving in certain ways for the good of science or country is all right, even though the behavior may transgress our own moral codes.

Milgram also found that a lack of clear authority immediately dropped the obedience rate. In this variation of the basic experiment, two experimenters were present and disagreed about continuance of the shock. Under these conditions the teacher quickly stopped shocking the learner.

Finally, Milgram has found that the obedience of others to an authority figure leads to the subject's increased obedience, whereas rebellion of others leads to rebellion by the subject, who refuses to deliver further shock. This effect is reminiscent of the deviant in Asch's experiments and suggests that conformity to group pressure is also involved in obedience to authority, in the sense that the authority figure represents the head of an accepted group.

Milgram believed that obedience to authority is a basic element of social living. Without obedience to accepted authorities, the very fabric of society would dissolve. Nevertheless, the same obedience that has helped humans to survive can also lead to atrocities such as occurred in the concentration camps of World War II and in such incidents as My Lai during the Vietnam conflict. It is frightening to realize that most of us are capable of committing such atrocities under the right conditions. Although we do not like to admit it, obedience to authority can override our ethics, morals, and sympathies toward our fellow human beings. Our cognitive processes allow us to rationalize away our own responsibilities to the point that we can self-righteously say, "We were only following orders." Finally, the very structure of our society, with its various divisions of labor, works against feelings of personal responsibility for our acts, as Milgram (1975) has so clearly pointed out. The person ordering an execution can disclaim responsibility for the death because he or she did not pull the trigger, while the executioner can likewise disclaim responsibility because he or she was only following the order of the judge. Also, when decisions are made by the "state," no one need feel responsible because the responsibility falls on a nonliving entity. In some respects it is perhaps surprising that atrocities are not more frequent.

Zimbardo's Mock Prison

As most people know, prisons do not work to reduce future crime, and although we talk about prisons as rehabilitation centers, they do not rehabilitate. Recidivism (i.e., being returned to prison after having been released and presumably rehabilitated) runs about 75% in U.S. prisons (Haney, Banks, & Zimbardo, 1976). It is very easy for most of us to believe that the stable (i.e., consistent) personality characteristics of criminals rather than situational factors are the cause of their return to a life of crime upon reentry into society; however, these assumptions are overly simple.

Phillip Zimbardo and his colleagues (Haney, Banks, & Zimbardo, 1976; Zimbardo, 1975) set up a mock prison environment in the basement of the psychology department at Stanford University in an attempt to determine how much of prison behavior (of both prisoners and their guards) could be attributed to personality characteristics and how much to situational factors that normally occur in prisons.

Volunteer subjects were paid $15 per day to play the role of either a prisoner or a guard. Subjects were randomly assigned one of the two roles and were carefully screened before the experiment for both physical and emotional stability. The 22 male subjects were normal, healthy college students from middle-class homes. Subjects chosen as prisoners were arrested by the Palo Alto Police Department at their homes, charged with suspicion of burglary or armed robbery, read their rights, searched, handcuffed, and taken to the police station. At the station a file was prepared on each subject; they were fingerprinted and placed in a detention cell. Subjects were then driven to the Stanford Prison (Zimbardo's experimental situation), where they were stripped, deloused, and given a prison uniform. The uniform, which consisted of a loose-fitting smock and a cap made from a nylon stocking, was designed to deindividuate the prisoners (i.e., reduce their feelings of self-identity). Subjects had to remain in the prison situation for 24 hours per day for an intended two weeks. Initiation of the experiment was thus quite similar to what one could expect in a real arrest situation.

Subjects chosen as guards were given an orientation meeting in which they were told to maintain order within the simulated prison. The guards, also explicitly instructed that they were not to physically abuse the prisoners, worked eight-hour shifts and could return to their homes when not on duty. Guards were issued khaki uniforms, a whistle, and a nightstick in order to enhance their identity. Although the guards believed that the study was primarily designed to observe the behavior of the prisoners, the study was actually concerned with the behavior of both prisoners and guards.

Results of the simulated prison experiment were quite startling. At the end of only six days, the study had to be stopped because of the rapid changes occurring in the behaviors of both prisoners and guards. Figure 10.3 profiles the kinds of behaviors in which both prisoners and guards engaged. As can be seen, guard behavior was typified by giving commands, insulting and threatening the prisoners, and engaging in both verbal and physical aggression against them. Prisoners were typified by a general lack of behavior, but when behavior occurred, it consisted mainly of either asking or answering questions. The verbal and physical aggression of the guards became greater as the study progressed. Though *each guard* was abusive at times, some guards were so abusive that Zimbardo characterized them as sadistic.

The emotionality of the prisoners became increasingly negative, with episodes of depression, extreme anxiety, psychosomatic illness, and thoughts of harming others. Their emotionality became so severe, in fact, that half the subjects had to be released from the experiment. Conditions had so degenerated in the mock prison that at a "parole hearing," three out of five subjects serving as prisoners were willing to give up the $15 per day in order to get out of the experiment—and this was after only four days. That the situation became a very real one for the prisoners was evidenced by the fact that 90% of their private conversations concerned the conditions of the prison rather than their real lives outside the experiment.

Thus both guards and prisoners apparently became very "caught up" in their roles, which largely determined their behavior. The guards behaved in the way they believed necessary to control the prisoners, and the prisoners behaved in ways highly similar to real prisoners in our penal system.

A battery of psychological tests had been given to both guards and prisoners before the experiment began. None of the tests predicted the differences seen between the behavior of the guards and that of the prisoners, nor, for that matter, between lenient and cruel guards. The situation of the model prison was apparently responsible for the large behavioral changes shown by these normal, healthy, middle-class college males. The guard group was all-powerful, and the prisoners

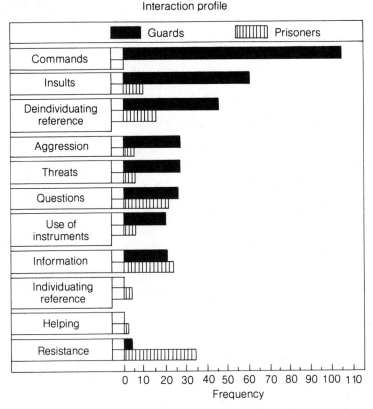

Figure 10.3 *Profile of the behaviors of guards and prisoners in Zimbardo's mock prison study. (From Zimbardo, 1975. Used by permission.)*

were helpless. As a result, their behaviors changed as a function of the situation in which they were immersed. Table 10.1 depicts some of the feelings expressed by the guards and prisoners concerning the experiment.

Zimbardo believed that the motive for power is the most important variable in social psychology (Zimbardo, 1975). Prisons contain groups of people with great power (e.g., guards) and others with no power (e.g., prisoners). To maintain the power structure, prisons dehumanize the prisoner by taking away his clothing and personal items and giving him a uniform and a number. Standard times for eating, sleeping, exercise, and so on also reinforce the power structure. The prisoner has no control over his environment. Under these conditions it is little wonder that people become passive, feel degraded, become depressed, and want to strike back at the society that put them there. Zimbardo's study suggests that the high rate of recidivism in our penal institutions may result, at least in part, from the very structure of the social situation that exists in prisons. If normal, well-adjusted students can become sadistic and brutal or passive and depressed in a mock prison situation lasting only six days, what can we expect

Table 10.1   Zimbardo's Guards and Prisoners

Guards' Comments	Prisoners' Comments
They [the prisoners] seemed to lose touch with the reality of the experiment—they took me so seriously.	The way we were made to degrade ourselves really brought us down, and that's why we all sat docile toward the end of the experiment.
I didn't interfere with any of the guards' actions. Usually, if what they were doing bothered me, I would walk out and take another duty.... Looking back, I am impressed by how little I felt for them.	I realize now (after it's over) that no matter how together I thought I was inside my head, my prison behavior was often less under my control than I realized. No matter how open, friendly, and helpful I was with other prisoners, I was still operating as an isolated, self-centered person being rational rather than compassionate.
They [the prisoners] didn't see it as an experiment. It was real and they were fighting to keep their identity. But we were always there to show them just who was boss.	I began to feel I was losing my identity, that the person I call____, the person who volunteered to get me into this prison (because it was a prison to me, it still is a prison to me, I don't regard it as an experiment or a simulation ...) was distant from me, was remote until finally I wasn't that person, I was 416. I was really my number and 416 was really going to have to decide what to do.
I was tired of seeing the prisoners in their rags and smelling the strong odors of their bodies that filled the cells. I watched them tear at each other, on orders given by us.	I learned that people can easily forget that others are human. (From Haney, Banks, & Zimbardo, 1976, p. 88. Reprinted by permission.)
Acting authoritatively can be fun. Power can be a great pleasure.	
During the inspection, I went to cell 2 to mess up a bed the prisoner had made and he grabbed me, screaming that he had just made it, and he wasn't going to let me mess it up. He grabbed my throat, and although he was laughing I was pretty scared. I lashed out with my stick and hit him in the chin (although not very hard), and when I freed myself I became angry.	

of less well adjusted individuals imprisoned for years?*

The study of social motivation leads us to consider the situational factors that influence our behavior. Just as the situational factors in Zimbardo's prison study appeared of paramount importance, they are also apparently involved in our coming to the aid of persons in distress. The presence of others appears to inhibit us from acting in emergencies. This study of helping behavior has been examined in most detail by Bibb Latané and John Darley. Their book, *The Unresponsive Bystander: Why Doesn't He Help?* (1970), has shed much light on the topic of bystander intervention.

BYSTANDER INTERVENTION

If you have ever had the misfortune of a car breakdown on an interstate highway (and you had no cellular telephone or CB radio), you al-

*The work of both Milgram and Zimbardo has raised questions about the ethics of psychological research (e.g., Baumrind, 1964). Subjects in Milgram's experiments were sometimes quite upset at their own behavior. Similarly, one might question the advisability of subjecting people to conditions leading to the kinds of behaviors found in Zimbardo's study. It is beyond the scope of this text to examine the ethics of psychological research, but it is important to note that researchers have recently become concerned with the possible side effects that some types of research may cause. The American Psychological Association (1973, 1982) has issued guidelines concerning the ethical considerations of research.

ready know how difficult it can be to get help from passers-by. As Latané and Darley have pointed out, it is not a question of people not helping others—because sometimes they do—but rather of the conditions under which helping behavior is likely to occur. This of course suggests that helping behavior depends less on the characteristics of the potential helper than on the characteristics of the emergency situation. Consider the following three examples from Latané and Darley (1970, pp. 1–2, reprinted by permission).

Andrew Mormille is stabbed in the stomach as he rides the *A* train home in Manhattan. Eleven other riders watch the 17-year-old boy as he bleeds to death; none come to his assistance even though his attackers have left the car. He dies.

An 18-year-old switchboard operator, alone in her office in the Bronx, is raped and beaten. Escaping momentarily, she runs naked and bleeding to the street, screaming for help. A crowd of 40 passers-by gathers and watches as, in broad daylight, the rapist tries to drag her back upstairs; no one interferes. Finally, two policemen happen by and arrest her assailant.

Kitty Genovese is set upon by a maniac as she returns home from work at 3 a.m. Thirty-eight of her neighbors in Kew Gardens come to their windows when she cries out in terror; none come to her assistance even though the stalker takes over half an hour to murder her. No one even so much as calls the police. She dies.

Latané and Darley determined to study the conditions leading to helping behavior or the lack of it. One of their first findings was that helping behavior depends to a certain extent upon what is being asked of the helper. In an initial study involving nonemergency situations, they had students at Columbia University in New York City walk up to people on the street and ask them for the time of day, directions, pocket change, a dime, or their name.

Results of the experiment showed that minor assistance (i.e., time, directions, or change) was rarely refused and that 85% of those requested provided assistance. Less than 40% of those asked gave the student their names, and only about 30% gave a dime when requested.

The manner in which the request was made also had a significant effect on receiving aid. For example, in the dime request condition, people were more likely to comply if the requesters first gave their own names (approximately 50% complied) or explained their reason for needing money (about 66% complied). Interestingly, the sex of the requester had no effect on receiving assistance in any except the dime condition. In that condition females were more likely than males to be given the money they requested.

These early studies indicate that one factor determining helping behavior (at least in nonemergency situations) is the amount of commitment that the helper must make. Minor or common requests are usually granted. Less common requests or requests that require the helper to make a larger commitment (e.g., giving money or one's name) are less likely to be granted unless some reasonable explanation is provided.

In emergency situations the commitment by the potential helper will be relatively large, perhaps leading to some reluctance in the potential helper to intervene. Latané and Darley pointed out that the very characteristics of emergency situations make them a "no-win" situation for the helper (e.g., the sometimes very real possibility of harm). There are also few tangible rewards for helping behavior (other than an occasional citation or news article). Thus we should not be too surprised that people hesitate to intervene.

A second problem with emergency situations is that they are, almost by definition, unusual events for which the potential helper is ill equipped. One is understandably reluctant to attempt a behavior that one is unsure how to perform. A third characteristic of emergencies is that they occur suddenly; if we are to react, we must do so immediately, without thinking through the best means of responding. We may thus hesitate in a state of indecision while the crucial time for action passes by. Finally, because we are generally unfamiliar with emergency situations, there is no handy list of how to behave or what to do in a particular emergency, and so we may not help because we simply don't know what to do.

"The picture is a grim one. Faced with a situation in which he can gain no benefit, unable to rely on past experience, on the experience of others, or on forethought and planning, denied the opportunity to consider carefully his course of action, the bystander to an emergency is in an unenviable position. It is perhaps surprising that anyone should intervene at all" (Latané & Darley, 1970, p. 31).

A Model of Intervention

Latané and Darley proposed that whether an individual intervenes or not in an emergency situation can be understood in terms of five factors, as shown in the flowchart of Figure 10.4. The pressure of others affects the decision process at each stage but is particularly important in the first three stages.

First we must take note of the situation; obviously we cannot react to an emergency of which we are unaware. Latané and Darley have found that the presence of other people around us, particularly strangers, reduces our

attention to the environment so that we take longer to notice a potential emergency situation.

In one experiment subjects were asked to report to a room to participate in an interview about urban life. The male students were given the room number and instructed to begin filling out some preliminary forms while they waited to be called to the interview. After the subject had been working alone for a few minutes, smoke began to filter into the room through a vent in one wall. The subjects, waiting alone, typically noticed the smoke soon after it began, quickly investigated it, and, finding no reasonable explanation, left their room to report it. Of the subjects in this condition, 50% reported the smoke within two minutes of its introduction, and 75% reported it within four minutes. Thus, subjects waiting alone reported the emergency quickly.

In a second condition, however, a subject, upon arrival at the designated room, found two other subjects already there and busily filling out forms (the two subjects already present were actually confederates of the experimenter). When the smoke was introduced into the room, the stooges were instructed to look up and notice the smoke but to continue working. Under these conditions only one out of ten subjects left the room to report the smoke, but the other nine continued to work on their questionnaires even as the smoke filled the room. Careful observation revealed that 63% of the subjects in the alone condition noticed the smoke within five seconds of its introduc-

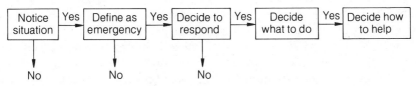

Figure 10.4 Schematic diagram of Latané and Darley's model of the intervention process. (Data from Latané & Darley, 1970.)

tion, while only 26% of the subjects in the room with others present noticed the smoke within five seconds.

These data indicate that one effect of the presence of others is a reduction in the amount of attention that we pay to our environment. The results suggest that when an emergency exists, we will be slower to notice it if others are present. This reduced attention to our environment may result from a tendency to maintain a certain psychological distance from others by avoiding eye contact. By avoiding looking at others, we also avoid observing much of our environment and thus notice potential emergency situations more slowly.

The smoke-filled-room experiment also demonstrates another factor involved in the inhibition of helping behavior. Emergency situations are often ambiguous, at least initially, and we are uncertain whether to consider the situation an actual emergency. When we are uncertain, we tend to look to those around us in order to test our ideas about the situation. The problem is that everyone else is doing precisely the same (i.e., looking at others). Because we don't want to embarrass ourselves by declaring an emergency when none exists, we tend to have calm, nonemotional expressions on our faces as we look around, and we see that everyone else also appears calm. Therefore we must be wrong; an emergency must not exist. Latané and Darley have labeled this behavior **pluralistic ignorance**. By remaining expressionless and unemotional as we survey the reactions of others, we "fool" each other into believing that an emergency does not in fact exist. Pluralistic ignorance seems to account for the cited fact that only one out of ten subjects in the second experimental condition reported the smoke during the entire six-minute test period. Referring back to Figure 10.4, the presence of others initially retards our noticing the situation, but the presence of others also creates a pluralistic

ignorance that retards our defining the situation as an emergency.

In another conceptually similar experiment, subjects filled out questionnaires in a room either alone or with another person. Some of the subject pairs were strangers, others were friends, and in one condition one subject was a confederate of the experimenter, as in the smoke experiment. A female experimenter, whom the subjects had met briefly, was heard to fall in the next room and moan that she had hurt her ankle. Latané and Darley found that 70% of the subjects alone in the room came to the aid of the female experimenter, while only 7% of the subjects paired with the confederate (who sat passively throughout) came to her aid. These latter subjects appeared uneasy and glanced often at the confederate, who continued to fill out the questionnaire.

For subjects paired with a stranger, only 8 out of 40 (i.e., 20%) intervened, demonstrating that the mere presence of another person tends to inhibit helping behavior. When two friends were paired in the room, helping behavior was approximately 70%—though friends, too, were slower to intervene than subjects in the alone condition. The friend condition, however, did create significantly faster intervention than the stranger conditions.

Latané and Darley believed that the results of this experiment can also be understood in terms of pluralistic ignorance. In both the passive confederate and stranger conditions, subjects looked furtively at one another while remaining outwardly calm. They were, in effect, creating a pluralistic ignorance that reduced the chances of their defining the situation as an emergency. Friends, however, were more likely to be open about their feelings, and this led to a reduction of the pluralistic ignorance created—although even in the friend condition, the reaction time to providing helping behavior was slower than in the alone condition.

When subjects were interviewed after the experiment, noninterveners were consistent in their interpretation of the situation as a nonemergency. Of some interest is that in both experiments, subjects were unaware that their behavior had been inhibited by the presence of others. Thus in an ambiguous situation, pluralistic ignorance apparently leads to cognitions that define the situation as a nonemergency, and behavior is inhibited.

Many situations, of course, cannot be ignored and are immediately defined as emergencies; yet even under these conditions, people may not intervene. This brings us to the third step in the intervention model shown in Figure 10.4: deciding if one is responsible for intervening.

Anyone who lives in a large metropolitan area and reads the newspaper or watches the news knows how common the examples of nonintervention have become. Why don't people intervene? For one reason, the cost of direct intervention can be high. If you intervene, for example, you may be attacked yourself; your altruistic behavior may be misunderstood by the victim, who may not want your help; you will probably be questioned by the police. There are good reasons, then, for not directly intervening. But what about some sort of indirect intervention such as calling the police? Yet even indirect intervention often does not occur.

Latané and Darley believed that the lack of intervention can be understood as resulting from a **diffusion of responsibility** because of the presence of others. In a situation where a person may already be reluctant to intervene, the presence of others takes the responsibility from the person's shoulders ("Surely someone has already called the police"). The problem is that each person is similarly influenced by this diffusion of responsibility so that many times

no one intervenes, as happened in the Kitty Genovese murder mentioned earlier.

Latané and Darley designed an experiment conceptually similar to the Kitty Genovese murder. Subjects were recruited to participate in a discussion of personal problems associated with college life. In order to reduce embarrassment (so the subjects thought), the participants were placed in individual booths with headphones and microphones for communicating with each other. After the experiment had begun, the subjects heard one of the participants fall into an epileptic seizure. In one condition each subject was led to believe that he or she was the only one aware of the seizure, while in a second condition each thought that four other participants could also hear the emergency. The seizure episode was actually a tape recording made to determine what percentage of people would seek help for the seizure victim.

Latané and Darley found that 85% of the subjects who thought they were alone sought help for the victim before the tape ended (125 seconds), while only 31% of the subjects who thought that four people could hear the seizure responded to the emergency. Eventually each of the subjects who thought they were alone sought help, and 62% of those in the second condition eventually reported it.

Those subjects who did not report the seizure were, however, anything but apathetic. They were very nervous and concerned about the seizure victim. Apparently, then, apathy and depersonalization resulting from city living are not adequate explanations for nonintervention in emergency situations. Instead, the presence of others not only reduces a scanning of the environment but also creates a pluralistic ignorance and finally diffuses the responsibility felt by any specific individual to the point that no help may be provided. These effects tend to be reduced if we are in the company of friends or are familiar with our surroundings, and they are exaggerated if we are in the company of strangers or are unfamiliar with our environment.

Personality characteristics do not as a rule seem related to the probability of helping behavior. Latané and Darley found no correlation between five different personality scales and helping behavior in the seizure study. Biographical background was also not predictive, with the exception that people who grew up in small communities were more likely to help than those who were reared in large metropolitan areas (see also Amato, 1983).

Latané and Darley's results thus suggest that situational factors (e.g., the presence of other people) are crucial determinants of helping behavior, while dispositional characteristics of the individual are less important. This is perhaps most clearly seen in an experiment by Darley and Batson (1976). Seminary students at Princeton University were asked to participate in a study on religious education and vocation. The subjects began the experiment in one room but were then asked to go to another building next door to finish the experiment by giving a short talk on either religious vocations or the parable of the Good Samaritan. Three conditions were run. In the first condition subjects were told that they were late for the second part of the experiment and should hurry across the alley to the second building. A second group of subjects were told that they had just time enough to make it to the other building, and a third group of subjects were told that they had plenty of time to get to the building for the second part of the experiment.

Subjects were directed to the building next door. Getting there required crossing an alley that ran between the buildings. In this alley a confederate of the experimenter was slumped against the wall and instructed to cough twice and groan as subjects passed him. The behavior of interest was whether stu-

dents in training for the ministry would stop to aid the victim and whether the type of talk they were about to give (i.e., religious vocation versus the parable of the Good Samaritan) and the degree of hurry (i.e., late, on time, or early) would influence the probability of their giving aid.

Results of the experiment are quite fascinating. The type of talk the seminarian was about to give (and thus was presumably thinking about on his way across the alley) had *no* effect on helping behavior. Subjects asked to talk on the parable of the Good Samaritan were no more likely to stop than those asked to talk on religious vocations. Thus thinking about helping others did not appear to increase the likelihood of lending aid to a victim. By contrast, the time constraints put on the subjects had a large effect on helping behavior. Subjects who thought they were late and were thus in a hurry were not very helpful; only 10% stopped to offer the victim aid. Of the subjects in the "on time" condition, 45% stopped to offer aid, while 63% in the "early" condition stopped. Clearly the situational factor of time can be crucial in determining helping behavior. Again we see the importance of situational factors in motivating behavior in social situations.

We have just reviewed considerable evidence that people are reluctant to help others in need. The factors identified as important in this reluctance have helped us to understand how tragedies such as the Kitty Genovese murder sometimes occur. Although these factors work against bystander intervention in an emergency, people nevertheless often do help others (Latané & Nida, 1981). Researchers have also looked at some of the motivational factors that lead to helping behavior (see, e.g., studies by Batson et al., 1981; Batson & Gray, 1981; Batson et al., 1983; Bauman, Cialdini, & Kenrick, 1981; Coke, Batson, & McDavis, 1978; Hoffman, 1981; Rutkowski, Gruder, & Romer,

1983; Schwartz & Gottlieb, 1980; Senneker & Hendrick, 1983; Toi & Batson, 1982; Weiner, 1980).

One thrust of this research has examined the idea that people are altruistic; that is, they provide help as a result of an unselfish concern for others. Others have suggested that helping behavior is never truly altruistic but is, rather, egoistic because helping another reduces the helper's distress that occurs when he or she sees another suffer. Alternatively, helping behavior may be viewed as egoistic if it leads to material, social, or self-rewards (Batson & Vanderplas, 1985).

Hoffman (1981), after reviewing evidence from the biological and psychological literature, concluded that altruism is a part of our makeup and can generate helping behavior. In support of Hoffman's argument, Batson and his colleagues have presented evidence that altruistic motivation is triggered by empathic emotions (feelings of sympathy or compassion for someone as a result of imagining how you would feel in the same situation). By manipulating empathic feelings, Coke, Batson, and McDavis (1978) found that subjects who experienced the most empathy also offered the most help. Toi and Batson (1982) designed an experiment in which egoistic helping could be tested against altruistic helping. Their subjects in the low-empathy condition helped less if escape from the situation was easy than if escape was difficult, suggesting that these subjects engaged in helping behavior egoistically to reduce their own distress. Subjects in the high-empathy condition, on the other hand, exhibited large amounts of helping regardless of the ease of escape, suggesting that their behavior was motivated altruistically.

The egoistic versus altruistic debate continues. Cialdini, Schaller, Houlihan, Arps, Fultz, & Beaman (1987) conducted two experiments whose results supported the egoistic interpretation of helping. Batson, Dyck, and associates (1988) performed five different experiments that supported the altruistic interpretation of helping. It seems likely, therefore, that helping behavior is sometimes motivated by egoistic needs and sometimes by altruism. Either may lead to helping behavior, and we can assume that helping behavior sometimes results from a combination of concern for others and a reduction of one's own distress.

Finally, it should be noted that being in a good mood appears to promote helpfulness (see, e.g., Berg, 1978; Isen, 1970; Rosenhan, Salovey, & Hargis, 1981; Weyant, 1978). Six differing hypotheses have been generated to explain why positive moods influence helping. Of these six hypotheses four have received support from a study by Carlson, Charlin, and Miller (1988): focus of attention, separate process, social outlook, and mood maintenance.

The **focus of attention** hypothesis proposes that good mood enhances helpfulness when positive events are directed toward the self. When something good happens to someone it is thought to confer a feeling of advantage to him or her. The recipient, in turn, tries to equalize the situation by helping others. If, on the other hand, someone else is the beneficiary of some good fortune, an individual feels disadvantaged and is less likely to provide help to others. Rosenhan, Salovey, and Hargis (1981) proposed the focus of attention hypothesis and provide evidence for its explanatory power in understanding the effects of mood on helping behavior. Carlson and associates (1988) provide further support for this hypothesis.

It has been known for some time that creating feelings of guilt in an individual can also increase the likelihood of helping behavior (Carlsmith & Gross, 1969; Carlson & Miller, 1987). Cunningham, Steinberg, and Grev (1980) propose that **separate neural processes** are responsible for guilt-induced helping and positive-mood-induced helping. Subjects in their experiment helped more either after experiencing a positive event (finding a dime in a pay phone) or a negative event (being led to believe they had broken a camera). Subjects who experienced both the positive and negative events helped no more than neutral-event control subjects. According to the separate process hypothesis, the motivational effects of experiencing both a positive and a negative event cancel each other out. The separate process approach, then, suggests that helping can be triggered by separate motivational processes that are mutually exclusive. Either process alone may trigger helping; however, if both are triggered simultaneously they reduce the chances of helping. The analysis of Carlson and associates (1988) found support for the separate process hypothesis.

The **social outlook** hypothesis suggests that helping behavior will be increased when information about the positive side of human nature is emphasized (Holloway, Tucker, & Hornstein, 1977; Hornstein, LaKind, Frankel, & Manne, 1975). According to this view, news that conveys information about human kindness and cooperation leads to increased helping even when mood is unaffected. In essence, the social outlook hypothesis suggests that prosocial behavior will promote helping more than neutral behavior, although this model does not indicate why such increases in helping occur. In their analysis of the mood/helping literature, Carlson and associates (1988) found support for the social outlook hypothesis. They suggest that the prosocial effect may result from a priming of thoughts involving a sense of community, or thoughts associated with attraction, empathy, or cooperation. An alternative explanation of the social outlook data is that prosocial behaviors promote helping because they provide a model for helping behavior. Such observational learning has been shown to be effective in other social situations (Bandura, 1977) and may be operative here also.

The **mood maintenance** hypothesis (Clark & Isen, 1982; Isen & Simmonds, 1978) proposes that good mood promotes helping behav-

ior because helping prolongs the positive mood state. Evidence that people who exhibit good feelings help more is provided by several studies (Forest, Clark, Mills, & Isen, 1979; Harada, 1983; Isen & Simmonds, 1978). Generally these studies have found that positive mood promotes helping when the helping task is pleasant but not when the helping task is unpleasant. Such a pattern of results makes sense if the effect of helping is to prolong an already existing positive mood. Carlson and associates (1988) also found evidence in their study for the mood maintenance hypothesis.

To summarize, considerable evidence shows that a person's mood influences his or her likelihood of helping. The analysis of Carlson and associates suggests that the mood-helping connection results from several factors. The most important of these factors would seem to be one's focus of attention onto one's self, the activation of separate motivational processes associated with positive and negative mood, one's social outlook, and the attempt to maintain positive mood.

The research we have examined so far in this chapter has shown the importance of social factors in motivation. We are socially motivated to conform to the desires of important reference groups, and we are strongly motivated to comply with the demands of authority figures. Similarly, social situations can work against helping behavior, and when we do come to the aid of another, it is often to reduce our own distress. We do seem to have, however, a genuine motive to help others that is triggered by or associated with the generation of our empathic feelings.

In the last section of this chapter we will also examine information that is usually categorized as belonging within the realm of social psychology; however, the research to which we now turn has emphasized the importance of our thoughts in generating behavior. Beliefs and attitudes that we hold about persons, places, and things can generate motives that direct our behavior in particular ways. One

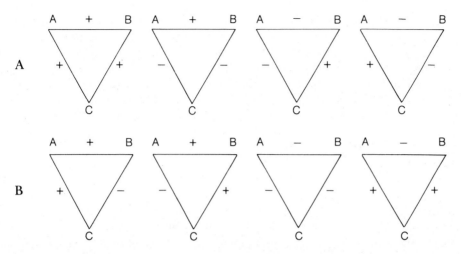

Figure 10.5 *Balanced and imbalanced relationships between triads. A, balanced relationships from the point of view of A; B, imbalanced relationships from the point of view of A.*

class of theory that has attempted to relate the role of our thoughts to the generation of behavior is called cognitive consistency theory.

COGNITIVE CONSISTENCY THEORY

Cognitive consistency theories of motivation begin with the idea that relationships between thoughts, beliefs, attitudes, and behavior can generate motivation. This motivation is often conceived as similar to a state of tension. It is aversive and activates behaviors that are designed to reduce tension. Consistency theories are thus homeostatic theories. As noted by McGuire (1966), about a half-dozen different consistency theories developed during the 1950s, all of which shared the basic idea that people will attempt to minimize internal inconsistency. Thus the optimal state for an individual is one in which one's thoughts, beliefs, attitudes, and behaviors are consistent with one another.

Cognitive consistency theory is usually regarded as beginning with the work of Fritz Heider (1946), but consistency theory's

emphasis on cognitive processes has been the further evolution of concepts promoted by both Tolman (1932) and Lewin (1938).

Balance Theory

Heider believed that a tendency exists for relationships between people, objects, or both to be balanced, and for this reason his approach is often termed **balance theory**.

In balance theory relationships between people and objects may be positive or negative. For example, a positive relationship might involve liking (e.g., John likes Gail) or belonging (e.g., Robert is a member of the Democratic party). Negative relationships can be similarly understood (e.g., Gail dislikes John, or Bill, a Republican, doesn't belong to the Democratic party). Heider analyzed the behavior of triadic (i.e., threes) situations in terms of balance. Figure 10.5 presents four balanced and four imbalanced relationships.

The positive and negative relationships discussed by balance theory are all "inside the head" of the person making the judgments. This suggests that balance may sometimes occur as a result of the perceptual distortion of the subject. For example, Levinger and Breedlove (1966) found that married partners assumed that their attitudes were much more similar than in fact they were. Thus spouses may distort their perceptions of each other's attitudes in order to maintain a balanced relationship.

The easiest way to determine if a relationship is balanced is to multiply the three signs together. If the result is positive, the relationships are balanced; if negative, an imbalance exists (Morrissette, 1958). When an imbalance occurs, motivation is triggered to return the relationship to a balanced state. Suppose, for example, that Bob and Shirley are looking for a house to buy. Now we can assume that Bob likes Shirley and if he finds a house that he likes but Shirley dislikes, a state of imbalance will exist, at least from Bob's point of view. Bob may try to restore the balance in one of several ways. For example, he might try to convince Shirley to like the house, or he might decide that Shirley is right and dislike the house too. Or, finally, he might end up disliking Shirley as a result. Any one of these methods could be used by Bob to restore balance to the situation.

Newcomb (1968) extended Heider's basic approach by emphasizing the idea that imbalanced relationships will lead to communications between individuals that are attempts to restore balance. Newcomb further suggested that when a negative relationship exists between two individuals, as in the third example of row B in Figure 10.5, there is no motivation toward change because if A dislikes B, A should not care what B thinks about C. Newcomb termed such a situation a **nonbalanced situation**. Present research on imbalanced versus nonbalanced situations seems unclear (see, e.g., Aronson & Cope, 1968).

Research on balance theory has generally supported the concept that imbalanced relationships are motivational. For example, Jordan (1953) found that people judged hypothetical imbalanced relationships to be more unpleasant than hypothetical balanced relationships. Further, Zajonc and Burnstein (1965) found that balanced relationships were more rapidly learned than unbalanced ones; interestingly, however, this was true only if the relationships tested were relevant for the individual. Irrelevant relationships that were balanced were not learned any faster than imbalanced relationships. Sentis and Burnstein (1979) have also obtained results suggesting that balance is important in the organization of memory.

Even though research was generally supportive of balance theory, the theory did not become the major explanation of motivation generated by cognitive inconsistencies. This was because several problems existed with the theory. In addition, balance theory was overshadowed by another theory known as **cognitive dissonance**. But before we turn to a consideration of cognitive dissonance theory, we will briefly note some of the shortcomings of balance theory.

Problems of Balance Theory   In our example of Bob and Shirley and the new house, we noted several ways in which Bob might restore balance to the situation. First, it is undoubtedly true that people resolve cognitive inconsistencies in various ways, but balance theory has little to say about how a person will resolve the imbalance. We cannot predict from balance theory how a specific situation is likely to be resolved.

Second, balance theory does not take into account the degree of relationship between the items out of balance. If Bob is strongly attached to Shirley, the relationship between them would probably not change as a result of a disagreement about liking the house. Clearly some relationships are more important than others, yet balance theory has little to say about how these differences influence the behaviors that occur.

A third problem involves the question of how much imbalance must occur before behavior is triggered. Some imbalances are relatively unimportant, while others are extremely important. Unfortunately, balance theory does not give us any direct way to gauge the degree or amount of the imbalance and remains unclear as to how much imbalance is required before behavior is triggered.

Some attempts have been made to resolve the second and third problems (Cartwright & Harary, 1956; Morrissette, 1958), and other problems might be noted (e.g., see Arkes & Garske, 1977; Korman, 1974). The three problems noted, however, are all part of a general problem—balance theory's lack of specificity. Balance theory, though useful in pointing out the general motivating property of imbalanced states, has not been specified in enough detail so that accurate predictions can be made.

Cognitive Dissonance

Undoubtedly, many of the problems with balance theory could have been worked out. At about the same time that balance theory was being studied, however, Leon Festinger (1957) proposed a far-reaching theory that has dominated research on cognitive consistency motivation. Festinger's theory is known as **cognitive dissonance**.

Cognitive dissonance as a concept stresses the idea that we attempt to maintain consistency of our beliefs, attitudes, and opinions with our overt behavior (Abelson et al., 1968). As long as consistency is maintained, no motivation is triggered.

Our cognitions about ourselves and the world around us can be related to each other in one of three ways. Cognitions can be consonant (i.e., consistent), irrelevant, or dissonant. According to dissonance theory, only when cognitions are dissonant is motivation activated to resolve the dissonance. When cognitions are dissonant, according to Festinger (1957), a negative motivational state is produced that is aversive, which in turn triggers specific mechanisms to reduce the dissonance. In this regard dissonance is often conceived to resemble a state of tension and seems to have many properties of drive (as discussed in Chapter Five).

Two cognitions are considered to be dissonant if, considered together, they represent an inconsistency. For example, suppose that we like to eat high-cholesterol foods but know that such foods increase the likelihood of stroke. The inconsistency of the two thoughts will generate some dissonance, which will in turn generate other thoughts or behaviors designed to reduce the inconsistency. We might reduce the dissonance in our example by altering our intake of foods high in cholesterol.

Festinger noted that dissonance may arise for several reasons. First, dissonance may result when an expected event turns out differently than we thought. Expecting an "A" on a test and receiving a "C" is a reliable dissonance-producing situation. Dissonance may also occur because thoughts are inconsistent with cultural mores (i.e., rules). For example, we might be strongly tempted to cheat on an exam for which we are unprepared. Our society frowns on cheating, and the person caught between the temptations to cheat and knowledge of society's rules will be in a state of tension. Dissonance may also occur as a result of inconsistencies between attitudes and behaviors, but only if the justification for behavior contrary to one's attitude is insufficient. To continue the cheating example, the person who cheats and who considers cheating a transgression of society's rules will experience considerable dissonance if he or she believes that there was insufficient justification for cheating. This might occur when a student is passing the course but has neglected to study for a particular test. On the other hand, no dissonance will be experienced if the student can internally justify the discrepancy between his or her attitudes and behavior. Such a case might occur if the student believes that the professor's tests are grossly unfair or that the test does not measure the student's abilities.

Dissonance, then, is believed to occur when inconsistency or conflict exists between cognitions. The total dissonance that an individual experiences depends upon the number of conflicting elements in relation to the number of consonant elements. Thus total dissonance equals dissonant elements divided by the sum of the dissonant and consonant elements ($D_{total} = D/D + C$). The more elements that are dissonant, the greater the overall dissonance. The strength of the dissonance created is also thought to depend upon the importance of the cognitive elements in conflict. The more important the elements are to the person, the larger the dissonance will be.

As with balance theory, there are several ways in which we can reduce dissonance. First, one may change one of the cognitions in order to reduce the dissonance. For example, the dissonance created by one's attitude against cheating and the knowledge of having just cheated on a test could be reduced by changing one's attitude (e.g., all's fair in love and war and college). This mode of dissonance reduction is particularly interesting because it suggests that if people engage in behaviors contrary to their beliefs or attitudes, and for which there is little justification, their attitudes should change. Several lines of evidence suggest that persuading people to engage in behaviors contrary to their attitudes does in fact lead to attitude change. For example, Cohen (1962) found that people who argued by request in favor of positions they personally opposed changed their attitudes.

A second way in which we can reduce dissonance is to alter behavior in order to reduce inconsistency between cognitions. Suppose I know that being overweight is harmful and increases the chance of heart attack and high blood pressure. This cognition conflicts with the knowledge that I love to eat. Changing my behavior by dieting to reduce weight and then eating sensibly would eliminate the dissonance.

A third way in which we can reduce dissonance is by introducing a third element that effectively reduces the dissonance without changing any of the conflicting elements. Suppose, for example, that you have just invested your bankroll in a new car. The day after you buy it, another dealer advertises the car for $500 less than you paid. Though you might be tempted to reduce the dissonance of this situation by returning the car, people often find additional reasons for sticking with the initial choice. You might, for example, note that the service at the dealer from whom you bought the car is superior to the one offering the lower price and that good service far outweighs the additional cost. Bringing in a third element is conceptually similar (if not identical) to the defense mechanism of rationalization. In rationalization we reduce anxiety by devaluing the original situation that led to the anxiety or by finding additional rewards in the situation different from those obtained.

How will an individual reduce dissonance? Dissonance theorists suggest that the method chosen will be whichever is easiest. For example, one who is publicly committed to a course of action different from one's accepted attitude will be more likely to change the attitude than the behavior in order to reduce the dissonance. On the other hand, if the behavior is a recurring one (e.g., studying for tests), changing the behavior when it conflicts with an attitude may be easier than changing the attitude. If you believe, for instance, that you are an "A" student and you received a "C" on the last test, you will probably reduce the dissonance of this situation by studying harder for the next test rather than by changing your opinion of your abilities. Finally, bringing in a third element may be easiest if changing either of the two elements is difficult. This is often the method chosen when the conflicting elements are important ones. Probably the most frequent example is heavy smokers who acknowledge the risk of cancer from smoking. A commonly heard rationalization is that by the time they actually contract cancer, science will have a cure for it.

Research on Dissonance

Cognitive dissonance has generated more research (and controversy) than any other cognitive consistency theory. We will not attempt to cover the entirety of this research but will focus on a few research areas most often cited as evidence of cognitive dissonance.

Forced Compliance One of the most cited examples of cognitive dissonance is the situation in which one publicly behaves in a manner contrary to one's privately held opinions (Festinger, 1957). Such a situation will lead to the production of dissonance if one is engaging in such behavior without sufficient justification for doing so. For example, one may publicly profess allegiance to a dictator for fear of punishment and yet hold a private opinion quite different from the public profession. Under these conditions little dissonance should occur because there is sufficient self-justification. However, if one is forced to behave in a particular way but cannot justify the conflict of the behavior with one's beliefs, dissonance should occur, and attitude change should follow. Such a situation is called **forced compliance**.

Festinger and Carlsmith (1959) tested the forced-compliance phenomenon by having three groups of subjects perform a repetitive, highly boring task (e.g., turning pegs in a peg-

board). After an hour of performing such tasks, the subjects of two such groups were asked by the experimenter to convince waiting subjects that the experiment was interesting. Subjects in one group were paid $20 for talking to the waiting individuals, while subjects in the second group were paid only $1. A third group served as a control; its members were not asked to convince anyone that the experiment was interesting.

The persons that the subjects were asked to convince, however, were confederates of the experimenter, and their purpose was to make sure that the subject actually tried to convince them that the experiment was interesting. After the subjects had completed their own bit of deception, they were asked to rate how interesting the experiment actually was to them.

The control group, as expected, rated the experimental task as boring. The subjects who were paid $20 also rated the experiment as boring, while the subjects paid only $1 rated the task as significantly more enjoyable than either of the other two groups.

According to dissonance theory, the $1 group should have had insufficient justification for engaging in behavior contrary to their attitudes about the experiment; that is, they believed that the experiment was dull but had just tried to convince someone that it was in fact interesting. The insufficient justification for their behavior, then, led them to alter their attitudes about the experiment so that they came to believe that the experiment was actually interesting and enjoyable. The subjects who were paid $20, on the other hand, could easily justify their counterattitudinal behavior on the basis of the money; therefore their attitudes did not change.

The generality of the forced-compliance type of experiment can be observed in punishment situations as well. For example, Aronson and Carlsmith (1963) designed an experiment in which children were shown desirable toys but were forbidden to play with one particular toy. Subjects in one group were threatened with strong punishment if they played with the forbidden toy, while a second group was only mildly threatened. After secretly observing the children to make sure that they did not play with the forbidden toy, the researchers asked the children to rate the attractiveness of each toy. The mildly threatened group rated the forbidden toy lower in attractiveness than did the strongly threatened group. The difference in attractiveness presumably resulted from dissonance created in the mildly threatened children. They did not play with the forbidden toy and did not have a sufficient external justification (as the strongly threatened group did) for their behavior. As a result, they rated the attractiveness of the toy lower in order to reduce their dissonance. Freedman (1965) replicated Aronson and Carlsmith's results and showed, in addition, that the devaluation that occurs can be quite long-lasting. Freedman found reduced playing with the toy more than two months after the initial experiment. Zanna, Lepper, and Abelson (1973) have extended these results a step further by showing that the more the child's attention is drawn to the dissonance-producing elements of not playing with the toy (when having been only mildly threatened), the greater the devaluation that occurs. Thus the more aware that one is of dissonance, the greater one's behavior change is apparently likely to be.

There is now considerable agreement about when dissonance effects are likely to occur in the forced-compliance paradigm. Dissonance occurs when the subjects feel that they are personally responsible for the consequences of their actions (Calder, Ross, & Insko, 1973; Collins & Hoyt, 1972). Thus the element of choice appears important to the production of dissonance.

Effort   In another often noted experiment

conducted by Aronson and Mills (1959), college women were asked to volunteer for a series of discussions on sex. Before they were allowed to join the discussion group, however, they first had to pass a "test" to determine if they were mature enough to handle the discussion material. One group of women was required to read aloud a list of sex-related words and some graphic descriptions of sexual activity in the presence of a male experimenter. A second group was required to read aloud only mildly sexual material. Both groups of subjects were then allowed to listen to a tape of what they thought was an actual discussion—but was actually a rather boring description of animal sexual behavior. Finally, the subjects in the two groups were asked to rate the discussion they had heard and their own interest in participating in future discussions. The group subjected to the "severe initiation" of reading lurid passages and four-letter words aloud rated the taped discussion as more interesting than did the "mild initiation" group. They also indicated more interest in future participation than did subjects in the mild initiation group.

Dissonance theory suggests that the severe initiation group experienced dissonance at the discrepancy between what they were required to do and the uninteresting nature of the supposed discussion. In order to reduce their dissonance, they came to believe that the discussion was interesting, and they indicated their desire for further participation.

One is reminded of the "hell week" activities of some fraternities and sororities and the secret initiations required of membership in some groups. All these activities should serve to create dissonance later if the individual's expectations are not met—and, as a result, lead the individual to value the membership more. Apparently one reason why we value things that we have worked very hard to obtain is to reduce the dissonance we experience when these things turn out to be less than we had hoped.

Postdecisional Dissonance and Selective Exposure to Information A third area of research on dissonance concerns the behaviors in which people engage after choosing among several alternatives. Suppose, for example, that you are trying to decide which of two highly desirable cars to buy. You like both cars for somewhat different reasons and of course can only afford to buy one. The choice that you eventually make between these two positive alternatives should create dissonance, which in turn should lead you to subsequently revalue the two cars. You will revalue the chosen car upward to reduce the dissonance the choice created, and you will revalue downward the car not chosen. In other words, after having made your choice, you will like your chosen car more and the unchosen one less. Additionally, dissonance theory predicts that you will selectively expose yourself to new information that reinforces your initial choice; that is, you will be sensitive to advertisements or information that supports your choice and will attempt to avoid information indicating that your choice was wrong. All these behaviors help reduce the dissonance created by your choice of one car over the other.

Research on postdecisional behavior has generally supported dissonance theory when certain additional factors are taken into account (Wicklund & Brehm, 1976). A study by Brehm (1956) found that if women were asked to rate products of similar desirability after they had been allowed to choose one to keep, the rating for the chosen object increased (relative to its prechoice rating), while the rating for the nonchosen object decreased (relative to its prechoice rating). Thus in this study, choosing between two products of similar value created dissonance, which in turn led to a change in attitude about the products, with the chosen one being more

highly valued. In Brehm's study a second group of women was asked to choose between two products of very different value. Because the alternatives were quite different in value and a choice was therefore easy, little dissonance was generated and, as a result, postdecisional attitudinal changes were small, as predicted by dissonance theory.

A series of studies reported by Festinger (1964) indicate, among other things, the importance of commitment to one's choice. It appears that dissonance reduction does not necessarily start as soon as a choice is made. If people believe that they can still obtain the unchosen alternative, then no dissonance develops. Unless a choice requires surrendering a valued alternative, no dissonance occurs to trigger postdecisional changes. Allen (1964), for example, found that only when a person made a choice that required surrendering another alternative did he or she rate the unchosen alternative as less desirable. Additionally, dissonance production and subsequent attitudinal change apparently depend upon the person's feeling personally responsible (Wicklund & Brehm, 1976) and able to foresee the possible consequences of the choice (for an interesting analysis of foreseeability, see Goethals, Cooper, & Naficy, 1979).

Evidence for selective exposure to new supportive information following a dissonance-producing choice has sometimes been difficult to obtain (Freedman & Sears, 1965). Wicklund and Brehm (1976) have noted, however, that the decision to expose ourselves to additional information about alternatives, after we have made a choice, is influenced by factors other than the development of dissonance. For example, **curiosity** may lead us to choose exposure to information about a nonselected alternative. Similarly, the **usefulness** of the new information may lead to exposure to nonsupportive information.

Suppose, for example, that I have decided, after much thought, to drive to a psychological convention in New York City rather than fly there from Baltimore. Dissonance theory suggests that I will selectively expose myself to information supportive of my choice and avoid nonsupportive information. Curiosity and usefulness, however, may lead me to seek out (or at least not avoid) information that does not support my decision. I might note a newspaper advertisement that gives the price for flying to New York, and I might talk to friends who have flown that airline about the airline's service. Such information, which may be nonsupportive of my decision to drive, is nevertheless likely to stimulate my curiosity because I had considered flying; further, such information may prove useful in the future should I decide to go to New York again. In the same newspaper I might also note an article on road construction on the New Jersey Turnpike, the route I plan to travel. Although this information would be nonsupportive of my decision to drive rather than fly (and therefore I should avoid reading it), it is nevertheless very useful and may cause me to select a different route to New York.

Wicklund and Brehm (1976) have noted that many of the studies of selective exposure to information following a choice have not eliminated various alternative reasons (such as curiosity and usefulness) for such exposure. In a review of the selective exposure literature, these researchers found that when alternative reasons for exposure were controlled or eliminated, support for selective exposure following a choice was obtained. Wicklund and Brehm also pointed out that the data, though strong for selective exposure to supportive information, are considerably weaker for avoidance of nonsupportive information. Apparently we seek out information that buttresses our choice but do not particularly try to avoid nonsupportive information.

An interesting study by Lord, Ross, and Lepper (1979) helps us understand why this might be the case. These researchers exposed two groups of subjects to identical information on capital punishment. Subjects in one group, opposed to capital punishment, viewed the information as supporting their position, while those in the other group, supportive of capital punishment, saw the same materials as supporting their point of view. Subjects in each group apparently extracted specific items of information that supported their position but were little influenced by nonsupportive items. We seem to be biased to give more weight to evidence that supports our point of view than to evidence that does not. The results of the Lord, Ross, and Lepper study may therefore help explain why we do not seem especially likely to avoid nonsupportive information; we do not give nonsupportive information much credence.

As the authors of the above study have carefully pointed out, their results have important implications for social policy. As students of psychology, we often assume that putting all the evidence before opposing groups of people will lead to enlightened decision making. But as this study shows, such a procedure can actually lead to a polarization of opinion among groups rather than to consensus.

When Prophecy Fails One of the most interesting aspects of dissonance theory is that it often makes nonobvious predictions. One such case involved a field study of a group of people who believed that their city was going to be destroyed by a great flood. The leader of the group had received a "message" from outer space telling her that the city would be destroyed on December 21. Festinger and his colleagues became aware of the group as a result of newspaper reports. Based on the cognitive dissonance formulation, they predicted that when the prophecy was disconfirmed, the group of believers would not forsake their beliefs but would try to win additional people to their cause in order to provide additional support for their initial beliefs. Festinger and his colleagues infiltrated the group so that they could study what happened when the predicted disaster did not occur. Their results are reported in the book *When Prophecy Fails* (Festinger, Riecken, & Schachter, 1956).

On the designated night, the small band of followers gathered at the prophet's home to await the disaster. Before their meeting, the leader had received a message telling the group that they would be saved by a flying saucer that would pick them up at midnight.

As the clock struck midnight, everyone waited expectantly, but after several minutes nothing had happened. After determining that the time was correct, everyone sat somewhat dazed. Then with despair they began to look at the messages again for some explanation. One could expect that at this point, considerable dissonance would be present in all the believers, because many had committed themselves wholeheartedly to their belief in the disaster by quitting their jobs and spending their money in expectation of the End.

In addition to considerable dissonance, there should also have been a reluctance to admit the disconfirmation. Given the degree of commitment and the social support provided by the other believers present, the dissonance should have been more easily reduced by some method other than admitting that the whole experience was not real.

The group's behavior provided striking support of Festinger's prediction (but not of their own). At 4:45 a.m. the leader informed the group that she had received another message. The message indicated that the group's belief had in fact saved the city from the flood. With this explanation, the dissonance could be reduced and the original beliefs kept intact. And the group became much more active in proselytizing people to its own beliefs.

Festinger's field study points out both how dissonance may be created by disconfirmation of our beliefs and how we often seek

the easiest solution for reducing the dissonance. For the group of believers, rejecting its belief in the disaster was not easy, given their involvement in terms of time, money, and so on. For the group it was easier to "discover" a new reason for the disconfirmation than to give up the old beliefs. In a much reduced degree, many of us seem to do the same when we rationalize our losses or shortcomings.

Dissonance theory continues to stimulate research (see, e.g., Baumeister & Tice, 1984; Croyle & Cooper, 1983; Frey, 1982; Steele, Southwick, & Critchlow, 1981); however, it has also generated considerable criticism. In the next section we will examine some of those criticisms.

Criticisms of Dissonance Theory

While dissonance theory has generated much research, it has also created large controversy. Perhaps the most important criticism of dissonance theory aims at its vagueness (McGuire, 1966). For example, Aronson (1968) pointed out that the theory is primitive and lacks precision. The imprecision of the theory makes the prediction of whether any two cognitions will conflict in a given individual virtually impossible. This of course means that we cannot accurately predict under what conditions a conflict in cognitions will occur. In this regard Aronson (1968) has suggested a general rule of thumb to be that violations of a person's expectancy usually lead to dissonance.

A second problem is one we have seen before. Dissonance (like balance) may be reduced in several different ways. The theory itself, however, does not provide any definitive statement about which particular way will be chosen in a given situation or by a given individual.

A third criticism of dissonance theory is that alternative explanations have not always been ruled out. For example, Chapanis and Chapanis (1964) noted that in the severe initiation experiment of Aronson and Mills (1959), the girls subjected to the four-letter words and vivid passages were possibly relieved to discover that the discussion group would not be more of the same, thus feeling pleasure rather than dissonance, and rated the tape session higher as a result.

Many of the early criticisms have been met by later research. For example, Gerard and Matthewson (1966) attempted to control alternative explanations in an experiment similar to that of Aronson and Mills. College females were again used as subjects and, as before, had to pass an "initiation" task in order to gain admittance to a group discussion on college student morality. As part of this screening task, all subjects were required to endure three electric shocks. Some subjects had strong shocks, while others got weak shocks. Then, as in Aronson and Mills's experiment, subjects listened to a taped discussion on cheating that was designed to be extremely uninteresting.

Gerard and Matthewson found that subjects who received the strong shock consistently rated the taped discussion higher than subjects who received weak shocks. Interestingly, control subjects given the shock procedure, but not as an initiation allowing them to join the group, rated the taped discussion lower if they had received strong shock. Thus the dissonance explanation was apparently supported while, at the same time, meeting many objections of the earlier Aronson and Mills study.

Despite the weaknesses of cognitive dissonance theory, it has had tremendous impact on cognitive consistency theories of motivation. The theory has generated a large body of research and has led to the examination of questions that might not otherwise have been asked. It is also a very appealing theory because of its simplicity and its ability to account for sometimes counterintuitive types of behavior.

Self-Perception Theory   Daryl Bem (1967) has proposed an alternative to dissonance theory emphasizing the idea that we observe our own behavior much as an outsider might do, then make judgments based on these observations. Bem's alternative is called **self-perception theory**. Bem argued that many of the experimental results quoted as supportive of a dissonance approach can in fact be explained through the concept of self-perception. He noted that the behavior measured in almost all dissonance studies is self-description of an attitude or a belief.

As just one example of how this might work, let's analyze the already mentioned Festinger and Carlsmith (1959) forced-compliance study. Recall that one group of subjects was given $20 in return for telling a waiting subject that the boring experiment was interesting, while a second group of subjects was paid only $1.

Bem noted that an outside observer who watched the experiment and behavior of the two groups would predict that the subjects paid $1 must have enjoyed the experiment because they weren't paid enough to lie about it; on the other hand, the observer would also predict that the subjects paid $20 behaved as they did because the amount of money was sufficient to justify their behavior. In other words, an observer of the total situation would attribute the $20 subjects' behavior to the money but would attribute the $1 subjects' behavior to enjoyment of the experiment. Carrying the analysis one step further, Bem argued that *we* are that outside observer of our own behavior; that is, we analyze our own behavior in the same fashion as we would analyze someone else's behavior. Thus a $20 subject, observing that he or she has just told the waiting subject that the boring experiment was interesting, decides that he or she behaved that way because of the money involved. The $1 subject, however, who observed the self-behavior concludes that the experiment was enjoyed because the money involved was not sufficient justification for lying about the experiment.

To test his hypothesis, Bem replicated the Festinger and Carlsmith experiment but had observers listen to communications between the subject who had just completed the task and the subject being convinced. Some observers were told that the communicator was being paid $20, while others were told that the payment was $1. In addition, the length of the communication was varied, being either extended (i.e., long-communication condition) or shortened. The long and short communications were used because Festinger and Carlsmith had found in the original study that in the $1 condition, the greater the number and variety of arguments used by the subject, the more favorably the subject rated the task. In the $20 condition just the opposite occurred. Thus if Bem's self-perception analysis was correct, outside observers should also rate subjects who were paid $1 as liking the experiment more if they presented a long argument about the experiment—while the opposite should occur for the $20 subjects.

The results of Bem's study replicated those of Festinger and Carlsmith, with $1 subjects (using long communication) being rated more favorable toward the experiment than those using short communications. As predicted, $20 subjects' attitudes toward the experiment were rated less favorably in the long-communication situation when compared to the short one.

Bem argued that the results of the forced-compliance type of experiment and his replications of it suggest that subjects simply make self-judgments based on the kinds of evidence publicly available to anyone, not as a result of aversive motivation generated by an inconsistency between attitude (i.e., the experiment was boring) and behavior (i.e., I've just told the new subject it was really interesting).

Bem's analysis does not require the development of a motivational state of tension that leads to changes in attitude or behavior but requires only that one analyze his or her own behaviors in the same way that one analyzes the behavior of others. Such an approach is called **attribution theory**, and we will look more closely at such approaches in Chapter Eleven.

Whether self-perception theory will replace dissonance as the explanation for behaviors such as noted here is hotly debated. Several lines of research suggest that self-perception theory may not account for observed behaviors in several of the basic dissonance paradigms (Fazio, Zanna, & Cooper, 1977; Higgins, Rhodewalt, & Zanna, 1979; Olson & Zanna, 1979; Zanna & Cooper, 1974, 1976). The research does seem to suggest, however, that both dissonance and self-perception processes may occur but under different conditions (Fazio, Zanna, & Cooper, 1977).

At present, consistency models of motivation, though intuitively appealing, are apparently becoming relatively less popular as explanations for motivation. At the same time, attribution explanations are becoming increasingly popular explanations of cognitive motivation.

General Problems of Consistency Theory

The relative decrease in popularity of consistency theories results, at least in part, from problems associated with this general approach rather than from specific consistency theories such as Festinger's. First, we have the conceptual problem of why inconsistency should be motivating at all (Singer, 1966). Very few consistency theories indicate why inconsistency is motivating; it just is. An exception is Festinger's cognitive dissonance theory, which conceptualizes dissonance as creating a drive state. However, the concept of drive itself suffers from many problems (see Chapter Five).

A related problem is that some organisms under some conditions seem to be **inconsistency seeking** rather than inconsistency reducing. Pepitone (1966) has noted several reasons why an individual might seek out inconsistency. For example, we might increase inconsistency so as to maximize our pleasure when the inconsistency is finally reduced. Sexual foreplay is sometimes used as an example of such a situation (Pepitone, 1966). Also, we may seek inconsistency in order to mask more serious or painful inconsistencies. Pepitone suggested that hypochondriacs who believe they are ill (although they are not) may be masking more serious inconsistencies that create anxiety. He also noted that we may seek inconsistency because the optimal level of stimulation may be higher than we often assume; that is, a certain amount of inconsistency may actually be beneficial in keeping motivational tension at some nonzero optimal level.

Finally, Pepitone noted that consistency theories do not consider the problem of uncertainty. Suppose, for example, that we are not certain of our attitudes about a particular set of cognitions. Though one might expect that uncertainty would lead to greater tolerance of inconsistent thoughts, consistency theory does not take ambiguous or uncertain situations into account.

Singer (1966) has pointed out that motivation generated from inconsistency of cognitions is not so strong that it overrules normal behavior. We do not, for example, stop eating until we have resolved the inconsistency between our attitude about our tennis game and the fact that we have just lost three straight sets. Similarly, if consistency motivation is important, why aren't our thoughts highly consistent? (See Korman, 1974.) Bem (1970) has in fact suggested that inconsistency may not be very important for some persons;

thus motivation generated by inconsistency may be more limited in scope than theorists had hoped. Finally, McGuire (1966) has noted that inconsistency may be dealt with in many ways and that consistency theories provide little help in predicting how a given individual will deal with the inconsistent relationship.

Consistency theories, which were developed to help us explain the motivational consequences of our cognitions, have proven less fruitful than we had hoped. The basic problem is apparently one of specification; the theories are presently too vague to be of much use. Also, many alternate explanations are possible. In all fairness to the consistency theorists, we should note that the complexity of consistency motivation is certainly part of the reason that the theories have not worked as well as hoped. Probably we must consider the links between several cognitions in most situations in order to understand the changes in behavior that occur. It is also reasonable to suppose that changing one relationship between two cognitions may change the relationship of those cognitions to other elements as well; one changed relationship may change a whole host of other relationships. Analyzing the relationships of cognitions to each other and to behavior is obviously extremely complex and deserves continued study.

SUMMARY

We have seen in this chapter that motivation is strongly influenced by the presence of others. The effect of others upon us has probably been adaptive and has aided in social interactions in those species (e.g., humans) who live in aggregations. In this chapter we have examined the motivational pressures exerted on each of us to conform to the rules of society. Data such as Asch's indicate that it is very difficult to go against group pressure. Milgram's experiments point out the difficulty that most of us have in refusing to carry out instructions, even those that may be morally reprehensible to us. These data on conformity and compliance are important because they help us understand how atrocities can occur. Because of our conforming tendency to obey authority figures, most of us have the potential to act in ways that we would judge immoral in others. Zimbardo's prison study is revealing because of the rapidity with which normal college students were changed by circumstances into brutal jailers and passive prisoners.

Even the likelihood of helping someone in distress is affected by the presence of others. Latané and Darley have found that the presence of others reduces our scanning of the environment so that we are slower to notice emergencies. We also tend to mask our true feelings while observing the expressions of others in an ambiguous situation. Masking our emotions leads to the creation of a pluralistic ignorance, in which we "fool" each other into defining the situation as a nonemergency, thus reducing the chances of intervention or increasing the time until intervention takes place. Finally, the presence of others diffuses the responsibility for action so that any specific individual feels less responsibility to act. Situational factors (e.g., being in a hurry) also reduce the probability of intervention in emergencies, while religious convictions appear to have little effect.

In this chapter we have also examined a major conception of motivation that emphasizes cognitive structures as important in the determination of behavior. Cognitive consistency theories such as balance theory and cognitive dissonance assume that inconsistencies between attitudes, beliefs, and behavior lead to a state of tension that generates a motivation to reduce or eliminate the inconsis-

tency. Dissonance theory has been the most popular consistency theory to date, but Bem and others have begun to question the usefulness of dissonance as an explanation of motivation. Self-perception and attribution explanations seem particularly able to account for some of the situations formerly explained by dissonance without having to assume the production of a negative motivational state. Our present understanding of the processes involved suggests that both cognitive dissonance and self-perception processes may occur but under differing conditions.

SUGGESTIONS FOR FURTHER READING

Festinger, L., Riecken, H. W., & Schachter, S. (1956). *When prophecy fails*. Minneapolis: University of Minnesota Press. This small book describes the field observations conducted by Festinger and his colleagues on the group that expected the world to come to an end. It is fascinating reading.

Latané, B., & Darley, J. M. (1970). *The unresponsive bystander: Why doesn't he help?* New York: Appleton-Century-Crofts. This book describes many of the initial experiments conducted by Latané and Darley on helping behavior.

Latané, B., & Nida, S. (1981). Ten years of research on group size and helping. *Psychological Bulletin, 89*, 308–324. This article provides a good overview of helping research in both laboratory and field settings.

Wicklund, R. A., & Brehm, J. W. (1976). *Perspectives on cognitive dissonance*. Hillsdale, N.J.: Erlbaum. This book summarizes the findings within the major areas of research in cognitive dissonance.

Chapter Eleven

Cognitive Motivation: Attribution Approaches

CHAPTER PREVIEW

This chapter is concerned with the following questions:

1. How can we explain the cause-and-effect relationships that people make concerning motivated behavior?

2. How are we biased in the attributions that we make?

3. How does analysis of dispositions and situations influence our attributions?

4. How does acting versus observing behavior influence our attributions?

5. How has attribution theory been applied to research on achievement?

In July 1984 a distraught, out-of-work man burst into a McDonald's restaurant in a San Diego surburb and began shooting the people eating there. Entire families died in the ensuing melee—men, women, and young children. The youngest to die was only eight months old; the oldest was in his seventies. Eventually a police sharpshooter brought this tragedy to an end by killing the gunman. Res-

cuers entering the battle zone discovered 22 dead and 19 wounded, one of the worst tragedies on record (see J. Leo, *Time*, July 30, 1984).

After the tragedy became known, the first question on most people's lips was *why*? What drove this man to kill people that he didn't even know? What explanation would help us understand how such an event could occur? We will probably never really understand why this man felt compelled to act the way he did on that July day in 1984, but the point of this chapter is that we all try to understand and make sense of the events around us, not only tragedies such as that described above but also everyday events such as why the paper is late this morning or why John said that to me.

The study of how we go about making decisions concerning the events we experience is called **attribution theory**. Social psychologists have examined how we make attributions about events; the following sections describe what they have found.

ATTRIBUTION THEORY

One aspect of socially motivated behavior that has received considerable attention is attribution theory, which primarily concerns factors assumed by the general public to cause people's behavior. People thus "attribute" the behavior of others to particular factors—usually either to consistent personality characteristics (termed **dispositions**) or to aspects of the social **situation** of the persons involved.

Attribution theory examines the cognitive explanations at which we arrive when we observe someone's behavior (or, for that matter, when we observe our own behavior) and relates these explanations to observable characteristics of the individual and the situation.

Though it is debatable whether the attributions we make are motivational in nature, it seems clear that attributions, once made, do serve to alter future behavior, rather like motivational variables are thought to do. Let us turn, then, to some of the major attribution theories that researchers have proposed.

Jones and associates (1972) pointed out that the study of attribution processes deals with rules that the average person uses to infer cause and effect. Heider (1958) called his analysis of attribution a **naive psychology** to emphasize that the attributions studied were those that normal people make, not what a trained observer might conclude.

Attribution theory rests on three basic assumptions (Jones et al., 1972). First, it assumes that we *do* attempt to determine the causes of both our own behavior and that of others. As part of this assumption, most theorists believe that we are motivated to seek out information that helps us make attributions about cause and effect. Note that this assumption does not require that we assign causes to all our behaviors or to all the behaviors of others. We do, however, seem most likely to attribute behaviors that have some importance to us. Interestingly, Pittman and Pittman (1980) have provided evidence that the motivation that impels us to make attributions is the need to control our environment. We will have considerably more to say about control

motivation in Chapter Twelve, but it is worth noting here that making accurate attributions about the events that happen around us should allow us to control those events better. Unless we know the causes of events, we are unlikely to be able to significantly influence them. Thus attributional processes may be seen as adaptive; they help us to understand and consequently control our environment.

Second, attribution theory rests on the assumption that the assignment of causes to behavior is not done randomly; that is, rules exist that can explain how we come to the conclusions we do about the causes of behavior. In this regard Beck (1978) has pointed out the conceptual similarity between expectancies and attributions. An expectancy, as he noted, is a belief (i.e., cognition) that one thing *will* follow from another (e.g., if I put 50¢ into the machine, I'll get a soda). An attribution is also a belief but is the reverse of an expectancy; that is, attribution is a belief that one thing *has* followed as a result of another thing (e.g., when my soda arrives, I attribute it to the 50¢ I put into the machine). Thus expectancies and attributions are generally the same. What differs is the time at which we regard the linked events. Before I put the money into the machine, I expect that money will *cause* a soda to appear. When I have the soda in hand, I attribute it to the causation of the money. All that differs is the time at which I consider the money-soda relationship; nothing else has changed.

Of course we also have expectancies that do not involve cause and effect. For example, I expect my car to be in the garage when I open the garage door, but I don't believe that my opening of the garage door caused the car to be there. Thus not all expectancies, apparently, are equivalent to attributions.*

---

*I thank Dr. Mark Lepper for pointing out this difference to me.

Nevertheless, Beck's analysis suggests that much of the research reported in Chapter Nine, where expectancy was emphasized as an important factor in behaviors such as achievement, could just as easily be analyzed from an attribution standpoint. That is exactly what seems to be happening, and later in this chapter we will briefly consider an attributional analysis of achievement motivation suggested by Weiner.

The final assumption that attribution theories rest upon is that the causes attributed to particular behaviors will influence subsequent emotional and nonemotional behaviors. The attributions we make, then, may activate other motives (e.g., we may become vindictive if we attribute someone else's behavior as spiteful). Attribution theories suggest that we are motivated to try to understand the environment in which we are immersed. This environment includes people with whom we interact and situations in which those interactions occur. Then our brains, having obtained sufficient information, cognitively process it according to relatively standard rules (most of them unknown) and make decisions (i.e., attributions) concerning how one event is related to another.

Attribution theory began with the work of Fritz Heider, whose theory we will now explore.

Heider's Naive Psychology

The origin of attribution theory is properly "attributed to" Fritz Heider, who, we discovered in Chapter Ten, was also responsible for balance theory. Heider (1944) first outlined some of his thoughts on the attribution of behavior in a review paper. Later he formalized his thinking into what he termed a *naive psychology* (1958). Heider chose the term *naive* to emphasize the point of his main interest—how the average person (who is presumably naive about how behaviors are objectively

determined) decides what are the causes of a behavior. Thus he was not interested in how an objectively trained observer might attribute behavior but how you and I in our everyday affairs attribute causality.

Heider pointed out that logically one could attribute behaviors either to forces within the individual (i.e., **dispositions**) or to forces external to the individual (i.e., **situational factors**). Dispositions include such factors as needs, wishes, and emotions, as well as abilities, intentions, and one's willingness to work (i.e., exertion). Dispositions have usually been divided into **abilities** and **motivations**, with motivation being further subdivided into **intention** (i.e., the cognitive plan to behave in a particular way) and **exertion** (i.e., the amount of effort that one is willing to put into the behavior).

Situational attributions include **task difficulty** and **luck**. Thus when we judge another's behavior (or our own), we may attribute the observed behavior to ability or lack thereof, intention, exertion, task difficulty, or luck. We might, of course, attribute a behavior to varying degrees of each of these, but Heider suggested that as a rule, we tend to attribute behavior to internal as opposed to external causes. According to Heider, the attribution rules are biased toward personal causation. The tendency to attribute behavior to stable, internal characteristics has been termed the **fundamental attribution error** (Jones, 1979; Ross, 1977) because our attributions clearly tend to be biased against situational explanations (see also Harvey, Town, & Yarkin, 1981; Reeder, 1982). Figure 11.1 depicts Heider's model. The attribution choice point represents the point at which the person is trying to decide how to attribute the behavior in question. The heavy arrow pointing toward dispositional attributions indicates the bias that exists toward choosing that alternative.

One suggestion (deCharms, 1968) is that our average bias toward dispositional attribu-

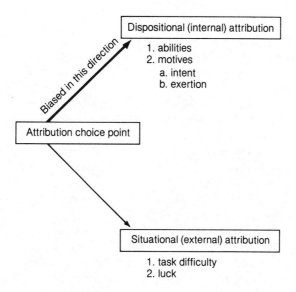

Figure 11.1 Diagram of Heider's attribution model.

tions may result from our own attempts to effect changes; that is, we consciously attempt to control our personal situations, and it is entirely reasonable for us to assume that others' behaviors are similarly caused. It is important to point out that our striving to control our environment does not mean that most of our behavior is actually dispositionally caused; in fact it is often situational. However, our attempts to control still tend to bias us toward dispositional explanations for both ourselves and others.

This bias toward dispositional attributions means that we will tend to misattribute behaviors that are situationally determined. Such misattributions can have future consequences because they will shape the way in which we behave in similar situations later. For example, the student who attributes his or her failure in college to lack of ability may end up in a boring work situation—when the poor grades may actually have resulted from an ill-advised course load or a bout of mononucleo-

sis. As students of the behavior around us, we should be careful not to make dispositional attributions about ourselves or others on little evidence—especially because attributions once made are apparently very difficult to change (Ross, Lepper, & Hubbard, 1974).

Heider's approach was the beginning of research on attribution theory. A major problem with his approach was that it did not generate specific hypotheses that were easily testable in the laboratory. His approach was, rather, a general framework that left the specific determinants of attributions unspecified.

The Jones and Davis Correspondence Theory

Jones and Davis (1965) have expanded Heider's approach in an attempt to make the components of dispositional attributions more specific. They suggested that people making a causal attribution look at the behavior in relation to other behaviors by that individual; that is, people observe a behavior, make an inference about the intent of the behavior, and then compare that intent against other behaviors of the individual that they have observed in the past. In making an attribution, then, Jones and Davis believed that we look for a **correspondence** between the observed behavior and the inferred intent of that behavior. For example, a person who is arguing angrily with a store clerk and who has acted similarly to others in the past is likely to have his or her hostile behavior attributed to a dispositional characteristic—because the inference is that the person's behavior results from an internal characteristic. In other words, if the correspondence between an observed and previous behaviors is high, Jones and Davis believed that we tend to infer dispositional attributions. On the other hand, when the correspondence is low (e.g., Jack is not himself today), we tend to make situational attributions.

Several factors may influence our interpretation of correspondence between behaviors. For example, socially desirable behaviors appear to be given less weight when we make dispositional attributions. **Social desirability** (i.e., behaving in ways that others or society expect of you), when inferred by an observer, reduces the chances that the behavior will be attributed to disposition. One way of thinking about social desirability is that the observer has an alternate explanation for the behavior (e.g., Joy acts the way she does because it's the social thing to do, not because she's really that way).

At the other extreme from socially desirable behavior is **nonnormative behavior**. Nonconforming or eccentric behavior is more likely to be attributed to dispositional characteristics than to situational influences. If the behavior is in opposition to what is socially desirable, the observer usually attributes the behavior to consistent characteristics of the individual (i.e., to dispositions).

Jones and Davis's analysis of attribution

processes suggested to them that one way we make decisions about the causes of behavior is by observing what they termed **noncommon effects**. Some parts of most behaviors that we observe are common to several alternative attributions. Other parts of an observed behavior, however, will be unique, and it is these unique aspects that allow us to make our attributions. In Jones and Davis's terms, the noncommon correspondences provide information to us about the causes of the behavior. Suppose for a moment that you are standing in a bank and you see a man enter. He walks to the shortest teller line and waits nervously. Up to this point, the man's behavior is common to several alternative attributions: he is late for an appointment, he is double-parked, he has bounced a check, and so on. When he pulls a gun and demands money from the teller, however, the attribution for his behavior is quite clear. The noncommon behavior allows us to attribute causality (as we back nervously out of sight).

Another factor that Jones and Davis believed is involved in attributions is our own personal involvement in the observed behavior. We are not usually passive observers of the world around us; we are both observing and interacting at the same time. Our involvement in the behavior that we are making attributions about will tend to increase the correspondences we observe and thus lead to increased dispositional attributions. Jones and Davis identified two categories of personal involvement that they believed are important: **hedonic relevance** and **personalism**.

Hedonic relevance refers to the possible extent of either a rewarding or punishing effect on us from an observed person's behavior. Suppose, for example, that after class you walk to the parking lot and discover that your car has a flat tire. A university security guard offers to change the tire. Because this is a rewarding situation for you (i.e., you won't be as late or get dirty), you will attribute the guard's behavior to some dispositional characteristic, such as "he's a nice person." (In fact, the behavior may be situational because the guard may have been instructed to help students with car trouble.)

Personalism involves the fact that our behavior influences the behavior of the person we are observing. The way the person reacts to us will lead to a high degree of correspondence and dispositional attributions. When I lecture, for example, I observe the faces of my students. Some smile and nod as I speak, while others may gaze out of the window or look bored. Based on my past experiences, I usually attribute the behavior of the attentive, nodding student to intellectual interest and understanding while attributing the window gazing or bored expressions to a disinterest in things academic (after all, who could find *my* lectures boring!). My dispositional attributions are often rudely disconfirmed after the first test. It is not unusual to discover that the "bored" student broke the curve and that the seemingly attentive student was simply conforming to my expectation and didn't understand a word I said. The point, nevertheless, is that the ways in which people react to our behavior influence the attributions we make, and their reactions tend to be interpreted in terms of their consistent characteristics.

Jones and Davis, then, attempted to specify some of the factors involved in making dispositional attributions. A major shortcoming of their theory, as well as of Heider's, is that it does not specify how we may make attributions about our own behavior.

Kelley's Theory

Kelley (1967, 1971, 1972, 1973) has developed an attributional theory that can account for the attributions we make concerning our own behavior as well as that of others. He believed that we have a need to control the environment in which we interact. In order to gain control, we must first gather information and determine what is causing particular changes to occur. In other words, attributions are attempts to specify how events are causally related to each other.

Causal attributions are regarded as the result of a complex interaction between several possible causal agents. Kelley argued that when we make attributions about events, we choose the explanations that "best fit" the observations. This is true whether we are making attributions about our own behavior or that of others. For Kelley, making attributions can be likened to generating a series of hypotheses concerning the causes of a particular event, then, through our observations and logical processes, eliminating alternatives until we reach the most logical "explanation" for the event. Kelley compared the attribution process to the way in which a scientist goes about testing an experimental question. Both attributions and scientific hypotheses are based on the logical elimination of alternatives.

Kelley argued that several principles guide our attribution decisions. A major principle used in the attribution process is that of **covariation**. Covariation across time is an important way in which we are able to make a judgment about causality. We notice that causes are related with particular outcomes over a period of time. Because there are usually several possible causes for any outcome, only those events that are consistently related to a particular outcome are causal. For example, suppose you receive an "A" on a test. The good grade may have been the result of luck, an easy test, or the fact that you studied. If you then take another test after not studying very hard and get a "C," the causal attribution "good grades result from studying" will be strengthened because studying and good grades have been linked. According to Kelley, we are sensitive to this covariation of cause and outcome. Across time the alternative hypotheses (e.g., luck) will be eliminated because they will not be consistently related to the outcome. In many situations, of course, we have only one instance from which to judge. Under these conditions Kelley (1972) argued that we rely on **causal schemata** to help us attribute events. A schema is a set of beliefs or ideas that an individual has about how certain causes lead to specific kinds of outcomes. Schemata develop as a result of our having experienced cause-and-effect relationships in the past.

Causal schemata have five basic characteristics. First, our causal schemata reflect our basic ideas about reality. For example, if we do not believe in ghosts, the creakings in an old house will more likely be attributed to stresses on the house by wind or trees rubbing against a window than to spirits.

Second, a schema provides a framework within which certain operations on the information can be performed. For example, if our schema says that gasoline engines don't run well with dirty air filters, we can replace the air filter on our car and see if it runs better. Without the framework provided by the schema, our attribution about why the car is running badly might be very different.

Third, schemata provide structure to ambiguous or minimal information. Thus when presented with confusing information, we attempt to fit it to whatever schema allows us to understand it best. This is probably why UFO sightings are either taken as evidence for extraterrestrial beings or rejected as natural phenomena. In the former case the individual has a schema that provides a framework for ambiguous lights in the sky as visitors from other worlds, while in the latter case the individual has a schema for explaining ambiguous lights in terms of natural events.

Related to the third characteristic of schemata is the fourth, which is that schemata contain assumptions about how the world is organized. For some people UFOs are not permitted within their assumed organization of the world, while for others UFOs are easily incorporated.

Finally, Kelley believed that schemata allow us to fill in "missing" data. Our observations of an event are often incomplete. Schemata help us figure out what probably occurred that wasn't observed, thus allowing us to make attributions based on incomplete information. It is probably fortunate that we can do so; otherwise we might have difficulty attributing the causes of a great amount of behavior.

In situations where only one observation is possible and several explanations present themselves as possible attributions, Kelley has identified two schematic principles that help us decide among the possibilities. The first is called the **discounting principle**, which says that a given cause will be discounted as producing an effect if other plausible causes are also present. Suppose that the lights in your home go out. It is possible that you've blown a fuse, but you also heard thunder from an approaching storm. The fuse attribution will tend to be discounted because of the presence of a plausible alternative—the approaching storm has knocked out lines between the power station and your house.

The discounting principle seems particularly important in decisions involving dispositional versus situational attributions. For example, if a person's behavior could be attributed to social desirability, this plausible external hypothesis should work to reduce the likelihood that the behavior will be considered dispositional. This is of course what Jones and Davis have already suggested, but Kelley's theory predicts the social desirability effect as one aspect of the discounting principle. The discounting principle can also work toward making dispositional attributions. If a plausible dispositional hypothesis exists as an alternative, situational explanations will be given less weight.

The second principle identified by Kelley

is called the **augmentation principle**. Augmentation occurs when a behavior exists even though present external conditions are such that they should inhibit the behavior. This might occur when an individual speaks out against a group decision, even though the person knows that doing so will incur the wrath of the group. The presence of the inhibitory condition augments (i.e., increases) the likelihood that the behavior will be attributed to dispositional characteristics. In the example just cited, we are likely to assume that the person willing to speak out against the group's decision feels strongly about the issue.

The attribution theories of Heider, Jones and Davis, and Kelley emphasize the information-processing aspects of human behavior. We accumulate information and, based on that information, attribute the causes of behavior in various ways. It is important to realize that we base our attributions on what we perceive the causes of behavior to be rather than on the objective causes of the behavior. These two are often but not always the same. In trying to understand the attribution process, we must take care to understand how the individual perceives the situation in question.

Research on Attribution

Much research has been conducted on attribution theory, and we will not attempt to cover it all, as several good books on the topic are available (e.g., Harvey, Ickes, & Kidd, 1976, 1978; Jones et al., 1972). However, we will examine some research suggesting that dispositional and situational attributions depend upon our point of view (literally). Then we will briefly examine attribution theory in regard to achievement motivation.

Actors and Observers   Much evidence exists that actors are more likely to attribute their own behavior to the demands of the situation, while observers of the same behavior are more likely to attribute it to dispositional characteristics of the actor (Jones & Nisbett, 1972). In one study Jones and Harris (1967) asked college students to judge the real opinions of other students who had been asked to read speeches on specific topics (e.g., a positive speech on Castro). The subjects were told in advance that the readers had no choice in the speech that they read. Nevertheless, the subjects still rated the speech readers as favoring the position that they had been required to present.

The "observing" students seemed to take the behavior they watched at face value as indicating consistent dispositions of the reader, despite the fact that they knew the speech readers had no choice in the matter. The results suggest that observers of behavior tend to make dispositional attributions. The actors, on the other hand, might be expected to judge their behavior more situationally. Why might actor and observer judge the same behavior differently? Jones and Nisbett pointed out that although behavior is always judged in relation to the situational context, the concept is different for the actor and the observer. The major difference lies, they believed, in the fact that the actor is aware of his or her own background and past experiences, while the observer must judge the behavior simply from what is observed. In the case of the speech readers, the actors would know quite well how they felt about Castro and also that they did not choose to read this particular speech. The observers, however, knew that people usually argue for positions they believe in; therefore the observers made dispositional attributions even though told that the actors did not choose the speech.

Jones and Nisbett noted that part of the difference between the attributions of the actor and observer results from a difference in what each attends to. The actor focuses attention on environmental cues because those are what must be attended to in order to interact successfully. At the same time, the actor will be relatively unaware of his or her own responses, because he or she cannot directly observe them. The observer, however, focuses attention on the actor because the actor is the focal point of the behavior being observed. Thus the observer may be quite unaware of the cues to which the actor is paying attention.

Consider a tennis player and an observer. The player is concentrating attention on the other player, the ball, the lines of the court, and so forth because these determine what the next response will be. At the same time, the player is usually unaware of his or her stance, movements, and appearance (my own experience is that attempts to pay such attention to personal details while playing tennis have disastrous results!). An observer of the tennis match sees the player moving back and forth, seemingly always knowing where the ball is going to be, and concludes that the player is a "natural athlete" (i.e., the observer makes a dispositional attribution). The player in fact had to learn all the various moves and has learned to focus attention on the opponent's eyes, feet, and racket in order to anticipate the next move. Players will tend to see their own behavior as resulting from these cues rather than from some dispositional characteristic.

Jones and Nisbett's analysis suggests that actors and observers attribute behavior differently because they perceive the behavior from different points of view. In a series of studies Nisbett and associates (1973) found that college students assumed that subjects who volunteered to help in one situation would be likely to do so in the future. The volunteers, on the other hand, did not rate themselves as more likely to help out in the future. Nisbett and associates also found that students described their friends' choices of college major and girl friend in terms of the dispositional characteristics of the friend, while describing their own choice of major and girl friend in situational terms. Thus even a single individual observing another's behavior (and one's own) seems to switch from dispositional to situational explanations depending on who is being observed. Again the difference seems to result from differences in perspective and amount of information available. We are more likely to attribute our own behavior to situational cues because we are aware of our past behavior.

Storms (1973) directly tested the perceptual question in an ingenious experiment. Subjects were asked either to engage in a short, unstructured conversation or to view someone else doing so. Subjects who participated in the conversation attributed more of their behavior to the situation than did the observers who watched them. Storms, however, also videotaped the conversation from two different points of view. One point of view was what the actor saw during the conversation, while the second was what the observer saw. In a second part of the experiment, a group of actors saw themselves from the viewpoint of the observer, and a group of observers saw the conversation from the viewpoint of the actor. Under these conditions the actors attributed more of their own behavior to dispositional characteristics than did the observers. Apparently the point of view (quite literally) of actor and observer is crucial in the attributions we make. Gilbert, Krull, and Pelham (1988) have also provided an interesting analysis of how attempting to regulate one's own behavior can influence how a person perceives others.

Achievement   Attribution theory has also appeared in the literature on achievement motivation. As we saw in Chapter Nine, much research has been conducted in an attempt to understand achievement motivation. Attribution theory may also be able to contribute to our understanding of this process.

Attribution theory has been applied most directly to achievement motivation by Bernard Weiner and his associates (Frieze, 1976; Weiner, 1972, 1974; Weiner et al., 1972; Weiner & Kukla, 1970; Weiner, Russell, & Lerman, 1978). Weiner argued that at least four elements are important in our interpretation of an achievement-related event. The elements are **ability, effort, task difficulty**, and **luck**. When we engage in achievement-related behavior, we will ascribe our success or failure at the task as a result of one or various combinations of these four elements.

Weiner's approach assumed that the inferences we make about our abilities primarily result from past experiences. Past successes will lead us to conclude that we have certain abilities in certain areas, while past failures will reduce our beliefs in our abilities. Our inferences about our abilities are not judged in a vacuum but in relation to the performance of others. If we succeed at a task in which others fail, we are likely to perceive ourselves as capable individuals.

We judge the effort that we have put into a task from such factors as time spent, muscular effort, and so on. Interestingly, we tend to perceive ourselves as having expended more effort when we are successful at a task (Weiner & Kukla, 1970). This suggests that we associate effort with a successful outcome because they tend to go together in our past experience. Both ability and effort can be regarded as internal characteristics. Thus we tend to regard our abilities and the effort we expend in working toward a goal as dispositional in character.

We apparently judge task difficulty primarily from social norms, though objective characteristics of the task also play a part. We infer the difficulty of a task by observing the percentage of other people who succeed.

When many or most others succeed, we judge the task to be easy; observing that most others fail leads us to infer that the task is very difficult.

Luck is assumed to be involved in a task when we have no control over the outcome of the task. For example, we tend to ascribe the attainment of a particular goal to luck when we can detect no relationship between our behavior and the successful attainment of that goal. Likewise, if we fail at a task but the failure seems unrelated to anything we have done, we tend to ascribe it to bad luck.

Both the difficulty of the task and luck can be considered situational factors (i.e., external to the individual). Thus attributions concerning our behavior that involve task difficulty or luck will tend to be situational rather than dispositional.

Weiner also argued that we tend to analyze our behaviors in regard to a dimension that he termed **stable-unstable**. Both ability and task difficulty can be regarded as relatively stable. Abilities do not swing drastically from moment to moment, nor does the difficulty of a task. Effort and luck, on the other hand, are rather unstable. We may work diligently on one project but put little effort into another. Likewise, luck fluctuates from moment to moment.

The four causal ascriptions and their two dimensions can be visualized as a fourfold square, as in Figure 11.2. The internal-external dimension varies along the top of the square, while the stable-unstable dimension varies along the side. Thus, for example, ability is regarded as internal and stable, while luck is considered external and unstable. Weiner's analysis of ability, effort, task difficulty, and luck as important factors in the causal attribution of behavior suggests that shifts in the expectancy of success (or failure) should depend upon the attributed source of the success or failure. For example, success

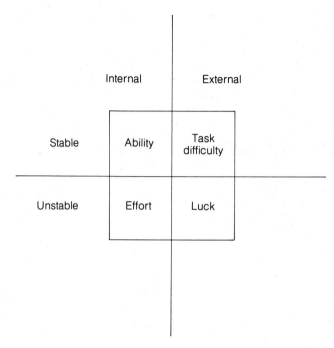

Figure 11.2   *The causal ascriptions of ability, task difficulty, effort, and luck as related to the dimensions of stability-instability and internality-externality. (Adapted from Weiner, 1974. Used by permission.)*

attributed to ability should lead to increased expectancy of success in the future, while success ascribed to luck should lead to little change. Also, attributing an outcome to a stable characteristic (i.e., ability or task difficulty) leads to greater expectancy shifts than when it is attributed to unstable factors such as effort or luck (Weiner, 1974).

Frieze (1976) investigated the possibility that other categories besides the four proposed by Weiner are relevant to the attribution of achievement behavior. Frieze found considerable support for ability, effort, task difficulty, and luck as causal attributions for success and failure; however, she also found evidence for the factors of **mood, effects of other persons**, and **incentive to do well**. Frieze's data suggest that success or failure at a task may be attributed to factors beyond those

suggested by Weiner and make the attribution process somewhat more complex.

Partially as a result of Frieze's study, Weiner has modified his attribution model (Weiner, Russell, & Lerman, 1978). One major change is the inclusion of a third dimension in his model that he called **intentionality**. The intentionality dimension takes into account that some causes of behavior may be intentional (e.g., teacher bias), while others (e.g., mood) are unintentional. As Weiner noted, intentionality was proposed as a factor in the attribution process by Heider in 1958 but was not incorporated into the attribution-achievement model until 1972 by Rosenbaum. Thus Weiner has broadened his attribution-achievement model to encompass factors beyond ability, effort, task difficulty, and luck. Some possible additional causal ascriptions for success and failure in achievement situations might include fatigue, mood, illness, and the biases of others (Weiner, Russell, & Lerman, 1978).

Perhaps the most interesting direction that Weiner's attribution research has taken is its investigation of the particular emotional labels associated with success and failure resulting from factors such as ability, effort, task difficulty, and luck.

In one study Weiner, Russell, and Lerman (1978) presented subjects with a brief story concerning success or failure that also contained the reason for the success or failure. The following is one of the story lines that Weiner used: "Francis studied intensely for a test he took. It was very important for Francis to record a high score on this exam. Francis received an extremely high score on the test. Francis felt that he received this high score because he studied so intensely. How do you think Francis felt upon receiving this score?" (Weiner, Russell, & Lerman, 1978, p. 70).

Subjects were asked to indicate the emotional reaction of the individual in the story by selecting emotionally toned words from a list prepared by Weiner. He presented ten different stories with ten different reasons for success. The results of the study indicated that some words reappeared in most of the ten causal attributions of success. Examples such as *pleased* and *happy* appeared on all ten, while *satisfied* showed up on eight and *contented* on seven. Six of the attributions seemed to generate specific emotions, as evidenced by the descriptive words chosen. For example, success attributed to unstable (i.e., intense) effort led to choices of words such as *uproarious, delirious, delighted, ecstatic*, and *elated* while success attributed to luck led to choices such as *surprised, astonished, wonderment, awe*, and *amazed*.

In a similar fashion, 11 stories were devised that attributed failure to various causes such as ability, mood, luck, fatigue, and so on. Several words showed up on several of the lists (*uncheerful* and *displeasure* on six lists, *upset* on five), but again it was possible to discriminate between attributions by the emotional words chosen. For example, failure resulting from lack of ability led subjects to choose words such as *incompetent, inadequate*, and *panic*, while failure attributed to luck led to choices such as *astonished, overwhelmed*, and *stunned*.

The results of Weiner's preliminary studies seem to indicate that different emotions are associated with different attributions for success and also for failure. Thus the view that success at achievement-related activities leads to feelings of pride and that failure leads to feelings of shame seems oversimplified. One may feel confident and pleased when success is attributed to ability while feeling surprised and astonished when success is attributed to luck. Likewise, failure does not always lead to feelings of shame. Failure resulting from lack of intense effort (i.e., unstable effort) elicits *ashamed* and *guilty* as emotionally toned associations, but failure as a result of others' efforts leads to aggressiveness, as evidenced by such words as *ferocious, revengeful,* and *furious*.

In 1985 Weiner proposed a modified attributional theory of achievement motivation which expanded upon his earlier work. In this model he proposed that the judgments about cause people make can be understood as belonging within three main dimensions: **locus, stability** (as noted in Figure 11.2), and **controllability**. (**Intentionality**, although suggested as a possible dimension earlier, is played down in this model. Weiner also suggests that **globality** is a possible further dimension of causality.)

After examining several studies (see Weiner, 1985, Table 2), Weiner concluded that controllability was necessary to describe the way people ascribed causality to their successes and failures, because causes falling within the locus and stability dimensions could also be categorized as either under or not under volitional control. Thus, for example, effort, which was classified earlier as internal and unstable, is also controllable, whereas mood and fatigue, which too are internal and unstable, are not normally controllable.

Weiner's model further attempts to relate the causal ascriptions that people make to their expectancies of future success or failure. Weiner's **expectancy principle** states: "Changes in expectancy of success following an outcome are influenced by the perceived stability of the cause of the event" (Weiner, 1985, p. 559). According to Weiner, three corollaries follow from the expectancy principle.

Corollary 1. If the outcome of an event is ascribed to a stable cause, then that outcome will be anticipated with increased certainty, or with an increased expectancy in the future.

Corollary 2. If an outcome is ascribed to an unstable cause, then the certainty or expectancy of that outcome may be unchanged or the future may be anticipated to be different from the past.

Corollary 3. Outcomes ascribed to stable causes will be anticipated to be repeated in the future with a greater degree of certainty than are outcomes ascribed to unstable causes. (Weiner, 1985, p. 559)

Let us take an example of causal ascriptions and see how Weiner's expectancy principle works. Suppose you have just received an "A" on your first laboratory report for a class in experimental psychology. You had expected to get only a "C+," so you are pleased and somewhat surprised by this outcome. The expectancy principle says that how you attribute your "A" will make a difference in your future expectations. If you attribute the grade to a stable cause such as your ability, then you are more likely to expect good lab grades on subsequent reports (corollaries 1 and 3). On the other hand if you attribute your grade to an unstable cause such as luck, corollary 2 says you will either not

change your future expectations about your lab grades (you will still expect "Cs" on subsequent labs), or you may expect the future to be different from the past (you will not expect to get another "A"). Thus according to Weiner, causal ascriptions can lead to changes in expectancies, which in turn influence future behavior.

Several studies have been conducted based on Weiner's 1985 model (de Jong, Koomen, & Mellenbergh, 1988; Weiner, Amirkhan, Folkes, & Verette, 1987; Weiner, Perry, & Magnusson, 1988). For example, Weiner, Perry, and Magnusson examined subjects' reactions to ten **stigmas**. A stigma is typically defined to be a mark or sign indicating a deviation from the norm. Ten stigmas were chosen for this experiment: AIDS, Alzheimer's disease, blindness, cancer, child abuse, drug addiction, heart disease, obesity, paraplegia, and Vietnam War syndrome. In the first of two studies they found that physically based stigmas were perceived as onset-uncontrollable and elicited pity and helping judgments. Stigmas that could be considered mental-behavioral were, however, perceived as onset-controllable and elicited anger and judgments not to help.

These researchers were also interested in determining how people's reactions to, and expectations of, helping would change if information was provided that changed the controllability dimension of the stigma. In the second of the two experiments they provided reasons for the stigmas such that half the time the stigmas were seen as controllable and half the time these same stigmas were seen as uncontrollable. Although the findings of this second experiment are complicated by the fact that not all stigmas are equally amenable to attributional alteration, the general finding was that stigmas presented as controllable (that is, as resulting from some mental-behavioral characteristic of the subject), led to judgments of more anger, less pity, and less helping than these same stigmas presented as uncontrollable. This study, then, is consistent in showing that controllability is an important dimension of the attributions we make and that these attributions have consequences for future behaviors such as helping.

The attributions we make about the causes of our successes and failures clearly influence our future expectancies of success; they also appear to influence the emotions we experience as a result of success and failure. Dweck and her associates have studied the attributions that people make after both success and failure experiences (Diener & Dweck, 1978, 1980; Dweck, 1975; Dweck & Reppuci, 1973). The Diener and Dweck studies are particularly interesting.

In the 1978 study children were tested for helpless or mastery orientation and were then asked to describe what they were thinking. Prior to performing a task (that they would subsequently fail), there were no differences between the attributions offered by the two types of children. Following the failure experience, however, the attributions made by the two groups were almost completely different. The children classified as helpless attributed their failure to uncontrollable factors; the mastery-oriented children did not appear to have defined themselves as failing at all but, from their verbalizations, appeared to be searching for solutions for their failure.

The emotionality generated by the failure task also differed for the two groups. The mastery-oriented children maintained positive attitudes about the task and continued to believe that they could do well in the future. The helpless children, on the other hand, developed negative attitudes about the task and sought to escape from the situation.

In their 1980 study Diener and Dweck examined the attributions of helpless and mastery-oriented children to successful experiences and once again found differences between the attributions made by the two

groups. The basic differences concerned how success was interpreted. The helpless children, for example, seemed to remember their successes less than the mastery-oriented children because they consistently underestimated the number of problems they had correctly solved. Additionally, the helpless children rated their success as lower than what they expected other children would do, while the mastery-oriented children rated their success as higher than that of most other children. This latter finding suggests that the helpless children attributed their success in such a way that it was not an especially rewarding event. Diener and Dweck have proposed that helpless children may compare themselves not to the average child of their peer group but rather to the "best" children. If such is the case, then to be truly successful these children would have to perform better than the "best" children in their reference group, a clearly difficult task.

Perhaps the most interesting difference between helpless and mastery-oriented children is that helpless children do not assume that present success is predictive of future success. Diener and Dweck suggested that this difference may result from different attributions about the causes of success. While mastery-oriented children are likely to attribute their successes to ability, helpless children are not. Furthermore, when helpless children experience success followed by failure, they discount the success more than do mastery-oriented children. The helpless children in the study, for example, were more likely to attribute their earlier successes to the ease of the task when asked about those successes after subsequent failure. Additionally, the helpless children lowered their expectancy of future success after failure, while the mastery-oriented children's estimates remained high. Helpless and mastery-oriented children, then, appear to view both success and failure quite differently. The helpless child seems to give more weight to failure in making attributions, while the mastery-oriented child pays more attention to success experiences.

Further research by Dweck and her colleagues (Dweck, 1986; Dweck & Leggett, 1988; Elliot & Dweck, 1988) has led to the hypothesis that helpless and mastery-oriented individuals differ in the **goals** they seek. According to Dweck and Leggett (1988), helpless individuals seek **performance goals** (defined as the gaining of favorable judgments of performance), while mastery-oriented individuals seek **learning goals** (defined as increasing one's competence). Their research suggests that these different goals lead to differing patterns of response, with failure in the pursuit of performance goals increasing one's vulnerability to helplessness, and failure at learning goals promoting behavioral strategies to turn the failure into success.

Dweck suggests that the pursuit of these two types of goals stems from differing implicit theories about one's intelligence. Some individuals seem to believe that their intellectual abilities are fixed, whereas others see their intellectual abilities as able to grow. Dweck's research (Dweck & Leggett, 1988; Leggett, 1985) indicates that subjects who viewed their intelligence as fixed tended to adopt performance goals in order to prove their ability. Individuals who viewed their intelligence as malleable, on the other hand, tended to adopt learning goals as a way of further developing that intelligence.

In light of Weiner's attribution model that emphasizes effort as one component of the attributions we make, it is also interesting to note that Leggett and Dweck (1986, as cited by Dweck & Leggett, 1988) have found that helpless and mastery-oriented children view effort differently. Helpless children perceive effort as indicating a lack of ability (e.g., if I have to work hard I must not be very smart), whereas mastery-oriented children view effort as one

strategy for demonstrating their competence.

The research of Dweck and her associates would appear to show that individuals' helpless and mastery-oriented behaviors can be traced to their different views about their abilities, which in turn lead to a focus on different goals. When these goals are not met the individuals' perceptions are quite different, leading to feelings of helplessness in some persons or more active problem solving in others.

The research of Dweck and her associates points out the importance of the attribution process in evaluating both success and failure—different people can attribute the same events in quite different ways. Further, these attributions will influence future expectancies of success and failure and will thus likely alter future motivation. Dweck's research also has important implications for education. She has shown, for example, that retraining helpless children's failure attributions leads to improved performance (Dweck, 1975). Similarly, Diener and Dweck have suggested that retraining helpless children to attribute success to stable characteristics (such as ability) should also be useful.

Fear of Success   As we saw in Chapter Nine, research on fear of success indicates that sex-role orientation is a good candidate for the differences in success imagery originally thought to result from a motive to avoid success (Horner, 1968, 1972).

Sex-role orientation and fear of success have both been examined from an attributional framework (Erkut, 1983; Zuckerman et al., 1980). In one study Erkut found that college men were more likely to attribute their grade-point averages to ability, while college women were more likely to attribute their averages to effort. In a second study, where attributions concerning the outcome of a midterm exam were investigated, both men and women attributed their exam grades to effort. The importance of effort in women's attributions implies that their expectancy of success is more situationally determined than is the case for men. Erkut further suggested that when men and women enter an achievement situation, they normally expect to succeed—men on the basis of ability and women on the basis of effort. As a result, women feel most confident when they believe that they have the ability to do well *and* are well prepared.

More importantly, Erkut found that sex-role orientation, as measured by the *Bem Sex Role Inventory* (Bem, 1974), was related to the actual grade received on the midterm exam, with high femininity scores being negatively associated with grade (that is, low grades were associated with high femininity scores and high grades with low femininity scores) for both men and women. Attributions were also related to sex-role orientation. Feminine women expected to receive lower grades, claimed they did not have the ability to do well, and expected the test to be hard. The attributions of feminine men also included test difficulty as a reason for the grade received; however, as noted by Erkut, feminine men do not seem to internalize failure information to the same degree that women do (as shown by the fact that the men's attributions about ability were not altered).

One reason that high femininity scores on the Bem Sex Role Inventory may have been related to low grades and debilitating attributions is the nature of the inventory. The inventory's adjectives indicative of femininity do not include items that one would normally associate with an achievement orientation. Thus, as Erkut pointed out, it may be better to consider the femininity scale, in the context of her study, as indicative of a nonachievement orientation.

Erkut's results are interesting and suggest that both achievement behavior and achievement-related attributions are linked to sex-role orientation for both men and women. The feminine orientation compared to the masculine, at least as measured by the Bem inventory, is associated with lower grades and different expectations. Further research is needed to clarify the relationships suggested by Erkut. In particular, it would be useful to use the fourfold classification suggested by Bem (1977), which divides scores on the inventory into four groups—masculine, feminine, androgynous, and undifferentiated. One could then examine achievement behavior and attributional responses, as Erkut did, for each of the four groups.

Zuckerman and associates (1980) examined the relationships between fear of success, intrinsic motivation, and attributions. Subjects were divided into high and low fear-of-success groups using the *Fear of Success Scale* (*FOSS*) developed by Zuckerman and Allison (1976). The subjects were given a series of timed puzzles to solve and were told that they had been either successful or unsuccessful relative to established norms. The results of the study showed that subjects who were told that they had been successful and who were low in fear of success showed more intrinsic motivation for the task and made more internal attributions for that success than did subjects who were high in fear of success. For subjects told that they had failed, no differences emerged between low and high fear-of-success subjects. The pattern of results in this study suggested to Zuckerman and associates (1980) that the high fear-of-success person uses a self-defeating strategy in dealing with achievement situations. High fear-of-success persons are less likely than others to strive for success to begin with and, when successful, are less likely to attribute that success to internal factors. Thus success seems to have a different effect on individuals high in fear of success than it does on individuals low in fear of success, in a manner reminiscent of Dweck's work with helpless and mastery-oriented children. In contrast to Dweck's research, however, Zuckerman and associates found no differences between high and low fear-of-success subjects when those subjects believed that they had failed. Zuckerman saw this lack of differences after failure as evidence against the idea, sometimes proposed, that fear of success and fear of failure are the same. Interestingly, Zuckerman and associates also found *no* sex differences in their study, further suggesting that fear of success is no longer exclusively a feminine phenomenon, as Horner had initially suggested.

Attribution and Learned Helplessness

In Chapter Six we examined the concept of learned helplessness, which Seligman and his associates believed analogous to depression in humans. Seligman has modified his theory (as it relates to depression) to take into account the importance of the attributions one makes about why one's behavior is ineffective (Abramson, Seligman, & Teasdale, 1978).

The "old" model of learned helplessness argued that helplessness and depression result from the perceived noncontingency between one's acts and the environment; that is, a person becomes helpless when he or she believes that he or she has no control over what happens to him or her. The early model of helplessness, however, had a number of problems. One was that it could not account for the depressed individual's generally low self-esteem; a second problem was the well-known fact that depressed persons typically blame themselves for their lack of control. The original learned helplessness theory of depression also could neither explain why some depressions are short-lived and why others continue for some time—nor why in some cases the observed helplessness is rather specific, while at other times it is quite general.

The reformulated model of learned helplessness relies on the type of attribution that the person makes to overcome these problems.

For example, Abramson, Seligman, and Teasdale argued that an individual may attribute his or her own lack of control to either external or internal events. Some situations over which we have no control are universal; that is, no one else has control over them either. A tornado that destroys our house is beyond our own control and that of others as well, while doing badly on a test may result from an internal characteristic (e.g., a perceived lack of intelligence) that other people can control. In this latter situation we perceive ourselves to be personally helpless (e.g., others do O.K. on tests), while in the case of the tornado we are universally helpless. Seligman and his associates argued that the type of attribution we make about our lack of control, either universal or personal, affects our self-esteem (Abramson, Seligman, & Teasdale, 1978). If we believe that we lack characteristics possessed by others that allow them to control their situations, this attribution of personal helplessness will lead to lowered self-esteem.

In attributions of both universal and personal helplessness, there will be motivational deficits, but only when attributions of personal helplessness are made will self-esteem be affected. According to Abramson, Seligman, and Teasdale, depressed individuals tend to attribute their lack of control to personal characteristics, and this attribution leads to feelings of low self-worth. The lowered self-esteem and self-blame of the depressed individual can be understood, Seligman argued, as the result of attributions of personal helplessness.

In a similar fashion the generality of helpless depression can be understood as a result of the type of attributions that a person makes. When people discover that their behavior has no discernible effect on the outcomes they are seeking, they may attribute it to specific circumstances or to a more global situation. If the attribution is to a specific circumstance (e.g., I don't do well in school), the individual is likely to demonstrate helplessness only in those specific situations. However, if the discovery of uncontrollability leads to a global attribution (e.g., failure on a test leading to the attribution that one is totally incompetent), many future behaviors will be affected by this global attribution.

The concept of specific versus global attributions regarding the lack of control over events may help explain why some depressions are characterized by little effort on the part of individuals to change their behavior; the depressed individuals tend to make global attributions and come to believe that nothing they do will have any effect on their environment.

The time course of depression can be understood, according to Seligman, by referring to the stable-unstable dimension of attributions, noted earlier in our examination of Weiner's attributional analysis of achievement. An individual, when perceiving that he or she has no control over events, may attribute this lack of control to stable factors (e.g., intelligence) or to unstable factors (e.g., I've had a run of bad luck). Helplessness that is perceived as the result of stable factors will greatly extend the time course of the helplessness, while attributions to unstable causes will be more transient. According to Seligman, the depressed individual's attributions tend to be stable and thus chronic.

Seligman was the first to admit that there are other causes of depression than helplessness. He argued, however, that helpless depression is one type of depression that occurs when people perceive their behavior as independent of the outcomes they seek. He suggested that the attributions made by this type of depressed person will determine whether the depression is long or short, specific to particular situations or more general, and whether he or she expresses feelings of low-esteem and self-blame or lacks these characteristics. Seligman suggested that some

depressed individuals tend to make personal (i.e., internal), global, stable attributions concerning their lack of control over events. Attributions of this type will lead to self-blame, lowered self-esteem, and to chronic and general depressions.

The attribution model of learned helplessness has generated a great deal of controversy (see, e.g., Alloy & Abramson, 1982; Baum & Gatchel, 1981; Boyd, 1982; Brockner et al., 1983; Danker-Brown & Baucom, 1982; Follette & Jacobson, 1987; Kuhl, 1981; Mikulincer, 1988; Mikulincer & Nizan, 1988; Raps, Peterson, Jonas, & Seligman, 1982). Though it is beyond the scope of this text to examine all the current research on learned helplessness, looking at a few of these studies is useful.

Wortman and Brehm (1975) proposed that the initial reaction to loss of control is not helplessness but reactance (i.e., a resistance to the loss of control with subsequent increased effort). If control is not regained as a result of reactance, *then* learned helplessness occurs. Raps and associates attempted to test this proposal by presenting people—who were either outpatients or had been hospitalized for one, three, or nine weeks—with a number of cognitive tasks. The rationale underlying their procedure was that hospitalization typifies a situation where a person has little control. If Wortman and Brehm's hypothesis is correct, then changes in performance on the cognitive tasks should occur. Patients hospitalized for a short time should show reactance and thus increased performance, while patients hospitalized longer should show increasing amounts of learned helplessness, as evidenced by a decrease in performance on the cognitive tasks. The results of the study indicated a steady decline in performance on the cognitive tasks as the length of stay in the hospital increased but no evidence of reactance. (The outpatients showed very little helplessness.) So these results support the proposed relationship between loss of control and learned helplessness but not between loss of control and reactance. Though Raps and associates conceded that the patient population they studied may have been particularly sensitive to learned helplessness manipulations (the patients were at a VA medical center), they argued that loss of control was the operative factor in the observed changes.

Although Raps and associates (1982) found no support for the reactance model, Mikulincer (1988) obtained evidence of both reactance and learned helplessness. In his study some subjects were exposed to one unsolvable problem while others were exposed to four unsolvable problems. For those subjects who had an internal attributional style, exposure to a single unsolvable problem led to reactance and better performance on a later task when compared to subjects who had an external attributional style. Internal-style subjects who were exposed to four unsolvable problems, however, exhibited stronger feelings of incompetence and showed a decrease in performance on a later task, much as learned helplessness would predict. Thus Mikulincer's study would appear to support the Wortman and Brehm reactance model.

In another study, Mikulincer and Nizan (1988) found that global attributions of failure led to an increase in what they termed off-task cognitions. These anxious thoughts interfered with subsequent performance. When instructions were given that discouraged off-task cognitions, the performance-decreasing effects of global attributions were eliminated. These researchers suggest that the performance deficits found with global attributions may result more from anxiety than from a change in motivational state as the learned helplessness model has proposed.

Baltes and Skinner (1983) have taken strong exception to the study by Raps and associates. These researchers point out that while the Raps study does not support the

Wortman-Brehm model of learned helplessness, it also does not necessarily support the learned helplessness model of Seligman and his colleagues. Baltes and Skinner noted that at least two other models could explain the deficits observed in the hospitalized patients—operant learning and role theory.

From an operant perspective, hospitalization presents a situation where reinforcement contingencies are such that independent, active, and control-taking behaviors are discouraged, while passive, dependent behaviors are encouraged. If rewards are consistently tied to passiveness and punishments to active control taking, then it is not surprising that as the length of hospitalization becomes greater, helpless behavior increases.

Role theory proposes that expectations, in the form of rules regarding appropriate behavior, can lead to behaviors appropriate for the role being played. As a result, when people play "patient," their expectations of appropriate patient behavior lead them to act in a passive and dependent way. Thus the subjects in the Raps study may have behaved passively because that is what they thought was expected of them.

In 1989 Abramson, Metalsky, and Alloy revised the 1978 learned helplessness model and termed their new model the **hopelessness theory of depression**. This more recent model proposes to explain a specific subtype of depression that they call hopelessness depression. This newer model also plays down the role of attributions in the understanding of this depression subtype. Hopelessness depression is, they believe, typified by two basic expectations: (1) highly valued outcomes are unobtainable or highly aversive outcomes cannot be avoided and (2) the individual is helpless to change these situations. Thus helplessness becomes a component of hopelessness in the new model.

Because the model deemphasizes the basic role of attributions in the promotion of depression, we will not further pursue it here. Future research will determine the usefulness of the model.

As you can see, the attribution model of learned helplessness has been both provocative and controversial. At present more definitive research is probably needed before we can determine the usefulness of the theory. Attributional approaches in general, however, are very popular. As we have seen, they have been applied to many different psychological phenomena, of which achievement and learned helplessness are only two examples. Attributional approaches tell us that we must understand how a person perceives cause and effect if we are to understand why that person behaves in a particular way. That is of course a difficult problem to solve, but it is one in which many researchers are currently engaged.

SUMMARY

One of the most important things we do is to make judgments about the causes of behavior. Attribution theory, originated by Heider to explain such judgments, has been expanded and refined by Jones, Kelley, and others. A major finding is that we overestimate the importance of dispositional characteristics and underestimate situational factors when making causal judgments, particularly when we judge the behavior of others. This fundamental attribution error may result in part from differences in what we attend to when observing others' behavior, as opposed to observing our own behavior.

Attribution theory has also been related to achievement. Weiner, for example, has investigated the various emotional ascriptions given to success and failure in achievement situations. Dweck has shown that the attributions of helpless and mastery-oriented children differ, and Seligman and his associates have reformulated their theory of learned helplessness to include the kinds of attribu-

tions people make when they discover that their behavior is unrelated to outcomes. These attributions in turn may influence the generality, time course, and self-blame that are often observed in depression.

Attribution theory emphasizes cognitive information processing as crucial to the understanding of behavior. Though in a sense nonmotivational, the attribution approaches generally acknowledge the importance of motives in generating attributions and, more importantly, the role of attributions in the future direction of behavior. Thus the attribution of past success to high ability probably serves to motivate future achievement behaviors.

If we are to understand why people behave as they do, we must understand the processes by which people attribute the causes of events, both within themselves and in others. Attribution theory attempts to help us gain such an understanding.

SUGGESTIONS FOR FURTHER READING

Abramson, L. Y., Metalsky, G. I., & Alloy, L. B. (1989). Hopelessness depression: A theory-based subtype of depression. *Psychological Review*, *96*, 358–372. The revision of the helplessness model is outlined here along with research support. For the advanced student.

Dweck, C. S., & Leggett, E. L. (1988). A social-cognitive approach to motivation and personality. *Psychological Review*, *95*, 256–273. Dweck and Leggett summarize the research that led them to propose the distinction between performance and learning goals. The concept of fixed versus malleable intelligence is also presented here.

Harvey, J. H., Ickes, W. J., & Kidd, R. F. (1976). *New directions in attribution research* (Vol. 1). Hillsdale, N.J.: Erlbaum.

Harvey, J. H., Ickes, W. J., & Kidd, R. F. (1978). *New directions in attribution research* (Vol. 2). Hillsdale, N.J.: Erlbaum. These two volumes provide a good overview of topics in attribution research.

Weiner, B. (1985). An attributional theory of achievement motivation and emotion. *Psychological Review, 92,* 548–573. This article presents Weiner's revised theory of achievement motivation, which stresses the idea of controllability.

Chapter Twelve

Cognitive Motivation: Competence and Control

CHAPTER PREVIEW

This chapter is concerned with the following questions:

1. What do Rogers's characteristics of the fully functioning individual suggest about motivation?

2. What is Maslow's approach to motivation?

3. What criticisms of the self-actualization approaches of Rogers and Maslow have been made?

4. How have the concepts of competence and personal causation been linked to behavior motivation?

The 15-month-old child tried for the fifth time to pull herself up onto the dining room chair. The seat of the chair, at eye level to the child, proved to be a formidable opponent. At last, after much struggling, the child managed to get a knee onto the seat and was able to push with one leg while pulling with an arm. The maneuver succeeded in getting the child onto "Daddy's" chair.

The child crowed with delight in herself and smiled broadly. Within a minute atop her perch, however, she began to whimper, demanding to be let down off the chair. The father, reading the evening paper, ignored the child's cries until they became louder and more persistent—he had played this game before. Putting down the paper and walking into the dining room from his easy chair, he gently removed the child from her perch and gave her an affectionate pat on the rear, admonishing her to "stay down." No sooner had the child's feet hit the floor, however, than she grabbed the chair and began her effort anew. After some struggle she again managed to pull herself onto the chair, and again her delight in this success quickly turned to demands to be rescued. This game continued until the child tired of the activity but began anew the next day. Eventually climbing the giant chair became easy, and the child lost interest in her conquest and turned to new challenges such as the several buttons on the stereo that controlled the music to which she danced.

This short "day in the life" of a typical 15-month-old child illustrates the major thrust of this chapter. Many researchers in the humanist approach to psychology have noted the persistent motive within individuals to become competent in dealing with the environment. Successful completion of a task, however, often seems to cause the task to lose some of its value, and new, more difficult challenges are undertaken.

Theorists and researchers in this area have described this persistent motive to test and expand one's abilities by a number of terms. Rogers has described this motive state as an attempt to grow and reach fulfillment, that is, to become a **fully functioning** individual. Maslow has described the process as a movement toward **self-actualization**, an attempt to become all that one can possibly become. White has suggested that a motive for **competence** exists in each of us, while deCharms has emphasized the idea that people strive to **control** their environment. Rotter has developed the concept of **locus of control**, and Deci, as well as others, investigated the concept of **intrinsic motivation**.

According to all these approaches, all of us, like the child and the chair, strive to reach our potential. Most of the theories examined in this chapter take the point of view that human behavior cannot fully be understood without some reference to this striving toward actualization or full functioning.

We shall see that although many of these theories are highly similar, each has approached the question from a slightly different point of view. We will begin our study of these approaches with the work of Carl Rogers.

CARL ROGERS AND POSITIVE REGARD

Carl Rogers is probably best known for the development of client-centered therapy. His therapeutic approach, however, is firmly based upon his ideas about the motives of individuals.

Rogers pointed out that life itself is an active, ongoing process and that the most basic characteristic of human behavior is a striving for wholeness. This concept of striving is important because it implies that the process of achieving wholeness is never complete; we change as we grow. Rogers has called this striving to become fully functioning the **actualizing tendency** and argued that it is innate in all living organisms (Arkes & Garske, 1977; Evans, 1975; Rogers, 1951, 1961; Schultz, 1977).

According to Rogers, there is only one motive—the basic motive toward growth. But this motive can be analyzed as consisting of attempts by an organism to maintain, enhance, and reproduce itself. The specific motives that other theorists discuss (e.g., hunger, thirst, sex, avoidance of pain) can be regarded as aspects of either maintenance or reproduction of the individual. Though we need to know under what conditions specific behaviors occur, we gain little, according to Rogers, by assuming the existence of specific motive states.

Rogers argued that our striving for fulfillment is importantly influenced by our environment. We are cognitive organisms, and our experiences (and their interpretations) can either help or hinder our attempts to grow. In this regard our interactions with others are particularly important. Rogers argued that experiences learned early in infancy influence our psychological growth. He saw the actualizing tendency as creating both a need for **positive regard** and a need for **positive self-regard**. A person's feelings of positive regard from others, as well as from oneself, come from interactions with his or her parents in what Rogers called **unconditional positive regard**. The basic idea is that a person is accepted and loved regardless of anything that he or she might do; hence one receives experiences that allow him or her to see that he or she is loved regardless of what he or she does. Under these circumstances, the actualizing tendency works toward growth because the person's own concept (i.e., the self) is consistent with the feedback received from others. Likewise, under these conditions, the person is open to change and is nondefensive, so that the self can change and grow. In Rogers's terms, the person is a "fully functioning individual."

Too often, however, positive regard is made contingent upon specific behaviors; that is, individuals are made to feel that they are worthwhile *only if* they behave in certain ways. According to Rogers, **conditional positive regard** leads to maladaptive behaviors because it creates anxiety. One feels loved only to the extent that one's behavior is correct. The anxiety triggers defenses so that the individual begins denying or distorting cognitions because they are inconsistent with one's self-concept.

When positive regard is made conditional, much energy of the self-actualizing tendency is channeled into the defenses that one uses to protect the self. Because the self is threatened, it is not free to grow and change in an atmosphere of acceptance and so becomes static. Lack of self-growth is maladjustive and limits the individual's attempts to become fully functioning.

Growth and change, then, are the basics for psychological health. According to Rogers's approach, the basic motive underlying all behavior is the actualizing tendency. To be fully functioning individuals, we must have unconditional positive regard so that we can "let down" our defenses and allow the self to change and grow. When we lose our defensiveness, we become aware of what is happening within us and can change. We can also learn to accept ourselves for what we are without the anxiety created by conditional positive regard.

The Fully Functioning Individual

Five basic characteristics define Rogers's concept of full functioning:

1. **Openness to experience**. Fully functioning individuals do not have to defend themselves against certain experiences; thus their perceptions of events are less distorted. They are aware of their own characteristics and are more flexible in being able to alter them. The fully functioning individual is usually *more* emotional than others, experiencing not only a wider range of emotions but also experiencing them more intensely.

2. **Existential living**. The fully functioning individual lives each moment to the fullest and does not concentrate on either the past or the future. The fully functioning person also has a general interest in life, and all aspects of life are experienced as new and rich. Rogers believed existential living to be the very core of the healthy personality.

3. **Trust in one's own organism**. Rogers described the fully functioning individual as one who often behaves in particular ways because it feels right rather than because it seems intellectually right. Thus fully functioning individuals are often intuitive because they are open and in touch with their innermost feelings. This trust in one's "gut reactions" may lead to spontaneous and sometimes impulsive behavior, but not at the expense of others. While intellectual decisions may be downgraded in importance, they are not ignored.

4. **Sense of freedom**. Fully functioning persons experience a sense of personal freedom in choosing what happens to them. They see themselves as having the personal power to determine what their futures will be. They regard themselves as in control of their lives rather than at the mercy of chance events.

5. **Creativity**. As might be expected, fully functioning persons are highly creative.

This creativity is also evidenced by their increased ability to adapt to change and to survive even drastic changes in their environment.

Fully functioning persons, as described by Rogers, have the power to control their own lives because they are free from the denial and distortions that produce rigid behavior. The fully functioning person is not in a "state" but is immersed in a "process," which causes one to strive continually to enhance oneself.

To be fully functioning does not mean that the person is in a constant state of ecstasy. Enhancing oneself is both difficult and painful as one grows. Full functioning does not promise happiness, although happiness often appears to be a byproduct of the process. The fully functioning person can be expected, however, to be more comfortable with life situations (whether happy or not) and to cope with situations in open and flexible ways.

Criticisms of Rogers's Approach

Rogers's view of human motivation is much more optimistic than most. He sees humans as motivated by the need to become fully functional in order to reach their ultimate potential. When we fail to reach our potential, it is because of experiences we have had in interacting with our parents or others where our self-worth has been made conditional.

Rogers's theory has been criticized on a number of counts (Arkes & Garske, 1977; Schultz, 1977). First, many of the terms that Rogers used are not operationally defined. For example, what is the self-actualizing tendency in operational terms? Where does it come from, and how does it promote one behavior as opposed to another?

Second, the environment is regarded as an important source of motivational change; yet it is unclear which environmental conditions will enhance growth and which will hin-

der it. In this regard a clearer distinction between situations that lead to unconditional versus conditional positive regard would help clarify the role of the environment in motivation.

A third criticism of Rogers's approach is that it implies a "me first" psychology. Rogers said little about how one's feelings of responsibility toward others may lead to growth. In light of Maslow's views on self-actualization (which will be discussed shortly), this seems a major omission.

Fourth, Rogers's approach does not emphasize to any great extent the goals toward which an individual may be striving. While he has emphasized the striving, he has largely ignored the end products of that striving as important determinants of behavior. As we saw in the work of Klinger (Chapter Seven), the goals toward which one strives can be very important determiners of behavior.

In summary, Rogers's theory is weak empirically. He has not specified the components of his theory in such a manner that it can be easily tested. One might also question the generality of conditional positive regard. We should probably make a distinction between situations in which a parent disapproves of a specific behavior in a child and situations in which the parent "rejects" the child. Disapproval of specific behaviors without rejection of the individual would not necessarily lead to stunting of the growth process. The dividing line between disapproval of specific behaviors and rejection is, however, difficult to determine, particularly from the child's point of view.

ABRAHAM MASLOW AND SELF-ACTUALIZATION

Abraham Maslow also developed a motivational theory that emphasizes the striving to reach one's full potential as basic to human motivation but also includes additional motives besides self-actualization.

Maslow (1943, 1959, 1965, 1971, 1973a, 1973b, 1976) argued that any comprehensive theory of human motivation must take into account the individual as a whole. One cannot hope to understand the complexities of the human condition by reducing behavior to specific responses in specific situations. The wholeness of behavior can also serve several motive states at once. Thus, for example, sexual behavior may serve physiological as well as psychological needs of belongingness and esteem.

Maslow argued that one must seek to understand the **ultimate goals** of behavior rather than the superficial or apparent goals, because the apparent goal for any observed behavior may be quite different from the ultimate goal. This implies, in a fashion similar to Freudian theory, that motivations for much of our behavior may occur at an unconscious level. Unlike Freud, however, Maslow saw the

unconscious in much more positive terms. Like Rogers, Maslow also regarded the striving for perfection or **self-actualization** as the ultimate purpose of behavior.

Maslow argued that human motivation can best be studied by observing human rather than animal behavior. His observations led him to the conclusion that human needs can be understood in terms of a **hierarchy of needs**. Needs lower on the hierarchy are **prepotent** (i.e., stronger) and must be satisfied before needs higher on the hierarchy will be triggered. Maslow did not, however, regard the hierarchy as totally rigid: one can partially satisfy lower needs, thus allowing higher needs to become partially active. Maslow regarded the satisfaction of needs on the hierarchy in a probabilistic manner. If a lower need is being satisfied most of the time (e.g., 85%), that need will have little influence on behavior, while other, higher needs that are less satisfied will have a larger influence on behavior. Figure 12.1 depicts Maslow's hierarchy.

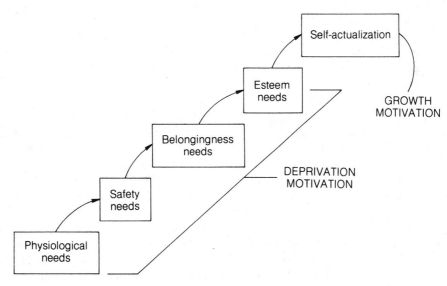

Figure 12.1   Maslow's hierachy of needs.

Hierarchy of Needs

Physiological Needs The first level of the hierarchy consists of physiological needs. If needs such as hunger or thirst are not adequately being met, the needs above them on the hierarchy are pushed into the background in terms of controlling behavior. The individual is in an emergency situation and his or her whole being is dominated by the need. For example, someone in a state of semistarvation will constantly think, dream, and talk about food.

Maslow felt that physiological needs are adequately met for most people in our society. When these needs are met, the next need on the hierarchy emerges as a dominant force in controlling and directing behavior.

Safety Needs These needs represent a need for safety or security in our environment. Like the physiological needs, safety needs are primarily triggered in emergency situations. Higher needs become unimportant when one's life is endangered, and our behavior reflects our attempts to remain secure. An example of this recently occurred when the remnants of a hurricane caused extensive flooding in my neighborhood. Some of my neighbors sustained thousands of dollars of damage to their homes; yet, at the time of the flood, their material loss was unimportant to them because escaping the flood was all that mattered.

Safety needs dominate our behavior primarily in times of emergency. Maslow, however, felt that working of the safety needs can also be seen in people's preference for familiar surroundings, secure jobs, savings accounts, and insurance. Safety needs are most evident in young children, as shown when an infant cries if it is dropped suddenly, is startled by a loud sound, or a stranger enters the room.

Maslow believed that the safety needs of most adults in our society are adequately met.

These needs do not, therefore, normally dominate behavior. Some types of neurosis, however, can be understood, according to Maslow, as the nonsatisfaction of these needs. In this nonsatisfied state one reacts as if one were continually in a threatening situation. Maslow proposed that obsessive-compulsive neuroses exemplify behavior generated by nonsatisfaction of the safety needs.

Love or Belongingness Needs When safety needs have been adequately met, they become unimportant in the direction of behavior, and the love or belongingness needs emerge. These needs involve a hunger for affectionate relationships with others, a need to feel part of a group, or a feeling that one "belongs." The love needs are not equivalent to sexual needs (which are physiological), though sexual intimacy can serve to satisfy one's need to belong. The love needs require both the receiving and giving of love—love from another and someone to love.

One may gain a sense of belonging in a number of ways. Marriage, a job, or admission to a select group such as a fraternity, sorority, or civic group can serve this need. According to Maslow, thwarting of the love needs leads to behavioral maladjustment and pathology and is the most common basis for behavioral problems in our society.

Esteem Needs If the love needs have been adequately met, they too slip into the background in relation to guiding behavior, and the esteem needs become dominant. These are needs for a positive, high evaluation of oneself. This evaluation can be broken down into two subcategories—a **need for self-esteem** and a **need for esteem from others**.

The need for self-esteem motivates the individual to strive for achievement, strength, confidence, independence, and freedom. The need for self-esteem seems to have at its core the desire to feel worthwhile and appears highly similar to Rogers's concept of positive regard. The related need of esteem from others involves a desire for reputation, status, recognition, appreciation by others of one's abilities, and a feeling of importance.

When the esteem needs are satisfied, one has feelings of self-confidence and self-worth and sees oneself as having a purpose in the world. When these needs are frustrated, maladjustment can occur, typified by feelings of inferiority, weakness, and helplessness. Lack of esteem leads the individual to feel inconsequential and to have little self-worth. One suspects that Maslow would regard depression as triggered by inadequate satisfaction of the esteem needs.

Deprivation Motivation The first four steps on Maslow's hierarchy constitute the needs that must be satisfied before one reaches the final level, the level of self-actualization. Maslow considered these needs to result from deficiencies in the person's life; that is, behaviors related to the first four categories are motivated by a deprivation of those things necessary for full development. Behaviors generated in attempts to fill these needs are therefore said to be activated by deprivation motivation (*D*-motivation).

Maslow pointed out that although the order of these four steps is correct for most people, there are exceptions. The most common exception is that for some people, esteem needs precede the love needs. For these people it is first necessary to feel worthwhile before they can satisfy the love needs.

Maslow also believed that for some individuals chronically deprived at the physiological level, the higher needs might never emerge. For these people it is sufficient simply to get enough to eat. On the other hand, Maslow also believed that people who have always had their basic needs satisfied will be less influenced by these needs later if the needs are suddenly no longer being met. This might

explain the behavior of martyrs who suffer deprivation because of lofty ideals. Maslow suggested that martyrs may be able to withstand deprivation better because their needs had usually been well met early in life, thus insulating them against these needs later. In this regard he felt that the first four years of life are particularly important in building resistance to later deprivation.

As mentioned earlier, each level of the hierarchy does not have to be perfectly satisfied. As lower needs are partially met, higher needs partially emerge. As the lower needs become more and more satisfied, the higher needs become more and more prominent in the control of behavior. Finally, Maslow suggested that most people are unaware of the need hierarchy; their needs are mostly unconscious.

Self-Actualization When one has satisfied the first four levels of need, the final level of development, which Maslow termed **self-actualization**, can be reached. At the self-actualization level, the person's behavior is motivated by different conditions than at the lower levels.

The self-actualized individual has satisfied all the deprivation needs of the first four levels of the hierarchy. The behavior of the self-actualized person is, as a result, motivated by a new set of needs, which Maslow termed the **being needs** (*B*-motivation, or metamotivation). These *B*-motives are values such as truth, honesty, beauty, and goodness, and they provide meaning to the life of the self-actualized individual.

The picture Maslow gives us of the self-actualized person is a very positive one. The self-actualized individual is no longer motivated by deficiencies but is motivated to grow and become all that he or she is capable of becoming. Self-actualization constantly stimulates people to test their abilities and expand their horizons.

Maslow suggested that the process of growth leading to self-actualization takes considerable time and that most self-actualizing persons are 60 or more years old. Maslow also believed that few people in our society reach self-actualization, estimating that fewer than 1% of the population could be considered self-actualized (Goble, 1970).

Characteristics of the Self-Actualized Person
Maslow spent considerable effort in attempting to define the major characteristics of the self-actualized individual (Lowry, 1973). He based his conclusions on his informal study of personal acquaintances, friends, and public and historic figures (e.g., Lincoln, Jefferson). The subjects of his study were considered to be possible candidates if neurosis, psychosis, or psychopathic personality traits were absent and positive evidence of self-actualization (roughly defined as the full use of one's talents) was present. Although Maslow was quite aware of the limitations and subjective nature of the methods he used, he believed that the information he obtained was of such value that it should be made public despite these limitations. The major characteristics he identified are listed below.

1. More efficient perception of reality and more comfortable with it

2. Acceptance of self, others, and nature

3. Spontaneous

4. Problem centering

5. Detached (need for privacy)

6. Independent of culture and environment

7. Freshness of appreciation

8. Mystic experience or oceanic feeling

9. Sympathy for humankind

10. Close interpersonal relations

11. Democratic character structure

12. Means and ends

13. Philosophical, unhostile, sense of humor

14. Creative

We will discuss *problem centering, freshness of appreciation, mystic experience*, and *means and ends* to help clarify Maslow's concept of the self-actualized person.

Problem Centering. The self-actualized individuals whom Maslow studied generally talked about important problems that they were concerned about solving. These problems were outside of themselves and represented something similar to a mission in life that they felt compelled to complete. Often the missions they described were not things they wanted to do but were things they felt obligated to do. Also, these tasks were not ego centered but usually related to some problem associated with the good of humankind. For example, a self-actualized person might try to find a cure for cancer and spend long hours in the laboratory, even though he or she preferred to do something else.

One aspect of this problem centering was also shown by the fact that self-actualized persons generally defined themselves in relation to what they did. Their work became a part of their identity; as a result their jobs were often independent of the external rewards they received. For example, a self-actualized person might choose to teach fourth-grade children rather than take a high-paying job simply because teaching was a part of that person's feeling of mission and identity.

Continued Freshness of Appreciation. Self-actualized persons had the ability to experience events intensely. They loved the basic experiences of life and did not grow tired of their beauty. For example, they saw the beauty of a dandelion on a fresh spring day (the rest of us just wish it would grow in our neighbor's lawn). This freshness of appreciation even extended to the work situation so that they could find joy and beauty in simply working. Their discovery of beauty in simple things was often childlike in its fascination with the world. Maslow noted, however, that these intense feelings experienced by self-actualized persons were occasional, not continuous in occurrence.

Mystic Experience or Oceanic Feeling. The self-actualized individual occasionally had experiences best described as mystic or profound in nature, termed **peak experiences**. Maslow believed that most people had peak experiences but that self-actualizers had them more often.

Peak experiences seem to involve a momentary loss of self or transcendence of self so that during the experience, one simply feels without relating the feelings back to one's self-concept. During a peak experience the person had feelings of limitless horizons opening up to view, of being simultaneously powerful and weak, of a loss of time and space, and of great ecstasy. The experience also usually led to the conviction that something important had happened that would have great effects on the future behavior of the individual. The following example, taken from Chiang and Maslow (1977), illustrates a peak experience.

Two years ago, while I was attempting to do some math problems in elementary calculus that I had for homework one night, I was following the long, involved procedure for finding the derivative of functions exactly the way my teacher had told me to do. I suddenly thought I saw a quick way of finding the answer. I tried my new method, which only required inspection rather than calculation, got an answer for the next few problems, then did them again the old way. I got the same answers, showing that my perceived relationships between function and derivative were indeed correct.

A day or so after this, going further in the math book, I saw an explanation of the way that I had

discovered for myself. Finding out that mathematicians had known this method before I stumbled upon it in no way marred my pleasure. Upon finding out that my method was correct, I became very excited. I felt very proud of myself, particularly because I had been having some trouble with math during the week or so before this experience.

I ran around the house until I found my parents and showed them my findings, then I sat down by myself and looked over my work again. I suppose I could say that I felt creative. I certainly felt as if I "belonged." I now saw myself as having a right to be in the advanced math class that I was in. I did not feel guilty any longer—there were no longer any nagging fears of inadequacy.

This was not just true of my mathematical ability—no sir. I felt confident and sure of myself with respect to all of my studies. I turned to working on the homework that I had in my other subjects, and the elation from the math carried over into everything I did. It helped me with my work, but occasionally I found myself thinking about what I had done and I would grin broadly, forgetting all about the work I was then attempting to finish. I began feeling "friendly" to the study of mathematics instead of, as before, hostile to it. I also saw it as having new importance and significance. It no longer seemed to me like a boring and unnecessary discipline. (From Chiang & Maslow, 1977, pp. 259–261. Reprinted by permission.)

Maslow noted that peak experiences appear to be triggered by certain situations. For example, his subjects indicated that peak experiences could sometimes be triggered by sexual orgasm or even by classical music. Maslow found that peak experiences for parents were sometimes associated with observing the birth of their child. Though peak experiences may be more common as a result of certain situations, they can apparently occur in almost any situation.

Means and Ends. Self-actualized individuals were interested in the goals toward which they were working, but in many instances the way in which the goals were pursued was itself a goal. They took satisfaction in both the doing and the product of that doing.

Maslow found that most of the self-actualized individuals he studied could be described as religious, though not in the sense of formal religion. Only one described himself as an atheist. To the self-actualized person, means and ends were importantly related to personal ethics and religious convictions.

The self-actualized person, then, is a person apart. He or she has mastered the deficiency needs and is motivated by what Maslow called **growth motivation**. These persons seek to solve problems outside themselves and reach for truth, beauty, justice, and other high values.

One should not, however, consider the self-actualized as perfect. Maslow pointed out that self-actualized individuals also have many of the lesser failings common to us all. They can be silly, wasteful, and thoughtless. They can also be boring, stubborn, and irritating. Self-actualized people often show superficial vanity concerning their own products and can occasionally exhibit ruthlessness. Because of their extreme abilities to concentrate, they sometimes appear absent-minded and can be impolite when thinking about a problem. They also feel guilt, anxiety, sadness, and conflict, but these arise from their realization that they are not all that they could be rather than from neurosis.

In his later writing Maslow (1971) came to the conclusion that there are actually two types of self-actualizing people, differentiated in regard to peak experiences. Some self-actualized persons rarely have peak experiences, while others experience peaks much more often. Those self-actualized individuals who experience peaks were called **transcenders** or **peakers**, and those who do not were called **nontranscenders** or **nonpeakers**. Both peakers and nonpeakers share all the characteristics of self-actualization with the exception of the frequency of peak experiences.

Maslow's description of the two types of actualizers suggests that self-actualization itself may contain two levels. The transcendent self-actualizers seem, if possible, more self-actualized than the nontranscendent. For example, peak experiences for the transcenders become the most important aspect of their lives. They are more consciously motivated by the B-values, and they think and talk in language concerned with honesty, truth, beauty, perfection, and so on. Transcenders see more fully the sacredness of all things and are more likely to be profoundly religious. They are also more wholistic in their approach to the world than nontranscenders and are more likely to be held in awe by others. Interestingly, Maslow believed that transcenders may be *less* happy than nontranscenders. He suggested that this is because of their ability to see the stupidity of people more clearly and to experience a kind of cosmic sadness for the failings of others.

Failure to Self-Actualize   If self-actualization is the ultimate level of being toward which we all strive, then why do most people fall short of this goal? Maslow believed that the tendency toward growth is weaker than the deficiency motives and can easily be stunted by poor environment or poor education. Maslow also believed that Western culture, with its emphasis on the negative nature of human motivation, has worked against our trusting of our inner nature. Our culture has emphasized that inner nature is bad (e.g., Freudian theory) and has been concerned with mechanisms of control. This has led many people to reject their inner experiences altogether.

Third, Maslow noted that growth requires the taking of chances, a stepping away from the secure and comfortable. It is not easy to take that step, which one must do again and again to grow, and many people choose security over growth. Maslow also believed that people are afraid of their own abilities. To become all that one is capable of becoming is frightening to many, and so people reject opportunities for growth. Maslow dubbed this phenomenon the "Jonah complex" after the Old Testament story of Jonah, who tried to run away from the purpose that God had planned for him.

Most people fall short of self-actualization for one or all of these reasons. Nevertheless, Maslow believed that to understand the potentialities of human behavior, one must study the truly exceptional individual rather than the average. Only in the self-actualized person can one see the full range of human motivation.

Criticisms of Self-Actualization Maslow's theory has not been free of criticism (Schultz, 1977; Geller, 1982). Perhaps the most common and damaging criticism has concerned the individuals Maslow studied who were self-actualized. Maslow began his study of self-actualization in an attempt to understand two friends whom he greatly admired. In talking with them he discovered that they shared many common attributes. This led him to study self-actualization more fully by examining friends, acquaintances, and public and historical figures. Many of the living individuals he studied preferred to remain anonymous, so other psychologists could not check the accuracy of Maslow's perceptions of these people. Also, the historical figures were dead, requiring reliance on written accounts, which are often self-serving. The major problem, then, is one of replicability. We are asked to take Maslow's word that the people he studied had the characteristics he described.

Second, Maslow's theory has sometimes been criticized as elitist. People confined by poor education, dead-end jobs, or societal expectations are unlikely to become self-actualized persons. Thus the elite seem to have a distinct advantage in obtaining self-actualization, so the theory may not describe people in general.

That so many people fail to become self-actualized has also suggested to some researchers that a motivation toward growth may not be as general as Maslow proposed. Perhaps the need to become all that one can become is idiosyncratic to some persons rather than present in all of us.

Finally, Maslow's theory has been criticized because of its vagueness in language and concepts and its general lack of evidence (Cofer & Appley, 1964).

Research on Self-Actualization Several research efforts have been completed since Cofer and Appley's criticisms, and to this research we now briefly turn.

Everett Shostrom (1964, 1966) developed an inventory designed to discriminate between self-actualized and non-self-actualized individuals. The inventory consisted of 150 two-choice value and behavior judgments; items were scored on two major scales plus ten subscales. Shostrom (1964) has shown that his inventory discriminates between people judged as self-actualized, normal, and non-self-actualized. His results indicate that self-actualized individuals appear to be less restricted by social pressures or conformity. The self-actualized person also appears to live in the present but can meaningfully tie past or future events to the present. One aspect of this **time competence**, as Shostrom terms it, is that the self-actualized individual's aspirations are tied to the goals toward which he or she is striving in the present. Shostrom's data also indicate that the self-actualized individual is more self-supportive than others. The self-actualized person is both inner-directed (in being free to behave in ways appropriate to his or her own standards) and other-directed (to the extent that he or she is sensitive to the feelings of others). Finally, the self-actualized person appears to have transcended the normal dichotomies that most people make. For example, the self-actualized make no distinction between work and play or between the needs of self and of others. Shostrom terms this **synergy**.

Shostrom's inventory has also been used by others to study various aspects of self-actualization. For example, Hjelle and Smith (1975) used it to divide females into self-actualized and non-self-actualized groups. These two groups were then given an inventory developed by Schaefer (1965a, 1965b) that assessed the memories that adults have of their parents. The self-actualized individuals, when compared to the non-self-actualized, reported significantly more memories of parental acceptance, independence, and low control. In contrast, the non-self-actualized reported significantly greater amounts of parental rejection, psychological control, and firmness.

Hjelle and Smith's data are interesting because they suggest that self-actualization, at least as measured by Shostrom's inventory, is correlated with perceived parental attitudes. Although the data are only preliminary, they do suggest that parent-child interactions may be an important component in the development of self-actualization. Proof of this would provide support for Maslow's contention that early experiences are important for the proper development of self-actualization.

Let us also examine a study by Rizzo and Vinacke (1975) as representative of research on self-actualization. This study also used Shostrom's scale to divide subjects into actualized and nonactualized groups. The inventory was given to three age groups: 18–25, 35–55, and 70–80. Based on Maslow's belief that self-actualization is a long-term process, one might expect to find more self-actualized persons in the older age groups. The subjects of the experiment were asked to think back over their lives and rank events that had happened to them in order of importance; they were further asked to describe what meaning these events had for them.

The results of this study were provocative on several counts. First, no sex differences were found on any of the 12 scales of Shostrom's inventory, indicating that men and women were very similar in regard to the measures of self-actualization employed on the scale. Age differences, however, were quite pronounced. College students (18–25) and mature adults (35–55) scored quite similarly in regard to self-actualization, but both groups were considerably *higher* than the aged group (70–80). Rizzo and Vinacke suggested that Shostrom's inventory may actually reflect attitudes or roles of the young adult rather than self-actualization per se. In support of their suggestion, they found that the scales appearing to fit Maslow's theory most closely did not show significant age differences. One must be cautious, however, in drawing too much from the data of the older group (70–80), because this group contained only 15 subjects, who were all residents of old-age homes and infirmaries. The lack of evidence for self-actualization in the aged group is not so surprising as it might seem. Clearly institutions for the aged (e.g., nursing homes) can have large effects on an individual's self-concept, esteem, love needs, and so on. The aged, in fact, may often find themselves placed into situations where their deprivation needs are no longer being adequately met. A sample of aged individuals living independently would of course provide some evidence for the generality of Rizzo and Vinacke's finding for their aged group.

Several interesting results were also obtained concerning the important experiences and their meaning in people's lives. Unhappy events were reported with twice the frequency of happy events. Events reported included deaths of loved ones, illnesses, love affairs, marriage, and personal accomplishments. College-age subjects typically reported events involving social or family concerns, while the adult groups most often reported events occurring during their adult years.

Childhood events for all groups were rarely mentioned.

Of particular interest was the finding that subjects who judged the meaning of an event as "happy," "positive," or "better" scored higher on the self-actualization inventory regardless of age. Because most of the events reported were not "happy" events, the data suggest that the ability to see the positive side of experiences, even initially negative ones, may be an important component of actualization. Rizzo and Vinacke noted that their data support Frankl's notion that actualization is associated with an ability to perceive the positive and meaningful aspects of events in our lives (Frankl, 1959).

Maslow's theory continues to stimulate research and discussion (Frick, 1982, 1983; Geller, 1982; Goebel & Brown, 1981; Haymes & Green, 1982; Mathes & Zevon, 1982; Privette, 1983). Several studies have examined the characteristics of peak experiences (see, e.g., Mathes & Zevon, 1982; Privette, 1983). Privette, for example, compared the construct of peak experience with the constructs of **peak performance** and **flow**. Peak performance has been defined as an episode of superior functioning, while flow has been defined as an intrinsically enjoyable experience. Peak experiences are largely passive; that is, one does not create a peak experience but rather senses them when they occur. Peak experiences would therefore appear to be largely perceptual, requiring no behavior of the individual and often leading to a reorganization of one's thoughts. Peak performance, however, *is* active, involving interaction with another person or with the environment. Flow, like peak performance, is active, but like peak experience, it is intrinsically enjoyable and leads to a fusion with the experience and subsequent loss of self.

In surveying the literature on these three concepts, Privette found many similarities and some differences among them. One quality common to all three is **absorption**. In peak experience, peak performance, and flow, an individual intensely focuses attention to the exclusion of other perceptual events. Further, in all three situations the individual spontaneously and effortlessly experiences events as they occur without trying to influence them in any way.

Privette has noted, however, that each concept also describes situations that have unique properties. Peak experiences, for example, usually have a mystical or transpersonal aspect that does not typically occur in either peak performance or flow. Indeed, in peak performance there is a strong awareness of oneself rather than a loss. "Flow is fun" (Privette, 1983, p. 1364)—people engage in activities that create a sense of flow because they are enjoyable. Additionally, people make some attempt to engage in activities that create flow, whereas peak experiences and peak performances are unplanned. Privette's topology is interesting and helps us sort out both the similarities and differences among these three constructs. Additional studies of peak experience, peak performance, and flow would be useful in further developing the ideas initially proposed by Maslow.

Research continues to be conducted on Maslow's theory. Although the evidence for the constructs proposed by Maslow is mixed, the idea that one source of behavior motivation is the need to expand one's potentialities and become all that one is capable of becoming has proven durable. In the next section we will examine two concepts related to actualization, the twin concepts of competence and personal causation.

COMPETENCE AND PERSONAL CAUSATION

Rogers's concept of full functioning and Maslow's construct of self-actualization both contain the idea that actualized individuals are free to control what happens to them. The concept of control is central to both theories and coincides with ideas generated by other theorists of human motivation. Control aspects of human motivation have been termed **competence** by some (White, 1959) and **personal causation** by others (deCharms, 1968). These theories imply that the basis for much of human behavior is **the need to be effective in controlling one's environment**.

Competence

Robert White (1959) has argued persuasively for the concept of **competence motivation**. As he defined it, competence is the capacity to interact effectively with one's environment. In a review of the theories popular in 1959, he showed how several lines of evidence from animal behavior, psychoanalysis, and related areas of psychology all pointed toward a motive that activated a striving for competence. White noted that this **effectance motivation**, as he termed it, was most clearly seen in the behavior of young children. The example at the beginning of this chapter concerning the child repeatedly climbing onto a chair can be viewed as the child's striving to gain control over her environment. In White's view the play behavior of children is serious business; it is triggered by the child's attempt to master the environment effectively.

White suggested that effectance motivation is normally seen when other homeostatic motives are at low levels. When, for example, children are neither thirsty nor cold, they will play in order to increase control over their world.

In the child effectance motivation is rather global, and the child's behavior is directed toward whatever aspect of the environment catches the attention. So, for example, the child may play with the buttons on the stereo, pushing them in and out, but a few moments later climb the stairs to turn the light switch off and on. These repeated behaviors can be quite exasperating to parents who are trying to keep the child away from the stereo, but they take on new perspective if seen as motivated by the need to control one's environment. In the adult competence behavior can become quite differentiated, so that one might even consider achievement behavior (as noted in previous chapters) as energized by effectance motivation, the control aspect in this case being to excel intellectually.

The goal of effectance motivation, according to White, is a feeling of efficacy (i.e., effectiveness), which satisfies much as physical goals satisfy physical needs. White also argued that competence behavior is adaptive. While the goal of effectance motivation is simply to have an effect on the environment and in turn discover how the environment affects us, the relationships we learn can serve us usefully later. For example, the child learning to climb a chair does so simply to be able to do it, yet he or she may use the information later to get a piece of fruit from a bowl. Clearly learning occurs during episodes of effectance motivation, and we can put this learning to good use at a later time.

Personal Causation

The concept of control suggested by White has been further extended by deCharms (1968). DeCharms argued that the primary motive in humans is to "be effective in producing changes in [their] environment" (p. 269). In other words, we strive for **personal causation** (i.e., to be casual agents in our environment).

Personal causation is not strictly a motive but a guiding principle upon which all other motives are built. As deCharms noted, we typically describe motivation in relation to the goals toward which a behavior leads: when hungry, we seek food; when thirsty, we seek water; and so on. Though we speak of the hunger motive, personal causation is the force requiring that we be able to respond in ways that will get us food. Thus deCharms saw personal causation as the underlying principle of all motivated behaviors. He also proposed that human behavior cannot be explained by referring to the goals we strive for or, for that matter, to the satisfaction experienced when a goal is reached. To comprehend human behavior fully, we must understand the individual's need to be an **origin of effects**.

Origins and Pawns DeCharms argued that people may be categorized as "origins" or "pawns." An origin believes that one's own behavior is controlled by one's own choices. A pawn, on the other hand, perceives one's behavior as being controlled by external forces over which one has no control. As you might guess, origins have strong feelings of personal causation, and much of their behavior is directed by these feelings of control. Pawns feel powerless, and their behavior is related to their perception of lack of control.

DeCharms's analysis is very similar to Rotter's locus-of-control concept, which we examined in Chapter Nine as an example of expectancy-value theory. Rotter's ideas concerning external and internal views of reward also fit nicely with the concept of competence developed by White. Though we will not repeat the coverage of Rotter's theory described earlier, the interested student may wish to reread that part of Chapter Nine describing Rotter's approach in light of the present discussion on competence and causation.

Intrinsic and Extrinsic Motivation Hunt (1965) was one of the first theorists to suggest that the assumption that all behaviors are controlled by external sources of reinforcement is inadequate (see also Berlyne, 1960). Hunt pointed out that when major needs are absent, organisms are still motivated. Under conditions of low need organisms still display exploratory behavior, curiosity, and manipulatory behaviors. These behaviors, according to Hunt, are intrinsically motivated. From Hunt's perspective, motivation exists whenever an incongruity occurs between past experience and new information. This incongruity triggers behaviors such as manipulation or exploration to resolve the incongruity. Small amounts of incongruity, such as in novel situations, were thought to be attractive, while large incongruities would lead to withdrawal from the situation. Thus Hunt suggested that intrinsic motivation results from relationships inherent in the information processing of the organism and that an optimal level of incongruity exists that is maximally attractive.

The concept of intrinsic motivation suggests that we may often be motivated in a task, not because of some external reward associated with the task but because the behavior itself is rewarding. Staw (1976) has in fact defined intrinsic motivation as the value or pleasure associated with an activity as opposed to the goal toward which the activity is directed. Extrinsic motivation, by contrast, emphasizes the external goals toward which the activity is directed.

Insufficient Justification and Overly Sufficient Justification What are the combined effects of intrinsic and extrinsic motivation on behavior? Logically we might expect that the addition of an extrinsic reward to a behavior that is already intrinsically rewarding would increase one's overall motivation for the task; that is, we might expect intrinsic and extrinsic motivation to summate. A number of studies, however, suggest that intrinsic and extrinsic motives act antagonistically under some conditions.

One example of such research involves experiments concerned with determining to what motivation one may attribute one's behavior when justification for the behavior is low. Remember Festinger and Carlsmith's (1959) experiment? Suppose that an individual is persuaded by an experimenter to tell a waiting subject that the experiment he or she is about to participate in is really interesting—when it is actually terribly boring. One person given $20 for this deception can justify his or her behavior extrinsically as a result of the external reward for such behavior. Another individual offered only $1 for the deception is less likely to attribute his or her behavior to the external reward. Under these conditions the person may reevaluate the intrinsic value of the experiment upward in order to justify saying that the experiment is interesting. In other words, the presence of extrinsic motivation may modify the amount of intrinsic motivation for a task in a downward direction, while the absence of extrinsic motivation may increase intrinsic motivation. Alteration in intrinsic motivation as a function of changes in extrinsic motivation is thus an alternative explanation for some types of cognitive dissonance phenomena. Intrinsic-extrinsic motivation explanations can also be regarded as attributional explanations of behavior.

Insufficient justification experiments suggest that the relationship between intrinsic and extrinsic motivation is sometimes negative. As extrinsic motivation increases, intrinsic motivation decreases, and vice versa. The hypothesis of a negative relationship between intrinsic and extrinsic motivation is further strengthened by research involving what has been termed *overly sufficient justification*. These experiments have usually involved adding an external reward to an already intrinsically motivating task.

Suppose that a young child sits and begins to color neatly in a coloring book. As the child's proud parent, you wish to reward this creative behavior, so you give the child 50¢ for his or her efforts. The presumed negative relationship between intrinsic and extrinsic motivation implies that this may be the wrong

thing to do if you want the child's creative behavior to continue. By giving the child an external justification for drawing (i.e., 50¢), you may have decreased the intrinsic motivation for the task.

Lepper, Greene, and Nisbett (1973) tested the negative relationship assumption in nursery school children. The children were allowed to draw with colored marking pens. One group of children was led to believe that it would receive a "good player award" as a result of its activity (i.e., the extrinsic motivation condition), while a second group was told about the award only after it had completed the activity. A third group performed the task without any reward. The groups of children were then allowed some free play time during the week following the task, when they could either play with the pens or with other toys. During this free play time, the children had no reason to suspect that any further tangible or social rewards would occur as a result of their activity. The experimenters found that those children originally given an external reward spent significantly less time playing with the pens during the free play period than those not rewarded. Receiving an unexpected reward (i.e., the second group) apparently does not decrease intrinsic motivation, because the researchers found that the expected reward group also played less with the pens than the unexpected reward group. This may suggest that the unexpected reward group had already attributed its behavior to intrinsic sources and was thus less influenced by the unexpected "good player award." Deci (1971) also found that adding an extrinsic reward to an already intrinsically interesting task decreases motivation for the task.

Staw, Calder, and Hess (1975) have carried the analysis of intrinsic motivation a step further by showing that one additional factor important to changes in intrinsic motivation as a result of extrinsic motivation is the *situation*. If the situation is one in which payment for a behavior is normal or expected, extrinsic reward does not seem to affect intrinsic motivation. But if the situation is one in which a reward would not normally be expected, its arrival leads to decreases in intrinsic motivation.

Why does extrinsic motivation seem to reduce intrinsic motivation in some situations? Staw suggested that intrinsic motivational factors are more ambiguous (i.e., less clear) to us than extrinsic factors. When we analyze our own behavior, we look for obvious extrinsic reasons for it. If we don't find extrinsic explanations, we will conclude that our behavior resulted from intrinsic factors. But if an extrinsic reward is added to a behavior that is already intrinsically motivated, we now have an obvious external explanation for our behavior, and intrinsic motivation for the task decreases.

The explanation offered above is the basic idea in Lepper, Greene, and Nisbett's (1973) **self-perception theory** of the overjustification effect. Their explanation is attributional (see Chapter Eleven for attributional explanations of motivation); that is, individuals viewing their own behavior discount intrinsic reasons for it if external factors such as reward are present. Because intrinsically motivated behaviors are thought to be inherently interesting, attributing our own behavior to external causes reduces the motivation to behave that way again, because we assume our behavior to result from the external reward rather than from internal interest.

Deci (1975) offered a second major explanation of the overjustification effect in his **cognitive evaluation theory**. We will look briefly at Deci's concepts regarding intrinsic motivation before we examine cognitive evaluation theory as an explanation of the overjustification effect.

Deci's Theory   Edward L. Deci (1975; Deci & Porac, 1978) has proposed a model of intrinsic motivation that is closely related to the concept of competence suggested by White (1959) and the concept of personal causation suggested by deCharms (1968).

Deci's theory emphasizes the dual themes of competence and control. He suggested that we need not only to control our environment but also to feel competent in our control. According to Deci, intrinsic motivation generates behaviors that cause a person to feel competent and self-determining. These behaviors are of two kinds. First, if stimulation is low, intrinsic motivation will generate behavior to **increase stimulation**. Second, intrinsic motivation will lead to behavior involved with **conquering challenges**. Deci argued that only by overcoming challenging situations can we feel competent.

Deci's model is cognitive because it emphasizes that we make choices from information available to us either from our environment or from memory. We base decisions not only on objective information but also on subjective states such as attitudes and feelings. Working with the cognitive representations of these states, we make choices concerning which behaviors will occur. Our choices of behaviors depend upon the goals toward which those behaviors lead. The goals themselves are cognitive expectations (i.e., beliefs that behavior A will lead to goal B).

In Deci's model motivation is triggered by cognitive representations of some future state. Thus one's expectation of receiving a college degree will motivate behaviors (e.g., studying) that will lead to the desired goal. According to Deci, the energy that drives our behavior is our awareness that goals can be obtained, and this awareness of potential satisfaction then activates behaviors designed to lead to the goal. Once a goal is obtained, reward occurs.

Rewards may be of three types: extrinsic, intrinsic, or affective. **Extrinsic reward** consists of some external object or situation that satisfies some expectation. Thus, getting a high-paying job as a result of four years of college could be an extrinsic reward. **Intrinsic reward** is different, involving the feeling of competence one obtains after successfully completing a task. Reaching the goal leads to the satisfaction of intrinsic motivation because one feels self-confident and able to control one's life. **Affective reward** involves the positive emotional experience that one gains when a goal is reached. For some behaviors, the affective experience may be the reward (e.g., sexual orgasm), while in other behaviors the affective reward may be only a small part of the situation (e.g., the warm glow you feel when you do well on a test). Theoretically Deci makes a distinction between intrinsic reward (i.e., feelings of competence) and affective reward (i.e., positive emotion), though practically these appear to be closely tied. Presumably, however, one could feel competent at some task without feeling good about it.

Research on the relationship of intrinsic and extrinsic reward has shown that extrinsic rewards do not always reduce intrinsic motivation. For example, in the Lepper, Greene, and Nisbett (1973) study, unexpected extrinsic reward did not influence motivation. External reward may also have a reduced effect on intrinsic motivation when it provides information concerning one's competence on some task (Boggiano & Ruble, 1979).

Cognitive evaluation theory proposes that external rewards will have differing effects on intrinsic motivation depending upon whether the reward has a *controlling* or an *informational* influence on the behavior. According to Deci, a reward used to control behavior effectively undermines intrinsic motivation because it reduces our belief in self-determination; that is, we feel controlled by the external reward. External reward used informationally, however, provides feedback about our competence. Such rewards tell us that we are doing a good job and lead to feelings of increased competence; consequently, such rewards usu-

ally increase intrinsic motivation. Research by Deci and others provides support for this interpretation (Anderson, Manoogian, & Reznick, 1976; Deci, 1971, 1972; Deci, Cascio, & Krusell, 1975; Deci, Nezlek, & Sheinman, 1981; Kruglanski, Freedman, & Zeevi, 1971; Zuckerman et al., 1978).

The overjustification effect continues to interest researchers. Extrinsic rewards have been shown to undermine intrinsic moral motivation (Kunda & Schwartz, 1983), to reduce the Zeigarnik effect (McGraw & Fiala, 1982), and to have differing effects when symbolic versus verbal rewards are used (Shanab et al., 1981; Vallerand, 1983). Additionally, developmental factors appear to influence the overjustification effect (Morgan, 1981); prior experiences with external rewards in a school setting alter the effect in children (Pallak et al., 1982); locus of control influences it (Earn, 1982); and even the characteristics of the person giving the reward can alter the intrinsic motivation of the person rewarded (Deci, Nezlek, & Sheinman, 1981). It is becoming increasingly clear that the relationship between intrinsic and extrinsic rewards is complex. Lepper and Greene (1978) have provided a number of perspectives on this literature, and additional models of the overjustification effect are beginning to appear (Williams, 1980; Pretty & Seligman, 1984). Pretty and Seligman, for example, have reported evidence suggesting that emotion may serve as a mediator in overjustification situations.

Feelings of competence, self-determination, and control have figured prominently in the theories and research noted in this chapter. One final point will end this discussion. What is important in any given situation is probably the perception of control rather than actual control. Several experiments have shown that perceived control leads to behavioral changes, even when actual control is nonexistent (Glass & Singer, 1972; Perlmuter & Monty, 1977; Perlmuter & Chan, 1983; Stotland

& Blumenthal 1964; Revesman & Perlmuter, 1981).

For example, Glass and Singer (1972) have shown that subjects exposed to noise perform better on a task if they have a button they believe they can push to stop the noise. Even though the button was never pushed, the subjects in this condition performed better than a control group not given the button. Apparently the perception of having the ability to control the noise was enough to allow the subjects to be less influenced by it than their counterparts without the button.

Similarly, Stotland and Blumenthal (1964) found that subjects who believed they were in control of a situation were less anxious than subjects who believed they had no control. Perlmuter and Monty (1977) have conducted several experiments on perceived control and have argued that while the perceived absence of control can be quite destructive, perceived control acts to enhance reinforcing situations. Their position is based on a series of experiments in which subjects were allowed to choose what materials they would learn. Subjects given a choice of materials learned significantly faster than a control group given the same materials but without any choice. In some of their experiments the subjects were told that they could control the materials to be learned even though they could not actually do so. Even under these conditions, performance was better than under conditions of no perceived control. Perception of control, then, may be more crucial than actual control (see Perlmuter & Monty, 1979, for a more complete discussion of perceived control).

The concept of perceived control, as briefly outlined above, supports and is supported by the research on learned helplessness discussed in Chapters Six and Eleven. As you may recall from the data presented in those chapters, considerable evidence exists that animals and humans "give up" when they perceive that they have no control over their environment. In a sense learned helplessness and perceived control are two sides of the same coin: lack of control has a demotivating effect on behavior, while perceived control (whether actual or not) has a motivating effect. The attempt to control one's environment, then, appears to be a general characteristic of many species and an important source of motivation. In humans the need to control the events of one's life may be especially strong.

SUMMARY

In this chapter we have reviewed data and theories suggesting that one very basic motive of human behavior is the need to control one's environment. Different theorists have approached this idea in slightly different ways, but all seem to share the conviction that healthy individuals need to perceive that they can affect their environment. In many respects the data and theories on learned helplessness also support the importance of perceptions of control.

Carl Rogers proposed that an individual is constantly striving for enhancement and growth. He argued that only one motive underlies all behavior—a motive for growth. Abraham Maslow proposed a very similar approach but also noted that certain deficiency needs must first be met before we can become all that we are capable of becoming. Nevertheless, the growth of the individual is the underlying theme of Maslow's theory too. Though not stated explicitly, the theories of both Rogers and Maslow seem to imply that the fully functioning or self-actualized person is both competent and in control of his or her environment.

Robert White and Richard deCharms have separately proposed models of human behavior emphasizing a striving for competence and self-determination as basic motives of human behavior. The concept of control as a motive force is seen in studies of intrinsic and extrinsic motivation. The attribution of motivation to an external source reduces intrinsic motivation in some situations. Examples of the interaction between intrinsic and extrinsic motivation can be observed in research on insufficient and overly sufficient justification.

Edward Deci has proposed a model for human motivation that emphasizes the cognitive information processing aspects of intrinsic motivation. His model suggests that motivation is generated by an awareness of possible satisfaction. Satisfaction can come from external sources in the form of rewards, from internal sources in the form of feelings of competence, or from affective sources in the form of positive emotional experiences. Deci's model emphasizes the importance of striving for self-determination as a basic motive of behavior. Finally, it appears that one's perception of control is more important than actual control. Perception of control enhances performance and reduces anxiety, while perception of lack of control decreases performance and increases anxiety.

In humans, then, the need to be competent, self-determining, in control, fully functioning, and self-actualizing is an important motivation of behavior. Although the terminology differs from theorist to theorist, the basic commonality is that people need to believe that they have an effect on the world around them.

SUGGESTIONS FOR FURTHER READING

Lowry, R. S. (Ed.). (1973). *Dominance, self-esteem, self-actualization: Germinal papers of A. H. Maslow.* Monterey, Calif.: Brooks/Cole. This book contains a collection of papers written by Maslow on the concepts involved in his theory of self-actualization.

Perlmuter, L. C., & Monty, R. A. (Eds.). (1979). *Choice and perceived control.* Hillsdale, N.J.: Erlbaum. This text contains chapters written by researchers interested in the effects of perceived control on behavior. It is a good cross section of research in the area.

Rogers, C. R. (1961). *On becoming a person: A therapist's view of psychotherapy.* Boston: Houghton Mifflin. This book provides a good overview of Rogers's ideas concerning full functioning.

V

APPLICATIONS OF MOTIVATIONAL THEORY

Chapter Thirteen

The Emotions as Motivators

CHAPTER PREVIEW

This chapter is concerned with the following questions:

1. How has the concept of emotion been explained by psychological theorists?

2. What is the role of biological forces in the expression of emotion?

3. What is the role of cognition in emotion?

4. Are there any universal emotions?

As an avid amateur athlete, I have watched various Olympic events with great interest and have vicariously experienced some of the emotional impact that success and failure brought to the participants. I have seen athletes receive gold medals with tears rolling down their cheeks. Are they sad? Hardly. Emotional? Definitely.

This chapter is about emotion. How can we explain not only the emotionality of the successful athlete but also our own emotions? Do emotions result from internal visceral changes, as suggested by James and Lange, or

do they result from cognitive appraisal of ongoing events? Are emotions innate and of limited number, or are they learned and multitudinous? These are a few of the questions research on emotion has attempted to answer. As we shall discover, the answers to such questions are difficult to obtain, and opinions differ widely.

Originally the word *emotion* meant to move, as in migrating from one place to another; however, the term later came to mean a moving or agitation in the physical sense. This usage was later broadened to include social and political agitation. Finally, the term came to mean an agitated or aroused mental state in an individual (Young, 1975). Thus the idea of emotion seems to imply that a person is moved, that is, changed from one state to another, as in from happy to sad or pleased to angry.

Researchers interested in the concept have attempted numerous definitions of emotion, but as noted by Mandler (1984), no commonly accepted definition has been provided. As we examine the various models of emotion presented in this chapter, it will become apparent that emotion can be conceptualized in many different ways, from physiological changes to cognitive appraisals to innate, fundamental facial expressions. Each approach has something to offer, and the lack of a generally acceptable definition of emotion probably results, in part, from the fact that emotion is multifaceted.

Over the years several traditions have developed in the study of emotion. One tradition is biological. Begun by Darwin (1872), the biological approach was further developed by James, Lange, Cannon, and more recently by the ethologists (as well as by many others too numerous to mention). In the first section of this chapter we will examine emotion from this biological perspective.

A second tradition has emphasized the role of learning processes in emotion. The drivelike qualities of emotion have been noted by Spence and Taylor, and the modeling of emotional behavior has been noted by Bandura. In the second section of this chapter we will briefly review some of the ways in which learning is involved with emotion.

In the third section of the chapter we will examine cognitive approaches to emotion. Theorists in this tradition have often emphasized cognitive appraisal as important to the experience of emotion. Several cognitive models will be examined.

In the final section of this chapter we will examine the idea that a limited number of emotions are universal. The theories typically propose that a small number of innate emotions have evolved because of their adaptive value to the individual. Further, facial musculature changes are often suggested as the way in which emotions are communicated to others and, indeed, to oneself. The fundamental emotions may be blended to produce an almost unlimited range of emotional experience.

As is evident from this short introduction,

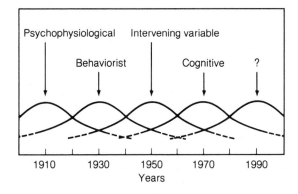

Figure 13.1 *Changing explanations of emotion during the twentieth century. (Adapted from Averill, 1983. Copyright © 1983 by the American Psychological Association. Reprinted by permission of the publisher and author.)*

research on emotion has provided no easy answers, and the disputes between theorists have sometimes been severe. In fact one explanation has tended to replace another about every 20 years (Averill, 1983). As shown in Figure 13.1, psychophysiological explanations seemed to peak around 1910; by 1930 behaviorist explanations dominated, and by 1950 emotion as an intervening variable was the preferred approach. By 1970 cognitive explanations dominated, and a question of some interest is what the next approach is likely to be. Averill has suggested that the next wave may concern social explanations, although a distinct possibility is the idea of biologically based, fundamental emotions expressed and experienced through bodily changes such as facial movements. In this chapter we will examine many of the approaches noted by Averill that have influenced our concepts about emotion. Let's start out at the beginning of modern approaches to the topic, that is, with Darwin.

EMOTION FROM A BIOLOGICAL PERSPECTIVE

Darwin

If you were to read Darwin's book *The Expression of the Emotions in Man and Animals* (1872), you would be struck by how modern much of it sounds. For example, he was aware that body movements and facial expressions (today called body language or nonverbal communication) communicate meaning between individual members of a species. He argued that much of this nonverbal communication transmits information about the organism's emotional state.

Darwin believed that both emotions and their expression are innate, though he allowed for the possibility that some types of emotional expression may be learned. Much of his analysis of emotion revolved around the manner in which emotions are expressed. He proposed three principles for understanding the expression of emotion in both humans and animals.

The Principles of Serviceable Associated Habits, Antithesis, and Direct Action of the Nervous System   In the principle of serviceable associated habits, Darwin proposed that the ways in which organisms express emotion have had survival value in the past. Thus a dog may bare its teeth when defending its master because, in the evolutionary past of canines, such behaviors increased the survival value of dogs that behaved that way. Baring the teeth should be adaptive for several reasons; for example, it can signal motivational readiness to attack, which in turn often causes the opposing animal to leave, and secondly, it prepares the dog for biting if necessary.

Darwin believed that emotional expressions were originally learned but had become innate over many generations; thus serviceable associated habits were learned behaviors

that became innate because of their usefulness. Because he did not know of the genetic work of Mendel, Darwin did not know how characteristics are passed from one generation to another, so he proposed that emotional expressions evolved from learned habits to hereditary traits over many generations. Today we know that evolution does not work that way. However, to bring Darwin's principle into line with modern knowledge of genetics, we need only note that certain genes "control" the development of particular emotional behaviors and that emotional expression (e.g., the dog baring its teeth) had survival value for organisms that possessed those genes.

In the principle of antithesis Darwin proposed that the expression of opposite emotions (e.g., anger and calm) involves opposite kinds of behavior. The "angry" cat crouches down, flattens its ears against its head, extends its claws, and opens its mouth to bite. The calm, "friendly" cat rubs against your leg with its tail and ears erect, mouth closed, and claws retracted. The behavioral expression of these two emotional states is very different and in many respects, opposite. Thus the principle of antithesis notes that behaviors associated with opposite kinds of feelings are also often expressed in opposite kinds of behavior (consider the upturned smile of the happy person and the downturned mouth of the sad person).

Darwin realized that he could not categorize all emotional behavior under the first two principles because some emotional behaviors appear useless to the organism and, in addition, often have no opposites. He therefore proposed the principle of direct action of the nervous system, which says that some emotional expressions occur simply because of changes in nervous system activity. Trembling when fearful or screaming when in agony might be considered as examples of this principle.

Darwin's first two principles seem more

relevant today than his third. It is generally believed that emotions and their expressions have been adaptive and are present today because they serve to communicate internal states from one individual to another. For example, how often have you glanced at someone and, without a word being spoken, known that something was wrong? Your recognition that something is amiss probably results from emotional signals you observed in the person's facial expression. Many modern theorists, following the lead of Darwin, also believe that emotions can be understood as consisting of polar opposites such as happy-sad, angry-calm, excited-bored, and so forth. As we shall see, however, there is much debate concerning unipolar versus bipolar dimensions in emotion. Darwin's third principle is currently not very popular. Trembling in fear, for example, can be understood as the result of activation of the sympathetic nervous system, and though activation of this system often accompanies emotion, it may not be the same as emotion. The trembling and the fear may result from activation of different systems. Likewise, screaming in agony may be an innate response to pain that is separate from concurrently experienced emotion.

Recognition of Emotional States   One way in which emotional behavior would have survival value for an individual is if it provided "clues" of that individual's emotional state to other members of its species. Darwin believed that expressive movements are recognized as being associated with particular emotional states by members of a species and that this recognition is itself innate. In other words, we recognize certain behaviors as indicating that an individual is in a particular emotional state, and we can thus alter our behavior accordingly (e.g., when Dad starts frowning and clenching his teeth, he is angry, so do as he says). Interestingly, Darwin noted that movements of the

eyebrows, forehead, and mouth are important signals of emotional state (the next time someone "gets mad" at you, note these facial regions).

Ethology

In Chapter Two we examined the proposal that motivation can be understood as the accumulation of energy associated with instinctive patterns of behavior, which are in turn released by appropriate key stimuli. This approach in its modern form has been argued most successfully by the ethologists. Just as the ethologists have emphasized the innate nature of motivational processes, so too have they argued for the innateness of emotion.

Following the lead of Darwin, ethologists have concentrated primarily on the study of the expressive movements of organisms. In fact the index of Eibl-Eibesfeldt's book *Ethology: The Biology of Behavior* (1970) does not contain emotion as a separate term. Motivation and emotion are seen as two names for the same concept: the buildup of action-specific energy.

Intention Movements   Ethological research has focused on the information conveyed by the expressive movements that accompany emotion. For example, Eibl-Eibesfeldt provided the following definition: "Behavior patterns that have become differentiated into *signals* are called expressive movements" (1970, p. 91, italics added). According to ethological analysis, these innate expressions of an animal's emotional state have evolved from intention movements, which (you may recall) are indicators of a behavior that an organism is about to make. Thus a dog's baring of the teeth is an expressive movement indicative of emotion and preparatory to biting. These expressive behaviors are often seen when opposing emotions are present and tend to be a mixture of behaviors involved in the conflicting states. For example, a male cat defending its territory against an intruding male may hiss and raise its fur and shortly thereafter turn away from the intruder. These expressive movements would seem to indicate hostility mixed with fear.

Intention movements will be informative to the extent that other members of the individual's group recognize them as a signal of behavior that may occur. Recognition of anger, for example, would help an individual avoid damaging fights; a fear response such as a cry could quickly bring an adult to the aid of an infant; and sensitivity to emotional cues would help males avoid wasting energy in making sexual overtures to unreceptive females. Intention movements thus serve the adaptive purpose of coordinating behavior between individuals so that they can exist in close proximity to others of their species and interact efficiently. Animals that live in groups, this also suggests, may have evolved ways of recognizing emotionally loaded signals and acting appropriately. Because humans as well as other primates typically live in small groups, it would not be surprising if both we and monkeys proved to be sensitive to emotional signals. Analysis of such nonverbal cues is considered in the following section.

Nonverbal Cues   Among the primates, facial expressions, gestures, and calls often accompany emotional behavior (Buck, 1976). Do these expressions, calls, and gestures serve as cues to the emotional state of an individual animal? Robert Miller and his colleagues have examined this idea in a series of experiments (Miller, Caul, & Mirsky, 1967). We will look at just one of them, as representative.

Miller put rhesus monkeys into an experimental situation in which they had to avoid shock by pressing a key whenever a light came on. This is a typical avoidance learning situation, and the monkeys had no trouble learning to avoid the shock. After he had shown that they could learn to avoid the shock, Miller altered the situation so that one monkey could see the lighted stimulus but could not avoid the shock directly because it had no key to press. A second monkey had the key but could not see the stimulus. This second monkey, however, could see the first monkey via a closed-circuit TV monitor that showed the first monkey's face. The question was: Would the first monkey alter its facial expression when the light came on? And could the second monkey perceive that change, press the key, and thus avoid shock for both of them?

The answer is yes. The first monkey's facial expression changed when the light came on, and the second monkey observed that change and learned to press the key to avoid the shock. Thus these monkeys could both "send" appropriate facial expressions and "receive" these expressions and alter their behavior as a result.

It should be noted that the sending monkey was not consciously trying to send information to the observing monkey. The sending monkey simply reacted to the light with a change of facial expression because the light indicated that shock was about to occur. The observing monkey was able to use this communication to press the key in order to avoid the shock. Likewise, the second monkey was not being altruistic by pressing the key so that both could avoid shock; it was simply pressing the key so that it would not get shocked. This experiment indicates that rhesus monkeys are sensitive to facial movements that may be expressions of emotion and can alter their behavior accordingly. If they can use this "emotional" communication in the sterile environment of the laboratory, they can probably also make use of facial expression in the natural environment.

In another part of this experiment, Miller, Caul, and Mirsky paired monkeys raised in isolation with normally reared monkeys and ran all combinations of senders and receivers. We have long known that monkeys isolated from other members of their species develop behavioral abnormalities, including self-clasping, rocking, and avoidance of social interaction. Miller found the isolates incapable as both reliable senders and observers. One effect of isolation, then, may be disruption of the ability to use nonverbal, emotion-produced cues. This disruption could be related to the bizarre behavior exhibited by isolated monkeys.

The ability to send and receive emotional cues may involve an interaction between innate and acquired patterns of behavior. Mason (1961) has suggested that many behaviors used by monkeys in communication are species specific (and therefore innate) but that the proper development of these behaviors depends upon adequate experience. Thus isolated monkeys may be deficient in emotional communication because their innate abilities have not had the proper social atmosphere to develop. If monkeys can communicate emotional states by facial movements, gestures, and calls, what about humans? Do they also communicate feelings through nonverbal cues?

Ross Buck has attempted to answer this question by adapting Miller's sender-observer methods for use with humans (Buck, 1976; Buck, Miller, & Caul, 1974; Buck et al., 1972). In Buck's experiments a subject viewed a series of slides that fell into various categories in relation to the emotional responses the subject was likely to feel when viewing them. The categories might include sexual, scenic, maternal, disgusting, and ambiguous slides. Another subject observed the facial reactions of the person viewing the slides and attempted to predict what type of slide the first person

was viewing and whether the emotion experienced was pleasant or unpleasant. If humans express emotion through facial movements, the observer should have been able to predict with some accuracy what type of slide the first person was watching and whether the person experienced it as pleasurable or unpleasurable.

In one study Buck found that an observer could predict at levels greater than chance the category of the slide that the sender was viewing. Although the prediction accuracy was statistically significant, it was not overwhelming, probably because different people reacted differently to the same stimuli. For example, one person might find nude photos pleasant, while another might find them distasteful. Accuracy of predicting categories of emotion, then, was marginal. In terms of pleasantness and unpleasantness, however, prediction was much better. Apparently we are pretty good at sending and receiving signals that reflect our general mood but not so good at indicating nonverbally why we feel that way do (i.e., the reasons for our pleasure or displeasure).

In all his studies Buck found that women communicated emotion nonverbally better than men—they were better senders—because they were more facially expressive (i.e., they made more facial movements). Buck has suggested that in our society little girls are taught that it is all right to openly express emotion, while little boys are taught that they must inhibit their expression of feelings. Thus women may be better at expressing emotion nonverbally because they are allowed to externalize their feelings, while boys are taught to internalize theirs. In a fashion parallel to the monkey data, the research by Buck implies that emotional expression is innate but can be altered by experience.

How early does emotional expression occur? Buck (1975) found that children as young as four reliably communicate emotion through facial expression. At this age, however, no reliable differences appeared between the sexes in sending ability, though girls still had a slight edge. Buck also found that the mothers of these children were most accurate at judging the categories and also the pleasantness of the emotion, though undergraduate observers also had some success in interpreting the children's facial expressions.

In all these studies the observers were better at judging the pleasantness or unpleasantness of the expressed emotion than they were at judging the particular category of the emotion. Emotional expression through facial movements, then, seems to generally indicate emotional mood but not the causes (category of slide) of that mood. In the last section of this chapter we will examine additional evidence that different facial expressions can accurately indicate specific emotions.

Robert Rosenthal has also been interested in understanding nonverbal communication. Rosenthal and his associates at Harvard have developed a device that they believe allows them to measure a person's sensitivity to nonverbal cues (Rosenthal et al., 1974). They measure reaction to such nonverbal cues as facial movement, body movement, voice tone, and so on by having a person choose, from a set of answers, the emotion that he or she believes is being conveyed. Their research indicates that most people can correctly identify various emotional states, even when given only very brief exposures ($1/24$ sec.) to the nonverbal cues.

Similar to Buck's research, Rosenthal and associates found that women were more sensitive than men to nonverbal cues, particularly body cues. According to the findings of Buck and Rosenthal, women are apparently better than men at both sending nonverbal information and detecting it in others. Although these researchers do not rule out learning, they suggest that some aspects of the ability to send and

detect emotional nonverbal cues may be innate.

A study of very young infants also bears on the question of the innateness of emotional expression (Haith, Bergman, & Moore, 1977). In Haith's experiment the visual fixation of faces by infants was examined. Infants three to five weeks old fixated the face of an adult only 22% of the time during testing, while seven-week-old infants fixated the face more than 87% of the time. The researchers also examined which facial features were fixated and found that the eyes attracted the most attention from seven weeks on. This was true even when the adult was talking (although one might have predicted that the infant would fixate the mouth region). Haith and his co-workers argued that the eyes become important fixation points because they serve as the source of signals or cues in social situations. Although this study does not show that gazing at the face is an innate response, it does suggest that fixating the face, particularly the eyes, begins at a very early age and may have some innate components (see also Field et al., 1982, for evidence that imitation of adult facial responses can occur as early as 36 hours after birth).

The studies of Haith, Rosenthal, and Buck indicate that humans are sensitive to the nonverbal expression of emotion and that while learning is undoubtedly involved in much of this ability, some components of emotional expression and recognition of the same are probably innate. Like other primates, humans apparently communicate affect nonverbally and "read" the nonverbal emotional signals of others.

EMOTION FROM A LEARNING PERSPECTIVE

In this section we will briefly look at some of the ways in which learning may contribute to emotionality. As was noted in Chapter Six, classical conditioning situations can lead to the development of emotionality to formerly neutral stimuli. It is also clear that emotions such as fear can lead to new instrumental behaviors that reduce or remove the organism from the emotion-producing situation. Because we have examined in some detail Hull's general theory of behavior (Chapter Five), let us begin our discussion by looking at how drive theorists dealt with emotion.

Emotion as Drive

Clark Hull was not particularly interested in emotion. The term *emotion* does not appear in the indexes of his 1943 and 1951 books. In 1952 Hull briefly mentioned emotion as being involved in the behavioral changes that follow shifts from large to small rewards (and vice versa). Because these behavioral changes result from contrasting changes in the incentive value of the goal, Hull apparently considered emotionality as partially responsible for incentive effects on behavior.

Kenneth Spence, a drive theorist at the University of Iowa, developed a more systematic approach to the study of emotion. Spence (1956, 1960) divided motivational events into two categories—appetitive and aversive. Appetitive states (e.g., hunger, thirst, and sex) involve situations that lead to approach behavior. Aversive states are situations that the organism attempts to withdraw or flee from. Pain is the most obvious aversive state and is also the most often studied.

In regard to aversive states, Spence argued that the drive that activates behavior results from the development of an internal *emotional* response in the organism. Thus the motivation that activates behavior in aversive situations was thought to be based on the development of emotionality. Spence also argued that this emotionality is aroused by an aversive stimulus (electric shock, tail pinch, and so on).

Spence also predicted that individuals would differ in the strength of the emotional response they would produce in the presence of an aversive stimulus. This suggests that highly emotional subjects should perform better than subjects lower in emotionality in an aversive situation, provided that the correct response has a high probability of occurrence, because high emotionality will lead to higher drive and more behavior. Janet Taylor, a student of Spence, developed a self-inventory to measure the emotional responsiveness of individuals. She chose anxiety as the basic process for study and developed the **Taylor Manifest Anxiety Scale** to measure it (Taylor, 1951, 1953).

In order to determine the effect of anxiety on behavior, Spence chose to study its effects on the classical conditioning of the human eyelid response to a puff of air. As you probably know, if a puff of air strikes your eye (e.g., when you round the corner of a building and turn into the full force of the wind), you automatically close your eyes. When a neutral stimulus is paired with a puff of air to the eye, a person will gradually begin blinking to the stimulus (e.g., a tone) even if the puff of air is eliminated on some trials. Spence wanted to test the idea that subjects high in anxiety, as measured by the Manifest Anxiety Scale, would show a greater percentage of conditioned responses than subjects low in anxiety. He predicted this difference between high- and low-anxious subjects based on the fact that the emotional response of anxiety would generate more drive in high-anxious than in low-anxious subjects. Because drive theory assumes that drive multiplies habit strength, the high-anxious subjects should show a higher percentage of eyelid closures in response to the conditioned stimulus.

Taylor (1951) first tested this idea. She

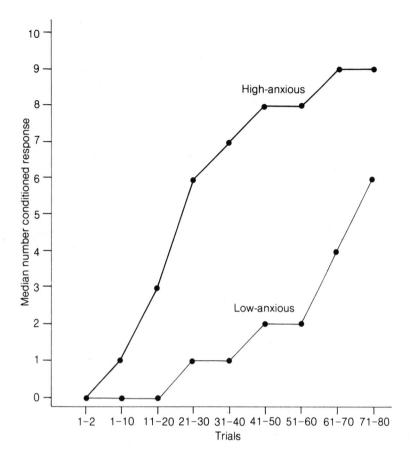

Figure 13.2 *Number of conditioned eyelid responses for high-anxious and low-anxious subjects. (Adapted from Taylor, 1951.)*

selected subjects for her high-anxious group who scored in the upper 12% of the Manifest Anxiety Scale distribution, while subjects for the low-anxious group were chosen from the lowest 9% of the distribution. Her results are shown in Figure 13.2. As expected, high-anxious subjects showed a greater number of conditioned responses than low-anxious subjects across training trials.

Many additional eyelid-conditioning experiments have been performed, and the findings are generally consistent: high-anxious

subjects show a greater percentage of conditioned responses than low-anxious subjects. The data obtained from classical conditioning situations, then, favor Spence's interpretation of emotionality as "adding to" the individual's general drive level. The eyelid-conditioning studies, however, represent a special situation in which the correct response (i.e., blinking the eye) is also the most probable response, so that increasing drive should lead to faster production of the response that the experimenter is testing. In more complex learning situations, where the correct response may not be the most probable one, the additional increment of drive added by emotionality will more likely interfere with performance of the correct response. This would happen if some noncorrect response was stronger than the one the experimenter was looking for; the increased drive would energize the strongest response, and this would cause high-anxious subjects to learn the correct response more slowly than low-anxious subjects. The results of several experiments using verbal materials associated with noncorrect, dominant responses have tended to confirm this hypothesis. When verbal items had no strong prior associations, high-anxious subjects learned the correct response more quickly than low-anxious subjects; when verbal materials did have strong prior associations, the correct response was initially learned more slowly by high-anxious subjects (Cofer & Appley, 1964; Spence, 1956, 1960).

The results of considerable research on the drive-producing properties of emotionality indicate that anxiety often seems to act like a drive. Increases in drive resulting from anxiety, however, produce mixed effects. In relatively simple situations where the required response has a high probability of occurrence, anxiety seems to facilitate performance. But when the correct response has a low probability of occurrence in comparison with competing responses, anxiety interferes with the proper performance of behavior. A familiar example of this phenomenon is test anxiety. A little anxiety prior to a test helps some students, presumably because they have learned the correct responses and the anxiety tends to activate these responses; however, such anxiety may completely interfere with the performance of other students because it triggers responses that are incompatible with test taking. The moral is clear: the better you learn the material, the less likely that test anxiety will work against you.

Spence's concept of emotionally based drive has not been without problems. As we saw in Chapter Three, emotionality generally causes complex physiological changes within the body. If the Manifest Anxiety Scale measures anxiety as it was designed to do, we should expect the correlation between it and measures of physical reactivity to be high and positive. The results of several studies, however, indicate that the relationship is small at best. These findings cast some doubt on the assumption that anxiety, as gauged by the scale, is measuring a drive. For example, correlations are often found between neurotic tendency and the scale (Cofer & Appley, 1964). That the scale may be measuring other factors besides anxiety means that these factors, rather than emotionally based drive, may be causing the behavior. This possibility seems more likely considering the problems that the drive concept has encountered (see Chapter Five for a discussion of the drive concept).

Emotional Modeling

The research discussed above suggests that emotion often has properties that lead to the production of behavior. Is emotionality innate, as Darwin and the ethologists argued, or can emotions be learned? Bandura (1971) argued that emotionality can be learned through the observation of others. According to Bandura, we are sensitive to the facial, vocal, and postural indications of emotional arousal in others, and we note them. If we later find ourselves in circumstances similar to those we have observed, we are likely to react in emotionally similar ways. As might be expected, we seem to be influenced more by the emotionality of models who are important to us—though probably part of the appeal of motion pictures, television, and plays is the actors' ability to arouse in us the emotions that we are observing.

Bandura (1969) has even suggested that

people may sometimes develop phobias not from direct experience but from seeing a model behave fearfully toward or be injured by some object (see the discussion on the preparedness of some phobias below for a somewhat different perspective). Bandura also pointed out that people may sometimes learn prejudices toward certain groups by observing a model who shows intense negative emotionality toward the group.

Though we may learn emotional behavior directly through classical or operant procedures, Bandura's analysis also makes it clear that through simple observation of emotional behavior, we can incorporate that emotionality into our own patterns of responding. We now leave emotional modeling to examine the idea that organisms have been specially adapted by evolution to associate emotion with certain classes of events.

The Preparedness of Emotional Learning

For many years theorists assumed that the rules by which learning occurs are fundamentally the same across organisms. This approach, termed **general process learning theory**, assumes that one response can be learned just as easily as any other. It now appears that the assumptions of general process theory may have to be modified. The response that we ask an organism to learn apparently makes a difference (Seligman, 1970; Seligman & Hager, 1972). Some responses can be learned very easily, while others may be learned only with considerable difficulty, and still others may be unlearnable. Such thinking was foreshadowed by Breland and Breland (1961); after many years of conditioning and observing thousands of animals, these researchers reluctantly concluded that one cannot adequately understand, control, or predict an organism's behavior unless one knows something about its instinctive pat-

terns, evolutionary history, and ecological niche.

Seligman (1970) suggested that the associability of events in the environment can be described as consisting of a continuum. At one end of the continuum are events that can be easily and quickly associated; these are said to be **prepared associations**. At the other extreme are associations that an organism apparently cannot learn; these are called **contraprepared associations**. Between these two extremes are said to be **unprepared associations**; these can be learned, but numerous experiences with the events are necessary for an association to be formed. The preparedness hypothesis argues that different species will have evolved different prepared, unprepared, and contraprepared associations as a result of the selective pressures of evolution. Thus one species may quickly learn a response to one set of environmental circumstances but not to another set because evolution has prepared one type of association to be easily formed while, at the same time, making other associations difficult or impossible.

Seligman (1971) has proposed that the development of phobias is an example of prepared learning in humans. A *phobia* can be defined as an unreasonable fear of some object, situation, or symbol that has no basis in fact. The presence of a phobic object leads to highly emotional behavior usually described as irrational fear. Many theorists have regarded the development of phobic behavior as an instance of classical conditioning. For example, a neutral stimulus such as an elevator might become associated with intense anxiety reactions triggered by a test. Subsequently, elevators could come to elicit a conditioned anxiety reaction too.

As noted by Seligman, however, several problems exist with this type of interpretation. First, phobias are very resistant to extinction, while normal laboratory conditioning of fear extinguishes relatively easily. Exposure to a stimulus that has elicited conditioned fear in the past without the fear now being present weakens conditioned fear. Presentation of phobic objects, on the other hand, usually does not diminish fear and may even enhance it.

A second problem with the conditioning explanation of phobias is that phobic reactions often appear to have been learned in as little as one exposure, while conditioned fear in the laboratory usually takes somewhere between three and six trials to become established. Thus phobias appear to be acquired much more quickly than conditioned fear reactions.

Third, conditioned stimuli are supposed to be arbitrary. Any neutral stimulus can become a conditioned stimulus if paired with some unconditioned stimulus (UCS), in this case an anxiety-producing UCS. But most common phobias appear to represent a nonarbitrary set of conditions (e.g., fear of heights, fear of the dark, fear of enclosed spaces, and so on).

Fourth, most phobic reactions are to objects of natural origin. The reasoning is that evolution has adapted us to be particularly sensitive to forming relationships between fearfulness and natural phenomena such as darkness and heights or organisms such as spiders and snakes because fearfulness of such things can be useful (some snakes and spiders are poisonous, darkness and heights increase the possibility of injury). This is not to say of course that all phobias are examples of prepared associations; some people are phobic of airplanes and even of symbols like the number 13 (White, 1964).

Phobias, then, apparently have many of the characteristics of prepared behaviors. Both phobias and prepared behaviors can be learned in one trial; both concern a nonarbitrary set of situations; both are very resistant to extinction; and both are probably noncognitive in nature. The overlap in the characteristics of phobias and prepared behavior is

indeed strong, and certain common phobias may develop because humans are prepared to make associations between fear and particular situations. Because phobias involve emotionally charged situations, one wonders whether, in a more general sense, humans are prepared to make emotional associations. Perhaps emotion has its impact precisely because it is easily associated with events. Future research may provide some answers.

EMOTION FROM A COGNITIVE PERSPECTIVE

Cognitive approaches to the understanding of emotion stress the importance of cognitive appraisal (Lazarus, 1982, 1984). According to this view, bodily changes are insufficient for the experience of true emotion; we must assess a situation as emotion producing before we experience emotion. Schachter's model (discussed in Chapter Three) was one of the first to suggest the importance of some sort of appraisal process. As you may recall, Schachter proposed that when arousal occurs, a cognitive label is attached to the arousal, and that both are necessary for the experienced emotion. Thus when we are aroused and the cues suggest pleasantness, we are happy; but the same arousal in the presence of different cues can make us feel angry. In Schachter's model the critical element determining the particular emotion experienced is the cognitive label; although arousal was deemed necessary, it was not thought to differentiate between the various emotions one could feel. Schachter's model has been criticized on a number of counts (see Chapter Three for a fuller discussion of both Schachter's evidence and the criticisms of his model), and cognitive theorists such as Lazarus have argued that cognition alone may be sufficient for the experience of emotion. For example, altering the appraisal process of subjects before viewing a gruesome film altered the quality and intensity of the emotions produced by the film (Lazarus, 1968). Emotional reaction to the film could be intensified by a soundtrack that emphasized the harmful consequences or decreased by a soundtrack that emphasized intellectual detachment. Lazarus's data argue for the primacy of cognition in the perception of emotion. Indeed Lazarus (1982, 1984) has strongly argued this point with Zajonc (1980, 1984), whose point of view we will examine in the next section.

The emphasis on the appraisal process in the experience of emotion is very similar to attribution approaches of motivation examined in Chapter Eleven. It should come as no surprise, then, that attribution theory has also been applied to the study of emotion. A study by Valins will serve as example.

Attribution of Emotion

Valins (1966) had male college students view slides of seminude females. While viewing the slides, the men were told that their heart rate was being monitored; in addition, they could also hear their heart beating as the slides were presented. The subjects did not realize that the heart rate feedback they were hearing was false; it was being controlled by the experimenter to indicate large increases or decreases for some slides and no change for others. Subjects were later asked to rate the slides in terms of attractiveness, and they judged the slides associated with a heart rate change (either up or down) to be more attractive than those associated with no change. In addition, Valins let his subjects take some of the slides home and found that the ones chosen were primarily those that had been associated with the heart rate changes.

Valins's data suggest that at least for ratings of liking, we form a hypothesis and then attempt to test it by searching for relevant cues

in ourselves or our environment. If this attribution process is an active one, as Valins suggested, then the rating may have been arrived at somewhat as follows: "My heart rate changed. Why? Because the girl in this photo is attractive." In a later study (Valins, 1974) subjects were debriefed and told that the heart rate feedback was false. Nevertheless, even after debriefing, the subjects still rated pictures associated with heart rate changes as more attractive than others not so associated. As with other research in attribution, once formed, emotions appear difficult to change.

Valins's research has generated a number of additional studies and debate—for his data seem to show that only the *belief* that one is aroused is necessary for the experience of emotion. Although Valins provided false heart rate feedback to his subjects, he did not actually measure their heart rate.

In a study conceptually similar to Valins's research, Goldstein, Fink, and Mettee (1972) showed male subjects male nudes and provided false heart rate information, but they also recorded actual heart rates. (These researchers expected the pictures to be disliked because of implicit homosexual connotations.) The false heart rate information provided by the experimenters was not related to the dislike of the slides as rated by the subjects, but the subjects' actual heart rate was. This result suggests that the attractiveness scores in Valins's studies may have resulted not only from the false feedback but also from actual physiological changes.

Further, Beck and Matteson (1982) have reported results suggesting that the false feedback effect may result from subtle cues provided by the experimenter that indicate to the subject how to respond. These **experimenter demand** characteristics, rather than an attribution that one is aroused, may therefore be responsible for the effects obtained in false feedback situations. Additionally, Parkinson and Manstead (1981) have provided evidence that attentional processes are important for Valins's effect. At present it seems best to leave open the question of whether emotion can result solely from attributions of arousal or whether some physiological changes are necessary.

Attribution theory is becoming increasingly important as theorists attempt to develop models describing how emotionality is influenced by the causes that we ascribe to events. Weiner (1985; Weiner, Amirkhan, Folkes, & Verette, 1987), for example, has broadened his original attribution theory (see Chapter Eleven) to include emotion. In this revised theory he argues that the perceived stability of the causes for behavior will influence one's expectancy of future success. In addition to the stability dimension, the locus and controllability dimensions of the causal ascriptions we make will influence the emotions we feel. Finally, expectancies and emotion are seen as guiding motivated behavior.

Suppose a friend you are supposed to meet for lunch stands you up. According to Weiner's theory, the reasons later given by your friend for breaking the engagement should influence your emotions toward that person and your future behavior toward him or her. The excuse "I missed our luncheon date because I went to lunch with John/Mary Doe instead" suggests that the reason for the missed date was internal and controllable (your friend decided he or she would rather go to lunch with someone else). Weiner's research has shown that internal and controllable excuses tend to produce aversive emotional reactions (you might become angry with your friend) and a desire for reduced social contact (you might not invite him or her out to lunch again). On the other hand, in the excuse "I missed our luncheon date because a truck backed into my car and damaged the radiator," the cause was external to the person, and un-

controllable. As a result of the second excuse you are much less likely to feel negative emotionality toward your friend, and your future desire for social contact with him or her will probably not be diminished.

Weiner and associates (1987) studied the excuses people give and found support for the analysis mentioned above. It would seem therefore that attribution theory can help us understand why our emotional reactions to various situations occur and, further, how those emotional reactions influence future behavior. Additional research on causal ascriptions and emotions is likely to help us understand, at least in part, the generation of emotion.

Indeed several researchers have suggested **attribution therapy** as a means of helping individuals. Davison (1966, cited by Valins & Nisbett, 1972), for example, used an attribution approach with a paranoid schizophrenic who believed that tics over one eye were being caused by an evil spirit. He showed the patient how to reduce the twitches by relaxing the appropriate muscles and gradually got the person to attribute the muscle spasms to tension rather than to spirits.

Valins and Nisbett (1972), following the lead of Maher (1970), proposed that delusional systems can be regarded as explanatory devices through which a troubled individual attempts to understand his or her own behavior. Maher had suggested that the sensory input of schizophrenics is distorted (perhaps because of biochemical malfunctions). But this distorted sensory information will be "real" to the schizophrenic, who may then develop delusional systems, or attributions, that attempt to explain the unusual sensations that he or she is experiencing.

Valins and Nisbett suggested that attribution therapy should first challenge the underlying attributions (often dispositional in nature) that the disturbed person holds. At the same time, more normal attributions should be suggested for the events being misattrib-uted. These new attributions should usually be more situational in nature and should lead to improvement because the new interpretations will not support the old anxieties that have maintained the disturbed behavior. Thus in the case of the paranoid schizophrenic who thought himself possessed, the attribution of the muscle twitches to tension led to a reduc-tion of the delusion of spirit possession.

Attribution therapy has not been free of criticism (see Miller & Berman, 1983, for a review); nevertheless, it does provide the pos-sibility of new techniques for the treatment of maladaptive behavior. Time will undoubtedly determine the usefulness of these techniques.

The Circumplex Model of Emotion

One cognitive approach to understanding emotion involves the examination of words we use when expressing emotional states. If we can determine how such labels are related to each other, we may gain insight into the emo-tional process itself. Several researchers have taken such a tack. Russell (1980), for example, has developed a model based on his research proposing that emotions fall along a circular path. As he noted, there have been two basic notions regarding self-reports of affective states. The first regards emotion as divisible into 6 to 12 independent factors, where each emotion represents a separate dimension (see, e.g., Nowlis & Nowlis, 1956; Nowlis, 1965). The second approach, in contrast, views emo-tions as consistently related to one another rather than independent. Specifically, Schlos-berg (1952) proposed that emotionality can be described by two dimensions, with emotional labels falling along a circle around them. Russell, in agreement with Schlosberg, also proposed two dimensions (pleasantness and arousal), with emotional words describing a cir-cle around these dimensions. Further, he ar-

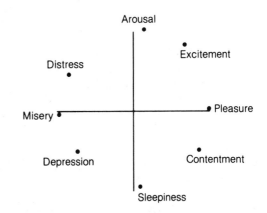

Figure 13.3 Circular arrangement of affect concepts around the dimensions of pleasantness (horizontal line) and arousal (vertical line). (Adapted from Russell, 1980. Copyright © 1980 by the American Psychological Asso-ciation. Reprinted by permission of the publisher and au-thor.)

gued that emotional labels describe a bipolar relationship among the emotions. Thus, as shown in Figure 13.3, the domain of affect can be represented by the circular arrangement of emotions around two bipolar dimensions.

Russell arrived at this model after con-ducting a series of studies to determine how subjects viewed 28 emotional words that repre-sented the range of emotionality. Using several sophisticated scaling techniques, Russell found that the ordering of the words was best repre-sented as falling along a circular path based on just two dimensions. Figure 13.4 shows the clustering of the 28 words. Notice that words expressing opposite emotional experience tend to fall opposite each other, supporting the no-tion that emotions can be regarded as bipolar.

Another interesting finding in Russell's results was that people sometimes placed a particular emotional word in more than one category and that these placements tended to be adjacent to each other. This suggests that an affective term (e.g., *pleased*) is essentially a label for a *category that is not clearly bounded* but

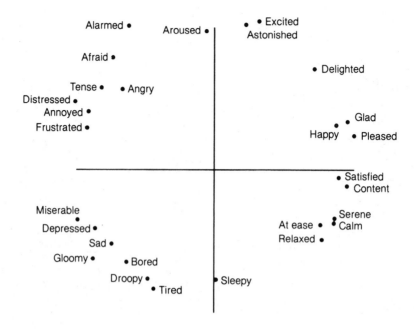

Figure 13.4 *Multidimensional scaling of 28 affect words. (Adapted from Russell, 1980. Copyright ©
1980 by the American Psychological Association. Reprinted by permission of the publisher and the
author.)*

is one in which the transition from membership to nonmembership is gradual. Such a category has been called a **fuzzy set** and appears generally characteristic of language categories. As noted by Russell, it is probably reasonable to consider the labeling of emotions as a mapping process whereby an internal emotional state is specified according to its degree of membership within a fuzzy set. Thus, for example, we can be a little happy, happy, or extremely happy—each term describing a different degree of membership within the fuzzy set "happy."

Russell (1980, p. 1176) concluded that "affective experience is the end product of a cognitive process that has already utilized that same cognitive structure for affect." He is therefore in agreement with Lazarus in regard to the necessity of cognition occurring before emotion. According to Russell, whatever cues

are used in the process of emotion, the cues themselves do not provide the experience of emotion. Instead, emotion is provided by the *interpretation* (a cognitive process) of those cues.

Additional support for Russell's circumplex model of emotion has been provided by three other studies (Daly, Lancee, & Polivy, 1983; Russell, 1983; Watson, Clark, & Tellegen, 1984). Russell (1983) found that emotional labels yield circular patterns in Gujarati, Croatian, Japanese, and Chinese as well as in English. Thus there seems to be cross-cultural evidence for the circular arrangement of emotion-related words. Watson, Clark, and Tellegen (1984), in a carefully conducted study, examined Japanese and American mood terms and found a remarkable convergence in the structure of emotion within the two languages. Further, their study supported a two-factor structure (which they labeled positive affect and negative affect). Although the two factors identified by Watson and co-workers are labeled differently than Russell's, and although these researchers argued for a simple two-factor model rather than a circular one, their data support the notion that emotion-related words may be reasonably described with only two dimensions (see also Mayer & Gaschke, 1988; Watson & Tellegen, 1985). Their data would also seem to support the idea that emotion-related words represent categories that define emotional states. The close similarity between these categories across Japanese and American cultures, together with the cross-cultural similarities found by Russell, suggest the interesting possibility that the categories of emotional experience may be universal in humans.

The study conducted by Daly, Lancee, and Polivy (1983) provides an interesting addition to Russell's model. These researchers, using multidimensional scaling techniques, replicated Russell's circular pattern of emotion-related words but also found evidence for a third dimension, representing the intensity of emotion. When this third unipolar dimension is added to Russell's circular pattern, a conical model is indicated (see Figure 13.5). In this model the tip of the cone represents neutrality, that is, no emotion. Intensity increases as one progresses toward the base of the cone (Russell's circle), reaching a maximum at the base. These researchers argued that their data provide a bridge between bipolar theories of affect such as Schlosberg's and Russell's and monopolar models such as those discussed in the next section. Although it is too early to judge the conical model's ability to integrate the findings of bipolar and monopolar emotion research, such attempts at integration are important steps toward a unified view of emotion. Without putting such attempts at unification aside, we will now examine

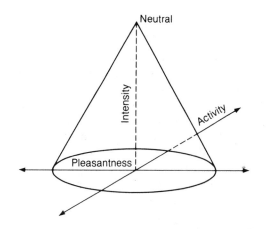

Figure 13.5 Conical model of emotion. Three dimensions—pleasantness, activity, and intensity—form the basis of the model. (Adapted from Daly, Lancee, & Polivy, 1983. Copyright © 1983 by the American Psychological Association. Reprinted by permission of the publisher and the author.)

research supportive of monopolar, independent dimensions of emotional experience.

EMOTION AS PRIMARY AND UNIVERSAL

Robert Zajonc has argued for the primacy of affect; that is, he has argued that emotion is independent of, and can occur prior to, any cognition. Zajonc and Lazarus have argued this point in several articles published in the *American Psychologist* (Zajonc, 1980, 1984; Lazarus, 1982, 1984). As we saw in the last section, Lazarus proposed that cognition must precede emotion, and indeed much research supports the idea that cognition is often involved in the experience of emotion. Zajonc proposed, however, that although cognition is often associated with emotion, emotion can occur without cognition and in fact prior to any cognitive processing.

Zajonc argued that **affect is basic**, that is, that emotion is universal among animal species. Because it is difficult to know whether animals other than humans cognitively process information, Zajonc reasoned that the system that generates affect must be independent of cognitive processing. Indeed, as Zajonc noted, a rabbit would rarely have time to assess all the attributes of a snake in order to decide whether to fear it; the rabbit feels fear and reacts. Such reactions may also occur in people. For example, a person may react to a dark leaf falling on his or her arm as if it were a feared insect when the movement is seen unclearly. Though we cannot rule out cognition in the human example, the fear and subsequent behavior generated by it are very quick, and closer analysis of the situation often seems to occur *after* the emotion is triggered.

A second argument in favor of the primacy of emotion is that **emotions are inescapable**. Affective reactions seem to occur whether we want them to or not. As noted by Zajonc, we can sometimes learn to control the expression of emotion (and society often demands this of us), but we do not seem able to control the feeling. Third, once an affective reaction occurs, subsequent instances of the emotion are very **hard to alter**. Zajonc suggested that we encounter great difficulty in trying to change an emotional reaction because emotional judgments *feel right*. Emotional reactions do not seem open to logic; if we don't like a particular piece of music, we simply do not like it, period. Similarly, an individual who finds oysters repugnant is not easily persuaded to eat them. According to Zajonc, if cognitive processing occurs prior to emotion, then logic should affect our emotional judgments.

Zajonc also noted that **emotional reactions are difficult to verbalize**. For example, when meeting someone for the first time, we know very quickly whether we like the person or not, but we often cannot say why we feel the

way we do. Indeed several lines of research suggest that the communication of emotion is largely nonverbal. Work reviewed in this chapter on intention movements and nonverbal cues represents part of that evidence. We will shortly examine research on the facial feedback hypothesis, which also bears on this issue. Zajonc proposed that our difficulty in verbalizing emotions suggests that emotion lies outside the cognitive system.

The points mentioned above are representative of Zajonc's view as expressed in his 1980 article. In the 1984 article he presented several additional points in support of the idea that emotion can occur without cognition. In both articles he presented numerous lines of evidence to support each point (but see Lazarus's 1982 and 1984 rebuttals of this evidence). Zajonc's view of emotion has been presented in some detail here because it represents a good overview of a particular approach to understanding emotion—the idea that emotions are evolutionarily adaptive, fundamental, and innate reactions. These reactions are usually seen as preprogrammed within the organism and consisting of a limited number of specific affective states. This view of emotion is ably represented by models developed by Tomkins, Izard, and Plutchik.

The Tomkins Model

Sylvan Tomkins (1962, 1963, 1979, 1981a) proposed that we have a limited set of emotions, which are genetically programmed into the brain and initiated by changes in stimulation. Specifically, changes in stimulation presumably cause changes in the neural firing pattern of circuits within the brain. These changed patterns in turn generate specific emotional states. Thus increased neural firing will lead to interest, fear, or surprise as the firing rate increases, while enjoyment is assumed to occur when the pattern of neural firing decreases. Distress and anger result from sustained levels of firing above some optimum level, with anger resulting from a higher sustained level than distress (Tomkins, 1979).

Although changes in the neural firing pattern are the triggering mechanism for innately programmed emotional reactions, our communication and experience of emotion come from feedback from facial expressions and voice. There is a preprogrammed set of facial muscle responses associated with each specific emotion. Similarly, for each emotion there is also a specific set of vocalizations so that there are "cries of joy, cries of distress, cries of anger, cries of excitement, cries of fear, and so on" (Tomkins, 1981a, p. 315). Thus we communicate our emotional state to others through facial expressions and voice inflections; however, we also *experience* emotion as a result of feedback from these responses. Although he originally emphasized facial musculature as important for the experience of emotion, Tomkins has more recently proposed that the important feedback signals for emotion come from changes in the stimulation of sensory receptors in the facial skin, in a manner analogous to the experience of orgasm resulting from changes in stimulation of skin receptors in the genital region.

One of the most interesting aspects of Tomkins's theory is his proposal that emotions serve to amplify drives. Although we may be aware of such drive states as hunger, thirst, and the need for sex, according to Tomkins, their urgency is provided by the emotional amplification of these conditions. In a very real sense for Tomkins, emotion provides the intensity factor in motivation and is necessary for the activation of behavior.

One final aspect of the theory deserves mention. Tomkins makes a distinction between innate emotion and what he calls **backed-up emotion**. The points we have examined above refer to innate emotion; however, as noted by Tomkins, every society puts constraints on the free expression of emotion because of its contagious quality and its power to generate behavior. As a result, many of the emotional reactions we observe in others are not innate but backed up, that is, voluntarily modified in some way. Often the modification of emotional expression is suppression, but people also feign anger, surprise, joy, and other emotions when they do not feel them. Tomkins argued that the backed-up expression of emotions is particularly common in anger.

Because we can suppress, augment, and disguise the emotional reactions we make, it is difficult for layman and scientist alike to clearly distinguish between true and backed-up emotion. This confusion may partially account for the many different models of emotion that currently exist.

Izard's Model

A model closely related to Tomkins's has been developed by Carroll Izard (1977, 1979), who, in agreement with Tomkins, argued that the fundamental emotions are innately programmed. Izard's **differential emotions theory** emphasizes the idea that specific emotions have distinct experiential qualities. As noted by Izard (1977), the theory is based on five assumptions.

The first assumption is that there are ten fundamental emotions: *interest-excitement, joy, surprise, distress-anguish, anger, disgust, contempt, fear, shame*, and *guilt*. Each emotion has three components—its own neural substrate, a characteristic expressive pattern (usually involving facial expressions), and a distinct subjective quality or feeling associated with it. None of these components by itself is an emotion; all three are required.

Izard's second assumption is that each emotion is inherently adaptive; that is, each emotion has unique motivational properties that are important for survival of either the individual or the species. Third, different emotions produce different inner experiences and are associated with different behaviors. Fourth, emotions interact with each other; that is, one emotion may activate, amplify, or reduce another. This assumption is important because it means that a particular emotional state may consist of a complex blend of fundamental emotions. Because the fundamental emotions can interact, the number of possible subjective emotional states is quite large.

Finally, according to Izard, emotions interact with and influence other important bodily processes such as homeostasis, drive, perception, cognition, and motor responses. This interplay makes emotion the principal motivational system for behavior. As is apparent in the following quote, emotion also provides the basis for personality. "The emotions are viewed not only as the principal motivational system but, even more fundamentally, as the personality processes which give meaning and significance to human existence" (Izard, 1977, p. 44).

Differential emotions theory argues that neurochemical activity, occurring in innate programs within the brain, causes facial and bodily changes. As these changes are fed back to the brain and made conscious, they produce one of the fundamental emotions. Because positive emotions such as interest or joy increase a person's sense of well-being, contact with the object or person generating the emotion is continued. Negative emotions such as fear or disgust, on the other hand, are aversive and generate withdrawal of contact if possible.

Other characteristics noted by Izard can also help us understand his conception of emotion. First of all, emotion is noncyclical. There does not appear to be any rhythm to emotions—we do not typically become interested or disgusted at certain times of the day independent of environmental stimulation. Second, emotions have almost unlimited generality. Although a relatively limited number of items will satisfy hunger or thirst, for example,

we can react with fear, joy, disgust, and so forth to an apparently unlimited number of things. The diversity of human personality structure may result in part from the flexibility of emotional associations. Third, according to Izard, the emotions serve as important regulators. In this regard an important function of emotion is to amplify or reduce the action of other motivational systems. Thus on the one hand, the sex drive can recruit an emotion such as interest-excitement and greatly increase sexual motivation, while on the other hand, the presence of fear can inhibit the sex drive completely.

From this brief survey of Izard's approach, it should be apparent that emotion is the primary motivator of behavior. It influences and is in turn influenced by the other systems. The emotions are fundamental and adaptive. Blends of emotion can and often do occur, making the possible number of emotional experiences quite large and varied. Finally, as noted by Izard (1977, p. 44), "The emotions are considered important both for behavior and for sensing, experiencing, and being."

Plutchik's Model

A third approach, closely related to those of Tomkins and Izard, has been proposed by Plutchik (1962, 1980, 1983), who argued that the emotions are associated with universal adaptive behaviors necessary for survival. Eight behaviors, identifiable at all phylogenetic levels, have corresponding primary or fundamental emotions. The eight primary emotions are *fear, anger, joy, sadness, acceptance, disgust, expectancy,* and *surprise*.

The emotional states that we both observe in others and experience within ourselves, however, are more complex than these eight fundamental emotions, because emotions can differ in intensity and persistence as well as combine with one another in complex blends.

In the realm of intensity, for example, a fundamental emotion such as sadness can vary from mild pensiveness to full-blown grief. Plutchik suggested that one reason why researchers have obtained differing results when studying emotion is that they have not equated intensity differences.

In regard to persistence, emotions may be short lived or long term. Laboratory studies usually examine short-lived emotional situations, while the emotion observed in clinical or therapeutic situations is more often long term. As Plutchik has noted, the effects of short-lived and long-term emotionality are quite different, so the correspondence between lab and clinical studies of emotion is not as high as one might expect.

The complex blending of the eight fundamental emotions leads to hundreds of different emotional states, particularly when one realizes that intensity and persistence differences are also involved. According to Plutchik, the great variety of individual differences in emotionality observed in human behavior results from this complex mixture of the fundamental emotions.

As you can readily see, the theories of Tomkins, Izard, and Plutchik share a common belief in the existence of a discrete number of fundamental, evolutionarily adaptive, and genetically determined emotions. All three also emphasize that combinations of these primary emotions can produce the complex variety of emotion that humans experience.

For Tomkins and Izard, emotion is the prime motivator, amplifying and interacting with other systems to produce behavior. Plutchik (1980), however, has maintained a distinction between the two concepts. His model reserves motivation for gradual and rhythmic internal changes that result from the absence of something, and it saves emotion for those situations normally aroused by the non-

rhythmic presence of some external stimulus.

Plutchik's theory would seem to differ from those of Tomkins and Izard in one other respect as well. While Tomkins and Izard have argued that emotion can occur prior to cognition, Plutchik's model assumes that some cognitive processing occurs prior to the experience of emotion. Plutchik's model, then, may be regarded as incorporating the concepts of innate and discrete emotions as well as the cognitivist's view that appraisal is a necessary component of emotion.

Facial Expression and Emotion

The theories of Tomkins and Izard have especially stressed the importance of facial changes in both the experience and communication of emotion. Unlike theorists who have stressed autonomic feedback as the source of differentiation between the various emotions, Tomkins and Izard have suggested that facial changes tell us what we are feeling. Tomkins originally proposed that feedback from the facial muscles provides the information necessary for the experience of the different emotions. More recently, however (e.g., Tomkins, 1981a), he has proposed that the essential information comes from changes in the facial skin. Izard has maintained the position that facial musculature changes are the feedback for emotional experience. The modern emphasis on facial changes in emotion is often traced to Darwin's (1872) book *The Expression of the Emotions in Man and Animals*, although others such as Sir Charles Bell and French physiologist Duchenne had commented on facial changes and emotion earlier (see Plutchik, 1980, chapter 15, for a short history of research on facial expression).

For both Tomkins and Izard, the existence of a fundamental set of emotions suggests that emotional expression should be similar across cultures. Although there has been a great deal of controversy concerning the universality of facial expression (see Ekman, 1972), it now appears that some expressions *are* universal and thus support the concept of innate, fundamental emotions. (As we will see, however, other facial expressions are clearly culture specific.) Early evidence for a correspondence between emotion and facial changes was provided by Tomkins and McCarter (1964), who found that observers could show high agreement in judging the emotion depicted in carefully selected photographs representing the fundamental emotions proposed by Tomkins.

Much of the initial work on the universality of facial expression was conducted by Ekman and his colleagues (see Ekman, 1972; Ekman and Oster, 1982, for reviews) and by Izard (1971). Ekman gathered data on the interpretation of facial expressions from five different cultures, while Izard gathered data from nine cultures. As noted by Ekman and Oster (1982, p. 147), "The majority of observers in each culture interpreted the facial expressions as conveying the same emotions." Thus careful research has reliably shown that facial expressions are judged as depicting the same emotion across various cultures.

People from diverse cultures not only judge specific facial expressions similarly, they also produce the same facial movements when asked to portray particular emotions. For example, Ekman and Friesen (1971) found that members of a preliterate New Guinea group showed the same facial movements as people in literate cultures when asked to pose specific emotions. Further, Ekman (1972) and Friesen (1972, as reported in Ekman, Friesen, & Ellsworth, 1982) found that Japanese and American individuals asked to watch films (some of which were stressing) showed the same facial expressions if alone.

Ekman and 12 other scholars from around the world (Ekman et al., 1987) have gathered additional evidence for the universal nature of facial expressions of emotion. Subjects from 10 different cultures (Estonia, Germany, Greece, Hong Kong, Italy, Japan, Scotland, Sumatra, Turkey, and the United States) were asked to judge the emotions depicted in pictures of a face. Subjects judged the primary emotion expressed and also secondary emotions that might also be present. In addition, subjects were asked to judge the intensity of the emotional expressions. Results of the study showed very good agreement across cultures in the interpretation of the emotions shown. Cross-culturally, subjects consistently agreed on which emotion was the strongest; they also agreed on which secondary emotion was being expressed for those pictures where more than one emotion was present; finally, there was also good agreement concerning the intensities of the emotions expressed. Ekman and associates view this study as providing strong evidence for the universal nature of facial expressions because many of the criticisms of earlier cross-cultural studies were controlled in their study.

A second important factor was also discovered in the Ekman and Friesen studies mentioned above. When an authority figure was present during the viewing of the films, differences in the facial expressions of the Japanese and American subjects became apparent. In particular the Japanese subjects showed greater control over their facial expressions (though they also smiled more than the American subjects under similar circumstances). The differences in facial responsiveness in the presence of an authority figure suggested to Ekman that although universal facial expressions are associated with specific emotional states, these expressions can be modified by what he calls **display rules**. Display rules are presumably learned early in life, and they determine which emotional expressions are appropriate in particular situations. An example of a display rule noted by Ekman is the masking of sadness in public by white urban males in the United States. (Similarly, women usually mask anger in public.) The modification of the fundamental emotional expressions by display rules is conceptually similar to Tomkins's concept of backed-up emotion. Ekman's research therefore supports both Tomkins's concept of primary emotions and his idea that primary emotions are often disguised.

The operation of display rules will of course vary from culture to culture and even within cultures to a degree. As Ekman (1972) pointed out, the contradictory findings of early studies on facial expression may have resulted from observation of facial changes that were modified, in part, by different display rules from one culture to another.

The role of facial expression in emotion has been pursued even further. Ekman, Friesen, and Ancoli (1980) presented films to subjects depicting happy events (a puppy playing with a flower, a gorilla in a zoo, ocean waves) and recorded the movements of the subjects' faces. In particular they wanted to determine if smiling associated with the action of the zygomatic major muscles corresponds with happiness. They based their analysis of this particular muscle group on observation, hunch, and the suspicion that it is involved with smiles of happiness, while other muscle groups are involved with other types of smiles.

Their results supported their predictions. Movement of the zygomatic major muscles was associated with self-reports of happiness. Seven of the subjects watching the films showed no movements of these muscles, and, interestingly, their happiness ratings were significantly lower than those subjects who showed zygomatic major muscle smiles. Further, the intensity of the zygomatic major muscle movements was an accurate predictor of which film was best liked by the subjects, indicating that movement of this muscle system is associated not only with positive feelings but also with the intensity of those feelings. Ekman and co-workers obtained similar correlations between other facial movements and negative

emotional states such as disgust. The study by Ekman, Friesen, and Ancoli (1980) is especially interesting because these researchers have gone a long way toward operationally defining the specific facial movements associated with some emotional states.

Ekman, Friesen, and O'Sullivan (1988) examined the physical differences between smiles that people give when genuinely happy and the smiles they give when they are not happy. In particular these researchers were interested in the subtle differences in muscle contraction that occur when people are asked to deliberately lie about their feelings of happiness.

Student nurses were shown either nature films designed to elicit pleasant feelings or gruesome films of amputations and burns. Subjects viewing the pleasant film were asked to describe their feelings honestly to an interviewer, while subjects viewing the gruesome film were told that it was important to mask their true feelings and to try to convince the interviewer that they had in fact just seen a pleasant film. They were told being able to mask their true feelings was important because they would encounter situations in their nursing career similar to those in the gruesome film and that revealing their true feelings to these patients would be unprofessional. Subjects' faces were videotaped during the sessions and their facial responses scored according to the Facial Action Coding System (FACS) developed by Ekman and Friesen (1976, 1978).

Results of the experiment showed that true smiles involved contraction of the outer muscles that orbit the eye (the orbicularis oculi) in addition to the contraction of the zygomatic major muscles. Smiles made while lying about their true feelings, however, showed a leakage (Ekman and Friesen's term) of other facial muscle activity (in addition to the zygomatic major muscle contractions) associated with the subjects' true feelings. For example, in some subjects minor muscle contractions associated with disgust were seen; in others traces of sadness were observed. Ekman and Friesen's data show that measurable differences between true happy smiles and masking smiles produced to cover true feelings can be found. The FACS measurement device would appear to be a useful procedure for studying the muscular changes associated with various emotional states and seems capable of measuring subtle differences as noted in the above experiment.

Aronoff, Barclay, and Stevenson (1988), in a study concerned with threatening facial stimuli as depicted in ceremonial masks, found evidence that the facial signals communicating threat and their correct recognition were similar across a number of differing cultures. Their study also found that these threat signals seemed to be based on a limited set of configural features which involved the geometrical patterns of diagonality and angularity. Thus anger was often displayed as the eyebrows drawn together in a downward direction.

The Facial Feedback Hypothesis

The models we have examined in this section emphasize the face as one important source of feedback to us about how we feel. The facial feedback hypothesis proposes that we know which emotion we are experiencing as a result of feedback from facial muscles or skin as emotion is expressed through these facial changes.

Tourangeau and Ellsworth (1979) attempted to test this hypothesis, but their study has been criticized on both methodological and theoretical grounds (see, e.g., Hager & Ekman, 1981; Izard, 1981; Tomkins, 1981b; and Ellsworth & Tourangeau, 1981, for a reply). Kraut (1982) designed an experiment in which he presented both pleasant and disgusting odors to subjects. The subjects smelled the odors over several trials during which their facial expressions were videotaped. Some trials recorded the subjects' spontaneous reactions to the smells. On other trials the subjects were in-

structed to compose their faces as if the odors were pleasant, and on still other trials they were told to act as if the odors were unpleasant. Subjects also rated each odor after each trial so that the experimenters could determine whether posing influenced the emotional evaluation of the odors.

Analysis of the data revealed that posing pleasant or unpleasant expressions led to evaluations consistent with the posed expression. In other words, the posed expressions influenced the emotion experienced, supporting the facial feedback hypothesis. Additionally, posing pleasant expressions increased the evaluation of an odor over its evaluation after nonposed trials; similarly, posing unpleasant expressions decreased the odor evaluations relative to nonposed trials. Kraut's study therefore provides limited support for the facial feedback hypothesis; however, as he has noted, the posing effect was small—the actual odors had a much larger effect on the subjects' emotional evaluations than did the posed facial expressions.

Research on the facial feedback hypothesis has exploded in recent years (Aronoff, Barclay, & Stevenson, 1988; Cacioppo, Martzke, Petty, & Tassinary, 1988; Cacioppo, Petty, Losch, & Kim, 1986; Ekman, Friesen, & O'Sullivan, 1988; Matsumoto, 1987; McCanne & Anderson, 1987; Strack, Martin, & Stepper, 1988; see also Adelmann & Zajonc, 1989, for a review of many additional studies relevant to the facial feedback hypothesis). The study by Strack and associates (1988) is ingenious in its attempt to test the hypothesis in an unobtrusive way.

Subjects were asked to hold a pen in their mouths in one of two different ways while viewing and rating cartoons for their humor content. One group held the pen between their teeth with their lips open so that they did not touch the barrel of the pen. Holding the pen in this manner contracts the zygomatic major and the risorius muscles that are involved in smiling. A second group held the pen with their lips only. Holding the pen in this manner contracts the orbicularis oris muscle, which should effectively prevent the contraction of the zygomatic major and risorius muscles. A third group of subjects served as a control by rating the cartoons while holding the pen in their nondominant hand.

A cover story concerning the use of pens by disabled individuals was developed in order to make the three various tasks appear reasonable to the subjects. Although the two experiments were considerably more complicated than presented here, the general outcome of the study was that subjects required to hold the pen between their teeth (and thus contract the muscles associated with smiling) rated the cartoons as more humorous than the control group, who held the pen with their nondominant hand. Those subjects asked to hold the pen with their lips (which prevented contraction of the muscles involved in smiling) rated the cartoons as less humorous than the control group. Thus the evidence suggests that the affective reaction to an emotional stimulus was intensified or weakened when the facial muscles associated with smiling were facilitated or inhibited, respectively. These findings provide good support for the facial feedback hypothesis and further suggest that recognizing the emotional meaning of the facial responses is not necessary in order for the emotion to be influenced.

When we consider the cross-cultural research showing the universality of certain facial expressions and, similarly, the universal recognition of the emotional states those expressions represent, the models proposed by Tomkins, Izard, and Plutchik gain credence. The work of Ekman that appears to have identified the specific muscles involved with such emotions as happiness and disgust further supports the models. These studies providing evidence for the facial feedback hypothesis also bolster the notion that some emotions are innate and universal. Taken as a whole, the research support for common patterns of emotional reaction is quite good, and the evidence continues to grow.

At the same time, however, it is clear that these primary emotions are easily modified by learned cultural influences. Tomkins has called the effect of this learning backed-up affect, while Ekman refers to such learning as display rules. That emotions can be suppressed, exaggerated, disguised, and combined to form blends makes the study of the universality of emotion extremely difficult. However, researchers are apparently beginning to tease apart the various factors contributing to the experience of emotion.

SUMMARY

In this chapter we have examined theories and research on emotion. As we discovered, Darwin's early emphasis on facial expression and body posture has its modern counterparts in the study of intention movements by the ethologists and research on the universality of facial movements by theorists such as Tomkins, Izard, and Ekman. Physiological explanations, popularized by the James-Lange theory and modified by research conducted by Cannon, find their modern counterpart in Schachter's cognitive-physiological model of emotion. Schachter's proposal that physiological changes by themselves are insufficient for the full experience of emotion has led to the development of several more fully cognitive explanations of the experience of emotion. These appraisal models, developed by researchers such as Lazarus, suggest that the cognitive component of emotion is primary and occurs before the full experience of emotion.

Researchers examining the words we use when expressing emotional states have provided evidence for both bipolar dimensions of emotion and circular descriptions of emotional experience. One of the most interesting proposals is that of Russell, who has argued for a circumplex model of emotion that describes a circular pattern of emotions around two major dimensions. Other researchers, adding the dimension of intensity to Russell's model, have suggested that emotional space is best described as cone shaped, with neutrality of emotion represented by the tip of the cone.

In contrast to strictly cognitive models of emotion, Zajonc has argued that emotion can precede and occur independent of cognitive appraisal processes. His argument for the primacy of emotion is supported by the research of Izard, Ekman, and others. In a sense the study of emotion has come full circle, starting with an emphasis on the bodily expression of emotion by Darwin and returning to similar analyses by theorists such as Tomkins, Izard, and Plutchik.

It should be obvious by now that the study of emotion is terribly complex and that theoretical explanations can and do differ widely. One reason for such divergence of opinion is that our emotional experiences are undoubtedly multiply determined. Some emotional feelings and their expression are probably innate and shared by all humans regardless of culture. Other emotional experiences consist of subtle interactions of the more primary emotions. Finally, still other emotional experiences may be altered by learned cultural display rules that limit emotional expression in many ways. Cognition must also play a part in our emotional lives, although the argument over the primacy of cognition is far from resolved. It is also clear that emotionality is strongly associated with physiological changes. Although our thinking has changed somewhat since James and Lange first suggested the importance of physiological change, alterations in the autonomic nervous system (particularly the sympathetic branch) usually accompany the experience of emotion. If emotion is multiply determined, as the evidence presented in this chapter seems to suggest, we should probably not expect one theory to encompass all we know. Rather, like motivation, emotion may be triggered by physiological change, learning, cognition, and perhaps by factors as yet undiscovered.

SUGGESTIONS FOR FURTHER READING

Adelmann, P. K., & Zajonc, R. B. (1989). Facial efference and the experience of emotion. In M. R. Rosenzweig and L. W. Porter (Eds.), *Annual Review of Psychology*, *40*, 249–280. This review provides a very complete analysis of the literature on the facial feedback hypothesis through 1988 for the advanced student.

Plutchik, R. (1980). *Emotion: A psychoevolutionary synthesis*. New York: Harper & Row. This text provides brief overviews of a large number of theories of emotion. In addition, it presents Plutchik's model of emotion and supportive data.

Young, P. T. (1975). *Understanding your feelings and emotions*. Englewood Cliffs, N.J.: Prentice-Hall. This paperback book provides a good introduction to the topic of emotion.

Chapter Fourteen

Conclusions

How does one pull together the research in a field as complex as motivation? Not easily. The research findings stretch from instincts to attitudes with many stops in between. The activation and the direction of behavior by motivational mechanisms are so complex because the relevant information cuts across all subareas within psychology. As a result, motivational explanations have varied depending upon the subarea within psychology from which the data were drawn. In order to attempt some conclusions, however, it seems worthwhile to return to concepts originally outlined in the beginning of this text.

As noted in Chapter One, motivation is a multidimensional phenomenon. Motive states such as hunger, thirst, and sexual activity are reasonably viewed from a physiological perspective. Neural circuits deep within the brain trigger appropriate motivation when internal changes are detected by monitoring systems. This neural circuitry often appears to be homeostatic, activating behavior to keep the body at an optimal level. In Chapter Four we reviewed much of the research pertaining to this view of motivation.

We covered a different type of physiological explanation in Chapter Three. There we

examined research suggesting that arousal mechanisms located within the brainstem are important for motivated activity. Researchers within this realm agree that understanding arousal mechanisms provides us with insight into motivated behavior, and behaviors as disparate as sleep and stress are viewed as different points on an arousal continuum.

Although physiological analysis helps us understand some types of motivated states, physiological explanations alone are inadequate. Humans clearly can override homeostatic mechanisms as a result of experience. Anorexics voluntarily starve, while bulimics gorge and then purge. History is full of examples of individuals who have denied physiological needs for political, philosophical, or religious purposes. Such examples suggest that other mechanisms must play a large role in the motivation of behavior.

Learning is certainly one such mechanism. In Chapters Six and Seven we examined the role of learning in the motivation of behavior, and we discovered that learning can result in the development of new motives not only through classical and operant conditioning but also through modeling. Further, and perhaps more importantly, learning plays a large

367

role in the goals that we pursue. For humans, learning processes lead to the development of incentive motivation, which in turn provides an important way in which environmental objects or goals stimulate and guide our behavior.

Cognitive mechanisms concerned with active information processing also provide an important source of motivation in humans. In Chapters Nine through Twelve we examined these sources of motivation. In Chapter Nine, for example, we noted the importance of expectancy in guiding behavior. In Chapter Ten we explored the important role that others play in motivating conformity and compliance in an individual. Additionally, we reviewed the concept of cognitive consistency. Consistency approaches propose that inconsistencies in our thoughts trigger motivation that brings them back into consistent relationships with one another. Consistency models, as represented by such theories as cognitive dissonance, suggest that our attitudes about ourselves, others, and events are an important source of motivation.

In Chapter Eleven we explored a line of evidence for attitudinal influences on motivation known as attribution theory. As noted, our attributions do alter our motivation; further, we appear to be biased in how we make those attributions. Clearly we cannot hope to understand human behavior unless we also understand both how attributions are made and how they change our motivation to behave in the future. Both social motivation and attribution approaches agree that our motivation is heavily influenced by the behavior of others. At this level of analysis, the group is sometimes the appropriate unit of study.

In Chapter Twelve we examined a somewhat different approach, one that might be considered as occurring at a philosophical level of analysis.

The concepts of the fully functioning individual and self-actualization introduced in Chapter Twelve are based on a positive point of view about human motivation—that we strive to become all that we can become. Because of difficulties in operationally defining such terms as *self-actualization*, data concerned with these approaches are often difficult to interpret. Nevertheless, these approaches have helped us describe human behaviors not easily accounted for by homeostatic or learned motives. As the title of Chapter Twelve suggests, common to many motivated human behaviors is the need to control one's environment. Considerable research on intrinsic motivation and perceived control suggests that competence in controlling the events of one's life is an important source of motivation. Perhaps self-actualization can be understood as a person's lifelong struggle to increase control over the events of his or her life. If one has good control over such basic needs as food, water, shelter, and so forth, then one can focus attention on gaining control over less immediate goals, such as the being needs proposed by Maslow.

In Chapter Thirteen, we used information gained in earlier chapters to examine theoretical approaches to emotion. Research explored in this chapter suggests that emotion, like motivation, is multidimensional. Physiological changes associated with the sympathetic nervous system and feedback from facial regions have both been implicated in the experience of emotion. Further, cross-cultural evidence supports the notion that some basic emotions are universal but can be overridden by cultural display rules. Analysis of emotional terms suggests that a model of emotionality incorporating the dimensions of arousal, pleasantness, and intensity may be able to account for much of emotional experience, although much more research clearly must be done to test the viability of such a model.

Other chapters not yet mentioned also contain important insights into the motivation of behavior. In Chapter Two, on instinct, we saw that the motivation of some animals is controlled by innate, genetically determined programs. Appropriate behaviors are released when specific stimuli are encountered, and while motivated, the animal need have no understanding of why it behaves the way it does. Research presented in Chapter Two suggests that some human behaviors may also be controlled in this way.

In Chapter Five, on drive, we presented theory and research on what for many years was the major concept in motivation. Beginning with Freud and culminating with the work of Hull, the drive model presented the view that physiological changes trigger a psychological state (drive), which then activates and directs behavior. Although drive theory has been replaced by more specific theoretical approaches, such as those outlined in the other chapters, it nevertheless stimulated much of the research upon which present theory is based.

In Chapter Eight we reviewed the concept of hedonism and tied it to work on the motivation for sensory stimulation. Research by Harlow and others has provided evidence of the importance of sensory input and the motivation to obtain it, while opponent-process theory has provided an updated version of hedonism that can help us understand such motivated states as drug addiction as well as other behaviors.

As noted at the beginning of this book, no single theory can account for all that we know about the motivation of behavior. Even a seemingly simple motivation like hunger can be influenced by physiological, cultural, learned, and social factors. Human motives appear to be multiply determined. Much of the complex interaction between the various factors that motivate us remains to be worked out. It is my hope that this text may stimulate some of you to help us tease apart those factors.

References

Abelson, R. P., Aronson, E., McGuire, W. J., Newcomb, T.M., Rosenberg, M. J., & Tannenbaum, P. H. (Eds.). (1968). *Theories of cognitive consistency: A sourcebook.* Chicago: Rand McNally.

Abramson, L. Y., Metalsky, G. I., & Alloy, L. B. (1989). Hopelessness depression: A theory-based subtype of depression. *Psychological Review, 96,* 358–372.

Abramson, L. Y., Seligman, M. E. P., & Teasdale, J. D. (1978). Learned helplessness in humans: Critique and reformulation. *Journal of Abnormal Psychology, 87,* 49–74.

Adelman, H. M., & Maatsch, J. L. (1955). Resistance to extinction as a function of the type of response elicited by frustration. *Journal of Experimental Psychology, 50,* 61–65.

Adelmann, P. K., & Zajonc, R. B. (1989). Facial efference and the experience of emotion. In M. R. Rosenzweig and L. W. Porter (Eds.), *Annual Review of Psychology, 40,* 249–280.

Adler, R., & Hogan, J. A. (1963). Classical conditioning and punishment of an instinctive response in *Betta splendens. Animal Behavior, 11,* 351–354.

Adler, T. (1989, August). Shy monkeys are born, not made. *American Psychological Association Monitor,* p. 5.

Adolph, E. F. (1939). Measurements of water drinking in dogs. *American Journal of Physiology, 125,* 75–86.

Ahsanuddin, K. M., & Nyeem, R. (1983). Fourth ventricle tumors and anorexia nervosa. *International Journal of Eating Disorders, 2,* 67–72.

Alcock, J. (1975). *Animal behavior: An evolutionary approach.* Sunderland, Mass.: Sinauer.

Allen, V. (1964). Uncertainty of outcome and post-decision dissonance reduction. In L. Festinger (Ed.), *Conflict, decision, and dissonance,* pp. 34–42. Stanford, Calif.: Stanford University Press.

Alloy, L. B., & Abramson, L. Y. (1982). Learned helplessness, depression, and the illusion of control. *Journal of Personality and Social Psychology, 42,* 1114–1126.

Allport, G. W. (1937). *Personality: A psychological interpretation.* New York: Holt, Rinehart and Winston.

Alpert, R., & Haber, R. N. (1960). Anxiety in academic achievement situations. *Journal of Abnormal and Social Psychology, 61,* 207–215.

Amato, P. R. (1983). Helping behavior in urban and rural environments: Field studies based on a taxonomic organization of helping episodes. *Journal of Personality and Social Psychology, 45,* 571–586.

American Psychiatric Association. (1980). *Diagnostic and statistical manual of mental disorders* (3rd ed.). Washington, D.C.: American Psychiatric Association.

American Psychiatric Association. (1987). *Diagnostic and statistical manual of mental disorders* (3rd ed., revised). Washington, D.C.: American Psychiatric Association.

American Psychological Association. (1973). *Ethical principles in the conduct of research with human participants.* Washington, D.C.: American Psychological Association.

American Psychological Association. (1982). *Ethical principles in the conduct of research with human participants.* Washington, D.C.: American Psychological Association.

Amsel, A. (1972). Behavioral habituation, counter conditioning, and a general theory of persistence. In A. H. Black & W. F. Prokasy (Eds.), *Classical conditioning II: Current research and theory.* New York: Appleton-Century-Crofts.

Amsel, A., & Roussel, J. (1952). Motivational properties of frustration: I. Effect on a running response of the addition of frustration to the motivational complex. *Journal of Experimental Psychology, 43,* 363–368.

Anand, B. K., & Brobeck, J. R. (1951). Hypothalamic control of food intake in rats and cats. *Yale Journal of Biological Medicine, 24,* 123–140.

Anderson, R., Manoogian, S. T., & Reznick, J. S. (1976). The undermining and enhancing of intrinsic motivation in preschool children. *Journal of Personality and Social Psychology, 34,* 915–922.

Andersson, B. (1971). Thirst and brain control of water balance. *American Scientist, 59,* 408–415.

Andrew, R. J. (1965). The origins of facial expressions. *Scientific American, 213,* 88–94.

Appley, M. H., & Trumbull, R. (1967). On the concept of psychological stress. In M. H. Appley & R. Trumbull (Eds.), *Psychological stress.* New York: Appleton-Century-Crofts.

Arkes, H. R., & Garske, J. P. (1977). *Psychological theories of motivation.* Monterey, Calif.: Brooks/Cole.

Arnold, M. B. (1967). Stress and emotion. In M. H. Appley & R. Trumbull (Eds.), *Psychological stress.* New York: Appleton-Century-Crofts.

Aronoff, J., Barclay, A. M., & Stevenson, L. A. (1988). The recognition of threatening facial stimuli. *Journal of Personality and Social Psychology, 54,* 647–655.

Aronson, E. (1968). Dissonance theory: Progress and problems. In R. P. Abelson et al. (Eds.), *Theories of cognitive consistency: A sourcebook.* Chicago: Rand McNally.

Aronson, E., & Carlsmith, J. (1963). The effect of severity of threat on the devaluation of forbidden behavior. *Journal of Abnormal and Social Psychology, 66,* 584–588.

Aronson, E., & Cope, V. (1968). My enemy's enemy is my friend. *Journal of Personality and Social Psychology, 8,* 8–12.

Aronson, E., & Mills, J. (1959). The effects of severity of initiation on liking for a group. *Journal of Abnormal and Social Psychology, 59*, 177–181.

Asch, S. E. (1952). *Social psychology*. Englewood Cliffs, N.J.: Prentice-Hall.

Asch, S. E. (1965). Interpersonal influence. In H. Proshansky & B. Seidenberg (Eds.), *Basic studies in social psychology*. New York: Holt, Rinehart and Winston.

Aserinsky, E. (1987, November 9). This week's citation classic. *Current Contents*, p. 22.

Aserinsky, E., & Kleitman, N. (1955). A mobility cycle in sleeping infants as manifested by ocular and gross bodily activity. *Journal of Applied Physiology, 8*, 11–19.

Atkinson, J. W., & Birch, D. (1978). *An introduction to motivation* (2nd ed.). New York: Van Nostrand.

Atkinson, J. W., & Litwin, G. H. (1960). Achievement motive and test anxiety conceived as motive to approach success and motive to avoid failure. *Journal of Abnormal and Social Psychology, 60*, 52–63.

Averill, J. R. (1983). Studies on anger and aggression: Implications for theories of emotion. *American Psychologist, 38*, 1145–1160.

Ayllon, T., & Azrin, N. H. (1968). *The token economy: A motivational system for therapy and rehabilitation*. New York: Appleton-Century-Crofts.

Azrin, N. H., Hutchinson, R. R., & Sallery, R. D. (1964). Pain aggression toward inanimate objects. *Journal of the Experimental Analysis of Behavior, 7*, 223–227.

Baerends, G. P. (1976). The functional organization of behavior. *Animal Behavior, 24*, 726–738.

Bailey, P., & Davis, E. W. (1969). Effects of lesions of the periaqueductal gray matter in the cat. In K. H. Pribram (Ed.), *Brain and behavior 1: Mood, states and mind*. Baltimore: Penguin.

Balkin, J. (1986). Contributions of family to men's fear of success in college. *Psychological Reports, 59*, 1071–1074.

Baltes, M. M., & Skinner, E. A. (1983). Cognitive performance deficits and hospitalization: Learned helplessness, instrumental passivity, or what? Comment on Raps, Peterson, Jonas, and Seligman. *Journal of Personality and Social Psychology, 45*, 1013–1016.

Baltimore Sun (1990, January 28). Girl recants testimony, freeing man from jail, p. 15A.

Bandler, R. J., & Flynn, J. P. (1974). Neural pathways from thalamus associated with regulation of aggressive behavior. *Science, 183*, 96–99.

Bandura, A. (1969). *Principles of behavior modification*. New York: Holt, Rinehart & Winston.

Bandura, A. (1971). *Social learning theory*. Morristown, N.J.: General Learning Press.

Bandura, A. (1973). *Aggression: A social learning analysis*. Englewood Cliffs, N.J.: Prentice-Hall.

Bandura, A. (1977). *Social learning theory*. Englewood Cliffs, N.J.: Prentice-Hall.

Bandura, A., O'Leary, A., Taylor, C. B., Gauthier, J., & Gossard, D. (1987). Perceived self-efficacy and pain control: Opioid and nonopioid mechanisms. *Journal of Personality and Social Psychology, 53*, 563–571.

Bandura, A., Ross, D., & Ross, S. A. (1961). Transmission of aggression through imitation of aggressive models. *Journal of Abnormal and Social Psychology, 63*, 575–582.

Bandura, A., Ross, D., & Ross, S. A. (1963). Imitation of film-mediated aggressive models. *Journal of Abnormal and Social Psychology, 66,* 3–11.

Bard, P. (1928). A diencephalic mechanism for the expression of rage with special reference to the sympathetic nervous systems. *American Journal of Physiology, 84,* 490–515.

Bard, P., & Mountcastle, V. B. (1964). Some forebrain mechanisms involved in expression of rage with special reference to suppression of angry behavior. In R. L. Isaacson (Ed.), *Basic readings in neuropsychology.* New York: Harper & Row.

Barfield, R. J., Wilson, C., & McDonald, P. G. (1975). Sexual behavior: Extreme reduction of postejaculatory refractory period by midbrain lesions in male rats. *Science, 189,* 147–149.

Barker, R. H., Dembo, T., & Lewin, K. (1941). Frustration and regression: An experiment with young children. *University of Iowa Studies in Child Welfare, 18,* 1–314.

Baron, R. A. (1974a). The aggression-inhibiting influence of heightened sexual arousal. *Journal of Personality and Social Psychology, 30,* 318–322.

Baron, R. A. (1974b). Sexual arousal and physical aggression: The inhibiting influence of "cheesecake" and nudes. *Bulletin of Psychonomic Society, 3,* 337–339.

Baron, R. A., & Bell, P. A. (1977). Sexual arousal and aggression by males: Effect of type of erotic stimuli and prior provocation. *Journal of Personality and Social Psychology, 35,* 79–87.

Bateson, P. P. G., & Reese, E. P. (1969). The reinforcing properties of conspicuous stimuli in the imprinting situation. *Animal Behavior, 17,* 692–699.

Batson, C. D., Duncan, B. D., Ackerman, P., Buckley, T., & Birch, K. (1981). Is empathic emotion a source of altruistic motivation? *Journal of Personality and Social Psychology, 40,* 290–302.

Batson, C. D., Dyck, J. L., Brandt, J. R., Batson, J. G., Powell, A. L., McMaster, M. R., & Griffit, C. (1988). Five studies testing two new egoistic alternatives to the empathy-altruism hypothesis. *Journal of Personality and Social Psychology, 55,* 52–77.

Batson, C. D., & Gray, R. A. (1981). Religious orientation and helping behavior: Responding to one's own or to the victim's needs? *Journal of Personality and Social Psychology, 40,* 511–520.

Batson, C. D., O'Quin, K., Fultz, J., Vanderplas, M., & Isen, A. M. (1983). Influence of self-reported distress and empathy on egoistic versus altruistic motivation to help. *Journal of Personality and Social Psychology, 45,* 706–718.

Batson, C. D., & Vanderplas, M. (1985). Helping. In D. Perlman & C. Cozby (Eds.), *Social psychology.* New York: Holt, Rinehart & Winston.

Baum, A., & Gatchel, R. J. (1981). Cognitive determinants of reaction to uncontrollable events: Development of reactance and learned helplessness. *Journal of Personality and Social Psychology, 40,* 1078–1089.

Baumann, D. J., Cialdini, R. B., & Kenrick, D. T. (1981). Altruism as hedonism: Helping and self-gratification as equivalent responses. *Journal of Personality and Social Psychology, 40,* 1039–1046.

Baumeister, A., Hawkins, W. F., & Cromwell, R. L. (1964). Need states and activity level. *Psychological Bulletin, 61,* 438–453.

Baumeister, R. F., & Tice, D. M. (1984). Role of self-presentation and choice in cognitive dissonance under forced compliance: Necessary or sufficient causes? *Journal of Personality and Social Psychology, 46,* 5–13.

Baumrind, D. (1964). Some thoughts on the ethics of research: After reading Milgram's "Behavioral study of obedience." *American Psychologist, 19,* 4211–4223.

Beach, F. A. (1955). The descent of instinct. *Psychological Review, 62,* 401–410.

Beach, F. A. (1967). Cerebral and hormonal control of reflexive mechanisms involved in copulatory behavior. *Physiological Review, 47,* 289–316.

Beach, F. A., & Jordan, L. (1956). Sexual exhaustion and recovery in the male rat. *Quarterly Journal of Experimental Psychology, 8,* 121–133.

Beck, A. T. (1967). *Depression: Clinical, experimental, and theoretical aspects.* New York: Harper & Row.

Beck, R. C. (1978). *Motivation: Theories and principles.* Englewood Cliffs, N.J.: Prentice-Hall.

Beck, R. C. (1983). *Motivation: Theories and principles* (2nd ed.). Englewood Cliffs, N.J.: Prentice-Hall.

Beck, R. C., & Matteson, N. (1982). False physiological feedback and emotion: An experimental artifact? Paper presented at the annual convention of the Southeastern Psychological Association, New Orleans.

Bedell, J. R., Giordani, B., Amour, J. L., Tavormina, J., & Boll, T. (1977). Life stress and the psychological and medical adjustment of chronically ill children. *Journal of Psychosomatic Research, 21,* 237–242.

Beebe-Center, J. G. (1932). *The psychology of pleasantness and unpleasantness.* New York: Russell & Russell. (Reissued 1966).

Bem, D. J. (1967). Self-perception: An alternative interpretation of cognitive dissonance phenomena. *Psychology Review, 74,* 183–200.

Bem, D. J. (1970). *Beliefs, attitudes, and human affairs.* Monterey, Calif.: Brooks/Cole.

Bem, S. L. (1974). The measurement of psychological androgyny. *Journal of Consulting and Clinical Psychology, 42,* 155–162.

Bem, S. L. (1977). On the utility of alternative procedures for assessing psychological androgyny. *Journal of Consulting and Clinical Psychology, 45,* 196–205.

Bemis, K. M. (1978). Current approaches to the etiology and treatment of anorexia nervosa. *Psychological Bulletin, 85,* 593–617.

Bennett, A. M. H. (1961). Sensory deprivation in aviation. In P. Solomon et al. (Eds.), *Sensory deprivation.* Cambridge, Mass.: Harvard University Press.

Benson, H. (1975). *The relaxation response.* New York: Avon.

Benson, H., Kotch, J. B., Crassweller, K. D., & Greenwood, M. M. (1977). Historical and clinical considerations of the relaxation response. *American Scientist, 65,* 441–445.

Bentler, P. M. (1968a). Heterosexual behavior assessment: I. Males. *Behavior Research and Therapy, 6,* 21–25.

Bentler, P. M. (1968b). Heterosexual behavior assessment: II. Females. *Behavior Research and Therapy, 6,* 27–30.

Berg, B. (1978). Helping behavior on the gridiron: It helps if you're winning. *Psychological Reports, 42,* 531–534.

Berkowitz, L., & Geen, R. G. (1966). Film violence and the cue properties of available targets. *Journal of Personality and Social Psychology, 3,* 525–530.

Berkowitz, L., & LePage, A. (1967). Weapons as aggression-eliciting stimuli. *Journal of Personality and Social Psychology, 7*, 202–207.

Berlyne, D. E. (1951). Attention to change. *British Journal of Psychology, 42*, 269–278.

Berlyne, D. E. (1958a). The influence of complexity and novelty in visual figures on orienting responses. *Journal of Experimental Psychology, 55*, 289–296.

Berlyne, D. E. (1958b). The influence of the albedo and complexity of stimuli on visual fixation in the human infant. *British Journal of Psychology, 49*, 315–318.

Berlyne, D. E. (1960). *Conflict, arousal, and curiosity.* New York: McGraw-Hill.

Berlyne, D. E. (1963). Motivational problems raised by exploratory and epistemic behavior. In S. Koch (Ed.), *Psychology: A study of a science* (Vol. 5). New York: McGraw-Hill.

Bermant, G. (1976). Sexual behavior: Hard times with the Coolidge Effect. In M. H. Siegel & H. P. Ziegler (Eds.), *Psychological research: The inside story.* New York: Harper & Row.

Bernstein, I. L. (1978). Learned taste aversions in children receiving chemotherapy. *Science, 200*, 1302–1303.

Berscheid, E., & Walster, E. (1974). A little bit about love. In T. L. Huston (Ed.), *Foundations of interpersonal attraction.* New York: Academic Press.

Bertini, M. (1973). REM sleep as a psychophysiological "agency" of memory organization. In W. P. Koella & P. Levin (Eds.), *Sleep: Physiology, biochemistry, psychology, pharmacology, clinical implications.* New York: Karger.

Bexton, W. H., Heron, W., & Scott, T. H. (1954). Effects of decreased variation in the sensory environment. *Canadian Journal of Psychology, 8*, 70–76.

Bieliauskas, L. A., & Strugar, D. A. (1976). Sample size characteristics and scores on the social readjustment rating scale. *Journal of Psychosomatic Research, 20*, 201–205.

Bieliauskas, L. A., & Webb, J. M. (1974). The social readjustment rating scale: Validity in a college population. *Journal of Psychosomatic Research, 18*, 115–123.

Bindra, D. (1968). Neuropsychological interpretation of the effects of drive and incentive-motivation on general activity and instrumental behavior. *Psychological Review, 75*, 1–22.

Bindra, D. (1969). The interrelated mechanisms of reinforcement and motivation, and the nature of their influence on response. In W. J. Arnold & D. Levine (Eds.), *Nebraska Symposium on Motivation.* Lincoln: University of Nebraska Press.

Bindra, D. (1972). A unified account of classical conditioning and operant training. In A. H. Black & W. F. Prokasy (Eds.), *Classical conditioning II: Current research and theory.* New York: Appleton-Century-Crofts.

Bindra, D. (1974). A motivational view of learning, performance, and behavior modification. *Psychological Review, 81*, 199–213.

Birch, D., Atkinson, J. W., & Bongort, K. (1974). Cognitive control of action. In B. Weiner (Ed.), *Cognitive views of human motivation.* New York: Academic Press.

Black, R. W. (1969). Incentive motivation and the parameters of reward in instrumental conditioning. In W. J. Arnold & D. Levine (Eds.), *Nebraska Symposium on Motivation.* Lincoln: University of Nebraska Press.

Blass, E. M. (1968). Separation of cellular from extracellular controls of drinking in rats by frontal brain damage. *Science, 162,* 1501–1503.

Blass, E. M., & Epstein, A. N. (1971). A lateral preoptic osmosensitive zone for thirst in the rat. *Journal of Comparative and Physiological Psychology, 76,* 378–394.

Blass, E. M., & Hanson, D. G. (1970). Primary hyperdipsia in the rat following septal lesions. *Journal of Comparative and Physiological Psychology, 70,* 87–93.

Blass, E. M., & Kraly, F. S. (1974). Medial forebrain bundle lesions: Specific loss of feeding to decreased glucose utilization in rats. *Journal of Comparative and Physiological Psychology, 86,* 679–692.

Blass, E. M., Nussbaum, A. I., & Hanson, D. G. (1974). Septal hyperdipsia: Specific enhancement of drinking to angiotensin in rats. *Journal of Comparative and Physiological Psychology, 87,* 422–439.

Blodgett, H. C. (1929). The effect of the introduction of reward upon maze behavior in rats. *University of California Publications in Psychology, 4,* 113–134.

Boggiano, A. K., & Ruble, D. N. (1979). Competence and the overjustification effect: A developmental study. *Journal of Personality and Social Psychology, 37,* 1462–1468.

Bolles, R. C. (1967). *Theory of motivation.* New York: Harper & Row.

Bolles, R. C. (1969). Avoidance and escape learning: Simultaneous acquisition of different responses. *Journal of Comparative and Physiological Psychology, 68,* 353–358.

Bolles, R. C. (1970). Species-specific defense reactions and avoidance learning. *Psychological Review, 77,* 32–48.

Bolles, R. C. (1974). Cognition and motivation: Some historical trends. In B. Weiner (Ed.), *Cognitive views of human motivation.* New York: Academic Press.

Bolles, R. C. (1975). *Theory of motivation* (2nd ed.). New York: Harper & Row.

Bolles, R. C., & Moot, S. A. (1972). Derived motives. In P. H. Mussen & M. R. Rosenzweig (Eds.), *Annual Review of Psychology, 23.*

Boring, E. G. (1950). *A history of experimental psychology* (2nd ed.). New York: Appleton-Century-Crofts.

Bovard, E. W. (1967). Invited commentary on psychophysiology and psychoendocrinology of stress. In M. H. Appley & R. Trumbull (Eds.), *Psychological stress.* New York: Appleton-Century-Crofts.

Bowlby, J. (1973). *Attachment and loss, Vol. II: Separation.* New York: Basic Books.

Bowlby, J., & Parkes, C. M. (1970). Separation and loss within the family. In E. J. Anthony & C. Koupernik (Eds.), *The child in his family.* New York: Wiley.

Boyd, T. L. (1982). Learned helplessness in humans: A frustration-produced response pattern. *Journal of Personality and Social Psychology, 42,* 738–752.

Bradburn, N. M., & Berlew, D. E. (1961). Need for achievement and English economic growth. *Economic Development and Cultural Exchange, 10,* 8–20.

Brecher, G., & Waxler, S. (1949). Obesity in albino mice due to single injections of goldthioglucose. *Proceedings of the Society for Experimental Biology and Medicine, 70,* 498.

Breedlove, C. J., & Cicirelli, V. G. (1974). Women's fear of success in relation to personal characteristics and type of occupation. *Journal of Psychology, 86,* 181–190.

Brehm, J. W. (1956). Postdecision changes in

the desirability of alternatives. *Journal of Abnormal and Social Psychology, 52,* 384–389.

Breland, R., & Breland, M. (1961). The misbehavior of organisms. *American Psychologist, 16,* 681–684.

Bremer, F. (1937). L'activité cérébrale au cours du sommeil et de la narcose. Contribution à l'étude du mécanisme du sommeil. *Bulletin de l'Académie Royale de Belgique, 4,* 68–86.

Brockner, J., Gardner, M., Bierman, J., Mahan, T., Thomas, B., Weiss, W., Winters, L., & Mitchell, A. (1983). The roles of self-esteem and self-consciousness in the Wortman-Brehm model of reactance and learned helplessness. *Journal of Personality and Social Psychology, 45,* 199–209.

Broughton, R., & Gastaut, H. (1973). Memory and sleep. In W. P. Koella & P. Levin (Eds.), *Sleep: Physiology, biochemistry, psychology, pharmacology, clinical implications.* New York: Karger.

Brown, J. S., Kalish H. I., & Farber, I. E. (1951). Conditioned fear as revealed by magnitude of startle response to an auditory stimulus. *Journal of Experimental Psychology, 41,* 317–328.

Brown, M., Jennings, J., & Vanik, V. (1974). The motive to avoid success: A further examination. *Journal of Research in Personality, 8,* 172–176.

Brown, R. (1965). *Social psychology.* New York: Free Press.

Brownmiller, S. (1975). *Against our will: Men, women, and rape.* New York: Simon & Schuster.

Bruch, H. (1973). *Eating disorders.* New York: Basic Books.

Bruner, J. S. (1961). The cognitive conse-quences of early sensory deprivation. In P. Solomon et al. (Eds.), *Sensory deprivation.* Cambridge, Mass.: Harvard University Press.

Buck, R. (1975). Nonverbal communication of affect in children. *Journal of Personality and Social Psychology, 31,* 644–653.

Buck, R. (1976). *Human motivation and emotion.* New York: Wiley.

Buck, R., Miller, R. E., & Caul, W. F. (1974). Sex, personality, and physiological variables in the communication of affect via facial expression. *Journal of Personality and Social Psychology, 30,* 587–596.

Buck, R., Savin, V. J., Miller, R. E., & Caul, W. F. (1972). Communication of affect through facial expression in humans. *Journal of Personality and Social Psychology, 23,* 362–371.

Buggy, J., Fisher, A. E., Hoffman, W. E., Johnson, A. K., & Phillips, M. I. (1975). Ventricular obstruction: Effect on drinking induced by intracranial injection of angiotensin. *Science, 190,* 72–74.

Bullen, B. A., Reed, R. B., & Mayer, J. (1964). Physical activity of obese and nonobese adolescent girls, appraised by motion picture sampling. *American Journal of Clinical Nutrition, 14,* 211–223.

Bunnell, D. E., Bevier, W., & Horvath, S. M. (1983). Effects of exhaustive exercise on the sleep of men and women. *Psychophysiology, 20,* 50–58.

Burghardt, G. M. (1973). Instinct and innate behavior: Toward an ethological psychology. In J. A. Nevin (Ed.), *The study of behavior: Learning, motivation, emotion, instinct.* Glenview, Ill.: Scott, Foresman.

Burish, T. G., & Carey, M. P. (1986). Conditioned aversive responses in cancer chemotherapy patients: Theoretical and developmental analysis. *Journal of Consulting and Clinical Psychology, 54,* 593–600.

Burish, T. G., Carey, M. P., Krozely, M. G., & Greco, F. A. (1987). Conditioned side effects induced by cancer chemotherapy: Prevention through behavioral treatment. *Journal of Consulting and Clinical Psychology, 55,* 42–48.

Buxton, C. E. (1940). Latent learning and the goal gradient hypothesis. *Contributions to Psychological Theory* (Duke University), *2,* No. 6.

Cacioppo, J. T., Martzke, J. S., Petty, R. E., & Tassinary, L. G. (1988). Specific forms of facial EMG response index emotions during an interview: From Darwin to the continuous flow hypothesis of affect-laden information processing. *Journal of Personality and Social Psychology, 54,* 592–604.

Cacioppo, J. T., Petty, R. E., Losch, M. E., & Kim, H. S. (1986). Electromyographic activity over facial muscle regions can differentiate the valence and intensity of affective reactions. *Journal of Personality and Social Psychology, 50,* 260–268.

Calder, B. J., Ross, M., & Insko, C. A. (1973). Attitude change and attitude attribution: Effects of incentive, choice, and consequences. *Journal of Personality and Social Psychology, 25,* 84–99.

Campbell, B. A., & Sheffield, F. D. (1953). Relation of random activity to food deprivation. *Journal of Comparative and Physiological Psychology, 46,* 320–322.

Cannon, W. B. (1927). The James-Lange theory of emotion: A critical examination and an alternative theory. *American Journal of Psychology, 39,* 106–124.

Cannon, W. B. (1929). *Bodily changes in pain, hunger, fear and rage* (2nd ed.). New York: Appleton.

Cannon, W. B. (1968). The James-Lange theory of emotion: A critical examination and an alternative theory. In M. B. Arnold (Ed.), *The nature of emotion.* Baltimore: Penguin.

Cannon, W. B., & Washburn, A. L. (1912). An explanation of hunger. *American Journal of Physiology, 29,* 444–454.

Cantwell, D. P., Sturzenberger, S., Borroughs, J., Salkin, B., & Green, J. K. (1977). Anorexia nervosa—an affective disorder? *Archives of General Psychiatry, 34,* 1087–1093.

Caplan, R. D. (1975). A less heretical view of life change and hospitalization. *Journal of Psychosomatic Research, 19,* 247–250.

Carlsmith, J., & Gross, A. (1969). Some effects of guilt on compliance. *Journal of Personality and Social Psychology, 11,* 232–239.

Carlson, M., Charlin, V., & Miller, N. (1988). Positive mood and helping behavior: A test of six hypotheses. *Journal of Personality and Social Psychology, 55,* 211–229.

Carlson, M., & Miller, N. (1987). An explanation of the relation between negative mood and helping. *Psychological Bulletin, 102,* 91–108.

Carlson, N. R. (1977). *Physiology of behavior.* Boston: Allyn & Bacon.

Cartwright, D., & Harary, F. (1956). Structural balance: A generalization of Heider's theory. *Psychological Review, 63,* 277–292.

Casper, R. C. (1983). On the emergence of bulimia nervosa as a syndrome. *International Journal of Eating Disorders, 2,* 3–16.

Cassel, J. C. (1976). The contribution of the social environment to host resistance. *Amer-*

ican Journal of Epidemiology, 104, 107–123.

Chapanis, N. P., & Chapanis, A. (1964). Cognitive dissonance: Five years later. *Psychological Bulletin, 61*, 1–22.

Chiang, H. H., & Maslow, A. H. (1977). *The healthy personality: Readings* (2nd ed.). New York: Van Nostrand.

Chung, S.-H., & Dickenson, A. (1980). Pain, enkephalin, and acupunture. *Nature, 283*, 243–244.

Cialdini, R. B., Schaller, M., Houlihan, D., Arps, K., Fultz, J., & Beaman, A. L. (1987). Empathy-based helping: Is it selflessly or selfishly motivated? *Journal of Personality and Social Psychology, 52*, 749–758.

Clark, M. S., & Isen, A. M. (1982). Toward understanding the relationship between feeling states and social behavior. In A. Hastorf & A. M. Isen (Eds.), *Cognitive social psychology*. New York: Elsevier.

Clark, T. K., Caggiula, A. R., McConnell, R. A., & Antelman, S. M. (1975). Sexual inhibition is reduced by rostral midbrain lesions in the male rat. *Science, 190*, 169–171.

Cleary, P. J. (1981). Problems of internal consistency and scaling in life event schedules. *Journal of Psychosomatic Reseach, 25*, 309–320.

Cobb, S. (1976). Social support as a moderator of life stress. *Psychomatic Medicine, 38*, 300–314.

Cofer, C. N., & Appley, M. H. (1964). *Motivation: Theory and research*. New York: Wiley.

Cohen, A. R. (1962). An experiment on small rewards for discrepant compliance and attitude change. In J. W. Brehm & A. R. Cohen (Eds.), *Explorations in cognitive dissonance*. New York: Wiley.

Cohen, S., & Wills, T. A. (1985). Stress, social support, and the buffering hypothesis. *Psychological Bulletin, 98*, 310–357.

Coke, J. S., Batson, C. D., & McDavis, K. (1978). Empathic mediation of helping: A two-stage model. *Journal of Personality and Social Psychology, 36*, 752–766.

Cole, H. W., Figler, M. H., Parente, F. J., & Peeke, H. V. S. (1980). The relationship between sex and aggression in convict cichlids *(Cichlasoma nigrofasciatum Gunther)*. *Behavior, 75*, 1–21.

Collins, B. E., & Hoyt, M. F. (1972). Personal responsibility for consequences: An integration and extension of the "forced compliance" literature. *Journal of Experimental Social Psychology, 8*, 558–593.

Cook, E. A., & Chandler, T. A. (1984). Is fear of success a motive? An attempt to answer criticisms. *Adolescence, 19*, 667–674.

Cook, K. S., Min, H. Y., Johnson, D., Chaplinsky, R. J., Flier, J. S., Hunt, C. R., & Spiegelman, B. M. (1987). Adipsin: A circulating serine protease homolog secreted by adipose tissue and sciatic nerve. *Science, 237*, 402–404.

Cooper, W. H. (1983). An achievement motivation nomological network. *Journal of Personality and Social Psychology, 44*, 841–861.

Costello, C. G. (1978). A critical review of Seligman's laboratory experiments on learned helplessness and depression in humans. *Journal of Abnormal Psychology, 87*, 21–31.

Cotton, J. L. (1981). A review of research on Schachter's theory of emotion and the misattribution of arousal. *European Journal of Social Psychology, 11*, 365–397.

Cowles, J. T. (1937). Food-tokens as incentive for learning by chimpanzees. *Comparative Psychology Monographs, 14*, No. 5.

Craig, W. O. (1918). Appetites and aversions as constituents of instincts. *Biological Review, 34*, 91–107.

Crandall, C. S. (1988). Social contagion of binge eating. *Journal of Personality and Social Psychology, 55*, 588–598.

Crespi, L. P. (1942). Quantitative variation of incentive and performance in the white rat. *American Journal of Psychology, 55*, 467–517.

Croyle, R. T., & Cooper, J. (1983). Dissonance arousal: Physiological evidence. *Journal of Personality and Social Psychology, 45*, 782–791.

Cunningham, M. R., Steinberg, J., & Grev., R. (1980). Wanting to and having to help: Separate motivations for positive mood and guilt-induced helping. *Journal of Personality and Social Psychology, 38*, 181–192.

Czeisler, C. A., Kronauer, R. E., Allan, J. S., Duffy, J. F., Jewett, M. E., Brown E. N., & Ronda, J. M. (1989). Bright light induction of strong (Type O) resetting of the human circadian pacemaker. *Science, 244*, 1328–1333.

Daly, E. M., Lancee, W. J., & Polivy, J. (1983). A conical model for the taxonomy of emotional experience. *Journal of Personality and Social Psychology, 45*, 443–457.

Danker-Brown, P., & Baucom, D. H. (1982). Cognitive influences on the development of learned helplessness. *Journal of Personality and Social Psychology, 43*, 793–801.

Darley, J. M., & Batson, C. D. (1976). From Jerusalem to Jericho: A study of situational and dispositional variables in helping behavior. In M. P. Golden (Ed.), *The research experience*. Itasca, Ill.: Peacock.

Darwin, C. R. (1872). *The expression of the emotions in man and animals*. New York: Appleton.

Darwin, C. R. (1899). *On the origin of species by means of natural selection* (6th ed.). Akron, Ohio: Werner.

Davenport, W. H. (1976). Sex in cross-cultural perspective. In F. A. Beach (Ed.), *Human sexuality in four perspectives*, pp. 115–163. Baltimore: Johns Hopkins University Press.

Davis, H., & Hurwitz, H. M. B. (Eds.) (1977). *Operant-Pavlovian interactions*. Hillsdale, N.J.: Erlbaum.

Davison, G. C. (1966). Differential relaxation and cognitive restructuring in therapy with a paranoid schizophrenic or paranoid state. *Proceedings of the American Psychological Association*, 177–178.

Dawkins, R. (1976). *The selfish gene*. New York: Oxford University Press.

deCharms, R. (1968). *Personal causation: The internal affective determinants of behavior*. New York: Academic Press.

deCharms, R., & Moeller, G. H. (1962). Values expressed in American children's readers: 1800–1950. *Journal of Abnormal and Social Psychology, 64*, 136–142.

Deci, E. L. (1971). The effects of externally mediated rewards on intrinsic motivation. *Journal of Personality and Social Psychology, 18*, 105–115.

Deci, E. L. (1972). Intrinsic motivation, extrinsic reinforcement, and inequity. *Journal of Personality and Social Psychology, 22*, 113–120.

Deci, E. L. (1975). *Intrinsic motivation*. New York: Plenum.

Deci, E. L., Cascio, W. F., & Krusell, J. (1975). Cognitive evaluation theory and some comments on the Calder and Staw critique. *Journal of Personality and Social Psychology, 31,* 81–85.

Deci, E. L., Nezlek, J., & Sheinman, L. (1981). Characteristics of the rewarder and intrinsic motivation of the rewardee. *Journal of Personality and Social Psychology, 40,* 1–10.

Deci, E. L., & Porac, J. (1978). Cognitive evaluation theory and the study of human motivation. In M. R. Lepper & D. Greene (Eds.), *The hidden costs of reward.* Hillsdale, N.J.: Erlbaum.

de Jong, P. F., Koomen, W., & Mellenbergh, G. J. (1988). Structure of causes for success and failure: A multidimensional scaling analysis of preference judgments. *Journal of Personality and Social Psychology, 55,* 718–725.

Delgado, J. M. R., Roberts, W. W., & Miller, N. E. (1954). Learning motivated by electrical stimulation of the brain. *American Journal of Physiology, 179,* 587–593.

Dement, W. C. (1972). *Some must watch while some must sleep.* San Francisco: Freeman.

Dewan, E. M. (1970). The programming (P) hypothesis for REM sleep. In E. Hartmann (Ed.), *Sleep and dreaming.* Boston: Little, Brown.

Diener, C. I., & Dweck, C. S. (1978). An analysis of learned helplessness: Continuous changes in performance, strategy, and achievement cognitions following failure. *Journal of Personality and Social Psychology, 36,* 451–462.

Diener, C. I., & Dweck, C. S. (1980). An analysis of learned helplessness: II. The processing of success. *Journal of Personality and Social Psychology, 39,* 940–952.

Dinsmoor, J. A. (1950). A quantitative comparison of the discriminative and reinforcing functions of a stimulus. *Journal of Experimental Psychology, 40,* 458–472.

Dinsmoor, J. A., Flint, G. A., Smith, R. F., & Viemeister, N. F. (1969). Differential reinforcing effects of stimuli associated with the presence or absence of a schedule of punishment. In D. P. Hendry (Ed.), *Conditioned reinforcement.* Homewood, Ill.: Dorsey.

Dinsmoor, J. A., & Sears, G. O. (1973). Control of avoidance by a response-produced stimulus. *Learning and Motivation, 4,* 284–293.

Dohrenwend, B. S., & Dohrenwend, B. P. (1974). A brief historical introduction to research on stressful life events. In B. S. Dohrenwend & B. P. Dohrenwend (Eds.), *Stressful life events: Their nature and effects.* New York: Wiley.

Dollard, J. C., Doob, L., Miller, N., Mowrer, O., & Sears, R. (1939). *Frustration and aggression.* New Haven, Conn.: Yale University Press.

Domjan, M., & Burkhard, B. (1982). *The principles of learning and behavior.* Monterey, Calif.: Brooks/Cole.

Domjan, M., Miller, V., & Gemberling, G. A. (1982). Note on aversion learning to the shape of food by monkeys. *Journal of the Experimental Analysis of Behavior, 38,* 87–91.

Donnerstein, E., Donnerstein, M., & Evans, R. (1975). Erotic stimuli and aggression: Facilitation or inhibition. *Journal of Personality and Social Psychology, 32,* 237–244.

Dorland's Illustrated Medical Dictionary (24th ed.). (1965). Philadelphia: Saunders.

Duffy, E. (1966). The nature and development of the concept of activation. In R. N. Haber (Ed.), *Current research in motivation.* New York: Holt, Rinehart & Winston.

Duke, M. P., & Lancaster, W. (1976). A note on

locus of control as a function of father absence. *Journal of Genetic Psychology, 129,* 335–336.

Dunham, P. J. (1968). Contrasted conditions of reinforcement: A selective critique. *Psychological Bulletin, 69,* 295–315.

Dweck, C. S. (1975). The role of expectations and attributions in the alleviation of learned helplessness. *Journal of Personality and Social Psychology, 31,* 674–685.

Dweck, C. S. (1986). Motivational processes affecting learning. *American Psychologist, 41,* 1040–1048.

Dweck, C. S., & Leggett, E. L. (1988). A social-cognitive approach to motivation and personality. *Psychological Review, 95,* 256–273.

Dweck, C. S., & Repucci, N. D. (1973). Learned helplessness and reinforcement responsibility in children. *Journal of Personality and Social Psychology, 25,* 109–116.

Earn, B. M. (1982). Intrinsic motivation as a function of extrinsic financial rewards and subjects' locus of control. *Journal of Personality, 50,* 360–373.

Eibl-Eibesfeldt, I. (1961). The fighting behavior of animals. *Scientific American, 205,* 112–122.

Eibl-Eibesfeldt, I. (1970). *Ethology: The biology of behavior* (trans. Erich Klinghammer). New York: Holt, Rinehart & Winston.

Eibl-Eibesfeldt, I. (1972). *Love and hate: The natural history of behavior patterns* (trans. Geoffrey Strachan). New York: Holt, Rinehart & Winston.

Eibl-Eibesfeldt, I. (1977). Evolution of destructive behavior. *Aggressive Behavior, 3,* 127–144.

Eibl-Eibesfeldt, I. (1979). *The biology of peace and war.* Britain: Thames and Hudson.

Ekman, P. (1972). Universals and cultural differences in facial expressions of emotion. In J. K. Cole (Ed.), *Nebraska Symposium on Motivation,* pp. 207–283. Lincoln: University of Nebraska Press.

Ekman, P., & Friesen, W. V. (1971). Constants across cultures in the face and emotion. *Journal of Personality and Social Psychology, 17,* 124–129.

Ekman, P., & Friesen, W. V. (1976). Measuring facial movement. *Environmental Psychology and Nonverbal Behavior, 1,* 56–75.

Ekman, P., & Friesen, W. V. (1978). *Facial action coding system.* Palo Alto, Calif.: Consulting Psychologists Press.

Ekman, P., Friesen, W. V., & Ancoli, S. (1980). Facial signs of emotional experience. *Journal of Personality and Social Psychology, 39,* 1125–1134.

Ekman, P., Friesen, W. V., & Ellsworth, P. (1982). What are the similarities and differences in facial behavior across cultures? In P. Ekman (Ed.), *Emotion in the human face* (2nd ed.), pp. 128–143. New York: Cambridge University Press.

Ekman, P., Friesen, W. V., & O'Sullivan, M. (1988). Smiles when lying. *Journal of Personality and Social Psychology, 54,* 414–420.

Ekman, P., Friesen, W. V., O'Sullivan, M., Chan, A., Diacoyanni-Tarlatzis, I., Heider, K., Krause, R., LeCompte, W. A., Pitcairn, T., Ricci-Bitti, P. E., Scherer, K. Tomita, M., & Tzavaras, A. (1987). Universals and cultural differences in the judgments of facial expressions of emotion. *Journal of Personality and Social Psychology, 53,* 712–717.

Ekman, P., Levenson, R. W., & Friesen, W. V. (1983). Autonomic nervous system activity distinguishes among emotions. *Science, 221,* 1208–1210.

Ekman, P., & Oster, H. (1982). Review of research, 1970–1980. In P. Ekman (Ed.), *Emotion in the human face* (2nd ed.), pp. 147–173. New York: Cambridge University Press.

Elliot, E. S., & Dweck, C. S. (1988). Goals: An approach to motivation and achievement. *Journal of Personality and Social Psychology, 54*, 5–12.

Elliott, M. H. (1928). The effect of change of reward on the maze performance of rats. *University of California Publications in Psychology, 4*, 19–30.

Ellsworth, P. C., Carlsmith, J. M., & Henson, A. (1972). The stare as a stimulus to flight in human subjects: A series of field experiments. *Journal of Personality and Social Psychology, 21*, 302–311.

Ellsworth, P. C., & Tourangeau, R. (1981). On our failure to disconfirm what nobody ever said. *Journal of Personality and Social Psychology, 40*, 363–369.

Engberg, L. A., Hansen, G., Welker, R. L., & Thomas, D. (1972). Acquisition of keypecking via autoshaping as a function of prior experience: Learned laziness? *Science, 178*, 1002–1004.

Entwisle, D. R. (1972). To dispel fantasies about fantasy-based measures of achievement motivation. *Psychological Bulletin, 77*, 377–391.

Epstein, A. N. (1982). The physiology of thirst. In D. W. Pfaff (Ed.), *The physiological mechanisms of motivation*. New York: Springer-Verlag.

Epstein, A. N., Fitzsimons, J. T., & Rolls, B. J. (1970). Drinking induced by injection of angiotensin into the brain of the rat. *Journal of Physiology* (London), *210*, 457–474.

Epstein, A. N., Kissileff, H. R., & Stellar, E. (Eds.). (1973). *The neuropsychology of thirst.* Washington, D.C.: V. H. Winston.

Epstein, A. N., & Teitelbaum, P. (1967). Specific loss of hypoglycemic control of feeding in recovered lateral rats. *American Journal of Physiology, 213*, 1159–1167.

Epstein, S. M. (1967). Toward a unified theory of anxiety. In B. A. Maher (Ed.), *Progress in experimental personality research* (Vol. 4). New York: Academic Press.

Erdmann, G., & Janke, W. (1978). Interaction between physiological and cognitive determinants of emotions: Experimental studies on Schachter's theory of emotions. *Biological Psychology, 6*, 61–74.

Erkut, S. (1983). Exploring sex differences in expectancy, attribution, and academic achievement. *Sex Roles, 9*, 217–231.

Eron, L. D., & Huesmann, L. R. (1984). The control of aggressive behavior by changes in attitudes, values, and the conditions of learning. In R. J. Blanchard and D. C. Blanchard (Eds.), *Advances in the study of aggression* (Vol. 1), pp. 139–171. New York: Academic Press.

Evans, R. I. (1975). *Carl Rogers: The man and his ideas.* New York: Dutton.

Faust, I. M., Johnson, P. R., & Hirsch, J. (1977a). Adipose tissue regeneration following lipectomy. *Science, 197*, 391–393.

Faust, I. M., Johnson, P. R., & Hirsch, J. (1977b). Surgical removal of adipose tissue alters feeding behavior and the development of obesity in rats. *Science, 197*, 393–396.

Fazio, R. H., Zanna, M. P., & Cooper, J. (1977). Dissonance and self-perception: An integrative view of each theory's proper domain of application. *Journal of Experimental Social Psychology, 13*, 464–479.

Feather, N. T. (1961). The relationship of persistence at a task to expectations of success and achievement-related motives. *Journal of Abnormal and Social Psychology, 63,* 552–561.

Feder, H. H. (1984). Hormones and sexual behavior. In M. R. Rosenzweig & L. W. Porter (Eds.), *Annual Review of Psychology, 35,* 165–200.

Feighner, J. P., Robius, E., Guze, S. B., Woodruff, R. A., Winokur, G., & Munoz, R. (1972). Diagnostic criteria for use in psychiatric research. *Archives of General Psychiatry, 26,* 57–63.

Festinger, L. A. (1957). *A theory of cognitive dissonance.* Stanford, Calif.: Stanford University Press.

Festinger, L. (Ed.). (1964). *Conflict, decision, and dissonance.* Stanford, Calif.: Stanford University Press.

Festinger, L., & Carlsmith, J. (1959). Cognitive consequences of forced compliance. *Journal of Abnormal and Social Psychology, 58,* 203–210.

Festinger, L., Riecken, H. W., & Schachter, S. (1956). *When prophecy fails.* Minneapolis: University of Minnesota Press.

Field, T. M., Woodson, R., Greenberg, R., & Cohen, D. (1982). Discrimination and imitation of facial expressions by neonates. *Science, 218,* 179–181.

Field, W. F. (1951). The effects of thematic apperception of certain experimentally aroused needs. Unpublished manuscript, University of Maryland.

Figler, M. H. (1973). The effects of chlordiazepoxide (Librium) on the intensity and habituation of agonistic behavior in male Siamese fighting fish. *Psychopharmacologia, 33,* 277–292.

Figler, M. H., Klein, R. M., & Thompson, C. S. (1975). Chlordiazepoxide (Librium)-induced changes in intraspecific attack and selected non-agonistic behaviors in male Siamese fighting fish. *Psychopharmacologia, 42,* 139–145.

Figler, M. H., Mills, C. J., & Petri, H. L. (1974). Effects of imprinting strength on stimulus generalization in chicks *(Gallus gallus).* *Behavioral Biology, 12,* 541–545.

Fillion, T. J., & Blass, E. M. (1986). Infantile experience with suckling odors determines adult sexual behavior in male rats. *Science, 231,* 729–731.

Fisher, A. E. (1964). Chemical stimulation of the brain. *Scientific American, 210(6),* 60–68.

Fisher, K. (1988, December). Researchers debate lifestyle, health links. *American Psychological Association Monitor,* pp. 13–14.

Fitzsimons, J. T. (1973). Some historical perspectives in the physiology of thirst. In A. N. Epstein et al. (Eds.), *The neuropsychology of thirst.* Washington, D.C.: V. H. Winston.

Fitzsimons, J. T., & LeMagnen, J. (1969). Eating as a regulatory control of drinking in the rat. *Journal of Comparative and Physiological Psychology, 67,* 273–283.

Fitzsimons, J. T., & Simons, B. J. (1969). The effect on drinking in the rat of intravenous infusion of angiotensin, given alone or in combination with other stimuli of thirst. *Journal of Physiology* (London), *203,* 45–57.

Flier, J. S., Cook, K. S., Usher, P., & Spiegelman, B. M. (1987). Severely impaired adipsin expression in genetic and acquired obesity. *Science, 237,* 405–408.

Flynn, J. P. (1969). Neural aspects of attack behavior in cats. In *Experimental approaches to* the study of emotional behavior: *Annals of the New York Academy of Sciences, 159,* 1008–1012.

Flynn, J. P., Vanegas, H., Foote, W., & Edwards, S. (1970). Neural mechanisms involved in a cat's attack on a rat. In R. E. Whalen, R. F. Thompson, M. Verzeano, & N. M. Weinberger (Eds.), *The neural control of behavior.* New York: Academic Press.

Follette, V. M., & Jacobson, N. S. (1987). Importance of attributions as a predictor of how people cope with failure. *Journal of Personality and Social Psychology, 52,* 1205–1211.

Ford, C. S., & Beach, F. A. (1951). *Patterns of sexual behavior.* New York: Harper & Row.

Forest, P., Clark, M., Mills, J., & Isen, A. M. (1979). Helping as a function of feeling state and nature of the helping behavior. *Motivation and Emotion, 3,* 161–169.

Fossi, L., Faravelli, C., & Paoli, M. (1984). The ethological approach to the assessment of depressive disorders. *Journal of Nervous and Mental Disease, 172,* 332–341.

Fowler, H. (1967). Satiation and curiosity: Constructs for a drive and incentive-motivational theory of exploration. In K. W. Spence & J. T. Spence (Eds.), *The psychology of learning and motivation* (Vol. 1). New York: Academic Press.

Fox, D. K., Hopkins, B. L., & Anger, W. K. (1987). The longterm effects of a token economy on safety performance in open-pit mining. *Journal of Applied Behavior Analysis, 20,* 215–224.

Franken, R. E. (1982). *Human motivation.* Monterey, Calif.: Brooks/Cole.

Frankl, V. E. (1959). *Man's search for meaning: An introduction to logotherapy.* New York: Simon & Schuster.

Freedman, J. (1965). Long-term behavioral effect of cognitive dissonance. *Journal of Experimental Social Psychology. 1,* 145–155.

Freedman, J. L., & Sears, D. O. (1965). Selective exposure. In L. Berkowitz (Ed.), *Advances in experimental social psychology* (Vol. 2), pp. 58–98. New York: Academic Press.

Freeman, G. L. (1940). The relationship between performance level and bodily activity level. *Journal of Experimental Psychology, 26,* 602–608.

Freud, S. (1915). Instincts and their vicissitudes. In *Collected papers of Sigmund Freud* (1949) (trans. J. Riviere, Vol. IV), pp. 60–83. London: Hogarth.

Freud, S. (1957). *The standard edition of the complete psychological works of Sigmund Freud* (trans. James Strachey, Vol. 14). London: Hogarth.

Frey, D. (1982). Different levels of cognitive dissonance, information seeking, and information avoidance. *Journal of Personality and Social Psychology, 43,* 1175–1183.

Frick, W. B. (1982). Conceptual foundation of self-actualization: A contribution to motivation theory. *Journal of Humanistic Psychology, 22,* 33–52.

Frick, W. B. (1983). The symbolic growth experience. *Journal of Humanistic Psychology, 23,* 108–125.

Friedman, M. I., & Stricker, E. M. (1976). The physiological psychology of hunger: A physiological perspective. *Psychological Review, 83,* 409–431.

Friesen, W. V. (1972). Cultural differences in facial expression in a social situation: An experimental test of the concept of display rules. Unpublished doctoral dissertation, University of California, San Francisco.

Frieze, I. H. (1976). Causal attributions and information seeking to explain success and failure. *Journal of Research in Personality, 10,* 293–305.

Fyans, L. J., Salili, F., Maehr, M. L., & Desai, K. A. (1983). A cross-cultural exploration into the meaning of achievement. *Journal of Personality and Social Psychology, 44,* 1000–1013.

Garcia, J., Ervin, F. R., & Koelling, R. A. (1966). Learning with prolonged delay of reinforcement. *Psychonomic Science, 5,* 121–122.

Garcia, J., & Koelling, R. A. (1966). Relation of cue to consequence in avoidance learning. *Psychonomic Science, 4,* 123–124.

Garcia, J., McGowan, B. K., & Green, K. F. (1972). Biological constraints on conditioning. In A. H. Black & W. F. Prokasy (Eds.), *Classical conditioning II: Current research and theory.* New York: Appleton-Century-Crofts.

Gardner, L. I. (1972). Deprivation dwarfism. *Scientific American, 227 (I),* 76–82.

Garrity, T. F., Marx, M. B., & Somes, G. W. (1977a). The influence of illness severity and time since life change on the size of the life change—health change relationship. *Journal of Psychosomatic Research, 21,* 377–382.

Garrity, T. F., Marx, M. B., & Somes, G. W. (1977b). Langner's 22-item measure of psychophysiological strain as an intervening variable between life change and health outcome. *Journal of Psychosomatic Research, 21,* 195–199.

Geen, R. G. (1972). *Aggression.* Morristown, N.J.: General Learning Press.

Geen, R. G., & Pigg, R. (1970). Acquisition of an aggressive response and its generaliza-tion to verbal behavior. *Journal of Personality and Social Psychology, 15,* 165–170.

Geller, L. (1982). The failure of self-actualization theory: A critique of Carl Rogers and Abraham Maslow. *Journal of Humanistic Psychology, 22,* 56–73.

Gerard, H. B., & Matthewson, G. C. (1966). The effects of severity of initiation on liking for a group: A replication. *Journal of Experimental Social Psychology, 2,* 278–287.

Gibbs, J., Young, R. G., & Smith, G. P. (1973). Cholecystokinin decreases food intake in rats. *Journal of Comparative and Physiological Psychology, 84,* 488–495.

Gilbert, D. T., Krull, D. S., & Pelham, B. W. (1988). Of thoughts unspoken: Social inference and the self-regulation of behavior. *Journal of Personality and Social Psychology, 55,* 685–694.

Glass, D. C., & Singer, J. E. (1972). Behavioral aftereffects of unpredictable and uncontrollable aversive events. *American Scientist, 60,* 457–465.

Glick, Z. (1982). Inverse relationship between brown fat thermogenesis and meal size: The thermostatic control of food intake revisited. *Physiology & Behavior, 29,* 1137–1140.

Goble, F. G. (1970). *The third force: The psychology of Abraham Maslow.* New York: Grossman.

Goebel, B. L., & Brown, D. R. (1981). Age differences in motivation related to Maslow's need hierarchy. *Developmental Psychology, 17,* 809–815.

Goethals, G. R., Cooper, J., & Naficy, A. (1979). Role of foreseen, foreseeable, and unforeseeable behavior consequences in the arousal of cognitive dissonance. *Journal of Personality and Social Psychology, 37,* 1179–1185.

Gold, R. M. (1973). Hypothalamic obesity: The myth of the ventromedial nucleus. *Science, 182,* 488–490.

Goldberger, L., & Holt, R. R. (1961). Experimental interference with reality contact: Individual differences. In P. Solomon et al. (Eds.), *Sensory deprivation.* Cambridge, Mass.: Harvard University Press.

Goldstein, D., Fink, D., & Mettee, D. R. (1972). Cognition of arousal and actual arousal as determinants of emotion. *Journal of Personality and Social Psychology, 21,* 41–51.

Goodwin, D. V. (1978, September 24). Dwarfism: The victim child's response to abuse. *Baltimore Sun.*

Gottlieb, G. (1972). Imprinting in relation to a parental and species identification by avian neonates. In M. E. P. Seligman & J. L. Hager (Eds.), *Biological boundaries of learning.* New York: Appleton-Century-Crofts.

Gould, J. L. (1982). *Ethology: The mechanisms and evolution of behavior.* New York: Norton.

Gray, D. S., & Gorzalka, B. B. (1980). Adrenal steroid interactions in female sexual behavior: A review. *Psychoneuroendocrinology, 5,* 157–175.

Gray, J. A. (1971). *The psychology of fear and stress.* New York: McGraw-Hill.

Greenberg, R. (1970). Dreaming and memory. In E. Hartmann (Ed.), *Sleep and dreaming.* Boston: Little, Brown.

Greenberg, R., Pearlman, C., Schwartz, W. R., & Grossman, H. Y. (1983). Memory, emotion, and REM sleep. *Journal of Abnormal Psychology, 92,* 378–381.

Greene, E. (1989). A diet-induced developmental polymorphism in a caterpillar. *Science, 243,* 643–646.

Grinker, J. A. (1982). Physiological and behavioral basis of human obesity. In D. W. Pfaff (Ed.), *The physiological mechanisms of motivation.* New York: Springer-Verlag.

Grossman, M. I., & Stein, I. F., Jr. (1948). Vagotomy and the hunger producing action of insulin in man. *Journal of Applied Physiology, 1,* 263–269.

Grossman, S. P. (1976). Neuroanatomy of food and water intake. In D. Novin et al. (Eds.), *Hunger: Basic mechanisms and clinical implications.* New York: Raven Press.

Guillemin, R., & Burgus, R. (1976). The hormones of the hypothalamus. In R. F. Thompson (Ed.), *Progress in psychobiology.* San Francisco: Freeman.

Gull, W. W. (1874). Anorexia nervosa. *Clinical Society of London.* Transactions. 7, 22–28.

Guyton, A. C. (1981). The adrenocortical hormones (Chapter 77). *Textbook of medical physiology* (6th ed.), pp. 944–958. Philadelphia: Saunders.

Hager, J. C., & Ekman, P. (1979). Long-distance transmissions of facial affect signals. *Ethology and Sociobiology, 1,* 77–82.

Hager, J. C., & Ekman, P. (1981). Methodological problems in Tourangeau and Ellsworth's study of facial expression and experience of emotion. *Journal of Personality and Social Psychology, 40,* 358–362.

Hailman, J. P. (1969). How an instinct is learned. *Scientific American, 221(6),* 98–106.

Haith, M. M., Bergman, T., & Moore, M. J. (1977). Eye contact and face scanning in early infancy. *Science, 198,* 853–855.

Halmi, K. A., Falk, J. R., & Schwartz, E. (1981).

Binge-eating and vomiting: A survey of a college population. *Psychological Medicine, 11*, 697–706.

Haney, C., Banks, W. C., & Zimbardo, R. G. (1976). Interpersonal dynamics in a simulated prison. In M. P. Golden (Ed.), *The research experience*. Itasca, Ill.: Peacock.

Harada, J. (1983). The effects of positive and negative experiences on helping behavior. *Japanese Psychological Research, 25*, 47–51.

Harlow, H. F. (1953). Mice, monkeys, men and motives. *Psychological Review, 60*, 23–32.

Harlow, H. F. (1958). The nature of love. *American Psychologist, 13*, 673–685.

Harlow, H. F., & Harlow, M. K. (1962). Social deprivation in monkeys. *Scientific American, 207(5)*, 136–146.

Harlow, H. F., & Harlow, M. K. (1966). Learning to love. *American Scientist, 54*, 244–272.

Harlow, H. F., Harlow, M. K., & Meyer, D. R. (1950). Learning motivated by a manipulation drive. *Journal of Experimental Psychology, 40*, 228–234.

Harlow, H. F., & Suomi, S. J. (1970). Nature of love—simplified. *American Psychologist, 25*, 161–168.

Harmatz, M. G., & Novak, M. A. (1983). *Human sexuality*. New York: Harper & Row.

Harris, B. (1979). Whatever happened to little Albert? *American Psychologist, 34*, 151–160.

Hart, B. (1967). Sexual reflexes and mating behavior in the male dog. *Journal of Comparative and Physiological Psychology, 66*, 388–399.

Hart, B. L. (1974). Gonadal androgen and sociosexual behavior of male mammals: A comparative analysis. *Psychological Bulletin, 81*, 383–400.

Hartmann, E. L. (1973). *The functions of sleep*. New Haven, Conn.: Yale University Press.

Harvey, J. H., Ickes, W. J., & Kidd, R. F. (1976). *New directions in attribution research* (Vol. 1). Hillsdale, N.J.: Erlbaum.

Harvey, J. H., Ickes, W. J., & Kidd, R. F. (1978). *New directions in attribution research* (Vol. 2). Hillsdale, N.J.: Erlbaum.

Harvey, J. H., Town, J. P., & Yarkin, K. L. (1981). How fundamental is "the fundamental attribution error"? *Journal of Personality and Social Psychology, 40*, 346–349.

Hashim, S. A., & Van Itallie, T. B. (1965). Studies in normal and obese subjects with a monitored food dispensing device. *Annals of the New York Academy of Sciences, 131*, 654–661.

Hayashi, Y., & Endo, S. (1982). All-night sleep polygraphic recordings of healthy aged persons: REM and slow-wave sleep. *Sleep, 5*, 277–283.

Haymaker, W., Anderson, E., & Nauta, W. J. H. (Eds.). (1969). *The hypothalamus*. Springfield, Ill.: Thomas.

Haymes, M., & Green, L. (1982). The assessment of motivation within Maslow's framework. *Journal of Research in Personality, 16*, 179–192.

Hebb, D. O. (1949). *The organization of behavior*. New York: Wiley.

Hebb, D. O. (1955). Drives and the conceptual nervous system. *Psychological Review, 62*, 243–253.

Hebb, D. O. (1966). *A textbook of psychology* (2nd ed.). Philadelphia: Saunders.

Heider, F. (1944). Social perception and phenomenal causality. *Psychological Review, 51*, 358–374.

Heider, F. (1946). Attitudes and cognitive organization. *Journal of Psychology, 21,* 107–112.

Heider, F. (1958). *The psychology of interpersonal relations.* New York: Wiley.

Heimer, L., & Larsson, K. (1966/1967). Impairment of mating behavior in male rats following lesions in the preoptic hypothalamic continuum. *Brain Research, 3,* 248–263.

Herberg, L. (1963). Seminal ejaculation following positively reinforcing electrical stimulation of the rat hypothalamus. *Journal of Comparative and Physiological Psychology, 66,* 388–399.

Heron, G., and Johnson, D. (1976). Hypothalamic tumor presenting as anorexia nervosa. *American Journal of Psychiatry, 133,* 580–582.

Heron, W. (1957). The pathology of boredom. *Scientific American, 196(1),* 52–56.

Heron, W. (1961). Cognitive and physiological effects of perceptual isolation. In P. Solomon et al. (Eds.), *Sensory deprivation.* Cambridge, Mass.: Harvard University Press.

Heron, W., Doane, B. K., & Scott, J. H. (1956). Visual disturbances after prolonged perceptual isolation. *Canadian Journal of Psychology, 10,* 13–18.

Herzog, D. B., & Copeland, P. M. (1985). Eating disorders. *New England Journal of Medicine, 313,* 295–303.

Hess, E. H. (1962). Ethology: An approach toward the complete analysis of behavior. In R. Brown, E. Galanter, E. H. Hess, & G. Mandler (Eds.), *New directions in psychology.* New York: Holt, Rinehart & Winston.

Hetherington, A. W., and Ranson, S. W. (1940). Hypothalamic lesions and adiposity in the rat. *Anatomical Record, 78,* 149–172.

Higgins, E. T., Rhodewalt, F., & Zanna, M. P. (1979). Dissonance motivation: Its nature, persistence, and reinstatement. *Journal of Experimental Social Psychology, 15,* 16–34.

Hilgard, E. R., & Bower, G. H. (1975). *Theories of learning* (4th ed.). Englewood Cliffs, N.J.: Prentice-Hall.

Himms-Hagen, J. (1979). Obesity may be due to a malfunctioning of brown fat. *Canadian Medical Association Journal, 121,* 1361–1364.

Hinde, R. A. (1966). *Animal behavior.* New York: McGraw-Hill.

Hinde, R. A. (1971). Critique of energy models of motivation. In D. Bindra & J. Stewart (Eds.), *Motivation* (2nd ed.). Baltimore: Penguin.

Hinkle, L. E. (1974). The effect of exposure to culture change, social change, and changes in interpersonal relationships on health. In B. S. Dohrenwend & B. P. Dohrenwend (Eds.), *Stressful life events: Their nature and effects.* New York: Wiley.

Hinton, B. L. (1968). Environmental frustration and creative problem solving. *Journal of Applied Psychology, 52,* 211–217.

Hinz, L. D., & Williamson, D. A. (1987). Bulimia and depression: A review of the affective variant hypothesis. *Psychological Bulletin, 102,* 150–158.

Hiroto, D. S. (1974). Locus of control and learned helplessness. *Journal of Experimental Psychology, 102,* 187–193.

Hirsch, H. V. B., & Spinelli, D. N. (1970). Visual experience modifies distribution of horizontally and vertically oriented receptive fields in cats. *Science, 168,* 869–871.

Hirsch, H. V. B., & Spinelli, D. N. (1971). Modification of the distribution of receptive field orientation in cats by selective visual exposure during development. *Experimental Brain Research, 13,* 509–527.

Hirsch, J., & Knittle, J. L. (1970). Cellularity of obese and nonobese human adipose tissue. *Federation Proceedings, 29,* 1516–1521.

Hjelle, L. A., & Smith, G. (1975). Self-actualization and retrospective reports of parent-child relationships among college females. *Psychological Reports, 36,* 755–761.

Hobson, J. A. (1977). The reciprocal interaction model of sleep-cycle control: Implications for PGO wave generation and dream amnesia. In R. R. Druke-Colín & J. L. McGaugh (Eds.), *Neurobiology of sleep and memory.* New York: Academic Press.

Hobson, J. A., McCarley, R. W., & Wyzinski, P. W. (1975). Sleep cycle oscillation: Reciprocal discharge by two mainstem neuronal groups. *Science, 189,* 55–58.

Hoffman, H. S., & Boskoff, K. J. (1972). Control of aggressive behavior by an imprinted stimulus. *Psychonomic Science, 29,* 305–306.

Hoffman, H. S., Eiserer, L. A., Ratner, A. M., & Pickering, V. L. (1974). Development of distress vocalization during withdrawal of an imprinting stimulus. *Journal of Comparative and Physiological Psychology, 86,* 563–568.

Hoffman, H. S., & Ratner, A. M. (1973). A reinforcement model of imprinting: Implications for socialization in monkeys and men. *Psychological Review, 80,* 527–544.

Hoffman, H. S., Searle, J. L., Toffey, S., & Kozma, F., Jr. (1966). Behavioral control by an imprinted stimulus. *Journal of the Experimental Analysis of Behavior, 9,* 177–189.

Hoffman, H. S., & Solomon, R. L. (1974). An opponent-process theory of motivation: III. Some affective dynamics in imprinting. *Learning and Motivation, 5,* 149–164.

Hoffman, J. W., Benson, H., Arns, P. A., Stainbrook, G. L., Landsberg, L., Young, J. B., & Gill, A. (1982). Reduced sympathetic nervous system responsivity associated with the relaxation response. *Science, 215,* 190–192.

Hoffman, L. Q. (1974). Fear of success in males and females: 1965 and 1971. *Journal of Consulting and Clinical Psychology, 42,* 353–358.

Hoffman, L. Q. (1977). Fear of success in 1965 and 1974: A follow-up study. *Journal of Consulting and Clinical Psychology, 45,* 310–321.

Hoffman, M. L. (1981). Is altruism a part of human nature? *Journal of Personality and Social Psychology, 40,* 121–137.

Hohmann, G. W. (1962). The effect of dysfunctions of the autonomic nervous system on experienced feelings and emotions. Paper presented at the Conference on Emotions and Feelings, New School of Social Research, New York.

Hokanson, J. E. (1969). *The psychological bases of motivation.* New York: Wiley.

Holloway, S., Tucker, L., & Hornstein, H. A. (1977). The effects of social and nonsocial information on interpersonal behavior of males: The news makes news. *Journal of Personality and Social Psychology, 35,* 514–522.

Holmes, T. H., & Masuda, M. (1974). Life change and illness susceptibility. In B. S. Dohrenwend & B. P. Dohrenwend (Eds.), *Stressful life events: Their nature and effects.* New York: Wiley.

Holmes, T. H., & Rahe, R. H. (1967). The social readjustment rating scale. *Journal of Psychosomatic Research, 11*, 213–218.

Holt, E. B. (1915). *The Freudian wish and its place in ethics.* New York: Holt, Rinehart & Winston.

Horner, M. (1968). Sex differences in achievement motivation and performance in competitive and non-competitive situations. Unpublished manuscript, University of Michigan.

Horner, M. S. (1972). Toward an understanding of achievement-related conflicts in women. *Journal of Social Issues, 28*, 157–175.

Hornstein, H. A., LaKind, E., Frankel, G., & Manne, S. (1975). Effects of knowledge about remote social events on prosocial behavior, social conception, and mood. *Journal of Personality and Social Psychology, 10*, 222–226.

Houpt, T. R., Anika, S. M., & Wolff, N. C. (1978). Satiety effects of cholecystokinin and caerulein in rabbits. *American Journal of Physiology, 235*, 23–28.

House, J. S., Landis, K. R., & Umberson, D. (1988). Social relationships and health. *Science, 241*, 540–544.

Hoyenga, K. B., & Hoyenga, K. T. (1979). *The question of sex differences: Psychological, cultural, and biological issues.* Boston: Little, Brown.

Hoyenga, K. B., & Hoyenga, K. T. (1984). *Motivational explanations of behavior: Evolutionary, physiological, and cognitive ideas.* Monterey, Calif.: Brooks/Cole.

Hsu, L. K. G., & Zimmer, B. (1988). Eating disorders in old age. *International Journal of Eating Disorders, 7*, 133–138.

Hudson, J. I., Pope, H. G., Jonas, J. M.,

Yurgelun-Todd, D., & Frankenburg, F. R. (1987). A controlled family history of bulimia. *Psychological Medicine, 17*, 883–890.

Hull, C. L. (1930). Knowledge and purpose as habit mechanisms. *Psychological Review, 37*, 511–525.

Hull, C. L. (1931). Goal attraction and directing ideas conceived as habit phenomena. *Psychological Review, 38*, 487–506.

Hull, C. L. (1943). *Principles of behavior: An introduction to behavior theory.* New York: Appleton-Century-Crofts.

Hull, C. L. (1951). *Essentials of behavior.* New Haven, Conn.: Yale University Press.

Hull, C. L. (1952). *A behavior system: An introduction to behavior theory concerning the individual organism.* New Haven, Conn.: Yale University Press.

Hulse, S. H. (1958). Amount and percentage of reinforcement and duration of goal confinement in conditioning and extinction. *Journal of Experimental Psychology, 56*, 48–57.

Hunt, J. McV. (1965). Intrinsic motivation and its role in psychological development. In D. Levine (Ed.), *Nebraska Symposium on Motivation.* Lincoln: University of Nebraska Press.

Isaacson, R. L. (1964). Relation between achievement, test anxiety, and curricular choices. *Journal of Abnormal and Social Psychology, 68*, 447–452.

Isen, A. M. (1970). Success, failure, attention, and reaction to others. *Journal of Personality and Social Psychology, 15*, 294–301.

Isen, A. M., & Simmonds, S. F. (1978). The effect of feeling good on a helping task that is incompatible with good mood. *Social Psychology, 41*, 346–349.

Isherwood, J., & Adam, K. S. (1976). The social readjustment rating scale: A cross-culture study of New Zealanders and Americans. *Journal of Psychosomatic Research, 20,* 211–214.

Izard, C. E. (1971). *The face of emotion.* New York: Appleton-Century-Crofts.

Izard, C. E. (1977). *Human emotions.* New York: Plenum.

Izard, C. E. (1979). Emotions as motivations: An evolutionary-developmental perspective. In R. A. Dienstbier (Ed.), *1978 Nebraska Symposium on Motivation,* pp. 163–200. Lincoln: University of Nebraska Press.

Izard, C. E. (1981). Differential emotions theory and the facial feedback hypothesis of emotion activation: Comments on Tourangeau and Ellsworth's "The role of facial response in the experience of emotion." *Journal of Personality and Social Psychology, 40,* 350–354.

Jackson, D. N., Ahmed, S. A., & Heapy, N. A. (1976). Is achievement a unitary construct? *Journal of Research in Personality, 10,* 1121.

James, W. (1884). What is an emotion? *Mind, 9,* 188–205. (Reprinted in M. Arnold [Ed.], *The nature of emotion.* Baltimore: Penguin, 1968.)

James, W. (1890). *Principles of psychology.* New York: Holt.

Jenson, W. R., Paoletti, P., & Peterson, B. P. (1984). Self-monitoring plus a reinforcement contingency to reduce a chronic throat clearing tic in a child. *Behavior Therapist, 7,* 192.

Johnson, C., & Larson, R. (1982). Bulimia: An analysis of moods and behavior. *Psychosomatic Medicine, 44,* 341–351.

Johnson, C. L., & Stuckey, M. K., Lewis, L. D., & Schwartz, D. M. (1982). Bulimia: A descriptive survey of 316 cases. *International Journal of Eating Disorders, 2,* 3–16.

Johnson, J. H., & Sarason, I. G. (1978). Life stress, depression and anxiety: Internal-external control as a moderator variable. *Journal of Psychosomatic Research, 22,* 205–208.

Johnson, L. C. (1983). Sleep deprivation and performance. In W. B. Webb (Ed.), *Biological rhythms and performance,* pp. 111–141. Chichester, England: Wiley.

Johnson, R. N. (1972). *Aggression in man and animals.* Philadelphia: Saunders.

Jones, A. P., & Friedman, M. I. (1982). Obesity and adipocyte abnormalities in offspring of rats undernourished during pregnancy. *Science, 215,* 1518–1519.

Jones, E. E. (1979). The rocky road from acts to dispositions. *American Psychologist, 34,* 107–117.

Jones, E. E., & Davis, K. E. (1965). From acts to dispositions: The attribution process in person perception. In L. Berkowitz (Ed.), *Advances in experimental social psychology* (Vol. 2). New York: Academic Press.

Jones, E. E., & Harris, V. A. (1967). The attribution of attitudes. *Journal of Experimental Social Psychology, 3,* 1–24.

Jones, E. E., Kanouse, D. E., Kelley, H. H., Nisbett, R. E., Valins, S., & Weiner, B. (Eds.). (1972). *Attribution: Perceiving the causes of behavior.* Morristown, N.J.: General Learning Press.

Jones, E. E., & Nisbett, R. E. (1972). The actor and the observer: Divergent perceptions of the causes of behavior. In E. E. Jones et al. (Eds.), *Attribution: Perceiving the causes of behavior.* Morristown, N.J.: General Learning Press.

Jordan, J. H. (1980). Trends in the work force: Individualism, inflation, and productivity. In C. S. Sheppard & D. C. Carroll (Eds.), *Working in the twenty-first century*. New York: Wiley.

Jordan, N. (1953). Behavioral forces that are à function of attitudes and cognitive organization. *Human Relations, 6,* 273–287.

Jouvet, M. (1976). The states of sleep. In R. F. Thompson (Ed.), *Progress in psychobiology*. San Francisco: Freeman.

Kagan, H. (1951). Anorexia and severe inanition associated with a tumor involving the hypothalamus. *Archives of Diseases in Childhood, 26,* 274.

Kagan, J., Reznick, J. S., & Snidman, N. (1988). Biological bases of childhood shyness. *Science, 240,* 167–171.

Kalat, J. W. (1981). *Biological psychology*. Belmont, Calif.: Wadsworth.

Kaplan, H. S. (1978). *Disorders of sexual desire*. New York: Simon & Schuster.

Karabenick, S. A. (1977). Fear of success, achievement and affiliation dispositions, and the performance of men and women under individual and competitive conditions. *Journal of Personality, 45,* 117–149.

Keesey, R. E., Boyle, P. C., Kemnitz, J. W., & Mitchell, J. S. (1976). The role of the lateral hypothalamus in determining the body weight set point. In D. Novin et al. (Eds.), *Hunger: Basic mechanisms and clinical implications*. New York: Raven Press.

Keesey, R. E., & Powley, T. L. (1975). Hypothalamic regulation of body weight. *American Scientist, 63,* 558–565.

Kelley, H. H. (1967). Attribution theory in social psychology. In D. Levine (Ed.), *Nebraska Symposium on Motivation* (Vol. 15). Lincoln: University of Nebraska Press.

Kelley, H. H. (1971). *Attribution in social interaction*. Morristown, N.J.: General Learning Press.

Kelley, H. H. (1972). Attribution in social interaction. In E. E. Jones et al. (Eds.), *Attribution: Perceiving the causes of behavior*. Morristown, N.J.: General Learning Press.

Kelley, H. H. (1973). The processes of causal attribution. *American Psychologist, 28,* 107–128.

Kissileff, H. R. (1969). Food-associated drinking in the rat. *Journal of Comparative and Physiological Psychology, 67,* 284–300.

Kissileff, H. R. (1973). Nonhomeostatic controls of drinking. In A. N. Epstein et al. (Eds.), *The neuropsychology of thirst: New findings and advances in concepts*. Washington, D.C.: V. H. Winston.

Kissileff, H. R., & Epstein, A. N. (1969). Exaggerated prandial drinking in the "recovered lateral" rat without saliva. *Journal of Comparative and Physiological Psychology, 67,* 301–308.

Klein, R. M., Figler, M. H., & Peeke, H. V. S. (1976). Modification of consummatory (attack) behavior resulting from prior habituation of appetitive (threat) components of the agonistic sequence in male Betta Splendens *(Pisces belongtiidae)*. *Behaviour, 58,* 1–25.

Kleinginna, P. R., & Kleinginna, A. M. (1981). A categorized list of motivation definitions, with a suggestion for a consensual definition. *Motivation and Emotion, 5,* 263–291.

Kleinke, C. L. (1986). Gaze and eye contact: A research review. *Psychological Bulletin, 100,* 78–100.

Kleitman, N. (1963). *Sleep and wakefulness* (2nd ed.). Chicago: University of Chicago Press.

Klinger, E. (1966). Fantasy need achievement. *Psychological Bulletin, 66,* 291–306.

Klinger, E. (1975). Consequences of commitment to and disengagement from incentives. *Psychological Review, 82,* 1–25.

Klinger, E. (1977). *Meaning and void: Inner experience and the incentives in people's lives.* Minneapolis: University of Minnesota Press.

Klopfer, P. H. (1971). Mother love: What turns it on? *American Scientist, 59,* 404–407.

Kluver, H., & Bucy, P. C. (1939). Preliminary analysis of functions of the temporal lobes in monkeys. *Archives of Neurology and Psychiatry, 42,* 979–1000.

Knowles, J. B., MacLean, A. W., & Cairns, J. (1982). REM sleep abnormalities in depression: A test of the phase-advance hypothesis. *Biological Psychiatry, 17,* 605–609.

Kobasa, S. C. (1979). Stressful life events, personality, and health: An inquiry into hardiness. *Journal of Personality and Social Psychology, 37,* 1–11.

Kobasa, S. C., Maddi, S. R., & Puccetti, M. C. (1982). Personality and exercise as buffers in the stress-illness relationship. *Journal of Behavioral Medicine, 5,* 391–404.

Köhler, W. (1925). *The mentality of apes* (trans. E. Winter). New York: Harcourt, Brace & World.

Kolata, G. (1983). Math genius may have a hormonal basis. *Science, 222,* 1312.

Kolata, G. (1985). Why do people get fat? *Science, 227,* 1327–1328.

Konishi, M. (1971). Ethology and neurobiology. *American Scientist, 59,* 56–63.

Korman, A. R. (1974). *The psychology of motivation.* Englewood Cliffs, N.J.: Prentice-Hall.

Kraly, F. S. (1981a). Pregastric stimulation and cholecystokinin are not sufficient for the meal size-intermeal interval correlation in the rat. *Physiology & Behavior, 27,* 457-462.

Kraly, F. S. (1981b). A diurnal variation in the satiating potency of cholecystokinin in the rat. *Appetite: Journal of Intake Research, 2,* 177–191.

Kraly, F. S. (1984). Physiology of drinking elicited by eating. *Psychological Review, 91,* 478–490.

Kraly, F. S., & Blass, E. M. (1974). Motivated feeding in the absence of glucoprivic control of feeding in rats. *Journal of Comparative and Physiological Psychology, 87,* 801–807.

Kraly, F. S., Carty, W. J., Resnick, S., & Smith, G. P. (1978). Effect of cholecystokinin on meal size and intermeal interval in the sham-feeding rat. *Journal of Comparative and Physiological Psychology, 92,* 697–707.

Kraut, R. E. (1982). Social presence, facial feedback, and emotion. *Journal of Personality and Social Psychology, 42,* 853–863.

Krueger, J. M., Pappenheimer, J. R., & Karnovsky, M. L. (1982). The composition of sleep-promoting factor isolated from human urine. *Journal of Biological Chemistry, 257,* 1664–1669.

Kruglanski, A. W., Freedman, I., & Zeevi, G. (1971). The effects of extrinsic incentive on some qualitative aspects of task performance. *Journal of Personality, 39,* 606–617.

Kubzansky, P. E., & Leiderman, P. H. (1961). Sensory deprivation: An overview. In P. Solomon et al. (Eds.), *Sensory deprivation.* Cambridge, Mass.: Harvard University Press.

Kuhl, J. (1981). Motivational and functional helplessness: The moderating effect of state versus action orientation. *Journal of Personality and Social Psychology, 40,* 155–170.

Kunda, Z., & Schwartz, S. H. (1983). Undermining intrinsic moral motivation: External reward and self-presentation. *Journal of Personality and Social Psychology, 45,* 763–771.

Kuo, Z. Y. (1921). Giving up instincts in psychology. *Journal of Philosophy, 17,* 645–664.

Kupfer, D. J. (1976). REM latency: A psychobiologic marker for primary depressive disease. *Biological Psychiatry, 11,* 159–174.

Labott, S. M., & Martin, R. B. (1987, Winter). The stress-moderating effects of weeping and humor. *Journal of Human Stress,* pp. 159–164.

Lacey, J. I. (1967). Somatic response patterning and stress: Some revisions of activation theory. In M. H. Appley & R. Trumbull (Eds.), *Psychological stress.* New York: Appleton-Century-Crofts.

Laessle, R. G., Kittl, S., Fichter, M. M., Wittchen, H.-U., & Pirke, K. M. (1987). Major affective disorder in anorexia nervosa and bulimia: A descriptive diagnostic study. *British Journal of Psychiatry, 151,* 785–789.

Lange, C. (1885). One leudsbeveegelser (trans. I. A. Haupt). In K. Dunlap (Ed.), *The emotions.* Baltimore: Williams & Wilkins, 1922.

Laségue, C. (1873). On hysterical anorexia. *Medical Times and Gazette, 2,* 265–266, 367–369.

Latané, B., & Darley, J. M. (1970). *The unresponsive bystander: Why doesn't he help?* New York: Appleton-Century-Crofts.

Latané, B., & Nida, S. (1981). Ten years of research on group size and helping. *Psychological Bulletin, 89,* 308–324.

Lazarus, R. S. (1968). Emotions and adaptation: Conceptual and empirical relations. In W. J. Arnold (Ed.), *Nebraska Symposium on Motivation,* pp. 175–266. Lincoln: University of Nebraska Press.

Lazarus, R. S. (1982). Thoughts on the relations between emotion and cognition. *American Psychologist, 37,* 1019–1024.

Lazarus, R. S. (1984). On the primacy of cognition. *American Psychologist, 39,* 124–129.

Lefcourt, H. M. (1966). Internal versus external control of reinforcement: A review. *Psychological Bulletin, 65,* 206–220.

Leggett, E. L. (1985, March). Children's entity and incremental theories of intelligence: Relationships to achievement behavior. Paper presented at the annual meeting of the Eastern Psychological Association, Boston.

Leggett, E. L., & Dweck, C. S. (1986). Goals and inference rules: Sources of causal judgments. Manuscript submitted for publication.

Lehr, D., Goldman, H. W., & Casner, P. (1973). Renin-angiotensin role in thirst: Paradoxical enhancement of drinking by angiotensin-converting enzyme inhibitor. *Science, 182,* 1031–1034.

Lehrman, D. S. (1970). Semantic and conceptual issues in the nature-nuture problem. In L. R. Aronson, E. Tobach, D. S. Lehrman, & J. S. Rosenblatt (Eds.), *Development and evolution of behavior.* San Francisco: Freeman.

Lenneberg, E. H. (1960). Language, evolution, and purposive behavior. In S. Diamond (Ed.), *Culture in history: Essays in honor of Paul Radin.* New York: Columbia University Press.

Lenneberg, E. H. (1967). *Biological foundations of language*. New York: Wiley.

Leo, J. (1984, July 30). Sudden death. *Time*, pp. 90–91.

Lepper, M. R., & Greene, D. (1978). *The hidden costs of reward: New perspectives on the psychology of human motivation*. Hillsdale, N.J.: Erlbaum.

Lepper, M. R., Greene, D., & Nisbett, R. E. (1973). Undermining children's intrinsic interest with extrinsic rewards: A test of the overjustification hypothesis. *Journal of Personality and Social Psychology, 28*, 129–137.

Levine, F. M. (1975). *Theoretical readings in motivation: Perspectives on human behavior*. Chicago: Rand McNally.

Levine, S. (1966). Sex differences in the brain. *Scientific American, 214 (4)*, 84–90.

Levine, S. (1971). Stress and behavior. *Scientific American, 224 (1)*, 26–31.

Levinger, G., & Breedlove, J. (1966). Interpersonal attraction and agreement: A study of marriage partners. *Journal of Personality and Social Psychology, 3*, 367–372.

Lewin, K. (1936). *Principles of topological psychology*. New York: McGraw-Hill.

Lewin, K. (1938). *The conceptual representation and the measurement of psychological forces*. Durham, N.C.: Duke University Press.

Lewith, G. T., & Kenyon, J. N. (1984). Physiological and psychological explanations for the mechanism of acupuncture as a treatment for chronic pain. *Social Science Medicine, 19*, 1367–1378.

Liberman, A. M., & Mattingly, I. G. (1989). A specialization for speech perception. *Science, 243*, 489–494.

Libet, J. M., & Lewisohn, P. M. (1973). Concept of social skill with special reference to the behavior of depressed persons. *Journal of Consulting and Clinical Psychology, 40*, 304–312.

Liddell, H. S. (1954). Conditioning and emotions. *Scientific American, 190 (1)*, 48–57.

Lindsley, D. (1950). Emotions and the electroencephalogram. In M. L. Reymert (Ed.), *Feelings and emotions*. New York: McGraw-Hill.

Lindsley, D. (1951). Emotion. In S. S. Stevens (Ed.), *Handbook of experimental psychology*. New York: Wiley.

Linville, P. W. (1987). Self-complexity as a cognitive buffer against stress-related illness and depression. *Journal of Personality and Social Psychology, 52*, 663–676.

Lipman-Blumen, J., Handley-Isaksen, A., & Leavitt, H. J. (1983). Achieving styles in men and women: A model, an instrument, and some findings. In J. T. Spence (Ed.), *Achievement and achievement motives: Psychological and sociological approaches*, pp. 147–204. San Francisco: Freeman.

Lockard, J. S., Allen, D. J., Schielle, B. J., & Wiemer, M. J. (1978). Human postural signals: Stance, weight-shifts and social distance as intention movements to depart. *Animal Behavior, 26*, 219–224.

Logan, F. A. (1968). Incentive theory and changes in reward. In K. W. Spence & J. T. Spence (Eds.), *The psychology of learning and motivation* (Vol. 2). New York: Academic Press.

Long, M. E. (1987, December). What is this thing called sleep? *National Geographic*, pp. 787–821.

Lord, C. G., Ross, L., & Lepper, M. R. (1979). Biased assimilation and attitude polarization: The effects of prior theories on subsequently considered evidence. *Journal of Personality and Social Psychology, 37,* 2098–2109.

Lorenz, K. (1950). The comparative method of studying innate behavior patterns. In *Symposia of the Society of Experimental Biology.* Cambridge: Cambridge University Press.

Lorenz, K. (1967). *On aggression.* New York: Bantam.

Lorenz, K. (1970). The establishment of the instinct concept. In *Studies in animal and human behavior* (Vol. 1, trans. Robert Martin). Cambridge, Mass.: Harvard University Press.

Lorenz, K. (1971a). A scientist's credo. In *Studies in animal and human behavior* (Vol. 2, trans. Robert Martin). Cambridge, Mass.: Harvard University Press.

Lorenz, K. (1971b). Part and parcel in animal and human societies. In *Studies in animal and human behavior* (Vol. 2, trans. Robert Martin). Cambridge, Mass.: Harvard University Press.

Lorenz, K. (1981). *The foundations of ethology.* New York: Springer-Verlag.

Lorenz, K., & Tinbergen, N. (1938). Taxis und instinkthandlung in der eirollbewegung der graugens. I. *Zeitschrift fur Tierpsychologie, 2,* 1–29.

Lowry, R. S. (Ed.). (1973). *Dominance, self-esteem, self-actualization: Germinal papers of A. H. Maslow.* Monterey, Calif.: Brooks/Cole.

Lubow, R. E., Rosenblatt, R., & Weiner, I. (1981). Confounding of controllability in the triadic design for demonstrating learned helplessness. *Journal of Personality and Social Psychology, 41,* 458–468.

Luria, Z., Friedman, S., & Rose, M. D. (1987). *Human sexuality.* New York: Wiley.

MacLean, P. D. (1969). The hypothalamus and emotional behavior. In W. Haymaker et al. (Eds.), *The hypothalamus.* Springfield, Ill.: Thomas.

Maddi, S. R., Bartone, P. T., & Puccetti, M. C. (1987). Stressful events are indeed a factor in physical illness: Reply to Schroeder and Costa (1984). *Journal of Personality and Social Psychology, 52,* 833–843.

Magoun, H. W. (1963). *The waking brain.* Springfield, Ill.: Thomas.

Maher, B. (1970, August). Delusional thinking and cognitive disorder. Paper presented at annual meeting of the American Psychological Association, Miami.

Maier, S. F. (1970). Failure to escape traumatic shock: Incompatible skeletal motor responses or learned helplessness? *Learning and Motivation, 1,* 157–170.

Maier, S. F., Anderson, C., & Lieberman, D. S. (1972). Influence of control of shock on subsequent shock-elicited aggression. *Journal of Comparative and Physiological Psychology, 81,* 94–100.

Malvin, R. L., Mouw, D., & Vander, A. J. (1977). Angiotensin: Physiological role in water-deprivation-induced thirst of rats. *Science, 197,* 171–173.

Mandler, G. (1967). Invited commentary on adaptive stress behavior. In M. H. Appley & R. Trumbull (Eds.), *Psychological stress.* New York: Appleton-Century-Crofts.

Mandler, G. (1984). *Mind and body: Psychology of emotion and stress.* New York: Norton.

Margules, D. L. (1979). Beta-endorphin and endoloxone: Hormones of the autonomic nervous system for the conservation or expenditure of bodily resources and energy in anticipation of famine or feast.

Neuroscience and Biochemical Reviews, 3, 155–162.

Margules, D. L., Moisset, B., Lewis, M. J., Shibuya, H., & Pert, C. B. (1978). Beta-endorphin is associated with overeating in genetically obese mice (ob/ob) and rats (fa/fa). *Science, 202,* 988–991.

Marler, P. (1970). Birdsong and speech development: Could there be parallels? *American Scientist, 58,* 669–673.

Marshall, G. D., & Zimbardo, P. G. (1979). Affective consequences of inadequately explained physiological arousal. *Journal of Personality and Social Psychology, 37,* 970–988.

Marshall, J. F., & Teitelbaum, P. (1974). Further analysis of sensory inattention following lateral hypothalamic damage in rats. *Journal of Comparative and Physiological Psychology, 86,* 375–395.

Marshall, J. M., & Karabenick, S. A. (1977). Validity of an empirically derived projective measure of fear of success. *Journal of Consulting and Clinical Psychology, 45,* 564–574.

Marx, J. L. (1982). Autoimmunity in left-handers. *Science, 217,* 141–144.

Maslach, C. (1979). Negative emotional biasing of unexplained arousal. *Journal of Personality and Social Psychology, 37,* 953–969.

Maslow, A. H. (1943). A theory of motivation. *Psychological Review, 50,* 370–396.

Maslow, A. H. (1959). *New knowledge in human values.* New York: Harper & Row.

Maslow, A. H. (1965). *Eupsychian management: A journal.* Homewood, Ill.: Dorsey.

Maslow, A. H. (1971). *The farther reaches of human nature.* New York: Viking.

Maslow, A. H. (1973a). Theory of human motivation. In R. J. Lowry (Ed.), *Dominance,* *self-esteem, self-actualization: Germinal papers of A. H. Maslow.* Monterey, Calif.: Brooks/Cole.

Maslow, A. H. (1973b). Self-actualizing people: A study of psychological health. In R. J. Lowry (Ed.), *Dominance, self-esteem, self-actualization: Germinal papers of A. H. Maslow.* Monterey, Calif.: Brooks/Cole.

Maslow, A. H. (1976). *Religion, values, and peak experiences.* Harmondsworth, England: Penguin.

Mason, W. A. (1961). The effects of social restriction on the behavior of rhesus monkeys: II. Tests of gregariousness. *Journal of Physiological and Comparative Psychology, 54,* 287–290.

Masters, W. H., & Johnson, V. E. (1966). *Human sexual response.* Boston: Little, Brown.

Masters, W. H., & Johnson, V. E. (1970). *Human sexual inadequacy.* Boston: Little, Brown.

Masters, W. H., & Johnson, V. E. (1974). *The pleasure bond: A new look at sexuality and commitment.* Boston: Little, Brown.

Mathes, E. W., & Zevon, M. A. (1982). Peak experience tendencies: Scale development and theory testing. *Journal of Humanistic Psychology, 22,* 92–108.

Matsumoto, D. (1987). The role of facial response in the experience of emotion: More methodological problems and meta-analysis. *Journal of Personality and Social Psychology, 52,* 769–774.

Mattingly, I. G. (1972). Speech cues and sign stimuli. *American Scientist, 60,* 327–337.

Maturana, H. R., Lettvin, J. Y., McCulloch, W. S., & Pitts, W. H. (1960). Anatomy and physiology of vision in the frog *(Rana pipiens). Journal of General Physiology, 43,* 129–175.

Mayer, D. J. (1983). Biobehavioral modulation of pain transmission. In National Institute on Drug Abuse, *Research Monograph Series, 45,* 46–69.

Mayer, J. (1955). Regulation of energy intake and the body weight: The glucostatic theory and the lipostatic hypothesis. *Annals of the New York Academy of Science, 63,* 15–43.

Mayer, J. D., & Gaschke, Y. N. (1988). The experience and meta-experience of mood. *Journal of Personality and Social Psychology, 55,* 102–111.

Mayr, E. (1974). Behavior programs and evolutionary strategies. *American Scientist, 62,* 650–659.

McCanne, T. R., & Anderson, J. A. (1987). Emotional responding following experimental manipulation of facial electromyographic activity. *Journal of Personality and Social Psychology, 52,* 759–768.

McCarley, R. W. (1982). REM sleep and depression: Common neurobiological control mechanisms. *American Journal of Psychiatry, 139,* 565–570.

McCarley, R. W., & Hobson, J. A. (1975). Neuronal excitability modulation over the sleep cycle: A structural and mathematical model. *Science, 189,* 58–60.

McClelland, D. C. (1961). *The achieving society.* New York: Van Nostrand.

McClelland, D. C. (1965). Achievement and entrepreneurship: A longitudinal study. *Journal of Personality and Social Psychology, 1,* 389–392.

McClelland, D. C. (1978). Managing motivation to expand human freedom. *American Psychologist, 33,* 201–210.

McClelland, D. C., & Atkinson, J. W. (1948). The projective expression of needs: I. The effect of different intensities of hunger drive on perception. *Journal of Psychology, 25,* 205–222.

McClelland, D. C., Atkinson, J. W., Clark, R. A., & Lowell, E. L. (1953). *The achievement motive.* New York: Appleton-Century-Crofts.

McClelland, D. C., Clark, R. A., Roby, T. B., & Atkinson, J. W. (1949). The projective expression of needs: IV. The effect of the need for achievement on thematic apperception. *Journal of Experimental Psychology, 39,* 242–255.

McClelland, D. C., & Pilon, D. A. (1983). Sources of adult motives in patterns of parent behavior in early childhood. *Journal of Personality and Social Psychology, 44,* 564–574.

McClelland, D. C., & Winter, D. G. (1971). *Motivating economic achievement.* New York: Free Press.

McDougall, W. (1970). The nature of instincts and their place in the constitution of the human mind. In W. A. Russell (Ed.), *Milestones in motivation.* New York: Appleton-Century-Crofts.

McGraw, K. O., & Fiala, J. (1982). Undermining the Zeigarnik effect: Another hidden cost of reward. *Journal of Personality, 50,* 58–66.

McGuire, W. J. (1966). The current status of cognitive consistency theories. In S. Feldman (Ed.), *Cognitive consistency: Motivational antecedents and behavioral consequents.* New York: Academic Press.

Mechanic, D. (1974). Discussion of research programs on relations between stressful life events and episodes of physical illness. In B. S. Dohrenwend & B. P. Dohrenwend (Eds.), *Stressful life events: Their nature and effects.* New York: Wiley.

Meddis, R. (1975). On the function of sleep. *Animal Behavior, 23,* 676–691.

Mehrabian, A. (1969). Measures of achieving tendency. *Educational and Psychological Measurement, 29,* 445–451.

Melzack, R. (1961, February). The perception of pain. *Scientific American,* pp. 3–12.

Melzack, R., & Wall, P. D. (1965). Pain mechanisms: A new theory. *Science, 150,* 971–979.

Melzack, R., & Wall, P. D. (1983). *The challenge of pain.* New York: Basic Books.

Metzger, R., Cotton, J. W., Lewis, D. J. (1957). Effect of reinforcement magnitude and order of presentation of different magnitudes on runway behavior. *Journal of Comparative and Physiological Psychology, 50,* 184–188.

Miczek, K. A., Brykczynski, T., & Grossman, S. P. (1974). Differential effects of lesions in the amygdala, periamygdaloid cortex, and stria terminalis on aggressive behavior in rats. *Journal of Comparative and Physiological Psychology, 87,* 760–771.

Mikulincer, M. (1988). Reactance and helplessness following exposure to unsolvable problems: The effects of attributional style. *Journal of Personality and Social Psychology, 54,* 679–686.

Mikulincer, M., & Nizan, B. (1988). Causal attribution, cognitive interference, and the generalization of learned helplessness. *Journal of Personality and Social Psychology, 55,* 470–478.

Milgram, S. (1963). Behavioral study of obedience. *Journal of Abnormal and Social Psychology, 67,* 371–378.

Milgram, S. (1965). Some conditions of obedience and disobedience to authority. *Human Relations, 18,* 57–76.

Milgram, S. (1975). The perils of obedience. In S. Milgram (Ed.), *Psychology in today's world.* Boston: Little, Brown.

Miller, N. E. (1948). Studies of fear as an acquirable drive: I. Fear as motivation and fear-reduction as reinforcement in the learning of new responses. *Journal of Experimental Psychology, 38,* 89–101.

Miller, N. E. (1963). Some reflections on the law of effect produce a new alternative to drive reduction. In M. R. Jones (Ed.), *Nebraska Symposium on Motivation.* Lincoln: University of Nebraska Press.

Miller, N. E., & Dollard, J. (1941). *Social learning and imitation.* New Haven, Conn.: Yale University Press.

Miller, R. C., & Berman, J. S. (1983). The efficacy of cognitive behavior therapies: A quantitative review of the research evidence. *Psychological Bulletin, 94,* 39–53.

Miller, R. E., Caul, W. F., & Mirsky, I. A. (1967). Communication of affects between feral and socially isolated monkeys. *Journal of Personality and Social Psychology, 7,* 231–239.

Miller, W. R., & Seligman, M. E. P. (1975). Depression and learned helplessness in man. *Journal of Abnormal Psychology, 84,* 228–238.

Mineka, S. (1975). Some new perspectives on conditioned hunger. *Journal of Experimental Psychology, 104,* 134–148.

Mineka, S., & Kihlstrom, J. F. (1978). Unpredictable and uncontrollable events: A new perspective on experimental neurosis. *Journal of Abnormal Psychology, 87,* 256–271.

Mineka, S., & Suomi, S. J. (1978). Social separation in monkeys. *Psychological Bulletin, 85,* 1376–1400.

Mineka, S., Suomi, S. J., & Delizio, R. (1981). Multiple separations in adolescent monkeys: An opponent-process interpretation. *Journal of Experimental Psychology: General, 110,* 56–85.

Miron, D. (1976). The economic effect of achievement motivation training for entrepreneurs in three populations. Unpublished manuscript, Harvard Graduate School of Education.

Mogenson, G. J. (1976). Neural mechanisms of hunger: Current status and future prospects. In D. Novin et al. (Eds.), *Hunger: Basic mechanisms and clinical implications.* New York: Raven Press.

Moltz, H. (1965). Contemporary instinct theory and the fixed action pattern. *Psychological Review, 72,* 27–47.

Money, J. (1977). The syndrome of abuse dwarfism (psychosocial dwarfism or reversible hyposomatotropinism). *American Journal of Disabled Children, 131,* 508–513.

Money, J. (1980). Endocrine influences and psychosexual status spanning the life cycle. In H. M. Van Praag, M. H. Lader, O. J. Rafaelsen, & E. J. Sachar (Eds.), *Handbook of biological psychiatry: Part III. Brain mechanisms and abnormal behavior—genetics and neuroendocrinology.* New York: Dekker.

Money, J., & Ehrhardt, A. A. (1972). *Man & woman, boy & girl.* Baltimore: Johns Hopkins University Press.

Money, J., & Wolff, G. (1974). Late puberty, retarded growth and reversible hyposomatotropinism (psychosocial dwarfism). *Adolescence, 9,* 121–134.

Montgomery, K. C. (1953). Exploratory behavior as a function of "similarity" of stimulus situations. *Journal of Comparative and Physiological Psychology, 46,* 129–133.

Morgan, C. T. (1943). *Physiological psychology.* New York: McGraw-Hill.

Morgan, C. T., & Morgan, J. T. (1940). Studies in hunger: II. The relation of gastric denervation and dietary sugar to the effect of insulin upon food-intake in the rat. *Journal of Genetic Psychology, 57,* 153–163.

Morgan, M. (1981). The overjustification effect: A developmental test of self-perception interpretations. *Journal of Personality and Social Psychology, 40,* 809–821.

Morris, D. (1967). *The naked ape.* New York: Dell.

Morrissette, J. O. (1958). An experimental study of the theory of structural balance. *Human Relations, 11,* 239–254.

Mortenson, F. J. (1975). *Animal behavior: Theory and research.* Monterey, Calif.: Brooks/ Cole.

Moruzzi, G., & Magoun, H. W. (1949). Brain stem reticular formation and activation of the EEG. *Electroencephalography and Clinical Neurophysiology, 1,* 455–473.

Moscovici, S., & Faucheux, C. (1972). Social influence, conformity bias, and the study of active minorities. In L. Berkowitz (Ed.), *Advances in experimental social psychology* (Vol. 6). New York: Academic Press.

Mowrer, O. H. (1947). On the dual nature of learning: A reinterpretation of "conditioning" and "problem solving." *Harvard Educational Review, 17,* 102–148.

Mowrer, O. H. (1960). *Learning theory and behavior.* New York: Wiley.

Moyer, K. E. (1971). *The physiology of hostility.* Chicago: Markham.

Moyer, K. E. (1975). The physiology of violence: Allergy and aggression. *Psychology Today, 9,* 76–79.

Murray, H. A. (1936). Techniques for a systematic investigation of fantasy. *Journal of Psychology, 3,* 115–143.

Murray, H. A. (1938). *Explorations in personality.* New York: Oxford University Press.

Myer, J. S. (1964). Stimulus control of mousekilling rats. *Journal of Comparative and Physiological Psychology, 58,* 112–117.

Myer, J. S., & White, R. T. (1965). Aggressive motivation in the rat. *Animal Behavior, 13,* 430–433.

Myers, H. H., & Siegel, P. S. (1985). The motivation to breastfeed: A fit to the opponent-process theory? *Journal of Personality and Social Psychology, 49,* 188–193.

Nash, L. T. (1978). The development of mother-infant relationship in wild baboons *(Papio anubis). Animal Behavior, 26,* 746–759.

National Safety Council. (1986). *Accident facts.* Chicago: National Safety Council.

Newcomb, T. M. (1968). Interpersonal balance. In R. E. Abelson et al. (Eds.), *Theories of cognitive consistency: A sourcebook.* Chicago: Rand McNally.

Nisbett, R. E. (1968). Taste, deprivation, and weight determinants of eating behavior. *Journal of Personality and Social Psychology, 10,* 107–116.

Nisbett, R. E., Caputo, C., Legant, P., & Marecek, J. (1973). Behavior as seen by the actor and as seen by the observer. *Journal of Personality and Social Psychology, 27,* 154–164.

Nisbett, R. E., & Valens, S. (1972). Perceiving the causes of one's own behavior. In E. E. Jones et al. (Eds.), *Attribution: Perceiving the causes of behavior.* Morristown, N.J.: General Learning Press.

Novin, D. (1976). Visceral mechanisms in the control of food intake. In D. Novin et al. (Eds.), *Hunger: Basic mechanisms and clinical implications.* New York: Raven Press.

Novin, D., Wyricka, W., & Bray, G. (Eds.). (1976). *Hunger: Basic mechanisms and clinical implications.* New York: Raven Press.

Nowicki, S., & Barness, J. (1973). Effects of a structured camp experience on locus of control orientation. *Journal of Genetic Psychology, 122,* 247–252.

Nowlis, V. (1965). Research with the mood adjective check list. In S. S. Tomkins & C. E. Izard (Eds.), *Affect, cognition, and personality,* pp. 352–389. New York: Springer.

Nowlis, V., & Nowlis, H. H. (1956). The description and analysis of mood. *Annals of the New York Academy of Sciences, 65,* 345–355.

Oakley, D. A. (1983). The varieties of human memory: A phylogenetic approach. In A. Mayes (Ed.), *Memory in humans and animals.* Wokingham, England: Van Nostrand Reinhold.

Odell, M. (1959). Personality correlates of independence and conformity. Unpublished manuscript, Ohio State University.

Oken, D. (1967). The psychophysiology and psychoendocrinology of stress and emotion. In M. H. Appley & R. Trumbull (Eds.), *Psychological stress.* New York: Appleton-Century-Crofts.

Olds, J., & Milner, P. (1954). Positive reinforcement produced by electrical stimulation of septal area and other regions of rat brain. *Journal of Comparative and Physiological Psychology, 47,* 419–427.

Olson, J. M., & Zanna, M. P. (1979). A new look at selective exposure. *Journal of Experimental Social Psychology, 15,* 1–15.

Oomura, Y. (1976). Significance of glucose, insulin, and free fatty acid on the hypothalamic feeding and satiety neurons. In D. Novin et al. (Eds.), *Hunger: Basic mechanisms and clinical implications*. New York: Raven Press.

Overmier, J. B. (1968). Interference with avoidance behavior. *Journal of Experimental Psychology, 78*, 340–343.

Overmier, J. B., & Lawry, J. A. (1979). Pavlovian conditioning and the mediation of behavior. In G. H. Bower (Ed.), *The psychology of learning and motivation* (Vol. 13), pp. 1–55. New York: Academic Press.

Overmier, J. B., & Seligman, M. E. P. (1967). Effects of inescapable shock upon subsequent escape and avoidance learning. *Journal of Comparative and Physiological Psychology, 63*, 23–33.

Ovsiankina, M. (1928). Die Wiederaufnahme von unterbrochener Handlungen. *Psychologische Forschung, 11*, 302–379.

Padgett, W. L., Garcia, H. D., & Pernice, M. B. (1984). A travel training program: Reducing wandering in a residential center for developmentally disabled persons. *Behavior Modification, 8*, 317–330.

Palca, J. (1989). Sleep researchers awake to possibilities. *Science, 245*, 351–352.

Pallak, S. R., Costomiris, S., Sroka, S., & Pittman, T. S. (1982). School experience, reward characteristics, and intrinsic motivation. *Child Development, 53*, 1382–1391.

Panksepp, J., & Trowill, J. (1971). Positive and negative contrast in licking with shifts in sucrose concentration as a function of food deprivation. *Learning & Motivation, 2*, 49–57.

Papez, J. W. (1937). A proposed mechanism of emotion. *Archives of Neurological Psychiatry, 38*, 725–743.

Pappenheimer, J. R. (1976). The sleep factor. *Scientific American, 235 (2)*, 24–29.

Parkinson, B., & Manstead, A. S. R. (1981). An examination of the roles played by meaning of feedback and attention to feedback in the "Valins Effect." *Journal of Personality and Social Psychology, 40*, 239–245.

Parlee, M. (1983). Menstrual rhythms in sensory processes: A review of fluctuations in vision, olfaction, audition, taste, and touch. *Psychological Bulletin, 93*, 539–548.

Patton, R. G., & Gardner, L. I. (1963). *Growth failure in maternal deprivation*. Springfield, Ill.: Thomas.

Pavlov, I. P. (1960). *Conditioned reflexes*. New York: Dover.

Pearlman, C. A. (1970). The adaptive function of dreaming. In E. Hartmann (Ed.), *Sleep and dreaming*. Boston: Little, Brown.

Peck, J. W., & Novin, D. (1971). Evidence that osmoreceptors mediating drinking in rabbits are in the lateral preoptic area. *Journal of Comparative and Physiological Psychology, 74*, 134–147.

Peeke, H. V. S. (1969). Habituation of conspecific aggression in the three-spined stickleback (*Gasterosteus aculeatus* L.). *Behaviour, 35*, 137–156.

Peets, J. M., & Pomeranz, B. (1978). CXBK mice deficient in opiate receptors show poor electroacupuncture analgesia. *Nature, 273*, 675–676.

Pepitone, A. (1966). Problems of consistency models. In S. Feldman (Ed.), *Cognitive consistency*. New York: Academic Press.

Peplau, L. A. (1976). Impact of fear of success and sex-role attitudes on women's competitive achievement. *Journal of Personality and Social Psychology, 34,* 561–680.

Perin, C. T. (1942). Behavior potentiality as a joint function of the amount of training and the degree of hunger at the time of extinction. *Journal of Experimental Psychology, 30,* 93–113.

Perlmuter, L. C., & Chan, F. (1983). Does control of the environment enhance the perception of control? *Motivation and Emotion, 7,* 345–355.

Perlmuter, L. C., & Monty, R. A. (1977). The importance of perceived control: Fact or fantasy? *American Scientist, 65,* 759–765.

Perlmuter, L. C., & Monty, R. A. (Eds.). (1979). *Choice and perceived control.* Hillsdale, N.J.: Erlbaum.

Peterson, C., Seligman, M. E., & Vaillant, G. E. (1988). Pessimistic explanatory style is a risk factor for physical illness: A thirty-five-year longitudinal study. *Journal of Personality and Social Psychology, 55,* 23–27.

Petri, H. L. (1974). Discrimination of schedules that predict reinforcement from nonpredictive ones and preference for less predictive schedules by rats. *Learning and Motivation, 5,* 336–351.

Petri, H. L. (1981). *Motivation: Theory and research.* Belmont, Calif.: Wadsworth.

Petri, H. L., & Mills, C. J. (1977). Effects of imprinting and isolation on aggressive responses in chicks. *Aggressive Behavior, 3,* 173–183.

Pfaff, D. W. (1982). *The physiological mechanisms of motivation.* New York: Springer-Verlag.

Pfaff, D. W., & Pfaffmann, C. (1969). Behavioral and electrophysiological responses of male rats to female rat urine odors. In C. Pfaffmann (Ed.), *Olfaction and taste.* New York: Rockefeller University Press.

Pfaffmann, C. (1958). *Flavor research and food acceptance.* New York: Reinhold.

Pfaffmann, C. (1960). The pleasures of sensation. *Psychological Review, 67,* 253–268.

Piliavin, J. A., Callero, P. L., & Evans, D. E. (1982). Addiction to altruism? Opponent-process theory and habitual blood donation. *Journal of Personality and Social Psychology, 43,* 1200–1213.

Pittman, T. S., & Pittman, N. L. (1980). Deprivation of control and the attribution process. *Journal of Personality and Social Psychology, 39,* 377–389.

Ploog, D. W., & Pirke, K. M. (1987). Psychobiology of anorexia nervosa. *Psychological Medicine, 17,* 843–859.

Plutchik, R. (1962). *The emotions: Facts, theories, and a new model.* New York: Random House.

Plutchik, R. (1980). *Emotion: A psychoevolutionary synthesis.* New York: Harper & Row.

Plutchik, R. (1983). Emotions in early development: A psychoevolutionary approach. In R. Plutchik & H. Kellerman (Eds.), *Emotion: Theory, research, and experience. Vol. 2: Emotions in early development,* pp. 221–257. New York: Academic Press.

Plutchik, R., & Ax, A. (1967). A critique of "Determinants of emotional states" by Schachter and Singer (1962). *Psychophysiology, 4,* 79–82.

Pomeranz, B. (1981). Neural mechanisms of acupuncture analgesia. In S. Lipton (Ed.), *Persistent pain: Modern methods of treatment.* London: Academic Press.

Pomeranz, B., Cheng, R., & Law, P. (1977). Acupuncture reduces electrophysiological and behavioral responses to noxious stimuli. *Experimental Neurology, 54,* 172–178.

Pool, R. (1989). Illuminating jet lag. *Science, 244*, 1256–1257.

Popkin, M. K., Stillner, V., Pierce, C. M., Williams, M., & Gregory, P. (1976). Recent life changes and outcome of prolonged competitive stress. *Journal of Nervous and Mental Disease, 163*, 302–306.

Powley, T. L. (1977). The ventromedial hypothalamic syndrome, satiety, and a cephalic phase hypothesis. *Psychological Review, 84*, 89–126.

Powley, T. L., & Keesey, R. E. (1970). Relationship of body weight to the lateral hypothalamic feeding syndrome. *Journal of Comparative and Physiological Psychology, 70*, 25–36.

Pressman, M. R. (1986). Sleep and sleep disorders: An introduction. *Clinical Psychology Review, 6*, 1–9.

Pretty, G. H., & Seligman, C. (1984). Affect and the overjustification effect. *Journal of Personality and Social Psychology, 46*, 1241–1253.

Privette, G. (1983). Peak experience, peak performance, and flow: A comparative analysis of positive human experiences. *Journal of Personality and Social Psychology, 45*, 1361–1368.

Rachlin, H. (1976). *Behavior and learning.* San Francisco: Freeman.

Rachman, S. (1966). Sexual fetishism: An experimental analogue. *Psychological Record, 16*, 293–296.

Rachman, S., & Hodgson, R. J. (1968). Experimentally induced "sexual fetishism": Replication and development. *Psychological Record, 18*, 25–27.

Rahe, R. H. (1974). The pathway between subjects' recent life change and their near-future illness reports: Representative results and methodological issues. In B. S. Dohrenwend & B. P. Dohrenwend (Eds.), *Stressful life events: Their nature and effects.* New York: Wiley.

Rajecki, D. W., Ivins, B., & Reins, B. (1976). Social discrimination and aggressive pecking in domestic chicks. *Journal of Comparative and Physiological Psychology, 90*, 442–452.

Ramirez, J., Bryant, J., & Zillmann, D. (1982). Effects of erotica on retaliatory behavior as a function of level of prior provocation. *Journal of Personality and Social Psychology, 43*, 971–978.

Ramsay, A. D., & Hess, E. H. (1954). A laboratory approach to the study of imprinting. *Wilson Bulletin, 66*, 196–206.

Raps, C. S., Peterson, D., Jonas, M., & Seligman, M. E. P. (1982). Patient behavior in hospitals: Helplessness, reactance, or both? *Journal of Personality and Social Psychology, 42*, 1036–1041.

Ravelli, G. P., Stein, Z. A., & Susser, M. W. (1976). Obesity in young men after famine exposure in utero and early infancy. *New England Journal of Medicine, 295*, 349–353.

Ray, J. J. (1982). Achievement motivation and preferred probability of success. *Journal of Social Psychology, 116*, 255–261.

Raynor, J. O. (1969). Future orientation and motivation of immediate activity: An elaboration of the theory of achievement motivation. *Psychological Review, 76*, 606–610.

Raynor, J. O. (1970). Relationship between achievement-related motives, future orientation and academic performance. *Journal of Personality and Social Psychology, 15*, 28–33.

Raynor, J. O. (1974). Future orientation in the study of achievement motivation. In J. W.

Atkinson & J. O. Raynor (Eds.), *Motivation and achievement.* Washington, D. C.: V. H. Winston.

Razran, G. (1961). The observable unconscious and the inferable conscious in current Soviet psychophysiology: Interoceptive conditioning, semantic conditioning and the orienting reflex. *Psychological Review, 68,* 81–147.

Reeder, G. D. (1982). Let's give the fundamental attribution error another chance. *Journal of Personality and Social Psychology, 43,* 341–344.

Renne, K. S. (1970). Correlates of dissatisfaction in marriage. *Journal of Marriage and the Family, 32,* 54–67.

Restle, F. (1957). Discrimination of cues in mazes: A resolution of the "place-vs.-response" question. *Psychological Review, 64,* 217–228.

Revesman, M. E., & Perlmuter, L. C. (1981). Environmental control and the perception of control. *Motivation and Emotion, 5,* 311–321.

Reynolds, G. S. (1975). *A primer of operant conditioning* (rev. ed.). Glenview, Ill.: Scott, Foresman.

Richter, C. P. (1927). Animal behavior and internal drives. *Quarterly Review of Biology, 2,* 307–343.

Riesen, A. H. (1961). Excessive arousal effects of stimulation after early sensory deprivation. In P. Solomon et al. (Eds.), *Sensory deprivation.* Cambridge, Mass.: Harvard University Press.

Rizzo, R., & Vinacke, E. (1975). Self-actualization and the meaning of critical experience. *Journal of Humanistic Psychology, 15,* 19–30.

Roberts, J. L., Chen, C. C., Dionne, F. T., &

Gee, C. E. (1982). Peptide hormone gene expression in heterogeneous tissues. *Trends in Neurosciences, 5,* 314–317.

Rodin, J. (1981). Current status of the internal-external hypothesis for obesity: What went wrong? *American Psychologist, 36,* 361–372.

Rogers, C. R. (1951). *Client-centered therapy: Its current practice, implication, and theory.* Boston: Houghton Mifflin.

Rogers, C. R. (1961). *On becoming a person: A therapist's view of psychotherapy.* Boston: Houghton Mifflin.

Rogers, R. W., & Deckner, D. W. (1975). Effects of fear appeals and physiological arousal upon emotion, attitudes and cigarette smoking. *Journal of Personality and Social Psychology, 32,* 222–230.

Roos, P. E., & Cohen, L. H. (1987). Sex roles and social support as moderators of life stress adjustment. *Journal of Personality and Social Psychology, 52,* 576–585.

Rosenhan, D. L., Salovey, P., & Hargis, K. (1981). The joys of helping: Focus of attention mediates the impact of positive affect on altruism. *Journal of Personality and Social Psychology, 40,* 899–905.

Rosenthal, R., Archer, D., DiMatteo, M. R., Koivumaki, J. H., & Rogers, P. L. (1974). The language without words. *Psychology Today, 8,* 64–68.

Roskies, E., Iida-Miranda, M., & Strobel, M. G. (1975). The applicability of the life events approach to the problems of immigration. *Journal of Psychosomatic Research, 19,* 235–240.

Ross, L. (1977). The intuitive psychologist and his shortcomings: Distortions in the attribution process. In L. Berkowitz (Ed.), *Advances in experimental social psychology* (Vol. 10). New York: Academic Press.

Ross, L., Lepper, M. R., & Hubbard, M. (1974). Perseverance in self-perception and social perception: Biased attributional process in the debriefing paradigm. Unpublished manuscript, Stanford University. (Cited by Hilgard, Atkinson, & Atkinson, *Introduction to psychology* [6th ed.]. New York: Harcourt Brace Jovanovich, 1975).

Ross, R. R. (1964). Positive and negative partial-reinforcement extinction effects carried through continuous reinforcement, changed motivation and changed response. *Journal of Experimental Psychology, 68,* 492–502.

Rosvold, H. E., Mirsky, A. F., & Pribram, K. H. (1954). Influence of amygdalectomy on social behavior in monkeys. *Journal of Comparative and Physiological Psychology, 47,* 173–178.

Rotter, J. B. (1954). *Social learning and clinical psychology.* Englewood Cliffs, N.J.: Prentice-Hall.

Rotter, J. B. (1966). Generalized expectancies for internal versus external control of reinforcement. *Psychological Monographs, 80,* 1–28.

Rotter, J. B. (1975). Some problems and misconceptions related to the construct of internal versus external control of reinforcement. *Journal of Consulting and Clinical Psychology, 43,* 36–67.

Rowland, N. E., & Antelman, S. M. (1976). Stress-induced hyperphagia and obesity in rats: A possible model for understanding human obesity. *Science, 191,* 310–311.

Rowland, W. J. (1989a). The effects of body size, aggression and nuptial coloration on competition for territories in male three-spine sticklebacks (*Gasterosteus aculeatus*). *Animal Behavior, 37,* 282–289.

Rowland, W. J. (1989b). The ethological basis of mate choice in male three-spine sticklebacks (*Gasterosteus aculeatus*). *Animal Behavior, 38,* 112–120.

Rowland, W. J. (1989c). Mate choice and the supernormality effect in female sticklebacks (*Gasterosteus aculeatus*). *Behavioral Ecology and Sociobiology, 24,* 433–438.

Roy-Byrne, P. P., Uhde, T. W., & Post, R. M. (1986). Effects of one night's sleep deprivation on mood and behavior in panic disorder. *Archives of General Psychiatry, 43,* 895–899.

Rozin, P., & Kalat, J. W. (1971). Specific hungers and poison avoidance as adaptive specializations of learning. *Psychological Review, 78,* 459–486.

Ruch, L. O., & Holmes, T. H. (1971). Scaling of life change: Comparison of direct and indirect methods. *Journal of Psychosomatic Research, 15,* 221–227.

Ruff, G. E., & Korchin, S. J. (1967). Adaptive stress behavior. In M. H. Appley & R. Trumbull (Eds.), *Psychological stress.* New York: Appleton-Century-Crofts.

Russell, J. A. (1980). A circumplex model of affect. *Journal of Personality and Social Psychology, 39,* 1161–1178.

Russell, J. A. (1983). Pancultural aspects of the human conceptual organization of emotions. *Journal of Personality and Social Psychology, 45,* 1281–1288.

Rutkowski, G. K., Gruder, C. L., & Romer, D. (1983). Group cohesiveness, social norms, and bystander intervention. *Journal of Personality and Social Psychology, 44,* 545–552.

Sackett, G. P. (1967). Some persistent effects of different rearing conditions on preadult social behavior of monkeys. *Journal of Comparative and Physiological Psychology, 64,* 363–365.

Sahakian, W. S. (1975). *History and systems of psychology.* New York: Schenkman.

Saito, A., Williams, J. A., Waxler, S. H., & Goldfine, I. D. (1982). Alterations of brain cholecystokinin receptors in mice made obese with gold thioglucose. *Journal of Neurochemistry, 39,* 525–528.

Sapolsky, B. S., & Zillmann, D. (1981). The effect of soft-core and hard-core erotica on provoked and unprovoked hostile behavior. *Journal of Sex Research, 17,* 319–343.

Sarason, S. B., & Mandler, G. (1952). Some correlates of test anxiety. *Journal of Abnormal and Social Psychology, 47,* 810–817.

Satinoff, E. (1987). Biology of drives. In G. Adelman (Ed.), *Encyclopedia of Neuroscience* (Vol. 1), pp. 342–345. Cambridge: Birkhauser Boston.

Sawyer, C. H. (1969). Regulatory mechanisms of secretion of gonadotrophic hormones. In W. Haymaker et al. (Eds.), *The hypothalamus.* Springfield, Ill.: Thomas.

Schachter, S. (1964). The interaction of cognitive and physiological determinants of emotional state. In L. Berkowitz (Ed.), *Advances in experimental social psychology* (Vol. 1). New York: Academic Press.

Schachter, S. (1971a). *Emotion, obesity, and crime.* New York: Academic Press.

Schachter, S. (1971b). Some extraordinary facts about obese humans and rats. *American Psychologist, 26,* 129–144.

Schachter, S., & Gross, L. (1968). Manipulated time and eating behavior. *Journal of Personality and Social Psychology, 10,* 98–106.

Schachter, S., & Rodin, J. (1974). *Obese humans and rats.* Hillsdale, N.J.: Erlbaum.

Schachter, S., & Singer, J. E. (1962). Cognitive, social, and physiological determinants of emotional state. *Psychological Review, 69,* 379–399.

Schaefer, E. (1965a). A configurational analysis of children's reports of parent behavior. *Journal of Consulting Psychology, 29,* 552–557.

Schaefer, E. (1965b). Children's reports of parental behavior. *Child Development, 36,* 413–424.

Schallert, T., Pendergrass, M., & Farrar, S. B. (1982). Cholecystokinin-octapeptide effects on eating elicited by "external" versus "internal" cues in rats. *Appetite: Journal for Intake Research, 3,* 81–90.

Schein, M. W., & Hale, E. B. (1965). Stimuli eliciting sexual behavior. In F. Beach (Ed.), *Sex and behavior.* New York: Wiley.

Schildkraut, J. J., & Kety, S. S. (1967). Biogenic amines and emotion. *Science, 156,* 21–30.

Schlosberg, H. (1952). The description of facial expressions in terms of two dimensions. *Journal of Experimental Psychology, 44,* 229–237.

Schmitt, M. (1973). Influences of hepatic portal receptors on hypothalamic feeding and satiety centers. *American Journal of Physiology, 225,* 1089–1095.

Schneiderman, N. (1973). *Classical (Pavlovian) conditioning.* Morristown, N.J.: General Learning Press.

Schroeder, D. H., & Costa, P. T. (1984). Influence of life event stress on physical illness: Substantive effects or methodological flaws? *Journal of Personality and Social Psychology, 46,* 853–863.

Schultz, D. (1977). *Growth psychology: Models of the healthy personality.* New York: Van Nostrand.

Schwartz, S. H., & Gottlieb, A. (1980). Bystander anonymity and reactions to emergencies. *Journal of Personality and Social Psychology, 39,* 418–430.

Scrima, L. (1982). Isolated REM sleep facilitates recall of complex associative information. *Psychophysiology, 19,* 252–259.

Sears, R. R., Maccoby, E. E., & Levin, H. (1957). *Patterns of child rearing.* Evanston, Ill.: Row Peterson.

Seligman, M. E. P. (1970). On the generality of the laws of learning. *Psychological Review, 77,* 406–418.

Seligman, M. E. P. (1971). Phobias and preparedness. *Behavior Therapy, 2,* 307–320.

Seligman, M. E. P. (1975). *Helplessness: On depression, development, and death.* San Francisco: Freeman.

Seligman, M. E. P. (1976). *Learned helplessness and depression in animals and man.* Morristown, N.J.: General Learning Press.

Seligman, M. E. P., & Hager, J. L. (1972). *Biological boundaries of learning.* New York: Appleton-Century-Crofts.

Seligman, M. E. P., & Maier, S. F. (1967). Failure to escape traumatic shock. *Journal of Experimental Psychology, 74,* 1–9.

Seligman, M. E. P., Maier, S. F., & Geer, J. (1968). The alleviation of learned helplessness in the dog. *Journal of Abnormal and Social Psychology, 73,* 256–262.

Selye, H. (1950). *Stress.* Montreal: Acta.

Selye, H. (1956). *The stress of life.* New York: McGraw-Hill.

Selye, H. (1973). The evolution of the stress concept. *American Scientist, 61,* 692–699.

Senneker, P., & Hendrick, C. (1983). Androgyny and helping behavior. *Journal of Personality and Social Psychology, 45,* 916–925.

Sentis, K. P., & Burnstein, E. (1979). Remembering schema-consistent information: Effects of a balance schema on recognition memory. *Journal of Personality and Social Psychology. 37,* 2200–2211.

Sevenster, P. (1961). A causal analysis of a displacement activity (fanning in *Gasterosteus aculeatus*). *Behavior Supplements, 9,* 1–170.

Seward, J. P. (1949). An experimental analysis of latent learning. *Journal of Experimental Psychology, 39,* 177–186.

Shanab, M. E., Peterson, D., Dargahi, S., & Derioan, P. (1981). The effects of positive and negative verbal feedback on the intrinsic motivation of male and female subjects. *Journal of Social Psychology, 115,* 195–205.

Shapiro, C. M. (1982). Energy expenditure and restorative sleep. *Biological Psychology, 15,* 229–239.

Shapiro, C. M., Bortz, R., Mitchell, D., Bartel, P., & Jooste, P. (1981). Slow-wave sleep: A recovery period after exercise. *Science, 214,* 1253–1254.

Sheffield, F. D. (1966a). A drive-induction theory of reinforcement. In R. N. Haber (Ed.), *Current research in motivation.* New York: Holt, Rinehart & Winston.

Sheffield, F. D. (1966b). New evidence on the drive-induction theory of reinforcement. In R. N. Haber (Ed.), *Current research in motivation.* New York: Holt, Rinehart & Winston.

Sheffield, F. D., & Roby, T. B. (1950). Reward value of a non-nutritive sweet taste. *Journal of Comparative and Physiological Psychology, 43,* 471–481.

Sheffield, F. D., Roby, T. B., & Campbell, B. A.

(1954). Drive reduction versus consummatory behavior as determinants of reinforcement. *Journal of Comparative and Physiological Psychology, 47,* 349–354.

Sheffield, F. D., Wulff, J. J., & Backer, R. (1951). Reward value of copulation without sex drive reduction. *Journal of Comparative and Physiological Psychology, 44,* 3–8.

Sherif, M. (1947). Group influences upon the formation of norms and attitudes. In T. M. Newcomb & E. L. Hartley (Eds.), *Readings in social psychology.* New York: Holt.

Sherrington, C. (1947). *The integrative action of the nervous system.* New Haven, Conn.: Yale University Press.

Shostrom, E. L. (1964). An inventory for the measurement of self-actualization. *Educational and Psychological Measurement, 24,* 207–216.

Shostrom, E. L. (1966). *Manual for the personal orientation inventory.* San Diego: Educational and Industrial Testing Service.

Siegel, S. (1975). Evidence from rats that morphine tolerance is a learned response. *Journal of Comparative and Physiological Psychology, 89,* 498–506.

Siegel, S. (1977). Morphine tolerance acquisition as an associative process. *Journal of Experimental Psychology: Animal Behavior Processes, 3,* 1–13.

Siegel, S., Sherman, J. E., & Mitchell, D. (1980). Extinction of morphine analgesic tolerance. *Learning and Motivation, 11,* 289–301.

Simmonds, M. (1914). Ueber embolische prozesse in der hypophysis. *Archiv fuer Pathologische, Anatomie, und Physiologie und fuer Klinische Medicin, 217,* 226.

Simmons, R. (1924). The relative effectiveness of certain incentives in animal learning. *Comparative Psychology Monographs, 2,* (7).

Simpson, J. B., & Routtenberg, A. (1973). Subfornical organ: Site of drinking elicitation by angiotension II. *Science, 181,* 1172–1175.

Simpson, M. J. A., & Simpson, A. E. (1982). Birth sex ratios and social rank in rhesus monkey mothers. *Nature, 300,* 440–441.

Singer, J. E. (1966). Motivation of consistency. In S. Feldman (Ed.), *Cognitive consistency: Motivational antecedents and behavioral consequents.* New York: Academic Press.

Skinner, B. F. (1938). *The behavior of organisms: An experimental analysis.* New York: Appleton-Century-Crofts.

Sluckin, W. (1973). *Imprinting and early learning.* Chicago: Aldine.

Smith, D. E., King, M. B., & Hoebel, B. G. (1970). Lateral hypothalamic control of killing: Evidence for a cholinoceptive mechanism. *Science, 167,* 900–901.

Smith, G. P. (1982). Satiety and the problem of motivation. In D. W. Pfaff (Ed.), *The Physiological mechanisms of motivation.* New York: Springer-Verlag.

Solbrig, O. T. (1966). *Evolution and systematics.* New York: Macmillan.

Solomon, P., Kubzansky, P. E., Leiderman, P. H., Mendelson, J. H., Trumbull, R., & Wexler, D. (Eds.). (1961). *Sensory deprivation.* Cambridge, Mass.: Harvard University Press.

Solomon, R. L. (1977). An opponent-process theory of motivation: V. Affective dynamics of eating. In L. M. Barker, M. R. Best, & M. Domjan (Eds.), *Learning mechanisms in food selection.* Dallas: Baylor University Press.

Solomon, R. L. (1980). The opponent-process theory of acquired motivation: The costs of pleasure and the benefits of pain. *American Psychologist, 35,* 691–712.

Solomon, R. L., & Corbit, J. D. (1974). An opponent-process theory of motivation. *Psychological Review, 81,* 119–145.

Spence, J. T. (Ed.). (1983). *Achievement and achievement motives: Psychological and sociological approaches.* San Francisco: Freeman.

Spence, K. W. (1956). *Behavior theory and conditioning.* New Haven, Conn.: Yale University Press.

Spence, K. W. (1960). *Behavior theory and learning.* Englewood Cliffs, N.J.: Prentice-Hall.

Spitz, R. A. (1946). *The psychoanalytic study of the child, II.* New York: International University Press.

Staddon, J. E. R. (1970). Temporal effects of reinforcement: A negative "frustration" effect. *Learning and Motivation, 1,* 227–247.

Stangler, R. S., and Printz, A. M. (1980). DSM III: Psychiatric diagnosis in a university population. *American Journal of Psychiatry, 137,* 937–940.

Starr, M. D. (1978). An opponent-process theory of motivation: VI. Time and intensity variables in the development of separation-induced distress calling in ducklings. *Journal of Experimental Psychology: Animal Behavior Processes, 4,* 338–355.

Staw, B. M. (1976). *Intrinsic and extrinsic motivation.* Morristown N.J.: General Learning Press.

Staw, B. M., Calder, B. J., & Hess, R. (1975). Intrinsic motivation and norms about payment. Unpublished manuscript, Northwestern University.

Steele, C. M., Southwick, L. L., & Critchlow, B. (1981). Dissonance and alcohol: Drinking your troubles away. *Journal of Personality and Social Psychology, 41,* 831–846.

Steers, R. M., & Porter, L. W. (1983). *Motivation and work behavior.* New York: McGraw-Hill.

Stellar, E. (1954). The physiology of motivation. *Psychological Review, 61,* 5–22.

Stellar, E., Hyman, R., & Samet, S. (1954). Gastric factors controlling water and salt solution drinking. *Journal of Comparative and Physiological Psychology, 47,* 220–226.

Stern, G. S., McCants, T. R., & Pettine, P. W. (1982). Stress and illness: Controllable and uncontrollable life events' relative contributions. *Personality and Social Psychology Bulletin, 8,* 140–145.

Stern, W. C. (1970). The relationship between REM sleep and learning: Animal studies. In E. Hartmann (Ed.), *Sleep and dreaming.* Boston: Little, Brown.

Sternglanz, S. H., Gray, J. L., & Murakami, M. (1977). Adult preferences for infantile facial features: An ethological approach. *Animal Behavior, 25,* 108–115.

Stevenson, J. A. F. (1969). Neural control of food and water intake. In W. Haymaker et al. (Eds.), *The hypothalamus.* Springfield, Ill.: Thomas.

Storms, M. D. (1973). Videotape and the attribution process: Reversing actors' and observers' points of view. *Journal of Personality and Social Psychology, 27,* 165–175.

Strack, F., Martin, L. L., & Stepper, S. (1988). Inhibiting and facilitating conditions of the human smile: A nonobtrusive test of the facial feedback hypothesis. *Journal of Personality and Social Psychology, 54,* 768–777.

Straus, E., & Yalow, R. S. (1979). Cholecystokinin in the brains of obese and nonobese mice. *Science, 203,* 68–69.

Stricker, E. M., & Bradshaw, W. G. (1976). The renin-angiotensin system and thirst: A re-evaluation. *Science, 194,* 1169–1171.

Stricker, E. M., Friedman, M. I., & Zigmond, M. J. (1975). Glucoregulatory feeding by rats after intraventricular 6-hydroxydopamine or lateral hypothalamic lesions. *Science, 189,* 895–897.

Stricker, E. M., & Zigmond, M. J. (1976). Brain catecholamines and the lateral hypothalamic syndrome. In D. Novin et al. (Eds.), *Hunger: Basic mechanisms and clinical implications.* New York: Raven Press.

Striegel-Moore, R. H., Silberstein, L. R., & Rodin, J. (1986). Toward an understanding of risk factors for bulimia. *American Psychologist, 41,* 246–263.

Suedfeld, P. (1975). The benefits of boredom: Sensory deprivation reconsidered. *American Scientist, 63,* 60–69.

Suedfeld, P. (1977). Using environmental restriction to initiate long-term behavior change. In R. B. Stuart (Ed.), *Behavioral self-management: Strategies, techniques and outcomes.* New York: Brunner/Mazel.

Suedfeld, P. (1980). *Restricted environmental stimulation: Research and clinical applications.* New York: Wiley.

Suedfeld, P., & Ikard, F. F. (1974). The use of sensory deprivation in facilitating the reduction of cigarette smoking. *Journal of Clinical and Consulting Psychology, 42,* 888–895.

Suedfeld, P., & Kristeller, J. L. (1982). Stimulus reduction as a technique in health psychology. *Health Psychology, 1,* 337–357.

Suls, J., & Mullen, B. (1981). Life change and psychological distress: The role of perceived control and desirability. *Journal of Applied Social Psychology, 11,* 379–389.

Swan, I. (1977). Anorexia nervosa, a difficult diagnosis. *The Practitioner, 218,* 424–427.

Symons, D. (1979). *The evolution of human sexuality.* New York: Oxford University Press.

Tanner, O. (1976). *Stress.* New York: Time-Life Books.

Tarpy, R. M., & Mayer, R. E. (1978). *Foundations of learning and memory.* Glenview, Ill.: Scott, Foresman.

Taylor, J. A. (1951). The relationship of anxiety to the conditioned eyelid response. *Journal of Experimental Psychology, 41,* 81–92.

Taylor, J. A. (1953). A personality scale of manifest anxiety. *Journal of Abnormal and Social Psychology, 48,* 285–290.

Teitelbaum, P., & Stellar, E. (1954). Recovery from the failure to eat produced by hypothalamic lesions. *Science, 120,* 894–895.

Thompson, W. R., & Melzack, R. (1956). Early environment. *Scientific American, 194* (1), 38–42.

Thorndike, E. L. (1913). *Educational psychology* (Vol. 2). New York: Teachers College.

Tinbergen, E. A., & Tinbergen, N. (1972). Early childhood autism: An ethological approach. *Beihefte zur Zeitschrift Tierpsychologie, 10,* 7–53.

Tinbergen, N. (1948). Social releasers and the experimental method required for their study. *Wilson Bulletin, 60,* 6–52.

Tinbergen, N. (1951). *The study of instinct.* New York: Oxford University Press.

Tinbergen, N. (1977). On war and peace in animals and man. In T. E. McGill (Ed.), *Readings in animal behavior* (3rd. ed.), pp. 452–467. New York: Holt, Rinehart & Winston.

Tinklepaugh, O. L. (1928). An experimental study of representative factors in monkeys. *Journal of Comparative Psychology, 8,* 197–236.

Toi, M., & Batson, C. D. (1982). More evidence that empathy is a source of altruistic motivation. *Journal of Personality and Social Psychology, 43,* 281–292.

Tolman, E. C. (1923). The nature of instinct. *Psychological Bulletin, 20,* 200–218.

Tolman, E. C. (1932). *Purposive behavior in animals and men.* New York: Appleton-Century.

Tolman, E. C. (1959). Principles of purposive behavior. In S. Koch (Ed.), *Psychology: A study of a science* (Vol. 2). New York: McGraw-Hill.

Tolman, E. C. (1967). *Purposive behavior in animals and men.* New York: Appleton-Century-Crofts.

Tolman, E. C., & Honzik, C. H. (1930a). Introduction and removal of reward, and maze performance in rats. *University of California Publications in Psychology, 4,* 257–275.

Tolman, E. C., & Honzik, C. H. (1930b). "Insight" in rats. *University of California Publications in Psychology, 4,* 215–232.

Tolman, E. C., Ritchie, B. F., & Kalish, D. (1946). Studies in spatial learning: II. Place learning versus response learning. *Journal of Experimental Psychology, 36,* 221–229.

Tolman, E. C., Ritchie, B. F., & Kalish, D. (1947). Studies in spatial learning: V. Response learning vs. place learning by the non-correction method. *Journal of Experimental Psychology, 37,* 285–292.

Tomkins, S. S. (1962). *Affect, imagery, consciousness. Vol. I. The positive affects.* New York: Springer.

Tomkins, S. S. (1963). *Affect, imagery, consciousness. Vol II. The negative affects.* New York: Springer.

Tomkins, S. S. (1979). Script theory: Differential magnification of affects. In R. A. Dienstbier (Ed.), *1978 Nebraska Symposium on Motivation,* pp. 201–236. Lincoln: University of Nebraska Press.

Tomkins, S. S. (1981a). The quest for primary motives: Biography and autobiography of an idea. *Journal of Personality and Social Psychology, 41,* 306–329.

Tomkins, S. S. (1981b). The role of facial response in the experience of emotion: A reply to Tourangeau and Ellsworth. *Journal of Personality and Social Psychology, 40,* 355–357.

Tomkins, S. S., & McCarter, R. (1964). What and where are the primary affects? Some evidence for a theory. *Perceptual and Motor Skills, 18,* 119–158.

Tourangeau, R., & Ellsworth, P. C. (1979). The role of facial response in the experience of emotion. *Journal of Personality and Social Psychology, 37,* 1519–1531.

Trapold, M. A., & Overmier, J. B. (1972). The second learning process in instrumental learning. In A. H. Black & W. F. Prokasy (Eds.), *Classical conditioning II: Current research and theory.* New York: Appleton-Century-Crofts.

Trayburn, P., Jones, P. M., McGuckin, M. M., & Goodbody, A. E. (1982). Effects of overfeeding on energy balance and brown fat thermogenesis in obese (ob/ob) mice. *Nature, 295,* 323–325.

Troland, L. T. (1932). *The principles of psychophysiology.* New York: Van Nostrand.

Udwin, O., & Yule, W. (1984). Spelling remediation: A single case study. *Educational Psychology, 4*, 285–296.

Ulrich, R., & Azrin, N. H. (1962). Reflexive fighting in response to aversive stimulation. *Journal of the Experimental Analysis of Behavior, 5*, 511–520.

Vale, W., Spiess, J., Rivier, C., & Rivier, J. (1981). Characterization of a 41-residue ovine hypothalamic peptide that stimulates secretion of corticotropin and B-endorphin. *Science, 213*, 1394–1397.

Valins, S. (1966). Cognitive effects of false heart-rate feedback. *Journal of Personality and Social Psychology, 4*, 400–408.

Valins, S. (1974). Persistent effects of information about internal reactions: Ineffectiveness of debriefing. In H. London & R. E. Nisbett (Eds.), *The cognitive alteration of feeling states*. Chicago: Aldine.

Valins, S., & Nisbett, R. E. (1972). Attribution processes in the development and treatment of emotional disorders. In E. E. Jones et al. (Eds.), *Attribution: Perceiving the causes of behavior*. Morristown, N. J.: General Learning Press.

Vallerand, R. J. (1983). The effect of differential amounts of positive verbal feedback on the intrinsic motivation of male hockey players. *Journal of Sport Psychology, 5*, 100–107.

Vanderweele, D. A., & Sanderson, J. D. (1976). Peripheral glucosensitive satiety in the rabbit and the rat. In D. Novin et al. (Eds.), *Hunger: Basic mechanisms and clinical implications*. New York: Raven Press.

Van Hemel, P. E. (1972). Aggression as a reinforcer: Operant behavior in the mouse-killing rat. *Journal of the Experimental Analysis of Behavior, 17*, 237–245.

Verney, E. B. (1947). The antidiuretic hormone and the factors which determine its release. *Proceedings of the Royal Society* (London), Series B, *135*, 25–106.

Vernon, W., & Ulrich, R. (1966). Classical conditioning of pain-elicited aggression. *Science, 152*, 668–669.

Veroff, J., Wilcox, S., & Atkinson, J. W. (1953). The achievement motive in high school and college-age women. *Journal of Abnormal and Social Psychology, 48*, 103–119.

Volicer, L., & Lowe, C. G. (1971). Penetration of angiotensin II into the brain. *Neuropharmacology, 10*, 631–636.

Wagner, A. R. (1961). Effects of amount and percentage of reinforcement and number of acquisition trials on conditioning and extinction. *Journal of Experimental Psychology, 62*, 234–242.

Wall, P. D., & Sweet, W. H. (1967). Temporary abolition of pain in man. *Science, 155*, 108–109.

Wang, G. H. (1923). Relation between "spontaneous" activity and oestrus cycle in the white rat. *Comparative Psychological Monographs, 2*, (6).

Wangensteen, O. H., & Carlson, A. J. (1931). Hunger sensation after total gastrectomy. *Proceedings of the Society for Experimental Biology, 28*, 545–547.

Warden, C. J. (1931). *Animal motivation: Experimental studies on the albino rat*. New York: Columbia University Press.

Warga, C. (1987, August). Pain's gatekeeper. *Psychology Today*, pp. 51–56.

Watson, D., Clark, L. A., & Tellegen, A. (1984). Cross-cultural convergence in the structure of mood: A Japanese replication and a comparison with U. S. findings. *Journal* of Personality and Social Psychology, 47, 127–144.

Watson, D., & Tellegen, A. (1985). Toward a consensual structure of mood. Psychological Bulletin, 98, 219–235.

Watson, J. B. (1914). Behavior, an introduction to comparative psychology. New York: Holt, Rinehart & Winston.

Watson, J. B., & Rayner, R. (1920). Conditioned emotional reactions. Journal of Experimental Psychology, 3, 1–14.

Webb, W. B. (1982). The sleep of older subjects fifteen years later. Psychological Reports, 50, 11–14.

Webb, W. B. (1986). Sleep deprivation and reading comprehension. Biological Psychology, 22, 169–172.

Webb, W. B., & Agnew, H. W. (1968). Measurement and characteristics of nocturnal sleep. In L. E. Abt & B. F. Riess (Eds.), Progress in clinical psychology (Vol. 8). New York: Grune & Stratton.

Webb, W. B., & Agnew, H. W. (1973). Sleep and dreams. Dubuque, Iowa: Brown.

Webster's New World Dictionary, College Edition. (1962). New York: World Publishing.

Weiner, B. (1972). Theories of motivation: From mechanism to cognition. Chicago: Markham.

Weiner, B. (1974). An attributional interpretation of expectancy-value theory. In B. Weiner (Ed.), Cognitive views of human motivation. New York: Academic Press.

Weiner, B. (1980). A cognitive (attribution)-emotion-action model of motivated behavior: An analysis of judgments of help-giving. Journal of Personality and Social Psychology, 39, 186–200.

Weiner, B. (1985). An attributional theory of achievement motivation and emotion. Psychological Review, 92, 548–573.

Weiner, B., Amirkhan, J., Folkes, V. S., & Verette, J. A. (1987). An attributional analysis of excuse giving: Studies of a naive theory of emotion. Journal of Personality and Social Psychology, 52, 316–234.

Weiner, B., Frieze, I., Kukla, A., Reed, L., Rest, S., & Rosenbaum, R. M. (1972). Perceiving the causes of success and failure. In E. E. Jones et al. (Eds.), Attribution: Perceiving the causes of behavior. Morristown, N. J.: General Learning Press.

Weiner, B., & Kukla, A. (1970). An attributional analysis of achievement motivation. Journal of Personality and Social Psychology, 15, 1–20.

Weiner, B., Perry, R. P., & Magnusson, J. (1988). An attributional analysis of reactions to stigmas. Journal of Personality and Social Psychology, 55, 738–748.

Weiner, B., Russell, D., & Lerman, D. (1978). Affective consequences of causal ascriptions. In J. H. Harvey et al. (Eds.), New directions in attribution research (Vol. 2). Hillsdale, N. J.: Erlbaum.

Weinstein, M. S. (1969). Achievement motivation and risk preference. Journal of Personality and Social Psychology, 13, 153–172.

Weiss, J. M., Krieckhaus, E. E., & Conte, R. (1968). Effects of fear conditioning on subsequent avoidance behavior. Journal of Comparative and Physiological Psychology, 65, 413–421.

Wershow, H. J., & Reinhart, G. (1974). Life change and hospitalization: A heretical view. Journal of Psychosomatic Research, 18, 393–401.

Weyant, J. M. (1978). Effects of mood states, costs, and benefits on helping. Journal of

Personality and Social Psychology, 36, 1169–1176.

White, R. W. (1959). Motivation reconsidered: The concept of competence. *Psychological Review, 66,* 297–333.

White, R. W. (1964). *The abnormal personality* (3rd ed.). New York: Ronald Press.

Wicklund, R. A., & Brehm, J. W. (1976). *Perspectives on cognitive dissonance.* Hillsdale, N. J.: Erlbaum.

Wiggins, J. S., Wiggins, N., & Conger, J. C. (1968). Correlates of heterosexual somatic preference. *Journal of Personality and Social Psychology, 10,* 32–90.

Wilcox, P. M., Fetting, J. H., Nettesheim, K. M., & Abeloff, M. D. (1982). Anticipatory vomiting in women receiving cyclophosphomide, methotrexate, and 5-FU (MF) adjuvant chemotherapy for breast carcinoma. *Cancer Treatment Reports, 66,* 1601–1604.

Wilcoxon, H. C., Dragoin, W. B., & Kral, P. A. (1971). Illness-induced aversions in rat and quail: Relative salience of visual and auditory cues. *Science, 171,* 826–828.

Williams, B. W. (1980). Reinforcement, behavior constraint, and the overjustification effect. *Journal of Personality and Social Psychology, 39,* 599–614.

Williams, D., & King, M. (1976). Sex role attitudes and fear of success as correlates of sex role behavior. *Journal of College Student Personnel, 17,* 480–484.

Williams, G. C. (1975). *Sex and evolution.* Princeton, N. J.: Princeton University Press.

Williams, H. L., Holloway, F. A., & Griffiths, W. J. (1973). Physiological psychology: Sleep. In P. H. Mursen & M. R. Rosenzweig (Eds.), *Annual Review of Psychology, 24,* 279–307.

Williams, S. B. (1938). Resistance to extinction as a function of the number of reinforcements. *Journal of Experimental Psychology, 23,* 506–522.

Willows, A. O. D. (1971). Giant brain cells in mollusks. *Scientific American, 224* (2), 68–75.

Willows, A. O. D., & Hoyle, G. (1969). Neuronal network triggering a fixed action pattern. *Science, 166,* 1549–1551.

Wirtshafter, D., & Davis, J. D. (1977). Body weight: Reduction by long-term glycerol treatment. *Science, 198,* 1271–1274.

Witt, E. D., Ryan, C., & Hsu, L. K. G. (1985). Learning deficits in adolescents with anorexia nervosa. *Journal of Nervous and Mental Disease, 173,* 182–184.

Wolfe, J. B. (1936). Effectiveness of token-rewards for chimpanzees. *Comparative Psychology Monographs, 12,* No. 60.

Wolff, G., & Money, J. (1973). Relationship between sleep and growth in patients with reversible somatotropin deficiency (psychosocial dwarfism). *Psychological Medicine, 3,* 18–27.

Wolgin, D. L., Cytawa, J., & Teitelbaum, P. (1976). The role of activation in the regulation of food intake. In D. Novin et al. (Eds.), *Hunger: Basic mechanisms and clinical implications.* New York: Raven Press.

Wolpe, J. (1958). *Psychotherapy by reciprocal inhibition.* Stanford, Calif.: Stanford University Press.

Wolpe, J. (1973). *The practice of behavior* (2nd ed.). New York: Pergamon.

Woodbridge, F. J. E. (1958). *Hobbes selections.* New York: Scribner.

Woods, S. C., Decke, E., & Vasselli, J. R. (1974). Metabolic hormones and regulation of body weight. *Psychological Review, 81,* 26–43.

Woodworth, R. S. (1918). *Dynamic psychology.* New York: Columbia University Press.

Woodworth, R. S. (1958). *Dynamics of behavior.* New York: Holt.

Woodworth, R. S., & Schlosberg, H. (1954). *Experimental psychology* (rev. ed.). New York: Holt, Rinehart & Winston.

Wortman, C. B. & Brehm, J. F. (1975). Responses to incontrollable outcomes: An integration of reactance theory and the learned helplessness model. In L. Berkowitz (Ed.), *Advances in Experimental Social Psychology* (Vol. 8). New York: Academic Press.

Young, P. T. (1961). *Motivation and emotion.* New York: Wiley.

Young, P. T. (1973). *Emotion in man and animal* (2nd ed.). Huntington, N. Y.: Robert E. Krieger.

Young, P. T. (1975). *Understanding your feelings and emotions.* Englewood Cliffs, N. J.: Prentice-Hall.

Young, P. T., & Falk, J. L. (1956). The relative acceptability of sodium chloride solutions as a function of concentration and water need. *Journal of Comparative and Physiological Psychology, 49,* 569–575.

Young, P. T., & Greene, J. T. (1953). Quantity of food ingested as a measure of relative acceptability. *Journal of Comparative and Physiological Psychology, 46,* 288–294.

Zajonc, R. B. (1972). *Animal social behavior.* Morristown, N. J.: General Learning Press.

Zajonc, R. B. (1980). Feeling and thinking: Preferences need no inferences. *American Psychologist, 35,* 151–175.

Zajonc, R. B. (1984). On the primacy of affect. *American Psychologist, 39,* 117–123.

Zajonc, R. B., & Burnstein, E. (1965). The learning of balanced and unbalanced social structures. *Journal of Personality, 33,* 153–163.

Zajonc, R. B., Heingartner, A., & Herman, E. M. (1969). Social enhancement and impairment of performance in the cockroach. *Journal of Personality and Social Psychology, 13,* 83–92.

Zanna, M. P., & Cooper, J. (1974). Dissonance and the pill: An attributional approach to studying the arousal properties of dissonance. *Journal of Personality and Social Psychology, 29,* 703–709.

Zanna, M. P., & Cooper, J. (1976). Dissonance and the attribution process. In J. H. Harvey et al. (Eds.), *New directions in attribution research* (Vol. 1). Hillsdale, N. J.: Erlbaum.

Zanna, M. P., Lepper, M. R., & Abelson, R. P. (1973). Attentional mechanisms in children's devaluation of a forbidden activity in a forced-compliance situation. *Journal of Personality and Social Psychology, 28,* 355–359.

Zeaman, D. (1949). Response latency as a function of the amount of reinforcement. *Journal of Experimental Psychology, 39,* 466–483.

Zeigarnik, B. (1927). Uber das Behalten von erledigten und unerledigten Handlungen. *Psychologische Forschung, 9,* 1–85.

Zeliger, H. P., & Karten, H. J. (1974). Central trigeminal structures and the lateral hypothalamic syndrome in the rat. *Science, 186,* 636–638.

Zilbergeld, B., & Ellison, C. R. (1980). *Principles*

and practice of sex therapy. New York: Guilford.

Zillmann, D., & Bryant, J. (1982). Pornography, sexual callousness, and the trivialization of rape. *Journal of Communication, 32,* 10–21.

Zimbardo, P. G. (1969). The human choice: Individuation, reason, and order versus deindividuation, impulse, and chaos. In W. J. Arnold & D. Levine (Eds.), *Nebraska Symposium on Motivation.* Lincoln: University of Nebraska Press.

Zimbardo, P. G. (1975). Transforming experimental research into advocacy for social change. In M. Deutsch & H. A. Hornstein (Eds.), *Applying social psychology: Implications for research, practice and training.* Hillsdale, N. J.: Erlbaum.

Zornetzer, S. F., Gold, M. S., & Boast, C. A. (1977). Neuroanatomic localization and the neurobiology of sleep and memory. In R. R. Drucker-Colin & J. L. McGaugh (Eds.), *Neurobiology of sleep and memory.* New York: Academic Press.

Zuckerman, M., & Allison, S. N. (1976). An objective measure of fear of success: Construction and validation. *Journal of Personality Assessment, 40,* 422–430.

Zuckerman, M., Larrance, D. T., Porac, J., & Blanck, P. D. (1980). Effects of fear of success on intrinsic motivation, causal attribution, and choice behavior. *Journal of Personality and Social Psychology, 39,* 503–513.

Zuckerman, M., Porac, J., Lathin, D., Smith, R., & Deci, E. L. (1978). On the importance of self-determination for intrinsically motivated behavior. *Personality and Social Psychology Bulletin, 4,* 443–446.

Zuckerman, M., & Wheeler, L. (1975). To dispel fantasies about the fantasy-based measure of fear of success. *Psychological Bulletin, 82,* 932–946.

Name Index

Subject Index